Advances in Object-Oriented
Database Systems

NATO ASI Series

Advanced Science Institutes Series

A series presenting the results of activities sponsored by the NATO Science Committee, which aims at the dissemination of advanced scientific and technological knowledge, with a view to strengthening links between scientific communities.

The Series is published by an international board of publishers in conjunction with the NATO Scientific Affairs Division

A Life Sciences	Plenum Publishing Corporation
B Physics	London and New York
C Mathematical and Physical Sciences	Kluwer Academic Publishers Dordrecht, Boston and London
D Behavioural and Social Sciences	
E Applied Sciences	
F Computer and Systems Sciences	Springer-Verlag Berlin Heidelberg New York
G Ecological Sciences	London Paris Tokyo Hong Kong
H Cell Biology	Barcelona Budapest
I Global Environmental Change	

NATO-PCO DATABASE

The electronic index to the NATO ASI Series provides full bibliographical references (with keywords and/or abstracts) to more than 30 000 contributions from international scientists published in all sections of the NATO ASI Series. Access to the NATO-PCO DATABASE compiled by the NATO Publication Coordination Office is possible in two ways:

- via online FILE 128 (NATO-PCO DATABASE) hosted by ESRIN, Via Galileo Galilei, I-00044 Frascati, Italy.

- via CD-ROM "NATO Science & Technology Disk" with user-friendly retrieval software in English, French and German (© WTV GmbH and DATAWARE Technologies Inc. 1992).

The CD-ROM can be ordered through any member of the Board of Publishers or through NATO-PCO, Overijse, Belgium.

Advances in Object-Oriented Database Systems

Edited by

Asuman Dogac

Software Research and Development Center
Middle East Technical University
TR-06531 Ankara, Turkey

M. Tamer Özsu

Department of Computing Science, University of Alberta
Edmonton, Alberta, Canada T6G 2H1

Alexandros Biliris

AT&T Bell Laboratories, Room 2C-221, 600 Mountain Avenue
Murray Hill, NJ 07974, USA

Timos Sellis

Department of Electrical and Computer Engineering
National Technical University of Athens, Zographou
GR-157 73 Athens, Greece

Springer-Verlag
Berlin Heidelberg New York London Paris Tokyo
Hong Kong Barcelona Budapest
Published in cooperation with NATO Scientific Affairs Division

Proceedings of the NATO Advanced Study Institute on Object-Oriented
Database Systems, held in Izmir, Kusadasi, Turkey, August 6–16, 1993

CR Subject Classification (1991): H.2, H.2.1–5, D.1.5

ISBN 3-540-57825-0 Springer-Verlag Berlin Heidelberg New York
ISBN 0-387-57825-0 Springer-Verlag New York Berlin Heidelberg

CIP data applied for

Typesetting: Camera ready by authors
SPIN 10130726   45/3140 - 5 4 3 2 1 0 - Printed on acid-free paper

Preface

Object-oriented database management systems (OODBMSs) have generated significant excitement in the database community in the last decade. This interest stems from a real need for data management support for what are called "advanced application areas" that are not well-served by relational technology. The case for object-oriented technology has been made on three fronts.

First is the data modeling requirements of the new applications. Some of the more important shortcomings of the relational systems in meeting the requirements of these applications include:

1. Relational systems deal with a single object type: a relation. A relation is used to model different real-world objects, but the semantics of this association is not part of the database. Furthermore, the attributes of a relation may come only from simple and fixed data type domains (numeric, character, and, sometimes, date types). Advanced applications require explicit storage and manipulation of more abstract types (e.g., images, design documents) and the ability for the users to define their own application-specific types. Therefore, a rich type system supporting user-defined abstract types is required.
2. The relational model structures data in a relatively simple and flat manner. Non-traditional applications require more complex object structures with nested objects (e.g., a vehicle object containing an engine object).
3. The relational model captures the factual data about applications, but not the "behavioral knowledge" or "domain-specific generic knowledge". This shortcoming was recognized quite early in the development of relational systems and various attempts were made to rectify it. For example, most of the commercial relational systems provide for stored procedures to capture behavioral knowledge, but this is only a half-measure.

The second area in which object-oriented technology is expected to be helpful is in facilitating better interfacing of the DBMS with the operating system at the bottom and the programming language at the top. The problem of building DBMSs on top of the existing operating systems are well-documented. The problems have to do with the closed nature of the operating systems and the unsuitability of the functions that they implement (e.g., file systems, buffer management, process scheduling) for data management. The common result is that DBMSs either bypass the operating system, treat the disk as raw disk, and implement their own functions thereby duplicating the some of the functions of the operating system, or they modify the operating system itself. Part of this problem is architectural and independent of the approach used to model system entities. However, as will be indicated below, object-orientation is expected to be of help.

At the programming language side, the "impedance mismatch" between the DBMS and the programming language has often been discussed. This problem arises because of the differences in the level of abstraction between the relational languages and the programming languages with which they interact. Relational systems provide a declarative and set-oriented language for accessing flat tables. The programming languages commonly used to implement applications, on the other hand, provide much richer structures (e.g., arrays and pointers) and operate in a record-at-a-time manner (i.e., the access is navigational). The applications mentioned above require richer database languages which overcome this impedance mismatch.

It has been suggested that these problems may be resolved by implementing an object-oriented DBMS on top of an object-oriented operating system which is accessed by an object-oriented programming language. Even though the potential exists for such a uniform treatment, this is easier said than done. The approach to object-orientation of these three systems are quite different.

The final reason for the interest in object-orientation is its potential for facilitating interoperability. In fact, many practitioners have pointed out that, in the long run, this may be the most important and most influential use of object-oriented technology. Object-orientation, with its encapsulation^j and abstraction capabilities, is expected to assist in providing interoperability.

Whether object-oriented technology will be able to meet all of these expectations remains to be seen. The market for OODBMSs is still small and there are a few, but fast growing number of, applications that use them. The technology is maturing, however, and with the emergence of new systems with full functionality (query languages, query optimizers, transaction managers) the number and variety of applications using OODBMSs is increasing. The research of the last decade is starting to generate results.

A NATO Advanced Study Institute was organized to review and discuss these advances in Kusadasi, Turkey, during August 6-15th of 1993. The Institute brought together 78 attendees. There were 18 presentations ranging from the basic principles to system implementation issues and prototype systems. This book brings together the text of these presentations. All of these papers were edited extensively following the Institute.

We would like to express our gratitute to all the authors who have agreed to revise their contributions based on the discussions during the Institute. We would also like to mention the extraordinary work of the volunteers from the Software Research and Development Center of the Scientific and Technical Reseach Council of Turkey and the Middle East Technical University in the local organization of the Institute. The final copy looks as nice as it does thanks to Anne Nield of the Laboratory for Database Systems Research at the University of Alberta. Finally, we would like to thank NATO, Scientific and Technical Reseach Council of Turkey, Middle East Technical University, Siemens-Nixdorf Turkey, Koc Unisys Turkey, Oracle Turkey, Login Turkey, IBM Turkey, and Software AG Turkey for their financial assistance.

June 1994

Asuman Dogac
M. Tamer Özsu
Alexandros Biliris
Timos Sellis

Table of Contents

SECTION 1
INTRODUCTION

What Makes Object-Oriented Database Management Systems Different?

Stanley B. Zdonik

Brown University, Department of Computer Science, Providence, RI 02912, USA

Abstract. In this paper, we briefly introduce the main features of an object-oriented database management system (OODBMS). We describe the typical architecture of OODBMSs and point out the differences between this architecture and that of a more conventional system (e.g., relational database). We discuss some of the issues involved in implementing this style of database system including the movement of data between client and server in a distributed setting. We also mention some of the unique aspects of querying an object-oriented database.

1 Introduction

The design of traditional database systems has largely been a response to the needs of typical business applications. Before commercial database management systems, each application program owned it's own set of files, each of which had its own idiosyncratic format and structure. Data in these file-based systems was often stored redundantly and, as a result, was difficult to keep consistent. Creating new applications required difficult extractions of information from many disparate sources. Programs were dependent on the structures of the stored data, making this structure difficult to change.

Database systems have improved the application development process in large data-intensive environments by providing a single, uniform view of data expressed in high-level terms. Their high-level linguistic features and their facilities for controlled sharing make it possible to create integrated applications more easily than before. This integration manifests itself through easy interchange of data among applications and an environment in which data consistency can be maintained.

The availability of high-performance graphics workstations has increased the complexity of applications. Complex data-intensive applications are being designed and built for application areas that include computer-aided design (CAD), computer-aided software engineering (CASE), and office information systems (OIS). For example, in electrical CAD, the typical design environment includes packages like schema capture editors, design rule checkers, and circuit layout programs. All of these systems, like their data processing predecessors, require massive amounts of persistent data; however, the level of complexity of these programs and this data has grown far beyond that which traditional database systems are prepared to handle. These advanced, design-support applications caused the database community to focus on solving the problems of efficiently handling complex information types and of managing system evolution. Research in the area of OODBMSs was a direct response to these needs.

Until recently, the application programs in design environments store their data in application-specific file structures. The state of the art here is roughly at the same stage that existed before the emergence of database technology in the data processing world. There has been agreement for some time that what is need is an extension of database technology that can provide the same advantages for the application development process that occurred in the data processing world. OODBMSs are a step in this direction.

Design applications must model very complex data and evolve without disruptive effects on the current application base. This places a requirement on the system to provide a mechanism that supports an appropriate level of extensibility in order to capture application-specific data semantics and a mechanism that allows for incremental development. The rest of this paper discusses these issues in detail.

One of the most important contributions of OODBMSs is support for type-level extensibility. New abstract data types can be added to the database system, and behavior for these new types is provided through new code in the form of methods. If this code is to be maintainable, good organization via modularity must be enforced at the system level. This is what abstract data types were designed to do. We might, therefore, say that one of the principal advantages of an OODBMS is that it supports the software engineering process at the level of the database for complex applications that require large amounts of persistent data.

2 Object-Oriented Data Models

In this section we will summarize the principle features that distinguish the data definition facilities of OODBMSs from that of their predecessors. This discussion is not meant to provide a detailed discussion of all of the variations in this technology. Instead, we will try to point out the principle themes.

In the mid- to late-seventies, there was a great deal of interest within the database research community in developing data models that were more expressive than the relational model. Semantic data models were a result of this work. Several models were proposed in the literature [HM81, MBW80, Shi81], but none were fully implemented. They all shared many features with current object-oriented data models, and as such were their spiritual forerunners. For example, object identity and class hierarchies were in evidence in these early models.

Unlike the relational data model, a single data model has not emerged from the object-oriented approach. Instead a family of models that have a set of features and goals in common have been proposed. Several research prototypes [BBG+88, CDF+86, Kin86, LRV88, LK86, MD86, RS87, ZW86] have been developed, and commercial products [AH87, MSOP86] have become available.

2.1 Type Extensibility

One of the key goals of object-oriented database system research is to provide a system in which the basic modeling primitives are *extensible*. This is a response to the requirement that new applications will involve unpredictably complex data and that the form of this data will evolve over time. Thus, a fixed set of data structuring primitives is not sufficient. An extension will provide new functionality to the data model and be at a level that is indistinguishable from the built-in mechanisms. In comparing the various object-oriented data models, it is worth asking "What can be extended?," "Who does the extensions?," and "When can the extensions be made?"

Relational databases present a view of the persistent data space to the programmer consisting of primitive values of integers, reals, and strings and requiring that all aggregate objects be represented as sets of tuples (i.e., relations) over these primitive values. This rather high-level view of data is very convenient for data processing applications that are principally concerned with producing reports. It is too restrictive, though, for systems programs that are at roughly the same level of complexity as an operating system or a compiler. These programs require tight control over how storage is used. They often need to be able to use data structures like stacks, queues, or streams of bytes. An OODBMS allows programmers to create abstractions that match the data structures that are needed for their intricate tasks.

The principle extension mechanisms is the creation of new *abstract types*. A type is a template for its instances. As such, a type indicates how its instances can be manipulated. One of the principle uses of types in programming languages is that of type checking. Type checking ensures that the types of expressions match the context in which they are used. For example, the type of an expression that is used as an actual parameter to a function, must match the type of the formal parameter in the function definition. An important question about the design of a type system is whether or not this type checking can be done at compile-time (i.e., static type checking) or whether some or all of it must be deferred to run- time (i.e., dynamic type checking). The TRELLIS/OWL language [SCB+86] combines strong typing, abstract data types, and subtyping such that the resulting language is statically checkable.

While the idea of creating new types is not new to the database field, the view that a type is really an abstract data type that encapsulates its implementation is unique to OODB's. Earlier database models provided the user with a fixed set of built-in types and a small set of type constructors (e.g., record). New types could be built with the type constructors, but these new types do not allow for operations that were different from the operations defined by the type constructor. For example, for records, the operations are the basic *get-value* and *set-value* operations on its fields. It is impossible in these models to add a more complex type like **Stack** with a *push* and *pop* operation.

Encapsulation is a very powerful system structuring technique in which a system is made up of a collection of modules that are accessible through a well-defined interface. Details of the implementation of a module are hidden from its users. The abstract data type approach defines the interface by a set of strongly-typed operation (or method) signatures. It also requires that each type define a representation (an instance of some other data type) that is allocated for each of its instances. This representation is used to store the state of the object. Only the methods are allowed to access the representation, thereby making it possible to change the representation without disturbing the rest of the system. If a change is made to the representation, only the methods would need to be recoded.

2.2 Subtyping

Another feature of object-oriented data models in general is a typing scheme that includes some form of *subtyping* or *inheritance*. Inheritance is a term that has come to describe many different mechanisms in which type definitions can be related to each other through a type lattice. The basic notion is that type definitions can be modified incrementally by adding subtype definitions that somehow modify the original type. The combination of the supertype and the subtype produces a completely defined new type.

Many variations on this idea have been proposed in the literature [WZ88]. Although it is beyond the scope of this paper, it is worth noting that care should be taken when discussing or comparing different languages with respect to the semantics of their subtyping mechanisms. There is likely to be subtle variation.

2.3 Object Identity

Object-oriented data models are also characterized by their ability to make references through an *object identity*. This requires that there be something about the object that remains invariant across all possible modifications of the object's value. This property has been a part of most modern programming languages for some time and has been a part of some early database models (e.g., CODASYL). Many modern database models (e.g., relational, logic-based), however, are value- based. In a value-based model, an object is identified by a subset of its attributes called its key. This leads to simpler computational structures, but makes some kinds of information difficult to express.

Although OODBMSs include the notion of identity,/indexidentity it is important to note that the way in which objects are related may or may not be based on this feature. References that make use of an object's identity directly are much like pointers in conventional programming languages. In an OODBMS it is possible to relate an object x to another object or set of objects S by storing the identity of S (or of the members of S) in x. However, since all access to an object x is through the methods defined on its type, computing the association between x and S must be done by a method. This method can make use of a stored identity, or it can use a value-based expression (e.g., a query) to compute the relationship. In this way, OODBMSs provide a framework for unifying value-based and identity based access.

A model like ENCORE [ZW86] has the ability to relate objects by means of properties. A property is a reflection of the abstract state of an object. As such, a property p relates an object x to a set of objects S without making any statement about how this relationship is computed. It could be computed by a direct reference to the identity of S (or its members), or it could be computed by a matching of values for some other properties as a join. Consider the following type definition:

Define Type Employee
Properties
  depts: **Set of** Department
  project: Project

Define Type `Department`

The `project` property which expresses the project that a given employee works on could be implemented by an imbedded object identifier. If the representations for both the Employee and the Department types are tuples in a relation, the `depts` property for a given employee, Smith, could be implemented by a relational query of the form:

Project$_{\text{Department}}$ (
  Select$_{\text{name}=\text{"Smith"}}$ (
    Join(Employee, Department)))

An OODBMS is based on the ability to define new abstractions and to control the implementation of these abstractions. From the above example, we can see that it is possible to combine both identity-based and value-based relationships at the implementation level while retaining the same abstraction at the logical level.

OODBMSs contain some features that are usually found in modern abstraction-based programming languages. This is a result of the fact that in this context the database can be programmed with a computationally complete programming language, thereby making it possible to include more of the execution of the application in the database itself. This presents an opportunity for using the knowledge of the database structures in the optimization and intelligent processing of the application code.

2.4 Objects vs. Values

Related to the issue of identity in object-oriented data models is the distinction between objects and values. In many cases, objects are simply defined to be values with an identity. Often, this identity is provided by a visible object identifier. This definition is simple and easy to understand in terms of structural data models based on records. The identifier can be thought of as an additional field in each record. This is reflected in models like the PROBE Data Model (PDM) and algebra [DS86a].

More abstractly, though, it is not a particular implementation of identity that distinguishes objects from values. It is rather based on whether or not an object can be shared and thus create aliased structures. Those that can be referenced from multiple places are called objects, and those that cannot support multiple references are called values.

We can further distinguish between *mutable* and *immutable* objects. First, we partition the methods on abstract type T into *observers*, *mutators*, and *creators*. The creators M_c create new objects; the mutators M_m change the state of existing objects; the observers M_o report on the state of an existing object without any side-effects. Objects that are defined by an abstract type T have an *abstract state* S. The abstract state S of an object x of type T can be defined to be a record containing the results of all of the observer methods on x.

$$S(x) = \langle a_1 : m_1(x), a_2 : m_2(x); \ldots, a_i : m_i(x) \rangle \tag{1}$$

where $a_i \in$ Strings and $m_i \in M_o$ and $a_i = \text{name}(m_i)$

This leads us to the observation that an immutable object that is shared is indistinguishable from an immutable object that is not shared. There is no way to detect the sharing in the first case. On the other hand, if the shared object is mutable, then it is possible to change it via one reference and observe the change through the other.

This distinction turns out to be very important in the development of query languages for OODBMSs since they must be sensitive to the question of whether or not sets (and other bulk types) are objects or values. We shall discuss bulk types in the next section, but for now, it is sufficient to note that different models take different positions on this question. For example, O_2 treats sets and tuples as values while ENCORE treats sets and tuples as first-class objects (and, therefore, mutable).

2.5 Bulk Types

Unlike programming languages, OODBMSs (and DBMSs in general) are very much concerned with detailed properties of and efficient access to the *bulk types*. A bulk type is one that has structure. That is to say, it contains other objects as components. Some common bulk types include **set**, **multiset**, and **list**.

Since databases are typically responsible for very large numbers of objects that are stored on relatively slow secondary storage media, it is natural for these systems to be concerned with the performance of retrievals over very large collections. It is not sufficient to be able to create these types and express computations over them. A database system must be able to optimize retrieval expressions over arbitrary sized bulk types. This task falls under the aegis of the query optimizer.

In a language like C++ or Smalltalk, it is possible to create abstract types that capture the interface behavior of just about any bulk type that could be imagined. However, from a database perspective, this is only half of the story. The database system itself must know about the algebraic properties of the operations over these types. It is only through this additional knowledge that a query optimizer can perform its task. The classic fact that *select* and *join* are commutative in the relational algebra exemplifies this kind of knowledge for sets.

There has been a great deal of interest lately in the modeling of advanced bulk types in an object-oriented context. This includes formal treatments of unordered bulk types such as **Set** and **Multiset**, but also of ordered bulk types such as **List** and **Array**. Another issue concerns the question of whether a fixed number of bulk types should be built into the language or whether users should be able to add new bulk types to meet the needs of their applications [MS91]. What kind of support can be given to these add-on bulk types?

3 Database Management Features

The relational model is very well accepted these days as the state of the art in the commercial database field. It is, therefore, worth trying to understand how OODBMSs differ from these systems. We have already indicated some of the technical features that underlie the object-oriented approach. Things like identity, abstract data types, and inheritance are all important distinguishing characteristics, but how do these characteristics relate to the ways in which these systems can be optimally used?

So far, we have briefly described the linguistic basis for object-oriented data models. As we have pointed out, there are many variations in the languages and models that underlie the current commercial systems as well as exisitng research prototypes. We must be careful to understand that the systems at hand are databases, and as such must provide the features and functionality that one has come to expect from modern database systems. These features are typically not found in the current breed of object-oriented programming languages (e.g., Smalltalk). Some of the features that are required of a database system are:

- Persistence
- Sharing
- Resiliency
- Consistency
- Associative access or query
- Views

We will briefly define what we mean by each of these terms. To a large extent, the experimentation and development of research systems is trying to answer the question of how well can a given mix of database features be implemented in the context of an object-oriented language, and still achieve an acceptable level of performance as a database system.

Persistence refers to the ability for objects to outlive the process that created them. A persistent object exists in a database that is not dependent on any single computational entity. It has the ability to store a very large number of objects, more than will fit into the virtual memory of a process. This memory space typically provides some special storage structures (e.g., B-trees) that allow this very large collection of objects to be searched and accessed efficiently.

The persistent memory space is shared by many concurrently operating processes. That is, the system must be designed to service requests from many application programs in such a way as to maximize the amount of concurrency. The level of sharing is usually the object.

The database must also be resilient or fault tolerant in the sense that if a system failure occurs (hardware or software) inconsistencies are prevented. The conventional approach to resiliency is to require that applications divide their work into transactions. The system will guarantee that a transaction either completes successfully or has no effect on the database at all. This guarantee is a logical result of the atomic nature of transactions. OODBMSs are no exception here. Their transaction models are very similar to those of relational DBMS's. A few have added some extensions to address the needs of cooperative transactions, but there is little agreement about how this should be done.

Databases are accessed by many programs each of which is a potential source of inconsistency if the author of a program does not exercise the proper care. In order to guard the database against such errors, one might describe to the database system a set of constraints that must always be satisfied. Any program that attempts to violate these constraints should be blocked by the system. These constraints are usually captured in terms of some predicate calculus based language. There is naturally an interest in enriching the type systems of object- oriented databases to incorporate this type of constraint knowledge. Object- oriented database systems do not support generalized constraint management; however, they often build in some useful constraints. For example, ObjectStore supports the automatic maintenance of inverse relationships.

Another characteristic that needs to be addressed by an OODBMS is that of associative access or query languages. Relational databases have been very successful at achieving this capability. Much current research is focused on the question of how OODBMSs can be as successful at the expression and efficient evaluation of queries. A query algebra is often viewed as a set of operations that are defined on collection types plus a sublanguage for constructing predicates over these collections. The difficult problem involves the optimization of queries in a context which is extensible and in which the details of storage are encapsulated or hidden from the interface. How can the optimizer discover equivalence preserving transformations when queries can contain arbitrary combinations of user-defined operations? How can the optimizer figure out when a transformation is cheaper than the original if the storage representation is hidden?

Finally, views are an important part of any relational database system. They provide an extra level of data independence and thus support schema evolution and application development. They are also used as a way to provide security by restricting what a user can access. These views are normally provided through declarative mappings specified using a query language.

OODBMS products do not typically provide such a view facility. There have been several proposals in the literature [AB91, Day89, HZ90, Cru92, Rud92], but there is little agreement here on how a view mechanism should operate. All of these proposals have something in common with our intuitive notion of views, but they also differ from each other in fundamental ways. The development of an object-oriented view capability is complicated by such model features as object identity. What are the identities of the objects in a view? Object-oriented view mechanisms are an important area for further research.

4 OODBMS Architecture

At this point, we might ask whether or not an OODBMSs are simply a fancier replacement for relational database system. Certainly, we have described many new features in the model that are distinct from their relational counterparts. For example, relational systems do not embrace such notions as object identity of inheritance. Some people have argued that the correct approach is to extend relational systems with these new features. We would then have a more expressive model that would be compliant with the systems that went before.

The rest of this section will examine this view. We will try to determine whether the extended relational approach gets us to the same point as an OODBMS. In order to do this we will look at some examples of the fundamental architectural assumptions of an OODBMS.

4.1 Problems with Conventional Approaches

Let us begin by considering the way in which relational database systems (In fact, all traditional database systems) work from the point of view of the application. An application program often sends a request in the form of a query to the DBMS as a request for data. This data is returned to the application and placed in its local virtual memory. The application then performs its computation and returns this data to the database upon completion.

If we look at Fig. 1, we clearly see that there are always two distinct memory spaces, one that corresponds to the virtual memory of the application and another that corresponds to the database or the disk. We will further note that each of these memory spaces has distinct functionality. The memory space of the database supports things such as concurrency control, recovery, and queries; however, it does not typically contain the power of arbitrary computation. The language of the database system is by design limited and is exemplified by a language like SQL. While SQL has many virtues, it is not computationally complete. On the other hand, the memory of the application has the power to perform arbitrary computation through a computationally complete programming language. It does not, however, support any of the database features listed previously.

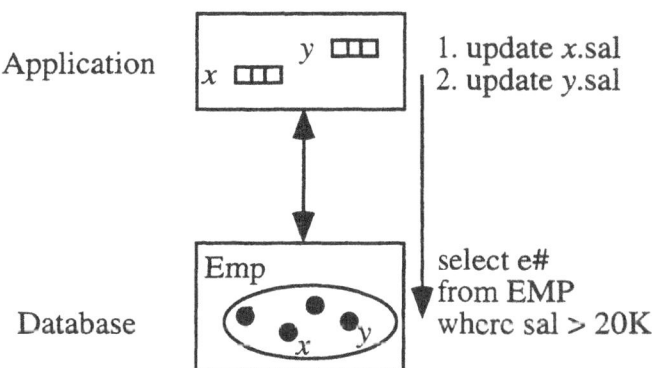

Fig. 1. The two memory space model

The fracture between these two memory spaces exists largely for historical reasons. The programming language world grew up around managing computations in RAM, while the database world concerned itself with protecting the concurrently accessed, persistent data on the disk. The result from the programmers point of view is additional complexity. The programmer must always be aware of where a given piece of data resides and what kind of computation is required of it. If the programmer wants to associatively search a huge amount of data, the database is likely to be the most efficient place to do that.

In the example of Fig. 1, the programmer wishes to first update the salaries of employees x and y. Perhaps the computation of their new salaries involves a complex calculation, something which is beyond the power of SQL. In this case, the data for x and y are read into the application program. Here, the computation is performed using a general-purpose programming language. Suppose that the next step is to find all of the employees who make more than $20K. This is a query and must be sent to the database system. If the programmer forgot to send the updates to x's and y's salaries back to the database, this query may get the wrong answer.

Fig. 1 also illustrates one additional disadvantage to this approach. Notice that the shape of x and y are different in the two memory spaces. This is meant to illustrate the fact that the type systems of these two memory spaces are different. Therefore, whenever data is moved between them, it must be translated. This difference in type systems is often called the *impedance mismatch* problem. It is undesirable because there is always some performance penalty to the translation process, and it is potentially error-prone.

4.2 Database Programming Languages

A better approach would be to create a single-level memory space. In this view, there is only one memory that supports all of the capabilities of both the database and the virtual memory in the previous model. That is, this store would support queries, concurrency control, recovery, consistency constraints, and general- purpose computation. Since there is only one store, there is only one type system, thereby eliminating the impedance mismatch problem. While this store might be supported by many different physical memories such as disks and RAM, from the programmer's point of view, there is a single memory abstraction (see Fig. 2).

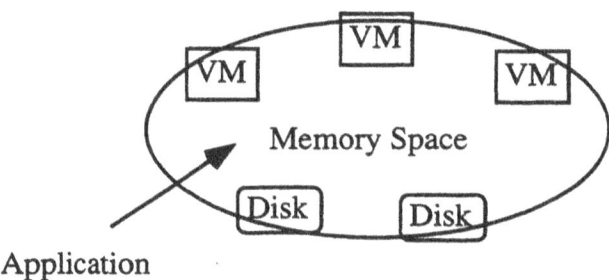

Fig. 2. Uniform memory space

If we, then, wrap the control structures of some programming language around this uniform memory space, we end up with what has been called a *database programming language* (DBPL). A DBPL is a programming language that contains database features embedded in it. The coupling between the database and the programming language in a DBPL is much tighter than in the conventional architecture.

A DBPL is a language that includes a way to create and manipulate persistent objects within the same type system as non-persistent objects. A DBPL, therefore, has a single type system that masks the existence of special mechanisms to deal with the disk.

The reason for all of this discussion is that if one looks at most of the commercial OODBMSs that are available today, one finds that they are, in fact, DBPL's. They are much more than a conventional database system that supports a more complex model. They are complete programming languages containing database features such as transactions and queries.

OODBMSs, then, are the first widely-accepted commercial DBPL's. (An exception to this is MUMPS, a non-object-oriented DBPL that has been used extensively in medical computing). The significance of the fact that object- oriented databases are really DBPL's is that they offer a better environment for crafting quality software for applications that need access to complex persistent data. As we will discuss later in this paper, though, there are serious problems with the current view of DBPL's.

5 Using an OODBMS

A type-extensible database system, such as the OODBMSs that we have been discussing, can provide the basis for an all-encompassing information *repository*. By this we mean a storage system that allows us to store all of our persistent information. The closest that we come to this currently is the file system. The main problem with a file system is that it does not view the contents of a file at a very high semantic level. To the file system, a file is a named collection of bytes. Some file systems support slightly more semantic content in the form of collections of records, but nothing more sophisticated than that.

5.1 A Generalized Repository

A repository must be able to store many diverse kinds of information within the same linguistic context. It must be possible to relate all objects using the same modeling mechanisms. A repository for a software engineering environment, for example, might want to store program specifications, code, documentation, employee records, and test plans. It should be possible to relate a code object to its specification using the same mechanism that we use to relate a piece of documentation to the employee who wrote it.

In this way, all persistent data can take advantage of the basic functionality of the database system. The concurrency control and recovery facilities are available for all objects. It should be possible to write a query that involves objects of many complex types - not just records. For example, one could ask for all programs that were written by John before last May that are documented in the User's Guide.

Adopting this point of view makes the file system unnecessary, at least at the level of the user. A file system might, however, provide the basic underlying support for the OODBMSs.

If we take the repository depicted in Fig. 3 and look below the interface, we might see something like Fig. 4. In this picture, the interface portrayed in Fig. 3 is at the top. The boxes labeled **Tuple, Set, String**, and **Stack** represent types. The dark circles beneath each of the types represent instances of that type. The **Stack** type is separated from the rest to indicate that it has been added by a user while the three types on the left are built-in types. The shaded boxes labeled **push** and **pop** represent the code for the methods of this new type.

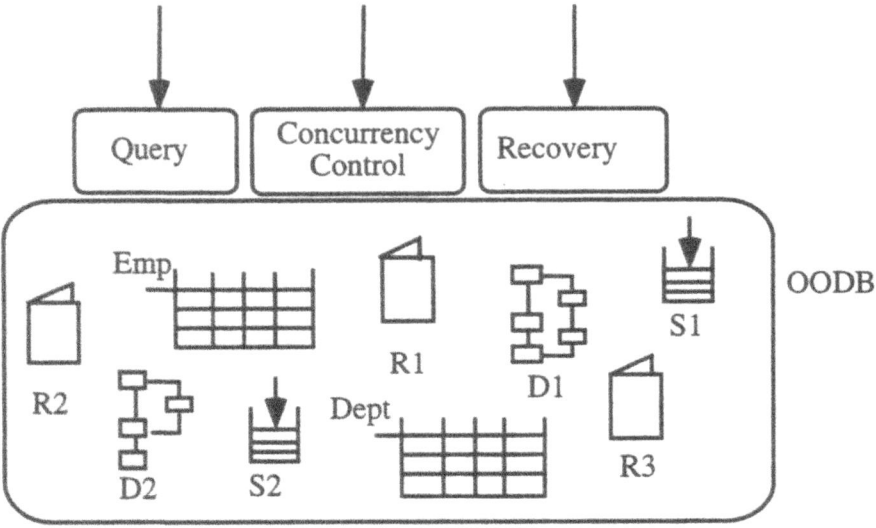

Fig. 3. A software environment in an OODBMS

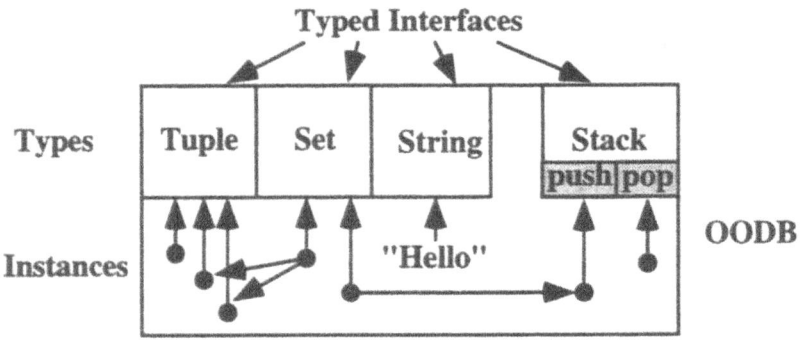

Fig. 4. Inside the repository

Notice that one of the two set instances points to two tuple objects. This represents a set of tuples or a relation. Similarly, the second set object points to a stack. This represents a singleton set of stacks. In this way, collection types can be used to aggregate both built-in and user-defined types. This preserves the *orthogonality* of the type system.

5.2 Code in the Database

As in Fig. 4, an OODBMS allows users to create new abstract types and to implement these types by writing programs that support their methods. These programs are placed "in the database" for the database management system to use. What does it mean, in this case, to have code in the database? It could certainly mean that the code is stored and managed by the database system instead of the file system, and this is true of some

OODBMSs. Code can be shared in the same way as data through the database interface, but is this all?

Code can also be shared and reused through a shared library. Is there a difference between a shared library and the method code in an OODBMS? The key to answering this question lies in the observation that the method code extends the available semantics of the database. It is now possible to do more things at a higher level of discourse. The importance of putting code in a database is not simply the potential for code sharing but rather the opportunity for the DBMS to use this additional semantics to reason more effectively about the data. As we add more semantics to the database, the database system can do more on our behalf.

If we look at the historical development of persistent storage systems, the level of stored semantics has been steadily increasing. As the semantics increased, so did the things that the DBMS could do. Consider the move from plain uninterpreted files to files with some structure (e.g., record-oriented file systems). This allowed the system to do useful things like the construction and maintenance of indices. Index maintenance can not have be contemplated without knowledge of the structure of the file.

When we moved to bona fide database management system like CODASYL or IMS, the DDL supported the specification of specialized integrity constraints. The system could, then, automatically maintain the invariants that they describe. For example, it is possible in CODASYL to describe set membership as *mandatory* or *optional*. If a set instance was created with no members for a mandatory set the system could detect this and raise an exception.

With relational systems and their declarative query languages, it became possible to reason about alternative query execution plans. This led to the very important technology of query optimization.

In general, it is better to put semantic knowledge closer to the data. Of course, this raises the question of whether or not the database system is up to the task of exploiting this information. This is really the challenge of making OODBMS technology work. As new types are added, how can more meaningful semantics for these types be described, and how can the system use this information to advantage?

OODBMSs already make good use of some of the knowledge that is embodied in abstract type definitions. For example, since they understand what constitutes an instance of a type and a method for objects of that type, they can decide whether to execute this method on the workstation or on the server. This could involve moving the method to the object or moving the object to the method. In either case, the OODBMS can make this decision independently of the user program.

Other examples of how OODBMSs make use of object semantics includes maintaining stored extents for certain types, maintaining inverse relationships, and managing the loading of client caches automatically whenever an object is referenced.

There are opportunities for exploiting this semantics to a much greater extent than it is being used today. For example, an OODBMS could allow more concurrency than can be achieved using simple read/write locks if the concurrency control manager has access to type-level semantics. This can be seen from the example in Sect. 8 on transactions.

The extent to which useful semantics of new types can be expressed in a form that the system can use is an important research question. Are there formalisms that can be used for this purpose? Currently, a type specification consists largely of syntactic signatures for the operations of that type. Research is needed to better understand type specification mechanisms that allow the system to do more sophisticated concurrency control, integrity management, or query optimization.

5.3 A *Gedanken* Experiment

Let us ask a question whose answer may never be realized in practice, but which might shed some light on this new technology. We have already established that application-level code might be used to extend the database system, but to what extent may this occur?

Consider a conventional database application with a relational database running in one process and an application running in another. Now, suppose that the conventional database is replaced by an OODBMS. At this point, someone notices that there is a piece of the conventional application that corresponds to an identifiable object type, say a **Stack**. The code is repackaged as an object type, removed from the application code, and moved across the boundary to the database process. Soon, someone else notices that other opportunities exist to move code in the form of new object types into the database. Slowly, the application code shrinks. This process is repeated until there is no longer any application code that lives outside of the database system. In other words, the database has subsumed all of the once external application code.

Is this possible in an OODBMS? The answer to this question has to be yes. It is not clear, however, that one would want to place all of the application code in the database in a real application. For example, the interface code that runs the display might make more sense to keep in a separate process, but, at least in theory, the database extensions could subsume the entire application. This idea is also consistent with the notion of a database programming language in which application development is done in a context that includes all of the database features.

6 Implementation Considerations

The object-oriented data model and the software architectures that support them present difficult implementation challenges. Some of these challenges have to do with providing traditional database services in the presence of an extensible data model. Other challenges are provided by the distributed client/server environments in which OODBMSs operate.

Like most DBMS implementations, OODBMSs tend to be composed of two logical components. The lowest level component is usually called the *storage* or the *object server*. It is responsible for moving data from the server disk into the workspace of the next level. The object server is also responsible for managing concurrency control and recovery. It typically supports a rather low-level data model, one that is much simpler than the full-fledged model of abstract types.

The layer above this is normally the *object model interpreter*. It is responsible for providing the semantics of the full data model. It is this layer in which types, methods, and inheritance are captured. The API of this layer is the one that is identified as the OODBMS and is accessed directly by application code.

The network connection must be accounted for somewhere in this architecture. It can occur at the border between the object server and the object model interpreter, but more commonly it divides one of these components. It could divide the object server, thereby putting a piece of the object sever on the workstation. It could alternatively divide the interpreter, thereby placing part of the interpreter on the server machine. Both of these alternatives have been proposed and implemented in practice.

The next few sections are not meant to be a catalog of OODBMS implementation techniques. They are simply meant to sketch typical issues that arise in making this model work.

6.1 Prefetching and Caching

For many design applications, being able to traverse a graph structure efficiently is of key importance. A CAD tool like a design rule checker requires that given a circuit component, connections to other components can be followed quickly. If a program accesses a circuit board, it will often next require the back plane to which the board is connected. Although this kind of access can be viewed as a degenerate query, other implementation techniques might be more useful than techniques that have been designed for queries over large sets.

One of the principal ways to improve performance in this situation is to minimize the probability that traversing an edge in the graph will cause a disk fault. This can best be done with intelligent prefetching. Often a scheme is used that allows that applications to create arbitrary sized collections of objects called segments that are stored contiguously on the disk. Whenever any object in a segment is accessed, the entire segment is read (prefetched) into the memory of the application. If the segments are set up properly, this will reduce the number of disk faults.

Determining how to configure automatically a set of segments for a particular pattern of accesses is an area that requires more research. Currently this is the job of the database type designer (formerly the DBA). If this person does a good job, performance will improve, but if they are not able to predict the future with a fair degree of accuracy, they can actually make matters worse.

Using learning algorithms to predict good clustering and/or prefetch units based on access histories is a promising new research direction. Experimental systems have been constructed with very encouraging results. FIDO [PZ91] was an experimental system that could learn prefetch patterns using a simple nearest-neighbor algorithm. It was able to improve performance on traces from a CAD tool by a factor of two. Another interesting experiment [CKV93, VK91] used compression algorithms and achieved a factor of three improvement on the same trace data.

6.2 Persistent Pointer Management

Pointers based on the identity of an object are critical to the implementation of any object model. However, object pointers are implemented differently in virtual memory than they are on disk. This is because in RAM, memory addresses are the most efficient choice. These addresses cannot, in general, be stored in the corresponding disk representation since next time the object is brought into virtual memory, it is unlikely that it end up in the same location or that the object to which it refers will be in the same location.

Most systems, then, use a different scheme for disk based pointers. A common choice uses the unique object identifier (oid) that is assigned to the object when it is created. In order to dereference this kind of pointer, the system must look it up in a hash table to determine its location on the disk. This can be somewhat expensive.

A major contribution to the implementation of these systems has come to be known as *pointer swizzling*. Pointer swizzling refers to the act of switching a virtual memory address for a disk based address when an object is brought into RAM and returning the disk-based pointer when it is written out again. In this way, the first access to a pointer will be expensive if the referenced object is not in RAM, but subsequent accesses to this pointer will run at standard memory speeds. This amortizes the cost of going to the disk and doing the hash over many uses of the reference.

6.3 Indexing

Another classic way to improve the performance of a database is to introduce auxiliary access methods that can be used to limit the amount of search that needs to be done. Indices have normally been used in this way to increase the ability of the system to process queries efficiently. Indices on method results introduce problems for OODBMSs [MS86, Zdo89]. Unless we restrict the kinds of indices that can be constructed, it is difficult to know when an index requires updating.

The reason for this last statement is that index maintenance is very difficult when it depends on the behavior of an arbitrary piece of code. Building the index I for a method m on set S is easy although it could take a large amount of time. A naive algorithm would simply apply the method m to every object in S and invert the results [KKM91]:

$$I(S, m) = \{(m(x), x)|x \in S\} \tag{2}$$

Since the computation of m can involve an arbitrary number of objects in the database, a change to any one of these objects can potentially invalidate the index. How is the system to know what indices might be invalidated when a given object is updated?

Path indices have been studied in the literature [KM90a, KM90b]. A *path expression* is equivalent to function composition. For example, if e is an employee, then *e.dept.manager* is a path expression that first applies the *dept* function to e and then applies the *manager* function to that result. The partial graph that is traversed in computing this result is called a *path*. A path index expresses the relationship between an object and an object that lies at the end or along a path. Indexes of this form can be useful in processing query expressions that involve path expressions in their predicates.

Index structures can be useful for managing large collections of objects or for handling single very large objects (e.g., bit maps). The EXODUS storage system [CDRS86] constructs a tree for large objects, thereby increasing the efficiency of retrieving smaller pieces. The tree structure allows us to access a sequence of bytes from the middle without having to read the entire object.

7 Query Processing

A query is a high-level specification of a set of objects of interest from the database. It is usually specified in a special language that describes what must be retrieved without requiring a statement of how to do it. The query processor figures out the most efficient plan for the retrieval. Query languages and their associated optimizers have been one of the major achievements of the relational approach. OODBMS products typically provide a simple query facility with some support for optimization [OHMS92]. However, there is still a great deal of research required to achieve the full potential of an extensible query facility.

Some extensions to existing relational query languages have been proposed [BKK88, CDV88] They embed object-oriented facilities in relational languages like SQL. Another approach is to propose a set of operations that can be applied to aggregate objects, thereby providing an object-oriented query algebra [Osb88, Zdo89, SZ90, SÖ90a, Abi90]. Once these primitive operations are well-understood, a more user-oriented language can be designed on top of them.

Non-first normal form relations (NF2) [DKA$^+$86, Kor88] were introduced to address the problem of expressing complex objects with components that can structured objects themselves. They extend the conventional relational model by allowing the value of an attribute (i.e., the contents of a cell) to be a record, a vector or another relation. OODBMSs solve this problem, but they also introduce ideas of identity, data abstraction and inheritance. In these models, additional operators to deal with the nesting of structure are added to the basic repertoire of relational operators. The most notable examples of this include the *nest* and *unnest* operators.

Queries in the object-oriented data model can be cast as expressions over special methods defined on the types that are defined for aggregating objects (e.g., **Set**, **List**, **Tree**). As a simple example, the Type **Set** would define a method *Select*: $S1$: *Set*(T) × P: *Predicate* → $S2$: *Set*(T). The predicate is a function of the form P: T → *Boolean*. The output $S2$ is a subset of the elements of the first input argument $S1$ such that they satisfy the predicate P. That is, $Select(S,P) = \{s \mid s \in S \text{ and } P(s)\}$. This *Select* operation would be part of an object-oriented query algebra, and is similar to the *Select* operation in the relational algebra.

Why is querying any different in an object-oriented data model than in the relational model? As mentioned above, we can construct an algebra for expressing queries over sets of objects. One problem involves the optimization of these expressions [MDZ94]. In the relational model, queries are cast in terms of well-defined operators over very simple structures (i.e., normalized relations). The predicates are boolean combinations of simple terms. In the object-oriented data models, queries can involve operators for newly defined abstract data types (typically in the predicates). Each new type, by introducing new operations, creates a new algebra whose properties are unknown to the query optimizer. Without knowing the algebraic properties of these new operators, it becomes difficult to transform query expressions into alternative equivalent forms.

This problem has been addressed in [GD87]. Here the optimizer is extended by supplying it with transformation rules to cover new data model features. These rules transform query trees with operations for internal nodes and stored data for leaf nodes into equivalent query plans. A plan is also a tree with lower-level access operators as

internal nodes and data sets as leaf nodes. Derivatives of this work have been applied
to the construction of real optimizers [BMG93].

Another approach to this problem is being explored by the EPOQ object-oriented
optimizer [MDZ93, MZD92]. The EPOQ architecture is extensible by being open. New
modules can be added to augment the repertoire of optimization techniques available to
the optimizer. The way in which the optimizer controls the use of these modules is also
extensible.

Another problem involves the information hiding presented by abstract types. Even
if we could produce transformed versions of queries, we need to be able to determine
the relative costs of processing these query expressions. Processing costs are typically
dependent on the underlying storage structures for the objects and their aggregates. For
example, if a given set S is implemented by a B-tree on some attribute A, then retrievals
over S on attribute A will likely be relatively inexpensive. Knowing about the existence
of such storage structures seems to be a violation of encapsulation. Although this is true,
encapsulation is a principle of good software structuring that is important to preserve
between application-level modules. The query optimizer is a trusted component of the
database system and can be allowed to look inside an abstract data type and determine the
implementation. There is still a question about how this can be effectively managed if the
implementation can be arbitrary other types. Recent work [GM88, Dan91] has suggested
a technique called revelation by which an abstract data type can reveal to the optimizer
details about its implementation. This revealed behavior is given as expressions that are
equivalent to pieces of the query but that are in terms of lower-level implementations.

Yet another problem is concerned with the need to query arbitrary aggregate or
bulk types. This might include unusual types such as lists, arrays, trees, or matrices. In
these cases, ordering and dimensionality present problems to the query formalisms that
were invented to deal with relations. Relational query languages like SQL do not have
facilities to deal with ordering, for example. This opens a new area for research. How
should ordering be reflected in a data model and in an algebra for querying it?

As an example of the problem, consider a bulk type called **List** that models un-
bounded, linear sequences. Since instances of this type contain elements that are ordered, we might reasonably want to retrieve subsequences that are sensitive to this order.
In other words, we need a predicate language that allows us to express patterns over
linear orders. As an example, perhaps we could use regular expressions as this pattern
language. Thus, we might be led to queries of the following form.

Select(Powerlist(L), $\lambda x.x \in ab * cd$)

This query would compute the set of subsequences of the sequence L that are in the
language specified by the given regular expression. The powerlist is defined to be all
possible subsequences of a list L. *Powerlist* is a useful construct for forming queries,
but would certainly never be generated in the actual computation. Notice that the result
does not record where the subsequence occurred in the original list. Additional operators
would be needed to provide this functionality.

Given such a query expression, the challenge becomes how to optimize its execution.
This would require special pattern indices on sequences or lists that record where patterns
of interest begin. The exact form of these indices is a research problem.

A query optimizer would also need transformation rules [BK90] that involve predicates that contain patterns. For example, if we assume that we have indices over patterns, it would be useful to have composition rules for pattern queries. For our example query given above, we might transform it into the following equivalent query.

Select (
  Maximal_Prefix(Powerlist(L), $\lambda p.p \in cd$), $\lambda x.x =? * ab * cd$)

The *Maximal_Prefix* operator applied to a list L and a pattern P returns the set of all sublists of L that begin at the beginning ofL and that contain the given pattern as its suffix. Thus,

Maximal_Prefix(L, P) =
  Select(Powerlist(L), $\lambda 1.1 = wp$ and $p \in P$ and Prefix(L, w))

The revised query will first find all the substrings rooted at the beginning of L that end in cd. This might be available from an index. Then, these lists are searched from the end to see if the cd is preceded by a sublist in the pattern $ab*$.

Augmenting our query formalisms to accommodate advanced bulk types and adding transformations like the one illustrated by the above example deserves further research. The previous example is offerred as an example of the kinds of things that we might like to do, not as a solution. This area also illustrates the need to include additional type-level semantics in our OODBMS so that they can perform more powerful reasoning for us.

8 Transactions

In order to preserve the correctness of the database in the face of concurrently executing processes, database systems support atomic transactions. Transactions are units of work that, when allowed to proceed concurrently, are guaranteed to produce results that are equivalent to the results produced by some serial execution. We say that any interleaving of operations that preserves this property is *serializable*.

There have been many implementations proposed that are guaranteed to produce serializable executions. These are largely based on read/write semantics. That is, reads and writes on a data item x are defined to conflict with other writes on x. The data manager can then make decisions (e.g., when to schedule a read or write) that will ensure serializability.

OODBMSs present an opportunity to do better than more traditional approaches [Wei88]. In the object-oriented approach, the database system knows more about the operations that are being performed. They are not simply reads or writes, but rather have more semantics. For example, for a **Queue** data type, we would have *enqueue* and *dequeue* operations. From some point of view, these operations can both be considered to be writes since they both modify the state of the queue. However, if we take the special semantics of these operators into account, we can achieve a higher degree of concurrency.

The **Queue** type models a simple FIFO data structure. There is an operation call $enqueue(Q, x)$ that puts a new data item x onto a queue Q and another operation called

$dequeue(Q)$ that removes and returns a data item from the other end of the queue Q. If we have a queue object Q and two transactions T_1 and T_2, and T_1 has done an enqueue on Q, then T_2 would be prevented from doing a dequeue on Q by common read/write semantics until T_1 has committed. However, if we notice that for non-empty queues, these two operations do not effect each other's result as expressed by the following commutativity axiom,

$$Notempty(Q) \Rightarrow enqueue(Q, x); dequeue(Q) = dequeue(Q); enqueue(Q, x) \quad (3)$$

we can allow them to proceed without a conflict. In this case, the concurrency control manager is able to exploit the commutativity semantics of these two operators.

For cooperative applications, like those seen in design environments the notion of serializability is too strong a correctness criterion [KS88]. Designers interact with many of the objects in their environment by using graphics-oriented editors. If we consider a session with an editor (or group of editors) as a transaction, serializability gets in the way. Designers do not serialize. They instead share information with each other in incomplete states. Furthermore, a single transaction T might touch objects that are connected through complex integrity constraints with a large number of other objects. If T is to check and adjust the state of these object such that they remain consistent, then T must acquire locks (read or write) on all of them. This reduces the amount of concurrency that is possible between long design transactions. Schemes have been proposed [NRZ92] to allow users to customize the correctness criteria that are imposed by the system.

The anticipated environment for these databases is in a network of workstations. Typically one of these workstations or some bigger machine (or machines) is designated as an object server which supplies objects to the workstations and their application programs as needed. Communication between the workstations and the server must be minimized. Most database systems require that the transactions that interact with it produce results such that the resulting schedule is serializable [BHG87]. Achieving this condition often requires a great deal of communication. At the end of each transaction, all objects that have been touched must be written back to the server.

In order to minimize the amount of communication between the client and the server and to facilitate more flexible sharing protocols, the ObServer system [HZ87] provides a rich set of lock types. The *notify* lock can be used by a process P to read a copy of an object x such that there is no guarantee that the state of the object remain stable. Instead, the system guarantees that if the state of x changes, P will be notified. P may then opt to reread the value of x. The write-keep lock can be used by a process P on an object x to indicate that it will not return this object to the server until some other process requests it. In this way, P is taking over the responsibility of the database system for object x. These two lock types provide a communication on demand situation between the client and server. It is possible to construct non-serializable interactions with primitives like these; therefore, they should be used with care.

9 Distributed Databases

OODBMSs have been designed to support complex applications like design that will largely run on high-performance workstations. Each designer will have a workstation that will interact with other workstations and a few larger server machines through a local-area network. Some data will be stored on shared data servers, while other data will reside locally on the secondary storage of the workstation. It is also unlikely that a single server will supply all of the data storage needs of a large design environment. We must therefore confront the additional problems presented by an environment that is inherently distributed. The Emerald system was an early attempt to introduce distribution into a distributed computing environment. THOR [LGJS90] is a research prototype that is currently under development. It is an object-oriented, distributed DBMS that concentrates on high-availability and high-reliability.

In order to simplify programming and preserve data independence, one of the goals of existing distributed database implementations is *transparent distribution*. That is, it should be possible to name the data in the same way as in centralized databases. The system is responsible for locating the required data items and for updating them atomically. In this way, programmers need only worry about logical issues. As the data is redistributed through the network, the programs remain invariant and the system can produce new optimizations for processing queries that require data from different sites.

Distributed databases have been discussed in the literature for some time, and they are now becoming a commercial reality. Previous discussion was largely in the context of relational systems. It is worthwhile asking if the object-oriented approach raises any additional problems or facilitates any new solutions.

One opportunity for better performance in an object-oriented framework comes from the fact that programs (i.e., methods or operations) are objects. As such they can be moved around the distributed database just like any other object. In performing a computation or processing a query, the system has the choice of moving the data to the programs or of moving the programs to the data. Often when executing a method M on a very large object x, it is more reasonable to move M to the machine on which x resides instead of moving x to the site of M.

Caching strategies are also relevant in a distributed system. As objects move from machine to machine, retaining local copies for some period of time can often shorten subsequent retrievals.

The interpretive nature of object-oriented systems can create performance problems that are particularly acute in the distributed environment if object placement is not done carefully. Late binding of method names to method bodies requires looking at several objects in order to determine what code needs to be run. Minimizing communications by careful object placement and by an intelligent planner will make a huge difference in the performance of a distributed OODBMS. The planner will determine the order in which to perform operations, the machine on which to perform them, and the location that should receive the result.

A major problem imposed by the application environment is one of interoperability among heterogeneous systems. This problem is exacerbated in a distributed environment because there is little control over the characteristics of the participating systems. This heterogeneity can take several forms. There can be differences in the underlying data formats of the participating tools and systems, differences in the languages used for developing applications, and differences in the way that designers need to share information.

OODBMSs might be used to address some of these problems of interoperability. Their abstraction mechanisms can be used to build bridges to existing data repositories. Consider an abstract type as depicted in Fig. 5(a). The type T supports three methods and stores its state in an internal representation that is pictured as a record labeled *rep*. Since *rep* is hidden, it can be any structure and it can be supported by any persistent storage system. Figure 5(b) shows the same type T supported by a *rep* that is stored in an external SQL database. From the point of view of an application program that uses T, there is no difference between Fig. 5(a) and Fig. 5(b).

In this way, a pre-existing data storage system can become the implementation vehicle for new abstract types. The representation for the new type could be a data structure that is supported by a foreign data repository. Whenever a method of this new type is invoked, the method code would make a call to the external repository in order to access the external representation. An old application would access and update persistent data in the same way as it always did, but new applications would access it through abstract types that are defined in the object-oriented schema (see Fig. 5). Although this might be somewhat slow, the ability to access data across different storage systems is a piece of functionality that is very valuable.

In Fig. 5(c), we have show an object-oriented database with an interface that consists of four abstract types. From the point of view of a new application using this database, everything looks very uniform. However, in reality, two of these types are supported by two different external databases and two of the types are supported by the persistent data structures of the object-oriented database.

10 Other Features

The literature on OODBMSs often discuss a few other features that are related to the requirements of design applications. It can be argued that these features are not required for a system to qualify as a an OODBMS. However, they would be very useful to any database system for CAD applications. A few of these features include version control, complex objects and long (and cooperative) transactions.

A version management facility within an OODBMS permits us to look at an object as a set of snapshots over time. Several proposals have been offered in this area [CK86, KL84, KC87, KSW86, Zdo86]. Several questions arise. One set concerns the basic structure of a set of versions. Can a version history branch when more than one competing proposal for an object update occurs, especially when these competing versions conflict on some basic assumptions? Notice that this is what most pessimistic concurrency control schemes are designed to avoid. If the version history is allowed to fork, are there mechanisms to allow these competing alternatives to be merged? That is, can a branch in a set of versions come back together? Another set of questions has to do with how the members of a set of versions that are representing an object are referenced? Are they referenced statically (e.g., by version number) or can they be referenced by a more dynamic mechanism (e.g., the latest version). Notice that the latter case is analogous to a query.

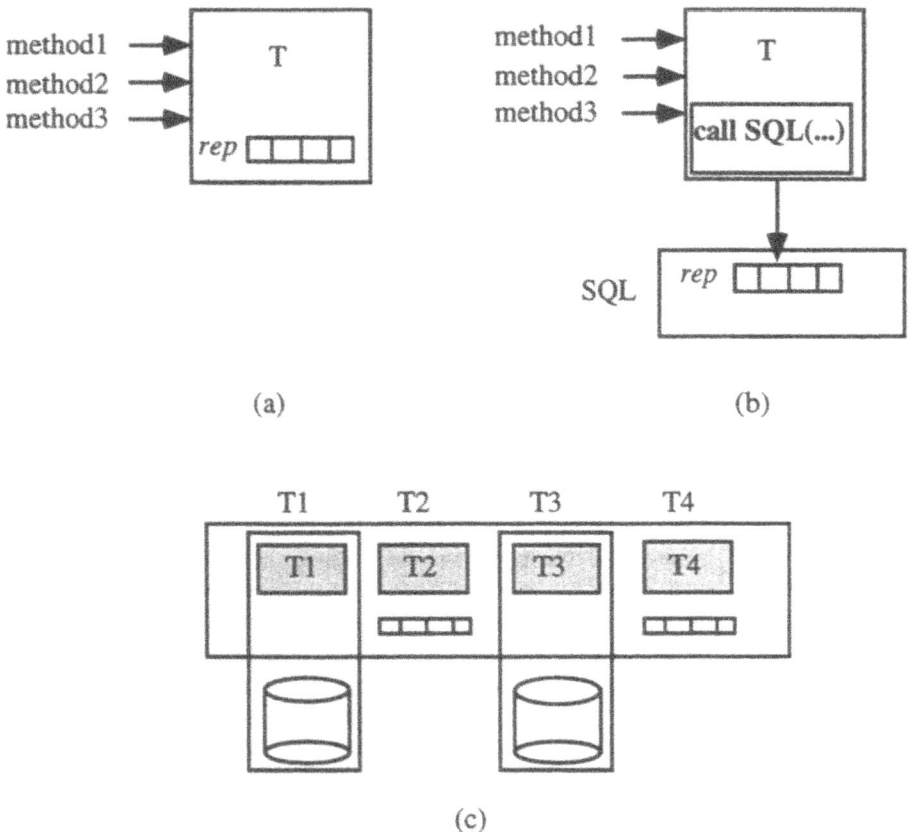

Fig. 5. Object-oriented approach to integration

Complex objects are an attempt to model objects that are built out of other objects [BK86, BB84, Day87b, KBC⁺87]. The crux of a complex object facility has to do with the semantics of the *part_of* relationship. Most work in this area is concerned with allowing the database system to ascribe additional behavior to the *part_of* relationship thereby affecting the behavior of other operations. An example of the kind of special behavior that one would want from such a facility is that when a containing object is deleted, the objects that are contained (i.e., objects that are related to it by the *part_of* relationship which we shall call components) should also be deleted. Furthermore, one might not be allowed to create the container without first creating its parts (or vice versa). The *copy* operation for a complex object might mean make a copy of the object plus all of its parts (i.e., components). [VKC86] investigates how access to complex objects can be optimized.

OODBMSs need good visual interfaces like other workstation software. How can one justify a textual interface like SQL in a world of windows, menus, and icons? Some work has been done on making database interfaces more accessible [GGKZ85, BH86, Cru92]. In some sense, hypermedia systems are really interfaces to large object bases.

Much of the work from this area could be transferred to general OODBMS interfaces.

The traditional notion of a database transaction is a very short piece of code that performed a very specific function on the database. The expected running time for such a transaction was likely measured in fractions of a minute. In the CAD world, a designer interacts with the database through some kind of graphical editor. If we view a session with one of these editors as a transaction, then we must face transactions whose running time might be measured in hours or days. This has an enormous impact on the kind of facility that we might want to manage transactions.

11 Summary

OODBMSs have been designed to meet some of the data handling needs of new, complex applications like those found in design environments. The data modeling facilities of these systems resemble on the surface many of the features found in object-oriented programming languages. It is important to note that these language features have to be embedded in a system that includes databases features like persistence, concurrency control, recovery, consistency management, and a query language. Often, the data model must be designed differently from the language counterparts in order to combine effectively database and programming language features. An example of this is the way in which the model incorporates constraints into an object-oriented type system.

The history of database management has seen many proposals for competing data models. Each model has its own set of strengths and weaknesses. The object- oriented approach has the ability to unify some of these dissimilar approaches by providing a model that is based on abstraction, and that allows type designers to use whatever technique best suits their applications as an implementation of basic functionality.

Based on the arguments in this paper, an OODBMS is more than simply a more powerful replacement for your current backend. Indeed, because of the tight coupling with a programming language and its extensibilty properties, an OODBMS presents a different paradigm for the development of data- intensive applications. In this paradigm, data and program are not as separate as they were in the past. Instead, they are designed, implemented, and used together.

We have seen that the field holds much promise for achieving a fully programmable database system. There are, however, research questions that still need to be addressed before the field can be considered mature. Research prototypes are being built to experiment with different ways of solving these problems.

SECTION 2

MODELS AND FORMAL LANGUAGES

Object-Oriented Data Model Concepts

Klaus R. Dittrich

Universität Zürich, Institut für Informatik, Winterthurerstrasse 190, CH-8057 Zurich, Switzerland

Abstract. A key concept of any database system is the data model it is based upon. Object-oriented data models (OODM) try to blend object-oriented concepts as they first emerged in programming languages with concepts from traditional (e.g. network or relational) data models, and at the same time respond to new requirements as they are posed by a variety of "nonstandard" application areas like CAD/CAM, geographic information systems, or office information systems. They are primarily used in object-oriented database management systems (OODBMS), but even traditional systems are about to adopt some of their features.

In this chapter, we first give a detailed explanation of the notion of data model in general, elaborate on the characteristics and shortcomings of "classical" data models, and motivate the introduction of OODMs. Afterwards, the mandatory and some optional ingredients of OODMs are explained. The chapter concludes by relating the data model to other issues in (object-oriented) database systems, and by discussing the state of the art and probable future developments.

It should be noted that the area of OODMs and systems is still in a phase of development where no general agreement on terms and concepts exists, and thus many variations for individual features can be found in the literature and in systems. The focus of this chapter is to give an introductory overview of the topic; it thus does not aim at a complete coverage of even all major approaches. It also describes the salient concepts in a rather abstract manner instead of referring to any particular system.

1 The Notion of "Data Model"

Automated problem solving requires the adequate representation of information about the relevant real world (usually called the "miniworld" or the "universe of discourse") in a form which can be "understood" and processed by the machinery to be used. In the case of digital computers, this *model* of the real world of interest has to be expressed by data which are coded and stored on appropriate devices, and by associated operations (programs) which determine how these data can be used in problem solving processes. Beyond, the expression of real world models in terms of data (and - even if often less explicit - operations) is also applicable for human communication, and indeed takes place in many cases.

Actually, there are two levels involved in data representations of a universe of discourse, the individual data themselves, and the structures into which these data are organized. As a matter of fact, we are often primarily interested in these structures, and only secondarily in the data it contains. Take for example the number "3000", which will probably only make sense to us if we know that it represents the salary of a specific employee (for whom also other data items like name, address, birthday, etc. are collected in a data structure).

In order for a machine (or another person!) to understand a model, it is essential that it is familiar with the repertoire of concepts used to build that model. In the context of computer programming and particularly databases, this is where the notion of "data model" emerges [Bro84]:

A *data model* is a set of conceptual tools for describing the representation of information in terms of data. It comprises aspects related to

- data types and structures,
- operations, and
- (consistency) constraints.

The specific description of a given miniworld in terms of a data model is called a *schema* (or data schema, database schema) for that miniworld. The collection of data themselves that represent the information about the miniworld forms the *database*. Thus we can also say that a schema describes a database (in that it reflects at least some of the "semantics" associated with these data). As a schema itself will have to be expressed by data, it is justified to speak about *metadata* .

Unfortunately, the notion of "data model" as it is now used in database technology has not been very well chosen: it is less a model itself than a framework to conceive models (of the real world). Nevertheless, as it is far too late to change terminology, we will stick to the given definition in the sequel. Whenever a "real" model is referred to, it will be clear from the context. Note, however, that other areas will make different use of terms (e.g. "enterprise data model" refers to the integrated, uniform schema for – ideally – all information available in an enterprise, and not to the data model in our sense used for such a description), which may easily lead to confusion.

Let us now explain the above-mentioned aspects of a data model in some more detail:

- **structural aspect:** We assume that our structural knowledge about miniworlds can be expressed in terms of the physical or logical "things" we can distinguish there (usually called "entities"), and in terms of associations (or relationships) among those entities.

  The structural part of a data model determines what kind of individual data items can be used in the description of database schemata, and how data can be organized into structures to model entities and their associations.

  Individual data items, also called *simple values*, include e.g. numbers like "7" or texts like "Kusadasi"; they will be used to represent individual properties of real world entities or associations. In a database schema, we have to specify a *value set* for each such property, and the data model tells us which value sets are at all available for this purpose. These value sets are either *predefined*, i.e., inherently incorporated in the data model, or *user-definable*, i.e., the data model provides means to specify them (e.g. by enumeration or by supplying some construction law).

Data structures or *composite values* are aggregations of other values; they will be primarily used to represent real world entities in their entirety (e.g. a specific employee who has various properties of interest), properties that are themselves composite (like e.g. the address of the employee), or associations among entities. In a database schema, we need to define the *structure type* (including the value sets it is built from) we want to use for the representation of composite properties, or of sets of entities or associations which have common properties (so-called entity types and association types). To this end, a data model provides some *constructors* that can be applied to build composite values (e.g. tuples, sets).

Since a data model is thought to describe entity and association types, the definition of individual value sets is only a means for the specification of structure types and does not make sense in its own right. Every data model thus has a notion of *"independently definable unit"* that determines which kinds of "first class" *elements* a corresponding database may contain.

Note that (simple and composite) values are principally *immutable*; any "modification" will result in a new value. As in a database we primarily want to deal with (changeable!) information about the **same** miniworld entities, data models (among other measures; see below) allow to associate names to (some) elements; a name may then refer to different values over time. This is similar to the distinction between constants and variables known from most programming languages.

Finally, for the practical use of a data model, some well-defined syntactical form is required to express the definition of schemata; a (sub)language serving that purpose is called a *data definition language* (DDL).

– **operational aspect:** This part of a data model determines how the defined values and structures can be operated upon; appropriate features are incorporated in *data manipulation* (sub)*languages* (DML).

Operations for simple values depend on the nature of the corresponding value set and include comparisons (e.g. "=", "≠", "<", etc.) and computations of new values out of given ones (e.g. "+", "-", etc. for numeric values). For composite values, access operations are provided to refer to their components. Furthermore, operations involving entire structures may exist, depending on the structure type (e.g. mathematical set operations).

For a database as a whole, the following four kinds of operations are required. They are partly based on the above-mentioned value operations and show considerable diversity in details from data model to data model; however, they are always based on the assumption that a database contains a potentially very large number of elements, out of which one or more have to be specified that are desired to be affected by those operations:

- **insertion** of new elements into the database (independently definable units in accordance with the data model and with the schema defined for the database),
- **deletion** of existing data elements,

- **modification** of existing data elements (i.e., replacement of individual values by other values),
- **retrieval** of existing data elements or parts thereof, based on various selection criteria to be specified.

Operations may be *generic* or (type-)*specific*. An operation is specific if it is defined for a particular value set or structure type, it is generic if it applies to **all** value sets/ structure types built by means of the same construction laws/constructors (e.g., tuple operators apply to any well-defined tuple, whatever the number, name and value set of the participating component attributes).

In a second dimension, we can further distinguish between *predefined* and *user-definable* operations. Predefined operations are a fixed part of the data model, user-definable ones can be introduced by users applying the data model; of course, those operations will be based on other (ultimately predefined) operations.

Finally, operations may refer to individual elements or to sets of elements. Especially for retrieval, we are often interested in finding the set of **all** elements meeting given selection criteria.

Combining user-definable value sets and user-definable type-specific operations, a data model may support the concept of *abstract data type* (ADT ; a more precise term is *user-defined data type* ; UDT). In this case, users associate specific semantics to "representational" values (mostly just byte strings) by defining interpretations in terms of operations for their use.

- **consistency aspect:** The choice of appropriate data structures together with the related operations of the data model will often be too coarse to exactly represent miniworld semantics. In this case, additional constraints (generally called consistency constraints or semantic integrity constraints) have to be specified, and a data model is required to provide appropriate support.

Consistency constraints can be classified along various dimensions. First, we distinguish between *internal* and *external constraints* : internal constraints are represented in one form or another in the database schema itself and thus need to be expressible in the data model, while external constraints cannot be expressed in the schema and thus remain under the responsibility of the application programmer. From a data model point of view, we are only concerned with internal consistency constraints.

Internal constraints can be further classified into inherent, implicit, and explicit ones. *Inherent consistency constraints* are directly built into the structural and operational features of a data model and do not require any direct specification during schema design (example: all values in a data model may be required to be atomic, i.e., not further divisible). *Implicit consistency constraints* are closely related to the structural and/or operational properties of a data model and can be specified during schema definition by means of the DDL. For example, an attribute in a tuple type may be defined to act as an identification key, which requires that at any time, no two tuples of that type in the database may have the same value for that attribute. *Explicit consistency constraints* include all other constraints that can be formulated within the framework of a data model, but will require a specific language (sometimes called a consistency definition language, CDL).

A second classification of internal constraints distinguishes between *static* and *dynamic constraints*. A static constraint always refers to a particular state of the database and determines whether it is admissible or not (e.g., "monthly salaries must not exceed US\$ 10.000"). In contrast, a dynamic constraint refers to the transition of the database from one state to another, and is thus closely tied to database operations (e.g., "salaries may never decrease"). While US\$ 7,000 and US\$ 6,500 would both be valid salaries under the first constraint, US\$ 6,500 is forbidden under the second constraint if the previous salary of the employee has been higher.

Obviously, it depends on the features available in a given data model whether some miniworld semantics can be expressed by internal constraints (if not by structural and operational features) or not. It is clearly desirable that the set of external constraints can be kept as small as possible for most applications.

The notion of data model as introduced above is purposely rather broadly defined. Depending on what kind of use they are thought for, three kinds of data models are usually distinguished [EN89]:

– conceptual data models,
– logical (or implementation) data models,
– physical data models.

Conceptual data models contain high-level features for modelling miniworlds irrespective of the concrete software to be used for implementation. Logical data models are those that are provided at the interface of software systems for data management; they still allow to describe the miniworld at a logical level. In contrast, physical data models are used for low-level descriptions of data referring to the physical storage and access structures available in a particular system. The level of abstraction provided thus decreases from conceptual via logical to physical data models.

The notion of data model is closely related to database management systems (DBMS) which provide standardized software for the reliable long-term management of large, integrated, multiuser databases. These systems support a logical data model and explicitly store the defined schemata together with the data themselves; it is thus not necessary to know any of the application programs to obtain information about what kind of data are in the database and what structures they are organized into. For the design of such databases, it is customary to use a conceptual data model.

Note, however, that the notion of data model is not necessarily confined to database systems. It also makes sense for example (though it is not very common) to talk about the data model of a programming language when considering its data declaration facilities and related operational aspects.

2 Traditional Data Models and their Shortcomings

Past and current mainstream DBMS-products typically implement one of the three "classical" approaches to data models, namely the hierarchical, the network, or the relational data model (or some derivative close in style and in the characteristics it offers). With respect to the issues discussed in the previous section, all these data models can be characterized as follows:

- structural aspect :
  - a (small) number of predefined (simple) value sets is provided, including e.g. various sorts of numbers, character strings, date, and time,
  - no user-definable value sets are supported,
  - a (small) number of constructors for composite values is provided, which can be applied in restricted ways only; for example, the relational model provides constructors for "set" and "tuple", however, only "sets of tuples of atomic values", called "relations", can be specified.
- operational aspect:
  - predefined type-specific and generic operations related to the given value sets and constructors, respectively, are provided, including appropriate insertion/deletion/modification/retrieval operations for databases,
  - no user-definable operations are supported.
- consistency aspect:
  - some inherent and implicit consistency features are supported,
  - typically no explicit consistency features are supported (though some systems have recently progressed into this direction [Ing89, Syb89]).

With regard to the first two aspects, these data models can be termed *record-oriented* in that they primarily support ("flat") records or homogeneous sets of such records, together with appropriate operations. However, more complexly structured information has to be split into smaller units during database design and operation. As a consequence, some salient semantics of appropriate applications cannot be expressed in the database, but will remain hidden in application programs. When operating on complexly structured data, they have to be (often repeatedly) reconstructed from the flat records during retrieval, which may lead to serious efficiency problems. A further loss of semantics (which may also lead to consistency problems) is incurred by the lack of user-definable operations for data structures. In fact, traditional data models do not directly support the representation of arbitrary information types; they rather include some preplanned "parameterized" structure types (like tuples where the user can decide on the number of attributes and the value sets admissible for them), and the desired types have to be expressed in terms of the provided ones. This again may result in more demanding database and application design, programming, and maintenance, and in efficiency problems during processing.

A further problem with traditional data models is that they are also *value- oriented*: all semantics are represented by the values of the stored data structures (and by the framework of these structures themselves). However, as values may be replaced by new values (and **any** value may, from the point of view of the data model), it may become difficult to recognize whether some modified data still represent the same real world entity (whose property values have changed), or some new entity that replaced a previously existing one.

This refers to the issue of *entity identity*: in the real world, every entity has its own identity, i.e. two distinct entities will always have an existence in their own right, even if they agree in the values of all their relevant properties (though it can be argued that there must be at least some property that allows to distinguish between the two - however, this property may be irrelevant from the applications' point of view, or even hard to detect;

see [Bee93] for a detailed discussion). Further, it is always possible in the real world to refer to the "same" object, even if some or all of its values change (because "identity" and "equality" are different concepts!).

In a value-oriented data model, it is difficult to maintain real world entity identity in the database. In fact, it is a matter of appropriate database design and operation, and the data model itself does not render specific services. Typically, one or more regular values will have to be used to represent entity identity. They can be designated as primary key, thus the data model will guarantee their uniqueness. However, applications still would have to make sure that such values are never changed as long as the represented entity exists in the database, or that it is possible by some other means to track the identity of an entity.

The features of traditional data models have proven to be rather adequate for many (also large-scale) applications in areas like administration and business data processing. However, the advent of numerous advanced database applications in areas like mechanical, electrical and electronic design (CAD-systems), manufacturing systems, software engineering (CASE-systems), office automation, knowledge engineering, and similar have clearly shown the shortcomings of traditional data models (see e.g. [Cat91] for examples and detailed discussions), and have been driving forces for new approaches. They include e.g. advanced semantic, functional, logic, and object-oriented data models (OODM). We will concentrate on the latter direction in the sequel which has proven to be the most fruitful area in the recent past.

3 The Quest for Object-Oriented Data Models

There are three major spheres of influence that fuelled the interest in OODMs:

- "academic curiosity" in regard of the advent of object-oriented systems in general, to exploit how those concepts transfer to the area of databases,
- the demand of object-oriented programming language users to store their data without suffering from the "impedance mismatch", and
- the shortcomings of traditional data models experienced in new advanced application areas, as explained above.

Beyond concepts of traditional and also extended semantic data models, the concepts of object-oriented systems in general as they mainly emerged from object-oriented programming languages have been most influential for OODM. In a nutshell, these concepts can be summarized as follows [Deu91a]:

- The universe of discourse is conceived and modelled as a collection of interrelated, possibly cooperating units, called *objects* .
- An object has a state (implemented by a data structure) and "understands" a number of *messages*; when it receives a message, it will execute an appropriate *method* (which may change the state and/or deliver some result to the sender of the message). With some simplification, we can regard messages and methods as the interfaces and implementations, respectively, of operations. While the state of an object and its methods are not visible for users of the object ("*encapsulation*", "information

hiding"), methods may include the sending of messages to other objects. Thus objects provide for *abstraction* and *autonomy*: they can be used without knowing more than their interface (users can abstract from all realization details), and they can be conceived without knowing about the environment of their future use (they are autonomous in how they provide their services).

- Similar objects are grouped into *classes*, and in fact classes are the units specified in an object-oriented system . A class acts as a pattern for the creation of its objects, and thus consists of a definition of the data structure used to represent the objects' state, a specification of the messages, and implementations for the methods. In addition to this intentional specification, the notion of class typically also refers to the extension, i.e. the set of objects of a class (often called its instances or members) available in the system at a specific point in time.

- Classes can be organized in a subclass/superclass structure to represent *taxonomies* in the real world. Subclasses *inherit* the properties of superclasses, i.e., instances of the subclass will also have the properties defined for the superclass.

Object-orientation allows to model systems in terms of units that closely resemble the units found in the miniworld. In particular, meaningful "higher-level" operations can be defined for classes that carry much more semantics than access-oriented operations in conventional data models. Thus object-oriented modelling provides for more "naturalness" of the abstract representation of real world information (as far as anything can be called "natural" when it comes to the use of computers!). Beyond, due to abstraction and inheritance in class hierarchies, object-orientation also supports evolutionary system design. New classes can be created by subclassing (and thus reusing) existing ones; thanks to the inheritance mechanisms, this "just" requires the realization of the new features that differentiate the new subclass from its superclass(es) ("incremental programming").

Though these advantages are first of all potential benefits that fully apply only if complemented by additional methodology and appropriate discipline, database researchers have soon become curious to see how object-oriented concepts blend with traditional database concepts. However, this scientific curiosity alone would not have been sufficient to explain the current popularity of OODM.

The demand for OODMs and, more importantly, appropriate DBMS stems from object-oriented programming languages. Generally, there has been a traditional "impedance mismatch" between programming and database languages, in that they have a different and unrelated historical background, and in that (at least part of) their concepts are not very well adjusted to each other [Ban88]. With the advent of object-oriented programming systems, it has been felt even more inconvenient to lose part of the advantages of object-orientation when it comes to the persistent storage of object data. Thus people got interested to combine object-oriented languages with DBMS features, or, regarded vice versa, to provide an OODM for database systems.

Finally, as detailed in the previous section, new advanced requirements demonstrated the shortcomings of traditional data models, and carefully conceived OODMs held out the promise to cure a major part of them.

4 Basic Properties of OODM

Unfortunately, in contrast to most previous data models, there was neither a clear-cut initial definition of an OODM (that could have been used as the basis for later implementations), nor a singular implementation (that could have been used as the basis for an abstract definition). Instead, numerous individual proposals for OODM have been made and prototypically (later on even commercially) implemented, each one addressing one or more of the above-mentioned issues, and of course each one with a different approach. Only later efforts commenced to work towards a common definition, but even today, there is no complete agreement on it. Rather, various people and organizations try to establish at least a framework for OODMs in order to clarify what features any OODM is required to have.

In this section, we discuss the basic properties of OODM, i.e. those properties that really make a data model deserve the attribute "object-oriented". In the next section, we will then introduce some further features that excellently go together with those presented here, but would also be useful as add-ons to traditional data models. Our discussion here is based on [ABD$^+$89] and also takes ideas from [L$^+$93] into account; in principle, also proposals published elsewhere (cf. e.g. [Kim90, ZM90a]) do not dramatically deviate from the material outlined here. Remember that we wanted to give an introductory overview of the topic instead of aiming at a complete coverage of even all major approaches. For that purpose, we also describe the salient concepts in a rather abstract manner instead of referring to any particular system. It also should be mentioned that the purpose of our presentation is clearly not to propose yet another OODM, but to give a general account of what such data models are all about.

The general idea of an OODM is to take the principal concepts of object-oriented systems in general, and to adjust them to and blend them with the salient features known from conventional data models. Thus an OODM is based on the notion of object (an object- oriented database consists of a collection of objects), and of class (a schema consists of a collection of class definitions).

An *object* in an OODM can be regarded as a quadruple
⟨ OID, value, state, class ⟩

and a *class* as an 11-tuple
⟨ class name, member value type, member state type, member messages,
member methods, class value, class state, class messages, class value
type, class state type, class methods ⟩

with the following characteristics (note that the individual components of these tuples are purposely not explained in the sequence of their appearance):

– An *object identifier* (OID) is a system-supported concept, separate from the value of an object, to support object identity, as discussed above (under the more general term of "entity identity"), within the database. To meet the requirements of object identity, an OID has to be system-wide unique, has to remain unchanged over the lifetime of the object, and **logically** cannot be reused for other objects [KC86].
Principally, the system will choose an OID meeting the above requirements for every object upon its creation. OIDs may be revealed to users (who may then use them in generic object operations, like comparisons or OID-based object retrieval,

but of course must not change them), or kept invisible inside the system. In the latter case, users may still use (temporary) "object handles" or may choose object names for some of their objects (it would be a tedious job to choose names for **all** objects!) for referring to particular objects. These handles/names system-internally have to be associated with OIDs; this allows to **physically** reuse OIDs of deleted objects (which in consequence allows for a more space-economic implementation), as it can be guaranteed that nobody outside the system will be aware that the same physical OID now refers to a different object than before.

It is also conceivable that, as an optional choice, an OODM allows class definers to select themselves an otherwise "regular" attribute to be used as an OID, if this is meaningful from an application's point of view (i.e. the values of that attribute in the miniworld would meet the requirements for OIDs anyway; [SRL+90]). Still, the system then has to guarantee the immutability of these values, on top of their uniqueness, while the non-reuse issues would typically be under the responsibility of the user.

- A *class name* is an identifier selected by the class definer (usually chosen mnemonically to meaningfully denote the real world concept modelled by the class). The class name can be used to represent the class, e.g. in the quadruple defining an object as above.

- An object has *structural* and *behavioral properties* (where, in accordance with the appropriate class definition, either of them may be missing). The structural properties are represented by an *(abstract) value*, whereas the behavioral properties are captured by *messages* the object is able to respond to. The set of messages applicable for an object can be inferred from its class.
  Structural and behavioral properties of an object (and possibly its OID, as explained above) are visible to its users.
  The visible properties of a class are its name, its value, and its messages.
  All other parts of objects and classes are *encapsulated* and thus invisible for the "regular" user (obviously, this is not true for the class designer during the design process).

- The value of an object is a tuple of values which may themselves be complexly structured (see the further discussion below). The *type* of these values is again determined by the object's class, more precisely, by the member value type defined there (note that in contrast to the more liberal use of some terms in the first sections, we now use "types" for values and states, and "classes" for objects; however, terminology for OODM is not at all consistent in this respect).
  Object values can be read and written freely by means of the regular access operations of their respective types. However, these values are abstract in that they do not entail any specific implementation by means of a data structure or other.

- The *state* of an object is a concrete data structure built in accordance with the member state type defined in the object's class. The abstract value of an object is then implemented by means of its state, either by directly matching value and state components, or by using methods to realize the appropriate read and write operations for component values on top of state components.

— Member *messages* specify the user-definable behavior of the objects of a class; a message has a name and a number of parameters (which may be objects and values). It is often implicitly assumed that the first parameter of a message indicates the object it is sent to. Member *methods* are implementations of messages (i.e., programs) and may also be used to realize abstract object values, as mentioned above. Methods perform their computations on the basis of the state of the respective object; we assume that the language provided for method programming allows to formulate any algorithm (*"computational completeness"*).

— Classes themselves may have a value, state and a set of messages **of their own** (which in turn requires the specification of appropriate value type, state type, and methods). While the **member** properties defined in a class refer to the objects of that class (they act as patterns for their creation), the **class** properties refer to the class as such (its extent). For example, "standard" class methods are those for the creation and deletion of their instances.

— Values and states may be composite (or "complex"), i.e. they may be built by applying constructors to other (ultimately simple) values. An OODM thus will provide a number of simple value types, not different from conventional data models (e.g. integer, float, character, string, date, time, ...). Next, it will also support a number of *value type constructors*. It is generally agreed that at least a tuple and a set constructor should be available; further constructors, e.g. for lists, bags, arrays, etc., will make the OODM more convenient for some applications. All constructors can be applied to simple value types, but also to the result of the application of other constructors or of themselves, allowing for the construction of arbitrary complex structures. Typically, it is required that the outermost constructor is a tuple.
Values and states of objects are also used to represent *object structures* and *complex (structured, composite, molecular) objects*. While both notions are often used synonymously, we are going to distinguish between them here.
In order to build general object structures, we need to be able to use a *reference* to an object (specified e.g. by a name, handle, or visible OID) as an additional simple value, which can then be included in the value or state of another object. This way, we are able to represent (in a unidirectional way) the fact that one object is associated with another one. In class definitions, the simple value type to be specified for that is of the form **ref** ⟨class⟩, where ⟨class⟩ is the name of another class (or the same, for recursive structures!).
In many miniworlds, especially in application areas OODMs are aiming at, it is rather frequent that objects are composed of other objects (by means of so-called "part of"-associations), and whole compositions have to be operated upon (e.g. when retrieving, copying, or deleting an object and all its component objects). Such situations can be supported by a special concept of complex object, which is different from object references. In a complex object, we directly **include** an object (again specified e.g. by a name, handle, or visible OID) in the value or state

of another object. The simple value type used to specify object inclusion in class definitions is just ⟨class⟩.

The difference between object inclusion and object reference is that for complex objects, we assume that also some generic "transitive" operations are provided whose effect will "propagate" from object to subobjects, and so forth. Of course, transitive methods may also be implemented. In contrast, references are not automatically exploited in operations. Applications would just be able to retrieve the knowledge that an object refers to another one, and if interested, would have to operate on the other object separately [Dit90].

Object inclusion and object reference can also be provided by making two different kinds of references available, as suggested in [Kim90]; we also talk about "loose" and "tight" associations between objects. [HGP92] contains a detailed discussion of various forms of part of-relationships. Due to the large diversity in detail, any OODM could possibly only provide a standard form of complex objects and require that users apply the other concepts to model the specific semantics they require. On the other hand, a number of rather early research prototypes have shown the viability and usefulness of complex objects in OODM (see e.g. [LP93], [DGL90]).

As a final characteristic of an OODM, it should also provide *class taxonomies* with *inheritance* as briefly explained in the previous section. To this end, class definitions may further include the specification of one or more superclasses, depending on whether just tree-like taxonomies (with "simple" inheritance) or general taxonomy hierarchies (with "multiple" inheritance) are supported.

Inheritance is in itself a rather complex issue which allows for many different semantics to be realized in a concrete OODM (see e.g. [US92] and the bulk of further literature cited there). For example, inheritance may either relate to the visible properties of objects, to their implementation, or to both. We may even obtain different taxonomy hierarchies for (value) types and for classes.

When messages are being inherited, an OODM would support *overloading* , i.e. messages in different classes in a hierarchy may agree in their interface. They may also be *overridden*, i.e. the message may be implemented by a different method at a lower level of the hierarchy than at the place where it has been "originally" defined. Technically, this requires *late binding* of the method to the message, as the class of an object the message is sent to often can be determined only at runtime. This also relates to the notion of "polymorphism": different objects (of different classes) may react differently when sent the same message.

Some OODMs do not support all of the features explained above. In particular, some OODM do not provide for messages and methods at all; on the other hand, they allow for arbitrarily complex values, including complex objects with transitive operations (*structural object-orientation*; [Dit91]). Other OODM do not support complexly structured values, and in particular just object references but no complex objects (*behavioral object-orientation*). Again other OODM would not support object values, but just messages ("strict encapsulation"; still, access to parts of the state may be provided anyway by generating explicit access functions, which would then be treated like messages at the interface).

On a last note, the OODM features introduced above do not mandate any specific implementation. Still, as in conventional data models, it is good practice to realize the metadata (in our case, class definitions) by the same concepts that are offered within the model itself. It is thus rather customary to represent classes (and their constituents) by other objects (whose classes then have to be predefined by the system). Furthermore, by using (some of) these system-defined classes as the top part of the class hierarchy where every user-defined class will inherit from, "generic" class messages like those for object creation, deletion, etc. can be provided as well.

In summary, we have shown that an OODM, in contrast to traditional data models,

- supports object identity
- provides various constructors for complex values, which can be applied recursively and in arbitrary combinations without further restrictions, item allows users to define operations for objects, and thus "arbitrary" classes,

and furthermore

- supports object structures and complex objects,
- supports class hierarchies with inheritance.

Its semantic expressiveness is thus considerably higher than known from previous kinds of data models.

5 Additional Properties of OODM

A number of further properties have been suggested for OODM, mainly to make them even more responsive to meeting the requirements of advanced applications. However, these properties are not really characteristic for the term "object-oriented", but could also be provided in an otherwise conventional data model. That is why we present them in a separate section here. Again, we only include some important features and do not want to give a complete overview of everything that has been proposed in the literature.

- **explicit relationships among objects**: Some OODM provide explicit relationships, much in the sense of the ER-model, among objects; they replace or complement object references. The advantages of such relationships are that they can associate any number of objects (not just two) in a symmetric way, that they can have a value of their own, and that they can be modelled and inspected independent of the objects they relate. In terms of consistency constraints, cardinalities may be assigned to relationships that will be enforced in the database.
  Generally, relationships can be considered as a special kind of objects bearing references to the objects they are supposed to relate. Depending on other mechanisms provided, it may however be difficult to guarantee referential integrity.

- **BLOBs (binary large objects)**: One of the ubiquitous database requirements mentioned for advances application areas is the support of large, unstructured byte streams (sometimes also called NCI — non-coded information), like e.g. the pixels of raster images, that are used chunk-by-chunk in a file-like manner in applications.

The technical solution for this requirement is an additional simple value type, called BLOB (binary large object, though it is certainly not an object in the sense of an OODM) or long field [LL89]. The operations provided for long fields are close to those known from direct files.

Values of type long field can then be used in object values and states (but could of course as well be provided for the domains in a relational model). By the way, OODM lend themselves easily to model the operations that recreate e.g. an image from the bytes stored in a long field as object messages.

– **user-defined value types**: An OODM might not only allow the definition of new classes, but also the definition of new value types. This is required as a separate feature if we want to avoid that any newly created concept that requires user-defined operations has to obtain the status of an object (and thus independent existence), although this would not be needed for reasons of the miniworld. User-defined value types are again also useful for traditional data models (and are in fact already offered by some systems, e.g. [Ing89]).

The definition of a new data type requires mechanisms to specify how its values should be represented (typically, byte strings will be used whose length has to be determined at definition time), to specify the operation interfaces, and to register implementations (programs) for the operations. This is in principle rather similar to the definition of new classes, though of course the general differences between objects and values apply.

– **object versions**: Versions are used to represent the temporal or causal development of real world entities and/or their relationships. Though users could principally model versions themselves by using the regular features of the data model at hand, it is more convenient, and more efficient if the data model directly includes appropriate concepts; furthermore, this is another issue where more real world semantics can be incorporated in the schema.

Version concepts are rather diverse even in the real world ([Kat90] gives an excellent overview of requirements and possible solutions). A data model looking for broad applicability will thus prefer to just support some basic concepts. First of all, class definitions have to differentiate between the "generic" part of an object (those properties that apply for all version alike, and where the previous state gets lost on updates) and its variant part (those properties whose changes are - individually or cumulatively - recorded such that previous states can be retrieved later on). Secondly, version graphs will typically be supported to organize the versions of an object. Thirdly, a set of specific generic operations is required to deal with versions and version graphs (and a version-free view of objects has to be available, too). Finally, as references/relationships/object compositions may refer to objects or individual versions of objects, the case where a version used in such an object structure is superseded by a new one has to be addressed with particular care.

– **rules**: The support of deductive [Gar93, CGT90] and active rules [Buc94, Day88] may also be considered as part of a data model, though it considerably exceeds traditional data model concepts. One approach is that deductive and active rules may refer to objects in an OODM, but are otherwise considered as orthogonal to objects and classes. On the other hand, classes might be enhanced by rules, which means that the internal functionality of their objects can be partly realized by those rules. Both approaches may also show up in combination.

We agree that it is disputable whether the features presented here are optional or mandatory for an OODM. However, we feel that it is anyway more important that users have adequate concepts at hand that meet their requirements, whatever such a data model is called.

6 The Relationship of OODM to Other DBMS Issues

A data model is only one, though decisive, feature of a full-fledged database management system. However, the concepts provided by the data model certainly influence other DBMS features. In this section, we briefly touch upon some issues which are particularly related to the fact that the data model is an object-oriented one. Further details for most of them can be found in anthologies and monographs like [BDK92, DDB91, Kim90, ZM90b].

Working with a database system always requires the retrieval of those pieces in the database that need to be processed. Conventional database systems have introduced *query languages* that allow to specify the desired part of the database descriptively, i.e. based on specific values or value ranges they are required to have; thus query facilities are closely related to the kind of data model supported. Though typical application areas often assumed for OODMs are mainly characterized by performing long and complex operations on database objects (often by sending them appropriate messages), they still require the comfortable and efficient retrieval of those objects, prior to making further use of them. Query languages are thus needed for object- oriented data models, too. According to our explanations in Sect. 4, queries will have to be formulated against the abstract value of objects, as their state is invisible to the outside; furthermore, they may also include messages.

Various other *language issues* are involved in OODMs. For one, we have already required a computationally complete language for method implementation. Furthermore, the question arises how a database system providing an OODM should be interfacing with a programming language for application development. Obviously, the "cleanest" and most elegant solution is to choose an object-oriented programming language and to use the same data model in the language and in the database system. In fact, this means that database and application classes are defined alike, and both systems can hardly be told apart any more - we just will have to deal with persistent and transient objects, respectively! This is clearly the case that makes the impedance mismatch completely disappear. Unfortunately, as a database is typically conceived to act as an enterprise-wide information repository, it is unlikely that all applications would use the same programming language. Thus other OODM/programming language couplings that provide more openness than the solution just outlined are required. In fact, the existence of an OODM in the database does not at all preclude to use rather conventional programming languages for application development, though in this case some sort of impedance mismatch will remain visible.

Database systems with record-oriented data models provide concepts like *views* or *subschemata* that allow to delimit and tailor the parts of the schema and/or database available for a given application or user. Similar features are certainly required for OODMs, though only few achievements into this direction have been made so far. Beyond the formulation of views based on queries against sets of objects, the existence of messages also has to be taken into account and may for example result in the exclusion of a particular message for a particular view, or in the inclusion of an additional (new) message.

Access control is also affected by moving from record-oriented to object- oriented data models, as the units to be authorized for access are now objects and classes. Again, the existence of messages will play an important role in the formulation of access control mechanisms and policies.

Schema evolution even occurs in conventional databases. In OODBMSs, it is expected to occur more frequently (due to the intended application areas), and it comprises more cases (e.g., a new class might get inserted "in the middle" of a class hierarchy). Hence, appropriate methods and mechanisms are required. For example, the schema itself might get versioned, and different parts of the database would relate to different schema versions (but should still allow to be queried comprehensively!).

It is sometimes argued that the use of OODMs would solve all consistency problems in databases. Unfortunately, though more advanced modelling capabilities and the availability of user-definable messages will certainly provide some relief, there are still numerous constraints that stretch across multiple objects, and thus cannot be treated locally within single objects. In consequence, there is still a need for explicit *consistency constraints* and their enforcement in OODBMSs.

New *transaction concepts* like various forms of nested and long-duration transactions have been proposed, often with the same application areas in mind that are also mentioned to motivate OODMs. Though objects can certainly be conveniently used together with such transactions, the two issues are nevertheless rather orthogonal to each other [Özs94]. Similarly, the *distribution* of databases across multiple nodes in a computer network is not directly influenced by the choice of the data model. Still, objects turn out to be a convenient unit for distribution, especially in client/server environments where distribution is not entirely transparent to applications. It is worth mentioning that object structures and their distribution (as well as their involvement in transactions) deserve special attention.

Finally, it should nearly go without saying that the *implementation* concepts and strategies used in a DBMS (e.g., storage and access structures, buffering, clustering) are also affected by the presence of an OODM.

7 Current State and Open Issues

OODMs are now being investigated since about ten years. They have been successfully provided in various DBMS that were particularly built for this purpose and sell under the name of OODBMSs since a couple of years. Beyond, many of the OODM-features have also been tried out as add-on features for relational data model, or they have been more closely merged with those.

Even the standards proposal for SQL3 currently under discussion includes many, if not all OODM-features discussed in this chapter [Gal92]. However, looking at the multitude of features suggested for SQL3 that seem to be only partly in accordance with one another, it seems more than doubtful whether it is really a wise idea to combine different approaches into one, at all costs. In this author's view, it is preferable to have multiple (probably just few) data models where each one is rather lean and concisely defined, and to have databases with different data models cooperate under a "common roof" (see below).

Standardization activities are also going on in the area of OODM and ooDBMS proper, mainly under the auspices of the Object Management Group (OMG) and the Object Database Management Group (ODMG ; [L+93]). Though there is considerable pressure from industry, it will probably take considerable more time to reach an agreement on **the** OODM (in contrast to a framework listing required and desirable features).

Current applications of OODM are mainly found in the areas mentioned in Sect. 2, but also in areas like management information systems, e.g. for decision support). In particular, two aspects seem to be characteristic for many current OODM-applications: they include some sort of complex network structure (e.g. for route planning, telecommunication network maintenance, facility management, etc.), or they involve large numbers of product variants (e.g. car sales support systems).

OODMs also play an important role in the construction of interoperable heterogeneous database systems, which is currently an important research area in itself. Features like the large variety of structures they are able to support (which acts more or less like a superset of structures provided in other models), definable messages (which may be used to perform conversions, calculate derived data and the like), and encapsulation make OODM unique candidates for the global data model in heterogeneous federations.

On the other hand, there are of course also various aspects which still need improvements or where viable solutions are still pending. For example, the right "mix" of concepts for representing various kinds of object structures still need some more consideration, also in the light of previous prototype work whose contributions have been overlooked in most products, for various reasons. Also, many implementation details need more advanced solutions to further improve the performance, but also the reliability of OODBMSs. Some other issues for further research have already been touched upon in the previous section.

Furthermore, formal foundations for OODM are way behind their practical exploitation. Fortunately, some progress can recently be seen in this area.

Finally, it is still a rather open issue how to do good database design for OODMs. Though (or probably even because!) an OODM offers much more elaborate concepts than a record-oriented data model, it is everything but straightforward to come up with a meaningful and "good" (whatever this means: what are the criteria?) schema. Like it previously happened for relational systems, it is just now that the technology has been made available, and it will take further time and hard work to also provide appropriate methods and tools to help us with its systematic use.

Query Languages for Models with Object-Oriented Features

Catriel Beeri

The Hebrew University, Institute of Computer Science,Jerusalem, Israel

Abstract. Query languages are the primary means for defining the declarative interface of a database system. While query languages for the relational model are well understood, such languages for object-oriented data models are relatively new. This paper suggests that to understand these languages, we need to consider languages for the so-called complex object model; languages for full object-oriented data models can then be obtained rather easily. The paper considers four query paradigms for the relational model, their evolution to the complex object model and their relationships: calculus, algebra, SQL and comprehensions.

1 Introduction

The relational model was the first data model to support the idea of declarative, or high level, query languages. In fact, these languages appeared in the database area with this model and contributed significantly to its success. The fact that the model is based on a single simple data structure was crucial — it permitted the development of simple yet powerful query paradigms, endowed with precisely defined semantics. However, in the last decade many other models, described as "advanced" but certainly less simple than the relational model, were proposed and studied. Noteworthy among those is the object-oriented data model (or paradigm), the OODM, that was introduced both to allow the representation of more domain semantics in the database, and to better support application development. The initial emphasis in its development has been on procedural programming, but more recently query languages for it have been studied and developed, utilizing the knowledge accumulated in the last decade in the development of such languages for a variety of "advanced" models.

The goal of this paper is the study of such languages and their properties. Our approach to the subject is incremental: we start from languages of the relational model, then add to the model features of the OODM, and consider the impact on the languages. This approach allows one to gain a better understanding of the requirements imposed by the various components of the OODM on its languages. As a matter of fact, we devote most of the paper to complex object languages (where "complex objects" actually mean complex values). We believe, and hope to convince the reader, that the transition from relational to complex objects is the crucial step; once the languages for complex objects are well understood, the generalizations needed to accommodate other features of the OODM are easier to work out.

The outline of the paper is as follows. In the rest of this section we recall some language design criteria and OODM fundamentals. In Sect. 2 we recall relational languages. Section 3 introduces the complex object model. The languages for the model are considered in Sect.s 4 and 5. Section 6 considers other features of the OODM, and Sect. 7 concludes. The discussion throughout is informal; more formal presentations abound in the literature. Also, the emphasis is on language design, not on implementation, although implementation issues are relevant for the design as well.

1.1 Language Design Criteria

Various criteria for query languages have been discussed in the literature, see e.g., [ABD+89, Dat84, HS91a]. We consider the following in our discussions. The *closure* property means that the result of a query should belong to the data model, hence can be an input to another query. In particular, queries should be closed under composition. In the relational model, this means that a query should return a relation. Another well-known requirement is *orthogonality*, meaning that one should be able to freely combine the available constructs. The relational model and its languages do not satisfy this requirement, and this was a strong motivation for considering various extensions. See, e.g., Date's criticism of the lack of orthogonality in SQL [Dat84]. A related property is *extensibility* namely the ability to accommodate extensions in the language, e.g., user-defined types. This is closely related to orthogonality.

Yet another requirement is *adequacy*, discussed in [HS91a]. It means that the query language should make use of all the features that exist in the underlying data model. In the relational model one may consider it trivially satisfied. As explained in [HS91a], closure and adequacy can be viewed as complementary requirements: that queries operate in the data model (closure), and use all of it (adequacy).

We finally mention *complexity* and *expressiveness* of languages, that provide upper and lower bounds on their expressive power. Although results on this topic abound, it is not emphasized here.

1.2 OODM Fundamentals

We now briefly consider some concepts and key features of the OODM, as background for the following discussion. These and others are discussed extensively in other papers in this volume, e.g., [Zdo94, Dit94, DOA+94] .

- **Complex values:** The relational model is based on one simple data structure — the relation, i.e. set of (fixed length) tuples, containing only atomic values. A generalization, directed by the principle of orthogonality, is to allow arbitrary applications of the tuple and set constructors . This led initially to the *nested relational* model [FT83, SS86], in which attribute values in a relation can be either atomic or relation-valued, and later to the *complex object* model, in which true orthogonality with respect to these two constructors is realized [AB88][1]. Many systems additionally support other data constructors, for example, *bags lists* and *arrays*.

[1] These "objects" are *not* real objects with identity; they are actually complex values.

- **Objects with identity:** Real-world entities have identities, that are invariant, in contrast to their properties that may change over time. Faithful modeling of reality requires that this concept also be present in the model. The relational model offers limited support in the form of keys, but their proper use is mostly the users' responsibility. The OODM supports the concept explicitly. This allows objects to be components of other objects, and supports sharing and cyclic relationships.

- **Extensibility:** A fixed set of data types supplied by the system may answer a variety of needs; still there exist situations where a user may want to define his/her own data types. Thus, it is desired to support a facility for defining new types, and for creating, storing and manipulating their instances. A basic requirement is that these should have the same status as the built-in types. The concept of orthogonality in the use of type constructors allows users to define new types by construction. The concept of behavior, described next, extends this facility.

- **Behavior and Encapsulation:** An inherent part of the object-oriented paradigm is the association of procedures, called *methods* with objects. The collection of methods associated with an object defines its behavior. In object-oriented database management systems (OODBMSs) behavior is associated with collections of objects (types or classes). Each object has an associated structure, where data is stored. The methods define the interface through which the data is accessed and manipulated. Direct access to the data is prevented by encapsulation — a mechanism that hides the internals of the object representation, and allows only the interface (i.e., public) methods to be used in accessing it.

- **Isa and inheritance relations:** These exist in the OODM in the form of subtype and subclass relations. Often these are accompanied by code inheritance with overriding.

As stated above, the discussion in this paper deals mainly with the first point. We consider some issues related to the other features very briefly.

2 Relational Query Languages

We recall here some relational query languages. For those that are well-known, details are mostly omitted.

2.1 Calculus and Algebra

The *relational calculus* is a straightforward adaptation of the elegant and well-understood formalism of first-order predicate calculus. Two versions, using tuple and individual variables, respectively, exist in the literature, and are equivalent in expressive power. (As argued later, adequacy would suggest using both types of variables.) Another well-known language is the *relational algebra*, which consists of a fixed collection of operations, that can be freely combined: *union, difference, product, selection, projection*. Others, such as *intersection, natural join* can be defined in terms of these five operations.

The complexity of both languages is known to be in LOGSPACE [Var82, Imm86].

2.2 SQL

Of special interest are the following sublanguages of the two languages. In the calculus, this is the class of *conjunctive queries*, which in the individual-variables version consists of the formulas consisting of a string of existential quantifiers followed by a quantifier-free body that is a pure conjunction, i.e., it contains no negations or disjunctions. To ensure domain independence, each variable is required to appear in an atom, a *range formula*, of the form $R(\overline{x})$. A generalization, that we assume from now, is that the body is a conjunction of two parts — a conjunction of atomic range formulas, and an optional part that may use any boolean combination of atomic formulas. In the tuple-variables version, since several individual variables are packed into a single variable, an explicit target list with components of the form $x.A$ is required, and existential quantifiers are needed only for the tuple variables that have no component in the target list. For example, given a relation $person(name, address)$, to list names of persons living in New York we write, using individual variables, $\exists a(person(n, a) \wedge a = NY)$ or, using tuple variables, $x.name \mid person(x) \wedge x.address = NY$.

In the algebra, it is the language that allows only *selection, projection, product*, often called the *SPJ* language. (The "J" is for *join*, which is expressible in the language, and is often considered more important than *product*.) The two languages are equivalent in expressive power. (The selection condition can use the three boolean connectives, but no quantifiers.) The algebraic language can be extended to *SPJU* by adding union, and the calculus language can be extended by adding disjunction. formulas. The resulting languages are also equivalent. For a discussion of relational languages see [Ull82, Kan90].

Another well-known paradigm is the language SQL. For our purpose, it is embodied in the *select-from-where* clause:

> **SELECT** $x_{i1}.A_1, \ldots x_{in}.A_n$
> **FROM** x_1 in $R_1, \ldots x_n$ in R_m
> **WHERE** p

(We regard the version without variables as an abbreviation.) Various deficiencies of SQL have been listed in [Dat84]. As one example, the FROM clause may contain only relation names, rather than arbitrary queries, as required by the orthogonality property. Also, although one can use *union* in SQL, its use is quite restricted. Since an SQL query with nested subqueries can be translated into a query without nesting [Kim82], these restrictions do not affect the expressive power; they are a language design issue.

Let us recall the relationships between these languages. It is well-known that the calculus[2] and the algebra are equivalent [Ull82]. Equivalence of languages means that we have succeeded to isolate an interesting concept, but nevertheless, the proof is often considered to be of theoretical interest only. Let us consider, however, the two sublanguages, the conjunctive queries and the *SPJ* queries, and also SQL (basic block only). The SQL query above may be written in the tuple calculus as

$$x_{i1}.A_1 \ldots x_{in}.A_n \mid \exists \overline{y}\,(R_1(x_1) \ldots R_m(x_m) \wedge p), \tag{1}$$

---

[2] The relevant notion of domain independence is not treated here.

where $\exists \overline{y}$ is optional, and contains only those variables among the x_i's that do not appear in the target list. This query is also equivalent to the algebraic query $\pi_{A_1\ldots A_n}(\sigma_p(R_1 \times \ldots \times R_m))$. Thus, we see that, first, the basic block of SQL can be seen as syntactic sugar for conjunctive queries; this part of SQL is a sublanguage of the calculus — a purely declarative language. We also see that the translation to the algebraic SPJ language, which is one direction of proof of equivalence of these languages, is a formal representation of a first step of compilation, translating a declarative query to an intermediate algebraic form, similar to that used in practice. In the other direction, an SPJ query can be rewritten as a product followed by a selection followed by a projection, by using the algebraic transformation laws [Ull82]. Thus, the core of SQL has the same expressive power as the SPJ language. We note that one can extend SQL with operations like *union*, *difference*, to obtain the full power of the calculus/algebra.

2.3 Comprehensions

We consider now the *comprehensions* language, less well-known in the relational literature. The notation of *list comprehension* has been quite popular in recent functional language literature [Pey87], and *set comprehensions* have been used in mathematics for decades. The language we consider is an adaptation of list comprehensions to the set-based relational model, following [Tri91]. The basic format is $\{t \mid q\}$, where t is a target list, and q is a *qualifier*, having the form $q_1, \ldots q_n$, where each q_i is an atomic qualifier. (If $n = 0$ it is empty). There are two kinds of atomic qualifiers: a *generator* has the form $x \leftarrow RE$, meaning that x ranges over the contents of the relational expression (i.e., query) RE; we also say that this qualifier *introduces* the variable x. The relational expression may be either a relation name R, or a comprehension query (orthogonality). Variables introduced in nested relational expressions are not visible outside. A *predicate* qualifier is simply a predicate as in the tuple calculus, involving qualified variables and constants. (A qualified variable is a term $x.A$, where x is a tuple variable.) The target list t may contain constants and qualified variables, using only variables introduced in the qualifier. (Orthogonality would suggest to allow also relational expressions, but the relational model does not allow set values.) It is not difficult to see that all predicates can be moved after all generators. This gives a form that is very close to SQL, except that in comprehensions *nested subqueries* are allowed.

The semantics of a comprehension query $Q = \{t \mid q_1 \ldots q_n\}$ can be defined either directly, as done for the other languages, or by translating it into either the calculus or the algebra. As a matter of fact, the similarity to SQL suggests immediately that this is essentially the same sublanguage of the calculus with one one important addition: rather to allow only atomic formulas of the form $R(x)$, now formulas of the form $RE(x)$ are also allowed. This is an application of orthogonality that corrects a flaw in the calculus. This view leads directly to a translation to a calculus with nested subqueries. These can be removed using the techniques of [Kim82], establishing a correspondence with the conjunctive queries. Alternatively, the correspondence with the SPJ language may be established by translating to this sublanguage of the algebra with nested subqueries, which can be "flattened" by pushing selections and projection outward [Ull82]. In any case, the language is clearly seen to be a syntactic variation on SQL (without *union*) having the same expressive power as the family of conjunctive/SPJ (or SQL) queries.

union can be added to achieve the power of *SPJU* queries. Of course, in the spirit of the language, it makes sense to allow using it also in nested subqueries.

2.4 Discussion

The complexity of all the languages considered above is low, as they are all sublanguages of the calculus or the algebra, which have complexity LOGSPACE. Why has SQL been preferred to either the calculus or the algebra in practice? After all, with additions like *union, difference* it can express the same class of queries. Essentially, this sublanguage of the calculus was chosen is because it is simple to understand and optimizable. Let us consider these properties in some more detail.

The calculus has probably been ruled out for several reasons. First, quantifiers are considered difficult to understand, especially when a query uses several of them. Second, variables, either free or bound, are not required to be associated with domains, and this makes it possible to write queries that are not domain independent. One needs to impose syntactic range restrictions — and this is one of the advantages of *SQL*. Finally, the calculus is quite neutral to the form of queries, but in practice there are certain forms that seem to be easier to formulate and understand.

Now, in SQL, there is a built-in preference to certain queries — those expressible by its basic block, and these seem to be more natural. Further, all variables are introduced with ranges, as part of the basic form; there is no need to worry about domain independence. Finally, only existential quantifiers are used, and a convention allows to omit them so no quantifiers at all are actually used in the basic form. Of course, the problems of quantification and domain independence do not exist in the algebra. SQL can thus be viewed as being close to, actually a sublanguage of the algebra, the only difference being its emphasis on a certain form — the combination of select, project, product as the basic "operation".

Regarding optimizability, we recall that a large class of algebraic transformation rules are known for the *SPJ* language, and can be used to optimize SQL queries. Similarly, cost-model based optimizations have been developed for the language. We know less about optimization if *union* is added, and almost nothing if *difference* is also added [Ull82]. Although we need these operations for the expressive power, optimization is normally performed independently on subqueries that do not use them.

The last point to be discussed here is the ability to nest subqueries. The ability to nest does not add to expressive power for the languages above, but is important in terms of language design, as it makes the language much easier to use. In the calculus there is no nesting, although it can be expressed in a roundabout way. Assume, for example, a database of suppliers and parts, with relations *SUPPLY(part#, sup#)*, *SUPPLIER(sup#, address)*, *FAST_SUPPLIER(sup#, phone)*, where each fast supplier is also a supplier. To find the part numbers of parts that are supplied only by fast suppliers we might write

$$
s.part\# \mid SUPPLY(s)
$$
$$
\land \{s1.sup\# \mid SUPPLY(s1) \land s.part\# = s1.part\#\}
$$
$$
\subseteq \{s2.sup\# \mid FAST\_SUPPLIER(s2)\} \tag{2}
$$

This is not a legal calculus query — subqueries are illegal, and $\subseteq$ is not in the language. The query can be expressed as

$$s.part\# \ | \ SUPPLY(s) \wedge \forall s1(SUPPLY(s1) \wedge s.part\# = s1.part\#$$
$$\rightarrow \exists s2(FAST\_SUPPLIER(s2) \wedge s1.sup\# = s2.sup\#)) \qquad (3)$$

One may argue about which formulation is easier to formulate and understand, but experience (with students in my case) seems to suggest the first is easier. We note that the first formulation is close to being a legal comprehension query — subqueries are legal in comprehensions. The use of $\subseteq$ is still problematic, since the relational model does not admit set values and their operations as first class citizens. Despite that, the obvious translation of this form of the query to SQL is legal in that language; the need to accommodate user convenience has been stronger than the desire to stay within the model.) Of course, these formulations are legal in the the complex object model, and more generally in OODMs, where set values and their operations are first class citizens. Anyway, the point is that the ability to nest offers to the user a wider range of language constructs to choose from to express the query. In many cases, a nested query can be unnested, that is flattened, using techniques such as those in [Kim82, Ull82]. However, this belongs to the realm of optimization, and is better left to the system. The users should not be restricted in how they formulate queries. This is a subtle difference between closure and orthogonality. The calculus has the first property, but not the second, whereas the algebra, and comprehensions have both.

2.5 Extensions

We briefly mention two practically important additions, that apply to each of the languages above, although the syntactic details may vary. We have allowed only constants and attributes (or qualified variables) as terms, and only equalities in selections. But, the underlying atomic domains such as the numeric domains and strings have various built-in functions and predicates. One may also want to allow user-defined ADT's as domains, and these also have functions and predicates. There is no difficulty in augmenting the set of terms to accommodate arbitrary functions, e.g. $3 + 2 \times A$. Such terms can be used, e.g., in selections, where arbitrary terms may be compared, and in projection and target lists[3]. This actually generalizes the notion of a projection — see the *map* operation in Sect. 5. Similarly arbitrary predicates can be used in selections.

While there is no inherent difficulty in this augmentation of the relational model and its languages, it brings to light an important point. Traditional treatments of relational theory push under the rug the fact that the universe of discourse is a *typed universe*, and accordingly, the languages should also be typed. Since one of our goals is to examine extensions of the model to more general type structures, we should consider typing as an important and explicit ingredient of our languages. Rather than elaborate this point here, we defer the discussion to Sect. 3.

Another practically important feature is *aggregations*. A collection of standard aggregates can be found in essentially each relational language. In contrast to scalar

---

[3] Since now they do not have attributes to name them, names must be supplied in the query.

functions, these additions are often ad-hoc, for a simple reason: Aggregates are functions defined on sets (or other collection types, such as bags and lists), but the relational model does not support set values. Hence, one often must define aggregates in a way that avoids explicit construction of the underlying sets.

3 The Complex Objects Model

During the 80's, several generalizations of the relational model have been investigated, the goal being to increase the expressiveness of the model. It was achieved by applying the orthogonality principle to the type constructors of the model. The *nested relational* model allows attribute values to be atomic or relations [FT83]. The *complex object* model[4] allows values to be constructed from atomic values by using tuple and set constructors in any order, so it allows also sets of sets and tuples of tuples [AB88]. In this model a set of values of a given type is a (generalized) relation, and a database is a finite collection of such relations. The model is very close to the nested relational model — any generalized relation in it can be easily transformed to a nested relation. We use it here since it uses two independent constructors, so it may lead to a better understanding of orthogonality and adequacy in query languages. The complex objects model is introduced below, and its languages are discussed in subsequent sections.

3.1 Types and Domains

As we mentioned above, even the relational model can be based on arbitrary domains, and can use their constants, functions and predicates. This also holds for the complex object model, as well for more general models. Additionally, we now also have type constructors. Thus, it is important to make types explicit. All the languages to be considered below are typed.

We assume that a collection of atomic domains is given, with a collection of constants, functions and predicates. This is described by a *signature* Σ, that includes: A set of domain names, or *atomic types*, and a function *type* that associates a domain name with each constant, and a (first-order) function/predicate signature with each function/predicate name. We assume Σ contains a type *unit* with a single element $[]$. This can be viewed as the empty tuple type. In the following, such a signature Σ is taken as a parameter of the model and its languages. That is, we are going to consider complex object databases constructed over arbitrary domains, and all the languages are frameworks that can accommodate arbitrary functions and predicates of Σ.

Given a signature Σ, the complex object model over it has all the domain names of Σ as *atomic* types. *Complex* types are constructed from them by applying the *tuple* and *set* type constructors. We assume a fixed, countable, collection of attributes used in tuple constructions. Assuming Σ is countable, we have a countable collection of types. A type is a *tuple/set type* if its primary constructor is *tuple/set*.

Given domains for the atomic types of Σ, and the two type constructors, what kind of universes do we have in mind? The answer is simple. The domain of a tuple type is obtained by a labeled cross product:

---

[4] As already noted, this is a model of complex values.

$$dom([A_1 : T_1 \ldots A_n : T_n]) = \{[A_1 : v_1 \ldots An : v_n] \mid v_i \in dom(T_i)\} \qquad (4)$$

The domain of a set type is obtained by a finitary powerset:

$$dom(\{T\}) = \{s \mid s \subseteq dom(T), s \text{ finite}\} \qquad (5)$$

Clearly, given the atomic domains, there is a well-defined domain associated with each type, and these domains are disjoint.

It is often convenient to be able to construct tuples without using attribute names. We will view the tuple $[t_1 \ldots t_n]$ as having (implicitly) the attributes $1st, 2nd, \ldots$.

In the following, we will often associate typing rules with language constructs, as done in the functional language literature, although we may omit some of the rules. Our assumptions leads to the following type *axioms*:

$$\overline{c : type(c)} \qquad \overline{[\,] : unit} \qquad \overline{f : type(f)} \qquad \overline{p : type(p)} \qquad (6)$$

These axioms state that each constant, function and predicate of the underlying domains has the type given to it by *type*.

3.2 Language Requirements

The structure of the model imposes certain requirements on the query languages, and on the kind of queries we want to express.

Values in this model may have a non-trivial nesting structure. The *nesting* in the data representation has to be reflected in appropriate mechanisms in the language, in two ways. First, we should be able to manipulate components of such values, i.e., use predicates on these components in selection conditions, or change their contents. Second, we should be able to create results with nested structure.

The last point is actually a special case. More generally we need to be able to change the format in which data is presented, i.e. perform *restructuring*. For example, we may want to convert from the type $[person\_name : string, children : \{string\}]$ to $[person\_name : string, parents : \{string\}]$. A simple restructuring operation changes the structure of each value in a set, and can be defined by a function that is to be applied to each value. In more complex cases, a single input value may create several values in the output (e.g., the *unnest* operation), or several input values are collected into a single output value (as in the *nest* operation). In this case, the restructuring can be expressed as a relationship between input and output values. What we need in the language, therefore, is (i) a facility to express restructuring functions and predicates, and (ii) a facility to use them in transformations of relations.

In the relational model the only elements are (flat) tuples, hence nesting is essentially a mute issue, and restructuring is limited to adding or deleting fields of tuples. In the more general models we consider now, these are important issues.

4 The Complex Object Calculus

We start the discussion of languages with a (predicate) calculus language. Although it is not a good user-level language, it serves as a simple vehicle for a discussion of types and of orthogonality and adequacy, and is a natural generalization of relational calculus. As already mentioned, traditionally the relational calculus has two versions: one that uses exclusively individual (i.e., atomic) variables, and another that uses only tuple variables. But here values may also be of other types, in particular of various set types. Evidently, a single variable kind is insufficient. Thus, we must realize that we are dealing with a typed universe, and to achieve flexibility and convenience in the expression of queries adequacy requires that we allow the use of variables for each type of value, thus having atomic, tuple and set variables. (The restriction to the flat relational model would then use, for the same reasons, both atomic and tuple variables.) We assume that each variable is associated with a type by an appropriate declaration[5]. In the logic literature, this is called a *many-sorted* calculus. Such a calculus is obtained from the simple uni-sorted predicate calculus by adding *sorts*, i.e., types, in precisely the same way that typed languages are obtained from untyped languages by adding types. We will use "type" rather than "sort" from now.

4.1 The Components

What kinds of additional functions and predicates, besides those of Σ, should we use? For the constructed domains, the key observation is that these are domains of data structures, and we should include *constructors* and *selectors* to allow us to construct and decompose values, just as *push, pop* and *top* are used for stacks. For convenience, we should also include additional functions (operations) on the values; the issue of which functions to include will be considered in depth here.

For tuples, the constructor is simply a tuple constructor for values. Since we have many tuple types, we have a parametrized family of constructors, where the parameters are attributes and their types. We represent a tuple constructor as $[\,]_{A_1:T_1,\ldots,A_n:T_n}$. Applying it to n terms $t_1,\ldots,t_n$, where each t_i is of type T_i, respectively, we obtain $[\,]_{A_1:T_1,\ldots,A_n:T_n}(t_1,\ldots,t_n)$, but as customary in the literature, we denote it $[A_1: t_1,\ldots,A_n:t_n]$. When the types are irrelevant, or known, we denote the constructor by $[\,]_{A_1,\ldots,A_n}$, and when we refer to the generic constructor, the attributes are omitted as well. For the case that $n = 0$, we obtain the empty tuple $[\,]$, the single element in the domain *unit*. As mentioned above, we allow also tuples without explicit attributes. The selectors for tuple types are the *attributes*: each attribute A is viewed as a unary function defined on every tuple type that has an A component. We may use either the customary function application notation $A(t)$, or the more familiar notation $t.A$. We do not propose additional functions for tuples; it seems that useful functions can be expressed in terms of the constructors and selectors.

For sets, the constructor(s) should be some function(s) that will enable us to construct finite sets of elements of any given type. One possible choice is to use $\{\,\}_n$ as an n-ary

---

[5] Practically, type indices on variables suffice, and furthermore in most cases even these can be dropped, and one can rely on type inference.

operator that takes a list of n arguments and creates a set. A cleaner approach is to use $\emptyset$ as a constant, $\{\ \}$, also called *single*, as an operation that creates a singleton set of a given element, and *union* as an operation that allows us to create larger sets. Again, we have one of these for each set type, but the type index is usually omitted. Other choices are possible, see e.g., [BTBN92].

One might object that *union* is an algebraic operation, so what is it doing in a calculus-based language? This argument is mute. An *algebra* is a domain of values, with a set of operations on them. The relational algebra is called by that name because relations are sets, and the language consists of a collection of operations on such values. We have here a many-sorted algebra in which set values are first-class citizens. Just as we use in the calculus the arithmetic operations for the numeric domains, we can use set operations on the set domains. As a matter of fact, we could use all the known complex object algebraic operations (presented below) as additional functions. The choice is a matter of language design rather than of expressive power — it is shown in [AB88] that, just as in the relational case, the calculus can express all the operations of the complex object algebra.

There are no deterministic selectors for sets, since there is no deterministic way to choose one element from a set, unless it happens to be a singleton. (Some language proposals use an operation *pick* that does just that.) We use instead the membership predicate, $\in$.

Finally, we allow the use of $\subseteq$ as an additional predicate. Although it can be expressed in a calculus that uses only $\in$, its use simplifies the expression of many queries. We discuss below the choice of functions and constructs for the language.

4.2 Terms and Formulas

The *terms* of the language are defined, as usual, as the smallest set that contains the *atomic constants* and *variables*, and is closed under the application of functions (conditional on the the typing rules). Terms without variables denote elements of the domains, e.g., $[name : Jack, children : \emptyset]$ or $\{Jack, Abe\}$. The term construction rules are embodied in *typing rules*, including those shown above for Σ, and the following:

$$\frac{t_1 : T_1 \ldots t_n : T_n}{[A_1 : t_1 \ldots A_n : t_n] : [A_1 : T_1 \ldots A_n : T_n]} \qquad \frac{t : [A_1 : T_1 \ldots A_n : T_n]}{t.A_i : T_i} \qquad (7)$$

$$\frac{t : T}{single(t) : \{T\}} \qquad \frac{t_1, t_2 : \{T\}}{t_1 \cup t_2 : \{T\}} \qquad \frac{f : T_1 \to T_2, t : T_1}{f(t) : T_2} \qquad (8)$$

These give the rules for tuple and set operations, and for function application[6]. Note that the rule for *single* could alternatively be written as $\overline{single:T \to \{T\}}$.

The definition of the language is completed in the standard way. Predicates include the built-in predicates of the atomic domains, the two set predicates $\in$, $\subseteq$ (actually two for each set type), an equality predicate for each type, and also a finite collection of *database predicates*, the names of database relations. Predicates applied to terms (with

---

[6] Note that $A : t$ in a tuple value means that the $A'th$ component is t; the : between a term and a type means that the term has this type.

the proper type restrictions) yield atomic formulas. General formulas are obtained by using the connectives and quantifiers.

A database assigns relations to the relation names, and is an interpretation for the language. Truth values for formulas can be defined in the standard way, when each of the free variables in a formula is assigned a value from its domain. Thus a formula can be viewed as a query, where the target list is its set of free variables. To make the notion of result well-defined, we may require that a query contains only one free variable, of a tuple type. It can be easily shown that every formula can be translated to satisfy this format.

4.3 Discussion

What kind of queries can we express with this language? It contains the relational calculus, so we can express all first-order queries. But, in our setting there are the additional requirements of nesting and restructuring. Both can be easily expressed in the calculus.

Example 1. Consider the relation schema (atomic domains are omitted for brevity)

$$people: \{ [name, \; children : \{ [name, \; birth\_date] \} \}$$

1. Select the persons that have children born after 23.10.67:

   $$people(p) \wedge \exists c(c \in p.children \wedge c.birth\_date > 23.10.67).$$

2. Select from *people* the tuples where the person's name is the same as the name of one of his/her children:

   $$people(p) \wedge \exists c(c \in p.children \wedge p.name = c.name).$$

3. Project out the names of children from the subrelations in people:
   Let n be a variable of type $[name, \; children\_b\_d : \{ \}]$.

   $$\exists p(people(p) \wedge p.name = n.name$$
   $$\wedge \forall d(\exists c(c \in p.children \wedge d = c.birth\_date) \leftrightarrow d \in n.children\_b\_d)).$$

   Note that the subformula starting after the first $\wedge$ can be viewed as expressing a function from the domain of p to the domain of n. The first part, $\exists p(people(p) \wedge$ is the "glue" that applies this function as a restructuring function on *people*.

4. Unnest *people*, that is convert it to a flat relation:
   Let f be a variable of type $[p\_name, c\_name, c\_b\_d]$.

   $$\exists p(people(p) \wedge p.name = f.p\_name$$
   $$\wedge \exists c(c \in p.children \wedge c.name = f.c\_name \wedge c.birth\_date = f.c\_b\_d)).$$

   Here also, we have a subformula that expresses a restructuring relationship between input and output values, and a "glue" that applies it on a relation.

5. We now show how a result with nesting different from that of the input can be created. We want to create a relation where each tuple has a child name, and a set of (at most two) its parents' names. For simplicity, assume that a child's name

uniquely identifies it among all children. Let c be a variable of the appropriate type:

$$\exists p \exists cs(people(p) \land cs \in p.children \land c.name = cs.name$$
$$\land \forall y(y \in c.parents \leftrightarrow \exists p1 \exists cs1(people(p1) \land cs1 \in p1.children$$
$$\land c.name = cs1.name \land y = p1.name)))).$$

As we can see, creation of a nested structure is possible by using variables with appropriate types, and describing their contents using a two-sided implication with a universal quantification. This is quite cumbersome[7]. It would be easier if we would allow in the language an additional construct — nested subqueries:

$$\exists p \exists cs(people(p) \land cs \in p.children \land c.name = cs.name$$
$$\land c.parents = \{p1.name \mid people(p1) \land \exists cs1(cs1 \in p1.children$$
$$\land c.name = cs1.name)\}).$$

Let us now consider the set of functions and predicates in the language. It is not minimal. Indeed, it is proven in [AB88] that if we augment the standard relational calculus with variables of any types, with the dot notation, and with the predicate $\in$, then we can express $\subseteq$, and also $\emptyset, single, union$, and even the tuple constructor. Further, the language can express all of the complex algebra operations. As seen above, it can also express nested subqueries. Thus, just for obtaining the expressive power we do not need the full set of constructors and selectors, and certainly no extra constructs. However, as seen in the final example above, adding features to a language often makes it much easier to use. Rather than striving for minimality in our presentation of the language, we have relied on the principle of adequacy: If the language has tuples and sets. it should have explicit facilities for manipulating them. We do not pursue this issue further here; we are not proposing the calculus as a practical language anyway.

The complexity of the relational calculus is in LOGSPACE. What can we say about this calculus? On this subject we have bad news. First, the calculus can express the *powerset* operation. That is, given a set, we can create its finitary powerset. This is an exponential increase in size! The expression is easy; for the relation *people* above, its powerset is $P \subseteq people$. Even if we exclude the $\subseteq$ operation, it can be expressed by using just $\in$. In [AB88] it is shown that the calculus can express the transitive closure query, and as a matter of fact any (Complex Object) Datalog query. This actually is not so surprising: it is well-known that all Datalog queries can be expressed in second-order predicate calculus. Our calculus has variables of arbitrary set types, which gives it the power of second order calculus for finite structures. Finally, in [HS91b] it is shown that the calculus can express all queries of elementary complexity (i.e., of complexity of any tower of exponentials.), even when the input and output of queries are restricted to be flat, i.e., relational. In this proof, queries with non-flat intermediate types are used. They also prove that increasing the set nesting of intermediate types increases the complexity of queries.

In summary, although the calculus seems to have the required functionality in terms of dealing with nesting and restructuring, the problems that we noted for the relational calculus still exist, and are actually aggravated. Several notions of range restrictions for

---

[7] Even students with a good background in logic take quite some time to formulate such a query.

variables are presented in [AB88]; in [GV91] it is shown that one such set of restrictions guarantee PTIME complexity. However, let us rather consider languages that embed such restrictions in a natural manner.

5 Algebraic and Functional Languages

We now consider an algebraic approach. An algebra is a functional language. In the functional approach there are no predicates as in the calculus above. The database relations are simply named constants (i.e., values) of certain given types. Thus, the treatment of sets is more uniform than in the calculus, and, additionally, it can be generalized to other bulk types, such as bags.

5.1 Preamble

What do we need to add to the relational algebra to obtain a complex object algebra? The answer is, as stated above, facilities to operate on nested substructures, and for restructuring. The relational algebra contains a restructuring operation — the *projection* operation — it allows one to decrease the width of tuples in a set. But we obviously need better facilities, e.g., to add components to tuples, or more drastically, to destroy or create sets, and so on. For the nested relational model, one of the proposed approaches was to add *nest* and *unnest* to the set of operations. To operate on or restructure a nested structure it was proposed to flatten a nested relation by using *unnest* repeatedly, then perform the access/restructuring, then restore the original shape, or any other desired shape, by using *nest*. There are some technical difficulties, caused by the fact that *nest* and *unnest* are not inverses, so if one uses *unnest* naively then nesting may not be able to restore the original relation. Surprisingly, despite that, the approach works, in the sense that the language has the desired expressive power. However, this is obviously not good language design. Nor is it easily extendible to other types.

Another approach, advocated e.g. in [Col90] is to allow recursive application of operations. For example, a projection list may contain also sublists for nested relations of depth one, and so on. But this has an ad-hoc flavor, and requires a separate mechanism for each operation, hindering extensibility. We follow the approach of [AB88, BTBN92]. It also aims at a recursive mechanism that will enable users to apply operations on nested substructures "in place", but it offers a general and extendible mechanism for that purpose. In this approach, the workhorse for restructuring is map[8], a well-known construct in functional programming. It is a *functional*, i.e., a *higher-order function*, that accepts a single function as a parameter, to yield another function. Its type rule is

$$\frac{f : T_1 \to T_2}{map(f) : \{T_1\} \to \{T_2\}} \tag{9}$$

Its effect is defined by: $map(f)(S) = \{f(s) \mid s \in S\}$. The facility to accept functions as parameters is crucial: it provides the key to applying operations on substructures. We start from map, and build the algebra by adding other functions and operations gradually.

---

[8] Called *replace* in [AB88]. A related operation ext, used in [BTBN92], is considered below.

We have the set of basic functions given with Σ, and for each such f we can now construct $map(f)$. By orthogonality, since $map(f)$ is a function, it can be an argument to map, that is map expressions can be nested. Recall that attributes are in our framework unary functions. Thus, $map(A)$ is a function that accepts a set of tuples and projects each on its A component. That hints that map is related to the relational *project*, and we show below that it is indeed a generalization of that operation. But so far we cannot even project on a set of attributes — and we need much more expressive restructuring functions. The solution is again found by applying the adequacy principle — we should include facilities for constructing and decomposing tuples and sets, namely constructors and selectors. Not less important, we need facilities, or a notation, for combining functions into more complex functions. As we are now in the realm of functional programming, we search in this realm for possible approaches.

There are at least two possible approaches to completing the language. One direction is to adopt a version of the λ-calculus for expressing functions. This approach leads to the language $\mathcal{MC}$ in [BTBN92]. Another approach, also taken in that paper, and in [AB88], is to stay in a pure algebraic framework. Note: In either case, we do not strive for the power of the full λ-calculus. We have our *data* types (called in [BTBN92] *object* types), and we want to be able to express functions from data types to data types, but no higher-order functions. These higher-order functions that are found useful for achieving this goal (like map) are explicitly included. Thus, a seen below, even the λ-calculus based language has an algebraic flavor.

Before presenting the details, let us briefly reconsider, actually redefine, what we mean by an algebraic framework. What we have in mind is a collection of functions, and also certain functionals that allow us to create new functions from existing functions. For example, *composition* is such a functional, and *map* is another. Each expression in the language denotes a function. There are no variables in such a language. This is more than the simple notion of algebra we had in mind so far, for example when we considered the relational algebra, in which only composition is used in combining functions (and it is implicit in the language definition, rather than being a named operation). A similar approach to functional programming appears in [Bac78]; a query language for the O_2 object-oriented database language based on this paradigm is described in [BJ91]. We recall a similar well-known concept in the domain of functional programming: The λ-calculus is one formalism for functional programming, but there is another, called *combinatory* calculus, that uses no variables, only constants, representing given functions, and combinators used to combine them. It is well known that the two languages are equivalent, and translating λ-calculus to combinatory calculus is an approach being investigated for the implementation of functional programming languages [Pey87]. What we show below is a simple case of these equivalences and translation.

5.2 The Core Algebras

We present now the two languages. The versions presented here are somewhat simpler than those in [BTBN92]. We first describe the (pure) algebra. Recall that we start from map. Certainly, we need to have the domains' constants. But in the algebra everything must denote a function, so we have for each constant c and type T the constant function

K_Tc, of type $T \rightarrow type(c)^9$. We also have the domain functions with their types, and for each attribute A, the function A. For sets, we have the function *single* with its type rule as given above for the predicate calculus, and an additional operation *set-collapse*, denoted μ, with the type rule $\frac{t:\{\{T\}\}}{\mu(t):\{T\}}$, that takes a set of sets into the union of its elements. (*single* increases set nesting, while μ decreases it, so in a sense they are complementary.) It turns out to be useful to have, for each type T, the identity function id_T. This concludes the list of functions. As for functionals, in addition to *map*, we have the functional $\circ$ denoting composition (typing rules for both omitted). Finally, we have a tuple constructor, [ ], but now it is a *function constructor (i.e., a functional)*! Its typing rule is

$$\frac{f_1 : T \rightarrow T_1, \ldots, f_n : T \rightarrow: T_n}{[A_1 : f_1 \ldots A_n : f_n] : T \rightarrow [A_1 : T_1 \ldots A_n : T_n]} \tag{10}$$

This completes the definition of the core algebra.

As a simple example, in particular to understand the use of the tuple constructor, consider the generalized projection of $R(A, B, C)$ (where A, B, C are of type *int*) on two attributes, the sum of A, B and the product of B, C. The expression for that is $map([S : + \circ [A, B], M : \times \circ [B, C]]) \circ R$. We explain how it is constructed: A and B are functions, hence so is $[A, B]$. The tuple constructor functional is applied here. Composition with the binary function $+$ yields a function that for every tuple argument with attributes $A, B, \ldots$ computes the sum of the A and B components. A similar construction is done for the product, and the two functions are again combined by a tuple construction. Then *map* is applied to the resulting function Finally, R is a constant, which in this case is a function $K_{unit}R$. We take it to be from *unit* to the type of R. This explains why we use $\circ R$, rather than (R). The type of the expression is $unit \rightarrow \{[S : int, M : int]\}$. In general, the type of a query in the algebra is $unit \rightarrow T$, for some T.

The above notation is quite cumbersome; we can simplify by using application and/or infix notation for arithmetic (and other parts of Σ). The query above would then be written as $map([S : A + B, M : B \times C]) \circ R$. One may be tempted to also replace $\circ R$ by (R). This is possible, as an abbreviation, but we point out below that, taking into account how the algebra will probably be used, there is a good reason to use $\circ R$.

The simpler projection of R on A, B is similarly written $map([A : A, B : B]) \circ R$. Note that A on the left names a position in the target list, the A on the right is a function. The simpler notation $map([A, B]) \circ R$ is an acceptable (and commonly used) abbreviation when the attribute name is the same as the function. This shows clearly that *map* generalizes the relational *project*.

Finally, we note that $map([A : A, B : B])$ (or the equivalent $map([A, B])$) is also a legal function expression; it is *polymorphic*, with many input types (all those that have the functions A and B defined on them).

It is worth noting here that we have seen three levels of tuple constructors, namely a type constructor, a function constructor and a value constructor. One could ask why do we need to have a function-level tuple constructor, rather than just a value-level

---

[9] For convenience we may still write c, leaving it to the language interpreter to interpret it as K_Tc, for an appropriate T.

constructor? And if we need a function-level constructor, why have we not elevated other functions, e.g., *single* to the function level? The example above illustrates how the function-level constructor is used. Could we express the idea 'take the functions $A + B, B \times C$, apply to an arbitrary object, and construct a tuple with attributes named S, M out of the results' without using it? We could try $[\,]_{S,M} \circ (A + B, B \times C)$, but that again uses a function-level tuple constructor, in the ( )! The issue is well-known: A theory or notation of functions and composition (but no application) works well for single-argument functions, but it is difficult to express composition of multi-argument functions. One well-know solution is to have the ability to create and decompose tuples. Then a multi-argument function is actually a single-argument function accepting tuple arguments (and accessing their components using selectors)[10]. Thus, the tuple constructor must construct tuples of functions. Once we have this ability, all other functions can remain regular functions and need not be elevated to the status of functionals. (We leave it to the reader to show that given *id* and ∘ and the tuple constructor, each of the function-level and value-level constructors can be expressed in terms of the other.) For example, we can write $single \circ [A : f_1, B : f_2] \circ R$, in which *single* is a function, or use it as a functional, as in $\{[A : f_1, B : f_2]\} \circ R$, The choice between these alternatives depends on the intended use of the language and is, to some extent, a matter of convenience.

Now for the calculus $\mathcal{MC}$. In the calculus, we use constants (with the typing axiom above), the functions of Σ, and also the following: the attributes, *map, single, set-collapse*. This is essentially a core it has in common with the algebra, except that constants are not functions now. Additionally, it has typed variables, and tuple construction (as a value-level constructor). Note that *id* and ∘ are *not* included. Instead, it has restricted first-order λ-abstraction and function application. (Expressing *id* and ∘ with these is easy.) The typing rules for the new constructs are:

$$\frac{x : T, t : T_1, \quad T, T_1 \text{ object types}}{\lambda x.t : T \to T_1} \qquad \frac{t_1 : T \to T_1, t_2 : T}{t_1 t_2 : T_1} \qquad (11)$$

The condition on λ abstraction explain why it is *first-order*. It can by used only to create functions from object types to object types. Recall that *object type* means a type of values. Thus, we cannot use λ-abstraction to create higher-order functions.

Note that this is not a standard λ-calculus. One one hand it has a set type constructor, the *single, set-collapse* operations, and the higher-order function, *map*. On the other hand it cannot use λ-abstraction for creating higher-order functions; *map* has to be used for that. Thus, a function to project on attributes A, B is represented in it as $map(\lambda x.[x.A, x.B])$, which is quite close to how this is represented in the algebra.

Remarks:

1. In [BTBN92], the calculus uses a functional *ext*, rather than *map* and μ, with the rule

$$\frac{t : T \to \{T_1\}}{ext(t) : \{T\} \to \{T_1\}} \qquad (12)$$

---

[10] In [AB88], another approach that uses a notation for composition of multi-argument functions is presented.

The meaning of ext is defined by: Given a function f from values to sets of T_1, the function $ext(f)$ extends it to sets of T. For a given set, f is applied to each element, so the result is a set of sets, then the union of all these sets is taken. Thus, obviously, $ext = \mu \circ map$, while $map = ext \circ single$ and $\mu = ext \circ id$. From these identities it follows immediately that the calculus, or the algebra, could contain either map and μ, or equivalently ext. The choice, for now, seems a matter of taste, and we will use both map and ext, as convenient.

2. We note an interesting remark on the calculus from [BTBN92]: It contains operations for creation and destruction of tuples and sets — the generic types of the model, and similarly function creation and function application (which can be viewed as function destruction). Each of these pairs is, in a sense, the minimum we need for the dealing with the corresponding type constructor. The language is obtained by adding to these the the constants and functions of the parameter signature Σ, the map/ext facility for extending functions to sets, so we can do restructuring, and allowing full orthogonality in how all those are combined. Thus, it is a small and clean language. A similar remark applies to the algebra.

5.3 Equivalence

We now briefly consider the correspondence between the $\mathcal{MC}$ calculus and the algebra. (Remember: this is not the predicate calculus, but rather a mix of algebra and some facilities of the λ-calculus.) First, both languages can express functions of arbitrary types $T \rightarrow S$ (where S, T are object types). What are the queries in each language? In the calculus, these are the expressions of any object type T. Recall that names of database relations are constants, and can be used in such expressions. Thus, a query is an expression e of type T. In the algebra we have only functions. Hence a query is an expression of type $unit \rightarrow T$. The correspondence between the languages associates calculus functions of type $T \rightarrow S$ with algebra functions of the same type, and also calculus queries of type T with algebra queries of type $unit \rightarrow T$. With this in mind, we can now state that the two languages are equivalent.

We show below a simplified (and partial) version of the translation from the calculus to the algebra. For the precise (more general, and different) formulation and details , see [BTBN92]. We denote by $tr(e)$ the translation of an expression e. We recommend that the reader checks the types of each expression and its translation.

Queries — expressions of object type:

1. The constant c is translated to $K_{unit}c$.
2. The function application $e_1 e_2$ is translated to $tr(e_1) \circ tr(e_2)$.

Functions:

1. Any function that exists in both languages is represented by its name in both. This includes domain functions, attributes, $single$ and μ, and also map.
2. The function $\lambda x_T.c$ is translated to $K_T c$.
3. The function $\lambda x.x$ is translated to id.

4. The function $\lambda x.e_1 e_2$ is translated to $tr(e_1) \circ tr(\lambda x.e_2)$. This translation is valid only provided that e_1 does not contain x free! As special cases, $tr(\lambda x.fe) = f \circ tr(\lambda x.e)$, where f is any of the functions that have names in both languages..

5. The function $\lambda x.[A : e \ldots]$ is translated to $[A : tr(\lambda x.e) \ldots]$. (Note that a value-level constructor is translated to a function-level constructor.)

5.4 Extending the Languages

The power of the language(s) is still a far cry from what we would like to have. We can express with it various kinds of projections. What else? Can we express, e.g., *product*? Recall that in the translation we assumed that if $\lambda x.e_1 e_2$ is a function expression, then the function e_1 does not contain x free. If e_1 itself was obtained by abstraction, as say, $\lambda y.e'$, then that means e' does not contain x free. If we allow in the calculus (as in [BTBN92]) function expressions with free variables[11], then we can also express *product*: Assume the input is a pair $w = [R, S]$. First, we define a function $f = map(\lambda y.[y, x])$, which when applied to a set R will replace each r in it by a pair $[r, x]$. As it has x free, denote it by f_x. Now $\lambda w.map(\lambda x.f_x(1st\, w))(2nd\, w)$ is a function that given a pair w as above, will replace each s in S by the set $f_s R$. To obtain the product, we apply μ to the result of the map. (Note that rather than using map followed by μ, we could simply use ext, and the function would then be $\lambda w.ext(\lambda x.f_x(1st\, w))(2nd\, w)$.) What we have done is to express *product* as a nested loop, with S on the outside. A translation to a nested loop with R on the outside is obviously possible.

How can we express product using the algebra we have so far? Our translation of the previous subsection does not work, since it does not deal with expressions like $\lambda y.[y, x]$. Assume we construct the pair $[R, S]$. The function f above can be expressed as $f = map([id, g])$, for some function g that still needs to be determined. Now, the application of f to R is expressed by $f \circ 1st$, and the application of that to elements of S by $map(f \circ 1st) \circ 2nd$. OOPS! This does not work; once we apply $2nd$, we have only S, and all other functions we want to apply next are interpreted in the context of S. It seems to be impossible to apply a function that uses one component of a pair to the other component. Let us try another direction. We start with $map([id, g]) \circ R$, which has the value $\{[r, g] \mid r \in R\}$. Now this is applied to S, with g being the identity on S, so we get pairs of the form $[r, s]$. After adding the μ, the expression is $ext(map([id, id]) \circ R) \circ S$. The problem here is that the first id is supposed to be the identity on R, the other the identity on S, but the expression does not say that! If the elements of R and S were of different types, then the type indices on the functions could help, but if they are of the same type then how can we distinguish between the two intended meanings of id? Thus, we need to extend the algebra. One possibility, considered briefly in [AB88] is to include a facility to rename functions, and a scoping mechanism to decide on the meaning of a function. We might write the query as $ext(let\ g = id\ in\ map([id, g]) \circ 1st) \circ 2nd$. The scope rule will associate g with the identity on $2nd$.

In [BTBN92] the solution is to include a new operation, ρ_2, that takes a pair consisting of an element v and a set S, and creates a set of pairs $\{[v, s] \mid s \in S\}$. This is essentially

---

[11] Permitting free variables in expressions of object type of the calculus (as necessary to express *product* and many other queries) complicates the translation to the algebra.

a tuple-level unnest; it allows one to refer to v as $1st$ and to s in S as $2nd$, so it indeed provides distinct functions to access them. Since projection functions and tuple construction allow us to permute tuples, we can easily express ρ_1 that operates on a pair $[S, v]$. The algebraic expression for the *product* given this operation is quite simple. If the input is the pair $[R, S]$, then the expression is $ext(\rho_1) \circ \rho_2$.

Both languages still cannot express many algebraic operations. One of the reasons [BTBN92] introduced this minimal language is to show (in)dependence of operations. Results on independence of operations are also presented in other papers, e.g., [BK90]. They show that the language above cannot express $\emptyset$ and *union*, and add them. Given the empty set, they use the type *set(unit)* as a boolean type: $\{[\,]\}$ represent *true* and $\{\,\}$ represents *false*. This gives a nice representation of *selection* using ext. Indeed, if a predicate applied to an element s returns true, i.e., $\{[\,]\}$, then a product of this result with $\{s\}$ gives $\{s\}$; if it returns $\{\,\}$, then the product returns $\{\,\}$. Then "pulling" this upward to operate on a set S with ext gives the desired result of the selection. That is, $\{\,\}$ with *product* acts as a black hole that swallows any element, while $\{[\,]\}$ leaves any element intact. The same idea can be used to implement domain-restricted existential quantification of the form $\exists x \in S.p$, by $ext(p)$. Then they show that if one also assumes an equality predicate on the atomic domains, then one can define equality on other set types, and then also *membership, subset, difference, nest* and a few other operations. For example, the membership predicate $x \in S$ is defined by $ext(\lambda y.x = y)$. These additions give the language the same power as the algebra proposed in [AB88] (without the *powerset* operation.) Both algebras now have *map* instead of the relational *project*, a *select* operation, the empty set, *union, difference, product*, — all the relational operations, and also the tuple and set operations and predicates and the machinery described above. A final augmentation in [BTBN92] is to allow an *if-then-else* construct, which they also show to be independent of the other operations.

5.5 Discussion

Let us now consider a few examples. We will use the same example scheme and queries used above for the predicate calculus. We use in the example a generalized version of the *product*, denoted Π, defined as follows: Let $R : unit \to \{T\}, f : \{T\} \to S$ be functions. Then

$$\Pi_{A,B}(R, f) = \{[A : r, B : y] \mid r \in R, y \in f(r)\}. \tag{13}$$

In the simple case, where f is the constant function S, we obtain the "standard" *product*: $\Pi(R, S) = \{[r, s] \mid r \in R, s \in S\}$. In both the algebra and calculus we include in some cases more than one solution.

Example 2.   1. Select the people that have children born after 23.10.67:

   Algebra:

   (i) $\sigma(\emptyset \neq \sigma(birth\_date > 23.10.67) \circ children) \circ people$.

   (ii) $map(P) \circ \sigma(C.birth\_date > 23.10.67) \circ \Pi_{P,C}(people, children)))$.

Note that, to adhere to the algebraic paradigm as it was described above, we should have treated the binary operations $\neq, >$ as prefix operations, and use a pair construction to convert their arguments into a single argument. We have used the common infix notation for convenience.

Calculus:

(i) $\sigma(ext(birth\_date > 23.10.67)(children))(people)$.

(ii) $\sigma(\sigma(birth\_date > 23.10.67)(children) \neq \emptyset)(people)$.

Note that, in the calculus version, the internal ext realizes a predicate of the form $\exists x \in S.p$, where p is the condition on the birth date, and S is the set of children.

2. Select from *people* the tuples where the person's name is the same as the name of one of his/her children:

Algebra:

(i) $\sigma(name \in map(name) \circ children) \circ people$.

Note the name clash here, which should be resolved by an appropriate scope rule, or by using ρ.

(ii) $map(P) \circ \sigma(C.name = P.name) \circ \Pi_{P,C}(people, children)))$.

Thus, one we have a *product* operation, resolution of names becomes much easier, since they can be associated with the different components of a tuple.

Calculus:

(i) $\sigma(\lambda x.name(x) \in map(name)(children))(people)$.

The explicit variable x helps to disambiguate the two uses of "name". Other possible versions:

(ii) $\sigma(name \in map(name)(children))(people)$.

(iii) $\sigma(\lambda x.ext(name(x) = name)(children))(people)$.

3. Project out the names of children from the subrelations in people:

Algebra:

(i) $map([name, children\_b\_d : map(birth\_date) \circ children]) \circ people$.

(ii) $map([P.name, C]) \circ \Pi_{P,C}(people, map(birth\_date) \circ children))$.

Calculus:

$map([name, children\_b\_d : map(birth\_date)(children)])(people)$.

4. Unnest *people*, that is convert it to a flat relation:

Algebra:

        let $g =$ let $p\_name = name$ in
        $map([p\_name, c\_name : name, c\_b\_d : birth\_date]) \circ children$
        in $ext(g) \circ people$

Calculus:

        let $h = \lambda x.map([p\_name : x.name, c\_name : name,$
                                   $c\_b\_d : birth\_date])(children)$
        in $ext(h)(people)$

5. Create a relation where each tuple contains a child name, and a set of (at most two)

its parents' names.

Algebra:

$$ext(map([name, f(name)]) \circ children) \circ people$$
$$\textbf{where } f(x) = map(x) \circ select(x \in map(name) \circ children) \circ people.$$

Calculus:

$$ext(map([name, f(name)])(children))(people)$$
$$\textbf{where } f(x) = map(x)(select(x \in map(name)children)(people)).$$

The examples illustrate that it is convenient to have nested subqueries, and even more convenient to define them separately, using a LET or a WHERE clause. As can be seen from the examples, most of them can be expressed in almost the same way in both languages, and most of them can be expressed very succinctly in the algebra with the generalized *product*. Finally, note that for internal representation of queries, the pure form of the algebra is actually superior to the calculus. Just replace ∘ by a dash.

An important property of this algebra, proved in [BTBN92] is that it is in PTIME. Note that [AB88] prove that their algebra without the *powerset* is equivalent to a strongly restricted version of the calculus, and this version is shown in [GV91] to be in PTIME. The current proof is more direct, and holds also when the *if-then-else* is added.

This work shows that the notion of an algebra can be generalized to the complex object model. For both languages it seems that the approach can be generalized to include other type constructors, and the close relationship with functional language notations should help us to draw on the technology of that domain. Still the language, in both its forms, seems to be too complex to be used as of a user-level query language. It is probably a reasonable language for internal representation, although more research is needed to understand its properties and use.

5.6 Comprehensions

Generalizing from the relational language, let us now consider the comprehensions notation for our model. Recall that we presented it as a succinct, precisely defined, equivalent of SQL. For an SQL-oriented language for an OODBMS, see e.g., [CDLR90].

Recall that a comprehension is defined by a target list t and a qualifier q consisting of a list of atomic qualifiers. Now, a qualifier may introduce a variable ranging over a set component of a previous variable, so it makes sense to require that each qualifier uses only variables introduced to its left. (The relationship to the Π operation is obvious.) Also note that now values of any types are first class citizens, so terms of set type can legally appear in the target list. In particular, comprehensions can appear in the target list, so the language supports complete orthogonality in the use of expressions. We illustrate with the same example queries:

Example 3.   1. Select the persons that have children born after 23.10.67:

$$\{p \mid p \leftarrow people, c \leftarrow p.children, c.birth\_date > 23.10.67\}.$$

2. Select from *people* the tuples where the person's name is the same as the name of one of his/her children:

$$\{p \mid p \leftarrow people, c \leftarrow p.children, p.name = c.name\}.$$

3. Project out the names of children from the subrelations in people:

$\{p.name, children : \{c.birth\_date \mid c \leftarrow p.children\} \mid p \leftarrow people\}.$

4. Unnest *people*, that is convert it to a flat relation:

$$\{p\_name : p.name, c\_name : c.name, c\_b\_d : c.birth\_date \mid$$
$$p \leftarrow people, c \leftarrow p.children\}.$$

Note how elements from different levels of the value are collected together, with no special operator like μ or ext.

5. Create a relation where each tuple has a child name, and a set of (at most two) its parents' names.

$$\{c.name, \{p.name \mid p \leftarrow people, c \in p.children\} \mid$$
$$p1 \leftarrow people, c \leftarrow p1.children.\}$$

Note how the subquery in the target list expresses a traversal of a link in the inverse direction.

Comparing the expressions in this example to those in the previous examples, it is clear that this language is a sublanguage of both the complex object calculus and the algebra. The relationship to the latter language is easily expressed with the generalized product. As in the relational case, it has the simple basic block, and eliminates the need for explicit quantifiers in many queries. Additionally, it expresses nests and unnests quite easily. Compared to the algebraic languages it has the advantage that it deals with *set-collapse* naturally, so in most cases there is no need to use it, resulting in further simplification of many queries. A translation from relational comprehensions to an algebra appears, e.g., in [Tri91], and several other recent works on comprehensions. Interestingly, ext is prominent in these translations, reflecting the fact that map and μ are often combined in a comprehension. A translation into the algebra with the generalized product has not yet been investigated and merits more attention; optimization of algebraic expressions also merits further attention.

6 Other OODM Features

6.1 Object Identity

Once identity is in the model, data is no longer hierarchical. It forms a directed graph, even cycles may exist. However, as noted in [AK89], when you start from any object, and consider the graph emanating from it, you have a (virtual) tree. Thus, a language that fits a hierarchical model can fit such a model quite well.

One impact of the fact that we have objects with identity is that operations now may return objects, not just values. Thus, $x.A$ may denote an object, so further use of dot notation as in $x.A.B$ is legal. Another issue is raised at the level of set operations. Returning objects seems fine for operations like selections, but is somewhat problematic for *projection* or *map*. If we have a set of objects with certain attributes, and we apply a *projection*, do we get back the same set of objects? If so, we still have access to the attributes, so what have we accomplished? Some researchers conclude that *project* returns a set of values. As a matter of fact, since we are talking here about a *query* language, we probably intend to present results on a screen or on paper, so results need to be values. To satisfy the closure property, one has then to include in the model not just objects and classes, but also values and relations. Although queries operate on objects, they usually return values. The languages we have described seem to be adequate for such a purpose.

Another approach, presented e.g., in [HS91a], relies on the adequacy principle, and claims that we should have two different kinds of projection. One indeed creates value tuples. The other kind, when applied to a class will create another class. Thus, given a class C with attributes A, B, a projection on A will create a new class, with attribute A only. Note that the new class has the same objects as C. Thus, we have here a totally new kind of operation: We are creating a new *type*, or *interface*, and we force accesses to the same objects, from the class C and from the new class to use different interfaces. This is more a schema-level operation than a data manipulation primitive. This kind of operations seems particularly useful when the query language is also used to define views.

Another interesting issue here is whether queries should only return existing objects, or should they also generate new objects. (See *object preserving, object generating* operations in [HS91a].) Again, if the interest is only in queries, there is no clear need to generate objects. But for view definition, part of the idea of restructuring that underlies the concept of a view is that the user's view of the world is changed, and that should include the generation of new objects. The theoretical implication of the ability to generate objects have been investigated in [AK89] and some subsequent papers. The practical aspects — incorporating the idea into a view definition facility, are still waiting.

6.2 Behavior and Encapsulation

Assume objects have methods associated with them, and access to the attributes is prevented by encapsulation. The question "Should the query language respect encapsulation" has been posed. My opinion on that is unconditionally "Yes". A user can access a database only through the provided interface. That is the only database he/she know about, and there is no reason to change that for a query language.

Is there any impact to the fact that now objects have methods rather than attributes? The answer seems to be that there arise some syntactic issues: rather than writing $x.A$, we may now write $x.m(y_1, ldots)$. Another issue that needs clarification is probably that of scope rules, to determine the meanings of the terms that appear as parameters of the method. A major problem here, not at the level of language design, is optimization.

Finally, objects and classes defined in a view need to have behavior too. That means that if the query language is used to define views, we need a facility for defining methods, possibly using the given methods of the database. The algebra seems like an interesting starting point, but this is still a virtually untouched research issue.

6.3 Isa and Inheritance

When a query is posed on a database with *subclass* relationships, it can be decomposed to a union of queries on the extents of classes. This has an impact on its optimization and execution. For recent work on this subject see [Cha92].

7 Conclusions

We have presented in this paper languages for a complex object model, and considered briefly possible generalizations, and problems to be solved, if one is interested in a full OODM. We hope the reader has been convinced that these languages are a good basis for languages for OODBMSs, so understanding them, and the problems involved in designing and implementing them, are important for OODBMSs.

As we have stated, we believe the algebra is a candidate for an internal language, while comprehensions/SQL are for the user-level. But these observations have to be substantiated. A major problem here is optimization. As we remarked, we know to optimize SQL as a relational language. But, in a complex object language, once we throw in equality on base types (and we certainly want that), we can express operations like *difference* and *nest*, and we do not know good optimizations for expressions involving these operations. Thus, even for the non-recursive algebra, a good clear theory of optimization is still missing.

While a good understanding of the languages we have described is important, they are essentially non-recursive languages. There exists a large body of literature on recursive languages and their optimization for the relational model. There has also been quite a lot of research on adding recursion to complex object languages. We note that recursion can also be easily added to comprehensions. In functional programming, recursion is added easily — one cannot really write good programs without using recursion. But in databases that is a major change of expressive power. Although there is a lot of knowledge about optimizing Datalog programs, there is, it seems, very little known about optimization for Datalog, or recursive comprehensions, for complex objects.

Adding aggregations adds another of level of complexity. Again, it is quite easy to augment comprehensions by aggregation facilities (as it is for any decent functional notation). However, general purpose aggregation facilities pose non-trivial semantic problems. See, e.g., [BS91]. This paper, along with many other recent papers, also considers the idea that the languages should support, rather than just sets, a large collection of bulk types.

Although we would like to borrow as much as possible from the elegant notations and constructs of functional programming for our query languages, we need to be careful, since constructs may have a cost in terms of too much expressive power. We have seen how to use only first-order λ-abstraction. A study of useful but manageable constructs and ideas from functional programming is needed.

Theoretical treatments of query languages often gloss over the naming issue. As we have seen, in a complex object model and certainly in other advanced model, a name may appear in different places and roles, so precise scope rules need to be provided.

Acknowledgments

This work was partially supported by a grant from GIF — The German Israeli Foundation for Scientific Research and Development, and by a grant from the Israel Ministry of Science for French Israeli Scientific Cooperation.

Functional Programming Formalisms for OODBMS Methods

Gerd Hillebrand, Paris Kanellakis, Sridhar Ramaswamy

Brown University, Department of Computer Science, Providence, RI 02912, USA

Abstract. Two well-studied functional formalisms in the theory of programming languages are (1) applicative program schemas and (2) typed lambda calculi. We relate these programming formalisms to object-oriented database management systems (OODBMSs) and in particular to the description of methods.

The language of method schemas (MS) is a programming formalism based on applicative program schemas with additional key object-oriented features such as classes, methods, inheritance, name overloading, and late binding. From [AKRW92], we present its syntax and semantics and survey the state-of-the-art of consistency checking or signature inference for this language, a problem which can be used in studying database schema evolution. We then relate MS with more conventional database query languages by showing that its expressive power over finite ordered databases is PTIME.

Despite its simplicity and applicability, MS does not directly model the tuple, set, and list complex structures that are quite common in databases. Also, it does not treat functions as objects, i.e., methods are different from objects. It is possible to achieve these two capabilities using the typed lambda calculus with equality (TLC$^=$) as a database query language, even without any object-oriented features. From [HKM93], we illustrate how this pure functional language subsumes most conventional database query languages including the relational calculus/algebra, Datalog (with or without negation), and the complex object calculus/algebra (with or without powerset).

In conclusion, we argue that the appropriate programming formalism for OODBs must be a functional language that combines the object-oriented MS with the expressive TLC$^=$ and facilitates operations on sets of objects.

1 Introduction

Object-oriented database managment systems (OODBMSs) represent a new generation of database technology, which has developed through a combination of advanced programming language features and successful relational/network database techniques, see [BDK92, KL89, ZM90b]. Both programming language theory and database theory have been proposed as starting points for OODB formal foundations. They are both legitimate starting points, but one should be aware that a naive synthesis of such distinct theories is not necessarily harmonious. For example, it is largely an open question how to match distinct programming paradigms in one language.

In this paper we explore the problem "what is the appropriate formal model for OODBs" from a functional perspective. We view the organization of data into *objects with methods* as the core new feature of OODBs. This is a function-centric (or method-centric) view of data as opposed to the structure-centric view of data in relational databases (e.g., in [Kan90, Ull82]).

Interesting functional approaches to database query languages have been advocated in the past, e.g., [BFN82, Shi81], but much remains to be done in this area. Because of the function-centric character of OODBs we believe that this is one of the most promising approaches to the problem of their formalization. Note that some of the actual query languages in OODB prototypes are functional [BDK92] and that recent research on complex-objects and types has emphasized functional models [BTBN92, BTBW92].

Two well-studied functional formalisms in the theory of programming languages are (1) applicative program schemas [Cou90, Gre75] and (2) typed lambda calculi [Chu41, Bar84, Bar90]. We relate these two programming formalisms to OODBs and in particular to the description of OODB methods.

In order to accomplish this: (1) We modify applicative program schemas into an OODB formalism called *method schemas* (MS) in [AKRW92]. We show that method schemas (over ordered databases) express exactly the PTIME queries. (2) We present the typed lambda calculus as a formalism for expressing a wide range of relational and complex-object database queries [HKM93]. In this case, the elementary time queries (which properly contain the PTIME queries) are expressible, because of a limited ability to create and manipulate list structures. So, in terms of expressive power, the typed lambda calculus is the more general (even if not the more convenient) framework.

By our overview of the approaches in [AKRW92, HKM93] and our new characterization of the expressive power of method schemas we demonstrate how *many notions from relational and object-oriented DBMSs can be formulated, with no loss of generality, in pure functional form*. More specifically, we proceed as follows.

MS is a simple programming formalism for OODBs, based on applicative program schemas with additional features such as *classes, methods, inheritance, name overloading*, and *late binding*. In Sect. 2.1, we explain the syntax and semantics of method schemas and motivate them with an OODB example. Method schema consistency is a form of "type inference," which involves deciding at compile-time whether a given method schema can lead to an inconsistency at run-time in some interpretation. A more precise term for this problem would be *signature inference*. The incremental version of consistency checking for method schemas is an algorithmic formalization of the database schema evolution problem [AKRW92, BKKK87, HTY89, SZ87, Wal91, Zic92]. In Sect. 2.2, we survey the state-of-the-art on consistency checking. We use various algorithmic techniques and techniques from the theory of program schemas, e.g., [AMP73, LPP70].

In Sect. 3, we examine the expressive power of MS by relating it to the more conventional formalisms of relational calculus [Cod72] and Datalog with negation [CH85, KP88, AV91]. For finite ordered interpretations this is a functional characterization of PTIME (analogous to the logical characterizations of [Imm86, Var82]). A different functional characterization in terms of equations is presented in [Gur83]. Note also that, Datalog with negation has been used in [ALUW93] to provide semantics to a number of variations of method schemas. In Sect. 3.1 we outline the input-output conventions, in Sect. 3.2 we argue that every PTIME query is expressible, and in Sect. 3.3 that only PTIME queries are expressible.

Our expressive power result indicates that MS is a syntactic variation on the very robust concept of PTIME database queries that is attractive because it incorporates many additional desirable object-oriented features. There are some disadvantages, however. Method schemas are an example of a practical functional framework but do not treat functions as objects, i.e., methods are different from objects. To achieve this uniformity one has to examine higher-order frameworks related to the lambda calculus. Another problem is that, as in Datalog, complex structures (such as sets, tuples or lists) are not directly part of the framework but have to be encoded (into relations for Datalog, into the class hierarchy and methods for MS). In typed lambda calculi we can use a simple type discipline to encode complex structures in a far more direct fashion. The notion of types here is structural and quite different from the notion of classes.

In Sect. 4, we present some basic background on the syntax, the operational semantics, and the types of the simply typed lambda calculus with equality (TLC$^=$). We refer to [HKM93] for how to remove equality from this calculus. For the problem of type inference we refer to [KMM91].

It is possible to "naturally embed" in the typed lambda calculus with equality many database query languages including the relational calculus/algebra [Cod72], Datalog (with or without negation) [CH85, KP88, AV91], and the complex object calculus/algebra (with or without powerset) [AB88, AK90]. We consider embeddings such that for each query expressed there is a lambda term which when applied to the input database (which is a list-of-tuples lambda term) normalizes to the output database; most importantly, if the query expressed is in PTIME then the normal form can be computed in a number of reduction steps polynomial in the size of input database.

In Sect. 5.1 we discuss the input-output conventions for representing sets, tuples and lists, as well as the important concept of list iteration. In Sect. 5.2 we present, as an extended example, the embedding of the relational algebra. Our analysis of the expressive power of the simply typed lambda calculus is based on the analysis of reduction sequences of [Sta79, Mai92b].

We refer to [HKM93] for the more advanced fixpoint and powerset features. Note that these features allow the embedding of higher-order queries, e.g., the second-order queries of [Fag74, CH82]. Note that we only use the very core of programming language type systems, i.e., only simple types without any polymorphism. It is interesting that the (otherwise very convenient) use of method names in method schemas and their recursive definition can all be simulated using the fixpoints of [HKM93] in the typed lambda calculus.

The embeddings we present form the first step in understanding the connections between functional programming and databases. Given the emphasis of database theory on efficiency, we can restrict ourselves to PTIME queries. For PTIME queries we present here a method schema framework (Sect. 3) and the basis for a lambda calculus framework (Sect. 5 and [HKM93]). For other functional characterizations of PTIME we refer to [Gur83, LM93].

In conclusion, in Sect. 6 we comment on the possible combination of MS with TLC$^=$ as well as some open research questions.

2 Method Schemas (MS)

2.1 Syntax and Operational Semantics

We assume the existence of the following disjoint countable sets of symbols: of *classes* $(c_1, c_2, \ldots)$ and of *methods* $(m_1, m_2, \ldots)$. For each method m, the arity of m is an integer greater or equal to zero. A *signature* is an expression $c_1, \ldots, c_{k-1} \rightarrow c_k$, where each c_i, for $1 \leq i \leq k$, is a class. For $k = 1$, the expression is $\rightarrow c_1$. In this formalism the signatures play the role of "types" (but since the word "type" has been misused in many different contexts we prefer to use the more precise term signature).

A *base definition* of m at $c_1, \ldots, c_{k-1}$, for $k \geq 1$ is a pair $(m, (c_1, \ldots, c_{k-1} \rightarrow c_k))$, where m is a method of arity $k - 1$ and the remaining part is a signature. (For $k = 1$, the method m is zero-ary.) A *coded definition* of m at $c_1, \ldots, c_k$, for $k \geq 1$ is a triple $(m, (c_1, \ldots, c_k), t)$, where m is a method of arity k, for $1 \leq i \leq k$, each c_i is a class, and t is a k-term (i.e., k-terms are our programming formalism).

A *k-term* for some $k \geq 1$ is a finite rooted ordered directed acyclic graph (dag) such that: (1) each vertex is uniquely labeled either by a method or by an integer in $\{1, \ldots, k\}$; (2) each vertex labeled by a method of arity j has j children which are ordered from left to right; (3) all vertices of out-degree zero are called *inputs* and each vertex labeled with an integer is an input; (4) the root is called the *output*; (5) the dag comes with a uniquely defined depth first search order going from left to right because the children of each vertex are ordered.

For example, the terms t and t' in Fig. 1 are 1-terms. They are, by definition, also 2-terms, 3-terms, etc. The idea is that k-terms represent functions of k arguments, where a copy of argument i is placed at each input labeled i. Vertices can also have outdegree zero and be labeled by zero-ary methods, i.e., they are constant inputs.

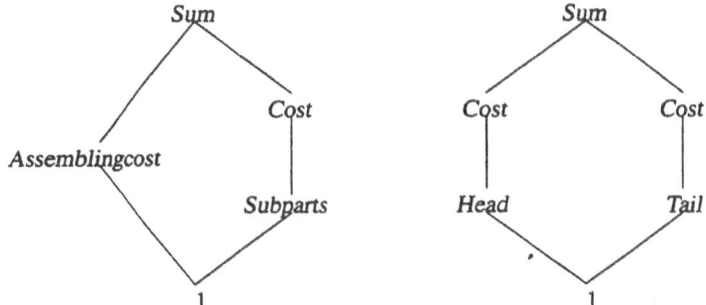

Fig. 1. Term t and t'

As an example, consider the following definitions:

$(Price, (Basepart \rightarrow Int))$

$(Cost, (Basepart), s)$

$(Cost, (Part), t)$

Let s be a single arc with tail labeled *Price* and head labeled 1, and t be as in Fig. 1. These definitions can be represented syntactically using an intuitive lambda notation— instead of the graphical k-term notation—as shown below. Note that we use the symbol colon (:) for representing base methods and the symbol equal (=) for coded methods.

$$Price \ @ \ Basepart : \ Int$$
$$Cost \ @ \ Basepart = \lambda x. \ Price(x)$$
$$Cost \ @ \ Part \quad = \lambda x. \ Sum(Assemblingcost(x), \ Cost(Subparts(x)))$$

Definition 1. A *method schema* is a 4-tuple $(C, \leq, \Sigma_0, \Sigma_1)$ where:

1. C is a finite set of classes and $\leq$ is a forest on C. We say that $c \leq c'$ if c is a descendant of c' in this forest. The partial order defined by $\leq$ is called the *Isa* relation.
2. Σ_0 is a set of base definitions with classes from C.
3. Σ_1 is a set of coded definitions with classes from C. Let M_0 be the set of methods defined in Σ_0 and M_1 be the set of methods defined in Σ_1. We require that $M_0 \cap M_1 = \emptyset$ and that the methods that appear in k-terms of Σ_1 are from $M_0 \cup M_1$.
4. Each method of arity k has at most one definition at $c_1, \ldots, c_k$ for each $c_1, \ldots, c_k$.

Example 1. Consider the class hierarchy of Fig. 2 and the terms t and t' in Fig. 1. Method definitions are presented in Fig. 3.

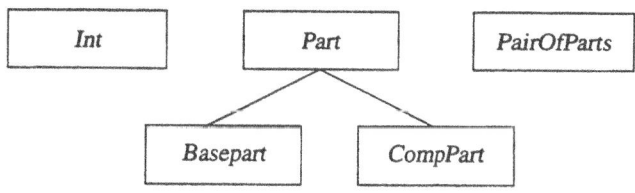

Fig. 2. An example *Isa* hierarchy

Let us briefly survey some important concepts in connection with method schemas.

Syntactically restricted families of method schemas: A schema is *monadic* if all its methods have arity 1. A schema is *recursion-free* if there is no directed cycle in the *method dependence graph*, where the vertices of the method dependence graph are the coded methods and there is an arc from m to n iff m occurs in some coded definition of n. (Note that, our definition of recursion-freeness is a reasonable syntactic way of avoiding recursion, but not necessarily the only one.) A schema is *simple* if only base methods occur in its coded definitions. Note that simple schemas are an important kind of recursion-free schemas.

Sum	@	*Int, Int*	: *Int*
Head	@	*PairOfParts* :	*Part*
Tail	@	*PairOfParts* :	*Part*
Price	@	*Basepart*	: *Int*
Subparts	@	*Part*	: *PairOfParts*
Assemblingcost	@	*Part*	: *Int*
Cost	@	*Part*	$= t$
Cost	@	*Basepart*	$= \lambda x.\, Price(x)$
Cost	@	*PairOfParts* $= t'$	

Fig. 3. Methods

For simple schemas, *covariance* is the following constraint on the signatures of base methods. A simple schema is covariant if for each m and for each pair

$$(m, (c_1, \ldots, c_k \to c)) \ ,$$
$$(m, (c'_1, \ldots, c'_k \to c'))$$

of definitions of a base method m, we have that $(\forall i\ c'_i \leq c_i) \Rightarrow c' \leq c$.

Method Inheritance: A method schema $(C, \leq, \Sigma_0, \Sigma_1)$ contains definitions of methods, i.e., Σ_0, Σ_1, which we call *explicit*. It is also used to define methods implicitly, through *inheritance*. This is for the convenience of code reuse. Therefore, in addition to the explicit definitions for a method, definitions are implicitly inherited along the class hierarchy. If a method m is explicitly defined at classes $c'_1, \ldots, c'_k$, then its definition implicitly applies at $c_1, \ldots, c_k$ where $c_i \leq c'_i$ for $i = 1, \ldots, k$.

Name overloading: Method inheritance implies that we can have several definitions for the same base or coded method at the same classes—although by condition 4 of the method schema definition there can be only one explicit definition. This creates overloading of names. To illustrate overloading, consider the method *Cost* in the example. That method is explicitly defined on *Part*, implicitly inherited by *Basepart* and *CompPart*, and explicitly redefined on *Basepart*; it is also explicitly defined for *PairOfParts*.

Resolution of name overloading: This consists of assigning to a given method and given classes, a unique definition. The resolution of a method m at some $c_1, \ldots, c_k$ is the explicit definition of m for the "component-wise smallest" tuple $c'_1, \ldots, c'_k$ at which m has an explicit definition and $c_i \leq c'_i$, for $i = 1, \ldots, k$ (if such a unique component-wise minimum exists). For example, *Cost* at *CompPart* is resolved to be the explicit definition from *Part*, whereas *Cost* at *Basepart* is *Basepart*'s explicit definition. If m has a resolution at $c_1, \ldots, c_k$, we say that m is *well defined* at $c_1, \ldots, c_k$. Otherwise, we say that m is *undefined* at $c_1, \ldots, c_k$. Non-definition can come either (1) because there is no definition of m above $c_1, \ldots, c_k$ or (2) because there is ambiguity of definitions above $c_1, \ldots, c_k$.

Example 2. Let c_1, c_2 be classes with $c_1 \leq c_2$ and consider the schema with explicit base definitions of m at c_1, c_2 and c_2, c_1. Then m is undefined at c_2, c_2 (no definition) and m is undefined at c_1, c_1 (ambiguity of definitions). For methods of arity 1, ambiguity (2) cannot arise because of the forest hierarchy, but we can have non-definition because of (1).

Object assignments: We assume the existence of a countably infinite set of *objects* $(o_1, o_2, \ldots)$ disjoint from classes and methods. We use object assignments [AK89] to provide semantics for classes with inheritance. The semantics of base methods is defined using partial functions satisfying certain signature constraints.

Definition 2. Given a method schema $(C, \leq, \Sigma_0, \Sigma_1)$, a *disjoint object assignment* ν for C is a total function from C to finite sets of objects such that distinct classes are mapped to disjoint sets of objects (sets with pairwise empty intersections). For each c, we define $\nu(c*) = \bigcup_{c_1 \leq c} \nu(c_1)$. We will refer to $\bigcup_{c \in C} \nu(c)$ as the set of objects in ν.

Definition 3. An *interpretation* of a schema $S = (C, \leq, \Sigma_0, \Sigma_1)$ is a pair $I = (\nu, \mu)$ where ν is a disjoint object assignment for C and μ a total function from the base methods M_0 in S to partial functions such that:

1. If m has arity k, $\mu(m)$ is a partial function from k-tuples of objects in ν to objects in ν.
2. For each $c_1, \ldots, c_k$, if m is undefined at $c_1, \ldots, c_k$, then $\mu(m)$ is undefined everywhere in $\nu(c_1) \times \cdots \times \nu(c_k)$. Otherwise, let the resolution of m at $c_1, \ldots, c_k$ be $(m, (c'_1, \ldots, c'_k \rightarrow c))$ where $c_i \leq c'_i$ for $i = 1, \ldots, k$. Then we have that $\mu(m)|_{\nu(c_1) \times \cdots \times \nu(c_k)}$ is a total function into $\nu(c*)$.

Intuitively, every class c is populated by a set of objects $\nu(c*)$, some of which are in this class exclusively (those objects that are in $\nu(c)$) and the rest belong to its "subclasses" c_1, where $c_1 \leq c$ and $c_1 \neq c$. When a base method is defined at a class c_1 with signature $c_1 \rightarrow c$ (or is inherited at c_1 with signature $c'_1 \rightarrow c$ such that $c_1 \leq c'_1$), then its meaning at c_1 is a total function from $\nu(c_1)$ to $\nu(c*)$. That is, given an object exclusively in c_1, return an object in c.

The semantics of coded methods is defined using the above semantics of base methods and a rewriting technique. Without recursion, this rewriting is equivalent to function composition.

Late binding: This is a result of the operational definition of rewriting. Let us first give some intuition for the rewriting of coded methods. Consider a k-term that is a single arc. Let its one internal node be labeled *Cost* and its input be replaced by an object o, as a "procedure call" to *Cost*. Based on the class of its argument, we can replace *Cost* either by some object/code if it is defined in a base/coded fashion, or by an error message if it is undefined. In general, we reduce the first method (first in the depth first ordering of the k-term we are processing) that has instantiated leaves as children. We continue this processing until we either obtain a result (i.e., an object), or reach an inconsistency. We might also not terminate. A partial sequence of rewritings for Example 1 is shown in Fig. 4, where o is in class *PairOfParts* and o', o'' are in class *Basepart*.

More formally, an *instantiated term* in interpretation $I = (\nu, \mu)$ is a k-term, whose integer labels have been replaced by objects. Let $c_1, \ldots, c_k$ be classes, m be a method

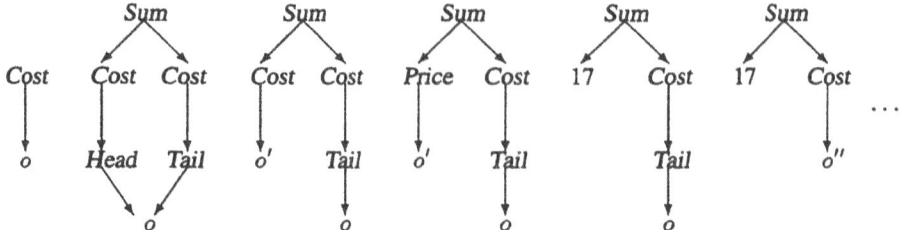

Fig. 4. A reduction sequence

of arity k, and for each i let $o_i \in \nu(c_i)$. Then the instantiated term consisting of a single vertex labeled m and k inputs labeled respectively $o_1, \ldots, o_k$ is said to be a *redex*. We define the *first reducible vertex* to be the uniquely determined first vertex in the depth first ordering of an instantiated term, which is the root of a redex.

Definition 4. Let I be an interpretation of method schema S, t be an instantiated term in I, w be the first reducible vertex of t, and m be the label of w. Let $o_1, \ldots, o_k$ be the labels of the children of w belonging respectively to classes $c_1, \ldots, c_k$. The *reduction* $I(t)$ of t in I is obtained as follows:

1. If m is undefined at $c_1, \ldots, c_k$ then $I(t)$ is a special symbol $\perp$.
2. If m is a base method well defined at $c_1, \ldots, c_k$, let its resolution there be $(m, (c'_1, \ldots, c'_k \to c))$. (This implies that $c_i \leq c'_i$ for $i = 1, \ldots, k$.) Then $I(t)$ is the instantiated term obtained by removing from w the outgoing edges and changing its label to $\mu(m)(o_1, \ldots, o_k)$. $\mu(m)$ is a total function from $\nu(c_1) \times \cdots \times \nu(c_k)$ into $\nu(c*)$. Therefore, $\mu(m)(o_1, \ldots, o_k)$ yields an object o such that $o \in \nu(c*)$.
3. If m is a coded method well defined at $c_1, \ldots, c_k$, then $I(t)$ is the instantiated term obtained by substituting, with the natural renaming of inputs, the vertex w by the dag s, where (m, σ, s) is the resolution of m at $c_1, \ldots, c_k$.

When I is clear from the context, we denote the reduction of t to $I(t)$ as $t \to I(t)$ and a finite sequence of reductions from t to t' as $t \xrightarrow{*} t'$.

2.2 Consistency and Signature Inference

We are interested in the rewriting sequences of a particular set of instantiated terms, i.e., these are the initial "procedure calls" that make sense according to a method schema. More formally we have the following: Let S be a method schema with interpretation $I = (\nu, \mu)$, $c_1, \ldots, c_k$ be classes in S, m a method of arity k well defined at these classes, and for each i let $o_i \in \nu(c_i)$. Then the instantiated term consisting of a single vertex labeled m and k inputs labeled respectively $o_1, \ldots, o_k$ is said to be a *start-redex*. We have an *inconsistency* in I if for some start-redex t we have $t \xrightarrow{*} \perp$.

Definition 5. A method schema S is *consistent* if for each interpretation I of S it is impossible to rewrite any start-redex into $\perp$ in a finite number of steps.

A variety of questions are important in this setting, e.g.: (1) Is a schema consistent? (2) Are there possible/certain diverging computations? (3) Is method m (at c) possibly/certainly "reachable" from m' (at c') [HTY89]? We concentrate here on (1) although most of the techniques that we develop can be used for studying other problems such as (2) or (3). Two properties simplify consistency checking: monadic arity and absence of recursion.

In an object-oriented context, it is not reasonable to recompile all methods each time the schema is updated. The problem is to obtain an *incremental* consistency checking algorithm that would avoid redoing the same verifications/computations. A solution that is adopted practically (e.g., [BDK92]) is to maintain a dependency graph of the methods and recompile only methods that may have been affected by the update. Of course, understanding what may be affected is the crucial part. We briefly summarize some results from [AKRW92] (on what may be affected) and some open questions. Let n be the size of method definitions in the input method schema and c the size of the class hierarchy.

In the general case of polyadic recursive schemas, consistency is undecidable. Both polyadic methods and recursion are necessary for this result. The proof is by reduction from results in [LPP70]. This undecidability result holds for schemas with methods of arity less than or equal to 3. The decidability of method schema consistency with methods of arity 2 is open.

In the case of monadic schemas, the set of possible computations can be described using a context-free language. An inconsistency may be reached if this language has a non-empty intersection with a particular regular language. To handle overloading, one can use a modification of a technique of [AMP73]. The decision procedure runs in $O(nc^3)$ time.

In the case of monadic and *recursion-free schemas*, checking a whole schema for consistency is logspace-complete in PTIME. This indicates that very efficient incremental solutions for even the simplest syntactic cases may be hard to obtain. One can focus on the key recursion-free case of a single coded method in the context of base methods. Checking a single coded method for consistency is logspace-complete in NLOGSPACE and can be done more efficiently than the recursive case above using finite state automata techniques (in $O(nc^2)$ time). Inheritance and overloading introduce some nondeterminism in the automata theoretic approach to consistency checking, but covariant signatures remove it. Consistency of a single coded method, assuming covariance, is in DLOGSPACE and can be checked in $O(n+c)$ time using a radix-tree data structure. We do not know whether this radix-tree data structure can be extended to solve the consistency of monadic, covariant, recursion-free schemas. We also do not know whether there are efficient incremental algorithms for any of the consistency problems. Since we know that the problem of consistency checking for monadic, recursion-free schemas is PTIME-complete, it would be interesting to know if there are good incremental algorithms for the simple, monadic or the covariant, monadic cases.

In the case of recursion-free schemas, the consistency problem is coNP-complete for a single coded method with two arguments. Some special cases can be shown to be in PTIME, using tree automata techniques. Covariance does not help in the recursive case. However, in the recursion-free covariant case there is a PTIME test for a fixed arity coded method. This is interesting in practice, because it motivates a heuristic for the general case.

In some proposals the class hierarchy is a dag and one has multiple inheritance. Also, in some proposals, it is required that the first argument, called the receiver, of a method must determine the resolution of name overloading. Each instance of a method is then viewed as "attached" to the class of the first argument. We believe that once the resolution mechanism is determined, the above techniques and results are directly applicable also to multiple inheritance and attachment to first argument.

3 The Expressive Power of Method Schemas

When considering method schemas in the context of finite databases, it is natural to ask what kind of queries can be expressed in the method schema framework. Of course, since method schemas are just *schemas*, one has to agree on the interpretation of the base methods in order to make this question precise. In this section, we describe a very simple way of encoding relations as interpreted base methods, and we show that under this interpretation, method schemas express exactly the PTIME queries. We assume some familiarity with Datalog terminology and notation from [Kan90, Ull82], e.g., rules, EDBs, IDBs etc.

3.1 I/O Conventions

We consider queries over finite ordered relational databases. The input of a query consists of a finite ordered universe U (w.l.o.g an initial segment of the positive integers) and some relations $P, Q, R, \ldots$ over U, and the output is another relation O over U. The arities and attribute names of the input and output relations are given by some fixed relational schema $\mathcal{S}$.

We encode these data in the method schema framework as follows. The elements of the universe are represented by objects of class *Number* and the ordering among them is given by a base method *Pred @ Number. Number* which computes the predecessor function. The initial element of the universe is represented by an object of class *Zero*, which is a subclass of *Number*. We capture the finiteness of the universe by providing its size as part of the input. More precisely, we provide as part of the input an object N of class *Number* such that N does not appear in the range of *Pred*. We assume that there is a unique object of class *Zero* and that there is at least one non-*Zero* element in the universe. When our interpretations satisfy these semantic conditions we will say that our language is *MS with order*.

A k-ary relation R is represented by a k-ary base method r whose signature is $r @ Number, \ldots, Number. Number$, such that $r(x_1, \ldots, x_k)$ returns an object of class *Number* if the tuple represented by $(x_1, \ldots, x_k)$ belongs to R and an object of class *Zero* if it does not. We will frequently write $r(\mathbf{x})$ instead of $r(x_1, \ldots, x_k)$ if the arity of the method does not matter.

For example, to encode the relation $R = \{(1, 1), (1, 2)\}$ over the universe $U = \{0, 1, 2\}$, we would populate the classes *Number* and *Zero* as *Number* $= \{1, 2\}$ and *Zero* $= \{0\}$, we would interpret *Pred* as *Pred*$(2) = 1$, *Pred*$(1) = $ *Pred*$(0) = 0$, and we would interpret r as $r(1, 1) = r(1, 2) = 1$, $r(x, y) = 0$ for all other x, y.

Queries are represented by coded methods q with a signature of the form $q @ \textit{Number}$, $\ldots, \textit{Number}. \textit{Number}$. If $q(\mathbf{x})$ reduces to an object of class $\textit{Number}$, then the tuple represented by $\mathbf{x}$ is considered part of the output; if $q(\mathbf{x})$ reduces to an object of class $\textit{Zero}$, then the tuple represented by $\mathbf{x}$ is not considered part of the output.

3.2 Expressing PTIME Queries

We show that under the input/output conventions given above, method schemas can compute inflationary fixpoints of Datalog$^\neg$ programs (see [Kan90] for a survey of these concepts). The results of Immerman [Imm86] and Vardi [Var82] then imply that method schemas can compute all PTIME queries over finite ordered databases.

To begin with, let us illustrate how to code simple Boolean and arithmetical functions. We represent the truth values $\textit{True}$ and $\textit{False}$ by the classes $\textit{Number}$ and $\textit{Zero}$. Any object of class $\textit{Number}$ (N, for example) represents $\textit{True}$, and the single object 0 of class $\textit{Zero}$ represents $\textit{False}$. (Note that we can compute 0 as $0 = \textit{Pred}^*(N)$, where $\textit{Pred}^* @ \textit{Number} = \lambda x. \textit{Pred}^*(\textit{Pred}(x))$ and $\textit{Pred}^* @ \textit{Zero} = \lambda x. x$.) We will often informally say that a method returns $\textit{True}$ when it returns a $\textit{Number}$ object, or $\textit{False}$ when it returns the $\textit{Zero}$ object.

The Boolean functions can be coded as:

$$
\begin{aligned}
\textit{Not} \ \ & @ \ \textit{Number} && = \lambda x. 0 \quad (\text{where } 0 := \textit{Pred}^*(N)) \\
\textit{Not} \ \ & @ \ \textit{Zero} && = \lambda x. N \\
\textit{And} \ \ & @ \ \textit{Zero}, \textit{Zero} && = \lambda xy. 0 \\
\textit{And} \ \ & @ \ \textit{Zero}, \textit{Number} && = \lambda xy. 0 \\
\textit{And} \ \ & @ \ \textit{Number}, \textit{Zero} && = \lambda xy. 0 \\
\textit{And} \ \ & @ \ \textit{Number}, \textit{Number} && = \lambda xy. N \quad (\text{and similar for } \textit{Or}) \\
\textit{Equal} \ & @ \ \textit{Zero}, \textit{Zero} && = \lambda xy. N \\
\textit{Equal} \ & @ \ \textit{Zero}, \textit{Number} && = \lambda xy. 0 \\
\textit{Equal} \ & @ \ \textit{Number}, \textit{Zero} && = \lambda xy. 0 \\
\textit{Equal} \ & @ \ \textit{Number}, \textit{Number} && = \lambda xy. \textit{Equal}\big(\textit{Pred}(x), \textit{Pred}(y)\big)
\end{aligned}
$$

We also need to extend the $\textit{Pred}$ function to k-tuples of objects. Below, we define methods $\textit{Pred}_i^k$ such that $\textit{Pred}_i^k(x_1, \ldots, x_k)$ is the ith component of the lexicographical predecessor of the tuple $(x_1, \ldots, x_k)$, for $1 \le i \le k$.

$$
\textit{Pred}_i^k @ \overbrace{\textit{Number}, \ldots, \textit{Number}}^{i-1}, \overbrace{\textit{Zero}, \ldots, \textit{Zero}}^{k-i+1} = \lambda x_1 \ldots \lambda x_k. N
$$

$$
\textit{Pred}_i^k @ \overbrace{\textit{Number}, \ldots, \textit{Number}}^{i}, \overbrace{\textit{Zero}, \ldots, \textit{Zero}}^{k-i} = \lambda x_1 \ldots \lambda x_k. \textit{Pred}(x_i)
$$

$$
\textit{Pred}_i^k @ \overbrace{\textit{Number}, \ldots, \textit{Number}}^{k} \qquad\qquad = \lambda x_1 \ldots \lambda x_k. x_i \quad (i \ne k)
$$

With this machinery in place, we can now code Datalog⁻ programs. For our purposes, we can think of a Datalog⁻ program as a relational expression $E(O; P, Q, R, \ldots)$ involving a designated output relation O, input relations $P, Q, R, \ldots$, and the operators *Union, Intersection, Complement, Times, Select,* and *Project.* The semantics of the program are given by the least fixpoint of the mapping $O \mapsto O \cup E(O; P, Q, R, \ldots)$. It is well known that the least fixpoint can be computed by iterating this mapping n^k times, where n is the size of the universe and k is the arity of O.

The relational operators can be coded as follows. Assume that r and s code relations R and S as described above, then:

$$
\begin{aligned}
Union(r, s) &\equiv \lambda\mathbf{x}.\, Or\big(r(\mathbf{x}), s(\mathbf{x})\big) \\
Intersection(r, s) &\equiv \lambda\mathbf{x}.\, And\big(r(\mathbf{x}), s(\mathbf{x})\big) \\
Complement(r) &\equiv \lambda\mathbf{x}.\, Not\big(r(\mathbf{x})\big) \\
Times(r, s) &\equiv \lambda\mathbf{x}\lambda\mathbf{y}.\, And\big(r(\mathbf{x}), s(\mathbf{y})\big) \\
Select_{i=j}(r) &\equiv \lambda\mathbf{x}.\, And\big(r(\mathbf{x}), Equal(x_i, x_j)\big)
\end{aligned}
$$

Projection is a bit more difficult, because it involves quantifier elimination. The projection of R onto its first $k - 1$ columns is encoded as:

$$
Project(r) \equiv \lambda x_1 \ldots \lambda x_{k-1}.\, r'(x_1, \ldots, x_{k-1}, N) \ ,
$$

where $r'(x_1, \ldots, x_{k-1}, y)$ is *True* if and only if there exists a $z \in \{0, \ldots, y\}$ such that $r(x_1, \ldots, x_{k-1}, z)$ is *True*. r' can be coded as follows:

$$
r' \, @ \, \overbrace{Number, \ldots, Number}^{k-1}, Zero \ = \lambda x_1 \ldots \lambda x_{k-1}\lambda y.\, r(x_1, \ldots, x_{k-1}, y)
$$

$$
r' \, @ \, \overbrace{Number, \ldots, Number}^{k-1}, Number =
$$
$$
\lambda x_1 \ldots \lambda x_{k-1}\lambda y.\, Or\big(r(x_1, \ldots, x_{k-1}, y), r'(x_1, \ldots, x_{k-1}, Pred(y))\big)
$$

Finally, we have to show how to compute fixpoints. Let $E(O; P, Q, R, \ldots)$ be a relational expression. Let k be the arity of O, let o be the base method representing O, and let e be the coded method corresponding to E. Then the fixpoint of E with respect to O is given by:

$$
Fix(o, e) \equiv \lambda x_1 \ldots \lambda x_k.\, o'(x_1, \ldots, x_k, \overbrace{N, \ldots, N}^{k}) \ ,
$$

where $o'(\mathbf{x}, \mathbf{n})$ is *True* iff $\mathbf{x}$ is in the image of the $\mathbf{n}^{th}$ iterate of the mapping $O \mapsto O \cup E(O; P, Q, R, \ldots)$, $\mathbf{n}$ being interpreted as a base-$(N+1)$ number. o' can be defined as follows:

$$o' \ @ \ Number, \ldots, Number, \overbrace{Zero, \ldots, Zero}^{k} \qquad = \lambda \mathbf{x} \lambda \mathbf{n}. \ 0$$

$$o' \ @ \ Number, \ldots, Number, \overbrace{Number, \ldots, Number}^{k} =$$
$$\lambda \mathbf{x} \lambda \mathbf{n}. \ Or\big(o'(\mathbf{x}, Pred_1^k(\mathbf{n}), \ldots, Pred_k^k(\mathbf{n})), \bar{e}(\mathbf{x})\big)$$

where the method $\bar{e}$ arises from e by replacing every occurrence of $o(\mathbf{x})$ in e by $o'(\mathbf{x}, Pred_1^k(\mathbf{n}), \ldots, Pred_k^k(\mathbf{n}))$.

Thus, for every Datalog⁻ program (interpreted in an inflationary fashion over an ordered input) one can construct a method schema with order (under the input-output conventions of Sect. 3.1) that computes the same query. First note that this method schema is consistent. Also note that, under the input-output conventions of Sect. 3.1, there is an easy to see one-to-one correspondence of finite ordered relational databases and method schema with order interpretations. We can conclude that,

Lemma 6. *Under the input output conventions of Sect. 3.1, MS with order can express every PTIME query.*

3.3 Simulating Method Schemas in Datalog

In this section, we show that the expressive power of method schemas over ordered finite interpretations is no more than that of Datalog⁻ over ordered input. This, combined with the previous reduction, allows us to deduce that method schemas express exactly the PTIME queries.

We will first explain the intuition behind the simulation. We capture the input/output characteristics of a method of arity k by means of a predicate of arity $k + 1$. The understanding is that the first k arguments of the predicate are the inputs of the method and the $(k + 1)$th argument is the output. Base methods correspond naturally to EDBs and coded methods to IDBs. The disjoint object assignment to classes in an interpretation of a method schema is simulated by means of a unary EDB predicate. The fact that the input is ordered is captured in the Datalog simulation by means of a special interpreted binary EDB predicate that orders the input.

Two technical problems arise with this approach. The first is that there will be input databases to the Datalog program that do not correspond to any interpretation for the method schema. In order to handle this case, we introduce rules that will "flood" the computation by deriving every possible fact if the input database does not correspond to a valid interpretation. The second technical problem is the issue of inconsistencies. In the case of method schemas, an inconsistency corresponds to an abnormal termination of computation. In the Datalog simulation, we simply fail when an inconsistency occurs in the corresponding method execution. The two cases are similar in the sense that no output is produced for the offending method call.

Consider a schema $S = (C, \leq, \Sigma_0, \Sigma_1)$. Since we are interested in data complexity, we will assume that the size of the method schema is fixed. We will also assume that there are no ambiguous method definitions. (This is a syntactic property that can be checked in constant time.) Further, we will also assume that all the method definitions are explicit at all the classes at which they are defined. This might increase the size of the schema by a factor of c^k where c is the size of the class hierarchy, and k the maximum arity of the methods. Since we assume that S is of fixed size, this does not matter. For the input method schema S, we will construct a Datalog program P_S such that the computations performed by S and P_S are equivalent in a sense which will be explained below.

P_S has the following predicates:

1. For each class $c \in C$, a unary EDB predicate Isa_c. The Isa_c predicates are meant to capture the meaning of the disjoint object assignment.
2. A special interpreted binary predicate $Pred$ that orders the input by providing the predecessor function. There will be objects o_0 (zero) and o_N (highest object) such that $Pred(o_0, o_0)$ is a fact and $Pred(X, o_N)$ is not true for any value of X. $Pred$ corresponds naturally to the interpreted base method $Pred$ in method schemas.
3. For each base method $m \in \Sigma_0$ of arity k, a $(k+1)$-ary EDB predicate m.
4. For each coded method $m \in \Sigma_1$ of arity k, a $(k+1)$-ary IDB predicate m.
5. An IDB predicate $Notequal$ that captures inequality between input objects. It is coded in terms of $Pred$.
6. A unary IDB predicate $Flood$ that will be used to check the validity of the input database.

For each method definition $m@c_1, c_2, \ldots, c_k = \lambda x_1, \ldots, x_k . m_1(\cdots)$ in S, the corresponding IDB predicate m has the following rule. The variables in the rule for m correspond to (1) the inputs to this code for method m and (2) the result and intermediate results of this code for method m.

$$m(C_1, C_2, \ldots, C_k, X) :\!- Isa_{c_1}(C_1), \ldots, Isa_{c_k}(C_k),$$
$$m_{i_1}(\ldots), m_{i_2}(\ldots), \ldots, m_1(\ldots, X);$$

The understanding here is that the first k predicates act as "guards" making sure that the "code" that gets executed has the arguments in the correct classes. After that, we have the method names that appear in the code of m sorted in left-to-right topological order. (This is the order of execution provided by the built-in interpreter in method schemas.) The arguments to these methods are arranged as they would be in a method schema execution.

We now write down the definitions for the $Flood$ predicate. There are four different ways in which the input database can be invalid. They are: (1) the disjoint object assignment could be invalid; (2) a base method could be undefined at some point where it is supposed to be defined (base methods correspond to *total* functions); (3) a base method could be multiply defined at some point; (4) a base method might produce a result of an invalid output class. We handle these one by one by means of the following rules. Before that, we need to code inequality among objects. This is easily done with the following rules:

$$Notequal(X, Y) :\!- Pred(X, X), \neg\, Pred(Y, Y);$$

$Notequal(X, Y) :\!\!- \neg Pred(X, X), Pred(Y, Y);$
$Notequal(X, Y) :\!\!- Pred(X, X'), Pred(Y, Y'), Notequal(X', Y');$

For every pair of classes c_1 and c_2 ($c_1 \neq c_2$), we use the following rule to enforce the disjoint object assignment:

$Flood(X) :\!\!- Isa_{c_1}(C), Isa_{c_2}(C);$

To make sure that every object belongs to a class, we use this rule:

$Flood(X) :\!\!- \neg Isa_{c_1}(C), \neg Isa_{c_2}(C), \ldots, \neg Isa_{c_l}(C);$

where $c_1, c_2, \ldots, c_l$ are all the classes in C. These rules ensure that whenever there is an object that does not belong to exactly one class, $Flood(X)$ is derived for all values of X.

We flood the computation by writing down rules of the following form for every IDB predicate p:

$p(X_1, \ldots, X_k) :\!\!- Flood(X);$

Next, if a base method m in S has the signature $m@c_1, \ldots, c_k : c_{k+1}$, we write the following rules that flood the computation if m is not defined everywhere in $\nu(c_1) \times \cdots \times \nu(c_k)$:

$Flood(X) :\!\!- Isa_{c_1}(C_1), \ldots, Isa_{c_k}(C_k), \neg m(C_1, \ldots, C_k, C_{k+1});$

Next, for a base method m in S with the signature $m@c_1, \ldots, c_k : c_{k+1}$, we write the following rule that floods the computation if m is multiply defined somewhere in $\nu(c_1) \times \cdots \times \nu(c_k)$.

$Flood(X) :\!\!- Isa_{c_1}(C_1), \ldots, Isa_{c_k}(C_k),$
$\qquad\qquad m(C_1, \ldots, C_k, C_{k+1}), m(C_1, \ldots, C_k, C'_{k+1}),$
$\qquad\qquad Notequal(C_{k+1}, C'_{k+1});$

Finally, for a base method m in S with signature $m@c_1, \ldots, c_k : c_{k+1}$, we write the following rule that floods the computation if m is improperly defined, i.e., the result belongs to an invalid class. Let $c_{k_1}, c_{k_2}, \ldots, c_{k_j}$ be the subclasses of c_{k+1}, including c_{k+1} itself.

$Flood(X) :\!\!- Isa_{c_1}(C_1), \ldots, Isa_{c_k}(C_k),$
$\qquad\qquad m(C_1, \ldots, C_k, C_{k+1}),$
$\qquad\qquad \neg Isa_{c_{k_1}}(C_{k+1}), \ldots, \neg Isa_{c_{k_j}}(C_{k+1});$

Since in this simulation we are interested in data complexity, the parameter of interest is the size of the input data which we measure by the size of the interpretation I. It is immediately clear that our representation of an interpretation in Datalog⁻ by means of the Isa_c, m, and Pred EDB predicates is the same size as the original method schema interpretation.

We now establish a one-to-one correspondence between interpretations for S and "valid" input databases for P_S.

Lemma 7. *Every interpretation for method schema S corresponds to an input database for P_S. Further, this input database is a "valid" input database in the sense that Flood(X) will never be derived for any value of X for such a database.*

Lemma 8. *Every "valid" input database for P_S (one in which Flood(X) is never derived for any value of X) corresponds to an interpretation for S.*

Now, we can use structural induction to show that S and P_S do indeed perform the same computations.

Lemma 9. *A call to method m with arguments $o_1, o_2, \ldots, o_k$ in an interpretation I terminates with a result o_{k+1} if and only if $m(o_1, o_2, \ldots, o_k, o_{k+1})$ can be derived in the corresponding input database in P_S. Further, Flood(X) will never be derived for any value of X in such an input database.*

Lemma 10. *If a fact $m(o_1, o_2, \ldots, o_k, o_{k+1})$ can be derived in P_S with a valid input database, then a call to method m with arguments $o_1, o_2, \ldots, o_k$ terminates with a result o_{k+1} in the corresponding interpretation for P.*

We put everything together in the following theorem:

Theorem 11. *Under the input output conventions of Sect. 3.1, MS with order expresses exactly PTIME.*

4 The Typed Lambda Calculus with Equality (TLC$^=$)

4.1 Language Definition

The syntax of *types* is given by the grammar $T \equiv t \mid (T \to T)$, where t ranges over a set of *type variables*. Thus, α is a type, as are $(\alpha \to \beta)$ and $(\alpha \to (\alpha \to \alpha))$. *Typed λ-terms* are given by the grammar $\mathcal{E} \equiv x \mid (\mathcal{E}\mathcal{E}) \mid \lambda x : T . \mathcal{E}$, where x ranges over a set of *expression variables*. As usual, $\alpha \to \beta \to \gamma$ stands for $\alpha \to (\beta \to \gamma)$ and PQR stands for $(PQ)R$.

Well-typedness of expressions is defined by the following inference rules, where Γ is a function from expression variables to types, and $\Gamma[x : \tau]$ is the function Γ' augmenting Γ with $\Gamma'(x) = \tau$:

(VAR)
$$\frac{\Gamma(x) = \tau}{\Gamma \vdash x : \tau}$$

$(\rightarrow\text{-INT})$

$$\frac{\Gamma[x:\tau] \vdash e:\tau'}{\Gamma \vdash \lambda x:\tau.\,e:\tau \rightarrow \tau'}$$

$(\rightarrow\text{-ELIM})$

$$\frac{\Gamma \vdash e:\tau \rightarrow \tau' \quad \Gamma \vdash e':\tau}{\Gamma \vdash ee':\tau'}$$

In what follows, we write "typed λ-term E" to mean E is well typed: $\Gamma \vdash E:\sigma$ is derivable by the above rules, for some Γ and σ.

The *order* of a type, which measures the higher-order functionality of a λ-term of that type, is defined as $o(t) = 0$ for a type variable t, and $o(\sigma' \rightarrow \sigma'') = \max(1 + o(\sigma'), o(\sigma''))$. We also refer to the order of a typed λ-term as the order of its type.

For well-typed λ-terms e, e', we write $e \rhd_\alpha e'$ (α-reduction) when e' can be derived from e by renaming of a bound variable, for example $\lambda x:\sigma.\,\lambda y:\tau.\,y \rhd_\alpha \lambda x:\sigma.\,\lambda z:\tau.\,z$. We write $e \rhd_\beta e'$ (β-reduction) when e' can be derived from e by replacing a subterm in e of the form $(\lambda x:\tau.\,E)E'$ by $E[E'/x]$ (E with E' substituted for all free occurrences of x in E). The fact that the subterm and its replacement have the same type is referred to as the *subject reduction theorem* [Bar90, Theorem 4.2.8]. We write $\rhd$ for the reflexive, transitive closure of $\rhd_\alpha$ and $\rhd_\beta$.

In this paper, we consider a mild modification of the standard presentation above, by enriching the simply-typed λ-calculus with a countably infinite set of constants of type O, and for some fixed type τ, introducing an equality constant $=_\tau:\text{O} \rightarrow \text{O} \rightarrow \tau \rightarrow \tau \rightarrow \tau$. For constants $a, b: \text{O}$, $a \not\equiv b$, we add to $\rhd_\beta$ the reduction rules $(=_\tau aa) \rhd_\beta (\lambda x:\tau.\,\lambda y:\tau.\,x)$ and $(=_\tau ab) \rhd_\beta (\lambda x:\tau.\,\lambda y:\tau.\,y)$.

The modified system enjoys the following well-known properties:

Theorem 12 (Church-Rosser property). *If $e \rhd e'$ and $e \rhd e''$, then there exists a λ-term e''' such that $e' \rhd e'''$ and $e'' \rhd e'''$.*

Theorem 13 (Strong normalization property). *For each e, there exists an integer n such that if $e \rhd e'$, then the derivation involves no more than n β-reductions.*

For more details, see for example [Chu41, Bar84]. In particular, [Bar84, Sect. 15.3] discusses the Church-Rosser property for the untyped λ-calculus enriched with equality. We refer to [HKM93] for how to remove equality from the language.

For results concerning the *type inference* problem for TLC and its extensions, i. e. the problem of deciding whether a given (untyped) term can be typed, see for example [KMM91]. The type inference problem for TLC$^=$ is equivalent to first-order unification.

Note that, the language presented above is the "simplest" typed lambda calculus. It has no type polymorphism and is a subset of the core-ML language of [Mil78] without *let* and without any explicit fixpoint construct.

5 The Expressive Power of TLC$^=$

The principal technical tool for this section is *list iteration*. Let us briefly review how it works and its limitations.

Let $\{x_1, x_2, \ldots, x_k\}$ be a set of λ-terms, each of type α; then

$$L \equiv \lambda c\colon \alpha \to \sigma \to \sigma.\, \lambda n\colon \sigma.\, cx_1(cx_2 \ldots (cx_k n) \ldots)$$

is a λ-term of type $(\alpha \to \sigma \to \sigma) \to \sigma \to \sigma$, for *any* type σ—in other words, L is a typable term no matter what type σ we choose (though one fixed term must be chosen). We abbreviate this list construction as $[x_1, x_2, \ldots, x_k]$; the variables c and n abstract over the list constructors *cons* and *nil*. List iteration implements primitive recursion.

For example, a standard coding of Boolean logic uses *True* $\equiv \lambda x\colon \tau.\, \lambda y\colon \tau.\, x$ and *False* $\equiv \lambda x\colon \tau.\, \lambda y\colon \tau.\, y$, both of type *Bool* $\equiv \tau \to \tau \to \tau$. Define the exclusive or as

$$Xor \equiv \lambda p\colon Bool.\, \lambda q\colon Bool.\, \lambda x\colon \tau.\, \lambda y\colon \tau.\, p(qyx)(qxy)$$

and the parity of a list of Boolean values as

$$Parity \equiv \lambda L\colon (Bool \to Bool \to Bool) \to Bool \to Bool.\, L\, Xor\, False \ .$$

Unlike circuit complexity, the size of the *program* computing parity is constant, because the iterative machinery is taken from the *data*, i. e., the list L.

On the other hand, to compute the length of a list, we define

$$Length \equiv \lambda L\colon (\alpha \to Int \to Int) \to Int \to Int.\, L(\lambda x\colon \alpha.\, Succ)\, Zero \ ,$$

where *Succ* $\equiv \lambda n\colon (\tau \to \tau) \to \tau \to \tau.\, \lambda s\colon \tau \to \tau.\, \lambda z\colon \tau.\, ns(sz)$ and *Zero* $\equiv \lambda s\colon \tau \to \tau.\, \lambda z\colon \tau.\, z$ code successor and zero on the Church numerals (of type *Int* $\equiv (\tau \to \tau) \to \tau \to \tau$).

These two simple examples point already to a restriction imposed by the simply typed lambda calculus: its lack of polymorphism. There are two facets to this problem.

(1) A list L of Booleans can be coded as a term of type $\mathcal{B} \equiv (Bool \to \sigma \to \sigma) \to \sigma \to \sigma$ for any type σ. To type *Parity L*, we must type L with *Bool* $\equiv \tau \to \tau \to \tau$ substituted for σ, which we write as $\mathcal{B}[\sigma := Bool]$. Similarly, to type *Length L*, we need to type $L\colon \mathcal{B}[\sigma := Int]$. Thinking of the type σ of L as an output type *variable*, in both instances we see that the output type must be "contaminated" or "raised" to provide the primitive recursive iterator. If we want the output type of input L to be fixed, and two different output types are needed to carry out the computation, this poses a problem.

(2) If we want the output type to remain σ, this poses yet another difficulty.

We point out that problem (2) can sometimes be handled by alternate encodings, for example

$$Length \equiv \lambda L\colon (\alpha \to \sigma \to \sigma) \to \sigma \to \sigma.\, \lambda s\colon \sigma \to \sigma.\, \lambda z\colon \sigma.\, L(\lambda x\colon \alpha.\, s)z \ ,$$

where L is used to iterate over objects of lower type. Problem (1) can be solved by defining the output type to be a suitably defined cross product of *Bool* and *Int*, and using this typing to iteratively generate two copies of the list, with respective output types *Bool* and *Int*.

These techniques, with elaborate variants, are exploited repeatedly in the following sections.

5.1 I/O Conventions

The paradigm we use is computation on finite structures, i. e., a λ-calculus for finite model theory. Inputs and outputs of a computation are *databases*, i. e., sets of relations, which are encoded according to the scheme below.

We start out with a countably infinite supply $o_1, o_2, \ldots$ of *constants*, of some base type o. We also fix, once and for all, a type variable τ.

Boolean values are represented by

$$\text{True:}\ \tau \to \tau \to \tau \ \equiv \ \lambda u : \tau.\, \lambda v : \tau.\, u \ ,$$

$$\text{False:}\ \tau \to \tau \to \tau \ \equiv \ \lambda u : \tau.\, \lambda v : \tau.\, v \ .$$

We abbreviate the type $\tau \to \tau \to \tau$ as *Bool*.

Tuples are represented in the standard way: if $x_1, \ldots, x_k$ are λ-terms of type $\alpha_1, \ldots, \alpha_k$, then

$$\langle x_1, \ldots, x_k \rangle : (\alpha_1 \to \cdots \to \alpha_k \to \tau) \to \tau \equiv$$

$$\lambda f : \alpha_1 \to \cdots \to \alpha_k \to \tau.\, f x_1 \ldots x_k$$

We abbreviate the type $(\alpha_1 \to \cdots \to \alpha_k \to \tau) \to \tau$ as $\alpha_1 \times \cdots \times \alpha_k$ or, if $\alpha_i \equiv \alpha$ for $1 \le i \le k$, as α^k. In particular, o^k is the type of a k-tuple of constants.

Lists are represented as described above: if $x_1, \ldots, x_k$ are λ-terms of type α, then

$$[x_1, \ldots, x_k] : (\alpha \to \tau \to \tau) \to \tau \to \tau \equiv$$

$$\lambda c : \alpha \to \tau \to \tau.\, \lambda n : \tau.\, c x_1 (c x_2 \ldots (c x_k n) \cdots)$$

We abbreviate the type $(\alpha \to \tau \to \tau) \to \tau \to \tau$ as $\{\alpha\}$. Note the difference between lists and tuples: a tuple represents a collection of a *fixed* number of terms of *varying* type, whereas a list represents a collection of a *variable* number of terms of a *fixed* type.

Relations are represented as duplicate-free lists of tuples of constants. Thus, the type of a k-ary relation is $\{o^k\}$. Note that, in all this development we use lists instead of finite sets, because finite sets are not available in the syntax of the λ-calculus; but we show how to eliminate duplicates.

Queries are represented as λ-terms of the form $Q \equiv \lambda R_1 \ldots \lambda R_k.\, M$, which when applied to encodings $\overline{r_1}, \ldots, \overline{r_k}$ of input relations, reduce to a normal form which is the encoding of the desired output relation. We measure the time complexity of computation by the length of reduction sequences, according to a fixed evaluation strategy, as a function of the database size.

It is interesting to observe that the "relations as iterators" convention above is equivalent to the "relations as characteristic functions" convention adopted in Sect. 3.1, *provided* that in the latter case, the input comes with a list of all the objects in the universe (the equivalent of the "size parameter" N in the method schemas case). Clearly, without any a priori knowledge of the universe, it is impossible to obtain a listing of a relation from its characteristic function.

However, if we assume the existence of an iterator U: $\{o\}$ representing the universe, then translations between the two conventions are easily furnished. Indeed, if R: $\{o^k\}$ is an iterator encoding a relation r, then

$$\chi_r: \overbrace{o \to \cdots \to o}^{k} \to Bool \equiv$$
$$\lambda x_1: o \ldots \lambda x_k: o.$$
$$\lambda u: \tau. \lambda v: \tau.$$
$$R(\lambda r: o^k. \lambda T: \tau. (Equal_k \, r\langle x_1, \ldots, x_k\rangle) u T) v$$

(where $Equal_k$, the equality predicate for k-tuples, is defined below) computes the characteristic function of r.

On the other hand, if $\chi_r: o \to \cdots \to o \to Bool$ encodes the characteristic function of a relation r, then

$$R: \{o^k\} \equiv$$
$$\lambda c: o^k \to \tau \to \tau. \lambda n: \tau.$$
$$U(\lambda x_1: o. \lambda T_1: \tau.$$
$$\quad U(\lambda x_2: o. \lambda T_2: \tau.$$
$$\quad\quad \cdots$$
$$\quad\quad U(\lambda x_k: o. \lambda T_k: \tau.$$
$$\quad\quad (\chi_r x_1 \ldots x_k)(c\langle x_1, \ldots, x_k\rangle T_k) T_{k-1}) \ldots T_1) n$$

is an iterator representing r.

Note that the characteristic function representation of a relation is simpler in the sense that its type is of order 1, whereas the type of an iterator is of order 2. It is possible to exploit this "order economy" of characteristic functions to provide an encoding of all PTIME computable queries in the typed lambda calculus of order 4. The (more simple) encoding given below uses types of order 5.

5.2 Expressing Relational Queries

In this section, we show how to express the relational algebra operators of [Cod72] in the simply typed lambda calculus with equality. Every operator is coded as a λ-term that takes one or two relations in the list-of-tuples format described in Sect. 5.1 as input and produces another relation in the same format as output. The homogeneity of the input and output format allows the result of one operator application to be used as input to another, so that arbitrary relational algebra expressions can be coded by nesting the λ-terms corresponding to the individual operators.

We begin with a λ-term $Equal_k$ that tests two k-tuples $\lambda f. f a_1 \ldots a_k$ and $\lambda f. f b_1 \ldots b_k$ for equality. The result of the comparison is a $Bool$, i. e., the term $\lambda u \lambda v. u$ if the comparison comes out true and $\lambda u \lambda v. v$ otherwise. The code depends on the arity of the tuples involved, so we use the subscript k to indicate that this particular term works for k-tuples.

$$Equal_k: o^k \rightarrow o^k \rightarrow Bool \equiv$$
$$\lambda t: o^k. \lambda s: o^k.$$
$$\lambda u: \tau. \lambda v: \tau.$$
$$t(\lambda x_1: o \ldots \lambda x_k: o.$$
$$s(\lambda y_1: o \ldots \lambda y_k: o.$$
$$((Eq\, x_1 y_1)$$
$$((Eq\, x_2 y_2)$$
$$\cdots$$
$$((Eq\, x_k y_k) uv) v) \cdots v)))$$

Here, Eq denotes the equality predicate for constants, of type $o \rightarrow o \rightarrow Bool$. Once t and s are instantiated with tuples $\lambda f.\, fa_1 \ldots a_k$ and $\lambda f.\, fb_1 \ldots b_k$, all $(Eq\, x_i y_i)$ terms reduce to either $True \equiv \lambda u.\, \lambda v.\, u$ or $False \equiv \lambda u.\, \lambda v.\, v$. Hence the "body"

$$\lambda u: \tau. \lambda v: \tau.$$
$$t(\lambda x_1: o \ldots \lambda x_k: o.$$
$$s(\lambda y_1: o \ldots \lambda y_k: o.$$
$$((Eq\, x_1 y_1)$$
$$((Eq\, x_2 y_2)$$
$$\cdots$$
$$((Eq\, x_k y_k) uv) v) \cdots v)))$$

of the $Equal_k$ predicate reduces to $\lambda u.\, \lambda v.\, u$ if $a_i = b_i$ for all i and to $\lambda u.\, \lambda v.\, v$ otherwise. Note that the final result is reached after $O(k)$ reduction steps (independent of the reduction strategy), which matches the time needed to compare two k-tuples in a procedural language.

The following term checks whether a k-tuple $\lambda f.\, fa_1 \ldots a_k$ is a member of a list $\lambda c \lambda n.\, ct_1(ct_2 \cdots (ct_m n) \cdots)$ of k-tuples by comparing the tuple to every element of the list.

$$Member_k: o^k \rightarrow \{o^k\} \rightarrow Bool \equiv$$
$$\lambda t: o^k. \lambda R: \{o^k\}.$$
$$\lambda u: \tau. \lambda v: \tau.$$
$$R(\lambda r: o^k. \lambda T: \tau. (Equal_k\, rt)uT)v$$

For example, $(Member_2 \langle 1, 2 \rangle [\langle 3, 4 \rangle, \langle 5, 6 \rangle])$ reduces to

$$\lambda u.\, \lambda v.\, (Equal_2 \langle 3, 4 \rangle \langle 1, 2 \rangle)u((Equal_2 \langle 5, 6 \rangle \langle 1, 2 \rangle)uv) \ ,$$

which in turn reduces to $\lambda u.\, \lambda v.\, v$, because both $(Equal_2 \ldots)$ terms evaluate to $False$. If the reductions are done according to an eager reduction strategy (which reduces a redex $(\lambda x.\ M)N$ only after fully reducing N), then the number of reductions needed to reach the normal form is $O(mk)$, where m is the length of the input list, and this again matches the time required by a straightforward procedural implementation.

Note that there are also "bad" reduction strategies which lead to an exponential number of reduction steps. This is due to the fact that the fourth parameter v of the $Equal_k$ predicate occurs k times in the body of the predicate. If a term with unresolved redexes is substituted for v (e. g., the term $((Equal_2 \langle 5, 6 \rangle \langle 1, 2 \rangle)uv)$ in the example above), then the number of redexes in the whole expression multiplies by k. Since this happens at every level of $Equal_k$ nesting, it is possible to reduce an expression $(Member_k \ tR)$, where R is of length m, to a term with $O(k^m)$ redexes by never evaluating the fourth argument to $Equal_k$ before substituting it.

With the aid of $Equal$ and $Member$, we can now code the set-theoretic operators of the relational algebra:

Intersection: To intersect two k-ary relations R and S, we build a new relation T by "walking down" R and testing each tuple for membership in S. If the tuple occurs in S, it is included in the output, otherwise it is ignored.

$$Intersection_k \colon \{\mathsf{o}^k\} \to \{\mathsf{o}^k\} \to \{\mathsf{o}^k\} \equiv$$
$$\lambda R \colon \{\mathsf{o}^k\}.\ \lambda S \colon \{\mathsf{o}^k\}.$$
$$\lambda c \colon \mathsf{o}^k \to \tau \to \tau.\ \lambda n \colon \tau.$$
$$R(\lambda r \colon \mathsf{o}^k.\ \lambda T \colon \tau.\ (Member_k \ rS)(crT)T)n$$

For example, $(Intersection_2 \ [\langle 1, 2 \rangle] \ [\langle 1, 2 \rangle, \langle 3, 4 \rangle])$ reduces to

$$\lambda c.\ \lambda n.\ (Member_2 \langle 1, 2 \rangle [\langle 1, 2 \rangle, \langle 3, 4 \rangle])(c \langle 1, 2 \rangle n)n\ \ ,$$

which further reduces to $\lambda c.\ \lambda n.\ c \langle 1, 2 \rangle n \equiv [\langle 1, 2 \rangle]$.

Set difference: This works like intersection, except that a tuple from R is included in the output if it does *not* occur in S.

$$Setminus_k \colon \{\mathsf{o}^k\} \to \{\mathsf{o}^k\} \to \{\mathsf{o}^k\} \equiv$$
$$\lambda R \colon \{\mathsf{o}^k\}.\ \lambda S \colon \{\mathsf{o}^k\}.$$
$$\lambda c \colon \mathsf{o}^k \to \tau \to \tau.\ \lambda n \colon \tau.$$
$$R(\lambda r \colon \mathsf{o}^k.\ \lambda T \colon \tau.\ (Member_k \ rS)T(crT))n$$

Union: The union of two k-ary relations R and S is formed by starting with S and adding those tuples of R that do not occur in S.

$$Union_k \colon \{\mathsf{o}^k\} \to \{\mathsf{o}^k\} \to \{\mathsf{o}^k\} \equiv$$
$$\lambda R \colon \{\mathsf{o}^k\}.\ \lambda S \colon \{\mathsf{o}^k\}.$$
$$\lambda c \colon \mathsf{o}^k \to \tau \to \tau.\ \lambda n \colon \tau.$$
$$R(\lambda r \colon \mathsf{o}^k.\ \lambda T \colon \tau.\ (Member_k \ rS)T(crT))(Scn)$$

(If we knew that R and S were disjoint, we could form their union by just concatenating them as follows: $\lambda c.\ \lambda n.\ Rc(Scn)$. In the general case, however, we need the more complex term above to ensure a duplicate-free output.)

Having dealt with the "set-oriented" operators, we now examine the "tuple-oriented" operators. We need two auxiliary terms first: The $Concat_{k,l}$ operator concatenates a k-tuple and an l-tuple to form a $(k + l)$-tuple, and the $Rearrange_{k;i_1,\ldots,i_l}$ operator takes a k-tuple and returns an l-tuple consisting of columns $i_1, \ldots, i_l$ of the input.

$$Concat_{k,l}: \mathsf{o}^k \to \mathsf{o}^l \to \mathsf{o}^{k+l} \equiv$$
$$\lambda t: \mathsf{o}^k. \, \lambda s: \mathsf{o}^l.$$
$$\lambda f: \mathsf{o} \to \cdots \to \mathsf{o} \to \tau.$$
$$t(\lambda x_1: \mathsf{o} \ldots \lambda x_k: \mathsf{o}.$$
$$s(\lambda y_1: \mathsf{o} \ldots \lambda y_l: \mathsf{o}.$$
$$f x_1 \cdots x_k y_1 \cdots y_l))$$

$$Rearrange_{k;i_1,\ldots,i_l}: \mathsf{o}^k \to \mathsf{o}^l \equiv$$
$$\lambda t: \mathsf{o}^k.$$
$$\lambda f: \mathsf{o} \to \cdots \to \mathsf{o} \to \tau.$$
$$t(\lambda x_1: \mathsf{o} \ldots \lambda x_k: \mathsf{o}.$$
$$f x_{i_1} \cdots x_{i_l})$$

Cross product: The Cartesian product of k-ary relation R and l-ary relation S is formed by a straightforward nested iteration, in which every tuple of R is concatenated with every tuple of S and appended to the output.

$$Times_{k,l}: \{\mathsf{o}^k\} \to \{\mathsf{o}^l\} \to \{\mathsf{o}^{k+l}\} \equiv$$
$$\lambda R: \{\mathsf{o}^k\}. \, \lambda S: \{\mathsf{o}^l\}.$$
$$\lambda c: \mathsf{o}^{k+l} \to \tau \to \tau. \, \lambda n: \tau.$$
$$R(\lambda r: \mathsf{o}^k. \, \lambda T: \tau.$$
$$S(\lambda s: \mathsf{o}^l. \, \lambda U: \tau.$$
$$c(Concat_{k,l} \, r s)U)T)n$$

For example, $(Times_{1,1} \, [\langle 1 \rangle, \langle 2 \rangle] \, [\langle 3 \rangle, \langle 4 \rangle])$ reduces to

$$\lambda c. \, \lambda n.$$
$$c(Concat_{1,1} \langle 1 \rangle \langle 3 \rangle)$$
$$(c(Concat_{1,1} \langle 1 \rangle \langle 4 \rangle)$$
$$(c(Concat_{1,1} \langle 2 \rangle \langle 3 \rangle)$$
$$(c(Concat_{1,1} \langle 2 \rangle \langle 4 \rangle)n)))$$

which further reduces to $[\langle 1, 3 \rangle, \langle 1, 4 \rangle, \langle 2, 3 \rangle, \langle 2, 4 \rangle]$.

Selection: To select tuples from a k-ary relation R according to a certain condition, say column i = column j, it suffices to iterate over R and include those tuples in the output that satisfy the condition.

$$Select_{k;i=j}: \{o^k\} \to \{o^k\} \equiv$$
$$\lambda R: \{o^k\}.$$
$$\lambda c: o^k \to \tau \to \tau. \lambda n: \tau.$$
$$R(\lambda r: o^k. \lambda T: \tau.$$
$$r(\lambda x_1: o \ldots \lambda x_k: o. (Eq\, x_i x_j)(crT)T))n$$

Projection: This is slightly tricky. The straightforward attempt to project onto columns $i_1, \ldots, i_l$ of a k-ary relation R,

$$SimpleProject_{k;i_1,\ldots,i_l}: \{o^k\} \to \{o^l\} \equiv$$
$$\lambda R: \{o^k\}.$$
$$\lambda c: o^l \to \tau \to \tau. \lambda n: \tau.$$
$$R(\lambda r: o^k. \lambda T: \tau. c(Rearrange_{k;i_1,\ldots,i_l} r)T)n \quad,$$

has the disadvantage that the output may contain duplicate tuples. To fix this, we include the projection t' of tuple t in the output only if t is the *first* tuple in R whose projection is t':

$$Project_{k;i_1,\ldots,i_l}: \{o^k\} \to \{o^l\} \equiv$$
$$\lambda R: \{o^k\}.$$
$$\lambda c: o^l \to \tau \to \tau. \lambda n: \tau.$$
$$R(\lambda r: o^k. \lambda T: \tau.$$
$$(First\, r\, R)(c(Rearrange_{k;i_1,\ldots,i_l} r)T)T)n \quad,$$

where $(First\, r\, R): Bool$ is an abbreviation for

$$\lambda u: \tau. \lambda v: \tau.$$
$$R(\lambda r': o^k. \lambda T': \tau.$$
$$(Equal_l(Rearrange_{k;i_1,\ldots,i_l} r)$$
$$(Rearrange_{k;i_1,\ldots,i_l} r'))$$
$$((Equal_k\, rr')uv)T')u \quad.$$

To see why this works, consider for example the query $(Project_{2;1}[\langle 1, 2\rangle, \langle 1, 3\rangle])$, which projects the relation $[\langle 1, 2\rangle, \langle 1, 3\rangle]$ onto its first column. The expression $(First\langle 1, 2\rangle[\langle 1, 2\rangle, \langle 1$ reduces to

$$\lambda u. \lambda v.$$
$$(Equal_1 \langle 1\rangle\langle 1\rangle)$$
$$((Equal_2\langle 1, 2\rangle\langle 1, 2\rangle)uv)$$
$$((Equal_1\langle 1\rangle\langle 1\rangle)((Equal_2\langle 1, 2\rangle\langle 1, 3\rangle)uv)u) \quad,$$

which further reduces to $\lambda u.\, \lambda v.\, u \equiv True$, whereas $(First\langle 1,3\rangle[\langle 1,2\rangle, \langle 1,3\rangle])$ reduces to

$\lambda u.\, \lambda v.$
$\quad (Equal_1\langle 1\rangle\langle 1\rangle)$
$\qquad ((Equal_2\langle 1,3\rangle\langle 1,2\rangle)uv)$
$\qquad ((Equal_1\langle 1\rangle\langle 1\rangle)((Equal_2\langle 1,3\rangle\langle 1,3\rangle)uv)u)$

and then to $\lambda u.\, \lambda v.\, v \equiv False$. Hence, the whole query reduces to

$\lambda c.\, \lambda n.$
$\quad (First\langle 1,2\rangle[\langle 1,2\rangle, \langle 1,3\rangle])$
$\qquad (c\langle 1\rangle((First\langle 1,3\rangle[\langle 1,2\rangle, \langle 1,3\rangle])(c\langle 1\rangle n)n))$
$\qquad ((First\langle 1,3\rangle[\langle 1,2\rangle, \langle 1,3\rangle])(c\langle 1\rangle n)n)$

and then to $\lambda c.\, \lambda n.\, c\langle 1\rangle n \equiv [\langle 1\rangle]$.

This completes the coding of relational algebra. It is straightforward to verify that every term given above is well-typed and, when applied to one (resp., two) relations coded in the format described in Sect. 5.1, reduces to a normal form which is the encoding of the desired output relation. Moreover, when the terms are reduced according to an eager reduction strategy (which reduces a redex $(\lambda x.\, M)N$ only after fully reducing N), the length of the reduction sequence is polynomial in the size of the inputs. (In fact, the length of the reduction sequence typically matches the running time of a naive procedural implementation of the operator in question.) Therefore, we have the following theorem.

Theorem 14. *Let $\phi(R_1, \ldots, R_l)$ be a relational algebra expression over relational schema $S = (R_1, \ldots, R_l)$. Then there exists a term ψ of the simply typed lambda calculus with equality such that for every instance $(r_1, \ldots, r_l)$ of S, the expression $(\psi\overline{r_1}\cdots\overline{r_l})$ reduces to $\overline{\phi(r_1, \ldots, r_l)}$, where $\overline{r}$ denotes the encoding of relation r as described in Sect. 5.1. Moreover, the normal form of $(\psi\overline{r_1}\cdots\overline{r_l})$ can be computed in a number of reduction steps polynomial in the size of $r_1, \ldots, r_l$.*

It is possible to extend the scheme above to an encoding of fixpoints and even Abiteboul's and Beeri's Complex Object Algebra [AB88]. This takes us from manipulating "flat" relations to more complicated data structures, namely arbitrary finite trees built from tuple and set constructors. The algebra under consideration is extremely powerful—in fact it expresses any "generic" (see [CH80]) elementary time computation on finite structures.

Theorem 15. *Let $\phi(R_1, \ldots, R_l)$ be a complex object algebra expression over the relational schema $S = (R_1, \ldots, R_l)$. Then there exists a term ψ of the simply typed lambda calculus with equality such that for every instance $(r_1, \ldots, r_l)$ of S, the expression $(\psi\overline{r_1}\cdots\overline{r_l})$ reduces to $\overline{\phi(r_1, \ldots, r_l)}$, where $\overline{r}$ denotes the encoding of relation r. Moreover, if the Powerset operator is not used, the normal form of $(\psi\overline{r_1}\cdots\overline{r_l})$ can be computed in a number of reduction steps polynomial in the size of $r_1, \ldots, r_l$.*

6 Conclusions and Some Open Problems

We have explored two functional formalisms, MS and TLC$^=$, in the context of expressing database queries or queries over finite structures. The main point of our exposition is that these formalisms can be related to traditional database query languages and can express all that is expressible using relational calculus/algebra, Datalog, etc.

We believe that the additional features of these functional formalisms (e.g., for MS classes, methods, inheritance, name overloading, late binding, and for TLC$^=$ higher-order functions and list, set, and tuple structures via typing) make them better vehicles for the formal study of OODBs. Thus, one can view our exploration as an attempt to change the vocabulary from a relational to a functional setting, while preserving some of the basic theorems of database theory. The following open problems highlight some topics for future research.

MS: We have investigated the consistency problem of method schemas as a form of signature inference and have highlighted a number of efficiently decidable cases. The decidability of the arity 2 case is still open, as well as many aspects of incremental consistency checking. In our formalization of method schema consistency, all base methods are uninterpreted. As we saw from the analysis of expressive power some degree of semantics, e.g., order, is useful. What about consistency then? For example, let us suppose that we have equality, with its normal interpretation, as a base method. This method will simply tell if the two arguments that it is supplied with are the same. Consistency checking becomes undecidable with monadic coded methods and polyadic base methods when augmented with equality. With equality, we can simulate the Lisp *car* and *cdr* functions so that we can "glue" and "unglue" arguments. However, the problem of checking consistency with monadic coded methods and polyadic base methods without equality is open.

TLC$^=$: The embeddings of database query languages in the typed λ-calculus that we present here are interesting for a number of reasons. They are "pure," without added constructs or added polymorphism. For example, the typed λ-calculus with equality is the simplest syntax to date, that can be used to describe the complex object algebra of [AB88]. In our embeddings we use lists of tuples and simulate sets by eliminating duplicates. In [AB88, BFN82, BTBN92] sets are used as basic constructs, and set iteration replaces list iteration in [BFN82, BTBN92]. One open question is: how can the λ-calculus syntax and semantics be augmented with set iteration? Not all database query languages can be embedded in the typed λ-calculus. Any computation that is not elementary is not captured by our framework. What should be added to the typed λ-calculus to capture exactly the more powerful database query languages such as the computable queries of [CH80, AK89]? The use of reduction strategies in these embeddings provides a link between complexity theory, finite model theory, and the typed λ-calculus, that should be further investigated.

MS+TLC$^=$: We believe that a synthesis of MS and TLC$^=$, with set-at-a-time instead of tuple-at-at-time evaluation, would be the appropriate formalism (or very close to it) for OODB querying. Such a formalism would have all the object-oriented features of MS and the expressibility and data abstraction capabilities of TLC$^=$. Given the organization of data into collections one would like the evaluation mechanism to emphasize sets, as in [AB88, BFN82, BTBN92]. Object-oriented dialects of Lisp [AR88] illustrate such linguistic syntheses (without sets and with a less clear type system). The challenge is to come up with a simply typed (and elegant) formal synthesis, that also facilitates the manipulation of collections of objects.

In our exposition we have explored the relationship with program schemas and simply typed calculi. This is a first step towards more complex database programming language models. For example, *let-* or ML-polymorphism [Mil78] is a very useful feature to include in a functional data model. The language ML has been the basis for many programming language investigations on structure and method inheritance. The literature is too extensive to even attempt a survey, but for pointers to the recent literature and for a programming language view of some of the issues raised here we recommend [Mit90, MHF93].

Acknowledgements

Research supported by ONR Contract N00014-91-J-4052, ARPA Order 8225.

A Formal Object-Oriented Query Model and an Algebra

Reda Alhajj and M. Erol Arkun

Bilkent University, Faculty of Engineering, Department of Computer Engineering and Information Sciences, 06533 Bilkent, Ankara, Turkey

Abstract. In this paper, we describe an object-oriented query model we have developed for object-oriented database management systems (OODBMSs). Our object algebra allows for the manipulation of existing objects as well as the creation of objects via the introduction of new relationships. As a result we have an object algebra that maintains the closure property in a natural way by having operands and the output from a query to have pairs of sets, a set of objects and a set of message expressions where a message expression is a sequence of messages. So, our object algebra handles objects as well as behaviour defined on them. Furthermore, our object algebra is at least as powerful as the relational algebra and the nested algebra. In fact, it is more powerful at least due to message expressions that handle both stored and derived values; hence give the user a full computational power without any need to have an embedded query language leading to impedance mismatch.

1 Introduction

Advances in database systems are being influenced by application requirements. Although the relational data model is suitable to handle conventional business applications, the first normal form restriction led to extensions to satisfy the requirements of new application areas, including Office Automation, Medicine, Geographical Information Systems, Artificial Intelligence applications and Engineering Design applications, e.g. CAD/CAM. Early extensions relaxed the first normal form by allowing set-valued attributes. Still a more advanced extension is based on complex objects where sets and tuples are arbitrarily nested. To satisfy object sharing within complex objects, object identity was introduced. A more advanced step towards satisfying emerging application requirements is the combination of object-oriented concepts [GR83, SB86] with the database technology [Dat90b, Dat90a] in developing object-oriented database management systems (OODBMSs), e.g. [BCG+87, CDV88, Deu91b, FBC+87, MS88, MD86, RS87].

It is necessary to have a query language present in any kind of database system [NS88]. Although the modeling power of an OODBMS presents implicit joins [Kim89] by allowing instances in a class to form the domain for an instance variable in another class and messages could be used to query the database, an explicit join is still necessary to introduce new relationships into the model [Shi81]; otherwise the manipulation power of the model will be restricted. Allowing an explicit join raises the closure property problem [ASL89]. Therefore, it is necessary to have an object algebra that handles the introduction of new relationships and maintains the closure property; otherwise the relational model will be more powerful.

Several query languages such as those of GemStone [MS88], O_2 [CD92], EXO-DUS [CDV88, VD91], IRIS [FBC$^+$87], ORION [BKK88, Kim89], OSAM* [ASL89], Postgres [RS87], PDM [Day89, MD86], ENCORE [SZ90] and the formal calculi and algebra developed by Straube and Özsu [SÖ90a] in addition to others [AB91, AK89, ACO85, BBKV87, KV84, Osb88, Zan83] have been proposed. Some of these query languages are extensions to relational languages such as SQL and QUEL. While EXO-DUS and Postgres provide QUEL based query language, IRIS and O_2 provide an SQL like interface. In IRIS queries are translated into relational algebra expressions which are executed. Therefore the underlying query processor of IRIS is purely relational, and so IRIS violates the encapsulation principle.

The algebra described in [VD91] has an equivalent expressive power as compared to the EXTRA query language described in [CDV88]; it assumes a data model in which several general type constructors are provided, and data structures are built through free composition of those constructors. The algebra of PDM [Day89, MD86] is based on a functional data model; it extends the relational algebra to handle functions. The algebra of ENCORE [SZ90], is based on a data model that has all types as abstract data types whose implementations are hidden from the algebra. ENCORE views everything as an object with an identity. An opposing view point [CD92, Deu91b] is that there is a distinction between objects, which possess identity and values which do not. Straube and Özsu developed a set-based object-oriented query algebra, and a corresponding calculus; also, they studied the problem of type unions in some details. However, their algebra does not handle the closure property and is less expressive compared to others described in the literature. The algebra of Osborn [Osb88] does not maintain the closure property; although the formation of new objects is allowed, however the output of some operations does not possess the requirements of an operand.

Some models described in the literature, e.g. [ASL89, CD92, MD86, RS87, SZ90, VD91], produce outputs that have the characteristics of a nested relation and hence force the latter as an input in satisfying the closure property. Other models, e.g. [BKK88, CDV88, MS88, SÖ90a], are based on retrievals without dealing with the closure property, and hence are not more powerful than the relational model when the introduction of new relationships is concerned. Our approach is to maintain the closure property without violating object-oriented concepts. One reason is that, we argue the requirement of a pure object-oriented model which may be combined with the relational model on need. An object-oriented model should be more powerful than the relational model at both the modeling and the manipulation phases. It is more powerful at the modeling phase due to the features of inheritance, encapsulation, identity and complex objects. It is more powerful at the manipulation phase due to the handling of both stored and derived values which result in a full computational power without any need to have an embedded query language leading to impedance mismatch.

In this paper we discuss the power of an object algebra we have developed for OODBMSs [AA92, AA93c, AA93a, AA93d, AA93b, Alh92]. To have an object algebra which is at least as powerful as the relational algebra, we support the five basic operators of the relational algebra with different operands, however. To catch the power of the nested algebra we add two operators, nest and one level project; although as we are going to show in the paper, the nest and the cross-product operations are equivalent under certain conditions. Also we have an operator that handles the application of aggregate functions with the output still having the characteristics of an operand; such an operand adds much to the power of the algebra.

Concerning the operands as well as the output from a query, they all have pairs of sets, a set of objects and a set of message expressions where a message expression is a sequence of messages. Message expressions are used in dealing with objects to maintain the encapsulation property and information hiding. They also provide a full computational power via handling both derived and stored values; a characteristic not satisfied by the relational model. Since the output from a query has the requirements of an operand, the closure property is maintained in a natural way.

We define a set of total instances for a class as the union of its instances with all the instances of its subclasses. Also a set of message expressions for a class can be derived starting from the set of messages used to invoke its methods. Therefore, a class having a set of objects and a set of message expressions, can be an operand in a query. Furthermore, it is possible to derive from any pair, a set of objects and a set of message expressions, the characteristics of a class [AA92, Alh92]. Such a possibility helps in making the output from a query persistent when required. This way, a view mechanism similar to that described in [AB91] can be supported in a natural way.

The paper is organized as follows. In Sect. 2, we briefly introduce the basic features of the data model on which the object algebra is based. The query model is discussed in Sect. 3. Sect. 4 includes some illustrating examples. Sect. 5 is the conclusions.

2 The Data Model

In this section we briefly describe the features necessary to be present in a data model for the sake of the object algebra. It is required to have objects, classes and methods. A class has a set of instance variables, a set of superclasses, a set of methods and a set of objects as its instances. To overcome duplication in definition, i.e., to benefit from reusability, inheritance is supported where a class is allowed to inherit the definition of one or more existing classes leading to multiple inheritance where classes are arranged in a lattice. This way, the definition of a class includes the union of those of its,superclasses.

Objects are collected into classes. An object, as an instance of a class, has a state and behaviour; the state is reachable via the behaviour. To maintain the object-oriented features, it is important for the object algebra to equally handle both the state and the behaviour of objects. An object has an identity that distinguishes it from other objects in the database and provides for object sharing [KC86]. We use $value(o)$ and $identity(o)$ to denote the state and identity of object o; the state of an object is a set of values, one for each of the instance variables of its class[1]. Two objects are said to be identical,

---

[1] The value of an instance variable may be either a single value or a set; *nil* is a value representing the empty set.

shallow-equal or deep-equal by having the same identity, the same value or their values include shallow-equal objects, respectively. A value is either an element or a subset of a domain. A domain is any of the atomic domains including integers, reals, etc, or a non-atomic domain which is formed by the total instances of some class.

A method is invoked via a corresponding message and retrieves either a stored value from an object, i.e., the value of an instance variable, or a derived value. We use messages(c) to denote the set of messages corresponding to methods of class c. The set of total instances of a class c, denoted by $T_{instances}(c)$, is defined to include instances in class c and all its subclasses; this is because the definition of a class is inherited by all its subclasses which implies that every object in a subclass should have values for the instance variables of any of the superclasses of its class.

Given a class c, we derive message expressions of class c, denoted by $M_e(c)$, as follows:

- messages(c) $\subseteq M_e(c)$
- if $x \in M_e(c)$ and the domain of the result of x received by an element
  of $T_{instances}(c)$ is $T_{instances}(c_1)$ for some class c_1, then
  $$(x \ messages(c_1))^2 \subseteq M_e(c)$$

We use len(x) to denote the number of messages constituting the message expression x. When received by an object, a message expression results in the execution of the methods underlying the constituting messages and in the same sequence. The underlying methods are executed as if they all form a single method invoked by the message expression, and hence behaviour construction is facilitated. Furthermore, a message expression returns either a stored or a derived value, a property that facilitates the invocation of behaviour and gives a full computational power to the user.

The name of an instance variable, actually a message, when sent to an object, returns the value of the instance variable in the receiving object. For instance, o_1 age() returns the age of object o_1, while o_2 works-in() returns the department o_2 is working at, and o_2 works-in() name() returns the name of the department o_2 is working at. Such methods return existing stored values while other methods that do not correspond to any instance variable return derived values, derived starting with existing stored values. According to the definition of a message expression, age(), works-in() and works-in() name() are examples of message expressions.

3 The Query Model

Although most of the existing query languages are devoted to the manipulation of existing objects without creating new ones, we and others [CD92, Kim89, MD86, Osb88, SZ90] argue the need for a more powerful query language that results in new objects in addition to the manipulation of existing others. This adds the flexibility of introducing relationships into the model making the manipulation more powerful.

Concerning our object algebra, an operand has a pair of sets, a set of objects and a set of message expressions. Since a class has a defined set of objects and a derived set of message expressions, a class can be an operand. The result of any query operation is also a pair of sets and can be made persistent in the lattice because it is possible to

---

[2] returns the concatenations of x with every element of $messages(c_1)$.

derive the state structure and behaviour definition of the result of a query from those of the operand(s); hence it is a class [AA92, Alh92].

Starting from a pair, a set of objects and a corresponding set of message expressions, it is possible to derive class characteristics. To remember, a class has a set of objects, a set of instance variables, a set of methods with corresponding messages in a one to one relationship, and a set of superclasses. A set of objects is given in the pair. So, finding a set of messages is equivalent to the finding of a set of methods and since an instance variable has a corresponding method to handle its value, and hence message, the set of instance variables is constructed by collecting those instance variables having a message in the calculated set of messages. The set of messages of a class is determined to include every message that appears as the first message in a sequence of messages constituting an element of the set of message expressions of that class. Finally, the set of superclasses is determined according to the applied operation as discussed in [AA92, Alh92].

Next we are going to discuss the power of our object algebra. Let A and B be defined to have pairs of sets, $\langle T_{instances}(A), M_e(A)\rangle$ and $\langle T_{instances}(B), M_e(B)\rangle$, respectively; A and B may be classes or the output from a query.

The selection operation is required to restrict objects in the output to those satisfying a given predicate. Although Straube claims in [SÖ90a] that his selection operation with multiple operands is more powerful than a selection operation with one operand, like that defined in [SZ90]. We do not agree with that, because he has the cross-product operation embedded within the selection and both operations are allowed in our model. He did that for not to get into the trouble of maintaining the closure property. In addition, we argue that the power of an algebra must be judged as a whole. The selection operation is defined in our model as:

$$A[p] = \langle \{o \mid o \in T_{instances}(A) \wedge p(o)\}, \quad M_e(A)\rangle \qquad (1)$$

where p is a predicate expression; although the set of objects in the output pair is restricted to those satisfying predicate p, however the same set of message expressions of the operand is still used in the output pair. A predicate expression is built using object variables, message expressions and constants; also quantifiers may be present in a predicate. One object variable is bound by $T_{instances}(A)$, i.e., the operand and other object variables are bound by other queries. An object variable followed by a message expression returns either a stored or a derived value. A returned value can be compared with another value or constant using conventional comparison operators in addition to $\subseteq$, $\nsubseteq$, $\in$ and $\notin$ added to support set-based comparisons and $=$, $\equiv$ and $\triangleq$ for identical, shallow-equal and deep-equal comparisons of objects, respectively. So predicates within an object-oriented context are more powerful than in the relational model where only atomic values are compared. Furthermore, extending predicates to allow quantifiers to propose the creation of objects does affect the query power. For example, $\exists s, s \subseteq T_{instances}(c)$ for some class c, binds s to a subset of $T_{instances}(c)$; the subset objects to which s is bound could be built by this query. Such object creation gives the algebra the power to do recursive queries by giving the ability to form a powerset [AB88].

The project operation is necessary in restricting the accessible part of each of the objects in the operand by eliminating some of the message expressions used in reaching the contents of an object; it is defined as:

$$A[M] = \langle T_{instances}(A), \quad M \rangle \tag{2}$$

where $M \subseteq M_e(A)$ specifies the behaviour of the result; the same set of objects from the operand is maintained in the result, i.e., concerning the project operation, only message expressions in M can be used to deal with objects in the result although those objects may include more values than those reachable by message expressions in M and even in $M_e(A)$; this is to maintain the encapsulation property and facilitate information hiding. In other words, the set of total instances of a class or the output from a query is in general heterogeneous and the only values reachable inside those objects are specified by the corresponding set of message expressions. Hence the object algebra deals with heterogeneous sets rather than being restricted to homogeneous sets like in the relational model [JS82].

On the other hand, it is necessary to facilitate the extension of the set of message expressions applicable to certain objects, i.e., it is necessary to have the inverse of the project operation. As it is possible to define such an operation in terms of others, we introduce it later in this section.

To be able to bring values found at different levels of nesting within an object to the same level of nesting, the one-level-project operation is defined. It is more powerful than the unnest operation of the relational model in being not only restricted to existing stored values, but derived values are also handled. In addition to that, not all the values at a certain level are unnested but selection of desired values is possible. In other words, using the one-level-project operation, it is possible to unnest selected values without any need to unnest all values then renest those not supposed to be unnested like in the nested relational model which is an exhaustive task. The one-level-project operation is defined as follows:

$$
\begin{aligned}
A![M_1] = \langle \{o \, | \exists o_1 \in T_{instances}(A) \wedge value(o) = (o_1 M_1)\}, \{x \, | \exists x_1 \in M_1 \\
\text{with } x_1 \text{ returning a stored value, } x_1 = (x_2 m) \wedge len(x_1) = len(x_2) + 1 \wedge \\
\exists x_3 \in M_e(A) \wedge x_3 = (x_2 x) \wedge x = (m x_4)\} \\
\bigcup \{x \, | \exists x_1 \in M_1 \text{ with } x_1 \text{ returning a derived value, } len(x) = 1 \wedge \\
\forall o_1 \in T_{instances}(A) \exists o \in T_{instances}(A![M_1]) \text{ such that} \\
o_1 x_1 = ox\} \rangle.
\end{aligned}
\tag{3}
$$

where $M_1 \subseteq M_e(A)$. While the Project operation does not evaluate any message expression, the one-level-project operation evaluates the provided message expressions resulting in new objects and a set of message expressions is derived to be used in dealing with those objects. In general, the one-level-project operation corresponds to a sequence of unnest followed by a projection in the nested relational model. The depth of nesting decreases as the length of the longest message expression in M_1 increases. In other words, the depth of nesting is inversely proportional to the length of message expressions in M_1.

The one-level-project operation does the function of Project and Image operations described in [SZ90], the Apply operation of [Osb88] and the Map operation described in [SÖ90a], however we maintain the closure property without additional constructs.

Although many relationships between objects are represented within the objects themselves, an explicit operation is required to handle cases when a relationship is not present in the model. Both the cross-product and the nest operations are defined to introduce such relationships. While the cross-product operation is defined to be associative, the nest operation is not. However, the two operations are equivalent under certain conditions [AA92, AA93c, Alh92].

The cross-product operation has four different forms depending on the domains of the instance variables of the operands. These four forms, given next, are necessary to have the cross-product operation associative; a property necessary for query optimization [AA92, AA93c, AA93b].

By assuming two messages m_1 and m_2 with domains being $T_{instances}(A)$ and $T_{instances}(B)$, respectively, the four cases are:

First case: if objects in each of $T_{instances}(A)$ and $T_{instances}(B)$ have all included values drawn from non-atomic underlying domains:

$$A \times B = \langle\{o | \exists o_1 \in T_{instances}(A) \exists o_2 \in T_{instances}(B) \wedge$$
$$value(o) = value(o_1).value(o_2)\}, M_e(A) \bigcup M_e(B)\rangle \qquad (4)$$

Second case: if only objects in $T_{instances}(A)$ include at least one atomic underlying domain:

$$A \times B = \langle\{o | \exists o_1 \in T_{instances}(A) \exists o_2 \in T_{instances}(B) \wedge$$
$$value(o) = identity(o_1).value(o_2)\}, (m_1 M_e(A)) \bigcup M_e(B)\rangle \qquad (5)$$

Third case: if only objects in $T_{instances}(B)$ include at least one atomic underlying domain:

$$A \times B = \langle\{o | \exists o_1 \in T_{instances}(A) \exists o_2 \in T_{instances}(B) \wedge$$
$$value(o) = value(o_1).identity(o_2)\}, M_e(A) \bigcup (m_2 M_e(B))\rangle \qquad (6)$$

Fourth case: if objects in each of $T_{instances}(A)$ and $T_{instances}(B)$ include at least one atomic underlying domain:

$$A \times B = \langle\{o | \exists o_1 \in T_{instances}(A) \exists o_2 \in T_{instances}(B) \wedge$$
$$value(o) = identity(o_1).identity(o_2)\}, (m_1 M_e(A)) \bigcup (m_2 M_e(B))\rangle (7)$$

By considering these four cases, the cross-product operation becomes associative [AA92, AA93c, AA93b]; an important property as query optimization is concerned.

The nest operation/indexnest operation takes two operands and adds a value to each of the objects in the first operand; the underlying domain being the objects in the second operand. It is a special case of the cross-product operation, but the difference is that here always the first operand is extended to include a reference to the second operand regadless of the underlying domains of the instance variables in the operands. It is defined as follows:

$$A >> B = \langle\{o|\exists o_1 \in T_{instances}(A)\exists o_2 \in T_{instances}(B) \wedge$$
$$value(o) = value(o_1).identity(o_2)\}, M_e(A)\bigcup(mM_e(B))\rangle \quad (8)$$

where the domain of m is $T_{instances}(B)$.

When combined with a selection operation, both of the cross-product and the nest operations result in a join operation. While the join due to a nest is an outer-join, the join due to a cross-product is an inner-join.

So using one-level-project, nest and cross-product operations, objects may be constructed out of existing ones. Also since the result of any operation including nest and cross-product, is defined to have a pair of sets, it ends up to have the characteristics of a class, derived from the pair. Therefore, we have the possibility of introducing new classes and hence supporting views via object algebra operations.

To drop a present relationship, we project on all message expressions of the operand except those related with the pair of the relationship to be dropped. For instance, to drop the relationship between A and B:

$$A << B = A[M_e(A) - (x\ M_e(B))] \quad (9)$$

where $x \in M_e(A)$ has underlying domain as $T_{instances}(B)$.

Remember that an operand has a pair of sets, a set of total instances and a set of message expressions. So, as we are dealing with sets, set operations are also supported. The union operation is defined as:

$$A\bigcup B = \langle T_{instances}(A)\bigcup T_{instances}(B),\ M_e(A)\bigcap M_e(B)\rangle \quad (10)$$

The intersection of the message expressions is taken because objects in the result will be heterogeneous and the only message expressions that can equally access those objects are found in the intersection of message expressions of the operands.

Under the condition that $M_e(A) - M_e(B) \neq \phi$, the difference operation has the following form:

$$A - B = \langle\{o \mid o \in T_{instances}(A) \wedge o \notin T_{instances}(B)\},\ M_e(A) - M_e(B)\rangle \quad (11)$$

However, if it occurs that $M_e(A) - M_e(B) = \phi$, then $M_e(A) - M_e(B)$ is replaced by $M_e(A)$ in the definition. This is done because any set of objects should have a non-empty set of corresponding message expressions in the same pair to support encapsulation and information hiding in accessing contents of the objects.

In terms of the difference we define the intersection operation as follows:

$$A\bigcap B = A - (A - B) \quad (12)$$

To have a more powerful object algebra, it is necessary to have the result of the application of an aggregate function used as an operand. The following operator is defined for that purpose:

Given $X \subseteq M_e(A)$ and $x_i \in M_e(A)$, the application of an aggregate function f is defined as:

$$A\langle X, f, x_i\rangle = \langle\{o\,|\,(o\,m_1) \subseteq T_{instances}(A) \wedge (o\,m_3) =$$
$$f(\{(o_1\,x_i)\,|\,o_1 \in T_{instances}(A) \wedge \forall o_2 \in (o\,m_1), (o_2 X) =$$
$$(o_1 X)\})\}, (m_1 M_e(A)) \cup \{m_3\}\rangle \qquad (13)$$

where $T_{instances}(A)$ is the domain of the result of message m_1, and the domain of the result of f is the domain of the result of message m_3.

The aggregation function is applied on A by evaluating the function f on the result of the message expression x_i for all objects that return the same values for elements of the set of message expressions X.

Finally the inverse of the project operation is defined at this point, as stated before, in terms of other operations:

To add a subset X of $M_e(B)$ to $M_e(A)$, we first nest A and B then do a one-level-projection to have all $M_e(B)$ and $M_e(A)$ together forming one set; after that we project on $M_e(A) \bigcup X$ to get the target set of message expressions in the resulting pair.

$$A]X[= (A >> B)\ ![messages(A)\bigcup(m_2\ messages(B))]\ [M_e(A)\bigcup X] \qquad (14)$$

where $X \subseteq M_e(B)$ is the set of message expressions to be added to $M_e(A)$, and m_2 is a message in the result of $A >> B$ with its domain being $T_{instances}(B)$.

Using the operators described in this section, we can form *object algebra expressions* since the closure property is maintained in having the output from a query as a possible input to another. Next in this section we are going to give the equivalence of some *object algebra expressions*.

3.1 Expressive Power of the Object Algebra

It is important to emphasize that, since we have the five basic operators of the relational algebra, the object algebra has at least the power of the relational algebra. In fact, our object algebra is more powerful because the relational algebra handles only atomic domains and only stored values can be retrieved which is nothing more than a restriction that necessitates an embedded query language and hence impedance mismatch in contrast to the object algebra which handles stored as well as derived values and hence satisfies computational completeness. Furthermore, the proposed model allows for set based predicates and quantifiers are allowed in predicates in contrast to only atomic predicates in relational algebra. Also we support encapsulation, object identity and inheritance. Generally speaking, the expressiveness of the constructors of an object-oriented data model do affect the expressiveness of the corresponding query language over the relational algebra. In other words, an object-oriented data model allows the definition of data through abstraction, supports derived data in addition to multivalued properties, complex objects, identity and inheritance. As a result the same real world situation can be expressed by a simpler object-oriented schema than the relational schema and hence all queries that are coded using the relational algebra could be expressed using an object-oriented query language; however, the reverse is not true. In addition to that, recursion is not supported by the relational algebra, however linear recursion is handled by the object algebra described in this work. Hence, an object-oriented query language is more expressive than the relational algebra for capturing the distinguishing properties of an object-oriented data model.

Concerning the nested relational algebra, although it handles non-atomic domains, it imposes the restriction of manipulating only stored values which is equivalent to having only message expressions that return stored values and excluding those that return derived values and hence does not overcome the impedance mismatch problem. Also, it does not support inheritance, neither identity nor encapsulation. In other words, the nested relational model aims to represent complex objects by nesting relations, but still they are value-based and record-oriented models. Next are the object algebra equivalents for the Nest and Unnest operations of the nested relational algebra. We assume that e_1 has a set of attributes N_1 and consider every element of N_1 as a message that returns the corresponding stored value in a receiving object (a tuple in a nested relation). Furthermore, we assume $T_{instances}(e_1)$ the same as the set of tuples in an equivalent nested relation and $M_e(e_1)$ has an equivalent calculation starting with attributes of e_1 and combining with nested attributes. Now given $N \subseteq N_1$:

$$\begin{aligned} \text{Nest}(e_1, N) = {}& (e_1[M_e(e_1) - \{x \mid x \in M_e(e_1) \wedge \exists m \in N \wedge x = (m\ x_j)\}] \\ & >> e_1[\{x \mid x \in M_e(e_1) \wedge \exists m \in N \wedge x = (m\ x_j)\}])\%s \\ & [\exists s_1 \in T_{instances}(e_1) \wedge s\ m_1()\ N = s_1\ N \wedge \\ & s\ (M_e(e_1) - N) = s_1\ (M_e(e_1) - N)] \end{aligned} \tag{15}$$

where $m_1()$ is a message added to the result of the nest operation ($>>$) to facilitate the access of objects in the second operand.

$$\text{Unnest}(e_1, N) = e_1\ ![messages(e_1) - \{m_2\} \bigcup (m_2\ messages(e_2))] \tag{16}$$

where $messages(e_2)$ corresponds to the set of attributes N and $m_2 \in messages(e_1)$ with underlying domain $T_{instances}(e_2)$.

So, the one-level-project operation corresponds to a sequence of Unnest followed by a projection in the nested relational model [AB88, JS82]. Also, the one level project operation does the function of *project* and *image* operations described in [MD86], the *apply* operation of [Osb88] and the *map* operation described in [SÖ90a], but we maintain the closure property without additional constructs.

As a result, the object algebra has the power of the nested algebra. It is more powerful due to the manipulation of stored and derived values, in addition to supporting the object-oriented features.

3.2 Equivalence of Object Algebra Expressions

In this section we are going to present some equivalences between object algebra expressions which are important in query optimization.

Let e_1, e_2 and e_3 be object algebra expressions, such that: $M_e(e_1) = X_1$, $M_e(e_2) = X_2$ and $M_e(e_3) = X_3$.

- Given two predicate expressions p_1 and p_2,

$$e_1[p_1][p_2] = e_1[p_1 \wedge p_2] = e_1[p_2 \wedge p_1] = e_1[p_2][p_1] \tag{17}$$

- Given $X \subseteq X_1$ and a predicate expression p_1,

$$e_1[p_1][X] = e_1[X][p_1] \text{ iff } \forall x \text{ appearing in } p_1, \text{ we have } x \in X \tag{18}$$

- For e_1 and e_2 as defined above

$$e_1 \times e_2 = e_2 \times e_1 \tag{19}$$

- For e_1, e_2 and e_3 as defined above

$$e_1 \times (e_2 \times e_3) = (e_1 \times e_2) \times e_3 \tag{20}$$

- For e_1 and e_2 as defined above

$$e_1 \bigcup e_2 = e_2 \bigcup e_1 \tag{21}$$

- For e_1, e_2 and e_3 as defined above

$$e_1 \bigcup (e_2 \bigcup e_3) = (e_2 \bigcup e_1) \bigcup e_3 \tag{22}$$

- Given $X_4 \subseteq X_1$ and $X_5 \subseteq X_1$,

$$e_1[X_4][X_5] = e_1[X_5] \text{ iff } X_5 \subseteq X_4 \tag{23}$$

- The following is true iff all instance variables in e_2 and e_3 have non-atomic underlying domains regardless of the domains of the instance variables in e_1:

$$e_1 \times (e_2 \bigcup e_3) = (e_1 \times e_2) \bigcup (e_1 \times e_3) \tag{24}$$

- The following holds iff all instance variables in e_1, e_2 and e_3 have non-atomic underlying domains.

$$e_1 \bigcup (e_2 \times e_3) = (e_1 \bigcup e_2) \times (e_1 \bigcup e_3) \tag{25}$$

- If p is a predicate expression

$$(e_1 \times e_2)[p] = e_1[p] \times e_2[p] \tag{26}$$

- Given a predicate expression p

$$(e_1 \bigcup e_2)[p] = e_1[p] \bigcup e_2[p] \tag{27}$$

– Given p_1 and p_2 as predicate expressions.

$$(e_1[p_1] \bigcup e_1[p_2]) = e_1[p_1 \vee p_2] \tag{28}$$

– For two predicate expressions p_1 and p_2

$$(e_1[p_1] - e_1[p_2]) = e_1[p_1 \wedge \neg p_2] \tag{29}$$

– If $X \subseteq (X_1 \bigcup X_2)$

$$(e_1 \times e_2)[X] = e_1[X] \times e_2[X] \tag{30}$$

– Given e_1, e_2, X_1 and X_2 as defined above

$$(e_1 \bigcup e_2)[X] = e_1[X] \bigcup e_2[X] \tag{31}$$

– If $X \subseteq (X_1 \bigcap X_2)$

$$(e_1 \bigcup e_2)![X] = e_1![X] \bigcup e_2![X] \tag{32}$$

The one-level-project and the project operations are equivalent when $M_1 \subseteq messages(e_1)$ and $X \subseteq M_e(e_1)$ such that elements of X return only stored values:

$$e_1[X] = e_1 ![M_1] \tag{33}$$

where $M_1 = \{m_1, m_2, ..., m_n\}$ and $X = \{x_1, x_2, ..., x_n\}$ with $x_i = (m_i \ x_{p_i})$ for $1 \le i \le n$ and arbitrary x_{p_i}.

The cross-product operation is equivalent to a combination of the nest, project and one-level-project operations as follows:

1. If all the stored values in $T_{instances}(e_1)$ and $T_{instances}(e_2)$ have non-atomic underlying domains:

$$e_1 \times e_2 = (e_1 >> e_2)![messages(e_1) \bigcup (m \ messages(e_2))] \tag{34}$$

where $T_{instances}(e_2)$ is the range (domain of the result) of the message m in the result of $e_1 >> e_2$

2. If only the stored values in $T_{instances}(e_2)$ have non-atomic underlying domains:

$$e_1 \times e_2 = e_2 >> e_1 \qquad \tag{35}$$

3. If only the stored values in $T_{instances}(e_1)$ have non-atomic underlying domains:

$$e_1 \times e_2 = e_1 >> e_2 \tag{36}$$

4. If at least one of the stored values in each of $T_{instances}(e_1)$ and $T_{instances}(e_2)$ has an atomic underlying domain:

$$e_1 \times e_2 = (e_1 >> e_2)[m] >> e_1 \tag{37}$$

where $T_{instances}(e_2)$ is the domain of the result of the message m in the result of $e_1 >> e_2$

Under this same condition, i.e. condition 4, we have:

$$e_1 >> e_2 = (e_1 \times e_2)[(m_1 \ messages(e_1)) \bigcup \{m_2\}] \tag{38}$$

where m_1 and m_2 are two messages in the result of the $e_1 \times e_2$ with their domains being $T_{instances}(e_1)$ and $T_{instances}(e_2)$, respectively.

Finally, the following properties of the object algebra are useful; given an object algebra expression e,

$$e[M_e(e)] = e, \tag{39}$$

$$e![messages(e)] = e. \tag{40}$$

The proofs of the given equivalences will be left out as they all follow from the definitions of the algebra operations already given in this section.

4 Illustrating Examples

Given the following classes based on which some illustrating examples are to be presented next in this section:

person$\langle \emptyset, name$:string,age:integer$\rangle$

employee$\langle \{person\}, salary$:integer,$works\text{-}in$:department $\rangle$

department$\langle \emptyset, name$:string,$manager$:employee$\rangle$

where any pair $iv : d$ represents an instance variable definition where iv is the instance variable name and d is the underlying domain. For instance, age has an integer domain.

The first argument in a class definition is a set with elements being classes from which inheritance is achieved. We say that person is a superclass of employee, while employee is a subclass of person. Any instance in employee is actually an instance in person but the reverse is not true. This is because in general, a subclass may include additional instance variables and behaviour definition. As inheritance is concerned, classes are arranged in a lattice with the general class object at the root, i.e., a direct or indirect superclass of all other classes.

Example 1. Find all employees managed by "Ali".

$S_1 = $ employee$\%e[e \ works\text{-}in() \ manager() \ name() =$"Ali"$]$

where % precedes a variable that should be bound to objects of the operand or by another query. The predicate expression, $e \ works\text{-}in() \ manager ()name() = $ "Ali", filters objects from the employee class which are to appear in the result. Due to the use of $=$, this query is evaluated on a temporary basis.

We differentiate between temporary and persistent evaluations of a query, where an assignment free query is always evaluated on a temporary basis while we use $=$ and $:=$ to differentiate between temporary and persistent based evaluations, respectively. While a temporary based evaluation of a query ends by finding the pair of sets in the result, a persistent based evaluation continues with the finding of class characteristics of the determined pair [AA92, AA93c, Alh92].

Example 2. Assume that the person *class is not present in the lattice and the* employee *class is defined as:*

employee⟨∅, *name*:string,*age*:integer,*salary*:integer, *works-in*:department⟩

To derive the person *class, we write:*

person:=employee [{*name*(), *age*()}]

The derived person class will be a direct superclass of the employee class. Presented elsewhere [AA92, AA93c, Alh92], we derive algorithms to maximize reusability while recognizing the derived person class as a superclass of the employee class and naturally placing it in the lattice.

Example 3. Find the names and managers of employees working in the "Accounting" department.

employee%e [e *works-in*() *name*() = "Accounting"]

![{*name*(), *works-in*() *manager*() *name*()}]

We first select employees working in the "Accounting" department, then one-level-project on the message expressions, {*name*(), *works-in*() *manager*() *name*()}, to get the result. Notice the use of the message expression, *works-in*() *manager*() *name*(), which is a concatenation of three messages, *works-in*(), *manager*() and *name*() are chosen from the employee, department and employee classes, respectively.

Example 4. Find all the employees managed by each manager.

(employee%e_1 >> employee%e_2)[∃ $d ∈$ department ∧ d *manager*() = e_1 ∧

e_2 *works-in*() = d]

We nest the employee class with itself by assigning to every employee the set of employees he/she manages.

Example 5. Find employees working at the same department as "Ahmet".

employee%e[∃e_1 ∈ employee ∧ e_1 *name*() = "Ahmet" ∧

e_1 *works-in*() = e *works-in*()]

Example 6. Find persons who are not employed by any department.

person − employee

Since M_e(person) − M_e(employee) = ϕ, because M_e(person) ⊆ M_e(employee), in the output pair M_e(person) is returned according to the definition of the difference operation given in the previous section.

Remembering that $T_{instances}$(employee) ⊆ $T_{instances}$(person), the same query can be coded using the select operation as follows:

person%p[p ∉ $T_{instances}$(employee)]

Example 7. Let net-salary(t) be a method defined in the employee *class to return the net salary of an employee after discounting taxes t. Assume t = 0.1 for employees working at the accounting department and t = 0.15 for other employees. To find the names and net salaries of employees, we write:*

employee%e[e *works-in*() *name*()= "Accounting"] ![{*name*(), *net-salary*(0.15)}]

⋃ employee %e[e *works-in*() *name*() ≠ "Accounting"] ![{*name*(), *net-salary*(0.1)}]

We first find employees working at the accounting department; then we apply one-level-project operation on the result with t=0.15; also, employees not working at the accounting department are selected and the one-level-project is applied on the result with t=0.1; finally, the union of both results is determined.

Example 8. Find employees working at the same department.

$$(\text{employee}\%e_1 \times \text{employee}\%e_2) \ [e_1 \ works\text{-}in() = e_2 \ works\text{-}in() \wedge$$
$$e_1 \ name() < e_2 \ name()]$$

Remember from Sect. 3 that, when combined with a selection operation, both of the cross-product and the nest operations result in a join operation. While the join due to a nest is an outer-join, the join due to a cross-product is an inner-join. Notice that the result of the query of Example 8 will be a direct subclass of the root because the *employee* class has some instance variables with atomic domains. However, using nest instead of cross-product forces the result to be a subclass of the *employee* class. The difference is due to the fact that while the nest operation will append to every employee a set of identities of related employees, the cross-product operation on the other hand forms, according to the definition of cross-product operation in Sect. 3, new values each consisting of the identity of an employee together with the set of identities of related employees [AA93c, AA93d].

Example 9. Find employees earning more than the average salary in their department.

$$\text{employee}\%e_1 >> \text{employee}\langle\{works\text{-}in()\}, average, salary()\rangle\%e_2$$
$$[e_1 \ salary() > e_2 \ avsalary()] \ [\{name()\}]$$

where *avsalary()* is a message to return the calculated average salary in the result of the aggregate function application; it is a concatenation of the first two letters of the applied function, *average*, with the first message in the used message expression, here *salary()*. We nest **employee** with the result of the application of the aggregate function *average* on **employee** grouped by *works-in()*, then we select those satisfying the given predicate and finally project on *name()*.

5 Conclusions

In this paper we discussed an object algebra we developed for OODBMSs. We support the encapsulation and information hiding features by deriving a set of message expressions to handle the set of objects in a class. We maintain the closure property by having the operands as well the output from a query to have a pair of sets, a set of objects and a set of message expressions. The operators of our object algebra handle both the objects and the message expressions of the operand(s) in producing objects and message expressions of the result. While doing this, heterogeneous sets are considered and this adds much to the power of the object algebra. Message expressions deal with both stored and derived values and hence provide a full computational power to the user without having an embedded query language leading to impedance mismatch. Not only the object-oriented data model is more powerful than the relational data model, we also have the object algebra more powerful than the relational algebra. Furthermore, our object algebra is more powerful than others described in the literature, e.g. [ASL89, BKK88, CDV88, CD92, Day89, FBC$^+$87, Kim89, MD86, Osb88, RS87, SZ90, SÖ90a, VD91], in supporting object construction, behaviour construction via message expressions and equally deals with the behaviour as well the state of objects in addition to handling the application of aggregate functions in a natural way.

SECTION 3

SYSTEM IMPLEMENTATION ISSUES

Optimization of Object-Oriented Queries: Problems and Approaches

Gail Mitchell[1], Stanley B. Zdonik[2], Umeshwar Dayal[3]

[1] GTE Laboratories Incorporated, 40 Sylvan Road, Waltham, MA 02254, USA
[2] Brown University, Department of Computer Science, Providence, RI 02912-1910, USA
[3] Hewlett-Packard Laboratories, Palo Alto, CA 94304-1120, USA

Abstract. An object-oriented data model can support features such as abstract data types, methods, encapsulation, subtyping (or inheritance), complex structures, and object identity. The processing of queries in such a model must incorporate support for these features. Query optimization will require new techniques for supporting the object-oriented features. Although some of the problems that must be solved by an object-oriented query optimizer are similar to problems solved by relational and extensible optimizers, there are also many problems that are unique to the object-oriented data model.

In this paper we explore some of the problems that are encountered when trying to optimize queries in an object-oriented database management system. We present each problem in the context of the object-oriented modelling constructs generating the problem. We also survey current approaches to solving some of these problems.

1 Introduction

A query is an expression describing information one wants to retrieve from a database. Such an expression is normally translated, by a query optimizer, into a series of database operations that yield the desired information.

The ability to do automatic query optimization is a strength of relational database systems. Relational query optimizers exploit the simple semantics of the model and the fixed sets of operators, storage structures, and implementation techniques for the operators. The designs of such optimizers differ and are specific to the system in which the optimizer is built [Dat90a, Ull88]. These optimizers generally embody a set of pre-defined manipulations on some internal query representation. These manipulations apply built-in heuristics to guide the discovery of efficient strategies for database access. The access strategies are evaluated according to some cost formula, and a best strategy is selected. The heuristics that are applied, the algorithms for searching for strategies, and the cost model upon which strategy evaluation is based, are all fixed and specific to the particular optimizer.

Most optimization strategies for relational optimizers focus on queries involving the *Select*, *Project* and *Join* operators (see [Ull88] for a discussion of the theory upon which such strategies are based). Further work in relational optimization looked at extending optimization to include other operators, for example aggregators, outerjoins, and nested subqueries [Day87a, GLR92, Kim82]. Optimization results have also been extended to include more expressive models, such as nested [Kor88, Saa89] and network models [Rie83, RR85].

A need for extensibility in data modelling and access led to the development of databases in which such aspects as the data types, operators, and access methods can be extended. Extended relational systems enhance the relational model with the ability to define new data types and operations, and new access methods for those types [HCF+89, SR86]. Here, extensibility refers to the ability to add new types defining data stored in relational tables. The underlying system model (i.e., relational) remains fixed, but the kinds of information that can be stored in the model can be extended.

Extensible systems are designed to allow flexibility in designing database systems for new and different applications. The term extensible refers to the idea that the system can be extended with new processing capabilities to respond to the requirements of different systems [CH90]. One approach to providing this extensibility is to provide a collection of tools that can be used to generate new database systems [BBG+88, CDF+86, GM93]. A more open approach is to build a database system that can be easily modified to incorporate new capabilities [Rei82, Sch86].

Optimizers for extensible systems are often based on transformation rules for a set of operators defined in the system [Bla94b, FG91, Gra87]. Extensibility of these optimizers results from the ability to augment the set of transformation rules. These transformations are applied to a query expression to generate equivalent, and hopefully more efficient, forms of the expression. A transformed expression often corresponds to many executable plans for database access. These plans are compared according to a cost model (which might also be extensible). The quality of the result produced by an optimizer depends on the completeness of the defined set of transformation rules as well as the cost model. The efficiency of the optimizer itself depends on the control strategies for selecting which transformations to apply and when to apply them.

Object-oriented database management systems (OODBMSs) respond to the needs of a variety of database applications by providing flexible database modelling capabilities [BDK92, BCG+87, MSOP86, MD86, ZW86]. There is much discussion about what constitutes a model for an OODBMS [ABD+89, Dit94, SRL+90]. Although there is no accepted common object-oriented data model, most agree that the data model should provide features such as data abstraction or encapsulation, complex object descriptions, types and subtyping, and object identity. However, different systems often place different meanings on these terms and provide differing amounts of support for some of the features.

OODBMSs are extensible systems; their extensibility is founded on the ability to extend the data model through abstract data types and the subtyping/inheritance structure [Zdo94]. In particular, the ability to define new abstract data types provides extensibility in the database modelled by the abstract data types and places a requirement on the database system to support the new model. Extensibility in OODBMSs is thus more fundamental to the underlying data model than in extensible relational systems and is also more dynamic than the extensibility provided by toolkit systems.

Research on query optimization for OODBMSs has followed two basic directions. One approach focusses on specific techniques that solve particular optimization problems. For example, one highly visible problem in optimization of object-oriented expressions is path expressions. Such expressions imply a navigation through objects to find the end of a path. Research in this area includes exploring indexing for paths [Ber93, KM90a, MS86, OHMS92], optimization in the presence of arbitrary methods along the path [Ber91, GM88, GW89, KKM91], and the use of clustering and other storage information to determine path accesses [CD92, JWKL90, LVZC91].

An alternative approach is to define a complete system for optimization. The application of algebraic transformations has formed the basis for the design of many query optimizers for OODBMSs [Bla94b, GLB89, Osb88, PHH92, SÖ89]. Algebraic transformations, however, do not always provide ways to deal with such problems as path expressions and method invocations. In addition, manipulations involving objects with identity complicate the definition of the equivalence of two query expressions thus complicating the application of transformation rules [SZ89]. Other proposals for optimizers allow combinations of algebraic transformation with other strategies for optimization [KMP93, LV91, MZD92].

In this paper we present some of the problems that arise when optimizing queries in an OODBMS. Although many of the problems that must be solved by an object-oriented query optimizer are similar to problems solved by relational and extensible optimizers, there are also many problems that are unique to the object-oriented data models. We look at problems that arise as a result of supporting different object-oriented features; in particular, abstract data types, complex structures, methods and encapsulation, and object identity. We discuss each problem in the context of the particular feature with which it is associated.

This approach provides important information for designers of data models and languages. It is also important to understand how existing optimization approaches can be applied to object-oriented query optimization, and where new approaches are required. A better understanding of the problems encountered can lead to the development of new (and better) techniques for optimizing object-oriented queries.

In the next section we review the data model and languages we will use to illustrate the problems. In Sect. 3 we discuss in detail some of the problems that must be addressed when optimizing object-oriented queries. In Sect. 4 we survey some of the techniques proposed for solving these problems and in Sect. 5 we describe some systems for object-oriented query optimization. In Sect. 6 we conclude with a brief summary.

2 Data Model and Query Languages

We use the ENCORE data model [ZM91] as the foundation for our discussion of problems in object-oriented query processing. The model incorporates data modelling features found in other object-oriented systems, such as abstract data types, subtyping (inheritance), encapsulation, complex structures, object identity, and late-binding of methods. Thus, problems in dealing with optimization in other models also arise in this model.

In Sect. 3 we express queries using a high-level SQL-like language and a query algebra. The high-level language is based on OSQL (Object SQL) [Lyn91]; the algebra used is EQUAL (Encore QUery ALgebra) [SZ90]. We quickly review ENCORE, OSQL, and EQUAL in this section.

2.1 ENCORE

The ENCORE object-oriented data model was developed at Brown University as a platform for experimentation with concepts related to object identity and abstract data types [ZW86]. The ENCORE model is based on data abstraction. An ENCORE type is an atomic type (Int, String, Boolean, etc.) or an abstract data type describing an interface and an implementation for instances of the type. An instance of a type is an *object*. The interface is a logical description of access to instances of the type; it describes methods that can be applied to objects. The implementation describes a physical representation for instances of the type and includes implementations for methods described by the interface. Abstract data types and encapsulation are synonymous in this model. Objects are encapsulated since all access is through the interface, and the representation of the data and implementation of the methods is hidden. A query is concerned with the interface of a type. However, processing of a query may need to consider the implementation.

Types are related to each other through subtyping. Subtyping requirements ensure that instances of a subtype can be substituted as instances of a supertype. All types are subtypes of type *Object*. This means that all types, and instances of types, are objects with unique identities.

Properties in ENCORE reflect the abstract state of an object. The notion of *property* is modelled by one or more methods (i.e., functions) defined on a type. A property value is accessed by a special observer method that is required to have no side-effects on the observable state of the object. This method for property P is called *Get_P*. For s an object of type T and q a property of T, we write q(s) to mean $Get\_q(s)$ — this can also be abbreviated using dot notation, e.g., $s.q$. The Get_Property_Value method can return the value of a stored field or it may perform a more sophisticated computation based on the stored representation of the object. A property P may also support another function called *Set_P* that allows the value of P to be changed.

The ENCORE model supports the construction of parameterized types. In the examples in this paper, we use the parameterized types Set[T], Bag[T], and Tuple[$< (A_1, T_1), ..., (A_n, T_n) >$]. A parameterized type is a metatype, and the type parameters are input arguments for that metatype's Create operation. For example, the metatype Set[T] defines a Create operation that takes a type T as an input argument and returns a new type as its output.

Parameterized type Set[T] declares T as the type, or supertype, of objects in a collection having type Set, and defines operations *in* and *subset_of* (among others). Type Bag[T] is defined similarly, and includes an operator *occurs* to return the number of occurrences of a particular object in a bag. Type T is called the *member-type* of the set or bag. Type Tuple associates types (T_i) with attribute names (A_i) and defines methods *Get_attribute_value* and *Set_attribute_value* for each attribute.

Abstract data types in ENCORE provide the ability to define logical complex structures. The properties of an abstract data type are similar to attributes in systems such as Orion [Kim89] or O$_2$ [KLR92] in that they give the ability to access state information about an object. The differences between properties and attributes is important to note however. Properties in ENCORE are objects, with methods that access their values. The properties of an object define a logical structure for the object. Attributes in other systems are names that have an associated stored value, thus they define a physical structure for objects. Tuple attributes in ENCORE are names with associated methods Get_attribute_value and Set_attribute_value that can compute values associated with the name.

An ENCORE database is a collection of typed objects. We generally query over collections of type Set[T],[4] where T is some data type, and return new objects having type Set[Q], where type Q is statically determined by the query. Duplication in set membership is determined using object identity; two members of a set cannot be identical.

The query operations support abstract data types. All access to objects in a collection is through the interface defined for the member-type of the collection.

2.2 OSQL

The OSQL language was developed at Hewlett-Packard Labs as a high-level language for OODBMSs that is independent of programming language and database implementation [Lyn91]. The language is a functional language, with a syntax that resembles that of SQL. In this section we look, in particular, at the OSQL query language as it can be applied to our data model.

The basic query statement in OSQL is the *Select* statement:

SELECT   *result specification*
FOR EACH   *variable declarations and bindings*
WHERE   *predicate*

The **FOR EACH** clause is the analog of the **FROM** clause in SQL, but more explicitly shows the semantics of set iteration. The **SELECT** clause specifies how to build objects to be returned by a query — for example, **SELECT** can specify a function (or functions) to be applied to an input object to produce a result. The Where predicate specifies criteria that must be met by objects included in the result.

For example, the following query returns the secretaries of all managers who work for 'GM':

SELECT   secretary(m)
FOR EACH   Manager m
WHERE   name(employer(m)) = 'GM'

The **FOR EACH** clause specifies a typed variable (or variables) that is bound at query execution to objects of the extent of the type. In the OSQL model, all types explicitly have an associated extent. This is not the case in ENCORE, so in order to apply the OSQL language to ENCORE we will assume, without loss of generality, that the For Each statement specifies a collection and a variable whose type is the member-type of the collection. For example, this query could contain the clause "**FOR EACH** Managers m" since Managers is the name we give to the set of all objects of type Manager (see Fig. 1).

---

[4] Queries may also be expressed over bags. In OSQL, queries are expressed over sets or bags, and return bags unless otherwise specified. In EQUAL, we assume queries return sets of objects.

Semantically, the above query states that for each manager in Managers, the name property (i.e., Get_name method) is applied to the result of the employer property applied to the manager, and compared to 'GM'. If the predicate is satisfied, the secretary property is applied to the manager and the result is added to the output. The result of a **SELECT** statement is, by default, a bag — secretaries who work for more than one manager will be referenced many times in the result. A set result is obtained using **SELECT DISTINCT**.

The output specification in the **SELECT** clause can also specify structured types of results — in particular, result tuples can be specified. For example, the clause

SELECT   ⟨ m, secretary(m) ⟩

specifies ordered tuples containing a manager (m) and secretary.[5] The same result can be specified as:

SELECT   m, secretary(m)

Here, the result tuple construction is implicit. This query form is more syntactically compatible with SQL.

Consider the query:

SELECT   cars(m)
FOR EACH   Manager m
WHERE   name(employer(m)) = 'GM'

For each manager employed by 'GM', the result contains a set of cars owned by that manager. However, an OSQL **SELECT** statement will never return a bag of bags, or a bag of sets (etc.) — such queries are automatically flattened. For example, the result of this query is a bag of cars.

Similarly, the OSQL model provides for polymorphic functions that can be applied to individual objects or sets of objects. For example,

SELECT   name(emps(d))
FOR EACH   Departments d
WHERE   name(mgr(d)) = 'Smith'

returns, for each department manager named "Smith", the names of all the employees in that manager's department. In OSQL, the Get_name function is applied to a set of employees by applying it individually to each employee in the set. Also, as noted earlier, the **SELECT** result will return a bag of names rather than a bag of sets of names.

In addition to **SELECT** and **SELECT DISTINCT**, the OSQL language provides **UNION, GROUP BY, HAVING** and **ORDER BY** clauses, as well as aggregate functions such as Avg, Sum, Max and Min. The *Union* operator combines the results of two

---

[5] Although OSQL only specifies ordered tuples, we will extend the result specification to allow unordered tuples with named fields. For example,

SELECT   ⟨ Manager: m, Secy: secretary(m) ⟩

has the semantics of the previous query, but specifies named fields in the result tuples.

queries to produce a bag containing no duplicates. The Union All operator concatenates two results — i.e., will contain duplicates. The rest of the operations work as in SQL, with the exception again that the operations apply functions to objects. For example, the query

> **SELECT** employer(m), AVG(salary(m))
> **FOR EACH** Manager m
> **GROUP BY** employer(m)

returns the employer and average salary of managers of that employer.

2.3 EQUAL

The EQUAL query algebra [SZ90] for ENCORE provides type specific operations against collections of objects with identity. The operations are concerned in particular with object identity; new objects with unique identities can be created and there are operators to manipulate the identities of objects.

EQUAL includes operations that are the analogs of relational algebraic operations as well as operations to manipulate the logical structure of ENCORE objects. The algebraic operations can be divided into two categories:

1) operations that retrieve data: *Select, Image, Project,Ojoin, Union, Intersection*, and Difference.
2) operations that support data retrieval through manipulation of result structure and object identity: *Flatten, Nest, UnNest, DupEliminate*, and *Coalesce*.

The operations in the first category are adaptations of operations of relational and complex object algebras to the semantics required to support the object-oriented data model. In particular, they are object-creating operations that can apply methods to database objects to retrieve information about the object properties and relationships. The *Flatten, Nest*, and *UnNest* operations are adapted from complex object algebras. Operations *DupEliminate* and *Coalesce* are included to deal with object identity and shared references.

The *Select* operation collects a set of database objects satisfying a selection predicate, i.e., $Select(S,p) = \{s \mid (s \in S) \land p(s)\}$. The *Project* and *Ojoin* operations can create new relationships not explicitly defined by the properties of the object types. These operations produce tuple objects to store the computed relationships. The *Project* operation creates one tuple for each object in the collection being queried, with the tuple storing selected relationships between components of the object, or relationships involving database objects from other collections. For example,

> *Project*(Employees,λe $\langle$ (E,e),
>
> (M,*Select*(Managers,λm m.salary < e.salary)))$\rangle$)

returns, for each employee, all managers who are paid less. The result is a collection of 2-tuples with attribute E of type Employee and M of type Set[Manager]. The value of each attribute E is obtained by applying the identity function (e) to an employee, and the value of each attribute M is obtained as the result of a query over Managers. *Project* can also act similarly to a relational *Project* by extracting only properties from the objects in the queried collection.

The *Ojoin* operator is an explicit join operator used to create relationships between objects from two classes in the database. For example, the matching of employees and managers could be accomplished using

$Ojoin$(Employees,Managers,E,M,λe λm m.salary $<$ e.salary)

where e and m represent objects in Employees and Managers, respectively. This result is stored as a collection of 2-tuples with one Employee type attribute and one Manager type attribute.

For sets of tuple objects, *Ojoin* is analogous to a relational *Theta-join*. When a Set[T] is involved in an *Ojoin* (for T some abstract, non-tuple type), it is treated as a set of single-attribute tuples Set[Tuple[A:T]].

The *Image* operation applies a function (which may be a property or an EQUAL operation) to each object in a set, collecting the results in a set object. For example,

$Image$(Managers,λm m.secretary)

applies the *secretary* property to each manager to yield a set of employees who are secretaries for some manager.

Union, *Difference* and *Intersection* are the usual set operations with set membership based on object identity. The result for all operations is considered to be a collection of objects of type T, where T is the most specific common supertype (in the type lattice) of the types of the objects in the operands.

The *Nest*, *UnNest* and *Flatten* operations work only with the structure of objects. *DupEliminate* and *Coalesce* manipulate identities of result objects. Operation *Flatten* takes a set of sets of objects (type Set[Set[T]]) and returns a set of objects (Set[T])[6]. *Nest* and *UnNest* extend the same operators for non-first normal form relations (see [JS82]) to sets of objects with identity. Sets of tuples can be unnested to convert a set-valued attribute to single-valued, or nested to create a set-valued attribute. Operation *DupEliminate* provides the option of eliminating duplicate copies of objects from a collection. Such elimination is automatic for identical objects (a set cannot have two identical members), but operations that can create new objects (such as *Project* or *UnNest*) may create objects that are equal-valued.[7]

Operation *Coalesce* can be applied to a set of tuples, and allows the removal of duplication in tuple attribute values; i.e., manipulates the structure of the tuples to provide aliasing of equal objects. For example, recall the query creating, for each employee, a set of managers who are lower paid. For each employee a new set is created to store the matching managers. So, for two equally paid employees, two set objects, each containing the same managers, will be created. Coalescing the result would ensure that employees having the same salary are paired with identical sets of managers.

---

[6] Recall that this is done automatically in OSQL.

[7] All duplicate elimination in OSQL was implicit. The assumption made in the OSQL model is that all structured types are literals; i.e., objects that are identified by their contents rather than by a unique identifier. Thus a *Select Distinct* operation that produces tuple results will not produce two tuples with the same values.

3 Problems in Object-Oriented Query Optimization

Although many of the problems that must be solved by an object-oriented query optimizer are similar to problems solved by relational and extensible optimizers, there are also many problems that are unique to the object-oriented data models. In this section we present some problems that arise when optimizing object-oriented queries. The problems are organized by the modelling feature that generates them.

In particular, we look at some problems that arise as a result of supporting abstract data types, complex structures, methods and encapsulation, and object identity. We discuss each problem in the context of the particular feature with which it is associated, and note any relationships between a problem being described for the object-oriented data model and problems encountered in relational optimization. For example, the nested queries common in object-oriented languages generalize nested queries in SQL. We also note proposed techniques for solving the problems, where applicable. We discuss these techniques in more detail in Sect. 4.

The examples in this section refer to the sample scheme of Fig. 1. The scheme represents a car-manufacturer database (similar to [BKK88]) in which companies have departments, and vehicles are manufactured by companies. There is also a hierarchy of people including employees, managers (specialized employees), and students who study at a company under the direction of a manager. Some students are paid while they study (type Student-Employee).

The schemes shown describe methods that can be applied to instances of a type to disclose state information (the *Properties*), the subtype lattice (*Supertypes*), and collections maintained by the database (the *Extents*). We do not show general operations over abstract data types in the scheme since we want to query without side-effects. The information shown is at the interface of the abstract data type. We assume no particular implementation or physical representation for the Properties.

The Properties of any type in the scheme include those explicitly listed for the type as well as all properties of its supertypes. For example, type Manager has Properties budget, secretary, employer, mgr, department, salary, name, age, cars and residences. Type Student-Employee has two different properties of type Company; Property *comp* is the Company inherited from type Student and represents the company at which the student studies, and Property *employer* is inherited from type Employee and represents the company that pays the student. Type Student-Employee also multiply inherits its *mgr* property. We are not concerned with the resolution of that conflict here.

Recall that the Properties of each abstract data type impose a logical structure on instances of the type. Since these are abstract data types, we do not know how the Properties are implemented. In general we assume properties are accessed with a Get_Property_Value method that may be implemented in any of many different ways. For example, access to the *dept* of a Manager m may be through a stored identifier for a department or may involve a computation such as searching through the Departments collection to find the one whose *mgr* field is m.

In Sect. 3.1 we discuss general problems that arise in supporting abstract data types and in Sect. 3.2 we look at problems that are specific to supporting the complex logical structures that can be built using an abstract type system. In Sect. 3.3 we discuss the problems related to supporting encapsulated methods. Finally, in Sect. 3.4 we examine

```
ADT Person                    ADT Vehicle
   Extent: People                Extent: Vehicles
   Properties:                   Properties:
          name: string                  vin: string
          age: integer                  manu_by: Company
          cars: Set[Vehicle]
          residences: Set[Address] ADT Company
                                    Extent: Companies
ADT Employee                     Properties:
   Supertype: Person                 name: string
   Extent: Employees                 emps: Set[Employee]
   Properties:                       depts: Set[Dept]
          employer: Company
          mgr: Manager           ADT Dept
          department: Dept          Extent: Departments
          salary: real             Properties
                                       mgr: Manager
ADT Manager                         emps: Set[Employee]
   Supertype: Employee
   Extent: Managers            ADT Address
   Properties:                    Properties:
          budget: real                  street: string
          secretary: Employee           city: string
                                         state: string
ADT Student                              zip: string
   Supertype: Person
   Extent: Students
   Properties:
          gpa: real
          comp: Company
          mgr: Manager

ADT Student-Employee
   Supertype: Student, Employee
```

Fig. 1. Example scheme

problems that arise when supporting object identity in an object-oriented database.

3.1 Abstract Data Types

In an object-oriented data model we need to incorporate optimizations for a changing variety of types. Queries may be based on operations over collections, but optimizations pertaining to sets (or bags or lists, etc.) need to be combined with optimizations over the types of the objects contained in the sets. Similarly, these optimizations can involve optimizations with the types of objects related to objects in the set (by properties, for example) and so on.

Type Specific Optimizations. An object-oriented query optimizer must be able to apply optimizations specific to the types, and optimizations that look at relationships between objects of different types. Such optimizations are similar to those examined in the area of semantic query optimization [Kin81, MZ87, SO87].

For example, suppose we have the query clause

$$e.employer.name = v.manu\_by.name$$

where e is an object of type Employee and v is a Vehicle, and suppose we can define the following axiom (analogous to a functional dependency) for abstract data type Company:

$$\forall c_1, c_2 : \text{Company} \quad c_1.name = c_2.name \implies c_1 = c_2$$

In other words, companies are constrained to have unique values for their *name* properties.

A type-specific optimization could note that e.employer and v.manu_by both refer to Company objects, and apply the axiom to the predicate to simplify it to

$$e.employer = v.manu\_by$$

The simplified expression would probably require fewer object accesses since the *name* properties of the Company objects no longer need to be computed.

This kind of simplification depends solely on the information about the abstract data type. It would be useful to incorporate such transformations into an object-oriented query optimizer. This additionally requires that the optimizer must be able to be extended with new transformations when new types and constraints are added to the system.

Subtypes and Subsets. An object-oriented query optimizer could also have opportunities to apply transformations that use knowledge about the abstract data type construct. For example, consider the query "Find all GM vehicles owned by GM employees". This query can be expressed in OSQL as follows:

SELECT DISTINCT v
FOR EACH Vehicles v
WHERE   name(manu_by(v)) = 'GM'
AND   v **IN SELECT DISTINCT** cars(e)
                FOR EACH Employees e
                WHERE   name(employer(e)) = 'GM'

This evaluation is represented in Fig. 2a, which corresponds to following sequence of algebraic operations:

GMemps	:=	*Select* (Employees,λe e.employer.name = 'GM')
GMempCars	:=	*Flatten*(*Image*(GMemps,λp p.cars))
Answer	:=	*Select*(Vehicles,λv v.manu_by.name = 'GM'
		$\land$ v $\in$ GMempCars)

The first *Select* operation creates a set of all GM employees. The *Image* operation extracts the cars for each employee — resulting in a set of sets which is then *Flattened*. The final *Select* chooses, from the set of all vehicles, those that are manufactured by GM and owned by GM employees. We would like the final selection to be simplified to:

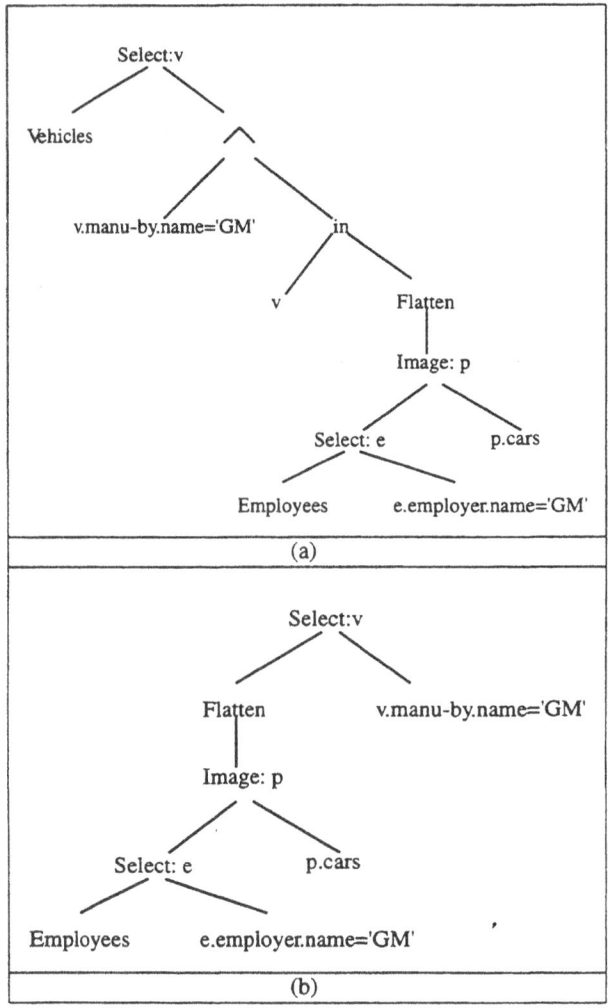

Fig. 2. Query – Find all GM vehicles owned by GM employees

Answer := *Select*(GMempCars, λv v.manu_by.name = 'GM')

This simplification, represented in Fig. 2b, could result from the knowledge that, in the data model, all sets with member-type T are subsets of the extent of T. Since GMempCars has type Set[Vehicle], it must be a subset of Vehicles (i.e., a subset of the extent of type Vehicle). This simplification is similar to the domain refinement technique in semantic query optimization [HZ80]. In our problem, however, the simplification is based on knowledge about set inclusion and abstract data types, not necessarily a particular ADT. Subtyping relationships give similar information about set inclusion relationships. For example, in most object-oriented data models, the set Managers is a subset of the set Employees. This results because Manager is a subtype of Employee, and the sets are both extents.

Subtyping and Static Type-checking. Subtyping information can also affect the applicability of transformations in a statically type-checked system. For example, consider the query *Union*(Students,Employees). In models without *Union* types, the application of this set operation, if it is even allowed, would normally result in a set having type Set[Person], where Person is the closest common supertype of types Student and Employee.[8] As a result, only properties of type Person are applicable, as far as static type-checking is concerned, to the result set. This modelling decision means that a query transformation distributing *Union* (or *Intersection* or Difference) over other operations is not applicable if static type-checking is required. In other words,

$$Union(\text{QueryOp}(S_1,p), \text{QueryOp}(S_2,p)) \neq \text{QueryOp}(Union(S_1,S_2),p)$$

since p may not be defined for the type of $Union(S_1,S_2)$.

For example, consider a query asking for the managers of all Students and Employees. This query can be expressed as

$$Union(Image(\text{Students}, \lambda s \text{ s.mgr}), Image(\text{Employees}, \lambda e \text{ e.mgr}))$$

but not as

$$Image(Union(\text{Students,Employees}), \lambda p \text{ p.mgr})$$

because the union result has (static) type Set[Person], and the *mgr* property is not defined for type Person. However, the *mgr* property could be applied to the union result because of late-binding of methods to the objects. If the intersection (i.e., objects of type Student-Employee) is large, the latter expression might be the most efficient to process; applying *mgr* after the *Union* would avoid applying it twice to objects in the intersection. The type inference mechanism of Straube and Özsu addresses this problem by inferring the methods (such as *mgr*) that can apply to the result of a *Union* (or other operation) [Str91a, SÖ90b].

---

[8] Of course, the closest common supertype can be ambiguous in systems that allow a type to have multiple supertypes (i.e., similar to multiple inheritance). Also, if closest common supertypes are used, set operations in a system with multiple supertypes will not be associative because the result types of different associations cannot be guaranteed to be the same.

Summary. These examples illustrate that knowledge about abstract data types and sub-typing in the object-oriented data model can affect query transformations. In order to support abstract data types an optimizer must be able to incorporate semantic query opti-mizations, such as those discussed here, while supporting standard query optimizations. An optimizer must also support the extensibility that is inherent in abstract data type construction. The addition of new types results in new operations and transformations that should be considered in the optimization process.

3.2 Complex Structures

The complex structure of objects means that languages to query the objects must have mechanisms for exploring their structure. In addition, languages that allow the creation of objects need mechanisms for building new structures. The exploration and creation of such structures can lead to the regular use of path expressions to navigate through a structure. Support for complex structures also results in languages that regularly use nested query expressions; i.e., variables from outer expressions are referenced in nested expressions.

Path Expressions. Path expressions imply an execution order for properties on the path. For example, the path $s.comp.name$, where s is in Students, corresponds to the execution $name(comp(s))$ – that is, apply the $comp$ method to s, then apply $name$ to the result.[9] This order may not, however, be the most efficient way to process the query. A path can sometimes be more efficiently processed using $Join$. For example, if there are very few companies it might be more efficient to first compute the $name$ property for each company and store this result in a tuple. The path from a student to a company name would then involve joining Students with the company/name tuples by matching the $comp$ property of a student with the company attribute of a tuple. An optimizer should be able to make (and evaluate) such transformations between path expressions and explicit joins. Such transformations are addressed by [JWKL90], [KM90a], [LVZC91], and [Rie83], for example.

Another difficulty with path expressions is the definition of indices for such expres-sions. For example, suppose an index from departmental secretaries to employees is required; i.e., the path $e.dept.mgr.secretary.name$[10] requires an index. One question that arises is how to store this index. For example, a single index from secretary name to employee could be maintained [BK89], or indices could be maintained for segments of the path and combined to give the whole path [KM90a, MS86, OHMS92].

Another problem arises when trying to maintain such an index. All steps of a path must be considered when updating an index; i.e., changes to an index can be necessitated by changes to more information than just the ends of the path. For example, changes to a department or manager, as well as changes to the employee or secretary, can affect the name-to-employee index. The presence of arbitrary methods in a path further complicates this problem, since the method results can be affected by changes to database information not apparent at the interface of the method. This is discussed more fully in the next section (3.3).

---

[9] These can be method applications, or just attribute references as in a complex object model.
[10] Assume there is no *mgr* property on Employees.

Common Subexpressions. In general we would like to optimize the use of common subexpressions in a query[11]. Many of these expressions will be path expressions. The use of common path expressions can complicate optimization because a common subexpression could be optimized differently over each instantiation of a common path. For example, consider the predicate

v.owner.residence.city = 'Boston' ∧ v.owner.employer.name = 'GM'

where v is a Vehicle.[12] The application of the *owner* method is common to both conjuncts of the predicate, and thus the expression *v.owner* is a common subexpression. However, if there is a path index on *v.owner.residence.city* we would not want to share the common path. Indeed, any transformation of v.owner on one path should not necessarily affect the other path. In general, any optimization of common subexpressions must determine whether the optimization transformation is applicable to a single path leading to the subexpression, or to all paths.

The formalism of Cluet and Delobel represents common subexpressions and optimizes them as single expressions [CD92]. To our knowledge, no research has been done to decide whether or not optimizations should be applied to every occurrence of an expression.

Nested Queries. A problem with nested query expressions is that query transformations may no longer be local transformations; they can involve query operators that are in different nesting levels. Consider for example a query to find the garaging locations for all Vehicles. The following EQUAL expression satisfies the query by storing a set of addresses with each vehicle.

Project(Vehicles,λv ⟨(V: v),
                        (G: *Flatten*(*Image*(*Select*(People,λp v ∈ p.cars),
                                                        λp p.residences))⟩⟩

This query is illustrated by the tree in Fig. 3a. In this query the variable representing a Vehicle is referenced in the nested *Select* query. The $v ∈ p.cars$ predicate indicates that there is a relationship between Vehicles (represented by variable v) and People (represented by variable p) that could be effected with a *Join* operation.

The query expression illustrated in Fig. 3b also satisfies the query. A difference in the solutions is that *Project* does a left outer join, so could result in vehicles related to empty sets of residences. In this example, the empty sets could easily be eliminated if necessary.[13]

The two query expressions differ significantly in their use of variables. In the first query, variable reference is nested, while in the second query all variables are local to the operation using them. The second query is similar to relational queries in which a *Join* of all relations assimilates the data, then a *Project* operation builds the result

---

[11] The detection of such expressions is discussed in Sect. 3.4.

[12] We change the scheme slightly here to illustrate the problem.

[13] There is a large body of research for dealing with outerjoin operations — e.g., [Day87a, GLR92, RGL90, RR84].

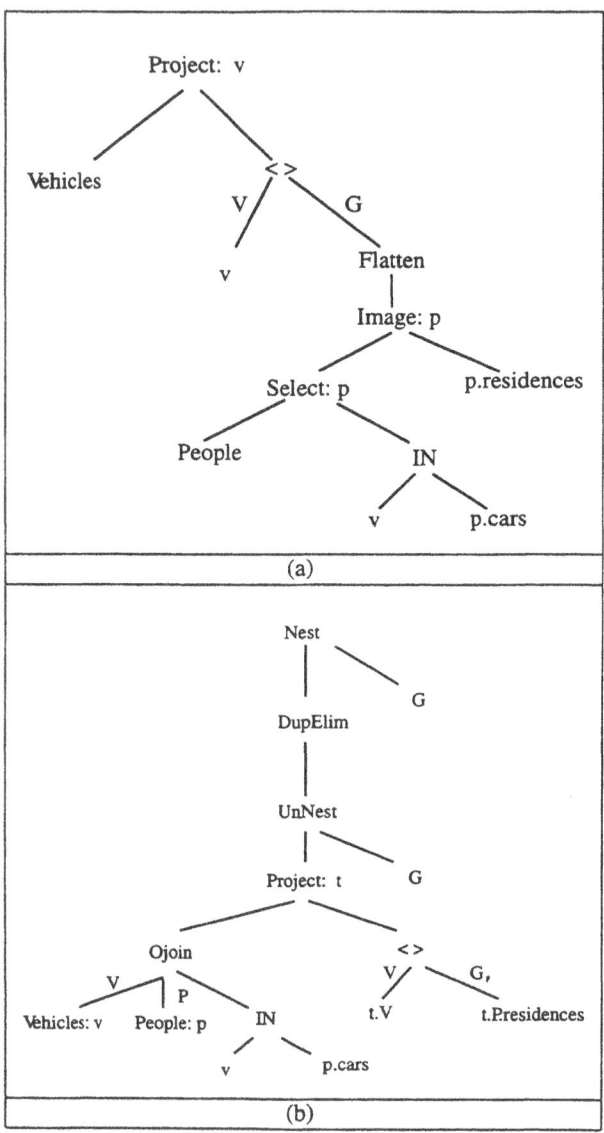

Fig. 3. Query – Find all possible garaging locations for each vehicle

relation. In this query, the data is basically collected using the *Join* operation, then the structure for the result is built with the *Project*, *Nest* and *UnNest* operations.

The transformation between the *Project* and *Join* versions of a query expression may require more than the application of context-free algebraic transformation rules. The arbitrary nesting of query expressions means that recognition of join relationships involves global knowledge about the expression. In addition, any transformations may have to preserve the structure of result objects. Again, producing such a structure requires knowledge which includes the effects of all parts of the query expression on that structure.

An optimizer should be able to generate, and work with, both the *Project* and *Join* query representations. The *Join* representation of the query might result, for example, from a mechanical translation from an SQL-like query. In this case it might be useful to translate to the *Project* version of the query to explore optimizations that cannot be recognized from the *Join* version. On the other hand, if the query is initially the *Project* expression it would be useful to generate the *Join* query, especially if there are efficient techniques for dealing with *Join* operations.

Processing of nested query expressions in SQL addresses situations where queries are nested in **WHERE** predicates [Day87a, GW87, Kim82, Mur92]. Proposals for handling nested queries in object-oriented SQL-like languages address nesting in **FROM** and **WHERE** clauses [CD92, PHH92]. The problem discussed here is equivalent to a query expression nested in an SQL **SELECT** clause. This problem is addressed by a new optimization strategy discussed in the example optimizer of [MDZ93].

3.3 Methods and Encapsulation

The applicability of algebraic transformations to object-oriented queries is complicated by the object model. In general, there are few universally applicable transformations; type and storage information about objects is necessary in order to decide the utility of an algebraic transformation. For example, in the object-oriented data model, the cost of applying a *Select* operation is an important factor when deciding whether to push the *Select* past a *Join*. Although this is also a recognized problem with relational queries, it is not as prevalent and, in the relational model, pushing a *Select* operation past a *Join* operation is generally accepted to be a useful transformation. However, the presence of methods in a selection predicate of an object-oriented query can mean that the cost of applying that operation depends on the cost of applying those methods.

Consider, for example, a query matching managers with budgets of over one million dollars with students, studying at the same company, with grade point averages of more than 3.5. An OSQL version of this query is:

SELECT   RichManager: m, GoodStudent: s
FOR EACH Managers m
             Students s
WHERE   budget(m) $\geq$ 1000000
             $\land$ gpa(s) $\geq$ 3.5
             $\land$ employer(m) = comp(s)

This corresponds to the algebraic expression:

> *Ojoin*(*Select*(Managers, λm m.budget ≥ 1000000),
>   *Select*(Students, λs s.gpa ≥ 3.5),
>   RichManager, GoodStudent,
>   λm,s m.employer = s.comp))

This query joins Managers with budgets of over one million with Students who have appropriate grade point averages, then selects over those pairs by matching the companies. The algebraic expression results from strategies that push selections (on *budget* and *gpa*, respectively) to the single relations to which they apply in an attempt to reduce the sizes of collections to be joined. The heuristic used is that joining is an expensive operation, but selections are straightforward or could even be done as part of the joining process.

However, consider the case where computing a manager's budget is an expensive operation. In this situation it could be more efficient to first join Students (perhaps selected by gpa, depending on the expense of that operation) with Managers by matching the companies. The join operation could reduce the number of managers to which the *budget* method must be applied.

This type of situation is certainly present in relational systems, but the presence of methods in the object-oriented data models — with possibly arbitrary computations implementing the methods — means that strategies such as pushing *Select* past *Join* will be less often applicable. One approach that avoids the cost of applying methods at query execution time is method precomputation [Ber91, KKM91]. An alternative strategy for is to consider cost in the application of rewrite transformations. This would require cost models for high-level expressions, as noted in [GCD+93].

Method Cost. The determination of the cost of a query, or query operation, is complicated by the presence of methods and encapsulation. A query optimizer needs a way to ascertain method cost in the presence of encapsulation. If the optimizer is allowed to break encapsulation and look at the implementation of a method, then it must be able to understand that implementation. For example, a method could be written in the query language understood by the optimizer. The method code could then be merged with the query and managed by the query optimizer [BK90]. This approach, of course, limits the expressibility of methods to that of the query language.

If the optimizer gathers cost information about a method by querying the method itself [GM88] then type Method must define an interface that can provide the required information. As a simple example, type Method would have a property named *cost* which, when applied to a method instance, would return an expected cost for executing the method.

An alternative to determining cost of method applications, of course, is to store precomputed results in tuples [Ber91, KKM91]. The costs of method application are then, in many cases, transferred to compile time.

Late-binding of methods also complicates the determination of method costs, since the implementation (and therefore the cost) of a method used in a query will not necessarily be known until query execution time. For example, suppose the *gpa* method for type Student directly accesses values in the representation of Student but the method is overridden in type Student-Employee by a more expensive method (perhaps computing an average using Student and Company information). The cost of applying the *gpa* method to members of Students can not be statically determined since some objects in the set could actually have type Student-Employee. The dynamic query evaluation plans of Graefe and Ward are designed to address this problem [GW89].

Indexing. The definition and maintenance of indexes is complicated greatly by the presence of methods. An index over even a single property implemented as a method could require the manipulation of arbitrarily many objects. This is similar to the problem with maintaining path indices discussed in Sect. 3.2. A method could be implemented as a path, or some other arbitrary computation, over many database objects. Modifications to any of those objects can change the method result, and thus the index value.

For example, suppose Managers are indexed by their *budget* property, and suppose that property is implemented as a computation that includes retrieving the salaries of all employees in the department. Clearly, a change to the salary of any employee will affect the index on Managers. The problem here, then, is defining indexes so the scope of changes that can affect the index is known and, perhaps, preventing the definition of indexes that will require extensive maintenance. The former problem is similar to the problem of determining when precomputed methods are invalidated [KKM91].

3.4 Object Identity

The identity of objects involves modelling and language decisions that can affect the optimization of queries. When objects have identities, there is a question as to what constitutes equality of two objects (see for example [KC86], [SZ89]). This carries over to the language, where equality operations are used in predicates and where a decision must be made concerning the creation of new objects by a query. The creation of new objects can lead to new definitions for equivalence of queries that affect the transformations available to an optimizer. An optimizer for object-oriented systems must be able to deal with the creation of new objects and with alternative definitions for equivalence.

Object Equality. Equality of objects in a query can refer to any definition of equality for type Object (e.g., identical, deep-equality) or to equality operations defined for a particular abstract data type. In a query language a variety of equality operations could be permitted in predicates. For example consider the operation $a.cars = b.cars$. Equality here might refer to identical sets (i.e., a and b reference exactly the same set of cars), to shallow equal sets (the sets of cars referenced by a and b contain exactly the same cars), or possibly even to sets with the same cardinality (if $=$ is defined as such for type Set[Car]). In the presence of object identity, an equality operation is actually a method, and will have to be treated as such by an optimizer.

Object Creation. A major language decision that affects the optimization of queries is whether a query language can create new objects and, if so, whether those objects can have identities. If the language does not create objects, new relationships between objects cannot be built by queries. If the language only creates objects without identities, then it must be able to work with those objects as well as with objects with identity. On the other hand, if the language creates objects with identity then it must have mechanisms to determine new identities and manipulate those identities. For example, the EQUAL query language provides *DupEliminate* as an operation to manipulate unwanted duplication in objects that may be created by a query [SZ90].

Query Equivalence. The creation of new objects with identity by a query can complicate the optimizer's task. For one thing, the optimizer may want a mechanism for deciding whether to create identities for objects in intermediate stages of a query. Also, the creation of objects with identity complicates the meaning of equivalence of two queries. The result of a query can be a new collection of objects with a unique identity, and as a result even two responses to exactly the same query are not identical. The creation of new objects by a query language means that the structure of results as well as the data retrieved by a query must be considered when defining equivalence.

Different equivalences that must be recognized by an optimizer working with a language that builds objects with identity are defined in [SZ89]. For example, a weak notion of equivalence states that two queries are equivalent if they respond with the same data, regardless of the logical structure of the objects returned. For example, the query "For each student find all employees in the same department" could be answered by a query returning Student/Employee pairs, or by a query returning Student/Set[Employee] pairs.

The ability to define these alternatives might allow the optimizer to choose a more efficient method for solving a query. It also might give the optimizer more latitude when working with nested queries. For example, consider the query:

SELECT   e
FOR EACH Students s
            Employees e
WHERE   mgr(e) = mgr(s)

which returns all employees who work for someone who also manages a student. Recall that the OSQL **SELECT** statement returns bags, so the result requested is a bag of employees. A straightforward translation of this query to EQUAL gives:

$Project(Ojoin(Students,Employees,S,E,\lambda s \; \lambda e \; s.mgr = e.mgr),$
$\qquad \lambda t \; \langle (Emps,t.E) \rangle)$

Note that this translation gives a return type of Set[Tuple[Employee]] rather than Bag[Employee]. This results because EQUAL does not deal directly with bags. However, each employee tuple in the EQUAL result will correspond to exactly one employee represented in the OSQL bag result; thus the EQUAL result is effectively a bag. This happens because the tuples in EQUAL are uniquely defined objects, so each time an employee object participates in the result it will be captured in a new tuple. If an *Select Distinct* operation is required instead of *Select*, then an *Image* operation would be chosen instead of the *Project* since the *Image* result will not contain duplicates of individual employees.

A query optimizer that has the ability to make transformations that manipulate result types might find them useful in providing further opportunities for optimization. For example, an optimizer that can deal with weakly equivalent transformations can transform the previous query by substituting a *Project* operation for the *Ojoin* giving

> *Project*(*Select*(*Project*(Students,λs
> $\qquad\qquad\qquad\langle$(S,s),(E,*Select*(Employees,λe s.mgr = e.mgr))$\rangle$),
> $\qquad\lambda$t NOT Empty(t.E)),
> $\quad\lambda$t $\langle$(Emps,t.E)$\rangle$)

The innermost *Project* operation finds, for each student, all matching employees. This is effectively the *Ojoin* operation, which finds student-employee pairs. The *Select* operation ensures that students that do not match any employee are not considered in the result.

A further transformation could commute the outer *Project* and *Select*, since the *Project* retains the information needed for the *Select*:

> *Select*(*Project*(*Project*(Students,λs
> $\qquad\qquad\qquad\langle$(S,s),
> $\qquad\qquad\qquad$(E,(*Select*(Employees,λe s.mgr = e.mgr))$)$,
> $\qquad\lambda$t $\langle$(Emps,t.E)$\rangle$,
> $\quad\lambda$t NOT Empty(t.E)))

The two *Project* operations can then be collapsed into one giving:

> *Select*(*Project*(Students,
> $\qquad\qquad\qquad\lambda$s $\langle$(Emps,*Select*(Employees,λe s.mgr = e.mgr))$\rangle$)
> $\quad\lambda$t NOT Empty(t.E))

The final result performs fewer operations than the original query, and also is concerned with fewer objects since there are no intermediate results. On the other hand, the final result has a different type than the initial query expression (i.e., Set[Tuple[Set[Employee]]] as opposed to Set[Tuple[Employee]]). The change in type information occurred when the *Project* was transformed to *Ojoin* using the weak equivalence. An optimizer could apply weaker equivalences to find better solutions, but must then be able to determine when such transformations are acceptable. This might involve the ability to restore the type of a result.

Common Subexpressions, Object Creation, and Equivalence. The creation of objects by a query complicates the determination of whether two query expressions can be considered to be the same — i.e., what are common subexpressions? If a query expression represents a constant (i.e., a named database object) or a variable, then it is straightforward to determine common subexpressions. For example, in the query

> *Ojoin*(People,People,A,B,some predicate)

it is clear that both references to People refer to the same database set. However, if a query expression represents a path, or a nested query, it is not always clear when two syntactically equivalent expressions yield identical results.

Methods called within expressions in the query (e.g., in path expressions) may create new objects as their results. Depending on the data model, methods can be written in arbitrary programming languages or may be queries. We assume that queries do not modify the database, but are providing information gathered from observations of the database. Thus, methods or queries are *observers*. However, we can identify two kinds of observers: 1) those that return only existing database objects and 2) those that generate new objects (e.g., queries). We call functions that return existing database objects *pure observers*. Functions that generate new objects are *generative observers* (or, simply, *generators*).

In a path expression containing methods that are generative observers, we have the query equivalence problem. For example, in the query

$$Ojoin(Q, Q, \text{etc.})$$

where Q is some nested subquery, the two executions of the Q subquery could create different objects, and would therefore not be considered to be common subexpressions. In general we would assume that an optimizer would ignore different objects generated by multiple applications of a query expression. On the other hand, it is possible that an optimizer could make use of such occurrences.

4 Optimization Techniques

In this section we look at some techniques proposed for dealing with individual problems in object-oriented query optimization. Much of the work in object-oriented query optimization techniques is devoted to finding efficient ways to access information referred to by a path expression. Research has explored the definition of indexes to speed the access through a path, clustering techniques that can be used to access portions of paths in few storage accesses, and manipulation of the path expression itself to find alternatives to navigation. We also review some of the proposals for rewriting algebraic query expressions, proposed cost models for query optimizers, and work in optimizing when query expressions invoke arbitrary methods.

4.1 Indexing

An early example of the use of indexing is in the Gemstone system [MSOP86]. In this system, paths follow a sequence of instance variables that are part of the structure (i.e., not behavior) of objects. Indexes are defined for each link in a path, and can be based on object identifiers or on values of the instance variables [MS86]. Indexes are implemented in B^+ trees and lookup of a path involves search through a sequence of trees.

Bertino and Kim [BK89] call the GemStone style of index a multi-index. Their work describes two other kinds of indexes for paths. A nested index uses a single index entry to denote the entire length of a path. As a result, one index access can find the beginning of a path given its endpoint. This is only useful when path uses can be predicted, though, and can be expensive to maintain. An alternative index method, the path index, associates the end of a path with all suffixes of the path. As a result, index manipulations involving subpaths can be performed.

The access support relations of Kemper and Moerkotte [KM90a] store in relations information that is equivalent to path indexes. Each column in a tuple represents a step in a path, and fields of the tuple contain object identifiers or data values. Using relations to store the paths generalizes path indexes to allow paths to traverse through sets. In addition, rewrite rules for relations can be used to manipulate the indexes during query optimization [KM90a].

The ObjectStore system allows the definition of indexes that are similar to path indexes [OHMS92]. They also have to contend with indexing collections that are not necessarily the extents of types.[14] Their optimizer generates code alternatives, and execution of a query determines whether an alternative that uses indexes is applicable.

For a more complete exposition and comparison of OODBMS indexing techniques see Bertino's survey [Ber93].

4.2 Clustering

Another approach that is used to speed access to paths is clustering of objects. Early work on object-based clustering strategies [HZ87, MSOP86] physically placed objects in clusters, or segments, according to specifications by an implementor. The implementor would use knowledge about which objects would be used together to ensure they would be stored and retrieved together.

Other work in clustering looks at grouping objects logically using information about the object's structural (component) relationships or also inheritance relationships [BD90, SS90b]. Recent research also addresses the dynamic re-organization of object clusters as structural object relationships change [CK89]. Related research dynamically determines prefetch units using pattern access histories [PZ91].

Cluet and Delobel [CD92] use clustering and index information to limit the search for equivalent queries during query rewrite. Lanzelotte et al. [LVZC91] represent clustering and index information in their physical database model, but then only use index information in the representation and manipulation of queries over that model.

4.3 Manipulating Path Expressions

Another approach to finding efficient ways to traverse paths is to transform the path navigation into join operations. This is the approach of Kemper and Moerkotte with their access support relations discussed earlier [KM90a], and is also the approach taken in the Adaplex optimizer [Rie83] and in distributed Orion [JWKL90]. In the latter, a path is represented as connections between sets of objects (classes) in a query graph. These graphs are manipulated to find efficient traversals (forward and reverse), with access techniques such as indexes, or merge-joins, applied to the traversals.

---

[14] The model of Bertino and Kim [BK89] assumes all collections are the extents of types. Indexing collections, as opposed to extents, is also discussed in GemStone [MS86].

In the Adaplex optimizer, query graphs represent nested loop accesses, quantifiers, some arithmetic expressions, and disjunctions, as well as a paths (i.e., function composition) [Rie83]. A path is represented in a graph by connections (between sets) that represent different kinds of join operations (e.g., cross product, natural join, outerjoin). As a result, paths are manipulated by the optimizer along with the other query constructs.

Lanzelotte et al. [LVZC91] propose an optimization approach that considers *Select* and join operations, as well as path expressions. They map a conceptual view of a query to a *processing tree* representing a more physical view of the query. In the tree, leaf nodes are physical database sets (or subsets) and interior nodes represent joins that are explicit (i.e., a join predicate is given), implicit (i.e., a path from an object to an attribute of the object), or implicit with a path index. Their optimizer manipulates the processing tree by applying tree transformation rules. These transformations can be applied using deterministic search strategies based on the cost of the query. The transformations can result in path traversals that can start from any point in the path (not just endpoints) and can be interleaved with other query operations. This work is extended to handle recursive queries in [LVZ92].

4.4 Algebraic Rewrite

A number of proposals have been made for o-o optimization based on the algebraic rewrite of query expressions [BK90, FG91, GLB89, KM90a, Osb88, SÖ89, Zdo89]. For example, Beeri and Kornatzky [BK90] provide an extensive set of rules for bulk data types that generalize existing axioms for object-oriented algebras, and assume the use of an extensible rule-based optimizer for processing the rules on a query.

Finance and Gardarin [FG91] present a rule language for specifying query rewrites that allows writing rules describing both syntactic and semantic transformations. They also have a meta-rule language that allows an implementor to define blocks of rules, iteration over blocks, and sequences of rules. The meta-rules help define which rules should be applied at any point, and therefore simplify the rule search strategy.

4.5 Cost Models

In general, assessing cost of access strategies in OODBMSs is modelled after relational cost models with enhancements for estimating path expression costs. For example, the cost model of Dogac et al. [DOA+94] uses information about classes, the representation of class instances, and information about attribute values (which can be references to other objects), along with disk access costs and index size estimates, to compute selectivities for attribute values and path expressions, and estimate costs of algebraic operations including joins.

The cost model of Bertino and Foscoli [BF92] uses similar information to compute estimated disk page accesses for forward and reverse path traversals. Their data and query models allow retrieval of objects from a single set, including semijoin retrieval — explicit join operations are not modelled.

The description of cost models that consider arbitrary methods in a query expression is still an open area of research. This is discussed further in the next section.

4.6 Optimizing with Methods

A recognized difficulty in applying query transformations is the problem of manipulating expressions containing references to arbitrary methods. Systems in which methods are written in the query language (e.g., [SR86]) can optimize the method code as a nested query. However, query languages in OODBMSs can access arbitrary methods defined for abstract data types; these methods may be written in languages not recognized by a query optimizer. The costs associated with the application of arbitrary methods need to be considered when manipulating query expressions to determine database access strategies.

Graefe and Ward [GW89] address this problem by statically generating query evaluation plans with alternatives. Information available about objects is used at execution time to choose among the alternatives and generate a final evaluation plan. More recently, Ioannidis et al. address the problem of parametric query optimization [INSS92].

The Revelation architecture describes an optimizer in which methods "reveal" information about their execution [Dan91, GM88]. The revealed information is used to expand the nodes of a query tree with execution information. The query tree, when fully expanded, could be input to a rule-based optimizer such as one generated by Volcano [GM93].

Bertino proposes to precompute the results of methods, and store those results using an index [Ber91]. A method over an object O can be written in an arbitrary language, but cannot have input parameters (other than O), cannot have side-effects, and must only use primitive properties of O (i.e., properties whose values are stored as part of O). These requirements are placed to allow the system to detect when a precomputed method is invalidated. Precomputed results, when still valid, are retrieved using the index. Invalidated results require the method be computed at query execution time.

A similar approach is taken by Kemper, Kilger and Moerkotte [KKM91]. In this system, precomputed function results are stored in relations (called *materialized functions*) along with validity flags for the data, and information about the objects contributing to a function result is maintained. The properties of types, encapsulation and object identity are used to minimize the amount of recalculation that is done when objects are updated. This approach to update management allows the system to handle arbitrary functions.

5 Some Object-Oriented Optimization Systems

Optimization techniques and results in relational and extensible databases form the basis for much of the current research in object-oriented query optimization. In this section we look at some object-oriented query optimization systems. In particular, we examine the optimization approach of Cluet and Delobel [Clu91, CD92], the query processing system of Straube and Özsu [Str91a, SÖ90a], the blackboard architecture proposed by Kemper, Moerkotte and Peithner [KMP93], and the Epoq architecture of Mitchell, Dayal and Zdonik [MZD92, Mit93].

5.1 Cluet and Delobel

Cluet and Delobel propose a formalism that provides for the integration of type-based path processing (e.g. [JWKL90]) with algebraic query rewrite [Clu91, CD92]. They present a model in which type information is added to a query to provide additional information for rewrite rules. The typed query can be represented as a query graph in which nodes represent sets and variables referenced in the query and are annotated with type information, and directed arcs represent operations. This graph is augmented with clustering and index information, and complemented by graphs of join and selection predicates for the query. The result is a model that integrates rewrite techniques for paths, algebraic query rewrite and common subexpression factorization, and also uses clustering and index information to reduce the search space for query transformations.

5.2 Straube and Özsu

Straube and Özsu apply relational techniques to produce a methodology for object-oriented query processing [Str91a, SÖ90a]. Their system takes a declarative object-oriented query to an access plan through the following series of steps: calculus-based optimization, transformation of calculus-based queries to algebraic form, type-checking of algebraic expressions, application of algebraic transformation axioms, and generation of access plans for the algebraic operations. They define a query calculus and an algebra that have only *object-preserving* operations; they cannot create new objects in response to queries.

The type-checking phase of optimization is new phase that determines type consistency when query results are input to further queries. Types that result from a query application can be inferred in order to ensure that further queries are well-typed.

Syntactic and semantic rewrite rules are defined for the object algebra. These rules can be applied by a rule-based transformation system. The application of these rules uses heuristics to produce a query expression that can be used to generate an access plan.

5.3 Blackboard Architecture

Kemper, Moerkotte and Peithner recently proposed a blackboard architecture that presents a novel approach to the generation of access plans in a query optimizer [KMP93]. The architecture is designed to be extensible, specializable, predictable, and tunable. Their systems generates an optimized query by processing a query in steps, where each step adds a piece to the plan.

The optimizer is organized as a ladder of *regions* on a blackboard. Between each successive pair of regions a *knowledge source* manipulates a query to move it from the lower region to the next higher region. There may be more than one knowledge source between any two regions, and any knowledge source can choose any query in the lower region to process. The processing of a knowledge source moves a query one region, but can access any of the information on the blackboard to provide additional information for its processing. All items in all regions have cost information that is used to assist the knowledge sources in their task.

Using this architecture, a query plan is generated in a fixed sequence of steps (from region 0 to region n) that can be only altered by a knowledge source that can move a query to a lower region without modifying it (giving iteration of plan generation). The extensibility in this optimizer comes from the ability to add additional knowledge sources between any two regions (although the control that decides between them is not specified) and the ability to add new regions. The latter extensibility could require a complete reworking of the optimization process though, since each region represents a different query form.

5.4 Epoq Architecture

The Epoq[15] architecture is motivated by the need to integrate a variety of strategies for solving different problems in query optimization [MZD92, Mit93]. An Epoq optimizer is a collection of concurrently available *region* modules, each of which embodies one strategy for the optimization of query expressions. Different regions often accomplish different query transformation tasks, but regions may also represent different strategies for accomplishing the same task in different ways. The Epoq architecture integrates the regions through a common interface for the region modules, and a global control that combines the actions of subordinate regions to process a given query.

The region modules are organized hierarchically, with a parent region controlling its subordinate regions as though they were a collection of transformations. The regions define, through their interface, the characteristics of queries they can process, goals for the transformation of queries, and the characteristics of result queries. A higher-level control uses this information to plan a sequence of region executions to process a given query expression. The control is a goal-directed planner that intermingles planning of the optimizer's processing with execution of region modules (i.e., query transformations), and uses execution results to direct further planning of the optimizer's processing [MDZ93].

The Epoq architecture integrates diverse strategies for query optimization and allows the addition of new strategies. Epoq expands the meaning of extensibility of query optimizers to include extending the collection of optimization strategies that can be applied to transform a query expression. Thus, an Epoq optimizer could incorporate new strategies that are developed to solve problems in query optimization such as those surveyed in this paper.

6 Summary

The features supported by a query language over an object-oriented data model are not necessarily supported by traditional query optimizers. However, the problems that arise from supporting these features must be recognized and managed during query optimization.

In this survey we noted some of the optimization problems that accompany support for abstract data types, complex structures, encapsulation and methods, and object identity. These problems need to be considered by designers of data models and languages, since support for a feature will require solutions to the problems accompanying that feature.

Solutions to some of the problems we have identified require optimization strategies that go beyond current relational optimization technology. We discussed some of the

---

[15] Pronounced as in epoch, Epoq provides extensible processing and optimization of queries.

current research in developing optimization strategies in Sect. 4. In particular we examined current research addressing problems in indexing and clustering, manipulating path expressions, optimizing expressions involving method applications, and rewriting algebraic expressions.

We also surveyed some systems that incorporate different strategies. These systems ranged from fixed architectures, that identify and address specific problems in object-oriented query optimization, to more open architectures that can accommodate the development of new strategies developed to address some of the problems surveyed here.

Acknowledgements

The preparatory work for this survey was performed while Umeshwar Dayal was affiliated with Digital Equipment Corporation, Cambridge Research Lab, and Gail Mitchell was affiliated with Brown University.

Partial support for this work was provided to Brown University by the Office of Naval Research and the Defense Advanced Research Projects Agency under contract N00014-91-J-4052 ARPA order 8225, and contract DAAB-07-91-C-Q518 under subcontract F41100.

Transaction Models and Transaction Management in Object-Oriented Database Management Systems

M. Tamer Özsu

University of Alberta, Department of Computing Science, Edmonton, Alberta, Canada T6G 2H1

Abstract. Transactions are important primitives to provide reliability and controlled access to shared databases. The theory and practice of conventional transaction management involving simple read/write transactions and enforcing serializability have already been developed. In the case of object-oriented database management systems, the traditional transaction management techniques are not sufficient and more powerful transaction models and more flexible correctness criteria need to be developed. The additional complexity of these systems proves to be a significant obstacle to their development. In this paper we review both the problems and the approaches that have been proposed to tackle these problems.

1 Introduction

A transaction is a basic, atomic unit of consistent and reliable computing, composed of a sequence of atomic operation executions. The original research on transactions and transaction management was done within the context of database management systems (DBMSs) and that is the main focus of this paper. Therefore, the more recent transaction-related work in the operating system (OS) and programming language (PL) communities (e.g., Camelot [EMS91], Argus [Lis88] and Quicksilver [SW91]) are not considered.

In the context of DBMSs, transaction management deals with the synchronization of concurrent accesses to a shared database. "Conventional" transaction management involves the synchronization of simple read/write access to a shared database in an environment that is not failure-free. Both the transaction models and the synchronization principles that are used in these environments are simple compared to those that are needed in object-oriented DBMSs (OODBMS). The complexity of the application domains that the OODBMS technology is expected to serve is reflected in the type of transaction management support that they require. In these systems there is a recognized need for more general and powerful transaction models (see, for example, [BBG89, ELLR90, Her90, GMK87, Mos85, PKH88, Wei89]).

In [BÖH$^+$92], a number of these "advanced" applications are analyzed and the transaction management requirements of OODBMSs are identified. The more important of these are the following:

- Conventional transaction management systems (TMS) synchronize simple read and write operations. However, TMSs for OODBMSs must be able to deal with *abstract operations*. It may even be possible to improve concurrency by utilizing semantic knowledge about the objects and their abstract operations.
- Applications supported by OODBMSs have different database access patterns than the conventional database applications where the access is competitive (e.g., two users accessing the same bank account). Instead, sharing is more cooperative as in the case of, for example, multiple users accessing and working on the same design document. In this case, user accesses need to be synchronized, but users are willing to cooperate rather than compete for access to shared objects.
- Conventional transactions access "flat" objects (e.g., pages, tuples) whereas transactions in OODBMSs require synchronization of access to composite and complex objects. Synchronization of access to such objects require synchronization of access to the component objects.
- These applications require the support of *long-running activities* spanning hours, days or even weeks (e.g., working on a design object). Therefore, the transaction mechanism must support the sharing of partial results. Furthermore, to avoid the failure of a partial task jeopardizing a long activity, it is necessary to distinguish between those activities that are essential for the completion of a transaction and those that are not, and to provide for alternative actions in case the primary activity fails.
- It has been argued that many of these applications would benefit from *active capabilities* for timely response to events and changes in the environment. This new database paradigm requires the monitoring of events and the execution of system-triggered activities within running transactions.

Similar requirements are discussed in [Kai89] within the context of software development systems. Five example applications are considered in [MP94]: (1) collaborative work in an office environment (the "shared desk top" metaphor), (2) a concurrent make facility, (3) editing a large document, (4) a CASE environment, and (5) cooperative arrangement of meeting rooms. A number of extensions to the traditional transaction model are identified from these examples categorized as those that *preserve transaction isolation* and those that *isolate cooperation*. The former class of extensions provide transaction properties more flexibly by capturing application semantics while the latter allow localized cooperation between a group of transactions. To preserve isolation, three specific extensions are proposed:

1. use of semantics-based concurrency control using commutativity of operations on objects;
2. identification of the layers of abstraction of a concurrent activity so that low level ordering dependencies can be ignored if higher level operations commute;
3. separation of the boundaries for failure atomicity and serializability to provide more flexibility.

To support isolation cooperation, the concept of *cooperative atomicity* is introduced. A group of concurrent activities is externally viewed as a single action and synchronized with respect to the group as a whole. Internally, the group of cooperating activities synchronize their own accesses to shared data.

The point of these analyses is that many of the properties that are commonly associated with transactions need to be revisited for OODBMSs. In this paper. we address the issues related to management of transactions in OODBMSs. We start, in Sect. 2, with a presentation of the fundamental transaction concepts. The purpose of this section is to make the paper self-contained, not to provide a detailed exposition of all of the issues. We assume the reader is familiar with basic transaction management issues at the level of [BHG87, GR93]. Two of the fundamental components of a TMS, namely correctness criteria and transaction models are topics of Sect. 3 and Sect. 4. We don't discuss the third component of a TMS, reliability issues, in this paper since most of the proposed approaches to OODBMS transaction management have employed well-known and standard recovery methods. We will introduce them as necessary. The relationship between some of the concurrency control algorithms and the reliability protocols is discussed briefly in Sect. 5 which is devoted to the management of transactions on abstract data types (ADTs). Section 6 presents a number of different algorithms that have been proposed to manage transactions in OODBMSs. Section 7 presents a brief overview of how transactions can be modeled as objects in OODBMSs that uniformly model every system entity as objects. We conclude in Sect. 8.

2 Fundamental Transaction Concepts

A transaction is defined as "an execution of a program that accesses a shared database" [BHG87]. A single database manipulation language statement or an entire user program containing a number of such statements can be encapsulated as a transaction to ensure its execution as a *consistent*, *atomic* and *reliable* unit of work.

Consistency is an important concept in transactions which needs to be defined precisely. We differentiate between *transaction consistency* and *concurrency transparency*. A consistent transaction is a correct program that maps a consistent database state to another consistent database state. A database is in a consistent state if all of the data objects that it stores obey all of the consistency (integrity) constraints explicitly defined over the database. State changes occur due to updates, insertions, and deletions. Although a database can be (and usually is) inconsistent during the execution of a transaction, it must be consistent when the transaction terminates (Fig. 1).

Concurrency transparency, on the other hand, refers to the actions of concurrent transactions. The database is expected to remain in a consistent state even if there are a number of transactions executing against the database. Various levels of concurrency transparency can be defined and enforced by TMSs [Gra79]. No concurrency transparency means that the TMS does not provide any facility to synchronize the operations of concurrent transactions whereas full concurrency transparency means that each user transaction seemingly executes alone in the system, without interference from others.

Reliability is another important term concerning transactions. It refers to both the resiliency of a system to various types of failure and to its capability to recover from them. A resilient system is tolerant of system failures and can continue to provide service even when failures occur. A recoverable DBMS is one that can get to a consistent

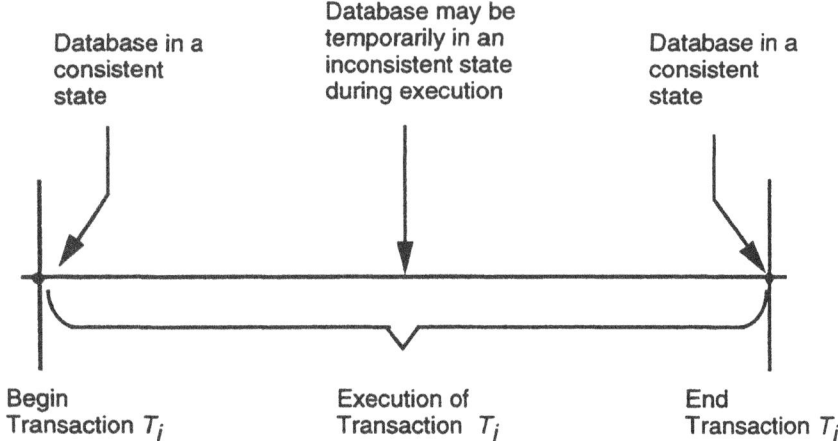

Fig. 1. Transaction execution

state (by moving back to a previous consistent state or forward to a new consistent state) following various types of failures. Failure atomicity refers to maintaining the database in a consistent state even when failures occur. Transaction management deals with the problems of enforcing concurrency transparency and failure atomicity. TMSs include schedulers and recovery managers that interact in implementing concurrency control algorithms to synchronize the concurrent operations on the database and recovery mechanisms for correct termination of transactions and to regain database consistency following failures.

2.1 An Example Transaction

Let us consider a simplified version of a typical airline reservation application, where a travel agent enters the flight number, the date, and a customer name, and asks for a reservation. The transaction to perform this function can be implemented as follows, where database accesses are specified in embedded SQL notation:

```
Begin_transaction Reservation                                          (1)
begin
   input(flight_no, date, customer_name);                              (2)
   temp ← Read(flight_no(date).sold_seats);                            (3)
   if temp = flight_no(date).maximum then                              (4)
   begin
      output ("no free seats");                                        (5)
      Abort                                                            (6)
   end
   Modify(flight_no(date).sold_seats, temp+1);                         (7)
   Insert(flight_no(date).cust_name, customer_name);                   (8)
end. {Reservation}                                                     (9)
```

Line 1 declares the beginning of the transaction (usually abbreviated as BOT). This is significant, because it notifies the transaction management system that the actions between this point and the "end" command in line 9 (usually called the **End_transaction** or EOT) are to be executed atomically obeying the properties specified in Sect. 2.2. Thus, lines 1 and 9 bracket the transaction.

Line 2 obtains flight information (flight number, date, and customer's name) from the customer. The seat information about this flight at the specified date is read in line 3 and compared with the maximum number of allowable seats on that flight (line 4). If there are no more seats, then the customer is informed (line 5) and the transaction is aborted (line 6). Aborting a transaction also terminates the transaction (equivalent to an exit).

If there are available seats (i.e., the transaction does not abort in line 6), the number of sold seats on that particular flight is incremented in line 7. The customer's name is added to the list of customers for that specific flight (line 8), and the transaction successfully completes in line 9. The "Modify" and "Insert" commands constitute the update (also called Write) operations on the database.

Aborting a transaction (as in line 6) is one of the termination conditions of a transaction. A transaction always terminates, even when there are failures (in fact, aborting is considered a transaction failure). Transactions may abort for a number of reasons. In the above example, the transaction aborts itself because of a condition that would prevent it from completing its task successfully. Additionally, the TMS may abort a transaction due to deadlocks or other conditions.

When a transaction is aborted, its execution is stopped and all of its previous actions are undone by returning the database to the state before their execution. This is known as rollback. When a transaction completes successfully, it is said to commit. The **end** command in line 9, in addition to syntactically bracketing the transaction definition, also serves the role of an implicit commit command. The importance of commit is twofold. First, the commit command signals to the TMS that the effects of that transaction should now be reflected in the database, thereby making it visible to other transactions which may access the same data. Second, the point at which a transaction is committed is a "point of no return." The results of the committed transaction are now permanently stored in the database and cannot be undone short of running another transaction to reverse its effects (usually called a *compensating transaction*). Thus, commitment implies permanence and visibility of results.

2.2 ACID Properties of Transactions

The concurrency transparency and failure atomicity of transactions are due to four properties: (1) Atomicity, (2) Consistency, (3) Isolation, and (4) Durability. Together, these are commonly referred to as the "ACID test" for transactions [HR83]. These properties, even though they are commonly used, are not orthogonal. We point out the strong interrelationships and comment on them at the end of this section.

Atomicity refers to the fact that a transaction is treated as a unit of operation. Therefore, either all or none of the transaction's actions are completed. This is also known as the "all-or-nothing property." A transaction builds a larger unit of atomic computation from smaller atomic operations. Atomicity requires that if the execution of a transaction is interrupted by any sort of failure, the TMS will be responsible for determining what to do with the transaction upon recovery from the failure. There are two possible courses of action: it can either be terminated by completing the remaining actions, or it can be terminated by undoing all the actions that have already been executed.

Typically there are two types of failures. A transaction itself may fail due to input data errors, deadlocks, or other factors. In these cases, either the transaction aborts itself, as we have seen in the example of the previous section, or the TMS may abort it while handling deadlocks, for example. Maintaining transaction atomicity in the presence of this type of failure is commonly called *transaction recovery*. The second type of failure is caused by system crashes, such as media failures, processor failures, communication link breakages, power outages, and so on. Ensuring transaction atomicity in the presence of system crashes is called *crash recovery*. An important difference between the two types of failures is that during some types of system crashes, the information in volatile storage may be lost or inaccessible.

As mentioned before, two consistency concerns need to be addressed: the consistency of individual transactions, and the consistency of the database under concurrent execution of transactions. These are rather different concepts, and the use of the term "consistency" is probably overloaded in referring to both of them.

Transaction consistency is inherent in the definition of a transaction in the sense that the TMS assumes that transactions are consistent and makes no attempt at verification. Verifying that transactions are consistent is the concern of integrity enforcement.

How one defines a "consistent" state under concurrent transaction access is dependent upon the correctness criterion that is used in developing concurrency control algorithms. We discuss this issue in more detail in Sect. 3.

Isolation is the property of transactions that requires each transaction to see a consistent database at all times. In other words, an executing transaction cannot reveal its results to other concurrent transactions before it commits.

There are a number of reasons for isolation. One has to do with maintaining the interconsistency of transactions (i.e., concurrency transparency). If two concurrent transactions access a data object that is being updated by one of them, it is not possible to guarantee that the second will read the correct value. If, for example, two deposits are made to the same bank account concurrently, one deposit may overwrite the other. This is referred to as the *lost updates* problem.

A second reason for isolation is *cascading aborts*. If a transaction permits others to see its incomplete results before committing and then decides to abort, any transaction that has read its incomplete values will have to abort as well. This chain can easily grow and impose considerable overhead on the DBMS.

It is obvious that the issue of isolation is directly related to database consistency and is therefore the topic of concurrency control.

Durability refers to the property of transactions that ensures that once a transaction commits, its results are permanent and cannot be erased from the database (i.e., failure atomicity). Therefore, the DBMS ensures that the results of a transaction will survive subsequent system failures. The durability property brings forth the issue of database recovery, that is, how to recover the database to a consistent state where all the committed actions are reflected.

As indicated at the beginning, the ACID properties of transactions are not orthogonal. They are interrelated in providing concurrency transparency and failure atomicity, suggesting that this set of properties may not be minimal in characterizing transactions. Nevertheless, they are useful in exposing the basic behavior of transactions and in defining the requirements for managing them. Transaction consistency requires integrity enforcement (which is not discussed in this paper) while concurrency consistency requires concurrency control algorithms. These algorithms enforce a well-defined *correctness criterion* (Sect. 3) to reason that concurrent execution of transactions is "correct" in some sense. Concurrency control algorithms also deal with the issue of isolation. Durability and atomicity properties of transactions require commit/termination protocols and recovery algorithms.

A categorization similar to ACID properties, with the four properties of visibility, failure atomicity, permanence, and consistency is used as the basis of the ACTA transaction metamodel [CR90]. The differences between these properties and the ACID properties are quite small, mostly terminological: visibility corresponds to isolation, failure atomicity is what we simply termed atomicity while permanence corresponds to durability.

3 Correctness Criteria

As indicated above, correctness criterion that is employed by the concurrency control algorithms indicates the notion of correctness that is employed to achieve a certain degree of *concurrency transparency* in the system. Full concurrency transparency means that each user transaction seemingly executes alone in the system, without interference from other transactions. The implication is that the result of concurrent execution of transactions should not compromise database consistency. In this context, the correctness criterion employed by a transaction management system determines the "acceptable" concurrent transaction executions. It is the responsibility of the scheduler to employ the necessary protocols to ensure that the executions are acceptable with respect to the chosen correctness criterion.

In this section we consider two correctness criteria: serializability-based, and non-serializable. Some of the commutativity-based serializability notions introduced in Sect. 3.1 are used in synchronizing operations on abstract data types (discussed in Sect. 5) and in OODBMSs (discussed in Sect. 6).

3.1 Serializability-Based Correctness

Basic Serializability Concepts. Discussion of serializability requires a definition of a few basic concepts. A *history* is defined over a set of transactions $T = \{T_1, T_2, \ldots, T_n\}$ and specifies an interleaved order of execution of these transactions' operations. Formally, it can be specified as a partial order over T. A *serial history* is one where the operations of various transactions are not interleaved (i.e., the operations of each transaction occur consecutively). Consider, for example, the following two transactions, where we place explicit "Commit" statements instead of the "end" statement to clearly indicate the termination condition:

T_1: Read(x) T_2: Write(x) T_3: Read(x)
      Write(x)   Write(y)   Read(y)
      Commit   Read(z)   Read(z)
                          Commit   Commit

The following history H_1, where R_i, W_i, C_i denote Read, Write and Commit operations of transaction T_i, is serial:

$$H_1 = \{W_2(x), W_2(y), R_2(z), C_2, R_1(x), W_1(x), C_1, R_3(x), R_3(y), R_3(z), C_3\} \quad (1)$$

If the transaction consistency is maintained by the system, then each transaction is a correct program in the sense that it takes a consistent database state and maps it to another consistent database state. That being the case, serial execution of a set of transactions (put differently, execution of a set of transactions that result in serial histories) will map a consistent database state to another consistent database state.

Serializability is a straightforward concept. It requires that any history of concurrent execution of a set of transactions be equivalent (in some sense) to a serial execution represented by a serial history. Since (by hypothesis) a serial history does not violate database consistency, any concurrent execution history that is "equivalent" to a serial history (i.e., a *serializable history*) would also maintain database consistency and enforce concurrency transparency. For example, history H_2 is serializable since it is "equivalent" to H_1 in terms of its effects on the database:

$$H_2 = \{W_2(x), R_1(x), R_3(x), W_1(x), C_1, W_2(y), R_3(y), R_2(z), C_2, R_3(z), C_3\} \quad (2)$$

Equivalence of histories will be defined more carefully in the next section as one of the bases of differentiating between various serializability-based correctness criteria.

Different Approaches to Attaining Serializability. A first order differentiation among serializability-based correctness criteria is introduced by variations in the definition of "equivalence" between histories. Two types of history equivalence that have been proposed are *view equivalence*, leading to *view serializability*, and *conflict equivalence*, leading to *conflict serializability* (or *conflict-equivalent serializability*). Since determining whether a history is view serializable has been shown to be NP-complete [Pap86], for practical reasons we are only concerned with conflict equivalence. Two histories are conflict equivalent if the relative order of conflicting operations is the same in the two histories. A history is said to be *conflict serializable* if it is conflict equivalent to a serial history. We refer to the *serialization order* of transactions to indicate the order in which the conflicting operations appear in the history. The serialization order of H_2 is T_3 followed by T_2 followed by T_1 (denoted $T_3 \rightarrow T_2 \rightarrow T_1$).

There are a number of serializability-based correctness criteria that basically differ in how they define a *conflict*. We concentrate on three criteria discussed in the literature: *commutativity* [Wei88, Wei89, FLMW89], *invalidation* [Her90], and *recoverability*[1] [BR87b].

---

[1] Recoverability as used in [BR87b] is different from the notion of recoverability found in [BHG87, Had88, BR87b].

Commutativity states that two operations conflict if the results of different serial executions of these operations are not equivalent. The traditional conflict definition is a special case of this. Consider the simple operations $R(x)$ and $W(x)$. If nothing is known about the abstract semantics of the read and write operations or the object x that they operate on, it has to be accepted that a $R(x)$ **following** a $W(x)$ does not retrieve the same value as it would **prior** to the $W(x)$. Therefore, a Write operation always conflicts with other Read or Write operations. The conflict table (Fig. 2) for Read and Write operations is, in fact, derived from the commutativity relationship between these two operations. This table is also called the compatibility table since two operations that do not conflict are said to be compatible. Since this type of commutativity relies only on syntactic information about operations (i.e., that they are Read and Write), we call this *syntactic commutativity* [BÖH+92].

	$Read_i(x)$	$Write_i(x)$
$Read_k(x)$	+	-
$Write_k(x)$	-	-

Fig. 2. Conflict (compatibility) table for commutativity of Read and Write (The subscripts indicate the transactions that the operations are part of and + indicates compatibility whereas − indicates incompatibility)

In Fig. 2, Read and Write operations and Write and Write operations do not commute. Therefore, they conflict, and serializability maintains that either all conflicting operations of transaction T_i precede all conflicting operations of T_k or vice versa.

If the semantics of the operations are taken into account, however, it may be possible to provide a more relaxed definition of conflict. Specifically, some concurrent executions of Write-Write and Read-Write may be considered non-conflicting. Consider, for example, an abstract data type (ADT) **set** and three operations defined on it: Insert and Delete, which correspond to a Write, and Member, which tests for membership and corresponds to a Read. Due to the semantics of of these operations, two Insert operations on an instance of set type would commute, allowing them to be executed concurrently. The commutativity of Insert with Member and the commutativity of Delete with Member depends upon whether or not they reference the same argument and their results[2]. *Semantic commutativity* (e.g., [Wei88, Wei89]) makes use of the semantics of operations and their termination conditions. It is also possible to define commutativity

---

[2] Depending upon the operation, the result may either be a flag that indicates whether the operation was successful (for example, the result of Insert may be "OK") or the value that the operation returns (as in the case of a Read).

with reference to the database state. In this case, it is usually possible to permit more operations to commute. For example, we indicated that an Insert and a Member would commute if they do not refer to the same argument. However, if the set already contains the referred element, then these two operations would commute even if their arguments are the same.

The intention of the work presented in [Wei88, Wei89] is to provide criteria that (a) consider the semantics of the operations, and (b) are based solely on information local to the individual objects. To achieve these purposes, [Wei88, Wei89] first defines atomicity or serial correctness of ADTs based on the sequences of operations allowed on a single ADT. An ADT is locally atomic if all operations of a serial execution on a single ADT obey the pre- and post-conditions defined on them.

Operation is defined as a pair of invocation and response to that invocation, e.g. x: [Insert(3),ok] is a valid invocation of an insert operation on set x that returns that the operation was performed correctly. A history consisting of these operations is said to be atomic if the committed transactions in the history can be expressed in some serial order with the same effect. Since the serial executions are characterized solely by the permissible operations defined for the objects, it depends only on the specifications of the objects whether the history is atomic or not. Because atomicity is defined in terms of operation sequences, it is first necessary to establish the correlation between operation sequences and histories:

Let H be a serial history with transactions $T_1, \ldots, T_n$. This history can be expressed as the concatenation of operations of each transaction:

$$H = H|T_1 \bullet H|T_2 \bullet \ldots \bullet H|T_n \tag{3}$$

This history is failure-free if the set of aborted transactions is empty. The operation sequence corresponding to a history, $OpSeq(H|T_i)$, is obtained from the restriction of H on T_i, $H|T_i$, pairing corresponding invocations and returns and eliminating commits and pending invocations. A serial, failure-free history H is acceptable at an object x if the restriction of H on x, $OpSeq(H|x)$, is an element of the serial specification of x.

Two histories H_1 and H_2 are equivalent, if every transaction performs the same steps (operations) in H_1 and H_2.

$serial(H|T)$ is the serial history equivalent to H in which transactions appear in the order T. H is serializable in T if T is a total order and $serial(H|T)$ is acceptable. Defining $permanent(H) = H|committed(H)$, i.e. as the set of committed transactions in the history, one can finally state that H is atomic if $permanent(H)$ is serializable.

A *local atomicity property* is defined as a property that guarantees, if every object in the system obeys this property, that every history in the system's behavior is atomic. One of these local atomicity properties is the notion of *dynamic atomicity*. Dynamic atomicity is a local atomicity property, i.e., it is solely based on local information, and states that a history is dynamic atomic if the set of committed transactions is serializable in every total order consistent with defined precedence relations. The precedence relation is defined as $(T_1, T_2) \in precedes(H)$ if and only if at least one operation invoked by T_2 responds after T_1 commits. The restriction $precedes(H|T_i)$ is a subset of $precedes(H)$.

A history H is dynamic atomic if $permanent(H)$ is serializable in every total order consistent with $precedes(H)$. The effect of dynamic atomicity is that different serialization orders are distinguishable by later transactions. This causes a problem when implementing this criterion, since for practical reasons a TMS wants to save only a single state that represents the committed transactions. Therefore, dynamic atomicity is further strengthened, and on-line dynamic atomicity is defined. the effect of on-line dynamic atomicity is that (a) regardless of which transactions commit, the resulting history will be dynamic atomic, and (b) future transactions cannot distinguish between two serialization orders.

If all histories satisfy the on-line dynamic atomicity property, then they are serializable. This is achieved using solely local information. This aspect is relevant in the context of object-oriented systems, since serializability can now be localized to objects. Another advantage of using serializability based on dynamic atomicity as a correctness criterion is that, as long as the objects involved in a transaction guarantee dynamic atomicity, it is irrelevant what specific algorithm is used to achieve this behavior. Therefore, it may be possible to use a number of type-specific concurrency control algorithms as long as each enforce dynamic atomicity.

The conflict relations defined in [Wei88] are binary relations between operations that consider both the operation and its result. Two different kinds of commutativity and their corresponding commutativity relation can be defined: *forward commutativity* and *backward commutativity*. Assume two operations P and Q and a state s of an object. Forward commutativity is then defined as follows: For every state s in which P and Q are both defined (individually), $P(Q(s)) = Q(P(s))$ and $P(Q(s))$ is defined (i.e., it is not the null state). The notation used means that if we apply first operation Q to state s and then operation P to that result, we obtain the same result as if we apply first P to state s and then operation Q to the result. Backward commutativity is defined as follows: For every state s in which we know that $P(Q(s))$ is defined (i.e., $Q(s)$ is defined but $P(s)$ may or may not be defined), $P(Q(s)) = Q(P(s))$. Of course, both forward and backward commutativity extends to the case where P and Q are sequences of operations rather than a single operation.

	[Insert(i),ok]	[Delete(i),ok]	[Member(i),true]	[Member(i),false]
[Insert(i),ok]	+	-	+	-
[Delete(i),ok]	-	+	+	+
[Member(i),true]	+	-	+	+
[Member(i),false]	-	+	+	+

Fig. 3. Compatibility table for forward commutativity in sets

It is important to notice the difference in the states over which the operations are defined. In forward commutativity, both operations are defined over the same initial state. Therefore, it makes no difference which operation is applied first, as long as the

	[Insert(i),ok]	[Delete(i),ok]	[Member(i),true]	[Member(i),false]
[Insert(i),ok]	+	-	-	-
[Delete(i),ok]	-	+	-	+
[Member(i),true]	-	-	+	+
[Member(i),false]	-	+	+	+

Fig. 4. Compatibility table for backward commutativity in sets

final result is the same. For example, if the initial state of the set object is $\{1,2,3\}$, and the first operation on that set object is the pair of invocation-response [Insert(3), ok], and the second operation is [Member(3), true], both operations are defined on $\{1,2,3\}$, and the result of applying them in either order is the same. However, if all we know is that the state is $\{1,2,3\}$ after applying the operation [Insert(3), ok], we cannot say whether the initial state was $\{1,2\}$ or $\{1,2,3\}$. Therefore, for a set object, the operations [Insert(x), ok] and [Member(x), true] do commute forward but do not commute backwards. The commutativity relations are given in Fig. 3 (forward commutativity for sets) and Fig. 4 (backward commutativity for sets). For set objects, the backward commutativity relation subsumes the forward commutativity relation. However, this is not true for all objects. In general, forward and backward commutativity relations are incomparable. To see this, the forward and backward commutativity relations for another abstract data type – a bank account – are given in Fig. 5 and Fig. 6. The operations are self-explanatory except for Post(i) which posts a given percentage i of interest to the account object. The argument of the operations are amounts of funds.

	[Withdraw(m),ok]	[Withdraw(m),no]	[Deposit(n),ok]	[Balance,r]	[Post(i),ok]
[Withdraw(m),ok]	-	+	+	-	-
[Withdraw(m),no]	+	+	-	+	+
[Deposit(n),ok]	+	-	+	-	-
[Balance,r]	-	+	-	+	-
[Post(i),ok]	-	+	-	-	-

Fig. 5. Forward commutativity table for a bank account object

The incomparability of these two relations and, as discussed in Sect. 5, their requirement of different recovery algorithms, causes difficulties in implementing TMSs

	[Withdraw(m),ok]	[Withdraw(m),no]	[Deposit(n),ok]	[Balance,r]	[Post(i),ok]
[Withdraw(m),ok]	+	-	-	-	-
[Withdraw(m),no]	-	+	-	+	+
[Deposit(n),ok]	-	-	+	-	-
[Balance,r]	-	+	-	+	-
[Post(i),ok]	-	+	-	-	-

Fig. 6. Backward commutativity table for a bank account object

that use them. Basically, one or the other has to be chosen for enforcement even though each permit certain operation histories that the other one rejects. Nakajima [Nak94] extends this work and defines a *general commutativity relation* which is a superset of both the forward and the backward commutativity relations. If $FC(o)$ and $BC(o)$ are the forward and backward commutativity relations, respectively, for object o, then the general commutativity relation is defined as $GC(o) = FC(o) \cup BC(o)$. The general commutativity relation for the bank account example is given in Fig. 7. Even though it seems preferable to use the general commutativity relation, as we will see in Sect. 5, enforcing it is not straightforward.

	[Withdraw(m),ok]	[Withdraw(m),no]	[Deposit(n),ok]	[Balance,r]	[Post(i),ok]
[Withdraw(m),ok]	+	+	+	-	-
[Withdraw(m),no]	+	+	-	+	+
[Deposit(n),ok]	+	-	+	-	-
[Balance,r]	-	+	-	+	-
[Post(i),ok]	-	+	-	-	-

Fig. 7. General commutativity relation for the bank account example

Invalidation [Her90] defines a conflict between two operations not on the basis of whether they commute or not, but according to whether or not the execution of one invalidates the other. An operation P invalidates another operation Q if there are two histories H_1 and H_2 such that $H_1 \bullet P \bullet H_2$ and $H_1 \bullet H_2 \bullet Q$ are legal, but $H_1 \bullet P \bullet H_2 \bullet Q$ is not. In this context, a *legal history* represents a correct history for the set object and is determined according to its semantics. Accordingly, an *invalidated-by* relation is defined consisting of all operation pairs (P, Q) such that P invalidates Q. The invalidated-by relation establishes the conflict relation that forms the basis of establishing serializability. Considering the Set example, an Insert cannot be invalidated by any other operation, but a Member can be invalidated by a Delete if their arguments are the same.

Recoverability [BR87b] is another conflict relation that has been defined to determine serializable histories. Intuitively, an operation P is said to be *recoverable with respect to* operation Q if the value returned by P is independent of whether or not Q executed before P. The conflict relation established on the basis of recoverability seems to be identical to that established by invalidation. However, this observation is based on a few examples and there is no formal proof of this equivalence. In fact, the absence of a formal theory to reason about these conflict relations is a serious deficiency that needs to be addressed.

3.2 Non-Serializable Correctness Criteria

Serializability requires that the execution of each transaction must appear to every other transaction as a single atomic step. This requirement may be unnecessarily strong for many applications. The semantic information about transactions and the objects that they operate on can be used to weaken serializability and achieve a higher level of concurrency. The semantic information, in this case, is the *application semantics* rather than the *data semantics* [SZR86] as is the case for the serializable approaches discussed above.

There have been a number of proposals along these lines. All depend upon establishing how transactions can interfere with each other between *steps*, which may consist of a single operation or a collection of operations. In [GM83] transactions are grouped into disjoint classes such that the transactions that belong to the same class are *compatible* and can interleave arbitrarily, whereas transactions that belong to different classes are *incompatible* and cannot interleave at all. Early use of the concept of transaction classes can be found in SDD-1 [BSR80].

The concept of compatibility is refined in [Lyn83] and several levels of compatibility among transactions are defined. These levels are structured hierarchically so that interleavings at higher levels include those at lower levels. Furthermore, [Lyn83] introduces the concept of *breakpoints* within transactions which represent points at which other transactions can interleave. This is an alternative to the use of compatibility sets.

Another work along these lines uses breakpoints to indicate the interleaving points, but does not require that the interleavings be hierarchical [FÖ89]. A transaction is modeled as consisting of a number of steps. Each step consists of a sequence of atomic operations and a breakpoint at the end of these operations. For each breakpoint in a transaction the set of transaction types that are allowed to interleave at that breakpoint is specified. A correctness criterion called *relative consistency* is defined based on the correct interleavings among transactions. Intuitively, a relatively consistent history is equivalent to a history that is stepwise serial (i.e., the operations and breakpoint of each step appear without interleaving), and in which a step (T_{ik}) of transaction T_i interleaves two consecutive steps $(T_{jm}$ and $T_{jm+1})$ of transaction T_j only if transactions of T_i's type are allowed to interleave T_{jm} at its breakpoint. It can be shown that some of the relatively consistent histories are not serializable, but are still "correct" [FÖ89].

Transaction groups are proposed in [SZR86] and [Ska89] as a way of dealing with the non-serializable execution of a set of *cooperating transactions* in a design environment. A transaction group coordinates the execution of its member cooperating transactions. Concurrent execution is controlled at two levels: at the level of a transaction group and at the level of individual objects. Object-level synchronization of operations are controlled according to a type-specific correctness criteria similar to semantic commutativity [Wei89] discussed earlier. Transaction group-level synchronization is performed according to a correctness criterion called *semantic patterns*. These are acceptable execution sequences of transaction operations. They are flexible in that a semantic pattern can be any arbitrary partial ordering of operations as long as one can construct a recognizer for it as well as a concurrency control algorithm that can enforce that pattern. In effect, patterns are user-defined correctness criteria [Ska91] that provide a high degree of flexibility in specifying what constitutes "correct" interleavings of the operations of a set of transactions.

Similar methods of specifying user-defined criteria have also been proposed by others. For example [BKK85] defines an invariant for each transaction. If the transaction execution fulfills this invariant, then the consistency of the database is guaranteed to be correct.

Another class of non-serializable correctness criteria has been defined in the context of multidatabase systems. In these systems there are two classes of transactions: *local* transactions are accepted directly by the individual, autonomous component DBMSs, and *global* transactions access multiple databases. This requires a two-level transaction mechanism. Each individual DBMS manages its local transactions together with the *subtransactions* of global transactions that are submitted to it, and the multidatabase software maintains the correctness of the global transactions. It has been suggested that the serializability theory may be inappropriate for multidatabase transactions since it does not differentiate between global and local transactions, thereby restricting the set of acceptable histories. Consequently, *quasi-serializability* [DE89] and *multidatabase serializability* [BÖ90] have been proposed as non-serializable correctness criteria for multidatabase environments. Both of these are equivalent and, in effect, require that all of the local histories be serializable and the global history be conflict-equivalent to a serial one. It has been shown that the set of quasi-serializable (or multidatabase serializable) histories is a superset of conflict-serializable histories.

3.3 Designing Concurrency Control Algorithms   ,

As indicated before, concurrency control algorithms enforce a particular notion of correctness in synchronizing concurrent transaction executions. Even though a number of concurrency control algorithms have been proposed, the most common class is locking-based algorithms. Very simply, these algorithms require transactions to place locks on data objects before they access them. There may be different types of locks, based on the operations defined on the objects and the conflict relationship among them. These locks can be characterized as *shared locks* and *exclusive locks*. For example, read locks are shared while write locks are exclusive. When a transaction issues an operation O against object x, the component of TMS known as the *scheduler* checks if another transaction currently holds a lock in an incompatible mode on x. If so, O

is usually delayed until the current lock is released. Otherwise, the scheduler sets a lock on object x on behalf of O in the appropriate mode. A scheduler which does not grant a lock request from a transaction after the transaction releases one of its locks guarantees serializability [EGLT76]. This is known as *two-phase locking* (2PL). Thus, the objective is to implement a concurrency control algorithm that will be implemented by the scheduler that obeys the 2PL rule which states that transactions can obtain locks during their *growing phase* but cannot obtain any further locks once they release one lock and thereby enter their *shrinking phase*.

Even though a 2PL algorithm enforces conflict serializability, it does not allow all histories that are conflict serializable. Consider the following history taken from [AE90]:

$$H = w_1(x)r_2(x)r_3(y)w_1(y) \tag{4}$$

H is not allowed by 2PL algorithm since T_1 would need to obtain a write lock on y after it releases its write lock on x. However, this history is serializable in the order $T_3 \rightarrow T_1 \rightarrow T_2$ [AE90]. Agrawal and El Abbadi observe that the order of locking can be exploited to design locking algorithms that allow histories such as these. We discuss the general idea in this section and its application in OODBMSs in Sect. 6.

The main idea is to observe that in serializability theory, the order of serialization of conflicting operations are as important as detecting the conflict in the first place and define locking modes to exploit this observation. Consequently, three lock modes are defined: *shared*, *exclusive* and *ordered shared*. Shared and exclusive locks have their ordinary meanings as discussed before. Ordered shared locking of an object x by transactions T_i and T_j have the following meaning: Given a history H that allows ordered shared locks between operations $o \in T_i$ and $p \in T_j$, if T_i acquires o-lock before T_j acquires p-lock, then o is executed before p. Consider the compatibility table between read and write locks given in Fig. 2. If the ordered shared mode is added, there are eight variants of this table. Fig. 2 depicts one of them and two more are shown in Fig. 8. In Fig. 8(a), for example, there is an ordered shared relationship between $Read_k(x)$ and $Write_i(x)$ [denoted as $Read_k(x) \Rightarrow Write_i(x)$] indicating that if T_i can acquire a write lock on x while T_k holds a read lock on x as long as the ordered shared relationship from $Read_k(x)$ to $Write_i(x)$ is observed. The eight compatibility tables can be compared with respect to their permissiveness (i.e., with respect to the histories that can be produced using them) to generate a lattice of tables such that the one in Fig. 2 is the most restrictive and the one in Fig. 8(b) is the most liberal.

In the above example, the write lock on behalf of T_i is said to be *on hold* since it was acquired after T_k acquired its read lock on x. The locking protocol that enforces a compatibility matrix involving ordered shared lock modes is identical to 2PL, except that a transaction may not release any locks as long as any of its locks are on hold. Otherwise circular serialization orders can exist.

4 Transaction Models

Transaction models, in one sense, specify the user interface to the TMS. The user is required to write the transactions according to the model restrictions. In another sense, the transaction model determines the capabilities of the TMS.

	$Read_i(x)$	$Write_i(x)$		$Read_i(x)$	$Write_i(x)$
$Read_k(x)$	$+$	$-$	$Read_k(x)$	$+$	$\Rightarrow$
$Write_k(x)$	$\Rightarrow$	$-$	$Write_k(x)$	$\Rightarrow$	$\Rightarrow$

(a)	(b)

Fig. 8. Commutativity table with ordered shared lock mode

As discussed in Sect. 1, the requirements of new application domains demand richer transaction models. These richer transaction models have to be connected to some correctness criterion to derive a concurrency control algorithm. Furthermore, transaction management design decisions have to be made to develop full-fledged transaction management systems. These design decisions are related to systems issues such as optimistic versus pessimistic concurrency control schemes, update scheme (deferred/immediate, in-place/private copy), the recovery methods, etc. In this section we do not address all of these these issues, but restrict our discussion to the model aspects.

There have been many advanced transaction model proposals in literature, which we classify along two dimensions: the *transaction structure* (the structure of the individual transactions allowed in the model) and the *object structure* (the structure of objects on which the transactions can operate). A few representative alternatives are depicted in Fig. 9. We discuss the basic ideas behind those approaches and the classification in the remainder of this section. Not all of the possible alternatives have been studied; most of the existing work have on models located close to one of the two axes.

4.1 Object Structure

Along the object structure dimension, we identify *simple objects* (e.g., files, pages, records), objects as instances of *abstract data types* (ADTs), *full-fledged objects*, and *active objects* in increasing complexity.

Current transaction management systems operate on simple objects, mostly on physical pages. There are systems that for provide concurrency at the record level, but the overhead is usually high and record operations alone are not atomic requiring synchronization at the page level as well. The characterizing feature of this class is that the operations on simple objects do not take into account the semantics of the objects. For example, an update of a page is considered a write on the page, without considering what logical object is stored on the page.

Abstract data types are programming language constructs that encapsulate the representations of a set of objects and a set of operations on these objects. The operations are the only means of accessing and manipulating the objects. From the perspective of transaction processing, ADTs introduce a need to deal with abstract operations. The operations of transactions that execute on ADTs are not simple reads and writes, but

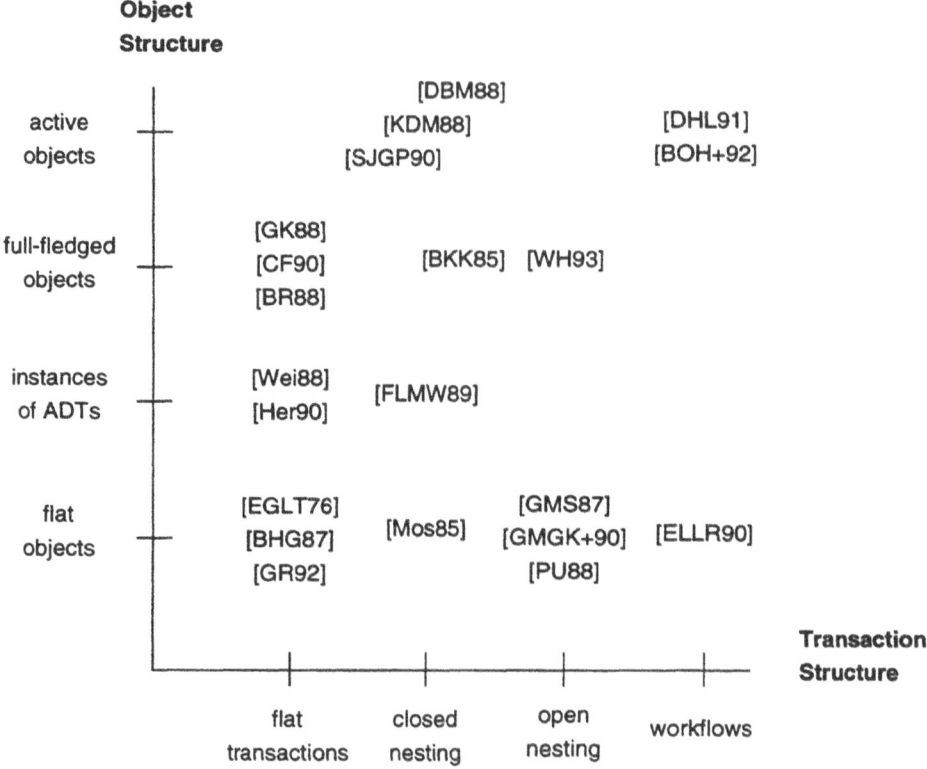

Fig. 9. Representation of transaction model space and examples

are more abstract, such as **Insert, Delete,** and **Member** for a set object. The execution of transactions on ADTs require a multi-level mechanism [BSW88, Wei91]. In such systems, individual transactions represent the highest level of abstraction. The abstract operations constitute a lower level of abstraction and are further decomposed into simple reads and writes at the lowest level. The correctness criterion, whatever it is, has to be applied to each level individually. In addition, abstract operations lend themselves nicely to the incorporation of their semantics into the definition of the correctness criterion, as discussed above.

We make the distinction between objects as instances of abstract data types and full-fledged objects to note that the latter have a complex structure (i.e., contain other objects) and their types participate in an inheritance lattice[3]. These are objects as found in object-oriented systems. They need to be treated separately due to of a number of considerations:

---

[3] Strictly speaking, abstract data types can have complex structures. However, the transaction work on abstract data types has consistently assumed a "simple" ADT structure. Our reference to "objects as instances of ADTs" should be understood within this context and with this qualification.

1. Running a transaction against one object may actually spawn additional transactions on component objects. This forces an *implicit nesting* [BR88] on the transaction itself (as opposed to explicit nesting that we discuss below). More importantly, the operations in these nestings are themselves abstract and need to be handled as multilevel transactions [WH93].
2. Inheritance involves sharing of state and/or behavior among objects. Therefore, the semantics of accessing an object at some level in the lattice has to account for this.

We also distinguish between *passive* and *active* objects. Although the approaches to the management of active objects vary, all proposals have in common that active objects are capable of responding to events by triggering the execution of actions when certain conditions are satisfied. The events that are to be monitored, the conditions that have to be fulfilled, and the actions that are executed in response are typically defined in the form of event-condition-action (ECA) rules [DBM88, KDM88]. Since events may be detected while executing a transaction on that object, the execution of the corresponding rule may be spawned as a nested transaction. Depending on the manner in which rules are coupled to the original transaction, different nestings may occur [HLM88]. The spawned transaction may execute immediately, it may be deferred to the end of the transaction, or it may execute in a separate transaction. Since additional rules may fire within a rule execution, nestings of arbitrary depth are possible.

4.2 Transaction Structure

Classifying transactions along this dimension is problematic. Many "extensions" to the standard transaction models (commonly referred to as "ACID transactions") have been proposed and there is no formal basis for comparing them. As indicated in [HOV93], unless the ACID properties are maintained, it is difficult to call these transactions; they are really coordinated activities. A large number of these extended transaction models are discussed in [Elm92]. We distinguish four broad categories in increasing complexity: *flat transactions*, *closed nested transactions* as in [Mos85], and *open nested transactions* such as sagas [GMK87], and *workflow models* which, in some cases, are combinations of various nested forms.

Flat Transactions. Flat transactions (see, for example, [EGLT76]) have a single start point (**Begin_transaction**) and a single termination point (**End_transaction**). Most of the transaction management work in databases has concentrated on flat transactions that operate on simple objects and use syntactic serializability as their correctness criterion. Excellent discussions of this work can be found in [BHG87] and [GR93]. Transaction models described in [HW88, Her90, Wei88, Wei89] are flat and operate on ADTs whereas those discussed in [BR87b, BR88] deal with flat transactions on complex objects. All of these use serializability-based correctness criteria, but differ in the way they define the conflict relation. On the other hand, [GM83, Lyn83, FÖ89] discuss the application of flat transactions to simple objects using non-serializable correctness criteria. All represent studies that go along the vertical axis in Fig. 9.

Nested Transactions. A nested transaction includes other transactions with their own beginning and termination points. These transactions that are embedded in another one are usually called *subtransactions*. Consider the airline reservation example that was presented in Sect. 2.1. It is quite common for travel agencies to make hotel and rental car arrangements together with airline reservations. It may be preferable to consider all three activities as one unit of execution instead of three separate transactions since they are related to each other. In this case, the reservation transaction would have the following structure:

> **Begin_transaction** Reservation
> **begin**
>   **Begin_transaction** Airline
>   ⋮
>   **end.** {Airline}
>   **Begin_transaction** Hotel
>   ⋮
>   **end.** {Hotel}
>   **Begin_transaction** Car
>   ⋮
>   **end.** {Car}
> **end.** {Reservation}

Nested transactions have received considerable interest as a more generalized transaction concept. The level of nesting is generally open, allowing subtransactions themselves to have nested transactions.

In this taxonomy, we differentiate between *closed* and *open* nesting because of their termination characteristics. Closed nested transactions [Mos85] commit in a bottom-up fashion through the root. The semantics of these transactions enforce atomicity at the top-most level. Significant work has been done in establishing the concurrency control aspects of closed nested transactions which use a serializable correctness criterion [BBG89]. Closed nesting for ADTs was reported in [FLMW89]. A variant of closed nesting with the possibility of making partial results selectively available to other transactions that are tightly structured into a transaction type hierarchy of transactions is discussed in [BKK85]. Closed nesting derived from the firing of rules occurs in active database systems. Representative approaches are [HLM88, KDM88, SJGP90]. They appear staggered in Fig. 9, because Postgres [SJGP90] provides only for immediate evaluation of a single rule. The triggering transaction is halted until the triggered transaction completes execution. This is a primitive type of nesting that has the behavior of a flat transaction. The most general approach is that taken by HiPAC [HLM88], which allows for arbitrarily deep nesting with immediate evaluation, evaluation at the end of the triggering transaction, or as a separate transaction, thus providing a form of execution outside the closed nesting. In all cases, serializability is the underlying correctness criterion.

Open nesting relaxes the top-level atomicity restriction of closed nested transactions. Therefore, an open nested transaction allows its partial results to be observed outside the transaction. Sagas [GMK87, GMGK$^+$90] and split transactions [PKH88] are examples of open nesting.

A saga is a "sequence of transactions that can be interleaved with other transactions" [GMK87]. The DBMS guarantees that either all the transactions in a saga are successfully completed or compensating transactions [GM83, KLS90] are run to recover from a partial execution. Two properties of sagas are: (1) only two levels of nesting are allowed, and (2) at the outer level, the system does not support full atomicity. Therefore, a saga differs from a closed nested transaction in that its level structure is more restricted (only 2) and that it is open (the partial results of component transactions or sub-sagas are visible to the outside). Furthermore, the transactions that make up a saga have to be executed sequentially.

The saga concept is extended in [GMGK$^+$90] and placed within a more general model that deals with long-lived transactions and with activities which consist of multiple steps. The fundamental concept of the model is that of a module which captures code segments that accomplish a given task and access a database in the process. The modules are modeled (at some level) as sub-sagas which communicate with each other via messages over ports. The transactions that make up a saga can be executed in parallel. The model is multi-layer where each subsequent layer adds a level of abstraction.

Another multi-layer model is the *multilevel transaction* model [Wei86, WS84, BSW88, Wei91]. Multilevel transactions "are a variant of open nested transactions in which the subtransactions correspond to operations at different levels of a layered system architecture" [WH93]. We introduce the concept with an example taken from [Wei91]. Since the concept was first developed within the context of relational DBMSs, the example will also assume a relational system[4]. However, we consider a transaction specification language which allows users to write transactions involving abstract operations so as to be able to exploit application semantics.

Consider two transactions that transfer funds from one bank account to another:

T_1: Withdraw(o, x) T_2: Withdraw(o, y)
        Deposit(p, x)   Deposit(p, y)

The notation here is that each T_i withdraws x amount from account o and deposits that amount to account p. The semantics of Withdraw is test-and-withdraw to ensure that the account balance is sufficient to meet the withdrawal request. In relational systems, each of these abstract operations will be translated to tuple operations Select (Sel), and Update (Upd) which will, in turn, be translated into page-level Read and Write operations. This results in a layered abstraction of transaction execution as depicted in Fig. 10 which is taken from [Wei91].

The traditional method of dealing with these types of histories is to develop a scheduler that enforces serializability at the lowest level (L_0). This, however, reduces the level of concurrency since it does not take into account application semantics and the granularity of synchronization is too coarse. Abstracting from the lower-level details can provide higher concurrency. For example, the page-level history (L_0) in Fig. 10 is not serializable with respect to transactions T_1 and T_2, but the tuple-level history L_1 is serializable ($T_2 \rightarrow T_1$). When one goes up to level L_2, it is possible to make use

---

[4] The extension of the concept to complex objects is given in [WH93] and discussed in Sect. 6.

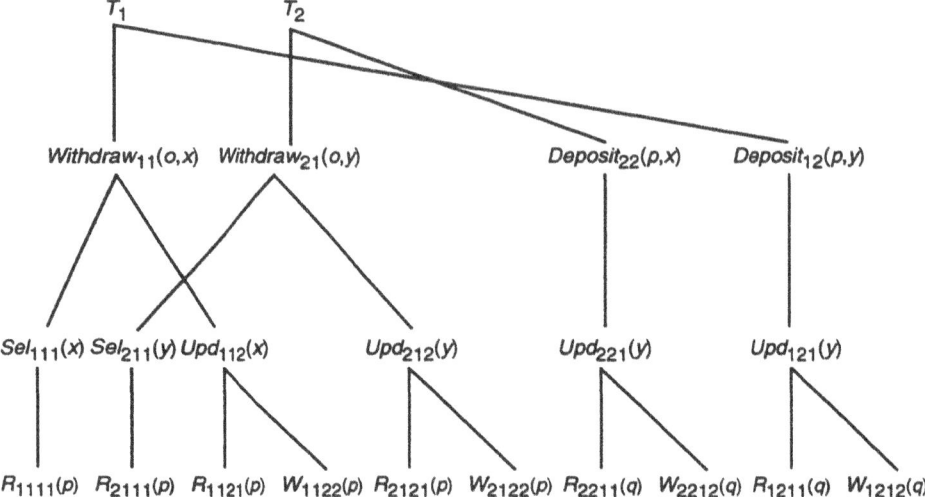

Fig. 10. Multilevel transaction example

of the semantics of the abstract operations (i.e., their commutativity) to provide even more concurrency. Therefore, *multilevel serializability* is defined to argue about the serializability of multilevel histories and *multilevel schedulers* are proposed to enforce it [Wei91].

Workflow Models. Traditional (or ACID) transactions model relatively simple and short activities very well. However, they are less appropriate for modeling longer and more elaborate activities.That is the reason for the development of the various nested transaction models discussed above. It has been argued that these extensions are not sufficiently powerful to model business activities: "after several decades of data processing, we have learned that we have not won the battle of modeling and automating complex enterprises" [MMWF93]. To meet these needs, more complex transaction models which are combinations of open and nested transactions have been proposed. There are well-justified arguments for not calling these transactions, since they hardly follow any of the ACID properties; a more appropriate name that has been proposed is a *workflow model* ([ELLR90, NZ90, ELLR90, BÖH⁺92, DHL91, Hsu93]). Various workflow models differ in a number of ways, but there is significant commonality among them. In this section we describe an abstract workflow model which is similar to the models of [BÖH⁺92, DHL91].

A workflow is modeled as an *activity* which has open nesting semantics in that it permits partial results to be visible outside the activity boundaries. Thus, components of an activity are allowed to commit individually. Components of an activity may be other activities (with the same open transaction semantics) or closed nested transactions (let us refer to them as *cn-transactions* for simplicity) that make their results visible to the entire system when they commit. Even though an activity can have both other activities and cn-transactions as its component, a cn-transaction can only be composed of other cn-transactions (i.e., once closed nesting semantics begins, it is maintained for all components). The structure of a workflow can be represented as a directed graph, even though some models may restrict it to be a hierarchy.

The cn-transactions commit according to the closed nesting semantics introduced earlier: all the components of a cn-transaction have to be ready to commit for the cn-transaction to commit, making the results visible. The abort semantics is such that if one component aborts, the entire cn-transaction aborts. Thus, a cn-transaction is the root of a tree of closed nested transactions through which the whole tree commits.

An activity also commits when its components are ready to commit. However, the components commit individually, without waiting for the root activity to commit. This raises problems in dealing with aborts since when an activity aborts, all of its components should be aborted. The problem is dealing with the components that have already committed. Therefore, *compensating transactions* are defined for the components of an activity. A compensating transaction effectively does the inverse of the transaction that it is associated with. For example, if the transaction adds $100 to a bank account, its compensating transaction reduces $100 from the same bank account. Thus, if a component has already committed when an activity aborts, the corresponding compensating transaction is executed to "undo" its effects.

Some components of an activity may be marked as *vital*. When a vital component aborts, its parent must also abort. If a non-vital component of a workflow model aborts, it may continue executing. A toptransaction, on the other hand, always aborts when one of its components aborts.

It is possible to define *contingency actions* or *contingency cn-transactions* for an action or a cn-transaction, respectively. These are invoked if their counterparts fail. For example, in the Reservation example presented earlier, one can specify that the contingency to making a reservation at Hilton is to make a reservation at Sheraton. Thus, if the hotel reservation component for Hilton fails, the Sheraton alternative is tried rather than aborting the entire activity.

These models also allow precedence relationships to be established between the components to determine the order of execution. For example, one may specify that the airline reservation component be tried before a hotel reservation is made. Precedence relationships allow the specification of control logic across components, but they also restrict the amount of parallel processing that is possible.

Workflow models are strongly related to rule systems and active DBMSs. For example, implicit nesting of transactions may occur because a rule may be fired from within a transaction and the rule may execute as a transaction. The structure of a nested transaction that results from the firing of a rule within another transaction depends on the *coupling mode* defined for the rule. The valid coupling modes are *immediate*, *deferred*, *detached*, or *causally dependent detached* [HLM88, CBB+89]. We do not discuss rule systems and the relationship of workflow models with active databases since this is the topic of another paper in this volume [Buc94].

5 Transactions on ADTs

In this section, we discuss the design of TMSs for ADTs which provide operations that are more complex than simple Reads and Writes. There are a number of proposals along these lines (e.g., [SS84, HW88, Her86, Her90]). The approach that we focus in this section is based on [Wei89]. This approach localizes synchronization decisions at individual objects.

The concurrency control algorithm that we describe is a rigorous two-phase locking (2PL) using forward commutativity relation for conflict definitions. The transaction model that is used is flat.

Rigorous 2PL concurrency control algorithms are introduced in [Geo90] as a restriction on the strict 2PL ones. The difference between the two is the following. Strict 2PL algorithms hold the read-locks on objects until the scheduler receives the EOT or Abort commands and releases them at that point. The write-locks are held until after the execution of the EOT or Abort command. Rigorous 2PL, on the other hand, holds **all** the locks until the transaction terminates (commits or aborts) [Geo90]. Thus the read-locks are held longer than is the case with strict 2PL. It has been shown [GRS91] that rigorousness facilitates the control of transactions running across multiple systems. In this case, each object is considered to be a separate system that locally coordinates its own activities.

Consider the actions performed on a data object x. The system must maintain information on state s of x, and on the status of the transactions that act on x. Specifically, it is necessary to keep track of the locks held by each transaction, the set of committed transactions and the set of the aborted transactions, a list of pending invocations to which responses must be generated, and the state the data object is in after execution of the transaction(s). To keep track of this information, the following five components of a state are defined:

- $s.permanent$ contains the state of a data object x after execution of the committed transactions;
- $s.pending$ is the list of all pending invocations to which responses must be generated;
- $s.log$ is the record of all the operations executed by transactions on x;
- $s.aborted$ is a list of aborted transactions that touched (i.e., performed any valid operation on) x; and
- $s.committed$ is a list of committed transactions that touched x.

When the data object receives a message or as long as there is a message in $s.pending$[5] it performs one of the following actions based on the type of the message: '

1. If the operation is any of the operations defined on the object, it writes the new pending invocation into $s.pending$. Next it acquires the appropriate lock by checking the conflict table. To test whether another active transaction holds a conflicting lock on the object, the log in $s.log$ is checked. If no conflicts exist, a response is returned, an entry of the operation is written to the log and the request is taken from the pending list. If a conflict exists the request remains in the pending list.

---

[5] Since the synchronization is localized at each object, there is a scheduler that carries out the synchronization. The scheduling function may be implemented either as part of the object's class-code (or its type) or the functionality may be defined at a higher level and inherited.

2. If the request received from the application is an EOT, the local commit phase begins. The transaction identifier is appended to the set of transactions that have committed at that object, i.e., *s.committed* is updated. All the operations that were previously logged are applied and *s.permanent* is rewritten.

3. If the request received is an abort, the transaction identifier is appended to the set of aborted transactions, i.e., *s.aborted* is updated.

Rigorousness is obtained in the above algorithm because lock conflicts are determined based on the operations of active (non-committed) transactions in the log. Therefore, every conflict is considered, unless the transaction has committed, i.e., the criterion for rigorousness.

For recovery, it is important to note that Weihl [Wei89] establishes a link between the choice of a concurrency control algorithm and the recovery protocol that can be used with it. Particularly, he notes that "deferred update" types of recovery mechanisms, which delay the application of updates to the database until commit time (such as intentions lists[6], can be used with concurrency control algorithms that enforce a conflict relation based on forward commutativity. Conversely, algorithms that use backward commutativity require a recovery method that updates the database buffers at the time the operation is executed. We call these protocols "immediate update" to contrast them with those that use deferred update mechanism[7] These two approaches are abstractions of various different recovery techniques and differ in two important ways. First, deferred update techniques reflect the effects of committed transactions on the database in the order transactions are committed whereas immediate update techniques reflect them in the order operations are received by the TMS. Second, deferred update techniques do not include the effects of non-committed transaction in the stable database whereas immediate update techniques may (depending upon how and when the buffer pages are moved to stable database) reflect them.

Since forward commutativity is used for conflict determination, a recovery algorithm based on intentions lists is implemented. Accordingly, if the recovery manager (RM) receives a message which is one of the operations defined on the data object x, it asks the buffer manager to bring x into the buffer if is not already there. The value of x is read, the operation is applied and the result is recorded in that transaction's intentions list (i.e., private log). Operations that "read" the value of x require some care. If an operation modifies the value of x and a later operation (belonging to the same transaction) needs to access the value to perform some other action (e.g., Insert(i) modifies the value of set object x which should be visible to a subsequent Member(i)) this value will not be found in the buffer since none of the changes have yet been applied. Therefore, operations that "read" the value of x need to check the transaction's private log as well as the buffer.

If the RM receives a Commit message, the RM installs the new copy, resets the

---

[6] An intentions list for a given transaction records all the updates of that transaction without making changes to the database buffers. When the transaction commits, the updates recorded in the intentions list is reflected in the stable database. If the transaction aborts, the intentions list is simply discarded.

[7] Weihl calls these types of recovery mechanisms "update-in-place", but this use of the term is different than its common usage which indicates that the changes overwrite the old values. Hence the change in terminology.

pointers to point to the new copy of the object, and frees the space used by the old object on disk and in the buffer. On the other hand, if the message is an Abort, the RM need not do anything, since no changes have been applied to the permanent copy. In this approach the scheduler has marked the transaction as aborted by writing its identifier into $s.abort$. The RM must only free the buffer space occupied by the copy of the object.

In Sect. 3.1 we introduced the general commutativity relation (see Fig. 7) which is a generalization of the forward and backward commutativity relations used in the above discussion. Since the general commutativity relation is a generalization of these two, and since forward and backward commutativity relations require different recovery algorithms, the implementation of a TMS based on this relation poses problems. Nakajima proposes an implementation based on *multiversion objects* [Nak94] which provide access to both committed states and current states of objects. As the name implies, each multiversion object consists of several versions, each one created whenever a method is executed that updates the object's state. Each object keeps all versions, ordered according to their creation times. These versions are classified into two categories: committed versions and uncommitted versions, corresponding to the state of the transactions that create them (Fig. 11). The most recent committed version of an object o [denoted $LCV(o)$] and the latest uncommitted version of the object [called the *current version* and denoted $CV(o)$] are identified. Using the histories of committed and uncommitted versions (more specifically, using $LCV(o)$ and $CV(o)$) Nakajima proposes a concurrency control algorithm as well as a recovery protocol that uses the general commutativity relation for determining conflicts. The general idea is to use $CV(o)$ to check for the backward commutativity part of the general commutativity relation and to use $LCV(o)$ to check for the forward commutativity part. For recovery – specifically, for transaction aborts – compensating methods are proposed to undo the effects of their corresponding methods.

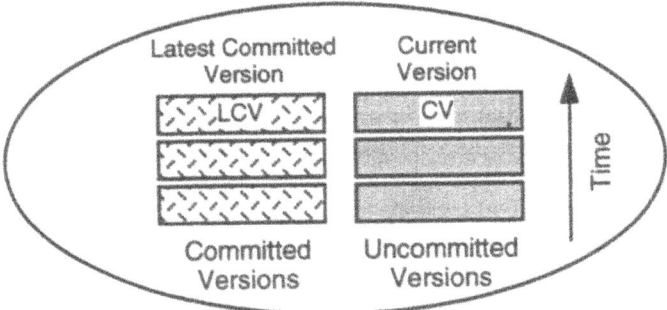

Fig. 11. Multiversion objects

6 Transactions Management in OODBMSs

As indicated in Sect. 4.1, transaction management in OODBMSs differs from systems that only support abstract data types in two major ways: objects may be complex and inheritance plays a role. These are represented by the following structures in OODBMSs:

1. *aggregation graph*, which shows the composite object structure[8]; and
2. *class (type) lattice*, which represents the IS-A relationship between objects.

The aggregation graph requires methods for dealing with the synchronization of accesses to objects which have other objects as components. The class (type) lattice requires the TMSs to take into account schema evolution concerns.

In addition to these structures, OODBMSs store methods together with data. Synchronization of shared access to objects needs to take into account method executions. In particular, transactions invoke methods which may, in turn, invoke other methods. Thus, even if the transaction model is flat, the execution of these transactions may be dynamically nested.

All of these factors introduce difficulties in executing transactions. Even the definition of conflicting operations become more involved. The conflict definition that we discussed earlier may no longer apply in OODBMSs. The classical conflict definition is based on the (non-)commutativity of operations that access the same object. In OODBMSs, there may be conflicts between operations that access different objects. This is due to the existence of the aggregation graph and the type lattice. Consider an operation O_1 which accesses object x which has another object y as one of its components (i.e., x is a composite or complex object). There may be another operation O_2 (assume O_1 and O_2 belong to different transactions) which accesses y. According to the classical definition of a conflict would not consider O_1 and O_2 to be conflicting since they access different objects. However, O_1 considers y as part of x and may want to access y while it accesses x, causing a conflict with O_2.

Schemes that are developed for OODBMSs need to take into consideration the issues that are introduced by these factors. In the remainder of this section, we present some of thc solution that have been proposed.

6.1 Synchronizing Access to Objects

The inherent nesting in method invocations is used by Hadzilacos and Hadzilacos [HH91] to develop algorithms based on the well-known nested 2PL and nested timestamp ordering algorithms. This study further takes not of the fact that there are additional concurrency possibilities by exploiting intra-object parallelism. In other words, attributes of an object can be modeled as data elements in the database whereas the methods are modeled as transactions enabling multiple invocations of an object's methods

---

[8] We distinguish between *composite objects* and *complex objects*. Composite objects depict referential sharing among objects whereas complex objects impose an IS-PART-OF constraint on the shared objects. Thus, all complex objects are composite objects, but the reverse is not true. Consequently, for complex objects, the aggregation graph is a hierarchy, but for composite objects in general, it is a graph

to be active simultaneously. This can provide more concurrency if special intra-object synchronization protocols can be devised which maintain the compatibility of synchronization decisions at each object.

Consequently, a method execution (modeled as a transaction) on an object consists of *local steps* which correspond to the execution of local operations together with the results that are returned, and *method steps* which are the method invocations together with the return values. A local operation is an atomic operation (such as read, write, increment) that affects the object's variables. A method execution defines the partial order among these steps in the usual manner.

One of the fundamental directions of this work is to provide total freedom to objects in how they achieve intra-object synchronization. The only requirement is that they be "correct" executions, which, in this case, means that they should be serializable based on commutativity. This is more flexible than the local atomicity property discussed in Sect. 5, which requires every object to sue the same synchronization mechanism. As a result of the delegation of intra-object synchronization to individual objects, the concurrency control algorithm concentrates on inter-object synchronization. The paper discusses various concurrency control algorithms.

An alternative approach based on multigranularity locking is used in ORION [GK88] and O_2 [9][CF90] even though they use different granularity hierarchies.

Multigranularity locking defines an hierarchy of lockable database granules (thus the name "granularity hierarchy") as depicted in Fig. 12. In relational DBMSs, files correspond to relations and records correspond to tuples. In OODBMSs, the correspondence is with classes and instance objects, respectively. The advantage of this hierarchy is to address the tradeoff between coarse granularity locking and fine granularity locking. Coarse granularity locking (at the file level and above) has low locking overhead since a small number of locks are set, but reduces concurrency significantly. The reverse is true for fine granularity locking.

Fig. 12. Multiple granularities

---

[9] Even though this technique has been proposed for O_2, the commercial implementation of the system uses a straightforward page-level locking scheme.

The main idea of multigranularity locking is that a transaction that locks at a coarse granularity implicitly locks all the corresponding objects of finer granularities. For example, explicit locking at the file level involves implicit locking of all the records in that file. To achieve this, two more lock types, in addition to shared (S) and exclusive (X) are defined: *intention* (or *implicit*) *shared* (IS) and *intention* (or *implicit*) *exclusive* (IX). A transaction that wants to set a S or an IS lock on an object has to first set IS or IX locks on its ancestors (i.e., related objects of coarser granularity). Similarly, a transaction that wants to set an X or an IX lock on an object must set IX locks on all of its ancestors. Intention locks cannot be released on an object if the descendents of that object are currently locked.

One additional complication arises when a transaction wants to read an object at some granularity and modify some of its objects at a finer granularity. In this case, both a S lock and an IX lock need to be set on that object. For example, a transaction may read a file and update some records in that file (similarly, a transaction in OODBMSs may want to read the class definition and update some of the instance objects belonging to that class). To deal with these cases, a *shared intention exclusive* (SIX) lock is introduced which is equivalent to holding a S and an IX lock on that object. The lock compatibility matrix for multigranularity locking is shown in Fig. 13.

	S	X	IS	IX	SIX
S	+	-	+	-	-
X	-	-	-	-	-
IS	+	-	+	+	+
IX	-	-	+	+	-
SIX	-	-	+	-	-

Fig. 13. Compatibility table for multigranularity locking

ORION's granularity hierarchy is given in Fig. 14. The lock modes that are supported and their compatibilities are exactly those given in Fig. 13. Instance objects are locked only in S or X mode, while class objects can be locked in all five modes. The interpretation of these locks on class objects is as follows:

– S mode: Class definition is locked in S mode and all its instances are implicitly locked in S mode. This prevents another transaction from updating the instances.
– X mode: Class definition is locked in X mode and all its instances are implicitly locked in X mode. Therefore, the class definition and all instances of the class may be read or updated.

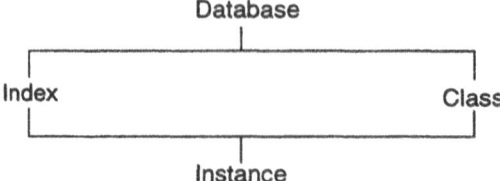

Fig. 14. ORION's granularity hierarchy

- IS mode: Class definition is locked in IS mode and the instances are to be locked in S mode as necessary.
- IX mode: Class definition is locked in IX mode and the instances will be locked in either S or X mode as necessary.
- SIX mode: Class definition is locked in S mode and all the instances are implicitly locked in S mode. Those instances that are to be updated are explicitly locked in X mode as the transaction updates them.

6.2 Management of Type Lattice

One of the important requirements of OODBMSs is dynamic schema evaluation. Consequently, the systems have to deal with transactions that access schema objects (i.e., types, classes, etc) as well as instance objects. The existence of schema change operations intermixed with regular queries and transactions as well as the (multiple) inheritance relationship defined among classes complicates the picture. First, a query/transaction may not only access instances of a class, but may access instances of subclasses of that class (usually called the *deep extent*). Second, in a composite object, the domain of an attribute is itself a class. So, accessing an attribute of a class may involve accessing the objects in the sublattice rooted at the domain class of that attribute. A further complication is introduced by versioning which (potentially) creates multiple schemas for different versions. We do not deal with the versioning issues in this paper, but a transaction management scheme that addresses versioning is given in [CW93].

ORION has dealt with these two problems again by the use of multigranularity locking. The straightforward extension of multigranularity locking where the accessed class and all its subclasses are locked in the appropriate mode does not work very well. This approach is inefficient when classes close to the root are accessed since it involves too many locks. The problem may be overcome by introducing *read-lattice* (R) and *write-lattice* (W) lock modes which not only lock the target class in S or X modes, respectively, but also implicitly lock all subclasses of that class in S and X modes, respectively. However, this solution does not work with multiple inheritance (which is the third problem).

The problem with multiple inheritance is that a class that has multiple supertypes may be implicitly locked in incompatible modes by two transactions that place R and W locks on different superclasses. Since the locks on the common class are implicit, there is no way of recognizing that there is already a lock on the class. Thus, it is necessary to check the superclasses of a class that is being locked. ORION handles this by placing *explicit* locks rather than implicit ones on subclasses. Consider the type lattice of Fig. 15 which is simplified from [GK88]. If T_1 sets an IR lock on class A and an R lock on C, it also sets an explicit R lock on E. When another transaction T_2 places an IW lock on F and a W lock on G, it will attempt to place an explicit W lock on E. However, since there is already a R lock on E, this request will be rejected.

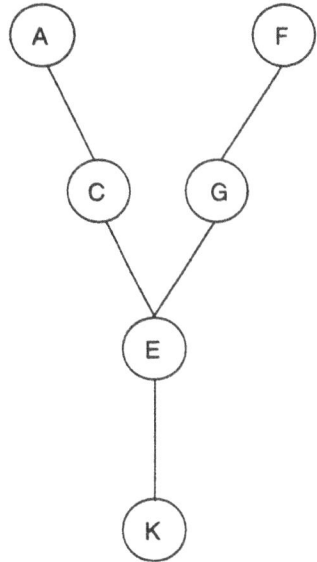

Fig. 15. An example class lattice

The approach followed by ORION sets explicit locks on subclasses of an class that is being modified. An alternative which sets locks at a finer granularity is proposed by Agrawal and El Abbadi [AE94] which uses ordered sharing as discussed in Sect. 3.3. In a sense, the algorithm is an extension of Weihl's commutativity-based approach to OODBMSs using a nested transaction model.

Classes are modeled as objects in the system similar to reflective systems that represent schema objects as first-class objects (e.g., TIGUKAT [PM93]). Consequently, methods can be defined that operate on class objects: $add(m)$ to add method m to the class, $del(m)$ to delete method m from the class, $rep(m)$ to replace the implementation of method m with another one, and $use(m)$ to execute method m. Similarly, atomic operations are defined for accessing attributes of a class. These are identical to the method operations with the appropriate change in semantics to reflect attribute access. The interesting point to note here is that the definition of the $use(a)$ operation for attribute a indicates that the access of a transaction to attribute a within a method execution is through the use operation. This requires that each method explicitly list all the attributes that it accesses. Thus, the following is the sequence of steps that are followed by a transaction, T, in executing a method m:

1. Transaction T issues operation $use(m)$.
2. For each attribute a that is accessed by method m, T issues operation $use(a)$
3. Transaction T invokes method m.

Commutativity tables are defined for the method and attribute operations. Based on these, ordered sharing lock tables for each atomic operation are determined as described in Sect. 3.3. Specifically, a lock for an atomic operation p has a shared relationship with all the locks associated with operations with which p has a non-conflicting relationship whereas it has an ordered shared relationship with respect to all the locks associated with operations with which p has a conflicting relation.

Based on these lock tables, a nested 2PL algorithm is used with the following considerations:

1. Transactions observe the strict 2PL rule and hold on to their locks until termination.
2. When a transaction aborts, it releases all of its locks.
3. The termination of a transaction awaits the termination of its children (closed nesting semantics). When a transaction commits, its locks are inherited by its parent
4. *Ordered commitment rule.* Given two transactions T_i and T_j such that T_i is *waiting for* T_j, T_i cannot commit its operations on any object until T_j terminates (commits or aborts). T_i is said to be *waiting-for* T_j if
   – T_i is not the root of the nested transaction and T_i was granted a lock in ordered shared relationship with respect to a lock held by T_j on an object such that T_j is a descendent of the parent of T_i; or
   – T_i is the root of the nested transaction and T_i holds a lock (that it has inherited or it was granted) on an object in ordered shared relationship with respect to a lock held by T_j or its descendents.

6.3 Management of Aggregation Hierarchy

Studies that deal with the aggregation hierarchy are more prevalent than others. The requirement for OODBMSs to be able to model composite objects in an efficient manner has resulted in considerable interest in this problem.

We start the discussion in this section by an overview of ORION's approach to managing the aggregation hierarchy, which is, once more, based on multigranularity locking. Two alternatives are identified. One is, as suggested in the previous section, to lock a composite object and all the classes of the component objects. This is clearly unacceptable since it involves locking the entire composite object hierarchy and thereby restricting the performance significantly. The second alternative is to lock the component object instances within a composite object. In this case, it is necessary to chase all the references and lock all those objects. This is quite cumbersome since it involves locking too many objects.

The problem is that the multigranularity locking protocol does not recognize the composite object as one lockable unit. To overcome this problem, three new lock modes are introduces: ISO, IXO, and SIXO corresponding to the IS, IX, and SIX modes, respectively. These lock modes are used for locking component classes of a composite object. The compatibility of these modes is given in Fig. 16. The protocol is then as follows. To lock a composite object, the root class is locked in X, IS, IX, or SIX mode and each of the component classes of the composite object hierarchy is locked in the X, ISO, IXO, and SIXO mode, respectively.

	S	X	IS	IX	SIX	ISO	IXO	SIXO
S	+	-	+	-	-	+	-	-
X	-	-	-	-	-	-	-	-
IS	+	-	+	+	+	+	-	-
IX	-	-	+	+	-	-	-	-
SIX	-	-	+	-	-	-	-	-
ISO	+	-	+	+	-	+	+	+
IXO	-	-	-	-	-	+	+	-
SIXO	N	N	N	N	N	Y	N	N

Fig. 16. Compatibility matrix for composite objects

The ORION concurrency control algorithms, based on multigranularity locking, enforce serializability. The recovery algorithm that is used is logging using no-fix/flush which requires undo but not redo.

An extension of multigranularity locking to deal with aggregation graph is discussed in [HDK+90]. The extension replaces a single static lock graph with a hierarchy of graphs associated with each type and each query. There is a "general lock graph" which controls the entire process (Fig. 17). The smallest lockable units are called *basic lockable units* (BLU). A number of BLUs can make up a *homogeneous lockable unit* (HoLU) which consist of data of the same type. Similarly, they can make up a *heterogeneous lockable unit* (HeLU) which is composed of objects of different types. HeLUs can contain other HeLUs or HoLUs indicating that component objects do not have to be all atomic. Similarly, HoLUs can consist of other HoLUs or HeLUs as long as they are of the same type. The separation between HoLUs and HeLUs are to optimize lock requests. For example, a set of lists of integers is, from the viewpoint of lock managers, treated as a HoLU composed of HoLUs which in turn consist of BLUs. As a result, it is possible to lock the whole set, exactly one of the lists, or even just one integer.

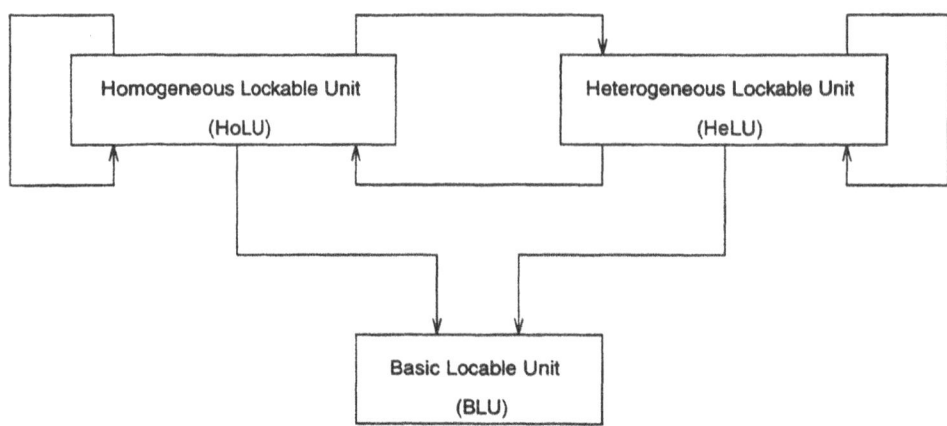

Fig. 17. General lock graph

At type definition time, an object-specific lock graph is created that obeys the general lock graph. As a third component, a query-specific lock graph is generated during query (transaction) analysis. During the execution of the query (transaction), the query-specific lock graph is used to request locks from the lock manager which uses the object-specific lock graph to make the decision. The lock modes that are used are the standard ones (i.e., IS, IX, S, X).

Badrinath and Ramamritham [BR88] discuss an alternative to dealing with composite object hierarchy based on commutativity. A number of different operations are defined on the aggregation graph:

1. examine a contents of a vertex (which is a class)
2. examine an edge (composed-of relationship)
3. insert a vertex and the associated edge
4. delete a vertex and the associated edge
5. insert an edge

Note that some of these (1 & 2) correspond to running object operators, while others (3–5) represent schema operations.

Based on these operations, an *affected-set* can be defined for granularity graphs to form the basis for determining which operations can execute concurrently. The affected-set of a granularity graph consists of the union of

- *edge-set*, which is the set of pairs (e, a) where e is an edge and a is an operation affecting e and can be one of *insert*, *delete*, *examine*.
- *vertex-set*, which is the set of pairs (v, a) where v is a vertex and a is an operation affecting v and can be one of *insert*, *delete*, *examine*, or *modify*.

Using the affected-set generated by two transactions T_i and T_j of an aggregation graph, one may define whether T_i and T_j can execute concurrently or not. Commutativity is used as the basis of the conflict relation. Thus, two transactions T_i and T_j commute on object K if $affected - set(T_i) \cap_K affected - set(T_j) = \phi$.

These protocols synchronize on the basis of objects, not operations on objects. It may be possible to improve concurrency by developing techniques that synchronize operation invocations rather than locking entire objects.

Another semantics-based approach is described in [MRW+93]. The distinguishing characteristics of this approach are the following:

1. Access to component objects are permitted without going through a hierarchy of objects (i.e., no multigranularity locking);
2. The semantics of operations are taken into consideration by a priori specification of method commutativities[10];
3. Methods that are invoked by a transaction can themselves invoke other methods. This results in a (dynamic) nested transaction execution even if the transaction is syntactically flat.

The transaction model that is used to support (3) is open nesting, specifically multilevel transactions as described in Sect. 4.2. The restrictions that are imposed on the dynamic transaction nesting are:

– all pairs (p, g) of potentially conflicting operations on the same object have the same depth in their invocation trees, and
– for each pair (f', g') of ancestors of f and g whose depth of invocation trees are the same, f' and g' operate on the same object.

With these restrictions, the algorithm is quite straightforward. A semantic lock is associated with each method and a commutativity table defines whether or not the various semantic locks are compatible. Transactions acquire these semantic locks before the invocation of methods and they are released at the end of the execution of a subtransaction (method), exposing their results to others. However, the parents of committed subtransactions hod a higher-level semantic lock which restricts the results of committed subtransactions only to those that commute with the root of the subtransaction. this requires the definition of a semantic conflict test which operates on the invocation hierarchies using the commutativity tables.

An important complication arises with respect to the two conditions outlined above. It is not reasonable to restrict the applicability of the protocol to only those for which those conditions hold. What has been proposed to resolve the difficulty is to give up some of the openness and convert the locks that were to be released at the end of a subtransaction into *retained locks* that are held by the parent. A number of conditions under which retained locks can be discarded for additional concurrency.

A very similar, but more restrictive, approach is discussed in [WH93]. The multilevel transaction model is again used, but restricted to only two levels: the object level and the underlying page level. Therefore, the dynamic nesting that occurs when transactions invoke methods which invoke other methods is not considered. The similarity with the above work is that page level locks are released at the end of the subtransaction whereas the object level locks (which are semantically richer) are retained until the transaction terminates.

---

[10] Commutativity test employed in this study is state-independent. It takes into account the actual parameters of operations but not the states. This is in contrast to Weihl's work[Wei88].

In both of the above approaches [MRW+93, WH93], recovery cannot be performed by page-level state-oriented protocols. Since subtransactions release their locks and make their results visible, compensating transactions need to be run to "undo" actions of committed subtransactions.

7 Transactions as Objects

One important characteristic of relational data model is its lack of a clear update semantics. The model, as it was originally defined, clearly spells out how the data in a relational database is to be retrieved (by means of the relational algebra operators), but does not specify what it really means to update the database. The consequence is that the consistency definitions and the transaction management techniques are orthogonal to the data model. It is possible – and indeed it is common – to apply the same techniques to non-relational DBMSs or even to non-DBMS storage systems.

The independence of the developed techniques from the data model may be considered an advantage since the effort can be amortized over a number of different applications. Indeed, the existing transaction management work on OODBMSs have exploited this independence by porting the well-known techniques over to the new system structures. During this porting process the peculiarities of OODBMSs such class (type) lattice structures, composite objects and object groupings (class extents), but the techniques are essentially the same.

It is our claim that in OODBMSs, it is not only desirable to model update semantics within the object model, but that it is indeed essential for the correct operation of these systems. The arguments are as follows:

1. In OODBMSs, what is stored are not only data but operations on data (which are called methods, behaviors, operations in various object models). Queries that access an object-oriented database refer to these operations as part of their predicates. In other words, the execution of these queries invoke various operations defined on the classes (types). To guarantee the safety of the query expressions, existing query processing approaches restrict these operations to be side-effect free, in effect disallowing them to update the database. This is a severe restriction that should be relaxed by the incorporation of update semantics into the query safety definitions.
2. As we discussed in Sect. 6, transactions in OODBMSs effect the class (type) lattices. Thus, there is a direct relationship between dynamic schema evolution and transaction management. Many of the techniques that we discussed employ locking on this lattice to accommodate these changes. However, locks (even multi-granularity locks) severely restrict concurrency. Definition of what it means to update an objectbase and the definition of conflicts based-on this definition of update semantics would allow more concurrency.

   It is interesting to note again the relationship between changes to the class (type) lattice and query processing. In the absence of a clear definition of update semantics and its incorporation into the query processing methodology, most of the current query processors assume that the database schema (i.e., the class (type) lattice) is static during the execution of a query[SÖ90a].

3. There are a few object models (e.g., OODAPLEX [Day89] and TIGUKAT [PÖS94]) that treat all system entities as objects. Especially in TIGUKAT, the object model treats the database schema (i.e., meta-objects) and queries as objects that can themselves be queried. This provides reflective capabilities to the model in that the model is defined within itself without any need for "out-of-the-model" constructs. Following this approach, it is only natural to model transactions as objects. However, since transactions are basically constructs that change the state of the database, their effects on the database need to be clearly specified.

Within this context, it should also be noted that the application domains that require the services of OODBMSs tend to have somewhat different transaction management requirements both in terms of transaction models and in terms of consistency constraints. Modeling transactions as objects enables the application of the well-known object-oriented techniques of specialization and subtyping to create various different types of TMSs. This gives the system extensibility.

4. Some of the requirements require rule support and active database capabilities. Rules themselves execute as transactions which may spawn other transactions. It has been argued that rules should be modeled as objects [DBM88]. If that is the case, then certainly transactions should be modeled as objects too.

As a result of these points, it seems reasonable to argue for an approach to transaction management systems that is quite different than what has been done up to this point. This is a topic of some research potential.

8 Concluding Remarks

Transaction management in OODBMSs is not a well-understood problem. Most of the current work extends the well-known transaction management schemes to the object-oriented domain. The commercial systems simply implement page-level locking and recovery mechanisms and may not even permit simple nested transaction semantics.

There are both application-driven requirements as well as system-dependent characteristics that dictate a different look at transactions. On one side, the applications that are claimed to require the sophistication of OODBMSs also require transaction models which are very different from what has come to be known as "ACID transactions." Much more flexible systems such as the workflow models discussed in this paper are required by these applications. Therefore, if OODBMSs are to serve the applications properly, they should also provide transaction services which meet the requirements. Clearly, simple transaction management schemes do not satisfy these requirements.

On the system-side, the encapsulation of methods with data in OODBMSs forces a clear definition of the updates semantics. Furthermore, since methods can be defined as transactions which are invoked by user-level transactions, the systems have to support some sort of nesting. Flat transaction models are simply the wrong model to force on these systems.

When these are coupled with the activeness of the system, it is not clear how much of the existing knowledge on conventional transaction processing would be applicable. The existing work on transaction management in OODBMSs should be considered as preliminary. A number of fundamental concepts such as nested transactions, semantic commutativity-based correctness, etc have emerged over the years. However, it is not clear if these are the sufficient primitives to work with nor is it clear what the best way of using these primitives are. In other words, "system integration" work of putting these pieces together into workable systems is relatively new. There are, for example, very few studies that even consider the performance aspects of various proposals.

Because of this, in this paper we concentrated on the problems and fundamental issues, and discussed a few proposals for putting the pieces together. We organized the discussion along a working classification of transaction models and correctness criteria. This classification identifies a rich design space, and our discussion has only concentrated on a few of the points in this space.

Acknowledgements

The material in Sect. 3 and Sect. 4 of this paper draws liberally from [ÖV91, BÖG91, BÖH+92].

The author's work is supported by the Natural Sciences and Engineering Research Council of Canada (NSERC) under the research grant OGP0951.

Object Storage Management Architectures

Alexandros Biliris[1] and Jack Orenstein[2]

[1] AT&T Bell Laboratories, 600 Mountain Avenue, Murray Hill, NJ 07974, USA

[2] Object Design Inc., One New England Executive Park, Burlington, MA 01803, USA

Abstract. This paper examines the architectural issues in building storage systems for object-oriented database management systems (OODBMSs) and persistent languages. We survey techniques for placing small and large objects on disk and disk space management, and we present client-server architectures for OODBMSs. We describe alternatives in making a programming language persistent and in particular, we discuss pointers and three pointer dereference mechanisms: import/export, software dereference, and hardware dereference.

1 Introduction

Relational database systems cannot meet the requirements of certain advanced database applications such as electronic CAD, mechanical CAD, geographic information systems and computer-aided publishing [Mai89]. These applications are characterized by extremely complex data structures, and complex patterns of computation and navigation. They are implemented in 3GLs such as FORTRAN, C, and C++, and because these applications are both computationally intensive and interactive, the performance demands are severe. The requirements of these applications are quite different from "traditional" ones, in which high throughput for simple manipulations of simple data models is the goal.

The data management requirements are similar to those of more traditional applications in that both persistence and transaction management are essential. Associative queries and related features such as views are useful but not essential. It is often the case that large volumes of existing code, (typically in FORTRAN and C) need to be supported, and of course there are no queries in this code. There is, of course, associative access, but it is coded in very low-level terms, e.g. a binary search subroutine. The acceptance of query processing, provided in the database language or in some sort of collection libraries, is a slow process by the developer's of these non-traditional applications.

Relational databases are not a good fit for the needs of these non-traditional applications. The modeling and performance requirements differ, as noted above. The separation of logical and physical schemas, supported by relational databases, is not so important for CAD applications – performance requirements are so stringent that concerns about representation are part of the application developers conceptual view. There is also a "cultural barrier". Developers of non-traditional applications either have no experience with database systems, or have been disappointed by the performance and modeling problems of relational database systems, (i.e. problems in applying these systems to their applications). Because of these problems, many developers have relied on "home-grown" data management systems. Many of these developers are now using or investigating OO DBMSs because they solve the same problems but have advantages in ease of use, performance, safety, or cost.

Like any relational DBMS, an OODBMS offers persistence, transaction management, and associative queries. An OODBMS also has the benefits of a programming language, namely generality (as opposed to an incomplete languages such as SQL or QUEL), low-level efficiency, and object-orientation [ABD+89].

In this paper we examine the architectural issues in building storage systems for object-oriented database systems and persistent languages. We start in Section 2 with techniques of placing small and large objects on disk, and disk space management. Section 3 describes client-server architectures. Section 4 describes alternatives in making a programming language persistent. Section 5 discusses pointer dereference mechanisms. Section 6 summarizes our work.

2 Organizing Objects on Disk

Most database systems store objects on *slotted pages* [ABC+76, SWKH76]. The basic idea is as follows. A slotted page contains a header and a variable size array of slots at the beginning and at the end of the page, respectively. The offset of each object from the beginning of the page is kept in one of the slots. When the first object is inserted into an empty page, it is placed right after the page header and slot[0] points to that location. Subsequent records are inserted right after the previous one, and their offsets are stored in the next slots (toward the beginning) of that page. So, as the page gets filled up, records and their slots grow towards each other and the free space is squeezed. Details for organizing and administering slotted pages vary considerably from system to system. For instance, slots can grow from left (right after the fixed-size page header) to right and objects from right (starting at the end of the page) to left.

The physical address of the object consists of the page number and the disk volume in which the object is stored and the slot number that contains the object's offset within the page. This way, objects can be shifted within the page, e.g., to make room for new objects when existing ones are deleted, without changing their address.

Object ids (oids) uniquely identify objects for the life of the database (sort of). In some systems, oids are the physical address of the objects. Other systems use logical oids, i.e., a value that maps through some kind of table to the actual location of the object. Physical oids are large and fast (no need for translation to locate an object) and logical oids are more flexible (allow free movement of objects). With physical oids, object can be moved too; however, the new address of the object must be kept in the original place so references to it can be forwarded to the new address. There are also combinations. In Mneme for example [Mos90], oids always name objects within a single file. So, if an object needs to refer to another one in the same file the oid of the referenced object would suffice to identify it. References to objects in other files are made with one level of indirection. In Section 4.1 we discuss the relationship between programming language pointers and oids.

In any storage system, there must be a mechanism that gathers "related" objects together; database *files* serve this purpose. On the physical level, a file consists of a number of pages and/or segments – a number of physically contiguous pages. Usually, pages and the objects stored on them belong to one file only but there are systems that allow object replication in many files [HZ87]. File organizations are classified according to the technique used to insert objects in them: in *unsorted* files a new object is placed in any of the file's pages or it is appended at the end of the file; in *key-based* files – such as sequential files, hash files, B-tree files – an attribute value of the object is used to determine the page in which the object is stored [GR93]. Note that in all key-based file organizations an object may have to be moved to a different page than it was originally assigned to. This limits their practicality because pointers that were pointing to the relocated objects become dangling. To avoid this problem, many systems use unclustered indices; i.e., indices that store a pointer to the object rather than the object itself.

At minimum, files must provide facilities for sequencing through the objects they contain. In addition, good object stores and the OODBMS language should allow applications to exercise some control over the physical placement of objects in a database. Although there are proposals for automatically clustering objects, what seems in practice to have most impact on performance is user specified clustering hints. Clustering hints may take the form "put the object near this object", "put the object on that disk volume", "do not put more objects on the page you place the new object", etc. For example, the latter may be useful in reducing contention because of locking for frequently accessed pages.

2.1 Large Objects

An object that can't fit entirely in a single page is termed *large*. Multimedia applications operate on very large objects such as digital images, continuous media (digital audio and video), documents and books. To display images, show movies, or play digital sound recordings, they require DBMSs to manipulate large objects as efficiently as possible [ACM91]. Large objects may also appear in other non multimedia kind applications.

There are several functional requirements imposed on a storage manager for manipulating large objects. First, ideally, the storage manager must have been designed in a way that can support objects of virtually unlimited size (within the bounds of the physical storage available). Second, the large object abstraction must support operations that deal with a specific number of bytes within the object: *read*, *write*, *insert*, *delete* bytes starting at arbitrary positions within the object, and *append* bytes at the end of the object.

There are also several performance requirements. First, the cost of allocating a large number of disk blocks must be minimal; this will reduce the cost of creating a large object. Ideally, the allocation cost should be 1 disk access regardless of the size of the requested space or the database size. The performance of successive appends at the end of the object is of particular importance since this is the expected way of creating very large objects.

Second, to perform a byte range operation we must first seek to a specific byte in the large object which requires efficient random access, i.e., the cost of locating any given byte within the object must be independent of the object size. This requirement by itself rules out simple solutions such linking in a linear fashion the pages on which the object is stored. After the first byte is located, we need to efficiently sequentially access the remaining bytes of the range to perform the operation. In turn, good sequential access performance means that the I/O rates in reading/writing a large chunk of bytes must be close to transfer rates. In other words, the cost of byte range operations must depend on the number of bytes involved in the operation rather than the size of the entire object. For this to happen, disk seek delays must be minimized which in turn requires that disk space is allocated in large units of physically adjacent disk blocks, rather than on a block-by-block basis.

Finally, regarding updates, small changes should have small impact; e.g., inserting few bytes in the middle of the object should not cause the entire object to be re-organized.

In early solutions to large object management [ABC+76, HL82, CDKK85], single disk blocks were used to store consecutive byte ranges of the object. The problems with the above schemes is lack of support for unlimited size objects and the loss of sequentiality. As a result, reads are slow because virtually every disk page fetch most likely results in a disk seek. More recent solutions store the object in segments of physically adjacent blocks [CDRS86, LL89, Bil92a]. From the latter three, EXODUS [CDRS86] uses fixed-size segments, Starburst [LL89] uses segments of fixed pattern of growth, and EOS [Bil92a] uses variable-size segments. Comparative performance results of the last three architectures are presented in [Bil92b].

In EOS [Bil92a], large objects of any size are stored in a sequence of variable-size segments allocated using the scheme discussed in Section 2.2. These segments are pointed to by a "count" B-tree-like structure. Each node of the tree contains a sequence of (page-no, cnt) pairs, indicating the child page id and the number of bytes stored under this child from the beginning of the node. Thus, the rightmost pair of a node gives the total number of bytes stored below it, and if the node is the root this value provides the total object size. When the object's size is known in advance, maximum size segments are used to hold the field. Otherwise, successive segments allocated for storage double in size until the maximum segment size is reached; then, a sequence of maximum size segments is used until the entire large object is stored. In either case, the last segment is trimmed, i.e., its unused blocks at the right end are freed. When updates (byte range deletes and inserts) are performed on the large object, segments may have to be broken up into smaller ones. If during an update operation, the two parts of a split segment are smaller than some user specified number of blocks, the segments are merged into a larger one.

2.2 Disk Space Management

Disk space management addresses the problem of allocation and deallocation of disk blocks to database files. There are two broad techniques, block-based and extent-based allocation.

In *block-based* allocation schemes each block is addressed individually (no notion of physical contiguity). Free blocks can be managed by a simple linear linked list. This is the approach taken by the design of Unix. The file directory contains an array (*inode*) of 13 pointers: Pointers 0 through 9 contain the addresses of the first 10 blocks. Pointer 10 points to a block that contains the addresses of the next n blocks, where n is the number of block addresses that can fit in a block. Pointer 11 points to a block that contains n pointers each of which points to a block with n block addresses (total n^2). Similarly for pointer 12. Total addressability: $10 + n + n^2 + n^3$. The expected performance for databases is going to be poor for two reasons. First, there is no notion of physical contiguity and second the scheme may lead to an unbalanced directory for large files.

In *extent-based* allocation schemes, disk space is allocated in chunks of contiguous blocks. An example of an extent-based allocation scheme is the one used in EOS [Bil92a] and it is based on the binary buddy system [Kot87]. Starburst uses a similar scheme [LL89].

A disk area is partitioned into a number of equal-size *extents*. An extent is a disk section of physically adjacent disk blocks. There is an allocation map directory associated with each extent that encodes the status (free or allocated) of each block in the extent. Disk space allocation is performed in terms of *segments* – variable-size sequences of physically adjacent disk blocks taken from one of the extents. For example, a 128-Mbyte disk volume could be partitioned into sixteen 8-Mbyte extents.

In the binary buddy system, segments of a given size can start only at blocks whose block number is divisible by the size of the segment. For example, a segment of size 8 can start only at blocks $0, 8, 16, ...$, etc. Suppose that a free segment of size $n = 2^t$ exists in the extent. In searching for this free segment, the buddy system always starts by checking the status of segment $S = 0$. If S is of size $m \neq n$, searching continues recursively at segment $S = S + \max(n, m)$ until the desired segment is located. Thus, in order to locate a free segment of a given size, there is no need to check every single byte of the allocation map.

If there is no free segment of size 2^t we find the smallest free segment of size 2^j such that $j > t$. Then this segment is split in half into two buddies each of size 2^{j-1}. One of these 2^{j-1} block segments is marked as free and the other is split up into two 2^{j-2} block segments. This process continues recursively until a segment of size 2^t is finally made up.

Conversely, on deallocation of a segment of size 2^t, the allocation map is updated to reflect the change. To avoid fragmentation, the buddy of the just deallocated segment is examined for possible coalescing. The buddy of a segment can easily be found by simply taking the exclusive OR of the segment address with its size. For example, the buddy of segment $6_{10} = 0110_2$ of size $2_{10} = 0010_2$ is segment $0110_2 \oplus 0010_2 = 0100_2 = 4_{10}$. If both of these 2-block buddies are free, they are merged into the larger free segment 4 of size 4.

Notice that whereas segments are internally managed as if their sizes are some integral power of 2, an application may request the allocation of a segment of any size. Details of the algorithms can be found in [Bil92a].

3 Client-Server Architectures

In a client-server architecture, the database resides on the database server machine. Objects in the shared database are accessed over computer networks by applications programs running on client workstations. Client/server architectures could be classified according to the way they perform the following functions.

- *Method execution process space.* This refers to whether database queries and object functions in general are evaluated on the server or client process space or both. Traditionally, relational systems do what is called *query shipping*: queries are shipped to the server and the query is executed there. On the other hand, most OODBMSs employ the *data shipping* approach: data is shipped to the client where queries as well as navigational type of operations are executed.
- *Unit of data transfer between the server and client.* Depending on the unit of transfer, we have *object servers* and *page servers* where the unit of transfer is an object and a page, respectively. In *file servers*, the client and the server communicate via a remote file system such as NFS [NFS88].
- *Caching and unit of data replication.* The goal of caching is to reduce the number of messages sent to and the need to obtain data from the server in the first place. Thus, during normal transaction execution, a portion of the database as well as locks are cached on the clients. Consequently, several copies of a shared object can exists in more than one application cache at the same time. The terms *intratransaction* and *inter-transaction* caching refer to caching within a transaction and between transactions, respectively. If we keep in the cache objects of committed transactions to be used by subsequent transactions we need to address the *cache consistency* problem. This is because between the time one transaction committed (and therefore all its locks are released) and a new one starts, the copy of the object on the server may have been updated by another transaction and so the object cached on the client becomes invalid.
- *Unit of locking and recovery.* Access to shared data must somehow be synchronized to ensure the ACID properties of transactions. Synchronization may occur at various granules such as files, pages, and objects.

Although the above functions are conceptually more or less orthogonal, the choice between the above approaches has significant impact on the overall design and implementation complexity of the system as well as performance. Usually, but not necessarily, the unit of transfer, locking and cache consistency is the same. For example, object servers employee object-level locking and cache consistency protocols, while virtually all existing page servers support locking and cache consistency protocols at the level of a page. Other combinations however are possible. For example, [MN91] proposed a scheme in the context of shared disk systems where two-phase locking is used on objects to ensure serializability and physical locks on pages for cache maintenance. Moreover, algorithms with adaptive granularity have been proposed in the context of shared disk systems [Jos91] and main memory databases [GL92b] that, properly modified, can also be used in a client server architecture. These algorithms use the idea of *lock de-escalation*: locks are obtained at some coarse granule and if, later on, data contention increases locks are de-escalated into finer-grained locks at the page or object level.

OODBMSs using the object server approach include the MCC's Orion1 [KGBW90], early versions of GemStone [CM84], a prototype of O₂ [VBD89], and Versant [Ver91]. Storage systems that can be classified as page servers are EXODUS [CFLS91], EOS [BP93], ObjectStore [LLOW91], O₂ [Deu91a], and GemStone [BOS91]. In the Ontos system [ONT92], users can choose between the object and page server approach; the choice is indicated statically on a per collection basis. Finally, Objectivity [Obj93] is a page server using NFS to transfer pages.

3.1 Query Execution Space

For a server to execute functions on objects it must understand the way objects are stored in the database as well as know about the types of objects. Basically, the functionality of the DBMS is replicated in both the server and the client. Since the server is aware of objects, it is capable to retrieve a query from the client that selects some objects from a collection of objects, process the query locally, and return the result to the client. The advantage of executing functions at the server is that if the result of the query against the collection is a small subset of the collection, it avoids the communication cost of transferring the entire collection to the client. As an example, consider an application that requires a full scan of all the fingerprints in the database so they can be compared with a target fingerprint. Transferring the target fingerprint to the server so it can be compared there is more efficient that transferring the available fingerprint collection to the client.

There are however several problems with this approach. First, for the server to apply methods on objects, user code has to be linked with the server's code which makes this scheme practically difficult to employ. Second, if methods can be applied on both the client and the server, their caches must be synchronized. This is because an object update performed on the client site must somehow become known to the server before the server applies methods to this object cached in its own pool. Third, if the server is not powerful enough, the scheme may face scalability problems. The server may become the bottleneck of the system, since most of the computations are carried out at the server side, while at the same time workstations remain underutilized.

3.2 Unit of Data Transfer

Page servers deal with pages only thus, knowledge of object structure or behavior is unnecessary. When the client needs an object it first searches its cache. If the object is not found, the page in which the object resides is requested from the server. The server sets the appropriate lock on the page, searches its own buffer pool and if the page is not there it is retrieved from the disk; then, the page is sent to the client. In this scheme, the server's cache consists of page frames. The client's cache can be organized in terms of objects, pages or both.

Object servers respond to object-based requests and thus they must understand the way objects are stored in the database. When the client needs an object it first searches its object cache. If the object is not found, the request is sent to the server. The server searches its own buffer pool and if the object is not there, the page in which the object resides is retrieved from the disk. The object is then extracted from the cached page and sent to the client.

One disadvantage of this scheme is increased communication cost for accessing objects on the client that might have been clustered in the same page. For instance, assume a program running at the client that retrieves all employee objects from a database collection and displays some of their fields on the screen. Although, there may be many such objects in the pages of the collection, the client has to initiate a request to the server for each one of them. Also, object-level transfer may not be appropriate for large objects. Even if the application intends to access a subset of the object's bytes, the entire object would need to be transferred. This is the case for example, when the object is a digitized movie stored at the server's side, and the client wants to display on the screen a frame of that movie at a time.

Finally, in file servers the DBMS runs on one machine and it access databases residing on a remotely mounted file system accessed via a remote file service such as NFS. Since NFS is part of the operating system, the DBMS can use this service directly to access database pages. The server however still has to provide concurrency control and recovery which are not usually provided by operating systems services. Thus to read or write a page, there must be two message requests. One message to the DBMS server to perform locking and recovery related activity, and the other to NFS to actually read or write the page, respectively. The latter – writing a data page on disk – actually involves an additional I/Os because the inode pointing to the block is written too.

A study that compares the performance of the above three architectures can be found in [DMFV90].

3.3 Caching - Data Replication

During transaction execution, objects fetched from the server as cached in a buffer pool. Typically, locks acquired on the server are also cached in some internal structures of the client. When the transaction commits, data and locks could be held for subsequent transactions. Caching items and/or locks on a client machine between transactions is generally referred in the literature as *inter-transaction* caching [WN90, WR91, CFLS91, FCL92, ÖDV94]. The following paragraphs elaborate on techniques with or without inter-transaction caching. We assume page-level locking.

2PL with no Inter-Transaction Caching. Let's assume that an application running on a client workstation consists of three transaction blocks, as shown in Fig. 1, that are executed sequentially. Suppose 2PL is used for concurrency with no intra-transaction caching. First time page requests require a round-trip message interchange between the client and the server. When the server receives the request, it first places the appropriate lock (read or write) on the page – i.e., a page requests implies a request for page locking so these two messages are combined into one. The client caches both the page and the lock mode acquired on it. Subsequent requests for pages that have already been cached do not require any interaction with the server as long as the lock mode held on the page is the same or stronger than the one required for the current access. Locks are held until

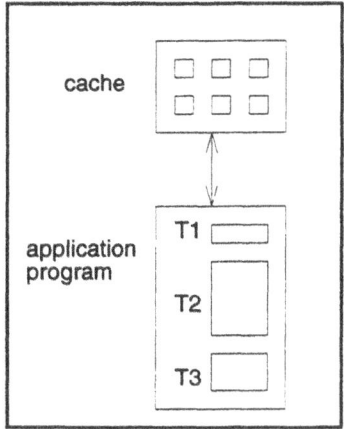

client workstation

Fig. 1. Caching.

the transaction terminates at which point the locks are released at the server and the client's cache is cleaned. Deadlocks are detected at the server using some centralized deadlock detection mechanism.

Referring to Fig. 1, when the transaction T1 commits, its locks are released at the server so that other transactions may access them. When the next transaction T2 begins, it sees a clean cache. Objects needed by this transaction must be requested from the server even if they were cached for the previous transaction. The server will have to acquire the appropriate locks on the objects before it transmits them to the client.

Data/No-Lock Cache 2PL. In this algorithm, pages cached in the client are retained across transaction boundaries. However, locks acquired during a transaction are released at the end of the transaction. When a transaction accesses, for the first time, a page cached in the client's pool by a previously running transaction, a read or write lock for this page must be requested from the server. The client is blocked until the server replies back that the lock is acquired. The page itself does not have to be sent to the client as long as the two copies on the client and the server are the same. If the server discovers that its local copy of the page is more recent than the one cached on the client, it sends the fresh copy to the client along with the reply.

For this scheme to work, for each page cached on a client workstation, the server must know the client that performed the last update on the page. If a client requests a lock on a page that has been modified by another client, the server attaches the page itself to the reply message.

This technique does nothing more than to essentially extend the available server pool to include the buffer pool space of all clients connected to the server. Thus, compared to non-caching 2PL this method reduces the number of I/Os for pages cached in the client but swapped out of the server's pool.

Data/Lock Cache 2PL (Callback Locking). In *callback locking* when a transaction terminates, pages used by the transaction as well as their lock modes are retained in the client's cache to be used for the next transaction. No interaction with the server is needed when a client accesses a cached page and the required lock is covered by the lock already held on the page. However, when a stronger lock is needed or a page is not present in the local cache, the server is contacted to place the lock, fetch the page or do both.

When the server gets such a message from a client, it broadcasts to all clients holding incompatible locks on the page, to give up their locks. If the client does not need the lock on the page – i.e., non of the currently running transactions holds the lock on the page – it releases the lock. On the other hand, if the lock is needed the client holds the lock until the transaction terminates. This mechanism is used in the Andrew File System [H+88] and ObjectStore database system [LLOW91].

Optimistic Locking. This technique assumes that a page found in the local cache is valid. That is, the application continues executing without being blocked when accessing cached pages. Lock upgrade requests are still sent to the server. At commit time, the server checks if conflicts developed during the normal transaction processing in which case the transaction is aborted [W+88]. In this algorithm, a transaction may continue executing even if the server knows the transaction will abort because of conflicts.

In a variation of the above algorithm, when the server receives a page updated by a committed transaction, it notifies all other clients holding copies of this page in their cache that the copy is invalid. This reduces the likelihood to abort a transaction at commit time. The server may also send the valid copy of the page along with the notification message.

4 Persistence and Programming Languages

The best OODBMSs combine influences from databases and programming languages in a clean way. Ideally, the same type system applies to both transient and persistent data. That is, any type may have both transient and persistent instances. This means that the application developer works with one data model (or type system) and language, not two – one for transient data such as C and another for persistent such as SQL. Finally, this means that there need be no translation between in-memory and on-disk representations. Or if there is such a translation, it is the responsibility of the OODBMS and not the application developer or the developer of each class that requires persistence.

An OODBMS can be viewed as a conventional programming language extended with persistence, (and other features). This view leads to the question: what is involved in adding persistence to a programming language?

In FORTRAN the basic types supported are numeric and string types, and the only structuring facility is provided by arrays. FORTRAN (up through FORTRAN-77) does not have pointers. Thus, it would be easy to add persistence to FORTRAN.

Adding persistence to PL/I is more complex, because in addition to the types provided by FORTRAN, there are pointers to deal with. However, some pointers can be handled easily: Objects allocated in an "area" which refer to one another via "offsets" can be made persistent easily. The entire area can be written to disk and read back. The pointers, which are relative to the beginning of the area, never have to be adjusted following retrieval. Ordinary pointers cannot be handled so easily.

In Smalltalk and Lisp pointers are not accessible by the programmer. A runtime system providing persistence has much latitude in how inter-object references are represented and manipulated. Absolute addresses (i.e. ordinary pointers) can be used; an area and offset scheme can be used; and there are other possibilities. It is even possible to use more than one approach, since the implementation is hidden in a way that is not possible with a language such as C.

In Pascal, Ada, C and C++, the programmer has direct access to pointers. Adding persistence to these languages is difficult. CAD applications spent much of their time traversing pointers, and the approach to persistence should not require any significant change in the way programmers use pointers, or increase the cost of dereference. What this means is that the languages most important for CAD and many other applications are precisely the languages that are most difficult to extend with persistence.

4.1 Pointers and Object ids

Pointers and object ids serve similar purposes – both serve to identify objects – but in different contexts. A pointer is valid only during the execution of a program; it specifies a location within a 32-bit address space; and operations on pointers are extremely efficient since they are supported directly by hardware. In order to be useful in an OODBMS, an object id has to be valid for the lifetime of the object, potentially beyond the lifetime of the process that creates the object. The address space is much larger, typically 64 to 128 bits, and access is usually slower. Object ids are not supported in hardware, so software mediation is required, and the dereference may involve an access to a disk or a request sent over a network.

In conventional application, (i.e., applications that don't use an OODBMS), connections between objects are represented by pointers, and networks of objects are traversed by dereferencing pointers. In OODBMS applications, objects are connected by object ids, and these object ids (oids, for short), have to be dereferenced. There is no question that oids, not pointers, must be stored in a database. The question is what the programmer deals with during the execution of an application. If the programmer is aware of oids, there are consequences for performance and ease of use. The programmer has to use an oid to refer to any potentially persistent object. If the programmer deals with pointers, then there must be a translation from oids to pointers and this raises questions about how in-memory and on-disk representations compare.

4.2 Object Layout

The in-memory and on-disk representations of an object may be the same or different. The former is determined by a compiler, (since the application is written in the language supported by the compiler), while the latter is under control of the OODBMS. The OODBMS may choose to store objects in some "neutral" format, (i.e. different from the layout generated by every compiler used to create an application accessing the database), or the layout may be identical to that of one compiler, (i.e. different from the layout generated by every compiler but one).

In many cases, the issue is decided by the approach taken to oids and pointers. If oids are stored in the database and pointers are used in the application, and if oids and pointers occupy different amounts of storage, then it is likely, but not certain, that the in-memory and on-disk representations differ. In general, some per-object processing is required in bring an object into memory. This processing may range from a mere transfer in the best case, to generating of an object with a different layout in the worst case. An intermediate case is one in which no reformatting is required, but some fixup is needed.

4.3 Retrieving and Updating Objects

Another key architectural issue is object retrieval. It is rarely a good idea to fetch a single object at a time. As we discussed in section 3, the request for an object typically may go out over a network and have to be serviced by retrieving an object from disk. Doing all this work for a single object is wasteful, so this raises the question of what other objects should be retrieved. The possibilities include the following: the requested object and connected objects, a logical cluster containing the requested object, or a physical unit containing the required object.

The retrieval may be implicit, triggered by a dereference, or explicitly requested by the programmer. When an object (or some larger unit) is going to be updated, it is necessary to record the fact for purposes of concurrency control and recovery. Ideally, the programmer would simply update the object and the OODBMS would note the update. Also, if writes have to be noted explicitly, this not only diminishes source compatibility, but introduces an opportunity for subtle errors.

One approach, followed in [LLOW91], is to detect updates automatically as a result of virtual memory protection violation, see section 5.3. Another approach, followed in [AG89a], is to have the compiler detect when an object becomes dirty, e.g., during an assignment, and pass flags to the underlying storage system.

5 OODBMS Architectures

An OODBMS architecture has to address all the issues identified above: what are the roles of oids and pointers? how are object retrieval and update specified and implemented? what are the in-memory and on-disk object representations? These issues are not completely independent of one another. This section will survey three OODBMS architectures to examine how these problems have been dealt with. The architectures to be surveyed are the following:

- Import/export object managers: Each type has functions for translating between in-memory and on-disk representations.
- Software dereferencing: Function call interface to all data management operations, possibly hidden by syntactic sugar.
- Hardware dereferencing: Data management functions triggered by hardware interrupts.

For each architecture, we will describe how it solves the problems of dereferencing, retrieval, update, and layout. We will describe the consequences of the solution:

- *Source compatibility*. How does a program that manipulates persistent data differ from the corresponding program for transient data? This issue is strongly related to ease of use. If persistent data and transient data are handled differently, then writing new code and migrating existing code will both be more complicated than would otherwise be the case.
- *Binary compatibility*. Does code have to be recompiled?
- *Performance*. When during execution does the overhead for persistence show up?

5.1 Import/export Object Managers

An import/export object manager depends on the presence of a pair of functions for carrying out translations between in-memory and on-disk representations. This approach is common in "home-grown" systems and, for example, the NIH class library.

Persistence is defined by reachability. That is, if object A refers to object B, and A needs to be persistent, then B has to be persistent also. (In some cases, the definer of type A may decide that the import/export functions do not need to propagate across certain pointers, e.g. if B is purely transient data that is only of interest within the scope of one process.)

In this architecture, only the import and export functions deal with oids, by turning them into ordinary pointers to ordinary transient objects. This means that object layout on disk is determined by the export functions. Retrieval is requested by the programmer, and the extent of the retrieval is determined by the import functions. Obviously, the finer the granularity, the more frequent are the requests for retrieval by the programmer. The request from the programmer may offer some advice about how much to fetch. Updates are also requested explicitly; updated objects are written to disk by running the export functions on updated objects.

Concurrency control, if implemented at all, is typically coarse-grain. Recovery is often not supported.

This approach to persistence treats class implementers and class users differently with respect to source compatibility. A class implementer must provide import and export functions and must therefore be aware of both representations. A user of this class need not be aware of the different representations, but need only initiate the retrieval or update. One aspect of representation that is relevant to the user of a class is the extent of the retrieval – when a retrieval occurs, the user must know how far traversal can proceed before another retrieval has to be issued. Binary compatibility is not an issue. Once an object has been imported, then already compiled code manipulating the object can be run without recompilation, provided the retrieval brings in all the objects that will be touched. For example, consider a linked list, composed of individual nodes. If there is a function that traverses the entire list, (e.g. mapcar), then this function can be applied to a persistent list following a retrieval that fetches the entire list. If retrieval of a node does not result in retrieval of a successor node, then the mapcar implementation will fail.

The performance of this approach depends on the granularity of retrieval. Import functions, which are written per type, determine the granularity of access, and this granularity may be too fine for some applications and too coarse for others. Each retrieval carries an overhead cost due to network and disk access costs, so if granularity is too fine, then performance will suffer due to the accumulation of these overhead costs. If granularity is too coarse, then performance can suffer due to unnecessarily high transfer times and the cost of reformatting objects.

5.2 Software Dereferencing

In a software dereferencing scheme, there are distinct types for pointers to transient objects and pointers to potentially persistent objects. The programmer must be careful to use the correct kind of pointer. A pointer to a potentially persistent object is dereferenced in software. This operation, sometimes called *swizzling*, checks to see if the target object is present in the applications address space [Mos92]. This involves at least a hash table lookup. If the target is not present, it is fetched. Once the object is present, the ordinary dereference, (the kind that occurs for ordinary transient pointers), can take place. In some implementations, the physical address is cached to optimize later dereferences.

In languages that do not provide direct access to pointers, (e.g. Smalltalk and Lisp), the distinction between transient and persistent pointers can be hidden. This is not possible in C and C++ because programmers have direct access to pointers. Persistent pointers appear to the programmer as a distinct type. Retrieval is triggered by the dereference of a persistent pointer. There are various policies that determine what should be retrieved. The options include retrieval of just the required object; objects in the same physical container, (e.g. a page); and objects reachable from the requested object.

The in-memory and on-disk object layouts are usually the same, but the architecture does not require this.

Transaction management relies on two-phase locking or optimistic concurrency control, and the unit of locking may be as small as a single object. Read sets are maintained during the software dereference. Write sets are more difficult to maintain this way, and if this can't be done, then the user has to indicate which objects have been modified by a transaction.

The software dereferencing scheme provides very poor source compatibility since it requires every variable and argument that could be bound to a persistent object to be declared as a persistent pointer. This is a serious problem when porting existing code. Binary compatibility is also poor, since code compiled to handle transient objects cannot manipulate persistent objects. Persistent pointers are typically larger than transient pointers. Typical CAD databases are so full of pointers that this results in a significant increase in storage requirements which in turn may lead to more I/Os [CDN93]. There is a time penalty also, as software dereferencing is slower than ordinary dereferencing.

One advantage of the software dereferencing scheme is that it permits dynamic reclustering. Because persistent pointers indirect through at least one table, when an object is moved, only the tables need be updated, not each pointer to the object.

5.3 Hardware Dereferencing

A hardware dereferencing scheme does not require custom hardware; just the ordinary virtual memory management hardware. In hardware dereferencing, there is only one kind of pointer, and it can be used to refer to both transient and persistent objects.

There are two variations of this idea. The simplest implementation just maps an entire database into virtual memory, (e.g. as if it were one big PL/I area). Pointers may have to be located and adjusted for the base address. This limits database size to the size of virtual memory, (typically no more than 2^{32} bytes). A more complex but more practical scheme maps portions of the database into virtual memory dynamically [SKW92, LLOW91]. This allows arbitrarily large databases, but limits the amount of storage that can be accessed in a single transaction to the size of virtual memory. The rest of this discussion will focus on the second variation.

The dynamic mapping scheme relies on the manipulation of memory protection bits. Objects that have been fetched reside in unprotected memory. Objects that have not been fetched but are pointed to by memory-resident objects lie in read-protected memory. An attempt to dereference such a pointer results in a protection violation. An interrupt handler fetches the protected unit of memory, e.g. a page, reduces protection to write-protection, and resumes the offending instruction. It may be necessary to read-protect more memory, to accommodate pointers on the retrieved page.

If, during a dereference, the target object has already been fetched, there is zero runtime penalty. The machine code sequence implementing the dereference is the same one used for an ordinary transient pointer. Indeed, transient and persistent pointers are identical.

In-memory and on-disk object representations are identical. It might seem that a pointer stored in the database would have to be larger than 32 bits, (since the address space of a database is not limited to 32 bits). This is not the case – conceptually the value stored in the pointer is used as a key to a table which contains the full oid. The implementation does not require a table with an entry for each object; large chunks of memory can be handled by a single table entry.

Transaction management is based on two-phase locking or optimistic concurrency control. Read and write sets are easy to maintain automatically. Violation of read protection yields read set information. The first write to a write-protected region of memory generates another interrupt. The handler for this interrupt reduces protection to unprotected, and maintains the write set.

Hardware dereferencing schemes provide nearly ideal source compatibility. There is only one pointer type, so no code that manipulates pointers has to be rewritten. Code written and compiled for ordinary transient data will also work on persistent data, as long as the access takes place in the scope of a transaction. The only caveat is that code doing allocation might have to be modified so that allocation in the database can be implemented. Write sets are maintained automatically, so no source modifications are required to indicate dirty data.

Hardware dereferencing swizzles each retrieved pointer exactly once, when the page is fetched. All subsequent dereferences proceed at full speed, (i.e. as if they were ordinary transient dereferences). In hardware dereferencing schemes, clustering is determined at the time of allocation. If dynamic reclustering is required, then it is implemented above the basic dereferencing scheme, in a library or in an application.

5.4 The C++ Hidden Pointers

Besides the problem of pointers discussed above, there are additional problems in making the C++ programming language persistent. In particular, some C++ objects contain special pointers which point to function tables implementing runtime dispatch of function calls. Such pointers are contained in C++ objects of types that have virtual functions or virtual base classes. The pointers are called *hidden* pointers [BDG93a] because they are not accessible to the user. In the case of virtual functions, the hidden pointer points to a virtual function table that is used to determine which function is to be called. In the case of virtual base classes, the hidden pointers are used for sharing base classes [Str91b].

Virtual functions are used for late binding. For example, a Person pointer p may point to a Student object. Assume that class Person defines a function address as virtual, and class Student defines its own version of address with a different body. Then when p->address() is invoked, the actual function body that is executed is determined at run time. If p points to a Person object, the Person's address function is invoked. If p points to a Student object, the Student's address function is invoked. The hidden pointers have to be handled specially, since the function tables are transient.

The basic scheme followed in [BDG93a] is to apply an overloaded operator new to invoke a constructor on an object that is just fetched from disk (and therefore the hidden pointers it contains are bad) to fix the hidden pointers. Note that the constructor must not initialize the values of the data members; it must have null body. For this to happen, the compiler generates a function for each class that sets the value of a global boolean variable to true before invoking the overloaded version of the new operator (the one that does not allocate any storage). The effect of the constructor invocation is simply that the hidden pointers are assigned the right values.

In ObjectStore [LLOW91] the schema records the layout of each object. This information is used when a page is mapped into the client's address space. Pointers are relocated, as described in section 5.3, so that they are consistent for the current address space. Schema generation is the process of analyzing class declarations (or some equivalent, e.g. debug information), to understand object layout. During schema generation, two notable events occur. First, pointers to virtual tables are noted. Second, a table mapping type identifiers to virtual table pointers is created. This table is filled in at link time. During relocation, virtual table pointers are filled in by consulting the table.

6 Summary

In this paper, we examined the architectural issues in building storage systems for object-oriented database systems and persistent languages. We discussed techniques for placing small and large objects on disk, disk space management, client-server architectures and mechanisms for caching data on the client workstation. Finally, we have described three pointer dereference mechanisms – import/export, software dereference, and hardware dereference.

Active Object Systems

Alejandro P. Buchmann

Technical University Darmstadt, Fachbereich Informatik, Frankfurter Str. 69a, 64293 Darmstadt, Germany

Abstract: Active database systems have been proposed to satisfy the requirements of applications that must react in a timely manner to events. Active object systems combine the properties of active database management systems and object-oriented database management systems (OODBMS). This chapter introduces a working model for active objects that attempts to unify the notions of active objects common in databases, operating systems and programming languages. It reviews their basic properties and presents an overview of current developments in active object systems. The structure of event-condition-action rules is presented. Event hierarchies and algebras, condition evaluation and action execution are discussed. The two basic components of the execution model of an active object system are presented: the coupling modes between triggering transaction and triggered rule, and transaction models. Architectural issues are briefly reviewed and correctness criteria and tools for rule definition and execution are discussed.

1 Introduction

Active database systems have been proposed recently as a new data management paradigm to satisfy the needs of many applications that require a timely response to critical situations. Typical examples are network management (both power and communication networks), computer-integrated manufacturing (CIM), commodity trading, air-traffic control, plant and reactor control, tracking, and many more. Common to all these applications is the need to respond in a timely manner to external events.

Consider a power-grid in which one power-generation node fails suddenly or is disconnected from the grid. This requires a response within seconds to compensate the sudden loss of capacity and rebalance the load. Within the required response time a large body of information must be analyzed. This information usually is collected continuosly over longer time periods or reflects long-term statistics. A failure to respond within the required time carries a high risk of causing additional failures through overload of backups and imbalance in the system, with the consequent massive losses.

In the area of trading and portfolio management active databases offer distinct advantages. They can monitor the market and initiate or suggest trades based on price developments. They also can be used, by virtue of temporal events, to time an investment to minimize taxes, or renew the maturing deposits. They are particularly useful in the area of commodity and currency trading, where timing is essential. It is interesting to observe that in financial applications earlier is not necessarily better. One often wants to wait as long as possible before carrying out an action.

Take flood control as a third example. Precipitation data and water-level readings are recorded in a database. There is no single externally-observable discrete event which causes a shift from a non-critical to a critical situation warranting an alert. Rather, the database system, as it collects water-level and precipitation data keeps analyzing their trends, to forecast, based on geographical and historical data, whether the observed accumulation approaches a critical situation. If so, the database system based on the integration of many discrete data initiates the appropriate action.

Conventional database management systems deal with such situations by polling the database at fixed time intervals and/or by embedding the situation monitoring capabilities and the corresponding actions in the application code. Polling may be rather wasteful, particularly if the required response time is short and the anomalous situation occurs seldom, as is the case in network management or plant control. Embedding the situation monitoring and the corresponding actions leads to redundant functionality, repetitive and possibly inconsistent condition/action specification and in general, to a loss of modularity and poor application maintainability. This situation is illustratd by Fig. 1.

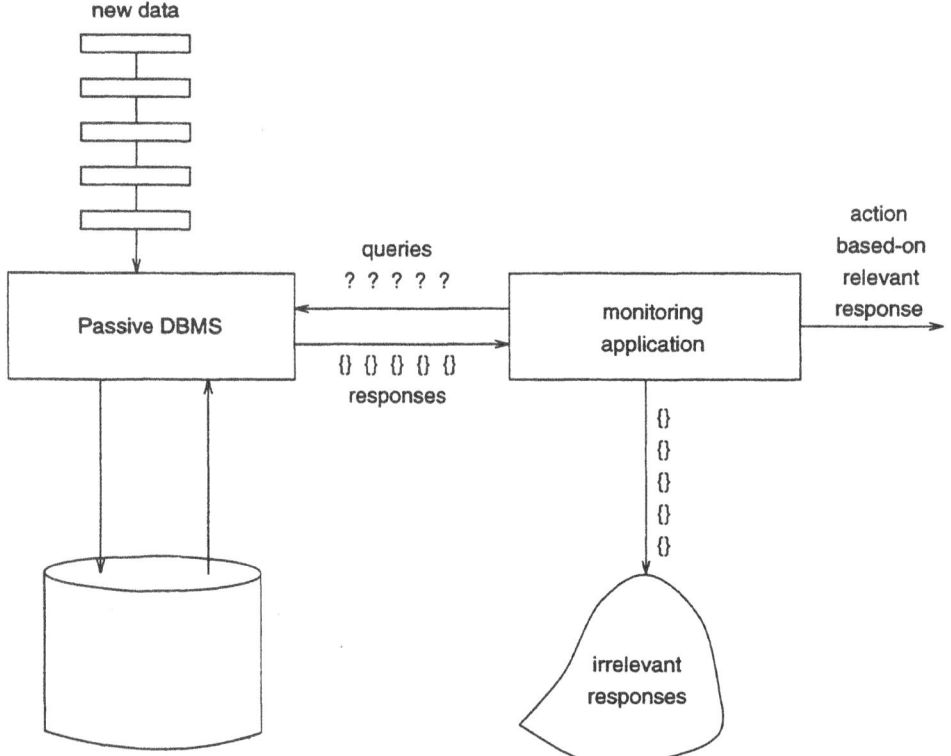

Fig. 1. Polling a passive DBMS by a monitoring application

An active database system, in contrast, manages an event-driven stream of activities in addition to the passive data structures, as shown in Fig. 2. This is accomplished by integrating event-condition-action (ECA) rules into the database [Day88, CBB⁺89, DPG91, HC88, Kot93, SHP88, WF90]. Active database capability does not depend on object orientation, but they are particularly compatible and complement each other well. This is also true because many applications benefitting from active database capabilities also handle data best represented in an object model. Therefore, it is just natural to combine both concepts into the notion of active objects.

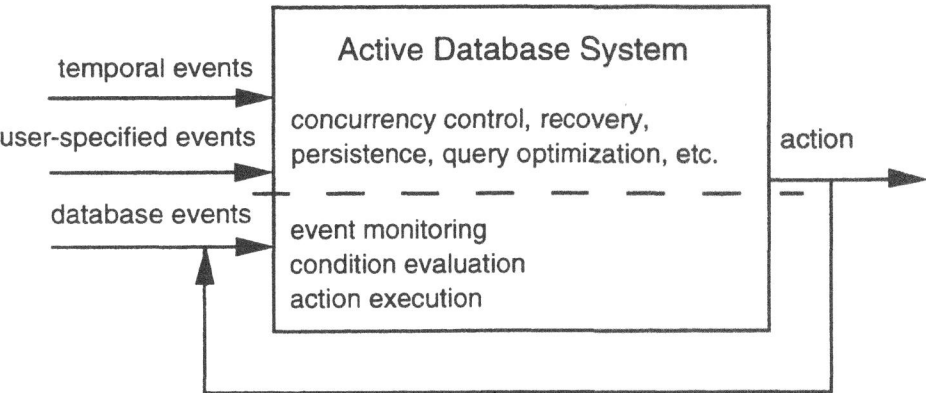

Fig. 2. Active database system with integrated ECA-rule evaluation

Active object systems have been proposed as mediator systems in the integration of heterogeneous environments. Their ability to represent complex and semantically rich structures and their capacity to react to external events makes them a powerful approach when trying to maintain consistency across heterogeneous databases, or as the support mechanism for access control in heterogeneous environments. DOM [MBH⁺92] and REACH [BBKZ92] are two examples of the use of active objects for the integration of heterogeneous environments.

2 Active Objects

The term *active object*, like so many in the object-oriented literature, has been applied to rather diverse notions. In the context of object-oriented programming languages it appears in the Actor-based languages Act1 [Lie87], Act2 [The83], Act3 [AH87b, AH87a] and their derivatives, for example, ABCL/1 [YBS86, YSTH87]; other languages using the concept are KNOs [TFGN87], Hybrid [Nie87, KNP88] and Orient84/K [IT86, IT87, TI86]. Unfortunately, the definition of active object has been vague and rather intuitive. The actor-based languages use a fairly primitive concept of active object, not much more than the object notion of other (passive) object-oriented languages but with asynchronous messages. At the other extreme one finds languages, such as Orient84/K, combining in a single language (and its objects) the notions of demons, declarative and procedural programming.

In the area of object-oriented operating systems, objects are often viewed as consisting of regions of data that the object serves to encapsulate, regions of code that are used to perform the operations defined on the object, and the control structures used by the kernel to manage the object. It is common that the structure of objects in object-oriented operating systems is very similar to that of a typical process since the mapping must be made to conventional, process-oriented hardware [Not87]. Most object-oriented operating systems center their notion of activity around threads. Some newer approaches try to bridge the gap between operating systems and programming languages. In the DaCapo project, for example, an active object is an encapsulation of state, thread, synchronization primitives, distribution capabilities, mobility aspects, and persistence [SHP89].

In the database context active objects are often referred to in an informal way as the objects in an active OODBMS capable of responding to complex events. These events may range from database updates, to temporal events and arbitrary, user-defined events. Events may also be composed. Given the nature of the events and the wide range of situations that can be monitored, rather complex execution strategies are required to insure the correct execution of rules while guaranteeing the basic database functionality of concurrency control and reocoverability.

The common theme in the various interpretations is that active objects have the capability of executing *autonomously* and *asynchronously* actions in response to the detection of *events*. Schematically, an active object can be represented as shown in Fig. 3.

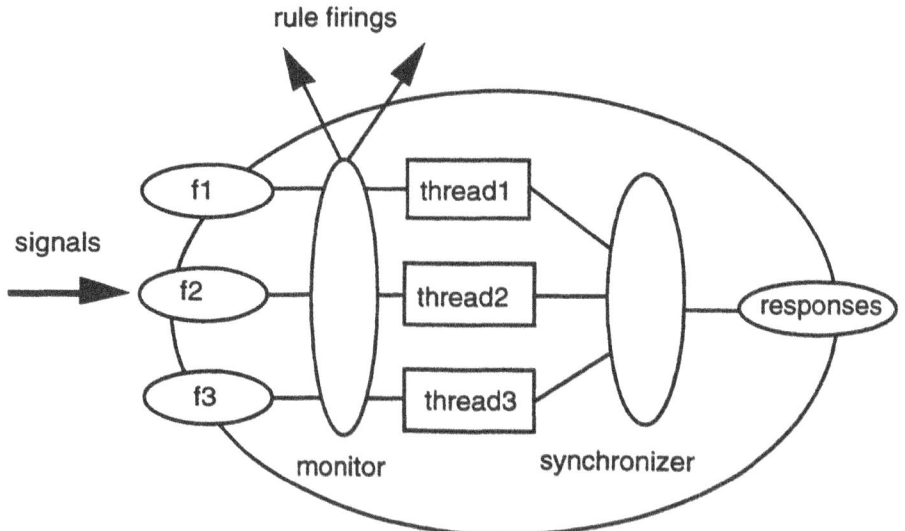

Fig. 3. Schematic representation of an active object

We can structure this intuitive understanding further by postulating some basic requirements for active objects based on [Buc90]:

1. An active object is capable of reacting autonomously to changes in its internal state and to events in its environment, including temporal events.
2. An active object is capable of executing multiple activities concurrently, of which one is necessarily event detection.
3. An active object may respond to detected events asynchronously.
4. An active object has to include the capability for defining the events that must be monitored, and how to react to them.
5. An active object knows its internal organization and is aware of its activity in order to manage it. Intra- and inter-object synchronization may be achieved by different mechanisms but must be subject to compatible correctness criteria.
6. An active object must provide persistence if required by its clients.

The capability of reacting autonomously sets active objects apart. Interaction among passive objects occurs via imperative messages. A message typically consists of a selector and a list of parameters and/or keywords. The recipient performs the operation specified in the message transparently to the invoker but has no autonomy to decide what action to perform. An active object can react just like a passive object to an imperative message, but it is also capable of responding to event messages, for example, a temporal event, or to extract an event from an imperative message. While response in a passive object system is typically synchronous, the response to events in an active object may be asynchronous.

To be able to respond to events, it is necessary to provide an ever-running event-monitoring capability. Since event-monitoring may be expensive, it may be delegated to specialized event monitors. Depending on the complexity of the events that must be monitored, the monitoring may be performed at various levels. For example, basic events may be monitored at the individual object level, composite events, however, might have to be monitored at higher levels. The level at which event monitoring is performed will ultimately define the granularity of an active object. The extremes are, on one end, an active object system in which all the monitoring is distributed and performed locally by the objects, and at the other end of the spectrum is an active database in which all monitoring is done centrally by a single event monitor.

An active object needs to have the capability for specifying its active behavior. The reactive capability of an active object is specified in the form of rules. It has become common to use event-condition-action rules as the mechanism for specifying the active behavior [DBM88, Kot93]. An event determines when the rule should be triggered, the condition states whether the action should be executed and the action part determines how the object should respond.

Active objects must be able to persist and to synchronize their actions. Persistence means that the state of an object should survive the session in which it was generated. It implies that the use of objects should occur within transactions in order to be able to guarantee both their correct concurrent use and their recoverability in case of failure, thus ensuring consistency. The activity of the objects means, in addition, that the responses to the events, i.e. the rule executions which are system-invoked, must be synchronized with the user-invoked transactions. This synchronization requires execution models which are different from those used in passive databases, both relational and object-oriented.

The remainder of this chapter deals with the above aspects of active object systems in more detail. Sect. 3 describes the rule classes, their structure and some important special cases. Sect. 4 deals with event mechanisms, event description, and monitoring of simple and complex events. Sect. 5 addresses the issues involved in condition evaluation, while Sect. 6 deals with the corresponding actions. Sect. 7 presents the need for an extended transaction model to properly synchronize rule executions and user transactions and discusses some open problems in this area. Sect. 8 deals with architectural issues influencing the implementation and functionality of active object systems. Finally, Sect. 9 addresses design issues, ranging from a discussion of some of the problems faced when designing an active object system, such as the halting problem and cycle detection, non-determinism, and conflicting rule specifications, to the need for design tools that are currently not available.

Simple trigger mechanisms are rapidly becoming a feature of many commercial DBMSs, such as Sybase and Ingres. Although the basic ideas have been around for a long time, it took almost 20 years to incorporate them into conventional database systems in a useful manner. Active object systems are an emerging area in the young field of OODBMSs. As such, the content of this chapter is based on research prototypes of the first generation of active OODBMSs. To focus the chapter we concentrate on object systems, leaving aside for the most part the work on active relational DBMSs. Many results are still tentative and will certainly be subject to revision in the future. This should be kept in mind when reading the remainder of this chapter which attempts to provide a summary and some structure for discussion of the main issues in this emerging and potentially important field.

3 Rule Classes

Rules are basic constructs of an active object system. We consider them here in their most general form, namely, event-condition-action rules. ECA rules are extensions of the procedural condition-action (CA) rules. The clear separation of event and condition was postulated in the HiPAC project [CBB+89, Day88, DBM88]. The general form of an ECA rule is

> **on** event **if** condition **do** action

- The *Event* of an ECA rule determines *when* a rule should be evaluated.
- The *Condition* of an ECA rule determines *whether* the action should be executed.
- The *Action* specifies the consequence of the condition being true, or *what* should be done.

We maintain that ECA rules are the most general construct under which other rule mechanisms can be subsumed by making simplifying assumptions about the events and the actions, and by using a particular formalism for specifying the condition part.

Let us begin with the formalism of the condition part. The condition can be expressed as a query in a language based on an algebra or calculus, or it could be expressed in a very general form as a statement in first order logic. The semantics of how a condition is interpreted depends on each particular case. In constraint-checking mechanisms used to enforce database consistency the (implied) action, an abort, is executed when the constraint's condition evaluates to FALSE. In most other cases, the action is executed if the condition evaluates to TRUE.

If the event is not specified, the ECA rule degenerates to a condition-action rule. Such a rule can be evaluated by running sequentially through a set of rules, or the event could be implicit and understood as any update event. The evaluation of these rules may be rather time-consuming, since the condition must always be checked. The action part of such CA rules may also be restricted. For example, it could be restricted to a transaction abort, the typical case in constraint checking mechanisms. It could also be restricted to testing membership in a relation, as is the case with Datalog. These examples show that ECA rules can be restricted and behave as declarative rules do.

Rules can also degenerate to event-action rules when no condition is specified at all. In that case, given an event, the action is always executed.

Most active object systems consider rules as first-class objects [DBM88, DPG91, BBKZ92, Kot93]. This means, that rules can be grouped in a class-hierarchy and can be inserted, deleted and modified as are all other objects. All rules belong to the class RULE. Rules may have attributes and methods defined on them, for example methods *fire, enable,* and *disable.* Rules are typically defined at the class level, i.e., they apply to all instances of a class. Some systems, like ADAM [DPG91], allow for selective deactivation of a rule for particular instances of a class. This can be used effectively for handling exceptions. It is also possible to define instance-specific rules. A mechanism for it is proposed in [Buc90]. It depends, however, on the manipulation of the oid structure. It is thus only implementable if the active object system is built from scratch. These issues are further discussed in Sect. 8.

It is common to consider the rule as a complex object consisting of an event object, a condition object, and an action object. Some systems [Kot93], in addition, group certain options, like execution mode, coupling mode, and execution order in a separate object that is referenced. The meaning of these options is explained as part of the execution model in Sect. 7. A simpler approach is taken in the ADAM system, where events are broken out as full-fledged objects but the condition and action parts are coded into the body of the rule.

ECA rules may be used for a variety of purposes. They can be used to implement part of the DBMS functionality, such as the control of materialized views, consistency enforcement, or access control. They can also be application-specific and are used to implement monitoring applications. Accordingly, rules can be classified based on their purpose, such as consistency rules, access control rules, transaction rules, or application-domain rules [BBKZ92, BBKZ93]. The rule class hierarchy can be further refined by specifying subclasses, for example, content-independent and content-dependent access control rules. These rules may then vary, among other things, in the events to which they respond and the point of the transaction at which they are executed. To stay with the previous example, content-independent access control rules may be evaluated before an access-operation is executed. In contrast, content-dependent access control rules must be evaluated after or while the access is processed. Fig. 4 shows the rule class-hierarchy currently being explored in the REACH project [BBKZ92]. This hierarchy includes flow-control rules needed for expressing complex transaction models via rules. Contingency rules are used for defining alternate actions that can be invoked whenever the primary task may fail, be it for timing reasons or lack of resources. The class ApplicationRule should further be refined as needed.

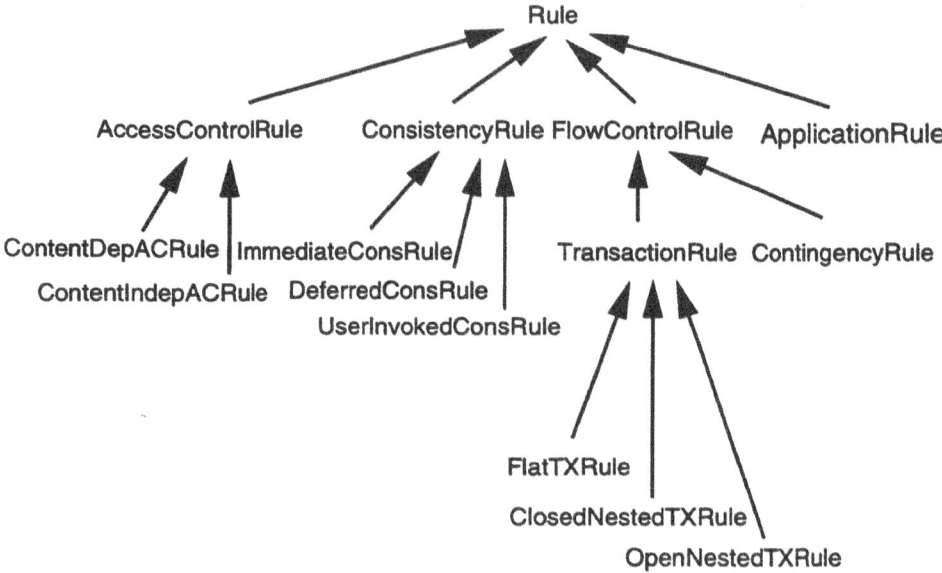

Fig. 4. A Rule hierarchy

4 Events

The clear separation of event and condition was introduced in [Day88]. This has a conceptual reason, since the event is the activator of a rule. It specifies when a rule should be evaluated. It also has a pragmatic reason, namely efficieny. Consider a tracking application that tracks ships moving in and out of a certain area. Whenever new position data comes in, a rule evaluates whether 5 or more ships are within 50 miles of a given point. If so, an alert is issued. To determine whether the condition is true, a spatial query must be evaluated. If event and condition are not separated, the updating transaction will be blocked until the spatial query is evaluated. This would cause unacceptable delays. By separating event and condition it becomes possible to fire the rule whenever the position update (the event) occurs, while the condition can be evaluated in a separate transaction.

Much of the expressive power of an active object system depends on the events that are supported and the mechanisms provided for their specification. Within a rule, an *event-class* is specified. A particular instance of that event class may cause the rule to fire.

Events may be either:

- the execution of methods,
- a state transition of the object space,
- temporal events,
- transaction and flow-control events,
- user-specified abstract events.

The following discussion is based largely on the events supported by SAMOS [GD93a, GD93b], SNOOP [CM91] and REACH [BBKZ92].

4.1 Method execution events

The invocation of a method can be specified as an event. Whenever that method is invoked, the corresponding event is raised. Since events are typically associated with a *point* in time but the execution of a method requires a time *interval*, method execution events require an additional, more precise specification. This is done through the use of modifiers such as BEFORE and AFTER, which specify, respectively, the point in time at which the invocation message was received or the point at which the method completed execution. Insertion and deletion of objects can also be modelled through method execution events raised by the corresponding costructor and destructor methods.

4.2 State transition (value) events

State transition events occur whenever the state of the object space is altered. This occurs typically through the execution of methods. However, some OODBMSs offer the possibility of handling values. The manipulation of these values through the generic accessor functions may raise the corresponding value events. To preserve encapsulation, some systems, like SAMOS, restrict the definition and use of rules containing value-events to the implementor of the class for which those rules are applicable.

4.3 Temporal events

Temporal events may be either absolute or relative. An absolute temporal event is specified by the corresponding date and time (to whatever granularity is desirable). For example, 93:08:27:15:00:00.

Relative temporal events may be specified by providing a time interval relative to another event, for example 10 seconds after commit. Therefore, they are considered composite events. They may also be periodic. In this case, the modifier EVERY is used, for example EVERY DAY 00:00:00 will be raised every day at midnight. This can be further refined by adding (optionally) a frequency and an interval to be able to specify such events as every 10th day during a year.

REACH recognizes a special type of temporal event, milestones [BBKZ93]. Mile-stones are specified to monitor the progress of a time-constrained process. If the mile-stone is not reached in time, the process is likely to miss its deadline. In that case a contingency plan is triggered. A contingency plan substitutes the original task for a faster task of less quality in order to finish on time.

4.4 Transaction and flow-control events

Most active object systems provide the basic transaction events, namely begin of transaction (BOT), end of transaction (EOT) and transaction abort (ABORT). REACH distinguishes between EOT and COMMIT. This distinction is necessary whenever a system is
to execute additional operations, e.g. constraint checking, after completing the execution
of a transaction and before the results of the transaction are committed. For implementation of distributed active-object systems additional events, such as pre-commits for
implementation of a two-phase commit protocoll will be required.

4.5 User-specified abstract events

While all other primitive events discussed so far are known by the system and can
therefore be recognized by it, there are situations in which additional abstract events
must be maintained. For example, when the user signals the active-object system that a
plane has taken off and that for this plane the rules applicable to airborne planes should
be enabled while those governing planes on the taxi- and runways should be disabled.
Abstract events can be specified and explicitly raised by the user. An abstract event has
a name and when raised it is instantiated and assigned a given point in time.

User-specified abstract events are not universally accepted as an essential, separate
class of events since their behavior can be provided through the definition of appropriate
database objects and the raising of method-invocation events.

4.6 Composite events

Many situations require more complex events than those described above. For example,
the sequence of a method-invocation event and an EOT event. For this purpose, primitive
events can be composed into more complex *composite events*. Event composition is done
through the use of *event constructors*. The set of event constructors and primitive events
form the *event algebra*. A composite event is then a regular expression built up from
the primitive events using the event constructors.

Events may also pass parameters to the rule they fire. In composing events it must
be established how the parameters of the component events shall be composed.

A simple event algebra was introduced in HiPAC [DBM88]. It consisted of three
event constructors: the *disjunction* of two events, the *sequence* of two events, and the
closure constructor.

The *disjunction* of two events, E1 and E2, is a composite event, E, denoted (E1 |
E2). The composite event E is raised when either E1 or E2 is raised. The parameters
of the occurring event, either E1 or E2 are bound to E, with the parameters of the
non-occurring event being set to NULL. The disjunction of events allows the succinct
definition of rules, since the same rule may be fired by either event, thus avoiding
unnecessary repetition. For example, if a rule is to check whether the relative distance
between a ship and a plane has changed, only one rule must be specified that may fire
when either the position of the plane or the position of the ship is updated.

The *sequence* of two events, E1 and E2, is a composite event, E, denoted
(E1 ; E2). E is signalled when E2 is signalled provided that E1 had been signalled

before during the same transaction or rule firing. The arguments of the composite event are in this case the union of the arguments of E1 and E2. For example, (Update_Inventory (I,A,S) ; EOT), where I, A, and S are parameters that are passed with the event. The sequence constructor is essential when trying to specify control-flow rules.

The *closure* constructor is used whenever an event should fire only once during a transaction considering the cumulative effect of all the operations that raise that event during a transaction. The closure of an event E is denoted E1*. For definiteness, the closure must be followed by another event, E2. Thus the composite event that is raised after an arbitrary number of occurrences of E1 is (E1*;E2). How the parameters of E are composed depends on the event E1.

The event algebra used in SAMOS [GD93a, GD93b] is an extension of the HiPAC algebra in that it includes these three constructors. Disjunction and sequence are defined with the same semantics. The closure operator of SAMOS is defined relative to a time interval and is raised the *first time* the primitive event occurs. The SAMOS event algebra adds three more: the *conjunction* of two events, the *negation* of an event, and a *history* event.

The *conjunction* of two events, E1 and E2, is denoted by (E1,E2). It is raised when both E1 and E2 occurred without consideration of the order in which they occurred. The composition of the arguments is the union of the arguments of the individual events.

The *negation* of an event is denoted as NOT E. It is raised when the event E did not occur in a defined time interval. The monitoring interval is defined separately. Through the use of the modifier *any* instead of a concrete event it is possible to raise a negative event if none of the events defined in the system has occurred in the monitoring interval. It is important to observe when dealing with the negation of events that a closed monitoring interval and a uniquely specifiable point at which the negative event is raised must always be specified. Otherwise the semantics of the negation of an event are ill-defined.

The *history* event counts the number of occurrences of a certain event and is raised if the primitive event occurred the specified number of times. It is represented as TIMES(n,E), where n denotes the number of occurrences of the event E that is needed before the history event is raised. A modification of the history event specifying a range of occurrences instead of a definite number, TIMES([n1-n2],E), is raised when within a specified time interval E occurred at least n1 times but at most n2 times. It is raised at the end of the time interval if the above condition is met.

The complexity of the composite events is even higher in other systems, such as SNOOP [CM91] and Ode [GJ91, GJS92a]. For example, SNOOP offers the possibility of defining composite events that are raised whenever a minimal number of events out of a larger set occurs, for example, two out of five possible. Ode takes the idea of making the event language more powerful to an extreme. It becomes possible to define complex conditions on the events thus almost obviating the condition part of the rule.

The Ode events are defined as mappings among histories and include, in addition to the constructors introduced above, such constructors as *prior, firstAfter, prefix,* and several others. We shall not elaborate further on the specific semantics of these constructors as it exceeds the scope of this paper and Ode will be presented at length in a companion paper. We only show in Fig. 5 in graphical form the event hierarchy currently defined in REACH, which is based on the SNOOP event hierarchy but introduces the milestone events and considers periodic and relative temporal events as composite instead of primitive events.

The comparison of the various event algebras illustrates some interesting points. A tendency towards more and more powerful (and complex) event algebras can be observed. While more powerful event algebras mean greater flexibility in expressing real-world situations, some of the original benefits of separating events and conditions are lost. Event composition appears increasingly to be a potential bottleneck. In addition to the performance problems, possible semantic ambiguities must be dealt with in the event algebras.

Semantically, event composition raises the following problems. Composite events are specified at the class level. If an event constructor like sequence or conjunction composing E1 and E2 is used, there is the possibility that the actual history of occurrence of events is e1,e1',e2, where e1 and e1' are two instances of the same event class. Each instance of E1 may have different argument values. The question is then, which instance of E1 should be used in the composition. The correct semantics may vary depending on the application domain. If we assume that the first occurrence should be used, then the question arises, how long an event should be kept waiting for the second event in the composition to occur. A possible solution is given in [Kot93], through the introduction of the notion of *grouped events*. Event grouping works similar to the transaction boundaries marked by a BOT,EOT pair. When events are grouped, the subsequent event must refer to the proper start event, similar to the transaction identifier. For example

$$OP\_A\_begin[1]; OP\_A\_begin[2]; OP\_A\_end[2]; OP\_A\_end[1]$$

Another semantic problem arises due to the use of absolute temporal events. If the event specifies that something must happen at 17:00:00 but there is a delay or the transaction must be aborted and rolled back because of a concurrency control problem, how should the absolute temporal event be treated during recovery? Initial thoughts on the recoverability of temporal events appear in [DHL91] and [BBKZ93].

From an implementation point of view, event composition may prove very expensive and crucial for the efficiency of the active object system. Most systems use some form of marked nets for implementing the event monitor. SAMOS uses Petri nets while SNOOP uses a RETE network. In Sect. 8 we analyze some architectural issues influencing the implementation strategy of the event monitor. In Sect. 9 we address some of the issues related to the specification of rules in general and events in particular as a part of the design of an active object system.

5 Conditions

The condition part of a rule can be viewed as a separate object consisting of a predicate or a (set of) querie(s) and the coupling mode. The coupling mode describes whether a condition should be evaluated immediately after the firing event has been raised or at another point in the transaction. Details of the coupling modes will be discussed in Sect. 7.

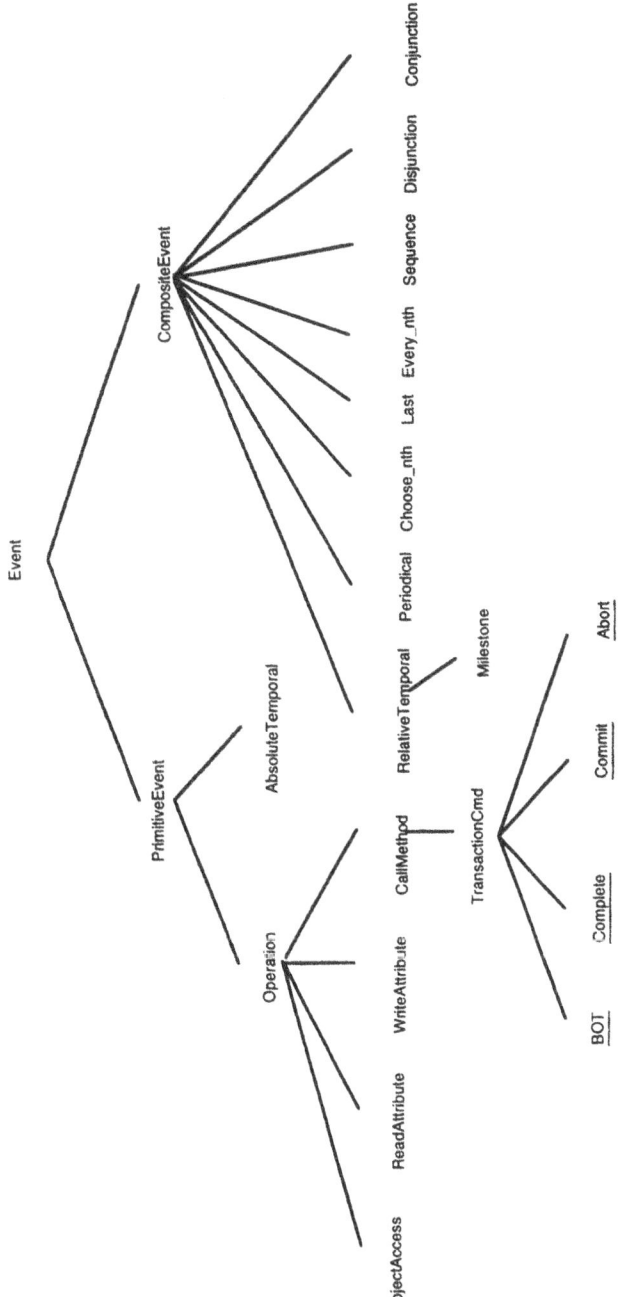

Fig. 5. The REACH event hierarchy

The actual condition is expressed differently in the various systems. In HiPAC [DBM88], the condition is viewed as a collection of queries. This collection of queries can be expressed in some query language. The condition is said to be satisfied if *all* the queries return *non-empty* answers. The main reason for expressing the condition as a collection of queries instead of a simple predicate is that the non-empty answers can be appended to the arguments passed by the event and made available to the action. The action can then refer to the bindings at event time, the state of the database at the time the condition was evaluated, or to the state at the time the action is carried out.

A much simpler approach is taken in [Kot93], where the condition is viewed as a boolean expression that is checked as a precondition of the action. A condition is described by a name, the boolean expression to be evaluated and an optional list of formal parameters.

6 Actions

The action of a rule may also be a complex object, consisting of a coupling mode between the transaction in which the rule was fired and the transaction in which the action is executed, and an operation to be executed in the action. Most active object systems are very liberal in their definition of action, i.e., what they allow an action to be. Actions may range from operations on the database (which may themselves trigger new rule firings), to arbitrary executable routines with or without visible side effects. It is here where many sources of potential problems lurk.

The fact that the action part may operate on other objects could cause an infinite chain of rule firings thus leading to the halting problem. Although this problem is difficult to solve in its most general form, there are approaches one could use to detect at the time a new rule is inserted, whether it is safe or potentially not. These issues are discussed in Sect. 9.

Actions on the database are, like any other database activity, recoverable if they are executed within a transaction. The situation changes when actions with external effects that may not be reversible are executed. For example, if a robot started cutting a piece of metal, that action cannot be rolled back. It is therefore, that the execution model governing the firing and execution of rules is so important.

7 Execution Models

The execution model of an active object system determines the correct synchronization of the user-submitted actions and the system-triggered rule executions. We will part from the assumption that every activity proceeds within transaction boundaries and later extend the approach to open systems. The execution model consists of two basic parts:

1. the specification of the coupling modes and the mapping of rule executions to transactions,
2. the structure of transactions and their synchronization.

The remainder of this section addresses each of these issues.

7.1 Coupling modes

The coupling modes determine the execution of rules relative to the transaction in which they were triggered. They further determine whether a rule is executed as a whole, or if the condition and action parts can be executed as distinct processing units.

The execution of a rule depends on the type of rule, and on the application domain. To illustrate this we shall examine the evaluation of consistency rules. If a consistency rule is specified over a single attribute of a single object it is best to evaluate this constraint during the time of the update. This strategy detects possible consistency violations with a minimum of wasted effort. On the other hand, if the consistency rule is defined over multiple objects that may individually be changed during a transaction, the correct time for evaluation of the rule is at the end of the transaction. Carrying this example further, if the consistency rule touches objects that are part of a design and some of them have not yet been instantiated, the rule cannot be evaluated at the end of the design transaction for the first object. It must be evaluated at a later point in time when all relevant objects have been instantiated.

The notion of coupling modes was introduced in HiPAC [Day88] to create a specification mechanism capable of describing the rule execution strategies required by a variety of applications. The HiPAC coupling modes are rather general and subsume those offered by most other active object systems. Therefore, we use them here to introduce the subject. The HiPAC coupling modes appear to cover all the relevant possibilities when dealing with a closed system, i.e., a system in which every action can be rollled back without visible side-effects. Recently, some extensions were proposed to deal with open systems, in which actions cannot be undone [BBKZ93]. The issues when defining a coupling mode are:

- when should rule execution begin?
- when should rule execution finish?
- must a rule be executed within the triggering transaction or may it run independently?

A rule-execution may begin:

- immediately after the event was detected,
- at the end of the user-transaction but just before it commits,
- after the triggering transaction committed, or
- in parallel with the user-transaction, i.e., the exact beginning of rule-execution is unimportant.

The completion of rule-execution may either be:

- before execution of the triggering transaction resumes,
- before the commit of the triggering transaction,
- after the commit of the triggering transaction, or
- after the abort of the triggering transaction.

Finally, a rule may execute either:

- as part of the triggering transaction (in the form of a subtransation), or
- it may execute in a separate transaction.

The possible coupling modes result from various combinations of the basic options listed above. We shall put them together now to obtain the main coupling modes. For the sake of simplicity, we consider first the condition and action to have the same coupling mode, although this is by no means a necessary condition.

The simplest coupling mode is the *immediate* coupling. Here, a rule is executed as soon as the triggering event is detected. After the condition and (if needed) the action have been executed, control returns to the point in the triggering transaction where the event was detected. This coupling mode is illustrated in Fig. 6(a). The rule is executed as a nested subtransaction or just as an extension of the original transaction (similar to query modification).

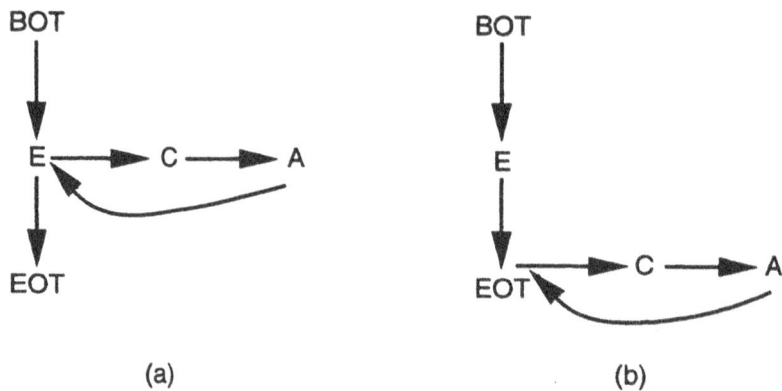

(a)   (b)

Fig. 6. (a) Immediate and (b) deferred coupling modes

The *deferred* coupling mode results from the execution of the rule after the user-submitted transaction has executed but before it commits. This case is shown in Fig. 6(b).

Sometimes it is possible to execute a rule in a separate transaction for efficiency reasons. For example, if monitored data come in at short intervals and every tenth update a rule is triggered. The evaluation of the condition may be rather time-consuming. In this case, the updating transaction should not be blocked while the rule is executed. Fig. 7 shows two rules that were triggered by events E1 and E2. Both rules start execution in a separate transaction some time after the event is detected. Triggered-transaction T1 completes execution before the triggering transaction commits, while triggered-transaction T2 finishes after the triggering-transaction's commit. Whenever rules are executed in separate transactions without any dependencies between the triggering and the triggered transaction we speak about *detached* coupling.

For some applications, additional restrictions must be imposed on rule execution in a separate transaction. For example, if a rule is fired that reorders a part whenever the

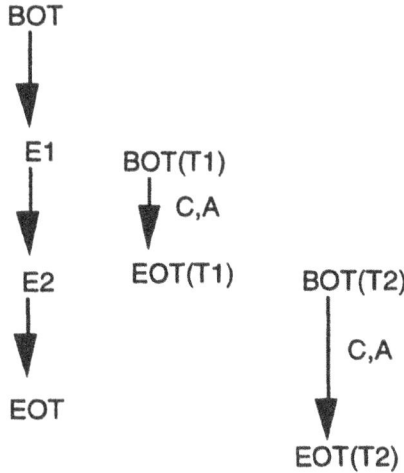

Fig. 7. Detached coupling mode

amount in the warehouse drops below the threshold value, this rule may start execution in parallel with the triggering transaction (e.g. a sale) but the rule transaction placing the order should only commit if the sale goes through. This situation is depicted in Fig. 8. A causal dependency exists between the two transactions. Therefore, this coupling mode is referred to as *detached causally dependent* in HiPAC [CBB+89]. The triggered transaction may begin execution in parallel. Therefore, it is also called *parallel causally dependent* [BBKZ93].

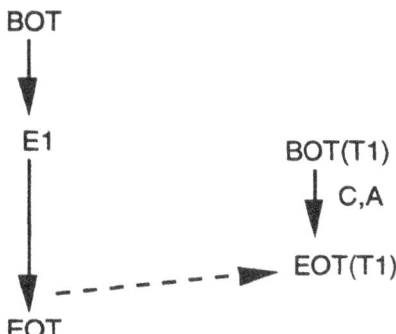

Fig. 8. Parallel detached causally dependent coupling mode

As long as the active system is closed and all objects follow the same database protocolls, these coupling modes appear to be sufficient. However, in the case of open systems in which certain actions may be non-database actions and where side-effects may be visible, additional restrictions must be placed on the detached transactions. For example, if the action part of the rule is an instruction to a robot to start cutting a piece of metal, the action may only start execution when the triggering transaction has committed. This results in *sequential causally dependent coupling* shown in Fig. 9.

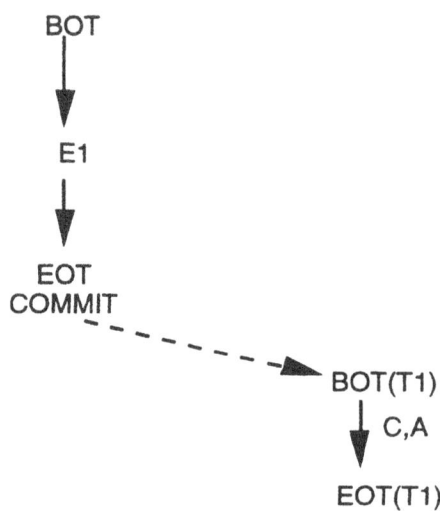

Fig. 9. Sequential causally dependent coupling mode

The second extension proposed in [BBKZ93] is a causally dependent execution, where the triggered transaction may start execution in parallel but may commit only in the case the triggering transaction *fails*. This coupling mode is called *exclusive causally dependent*. We introduced contingency rules in Sect. 3. They have been proposed to execute alternate processes that return results of lesser quality but in a timely manner in environments in which timeliness is critical. Such a rule may be triggered by a milestone event, i.e., whenever the system detects that it fell behind in the execution of a task and runs the risk of missing the deadline, it may invoke a contingency plan if it exists. Such a contingency plan must begin execution in parallel but may actually be thrown away if the primary task can be completed in time. Fig. 10 illustrates the exclusive causally dependent coupling mode.

So far, we considered the execution of condition evaluation and action together. They may actually be executed as separate transactions. The same way the coupling mode specifies the relationship between the event detection and the condition evaluation, a coupling mode can be specified between condition evaluation and action. By considering condition evaluation and action as a block, we tacitly specified the immediate coupling mode between condition and action. The basic coupling modes introduced above may be applied to the action relative to the condition evaluation.

Coupling modes specify the conditions under which execution should begin and end, as well as the transaction in which rule execution should take place. We summarize them in Table 1. Systems that do not explicitly include the coupling mode as part of

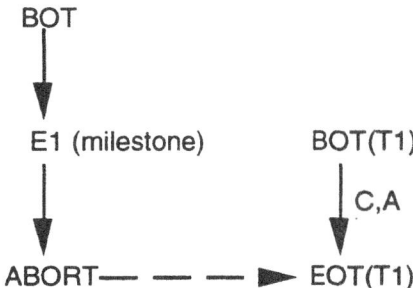

Fig. 10. Exclusive causally dependent coupling mode

their constructs typically represent the starting point of rule execution through complex events involving the EOT or COMMIT events of the triggering transaction. They make simplifying assumptions about the transaction in which the rule executes, using as a default an extension of the triggering transaction. Most systems that do not provide explicit coupling modes limit the choice to immediate and/or deferred coupling.

	BEGIN				COMPLETION				TRANSACTION	
	Event Detection	EOT	After Commit	Parallel to user-transact.	Before Resume user-TX	Before Commit user-TX	After Commit user-TX	After Abort	Sub-TX	Separate TX
Immediate	X				X				X	
Deferred		X				X			X	
Detached				X						X
Parallel Causally Dependent				X			X			X
Sequential Causally Dependent			X				X			X
Exclusive Causally Dependent				X				X		X

Table 1. Summary of possible coupling modes

7.2 Transaction structure

The transaction structure that results when the coupling modes that were described in Sect. 7.1 are implemented is a *nested transaction* structure. For immediate and deferred coupling mode each rule (or part of a rule if condition and action are separated) executes as a subtransaction of the triggering transaction. When the action of a rule can trigger another rule, this second rule is again executed as a (next-level) subtransaction. The result is a transaction tree, exemplified in Fig. 11. The semantics typically given to these nested transactions are the semantics of *closed nesting* first formalized by Moss [Mos85].

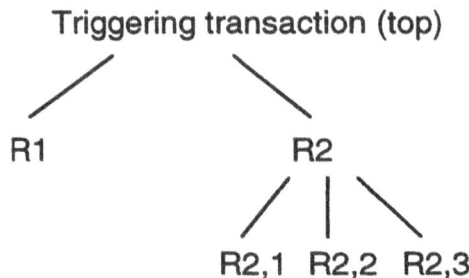

Fig. 11. Nested transaction structure

Transactions in such a closed nesting always commit through the top. This means, that no results of a subtransaction will be visible to the outside world until the top transaction commits. Among siblings, no subtransaction may view the results of a sibling, unless that sibling transaction has committed and passed its results to the parent. In Fig. 11, R2,1 may only see the results of R2,2 when R2,2 commits. R1, however, may not see any of the results of R2,2 until R2 commits and makes its results available through the triggering (top)-transaction.

If all the rules are executed in the immediate coupling mode, the transaction tree is executed exactly according to the traditional (Moss-style) closed nested transaction model.

The execution of deferred rules may occur either sequentially or parallel. In the sequential case, supported for example by STARBURST [WF90], all the rules that are triggered are placed in a pool from which one is selected and executed. If the rule triggers another rule it is added to the pool of rules awaiting execution. Rules whose condition part becomes invalid due to another rule's execution are eliminated. In the parallel case, supported by HiPAC, deferred rule execution occurs in cycles. It is delayed until the end of the user's top transaction. This point is called the *cycle-0 end* in [DHL90, DHL91]. When this point is reached, execution of all the deferred rules triggered so far begins. If more than one deferred rule was triggered, they can all execute in parallel as concurrent subtransactions in cycle 1. Any rules triggered during the execution of cycle 1 are either executed immediately (for immediate coupling) or collected for execution in cycle 2 after the end of cycle 1 (for deferred coupling). Execution stops when no more rules have been triggered.

For the detached coupling mode it is possible to create separate top transactions from within a nested transaction. Such a top transaction may execute independently of the spawning transaction and may be nested itself.

For the causally dependent coupling modes separate top transactions can be created, but these are subject to the dependencies specified by the corresponding coupling mode.

In establishing the execution model of an active object system we make the assumption that everything runs within transaction boundaries. This holds even for external components which may not know the semantics of transactions. However, we can define within the active object system a placeholder for every external system. The placeholder is an active object that follows all the protocols of the active object system. By doing this we can "wrap" the external components into full-fledged active objects. Access to the external component is through the active object.

When the active object system is used as a mediator system in the integration of heterogeneous components, the results of some subtransactions may be visible to the outside world. In this case, we speak about *open nesting*. The transaction model used in such an active object system must combine both closed nesting and open nesting. The global transaction, or multitransaction, consists of several openly nested component transactions. Each of these component transactions may be a nested transaction itself, since the active object that acts as the placeholder may trigger rules. Examples of transaction models that combine the closed nesting for rule execution with the open nesting of mutitransactions are the DOM transaction model [BÖH+92, MBH+92], and the Transaction Activity Model (TAM) presented in [DHL91].

8 Architectural Issues

The implementation of an active object system requires several changes or additions to an OODBMS. In extending the OODBMS with active capabilities one should observe the principle that says, one should only pay for the services one uses. This means in an active object system, that passive objects should not pay the overhead for services that are specific to active objects, such as event monitoring. How easy or difficult this is depends largely on the access one has to the internals of the OODBMS. The extremes in the spectrum of possible implementations are:

1. A layered architecture, defining the active capabilities on top of an OODBMS without the possibility of changing any of the internals of the OODBMS, and
2. an integral approach, reimplementing portions of the basic functionality of the OODBMS to embed the active capabilities and support mechanisms within it.

An excellent description of the layered approach on top of Gemstone is given in [Kot93]. An interesting example of a system that was developed from scratch is Ode [GJ91, GJS92a].

It is interesting to analyze what factors may influence the implementation of an active object system and what limitations the characteristics of the underlying OODBMS impose. Some of the relevant issues are:

- structure of oids and access to it,
- implementation of method invocation,
- communication mechanism, and
- supported transaction model.

One of the most efficient ways of detecting whether an object is active or not is by marking the oid. Many systems use a few bits in the oid to represent relevant information. Being able to recognize whether an object is active or not by accessing only the oid saves many additional lookups.

In a layered architecture one has no access to the structure of the oid and cannot use any portion thereof to mark objects as active. In a layered architecture the fact that an object is active can be implemented by defining a class active_object and inheriting from it. If the system does not provide multiple inheritance, all the system-defined classes must be reimplemented, since it would not be possible to inherit from active_object and a system-defined class, such as array. A major problem of the layered architecture is that inheritance of rules is usually not possible.

The access to the method invocation mechanism is also crucial. Method wrappers can be placed around the methods of the active-object classes. The method wrapper contains the detection capability to raise the corresponding primitive method-access events at the begin and at the end of a method execution. While it was shown in [Kot93] that it is possibe to define the ability to define the wrappers in the class active-object and to create the method wrappers dynamically as soon as a rule refers to a method, it would be much more efficient if this functionality could be implemented at a lower level.

The communication mechanism has an impact on the cost of propagation of events. For efficiency reasons, one would like to avoid a single, monolithic event monitor and have the primitive events detected at the object level propagated directly to the rules that depend on them. Similarly, primitive events should be propagated to the composite event objects, that will compose their own small state diagrams. This propagation should not be done through a global broadcast but rather through a multicast mechanism.

Finally, the execution of rules requires a nested transaction model. Most OODBMSs offer only flat transactions, thus requiring external control mechanisms to provide the nesting at a higher level. Since the systems treat the transaction manager frequently as a black box, it is not possible to implement all the coupling modes described in Sect. 7. Therefore, the OODBMSs that support a nested transaction model are better suited as a platform for a layered architecture.

9 Design Issues

From the point of view of the user, the availability of active object systems raises a new set of design challenges. Some of the design problems are specific to active object systems, others existed all along but were not as visible, because the conflicting information was buried in the application code. Making the conflicts visible may be the first step towards their solution. Some of these problems are well-known from integrity management in traditional databases. [Etz90] provides a good overview of some of the problems that may arise when defining ECA rules. Four problems were selected as an illustration here:

1. The multiple relationship problem:

$$Y := X + 3 \tag{1}$$
$$Y := X + 5 \tag{2}$$

2. The conflict resolution problem:
$$Y := X + 3 \text{ when } Z > 0 \tag{3}$$
$$Y := X + 5 \text{ when } Z > 5 \tag{4}$$

3. The non-determinism problem in which Y is defined by two unrelated rules:
$$Y := X + 3 \tag{5}$$
$$Y := Z + 1 \tag{6}$$

4. The halting problem due to cycles:
$$Y := X + 3 \tag{7}$$
$$X := Y + 4 \tag{8}$$

This partial list illustrates some of the problems that may arise when defining ECA rules. We require tools that assist the designer. [Kot93] provides a list of desirable tools.

Design tools could be used to deal with one of the main problems when designing an active object system, namely the infinite firing of rules due to the occurrence of cycles. It is possible to detect potential cycles at the class level, as has been illustrated for the relational case in [AWHJ92]. However, some additional problems arise in object systems due to the richness of actions that is possible. Objects may send messages to other objects while executing a method. For the user it is not possible to detect what messages are sent due to encapsulation. However, for the database designer it is possible to use compiler technology to trace the execution of methods.

Detection of cycles among rules can proceed similar to the detection of conflicts in a serializability graph. Two possible structures have been proposed. The first is an *execution graph* in which the nodes are states and the edges represent rules. Paths in the execution graph represent possible processing sequences. Branches in the execution graph represent valid alternatives in choosing the next rule to be executed. Infinite paths, due to cycles, represent non-terminating rule sets.

Another structure that can be used is a *triggering graph*. Nodes in the triggering graph are rules, while the edges of the graph represent the triggering of one rule by another. If there are no cycles in the triggering graph it can be stated that the rules in the rule set are guaranteed to terminate.

One of the major problems when dealing with rule executions in an active object space is the non-determinism of the execution of multiple rules of equal priority. The execution of two rules of equal priority in different order may lead to different final states of the object space. Three possible solutions can be envisaged. The first solution, totally ordering the rule execution, is impractical for most situations. As a second criterion, confluence has been proposed. Confluence is a conservative criterion that allows us to determine whether the final state is independent of rule ordering or not [AWHJ92]. For practical reasons, edge-confluence is used. If two rule orderings could yield different states, the user may either check the commutativity of the conflicting rules, may specify new priorities to uniquely order the conflicting rules, or may remove previously specified priorities from the conflicting rule sets. A third possibility, which is an open research problem, is the definition of a correctness criterion for rule execution that is equivalent and equally potent as the notion of serializability. Under the criterion of serializability, transactions may execute in different order and we only require that the execution be equivalent to one serial ordering. Similarly, a correctness criterion for the execution of rules is needed, in which equivalent execution orders can be defined that are all correct, even though they may lead to different final states.

Support is also necessary to detect inconsistencies in the event specification and the coupling modes. It is difficult for the user, even a rather sophisticated one, to specify events and coupling modes correctly. Therefore, a variety of efforts are currently under way to exploit the power of the ECA rules as an operational mechanism but providing user interfaces that are easier to use. By fixing some parameters and giving defaults, it is possible to cover quite a few important applications with a restricted rule mechanism.

A *rule browser* is needed that allows one to group and retrieve rules based on various criteria. These may range from the event that triggers them, to all the rules of a class, and all rules that may be involved in a cycle.

A *rule simulator* or debugger [DJP93] that visualizes the effects of changes to the database under the existing rules without applying any of the changes to the database would be very useful.

Finally,an *event log* and a *rule tracer* to keep track of all the rule invocations would round off a useful suite of tools.

10 Conclusions

Active object systems have great potential to become a standard processing paradigm for many applications. The field is, however, at the beginning of its development and no commercial systems are available yet. Therefore, we presented an overview of the issues based on some of the available prototypes.

Object-Oriented Rule Languages and Optimization Techniques

Georges Gardarin

MASI CNRS and University Paris VI, 78035 Versailles Cedex, France, and
INRIA RODIN 78153 Le Chesnay, France

Abstract. In a first part, this paper reviews rule languages that have been proposed for relational and object-oriented database management systems (OODBMSs). Relational languages based on extensions of Datalog are analyzed. Then, we concentrate on rule languages for OODBMSs. We focus on the ROL rule language, a rule language that we propose to handle persistent C++ databases. In a second part of the paper, optimization techniques for object-oriented rule language compilers are summarized. Possible transformations of algebraic trees include operation permutation, fixpoint reduction, integrity constraint addition, predicate simplification and method call optimization. Some of them are exemplified using ROL as a language to optimize itself. In case of recursive updates, additional memory-based nets are useful to accelerate query evaluation. Possible choices are Rete, Treat or Cosma networks. We discuss and compare these types of accelerators. The search strategy component is in charge of determining the best choice in the solution space of all evaluation approaches and access plans. Finally, we conclude by discussing engineering techniques to develop an integrated optimizer.

1 Introduction

It is well recognized that integration of the object-oriented and logic paradigms should become a basis for real implementation of database programming languages [BM92]. Object-orientation will provide its ability to support reusability, extensibility and data hiding. Logic will bring its formal basis, declarativeness, modularity and readability. Thus, several attempts to combine object-oriented and logic database languages have been reported in the literature [BK86, Mai86, CG88b, KL89, Abi90]. Most of these proposals are first approaches and seem rather far from real applications. Two of the most advanced proposals are IQL [Abi90] and LOGRES [CCCR+90]. A more recent paper suggests a rule object language called ROL based on production rules and object encapsulation [GF92]. Such languages are current in expert system shells and have demonstrated their capabilities in applications.

To illustrate the rule languages surveyed in this paper, we introduce a database whose schema is given Fig. 1 using an entity-relationship approach. It is composed of a road relationship between cities and maps defined by their borders. The ROAD relationship contains tuples describing the main roads between the capitals in Europe. Each road is described by a number, a reference to the city (obj(X) denotes a reference to object X) where it comes from, a reference to the city where it goes to and a map that represents graphically the roads as a list of lines. The database also contains a city entity whose objects describe each city referred to in the road relationship. The attributes of the city entity give the name of the city, its role in the state (i.e., capital, subcapital or normal), its population and a reference to a graphical representation of the city state. Each border is described in the border entity by a color chosen from among green, blue and red, and a list of lines, each being defined by a list of points.

```
Entity CITY (NAME:string, ROLE:FUNCTION, POP:int,
STATE:obj(BORDER))
Entity BORDER (COLOR:PALETTE, FORM:List of  LINE)
Relationship ROAD (RN:int, FROM:obj(CITY), TO:obj(CITY),
MAP:obj(BORDER))

Type FUNCTION : Enumeration of (Capital, Subcapital, Normal)
Type LINE : List of POINT
Type POINT : Tuple of (X:real, Y:real)
Type PALETTE : Enumeration of (Green, Blue, Red)
```

Fig. 1. An extensional database schema

A deductive database also includes an intentional database. The intentional database is defined by a set of rules of the form: $\langle action \rangle \leftarrow \langle condition \rangle$ (sometimes written in reverse direction $\langle condition \rangle \rightarrow \langle action \rangle$). A set of related rules are generally grouped into a rule module. Rule modules compute deduced tables from the extensional database. Deduced tables can be queried as normal ones. The role of the deductive DBMS is to instantiate part (as small as possible) of deduced tables necessary to answer queries. Figure 1 gives the schema of a deductive database constructing a path relationship and a state entity, derived from the extensional database given in Fig. 1. Queries can transparently reference both the extensional and the intentional database.

```
Entity STATE (CAPITAL:string, FRONTIER:obj(BORDER),
SURFACE:real)
Relationship PATH (FROM:string, TO:string, LENGTH:real)
```

Fig. 2. An intentional database schema

The implementation of object-oriented rule languages requires compiling rule modules in optimized programs of an object algebra. Translating rule programs in a graph of algebraic operators is a fairly simple task. Optimizing the graph is more difficult. Query optimization includes syntactic transformations such as operation permutation, redundant sub-query elimination, select migration through join and fixpoint using methods such as Magic Sets or Alexander [BR87a], etc. It may also include semantic transformations such as query simplification using integrity constraints [SO87] and operator properties (e.g., transitivity of equality). Recursive update optimization is one of the most difficult problem. Several methods have been proposed to optimize updates. Most of them implement a rule representation net to propagate differentially updates. RETE, TREAT and COSMA techniques are the most well known. A survey of these techniques shows that the selection of the net structure to optimize recursive update propagation should be part of the query optimization process.

This paper is organized as follows. After the current introduction, Sect. 2 gives an overview of rule languages for relational databases. Then, in Sect. 3, rule languages devised for OODBMSs are surveyed. The ROL rule language integrates the essential concepts of IQL and LOGRES, but is built for the C++ data model. The target language of a rule language optimizer is an object algebra, as detailed in Sect. 4. Section 5 reviews the various transformation techniques that should be integrated in the query optimizer. It includes syntactic and semantic transformations. Section 6 concentrates on recursive update optimization techniques, including an overview of RETE, TREAT and COSMA. Section 7 gives an overview of search strategies that can be used to select the best query graph with additional update propagation nets: exhaustive search, iterative improvement and simulated annealing are surveyed. Section 8 concludes the paper.

2 Relational Rule Languages

In the database world, rule languages have first been introduced in relational systems. In this section, we summarize and compare rule languages for relational and extended relational systems.

2.1 Overview of Languages

The basic relational rule language is DATALOG. DATALOG is a formal language derived from Horn Clauses with a fixpoint or a logic semantics. The fixpoint semantics is defined by iteration of an operator up to saturation. The logic semantics is defined as a minimal model of a set of Horn clauses. They both coïncide for pure DATALOG programs. DATALOG has been extended with negation, sets and functions. Several prototypical implementations of pure DATALOG have been done, among them [Ull88, Abi90]. DATALOG has also been extended for handling complex values in [BK86, Kup87, CG88b].

The most well known rule languages for extended relational systems is LDL, developed at MCC [Zan88, NT89]. LDL is a declarative language based on the logic programming paradigm [Llo87] with a logic semantics. It supports a rich data model that includes atoms, lists and sets. It also supports negation and updates with some form of user control. Although it can be seen as derived from PROLOG, LDL is declarative in nature while PROLOG is procedural. Thus, rules in LDL (as in the other languages studied here) are basically not ordered by the user. While the LDL compiler was designed for working with disk databases, its current implementation only works on hashed files in main memory.

Another well known rule language is RDL. It was developped on top of the SAB-RINA extended relational system [G. 86] at INRIA in France. The language was initially derived from production rule systems [BFKM85]. Thus, conditions and actions are more general than Horn clauses: conditions may include full logic formulas with disjunctions and quantifiers, and actions may be multiple. Also, RDL integrates a rich abstract data type sub-system, which allows the user to define complex values and associated methods with an inheritance facility. RDL1 is currently operational as a teaching tool and integrated in a relational database system [KMS90].

EKS is a knowledge base management system developed at ECRC. The EKS language is logic based. It uses general conditions with and/or connectives and for all/exists quantifiers. EKS also supports aggregate functions and integrity constraints. Integrity constraints are closed formulae of the language, which must remain satisfied when an update is performed. The system also offers guarded updates, with pre-condition or post-condition. A working prototype of EKS is operational in a Prolog mono-user environment [Vie90].

2.2 Comparison of Syntactical Constructs

All rule languages are derived from first order logic. As such, they use constants and variables. In DATALOG and LDL, constants are atoms and variables refer to domain values. Predicates are either relational predicates or comparison predicates. With EKS, variables also refer to domain values, but they are denoted with a full name starting with an upper-case letter. On the opposite, RDL is based on the tuple relational calculus (as SQL). A constant may be considered as a tuple (an atom is a tuple with one attribute) and variables refer to tuples in relations. The projection function is integrated in the language: X.A denotes the projection of tuple variable X on the attribute A. DATALOG and LDL are derived from pure logic programming. Thus, a rule is basically a Horn clause. On the contrary, RDL and EKS support general conditions with disjunctions and quantifiers.

With DATALOG, EKS and LDL, actions are defined by a unique predicate. Two actions require two rules. However, EKS also supports side effects in the action part, such as tuple insert. RDL is much more general and supports multiple actions. Actions are of two types : addition of tuples to database transient or persistent relations (denoted +) and deletion of tuples from database transient or persistent relations (denoted -). Full updates are considered as deletion followed by addition and denoted ±.

Figure 3 gives examples of rules in DATALOG, EKS and RDL. LDL will be similar to DATALOG for this example. The given rules construct the PATH relation derived from the ROAD relation, whose schemas were defined in Fig.s 1 and 2. They all assume the existence of an external function (flength) computing the length of a list of lines. An additional rule to replace all path going through an isolated city (a city with no other road going in or out) is added to illustrate quantification and update when possible.

DATALOG PROGRAM :

$PATH(x, y, l) \leftarrow ROAD(-, x, y, b), l = flength(b)$

$PATH(x, z, l) \leftarrow PATH(x, y, m), ROAD(-, y, z, b), l = m + flength(b)$

EKS PROGRAM :

$PATH(Origin, Extremity, Length) \leftarrow ROAD(-, Origin, Extremity, Border),$

$Length = flength(Border)$

$PATH(Origin, Extremity, Length) \leftarrow PATH(Origin, Intermediate, Lengthint),$

$ROAD(-, Intermediate, Extremity, Border), Length =$

$Lengthint + flength(Border)$

EKS Quantification and Side Effects :

$Del(PATH(Origin, Intermediate, -)), Delete(PATH(Intermediate, Extremity, -))$

$Ins(PATH(Origin, Extremity, Lenght1 + Lenght2)) \leftarrow$

$PATH(Origin, Intermediate, Length1), PATH(Intermediate, Extremity, Lenght2),$

$\neg(\exists(PATH(Origin2, Intermediate, -) or PATH(Intermediate, Extremity2, -)))$

RDL PROGRAM :

$ROAD(X) \rightarrow +PATH(X.FROM, X.TO, flength(X.MAP))$

$PATH(X) and ROAD(Y) and X.TO = Y.FROM \rightarrow$

$+PATH(X.FROM, Y.TO, X.LENGTH + flength(Y.MAP))$

RDL Quantification and Updates :

$PATH(X) and PATH(Y) and X.TO = Y.FROM and$

$(\forall PATH(Z) (X.TO \neq Z.FROM) or (Z = Y)) and$

$(\forall PATH(Z) (Z.TO \neq Y.FROM) or (Z = X)) \rightarrow$

$-PATH(X) - PATH(Y) + PATH(X.FROM, Y.TO, X.LENGTH + YLENGTH)$

Fig. 3. Example of DATALOG and RDL programs (*Del* stands for *Delete*, *Ins* stands for *Insert*)

2.3 Logic versus Fixpoint Semantics

Several equivalent semantics have been defined for rule languages. The logic semantics is derived from the minimal model approach: the semantics of a rule program is the minimal interpretation which satisfies all formulae, including the extensional facts. The membership of a fact in the minimal model of a rule program can be calculated using the proof theory approach (SLD resolution) for positive facts. SLD resolution must be extended to SLDNF (SLD resolution with negation by failure) to support negative facts and formulae.

In most rule languages (e.g., RDL), the semantics of a program P is not defined using SLDNF (this is only the case for languages derived from PROLOG [Vie86], such as the EKS's language), but as the least fixpoint of a bottom-up operator TP. TP is the immediate consequence operator. Let F be a set of facts. $TP(F)$ acts as follows:

1. Select a rule of P whose condition is satisfied in F.
2. Instantiate the variables with tuples satisfying the condition in F.
3. Apply the action for the instantiated variables.
4. Add the generated facts to F.

With pure DATALOG, TP is a monotonic operator, which yields a fixpoint from any given set F. Applying TP to the empty set yields $TP(\emptyset)$, which are the facts of P. Then, $TP(TP(\emptyset))$ are the facts of P, plus the first level consequences of the rules. Finally, the semantics of P is defined as $Sem(P) = \lim TP^n(\emptyset)$, that is the fixpoint of TP. With the current definition of RDL (called RDL1), TP is slightly modified to act as a set oriented operator. In fact, TP processes a set of tuples at a time; thus, step 2 is replaced by: "Extract the set of tuples satisfying the condition". Set and tuple semantics coincide for programs without deletion in rule actions and without negation and universal quantification in rule bodies. However, they are in general distinct.

2.4 Handling of Negation

In LDL, RDL and EKS, negation of predicates can be introduced in rule conditions. For example, if one wants to define $LongPath$ as paths that are not direct roads, one can use the following DATALOG program:

$$Path(x, y) \leftarrow Road(-, x, y, -)$$
$$Path(x, z) \leftarrow Road(-, x, y, -), Path(y, z)$$
$$LongPath(x, y) \leftarrow \neg Road(-, x, y, -), Path(x, y)$$

To define the semantics of programs with negations in rule conditions, the immediate consequence operator TP must be extended. A condition is true iff for given values of variables (e.g., $x = a, y = b$):

1. the positive facts belong to F (e.g., $Path(a, b) \in F$);
2. the negative ones do not belong to F (e.g., $Road(-, a, b, -)$ not $\in F$).

Unfortunately, with such a fixpoint operator, the semantics of a program may be non-unique. For example, the previous program completed with the rule:

$$ShortPath(x, y) \leftarrow Path(x, y), \neg LongPath(x, y)$$

may lead to different fixpoints if the rule defining $ShortPath$ is applied before the one defining $LongPath$, or reverse.

The solution to this problem is the introduction of the stratification condition. Stratification is used in LDL and RDL. It is simply a meta-rule, which says "Compute a predicate before using its negation". For instance, in the previous example the $LongPath$ predicate must be computed before applying the last rule computing $ShortPath$.

Problems arise when negation crosses recursion. For example, with the program:

$$Even("Paris")$$
$$Even(y) \leftarrow Road(-, x, y, -), \neg Even(x)$$

one cannot compute Even before using it. Such a program is not stratifiable. However, this program may have a meaning: assuming that Paris is even, it could compute all cities which can be reached by crossing an even number of roads from Paris.

Theoretical solutions have been proposed, such as inflationary or well founded semantics or preference models (see [Bid91] for a survey). Most DATALOG implementations reject such non-stratifiable programs (i.e., programs in which a predicate is defined in terms of its negation through one or several rules). RDL accepts them but gives an undetermined result.

One of the most interesting semantics to give sense to rule programs in which negation crosses recursion is the well founded semantics [GRS88]. This semantics is defined from the observation that to apply a rule with negation, it is sufficient to know an underestimate of the negative facts. One is well-known, it is the empty set. Thus, starting from $\emptyset$ as a first underestimate of the negative facts, it is possible to apply iteratively the following sequence of computation:

1. Apply the rule from the underestimate of the negative facts to compute an underestimate of the positive facts.
2. By negation of the underestimate of the positive facts, get an overestimate of the negative facts.
3. Apply the rule from the overestimate of the negative facts to get an overestimate of the positive facts.
4. By negation of the overestimate of the positive facts, get a new underestimate of the negative fact.

Beautifully, the iterative application of this procedure converges towards the computation of the negative and positive facts.

2.5 Support of Updates

LDL and RDL allow updating of the fact database. Insertion is rather straightforward in RDL: a positive predicate in the head of a rule is interpreted as an insertion action in the corresponding relation, which can be either a base or a derived relation. To focus on this semantics, RDL imposes to write a + in front of each positive predicate (+ means insert in). For example, one can write a rule as:

$$Road(X) \rightarrow +Road(X.RN, X.TO, X.FROM, X.MAP)$$

which adds reverse direction roads to the road relation.

Strangely, LDL does not permit insertion in a base relation in a rule conclusion. Rather, updates must be expressed in rule conditions, using the + prefix. For example, adding reverse direction roads in the road relation will be done using the rule:

$$Done(r) \leftarrow Road(r, x, y, z), +Road(r, y, x, z).$$

This approach probably comes from the PROLOG origin of LDL, with backward interpretation of rules.

Deletion, which removes tuples from base relations, is written in rule heads in RDL. It is a special action denoted with a minus. Thus, suppressing reverse roads in the road relation is done with the rule:

$$Road(X) \rightarrow -Road(X.RN, X.TO, X.FROM, X.MAP).$$

In LDL, deletion are written in rule conditions, as follows:

$$Done(r) \leftarrow Road(r, x, y, z), -Road(r, y, x, z).$$

Note that in RDL, deletion can be seen as negation in rule heads. The fixpoint operator TP must be extended to capture deletion and more generally updates. It can be extended by deleting the generated facts in the head or tail predicates prefixed by minus. Unfortunately, TP is no longer monotonic, which yields undeterministic semantics. The fixpoint may depend on the rule application order (procedurally); even worst, the fixpoint may not exist (loop), as for example with the rules:

$$ROAD(X) \rightarrow +ROAD(X.RN, X.TO, X.FROM, X.MAP)$$
$$ROAD(X) \rightarrow -ROAD(X.RN, X.TO, X.FROM, X.MAP)$$

The determinism of RDL1 programs has been studied in [Abi90].

An additional feature of both RDL and LDL is that multiple updates are possible in rules. While LDL offers special control structures to sequence updates (denoted by a semi-colon: $u1; u2$ means apply update $u1$ before update $u2$), RDL defines a set oriented semantics for updates, which is order independent. When applying an action expression $+u1 - u2$ to a relation R, the RDL interpreter computes the set of tuples to insert in R (denoted R^+) and the set of tuples to delete from R (denoted R^-). It then performs:

$$R := R - R^- \cup (R^+ - R^-)$$

independently of the order of the update specifications. This is powerful and makes updates order independent.

2.6 Support of Complex Values

Various extensions of DATALOG for supporting complex values have been proposed [BK86, Kup87, CG88b]. Complex value support is a step towards development of languages for OODBMSs. However, these systems require the support of object identity, which is not integrated in the languages studied in this section. As an example, LDL supports multi-valued attributes, which can be implemented as sets or lists. Sets are derived from relations using the grouping construct, denoted $\langle \rangle$ in rule heads. For example, the nesting of a relation B on attribute x is performed by the rule : $P(x, \langle y \rangle) \leftarrow B(x, y)$. Special predicates, such as set equality, membership, union, etc., are built in LDL. LDL also supports lists. Lists are manipulated through the usual functors car and cdr, denoted $[car \mid cdr]$. External functions are also possible in LDL (written in C). They can be used to manipulate complex objects.

LDL offers an abstract data type (ADT) toolbox to define and manipulate complex values [GV89]. The ADT toolbox allows users to specify complex domains for relations using the list constructor and the LISP or C languages. Complex domains are built with the list constructor and are defined within an inheritance hierarchy. Functions associated with a complex domain are programmed in LISP or C and recorded in a function database. A library of predefined complex domains and associated functions comes with the system, including sets with special functions defined on them: equality, membership, union, intersection , etc.

2.7 Rule Execution Control

DATALOG is a theoretical language, which does not offer any control structure to the user, as the cut in PROLOG. However, LDL, which handles practical applications, feels the need for user control. User control is introduced in LDL as compound predicates. This includes the following constructs:

1. sequence: $p \leftarrow p1; p2$
2. conditional: $p \leftarrow if(c \ then \ p1 \ else \ p2)$
3. saturation: $p \leftarrow forever(p1, p2)$
4. choice: $OnePath(x, y) \leftarrow Path(x, y), choice((x), (y))$

In a more general way, RDL supports user control as meta- rules. Each rule in RDL is given a name. A meta-rule may be associated to a rule module to describe an explicit ordering among rules. The $BLOC(rule1, rule2, \ldots)$ construct specifies that the given rules must be executed up to fixpoint without any pre-imposed order whereas the $SEQ(rule1, rule2, \ldots)$ construct specifies that the given rules must be executed up to fixpoint in the given order. The $BLOC$ and SEQ constructs can be nested to specify a sequence of rules or blocks of rules. For example, a valid RDL program is:

$$r1 : p1 \rightarrow +p$$
$$r2 : p2 \rightarrow +p$$
$$r3 : p3 \rightarrow -p$$
$$SEQ(BLOC(r1, r2), r3)$$

The meta-rule specifies that $r1$ and $r2$ can be executed in any order, but that $r3$ must be executed after $r1$ and $r2$.

2.8 Summary

Figure 4 summarizes the main features of the languages discussed above. Clear differences appear, mainly at a syntactical level. Pred means simple predicate, while Side means side effects through specific commands (e.g., insert).

3 Object-Oriented Rule Languages

A great number of attempts to combine object-oriented and deductive databases have been reported in the literature [Mai86, CG88b, KL89, Abi90]. Most of these proposals are first approaches and do not support full object orientation; furthermore, some seem far from a possible implementation and are even not fully specified. Recently, three rule languages have been proposed that seem to integrate in a cleaner way the object-oriented and deductive paradigms. In the sequel, we concentrate on these three languages, which are IQL [Abi90], LOGRES [CCCR+90] and ROL [GF92]. While IQL and LOGRES are object-oriented extension of DATALOG, ROL is a rule language derived from RDL extended to support object orientation with a C++ data model.

Features	DATALOG	LDL	RDL	EKS
Class	N	N	N	NÉ
Relation	Y	Y	Y	Y
List	N	Y	Y	N
Set	N	Y	N	N
Variable	Domain	Domain	Tuple	Domain
Condition	Horn	Horn	General	General
Action	Pred	Pred	Expression	Pred or Side
Update	N	Condition	Action	Side
Control	N	Compound	Meta-rule	Guards
Semantics	Fixpoint	Fixpoint Strat.	Fixpoint Strat.	SLDNF

Fig. 4. Comparison of rule languages for relational databases

3.1 Object Model

A database schema is a specification of a set of types and object extensions (i.e., containers). IQL and LOGRES integrate their own object model to define database schema. This model includes both values and objects. ROL is based on the C++ object model. C++ uses the class construct to support both types and extensions. In IQL and LOGRES, a type is built using a type expression from a set of primitive types, e.g., integer, real, string and Boolean. Type expressions apply type constructors to existing types to derive new types. A constructor is a generic type, i.e., a type parametrized by other types. Classical type constructors are the tuple, set, bag (or multiset) and list (or sequence) templates. For example, one may define a line as a list of tuples with two attributes (X and Y) using a similar syntax in LOGRES and IQL:

$$LINE = \langle [X : Real, Y : Real] \rangle.$$

In addition, IQL supports the union or intersection of types to define new types.

Containers in IQL are either classes or relations. A class is a container for a set of object identifiers, the objects having values of the class type. A relation is a container for a set of tuples of the corresponding type. LOGRES is very similar, except that relations are considered as associations between objects. Classes and associations are declared in separated sections rather than using the class and relation key-words. Associations correspond to relationships between objects and enforce referential integrity. For example, declaring a class CITY and a relation ROAD (maps are omitted for simplicity) will be done as follows in LOGRES:

```
Classes section
CITY = (NAME : String , POP : Int )
Association Section
ROAD = (RN : Int, FROM : CITY, TO: CITY, LENGTH : Real).
```

In a simpler way, ROL uses the class construct of C++. Thus, a full definition of the types and extensions of our example database will be done as follows in ROL:

```
Class ROAD int RN, CITY* FROM, CITY* TO , BORDER* MAP;
Class CITY  String NAME, FUNCTION ROLE Int POP, BORDER*
                    STATE;
Class  BORDER PALETTE COLOR, List<LINE> FORM;
Class LINE  List<POINT> POINTS;
Class POINT Real X, Real Y;
        Enum Capital, Subcapital, Normal FUNCTION ;
Enum Green, Blue, Red PALETTE.
```

3.2 Handling Inheritance

In object oriented-databases, methods are polymorphic functions which apply to objects of certain classes. Methods can be attached to classes or defined independently of them. Methods are appropriate over a range of parameter types. Overloading resolution chooses the appropriate method based on the runtime type of arguments. In IQL, ROL and LOGRES, methods are functions attached to classes satisfying the typing constraints given as the method signatures. In all languages, method can be set-valued.

Problems arise with methods when inheritance is introduced. In IQL and LOGRES, inheritance is a relationship established between classes. In LOGRES, "$C1$ ISA C" means that the objects of the sub-class $C1$ are also objects of the super-class C. IQL may also handle inheritance through union types, specifying for example that class C is equal to $C1$ union $C2$. In all languages, objects of class $C1$ may have more properties than objects of class C. In all languages, the inheritance is structural and behavioural, which means that $C1$ inherits both the structure and the methods of C. To illustrate that kind of inheritance, let us introduce two sub-classes of $BORDER$ representing circular borders ⟨ CIRCLE ⟩ and polygonal borders ⟨ POLYGON ⟩. In IQL and LOGRES, one should declare:

CIRCLE ISA BORDER
POLYGON ISA BORDER

while it should be done when defining the subclass in ROL:

CLASS POLYGON : BORDER { ...}.

Circles and polygons will then be encoded as list of lines, with a color. It is possible to add more attributes to circles or polygons, for example:

CIRCLE { POINT CENTER },

which states that a circle has a center.

An important property for an object-oriented rule language is the ability to perform type checking at compile time, i.e., static type checking. Checking that a method call is defined for all possible parameter types and subtypes at compile time avoids runtime errors and enables efficient execution. IQL seems to be the only type safe object-oriented rule language, at least on paper.

3.3 Deductive Rules

In LOGRES and IQL, rules are constructed in the standard way, using positive or negative literals $L, L1, L2, ..., Ln$. The structure of a rule is:

$$L \leftarrow L1, L2, ..., Ln.$$

Positive literals are truth-valued predicates obtained from terms using various types of equality, such as:

- $t1 = t2$ for value equality,
- $t1 == t2$ for object identity.

or membership, such as:

- $t1 \in t2$ for set membership,
- $t2(t1))$ for complex term membership.

A term is either a constant of a primitive type, or a variable, or any method or constructor applied to a term. Terms are typed; correct typing is required for constructed terms. LOGRES and IQL seem very similar for rules.

On the opposite, rules in ROL are perceived as productions of the form:

$$L1, L2, ..., Ln \rightarrow L.$$

L can be positive (denoted $+C$) meaning an insertion in class C through the object constructing method (i.e., new), negative (denoted $-C$) meaning a deletion through the delete method, or neutral (i.e., $\pm C$), which means a replacement of all objects that satisfy the condition by the new objects created in class C; the latter facility gives ROL the possibility of supporting rewrite rules. Collection valued attributes are handled through built-in methods attached to the collection template (e.g., Contains for Sets).

A few differences can be isolated between IQL and LOGRES, which both are based on domain calculus and domain variables. LOGRES requires the naming of attribute variables in associations or classes; variables without names are considered as tuple or full object variables. IQL links variables to attributes through positions, as DATALOG. In LOGRES, object identifier variables are defined using a special attribute name, denoted self. Object identifiers are denoted by a variable prefixed by a star in IQL. Object creation is done through non ranged variables.

On the contrary, full object variables are natural in ROL. Attributes may be reached using the attribute name as a projection function, e.g., $X.A$, where X is a variable and A an attribute. However, as a term may be a data construction using any template, domain variables can be used, e.g., inside a tuple construction. This approach is more general than that of LOGRES; a variable may refer to any data construction, going from a primitive ADT sort to complex constructions.

To illustrate the power of object oriented rule languages such as IQL, one may construct a derived class which gives the set of first points of border lines corresponding to a given color. The structure of the derived class is:

$SAMECOLOR\,[COLOR : PALETTE, POINTS : \{POINT\}].$

The IQL rules deriving objects in SAMECOLOR may be written as follows:

$SAMECOLOR(*o, C, X) \leftarrow BORDER(C, Y), X = \emptyset$
$SAMECOLOR(*o, C, Z) \leftarrow SAMECOLOR(*o, C, X), BORDER(C, B),$
$\quad B = [H \mid T], H = [P \mid S], Z = X \cup \{P\}$

The first rule constructs an object of a given color extracted from BORDER, with a corresponding empty set of points. It illustrates object creation, known as object invention in IQL. The second rule extracts in a recursive manner the first point of the first line of each border and adds it to the correctly colored set of points (using the Union operator). The ROL declarations and rules to derive the same class are the following:

$class\,SAMECOLOR\,\{PALETTE\,COLOR, Set\langle POINT \rangle\,POINTS\}$
$BORDER(B) \rightarrow +SAMECOLOR(B.COLOR, \emptyset)$
$SAMECOLOR(S)\,and\,BORDER(B)\,and\,S.COLOR = B.COLOR\,and$
$P = First(First(B.LINES)) \rightarrow \pm SAMECOLOR(S.COLOR, \{P\})$

Object invention being clearly an insertion of an object denoted by $+$, no token variable is necessary in ROL.

3.4 Updates

The three rule languages that have been considered allow for full updates, i.e., insertion, deletion and modification of values and objects. In IQL and LOGRES, values are deleted using negative predicates in rule heads. New objects are created through the use of invented object identifiers, which are unbound object type variables in rule heads (denoted self in LOGRES and $*x$ in IQL). Note that a new object is created only if no object satisfies the requirements (i.e., the other property values). Existing objects are deleted using negation of classes in rule heads. In a cleaner way, ROL uses predicates prefixed by $+$ to create a new object, by $-$ to delete an existing object and by $\pm$ to replace one or more objects. This makes explicit the semantics of object invention, rather than using unbound variables and gives the language the possibility of supporting rewrite rules.

All languages support the notion of modules. LOGRES introduces interesting modes for applying modules to a database state. The RIDI (Rule Invariant Data Invariant) mode corresponds to normal query processing. The RADI (Rule Addition Data Invariant) mode is used to add new rules to the database. The RIDV (Rule Invariant Data Variant) mode is used to update the extensional database. The RADV (Rule Addition Data Variant) mode is used to add new rules and to update the extensional database. Rule deletion modes are also considered in LOGRES.

3.5 Semantics

The semantics of an object-oriented rule program is defined similarly that of a DAT-
ALOG rule program, i.e., through a fixpoint computation. For handling negation and
collections, stratification is generally admitted. When updates and modules are supported, defining the semantics of a rule program becomes a complex issue. It can be
computed as follows. Let E be extensional database states and I intentional database
states. The semantics of a rule module is defined as the binary relation $W(E, I)$, which
is unchanged when applying the immediate consequence operator (i.e., a rule with a
valuation satisfying the condition variables) to all Is. A program is defined as a set of
modules, with an order of application. The semantics of a rule program may be seen as
some composition of the W's binary relations. It is deterministic if E functionally determines I. To avoid ambiguities in programs without updates and make W a function,
it is possible to stratify rule modules. Stratification consists in ordering rules such that
rules computing positive predicates and collections (e.g., sets, lists) be applied before
using negation of these predicates or collections.

4 Object-Oriented Target Algebra

Traditionally, a query optimizer translates a rule program (e.g., a DATALOG program)
in a tree or a graph of relational algebra operations and optimizes the graph by successive
transformations. Most authors propose a similar approach for an object-oriented rule
compiler-optimizer. However, the algebra has to be extended to support complex objects
and methods. In this section, we propose an object-oriented target algebra, which is called
OOA (Object-Oriented Algebra). OOA is an extended relational algebra to support
method calls and objects. This language has been chosen for its power of abstraction from
the physical implementation and from the query. OOA operators can easily represent
rule programs. For example, a ROL query is an OOA expression that maps collections
into a collection as defined in [SLPW89].

4.1 Valuable Expressions and Conditions

The Codd's relational algebra allows the user to reference attribute expressions in query
results or conditions. In an object-oriented environment, it is necessary to extend attribute
expressions to path expressions and method calls. A path expression is a sequence of
attributes of the form $A_1.A_2 \ldots A_n$ such that A_i is a pointer to objects of the class whose
A_{i+1} is a member. A method expression is a sequence of the form $F_1.F_2 \ldots F_n$ that is
applied to objects, where F_i is a method returning an object to which F_{i+1} applies. A
method expression is a generalization of a path expression. More generally, the algebra
refers to valuable expressions, which are either constants, attribute names, or method
expressions applied to object pointers. Arithmetic expressions can be used as specific
cases of methods. Examples of valuable expressions are:

```
C.Name // Simple attribute expression
B.Form.First // Simple method expression
C.State.Form // Path expression
C.State.Form.First.First // Method expression
```

An elementary condition is either a Boolean valuable expression or a predicate of the form $\langle ValuableExpresssion\rangle\langle Comparator\rangle\langle ValuableExpression\rangle$. A comparator is chosen among $\{=, <, \leq, >, \geq, \neq, like, in, between\}$. A complex condition is a conjunction of disjunction of elementary conditions.

4.2 Basic Operations

The basic operations of the proposed algebra are extensions of Codd's algebra with path and method expressions, as defined for example in [GV89]. They apply to collections of objects (i.e., set, list, etc.) or to class extentions being considered as a special type of collections. These operations are:

1. Restrict which produces, from a collection, a collection of the same type and whose objects satisfy a (possibly complex) condition.
2. Project which produces a new collection from a given one by computing the expressions of source attributes as target attributes.
3. Join which may be defined as a Cartesian product of two collections followed by a restrict.
4. Set operations including union, difference, and intersection.

Sometimes a sequence of basic operations can be implemented efficiently in a single algorithm (e.g., restrict followed by project and n-ary join). Consequently, we define a macro algebra with compound operations. The compound operations are the n-ary union (denoted union*, which performs the union of N collections) and the n-ary join (denoted join*, which performs the Cartesian product of N collections followed by a restriction). They also include the search operation, which is a composition of restrictions, n-ary joins and projections. These compound operations are close to generalized tuple calculus expressions referring to collections of objects and methods. They provide the optimizer with the necessary degree of freedom to optimize correctly the queries. Logic calculus is a good starting point for query optimization since it provides an optimizer with only the basic properties of the query; optimization opportunities may become hidden in a particular sequence of algebra operators like projection, restriction, join [JK84].

One question which arises when dealing with collections of objects is the identification of the objects resulting from an algebraic operation. We choose the view that classes are object factories while normal collections (i.e., set, list, bag, array) are not. Thus, if the result is declared as a class, new object identifiers are created using the new method of the class. On the countrary, objects in normal collections are not identified by new identifiers. Operations between collections and classes are possible: object identifiers are created if the result is a class, ignored otherwise.

4.3 Iterative Operation and Fixpoint

Recursive queries can be easily expressed by a fixpoint operator as shown in [Ull88, CGL86, IW87]. This operator simply produces the saturation of a collection computed recursively by an algebra expression. More generally, iterative algebra expression computes recursively a collection by applying at each cycle a sequence of OOA operations.

The stop condition is the saturation of a collection that may be expressed as the absence of objects in a differential collection. We introduce a specific method IsEmpty to check wether a collection is empty. A stop condition in a fixpoint is more generally a logical expression (using not, and, or) of Boolean method calls. Thus, the syntax of a fixpoint operation is:

$$\langle OutputCollection \rangle = FIXPOINT(\langle InputCollection \rangle; \langle StopCondition \rangle)$$
$$DO \{\langle OOAOperations \rangle\};$$

For example, the fixpoint of the PATH class may be computed by the program of Fig. 5.

```
class PATH (ROAD* FROM, ROAD* TO);
set NEW, NEWD (ROAD* FROM, ROAD* TO);
PATH =  ∅ ;
NEW = PROJECT(ROAD R; R.FROM, R.TO) ;
BETTER-THAN = FIXPOINT(PATH, NEW;  Not NEW.IsEmpty)
DO  PATH = UNION(PATH, NEW) ;
    NEWD = JOIN(PATH P, ROAD R;P.TO=R.FROM;P.FROM, R.TO);
    NEW = DIFFERENCE(NEWD; PATH) ; ;
```

Fig. 5. A fixpoint computation program

4.4 Query Graph

An OOA program can be represented as a query graph, which is a generalization of a relational algebra tree. Edges represent persistent or transient collections moving from nodes to nodes. Nodes represent operations such as restrict, project, join, union, etc., and more generally search. An operation has a list of input edges that correspond to persistent or transient classes or collections generated by previous operations. An operation has also a list of output edges that correspond to generated results. A fixpoint operation is translated as a cycle.

To be able to manipulate a query graph using a rule language such as ROL, we represent it using three classes:

- The NODE class represents nodes with input and output edges, with further references to node descriptors.
- The QUALIFICATION class represents the qualification of operations such as JOIN and RESTRICT.
- The EXPRESSION class represents method expressions resulting from operations such as PROJECT.

Node descriptors are references to object in the QUALIFICATION or EXPRESSION classes. Figure 6 gives a definition of the GRAPH class. It will be used in the following to illustrate rules written in ROL to transform query graphs.

```
Class NODE
    Operation OPER ;  // Operation code of a node
    Set<NODE*> Input ; // Input edges
    NODE* Output ; // Ouput edge
    QUALIFICATION* Qual ; // Operation qualification if any
    EXPRESSION* Exp ; // Result expression if any
```

Fig. 6. Possible representation of a query graph

5 Transformations to Optimize OOA Programs

In this section, we survey the query optimization techniques that have to be integrated within an object-oriented rule compiler. A query and its associated set of rules is first transformed in an OOA graph. Logical query optimization consists in transforming the query graph using syntactic or semantic transformation rules. Physical query optimization annotates the query graph with selected indexes and algorithms at each node. We only review the logical optimization techniques.

5.1 Syntactic Transformations

Logical query optimization requires to transform the graph to generate equivalent graphs that might be more efficiently executed than the original one. Syntactic transformations concentrate on the ordering of operations, without any knowledge of the semantics of methods and operators. In this section, we review the main syntactic transformation rules.

Composition and Decomposition of Operations. Search operations are complex operations that can be decomposed in more elementary operations such as union, restrict and join. Even a restrict operation with a complex criteria involving conjunctions and disjunctions can be decomposed in cascading restrictions or unions of restrictions. In the reverse direction, simple operations can be composed in complex search. Composition and decomposition of operations generate various execution plans. Simple heuristics may be used to reduce the number of combinations, such as grouping the operations dealing with the same class, etc.

Permutation of Operations. Permutation rules push constraints on classes stored in the database and focus the query on relevant facts. Permutation rules are heuristic and do not guarantee a better processing plan; their role is to propagate constraints on base relations as much as possible. They correspond to well known heuristics such as apply selections before joins. Joins can also be permuted. It is more difficult to choose the right ordering of joins, although semi-joins can be performed first. Permutation techniques are not different from well known relational optimization techniques [GV89]. Figure 7 illustrates the rule pushing search through union in the ROL rule language. Note that in ROL, variables can be used to refer objects created in rule heads.

```
Search-through-Union -Pushing-Rule :
if    NODE(X) and NODE(Y) and X.OPER = SEARCH and
      Y.OPER = UNION and Y.Output = X
then   R = NODE( UNION,   U,V, X.Output)
     + U = NODE(SEARCH, Choice(Y.Input),R,X.Qual,X.Exp)
     + R = NODE(SEARCH, Rest(Y.Input),R,X.Qual,X.Exp)
```

Fig. 7. Example of search and union permutation rule

Common Sub-Query Isolation. Common sub-queries correspond to pending part of the query graph that are duplicated. They should be isolated and replaced by a common sub-graph with a unique output to avoid performing twice the same work. One difficulty is that common sub-query can be generated when decomposing search expressions.

Fixpoint Reduction. In the case of recursive predicates, the permutation between operators cannot be done so easily. However, in cases where a restrict qualification is not conflicting with joins involved in the fixpoint loop (i.e., when the restricted attributes are not involved in joins), a simple push of restriction before recursion is possible using the Aho and Ullman's method [UA79]. In more complex cases, the application of a rewriting method such as Magic Sets [BMSU86] or Alexander [RLK86] is recognized as useful. They transform recursive expressions into expressions that focus on relevant facts. Such methods can be implemented directly on the operation graph [FG91]. This avoids unnecessary translation from algebra to logic, and from logic to algebra. The transformation method is applied to an algebraic expression E(R). As stated in [IW87], an algebraic structure so obtained enables us to get more information about the mechanisms of recursion, and to get more properties of operations. Note also that the composition of operation rule (e.g., the search merging rule) is a typical case of rule that takes advantage of being applied more than once (e.g., before and after pushing selections through fixpoints).

One difficulty with fixpoint reduction in an object-oriented context is dealing with methods. When restrction conditions bears upon result of methods, it is very difficult to push restrictions before recusion. The transformation should take into account the semantic of the method. For example, in the case of path computation, if the condition is $path.lenght < 50$ and if the recursion only increases the lenght attribute, it is not necessary to take into account initial path with lenght greater than 50. Thus, the restriction can be pushed before recursion. More general results are needed concerning this problem.

5.2 Semantic Transformations

Traditionally in query optimizers, decisions are made mainly based on syntactic knowledge and data structures. However, this is not sufficient in OODBMSs, where users can define their own structures, their own methods and even their own operators. Thus, it is useful that the query optimizer support the introduction of new query transformation rules. In this section, we briefly demonstrate through examples that several types of semantics rules should be introduced as transformation rules on query graphs and search qualifications.

Abstract Data Type Function Rewriting. Certain queries are expressed over well-understood generic abstract data types, such as sets, lists, arrays and bags. These structures have natural algebraic operations (e.g., inclusion, intersection, etc.), and privileged predicates (equality, membership, etc.) associated with them. The properties of these algebraic operations and predicates comprise the implicit semantic knowledge. It defines properties of system constructs, which can be known in the system Let us assume for example that a Min method is defined on sets to compute the minimum value of a set. Then, it is well known that the minimum of the minimums of two sets is the minimum of the union set.

Semantic properties of user defined methods can also be introduced as rewriting rules [GL92a]. One further difficulty is estimating the cost for method computation. A cost estimate could be given by the method implementor. In a more sophisticated system, it could be derived from the method code or from execution samples.

Integrity Constraint Based Enrichment. A second kind of semantic knowledge concerns integrity constraints. Choosing appropriate integrity constraints that simplify query processing is a difficult task. Integrity constraints may be added to queries as additional restrictions. For example, to add a constraint specifying that the lenght method applied to a border gives a result between 0 and 120, we simply add the restriction $Border.Length > 0$ and $Border.Length < 120$. The problem is then to determine if a query graph with this restriction (or part of it) is less costly than a query graph without it. Whether it is useful or not to add integrity constraint equation(s) should be determined when choosing a query graph in the search space of all possible query plan. Note that adding integrity constraints may further make applicable certain transformation rules. For example, if the query also state $Border.Length > 120$, then an operator simplification rule should infer an empty answer.

Operator Property Based Simplification. A third kind of semantic knowledge concerns the semantic of operators. In object oriented systems, operators can be overloaded or specific operators can be defined. Thus, it is useful to be able to introduce rules to use the properties of operators in query optimization. An example of such a rule is the transitivity of equality. It can be introduced by the knowledge plugged in the system that $a = b$, and $b = c$ is equivalent to $a = b$ and $a = c$. Such transformations greatly increase the search space of the optimizer.

6 Recursive Update Optimization

A rule program performing updates (i.e., insertions or deletions) of classes that appear in rule conditions is said to perform recursive updates. The naïve evaluation of recursive updates requires recursive evaluation of rule conditions for modified classes. Data structures to memorize temporary results of rule conditions and to propagate updates have been proposed in the literature. They may be viewed as data flow graphs where input nodes are classes that correspond to predicates in the bodies of rules and output nodes correspond to predicates in rule heads. In an object-oriented environment, instances of such predicates can be maintained in main memory as lists of object identifiers with possibly associated attribute values.

6.1 Principles of Memorization Algorithms

Algorithms that use a memorization structure to propagate updates implement a generalization of semi-naive evaluation. They differ from one another by the choice of the memorised temporary predicates and by the mechanism of propagation in the graph. More precisely, the choice of the memorized temporary relations may be:

- Condition oriented. Some heuristics determine the memorized nodes without taking into account the foreseeable migrations of data w.r.t. the rule heads.
- Action oriented. The choice of memorized data is advised by updated predicates in rule heads and migrations of data.

The propagation mechanisms may be:

- Static. The materializations are performed before the execution. When the program runs, changes are automatically propagated in the entire structure.
- Dynamic. The materializations are deferred and only performed when required for the first time; propagation of the changes takes into account the control strategy.

In the following, we present some algorithms that use memorization techniques. They are devoted to optimize incremental computation of extensions of Datalog programs with non-deterministic semantic. RETE and TREAT are condition oriented, and use static propagation; COSMA is action oriented and use dynamic propagation.

6.2 The RETE Algorithm

The RETE match algorithm [For82] has been proposed to optimize the execution of the AI production rule programs in main memory. Several algorithms such as DBRete and DBCond [SLR88] have adapted RETE to the execution of production rule programs in the database context. These RETE like algorithms use a data flow network in which the inputs are the classes invoked in the bodies of the rules. For each rule, selection conditions in the body are evaluated against the database. The corresponding nodes in the network are associated with materialized temporary classes. When an elementary condition is common to several rules, it is only materialized once.

More precisely, let r be a rule with a conjunctive condition, $(c_0, c_1, \ldots c_n)$ an evaluation order of the elementary conditions of its body and $(C_0, C_1, \ldots C_n)$ the sequence of associated base classes. For i varying from 0 to n, RETE materializes the set of objects satisfying the select operation defined by c_i in a structure referred as α-memory. Let α_i be this memory. These α-nodes are entries to a "comb-like" data structure. A binary operation node in that comb is associated to a β-memory materializing the class bi defined by $(c_0, \ldots, c_{i-1}) \wedge c_i$. When an update to C_i arises, it is propagated to all β-memories, on the path $(\alpha_i, \beta_i, \ldots, \beta_n)$. The propagation mechanism is static as defined above.

The RETE algorithm is interesting to avoid evaluating several times queries against databases when classes referenced in conditions are updated. It can be extended to complex conditions involving methods. However, it is costly in memory. Thus, a rule optimizer could choose a more sophisticated algorithm that does not instantiate all conditions in main memory.

6.3 The TREAT Algorithm

The TREAT algorithm [Mir87] uses a data flow network similar to RETE. This network has the same inputs and outputs as a RETE network. However, there is no intermediate node. Only the initial selections and the final condition are memorized. The algorithm makes assumption that the system supplies object identifiers. Object identifiers of the source objects are recorded with the objects satisfying the final condition, which allows a direct propagation of deletions. The propagation mechanism is static. The changes on the inputs are propagated one by one.

More precisely, let r be a rule with elementary conditions $\{c_0, c_1, \ldots, c_n\}$ in the body. TREAT memorizes $\{\alpha_0, \alpha_1, \ldots, \alpha_n\}$, the set of associated α-memories, plus the set γ of instantiations of the body of r. When a change arises on some entry, say α_i, γ is updated. If the change is a deletion, then using object identifiers of the deleted objects, γ is directly modified. Else, the changes induced on γ are computed from the change on α_i and the set α_j, $j \neq i$ of the other α-memories.

The main advantage of the TREAT algorithm with respect to RETE is to reduce the amount of required memory. However, it requires recomputation of intermediate join. This can be very costly, for example in the case of rules with methods.

6.4 The COSMA Algorithm

The COSMA algorithm [FRS92] uses a data flow network that is similar to the previous ones. However, only effective modifications are recorded in output nodes, which requires a slight extension of the RETE network. For each rule, the inputs are both the classes associated with the elementary conditions in the body (restricted input classes) and the predicates in the head (output classes). Each rule is associated with output nodes that memorizes the effective set of objects to insert or delete for each updated predicate.

The choice for memorizing some intermediate temporary classes in the graph is action oriented and takes into account the explicit control (if any). As TREAT, the algorithm assumes that the system supplies tuple identifiers. Thus, COSMA can be seen as a kind of dynamic TREAT.

More precisely, let r be a rule. A network is created with the rule body and head predicates, making possible the maintenance of α_i memories. δ_k memories may be maintained for head predicates, to memorize the effective updates to perform. A preprocessing phase analyzes how do variables migrate within predicates from the heads to the body of r. This syntactic information advises the memorization heuristic. It allows to isolate subexpressions in the rule body that produce a result useful for the computation of the output memory and that can be efficiently maintained when changes arise on the input classes of r.

6.5 Choice of Classes to Materialize

As shown above, recursive updates may benefit from the maintenance of intermediate memories, say α_i for selection conditions, β_j for join conditions, γ for the whole rule condition and δ_k for the rule heads effective updates. The choice of instances to maintain in main memory is not obvious. It depends on the rule program and the available propagation algorithms.

More simply, given a query graph representing a rule program with recursive updates, each node corresponding to a transient class can be maintained in main memory. When a class is materialized, object identifiers of the source objects can be maintained. Thus, if a deletion of a source object appears, the deletion can be directly propagated. More generally, materializing a temporary class avoids full recomputation of a condition against the database when a recursive update occurs. However, materializing a class incurs an additional cost in memory. Thus, the choice of materializing a class is a tradeoff between time and space.

As a synthesis, we could consider that a given query plan can be extended with materialization annotations. A materialization annotation attached to an intermediate class means that the objects of that class with source object identifiers should be maintained in main memory using differential propagation algorithms. Materialization annotations are similar to access path annotations and may change the cost of a given query plan. They should be considered for query plan optimization.

7 Search Strategies to Select a Query Plan

A query plan can be perceived as a query graph with physical annotations. Annotations describe the materialization policies and the selected access methods with indexes for each class edge; they specify the selected algorithms for each operation node. With all the possible logical optimizations and the possible variations in annotations, the number of query plans corresponding to a given query over a large set of rules is in general very large.

The problem of query optimization is to find the best query plan. It can be decomposed in two sub-problems. The first sub-problem consists of generating query plans.

This can be done using a transformative approach, which starts with a given query plan and transforms it by applying rules. An alternative is to use a generative approach, which generates directly good plans. The second sub-problem is to select the best plan among those generated. The plan selection component of a query optimizer is basically a search algorithm in the space of query plans. A plan can be generated by transforming a current plan using a set of transformation rules; a cost can be given to a plan using a cost function. Specifying the cost function is beyond the scope of this paper. The problem we would like now to address is that of selecting the best plan.

Several search strategies have been proposed to explore the search space of query plans [SG88, IC90]. Object-oriented implementations of several of them are nicely described in [LV91]. In exhaustive search, the entire search space is investigated for the optimal solution. The system R optimizer [SAC$^+$79] exemplifies a restricted case of exhaustive search in which only binary trees without Cartesian products are considered for joins. The search strategy is improved using a branch and bound algorithm. In randomized search, start solutions are first selected to sample the search space. Then, the start solutions are improved until a local optimal solution is obtained. Two variations of randomized search are iterative improvement [SG88] and simulated annealing [IW87]. In the following, we give specific methods for implementing variations of exhaustive search, iterative improvements and simulating annealing.

7.1 Exhaustive Search

Full exhaustive search starts from the initial plan derived from the parser, then applies all possible transformations in sequence and finally select the best plan among all the generated ones. An algorithm performing some kind of exhaustive search is given in Fig. 8. The Optimal method is supposed to return the plan having a minimum cost among those considered. However, the search time must be limited to avoid looping, for example by the maximum time allowed to the exploration of the search space. StopCond returns true when the search time is exhausted.

```
Function Exhaustive(Query)
 { p:=Parse(Query); //Set the intial plan
   S:=p; //S is the set of  all investigated plans
   while not StopCond()
   { p':=Transform(p); //Apply a transformation rule
     if  p' not in S then
     { p ::= p';
        Insert(S,p'); //Maintain the set of investigated plan
     }
   }
   return Optimal(S); //Select best among all generated plans
}
```

Fig. 8. Exhaustive search algorithm

7.2 Iterative Improvement

Iterative improvement selects initial plans at random in the search space. From an initial state, it applies profitable transformations also selected at random from the applicable rules, to reach a local minimum. The best traversed plan is kept as the optimum The selected initial plans must represent a good sample of the search space. Several solutions exist to generate the initial plans. The algorithm corresponding to iterative improvement is given in Fig. 9. We start from the plan generated by the parser; the next plan to explore is generated by a random perturbation of the parsed query (Random method). As with exhaustive search, StopCond returns true when the maximum allowed search time is exhausted. The number of profitable transformations that can be applied is limited to MaxMoves, which can depend on the complexity of the query.

```
Function Iterative(Query)
 { p:=Parse(Query);  //Set the initial plan
   S:= ; //S is the set of locally optimum plans
   while not StopCond()
   { nmoves:=0;
      while nmoves < MaxMoves(Query)
      { p':=Transform(p); //Apply a transformation rule
         if  Cost(p') < Cost(p) then
         { p::=p';
            nmoves::=nmoves + 1;
         }
         Insert(S, p'); //Maintain the set of interesting plans
         p:=Random(Parse(Query)); //Generate a new initial plan
                                  //at random
      }
   }
   return Optimal(S); //Select best among all generated ones
 }
```

Fig. 9. Iterative improvement search algorithm

7.3 Simulated Annealing

Simulated annealing starts from the initial plan and tries to improve it as iterative improvement does. However, a temporary deterioration in cost of the plan is permitted to explore in a better way the search space. A temperature is defined for the modified plan, which varies from a maximum value to 0. At 0, the system is frozen and only profitable moves are accepted. A possible choice for the temperature of a plan p is $MaxMove - nmove$. Before the system being frozen, the criterion for accepting a transformation is different from that of iterative improvement: a transformation is accepted if it is profitable, but also if it is not with a probability that depends on the temperature and the augmentation of cost. The basic idea is to accept a move that deteriorates the cost with a threshold depending on the system temperature. For example, the probability to accept a bad move may be given by the formula where $temp$ denotes temperature [IW87]:

$$Prob(temp, CostBefore, CostAfter) = e^{-(CostAfter-CostBefore)/temp}. \quad (1)$$

Figure 10 gives the algorithm that implements simulated annealing. MaxTemp is a method setting the initial temperature, which can depends on the query. Equilibrium is a counter that counts the number of successive unchanged states in the inner loop. Prob(x) is a Boolean function that returns true with a probability given by the argument. To fix ideas, we set the frozen temperature to 0.1 and the maximum number of unchanged states to 4. These could be parameters depending on the query complexity.

```
Function Annealing(Query)
 {  p:=Parse(Query); //Set the initial plan
    temp:=MaxTemp(Query); //Set the temperature at maximum
    S:={}; //S is the set of locally optimum plans
    equilibrium:=0 ; //Count no. of successive unchanged states
    while temp  > 0.1 and equilibrium < 4
    { nmoves:=0;
        while nmoves < MaxMoves(Query)
        { p':=Transform(p); //Apply a transformation rule
           if Cost(p')<Cost(p) or Prob(e**-(Cost(p')-Cost(p))/temp)
           then
           { p::=p';
              nmoves::=nmoves+1; //One more move
              equilibrium:=0; //Plan have been changed
           }
           else equilibrium:=equilibrium+1; //No change
           Insert(S, p'); //Maintain the set of interesting plans
           temp:=0.95*temp; //Decrease temperature
           }
    }
    return Optimal(S); //Select best among all generated ones
 }
```

Fig. 10. Simulated annealing search algorithm

8 Conclusion

An overview of rule languages for relational and relational DBMSs was first presented. Then, the extensible techniques required for compiling such rule languages were studied. They include techniques for compiling rule programs into object-oriented algebra graphs, traditional syntactic query graph transformations, less traditional semantic based optimization and materialization of recursively updated classes. All these techniques should be integrated in an intelligent optimizer as transformation rules for algebraic expressions. These rules can be easily expressed using rewriting systems, as supported by the ROL rule language.

One of the main problem of the optimizer is to include a good search strategy. Examples of the most well known strategies were given as typical programs. Chosing one strategy is probably difficult, although exhaustive search is surely not viable. Organizing query processing knowledge in transformation rules whose application is directed by a strategy component for each module yields a modular architecture for the query optimizer. Our experience in the EDS ESPRIT project demonstrated the validity of the approach for logical optimization [FG91].

Further research is necessary to better understand what can and cannot be done. Very powerful rules and strategies can be integrated within the optimizer. Such rules may lead to long processing if the limits in number of moves and elapsed time are too high. If one stops too early (low limits), then the optimization can be very poor. Thus, a tradeoff has to be found. The limits given to the optimizer could also be allocated dynamically, according to the complexity of the query. Incremental compilation of rule programs could also be considered. Several queries can be issued on the same deduced class. Thus, the same rule program can be considered several times when compiling similar or different queries. More research is required to know what optimized plans can be reused. This could be integrated in the search strategy component, as already known "good" starting plans for the optimization process.

Acknowledgements

The author is indebted to Rosana Lanzelotte for pointing out the problem of extensible search strategies. He wishes also to thank Béatrice Finance, Françoise Fabret, Eric Simon and Patrick Valduriez for helpful discussions on topics covered by this paper.

The Promise of Distributed Computing and the Challenges of Legacy Information Systems*

Michael L. Brodie

GTE Laboratories Incorporated, 40 Sylvan Road, Waltham, MA 02254, USA

Abstract. The imminent combination of computing and telecommunications is leading to a compelling vision of world-wide computing. The vision is described in terms of next generation computing architectures, called Enterprise Information Architectures, and next generation information systems, called Intelligent and Cooperative Information Systems. Basic research directions and challenges are described as generalizations of database concepts, including semantic aspects of interoperable information systems. No matter how compelling and potentially valuable the vision may be, it is of little use until the legacy problem is solved. The problem of legacy information systems migration is described, in the context of distributed computing, and is illustrated with lessons learned from actual case studies. The basic research directions and challenges are recast in the light of actual legacy information systems. Recommendations for both realizing the vision and meeting the challenges are given, including the search for the elusive Killer Application and one fundamental challenge for future information systems technology.

1 World-Wide Computing

My professional goal is to contribute to making the world a better place by providing solutions to significant, practical problems (see Appendix). As a computer science researcher, this means that I want to produce the highest quality research and technology that is ultimately applicable to real problems so that the results are consistent with my beliefs. In this regard, I have high hopes and expectations for the potential benefits of world-wide computing. The vision is that problems or questions posed by one or more agents (e.g., humans or computer) can be solved as automatically and transparently as possible. Automatically means that the necessary computing resources [e.g., programs, information bases, information systems (ISs)] are identified and caused to interact cooperatively to effectively and efficiently solve the problem. Transparency means that all unnecessary details are not seen by the agent (e.g., locations and nature of the participating resources).

---

* This paper originally appeared in D.K. Hsiao, E.J. Neuhold and R. Sacks-Davis (eds.), *Interoperable Database Systems (DS5)*, North-Holland, 1993.

In this section, I describe a world-wide computing vision in terms of cooperation amongst ISs augmented by a telecommunications vision that provides communication on a scale previously unthinkable by computer scientists.

1.1 The Vision

The vision of distributed computing is compelling. It says that soon the dominant computing paradigm will involve large numbers of heterogeneous, intelligent agents distributed over large computer/communication networks. Agents may be humans, humans interacting with computers, humans working with computer support, and computer systems performing tasks without human intervention. Work will be conducted on the network in many forms. Work task definition will be centralized (e.g., a complex engineering task) and decentralized. Tasks will be executed by agents acting autonomously, cooperatively, or collaboratively, depending on the resources required to complete the task (e.g., monitoring many systems of a patient or many stations in a factory). Agents will request and acquire resources (e.g., processing, knowledge, data) without knowing what resources are required, how to acquire them, or how they will be orchestrated to achieve the desired result. A goal of this vision is to be able to use, efficiently and transparently, all computing resources that are available on computers in large computer/communications networks.

Cooperative Work. Computers should support humans and organizations in their natural modes of thinking, playing, and working. Consider how complex activities are in human organizations such as a hospital (Fig. 1). Each human agent (e.g., doctor, technician, nurse, receptionist) provides capabilities to cooperatively achieve a goal (e.g., improve the health of a patient). For a doctor to complete an analysis of a patient, the doctor may need the opinion of another doctor, the results of a laboratory test, and personal information about the patient. In general, the analysis is broken into sub-activities and appropriate agents are found for each sub-activity. Each sub-activity is sent to the appropriate agents together with the required information in a form that the agent can use. Cooperating agents complete the sub-activities and return the results in a form that the doctor can use. The doctor then analyzes the results and combines them to complete the analysis, possibly by repeating sub-activities that were not successful or by invoking new sub-activities.

Such cooperative work requires considerable intelligent interaction among the agents using knowledge of who does what, what information is required, the form in which it is required, scheduling requirements or coordination of tasks, how to locate agents, how to request that sub-activities be done, etc. The cost and quality of products of most human organizations depend on the effectiveness of such cooperation. In hospitals, the quality and cost of health care depend on effectiveness and speed of cooperation. Aspects of the cooperation can be seen as effective parts of the work being done (e.g., doctor's interaction to solve life critical problems), while others may be seen as counterproductive (e.g., converting patient chart information into multiple computer formats for automated analysis steps). The cost and complexity of interactions in a hospital argue for their optimization. What cooperation aspects are effective and should be encouraged, and which should be diminished?

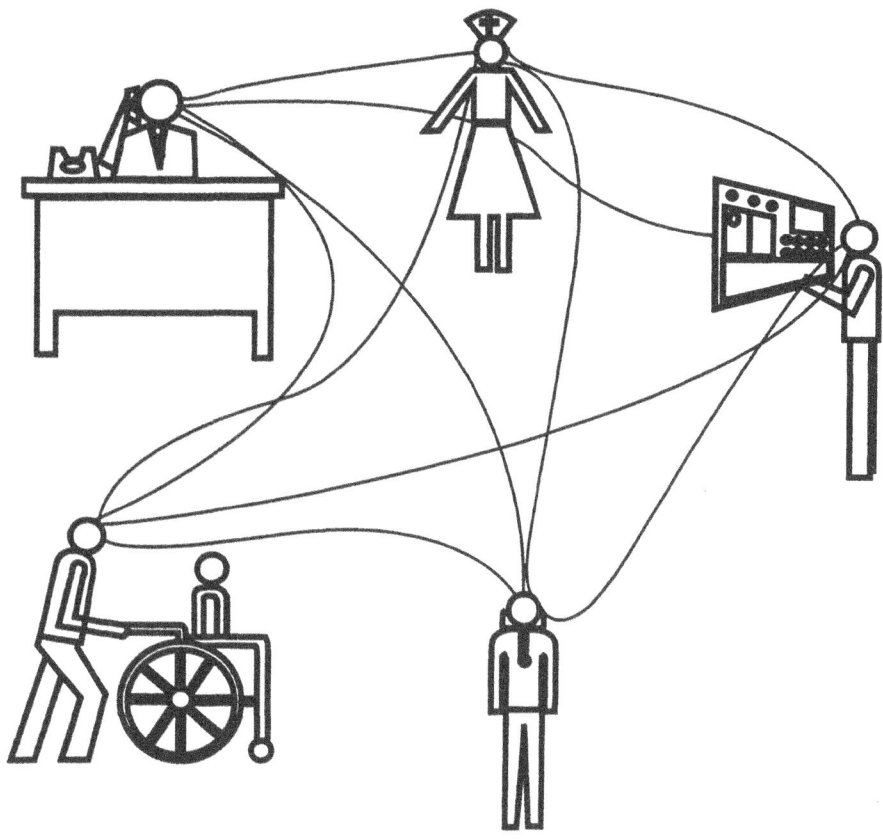

Fig. 1. Cooperating agents in medical care

Intuitively, it seems that the distributed computing vision could meet many requirements of cooperative work. The cost of an activity could be reduced by a computing infrastructure that makes appropriate interactions transparent to the agents. Computers could contribute to more productive (e.g., effective and efficient) work by intelligently supporting cooperation. In the next section, I examine forms of intelligence and cooperation that computers might support. I limit my scope to the cooperative work that might be supported by cooperating ISs and the resulting requirements on the computing infrastructure, or systems technology.

Intelligent and Cooperative Information Systems. Intelligent and Cooperative Information Systems (ICISs) are seen as the next generation of IS, 5-10 years in the future [BC92]. ICISs are collections of ISs that exhibit forms of cooperation and intelligence. Cooperation is supported by interoperability (the ability to interact effectively to achieve shared goals, e.g., a joint activity). Intelligent refers, in part, to the ability to do this efficiently (i.e., have the system find, acquire, and orchestrate resources in some optimal fashion) and transparently (with the least human effort). The goal is that any computing resource (e.g., data, information, knowledge, function) should be able to transparently and efficiently utilize any other. Although some features of such systems are agreed upon, no one knows the exact nature of these systems. This sub-section illustrates and suggests some initial ideas for ICIS functionality.

Most organizations have developed many application-specific but independent ISs and other computing resources. They soon find that almost all ISs must interact with other ISs or resources, just as the people in their organizations need to interact. Such organizations have vast investments in valuable resources that cannot be used together without great cost. For example, valuable data is bound to applications and is not available to others. There is a growing need for vast numbers of disjoint information/computing resources to be used cooperatively, efficiently, transparently, and easily by human users (e.g., clerks, scientists, engineers, managers). Consider, for example, the different ISs that must interact to support the functions of a hospital (Fig. 2). To produce a patient bill, the billing system must obtain information from many hospital ISs (e.g., nursing records, doctors' bills, pharmacy, radiology, lab, ward, food services).

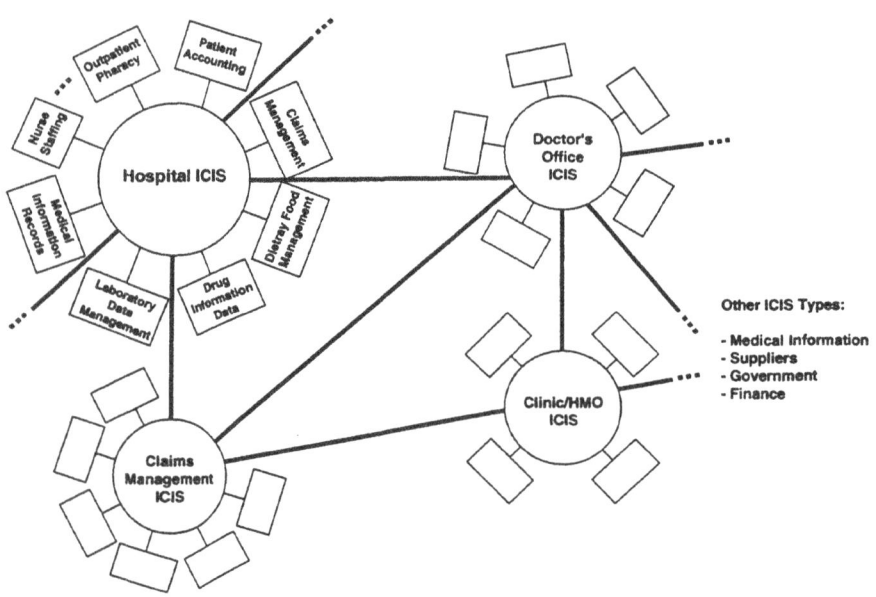

Fig. 2. Health Care ICIS

Let's call such an effective combination of systems, a Health Care ICIS. The Health Care ICIS requires access between multiple, heterogeneous, distributed ISs that were independently designed to be used in isolation.

I consider two or more ISs that execute joint tasks to form a larger IS, called a *cooperative IS*. I call an individual IS within a cooperative IS a *component IS*. With various forms of transparency, a cooperative IS can act as, and be considered as, a single IS (e.g., the hospital billing system accesses of multiple ISs should be transparent to the user). A common requirement for component ISs is to maintain autonomy while cooperating within the cooperative IS.

Intelligent features could be added to a cooperative IS. These features require of technology, or provide users with, more *intelligence* than do conventional ISs. Intelligence has a potential role in user interaction between the user and the component ISs to enhance the quality of interaction. Examples of such features include presenting an integrated view of the multiple ISs; explanation; intentional queries; and presenting functionality through graphic, visual, linguistic, or other support (e.g., use of icons, templates, graph representations).

Intelligence also plays a role in enhancing IS functionality. Examples include the following:

- Enhanced decision making or reasoning capabilities (e.g., incorporate hospital rules into the Health Care ICIS).
- (Re)Active (e.g., when a new patient is registered, a transaction is triggered that checks the availability of rooms in wards and orders needed supplies).
- Nondeterminism (e.g., give me any one of the possible teams that has two doctors from cardiology, an anesthetist, and three nurses who are not already booked).
- Nondeductive forms of inference (e.g., induction such as learning rules or constraints from databases, reorganizing a schema based on current extensions of different classes, redistributing information based on access patterns; case-based reasoning, where information is structured according to *cases* and new situations are dealt with by finding similar ones in the information).
- Maintaining integrity constraints.
- Introspection: reasoning about meta-knowledge (e.g., a Health Care ICIS component reasoning about what it can and cannot do in the face of a request).

The Global Computer. In a separate universe far away, or so it seems, a vision for the next generation telecommunications technology is taking shape. It intends to permit any information to be communicated anywhere, at any time, in any form, to any agent (human or machine). The key technologies include ubiquitous, broadband, lightning fast intelligent networks enabling universal information access to support information malls, multimedia communications, and business enterprise integration. This will require all-digital, broadband transport and switching; distributed intelligence and high-speed signaling; geographic independence for users and services; interoperability of diverse networks and equipment; transparency via common look and feel interfaces; etc. Sound familiar? Just as computing technology [e.g., database management system (DBMS)] is being extended from computing with text and integer data to computing with all types of objects, telecommunications technology is being extended from communicating voice to communicating all types of information.

The telecommunications vision does not consider only agents in hospitals. A significant difference with the computing vision is the world-wide scale of telecommunications. Figure 3 illustrates agents interacting with agents across Europe and North America.

Current telecommunications advances involving cellular communications and satellites will soon permit point to point communication anywhere in the world, with or without old-fashioned wires or new-fangled fiber optics.

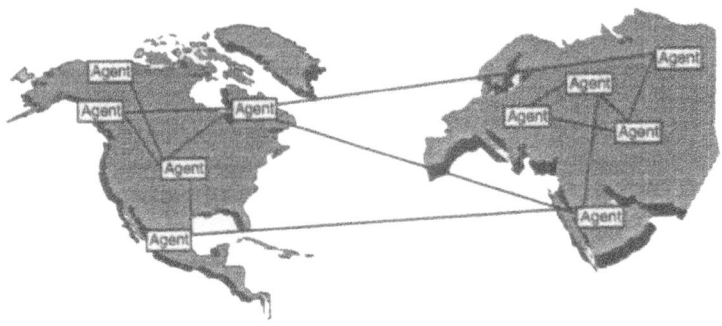

Fig. 3. Agent interaction in telecommunications

There are striking similarities between the computing and telecommunications visions [WA91]. The motivations are very similar, in terms of both applications (i.e., business) and technology. They both rely on similar technological advances. Indeed, the telecommunications vision, underlying Bellcore's Intelligent Network Architecture (INA) program is stated simply and compellingly as the addition of a distributed computing environment (DCE) or distributed processing environment (DPE) to the public network (i.e., the world-wide telephone system).

The vision of world-wide computing results from the combination of the computing and telecommunications visions. In this vision, the device (e.g., telephone, computer, FAX, television, answering machine) on your desk or in your pocket can be connected to the world-wide public telecommunications/computing network. It has transparent access to all allowable resources in the network. Your computer just became a global computer. You can transparently participate in ICISs world-wide, as illustrated in Fig. 4. Figure 4 illustrates Motorola's Iridium project, which will place over 75 satellites in earth orbit to provide ubiquitous telecommunications. In computing terms, the scale is unimaginable, at least for me. There is currently approximately one device per citizen (i.e., 10^8) on the public network in the United States. How many devices would there be in the global computer?

The telecommunications vision critically depends on computing and *vice versa*. The implications of merging telecommunications and computing are profound. An obvious change will be a lack of distinction between computing and telecommunications technologies and businesses. The world-wide public telephone system becomes a universally accessible DCE/DPE. In broad terms, these visions are widely agreed to. It is not news. Although [Kap92] predicts that the revolution is at hand[2], it is taking a

---

[2] "As a result of rapid technological developments in the computer software and hardware,

long time to realize the visions. New technology facilitates revolutions; it seldom brings them about. These visions are currently solutions looking for problems. For example, two major telecommunication/computing experiments in the United States have no compelling applications to drive them. The most advanced technology is being used to support computing and communicating hospital imagery and visualization of scientific data. These are not the *killer applications* that are in such great demand that they alone will force the realization of the visions. Other problems concern unreliability, privacy, security, fraud, and hype.

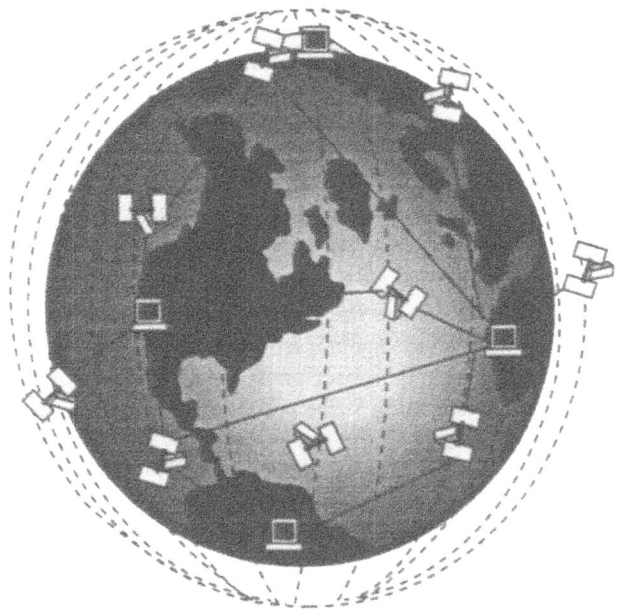

Fig. 4. World-wide computing

The remainder of the paper addresses technical ideas and challenges in the realization of the distributed computing vision, possibly on the scale of world-wide computing. In addition to basic research challenges, there are the critical challenges of evolving the current technology base, including existing or legacy ISs, towards the vision. I return at the end of the paper to the lack of killer applications.

1.2 The Technology

The motivations for the telecommunication and distributed computing visions are similar. The primary motivation is for users to gain control of their technology/networks

consumer electronics, and telecommunication industries, we believe a true revolution in the delivery of entertainment, information, transactional, and telecommuncation services may be at hand."

(e.g., distribution and deployment of their data and applications). In the past, hardware, and to some extent software, vendors had control (e.g., use any system or computer you like as long as it is Blue). A current goal is vendor independence as expressed in the ill-defined phrase *Open Systems*. Another motivation is the dramatic cost reductions possible in moving computing from costly mainframes to workstations/minicomputers. These strategic motivations relate to key technical motivations such as interoperability and reuse of interchangeable components. The potential magic of these trends towards open, distributed computing/telecommunications is that they potentially support what appears to be more natural modes of working/playing for humans and organizations (i.e., cooperative work). The magic is still potential due to the lack of killer applications. This sub-section describes a pervasive vision of next generation computing architectures, the generalization to this environment of database concepts, and consequent research challenges. This sets the stage for the subsequent section, which poses the challenges of legacy ISs in the face of this vision.

Next Generation Computing Architecture and Object Space. The agent-oriented, cooperative work described above will be supported by a global object space, as illustrated in Fig. 5. Cooperating agents (e.g., resources such as humans, computers, information bases) will interface to the global object space via a human or systems interface, depending on whether the agent is a human or a system. Each agent may request or provide resources to the global object space (e.g., may be a client or a server). As a server, the agent may provide all or some subset of its capabilities. The interface layer will provide transparent access to the object space by mediating between the agent's languages, formats, etc., and those of the object space. By the mid 1990's, the notion of a global object space will become an architectural paradigm which will provide the basis of next generation computing environments. These environments will provide practical interoperability with limited transparency, efficiency, intelligence, and distribution.

The object space can be considered a logical extension of a database. A database consists of data elements. Using the object-oriented approach, data and operations are encapsulated so that all computing resources (e.g., data, information, programs, knowledge) can be seen as objects. Data management concepts are being extended to manage objects. Hence, the global object space provides a challenging opportunity for extending database technology to global object management. Given the world-wide computing vision, the scale of the challenges is enormous. The opportunities for distributed computing are compelling.

The global object manager could potentially offer access to any subset of the union of the resources provided by the agents (e.g., agent-specific object spaces or object views). The object space may be largely virtual since it is an implementation detail as to how the objects (i.e., agent-provided resources) are managed, stored, and accessed. A global object manager will support efficient and intelligent (e.g., transparent) interoperability between all objects. Hence, resources can be combined in unanticipated ways to meet new application requirements and opportunities. The object space will be based on the object-oriented approach and will be supported by a generic technology which will provide tool kits for combining computing components in arbitrary ways. In this context, the notion of a single DBMS as a separate component serving a wide range of

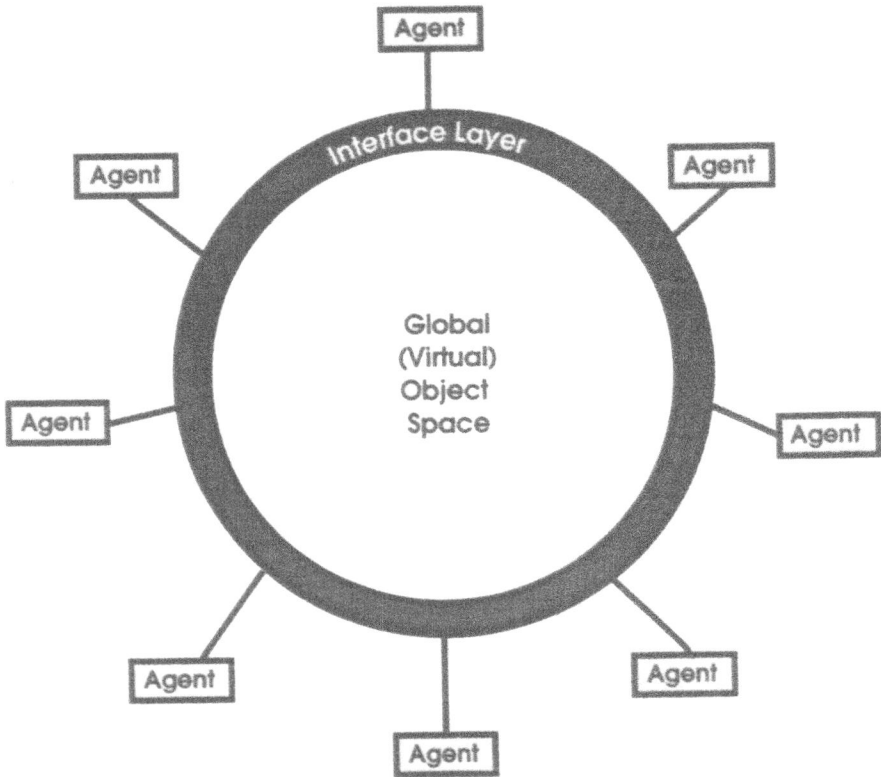

Fig. 5. The global object space

applications will cease to exist. Instead, DBMSs become cooperating agents. Database interoperability will be supported by the global object space manager just as it supports interoperability between all agents.

Object space management technology is only one of many systems technologies necessary to support the vision. The remarkably successful database notion of extracting as much data management functionality from applications as possible and providing it in a generic DBMS (Fig. 6) has been extrapolated to many computing services to arrive at a distributed computing architecture, illustrated in Fig. 6. The resulting architecture separates four systems functions:

- User interfaces
- Applications (the minimum code necessary for the application semantics)
- Shared distributed computing services (e.g., global object space management)
- A global object space

The most compelling idea of the distributed computing architecture (also referred to as the Enterprise Information Architecture) is the concept of shared, distributed

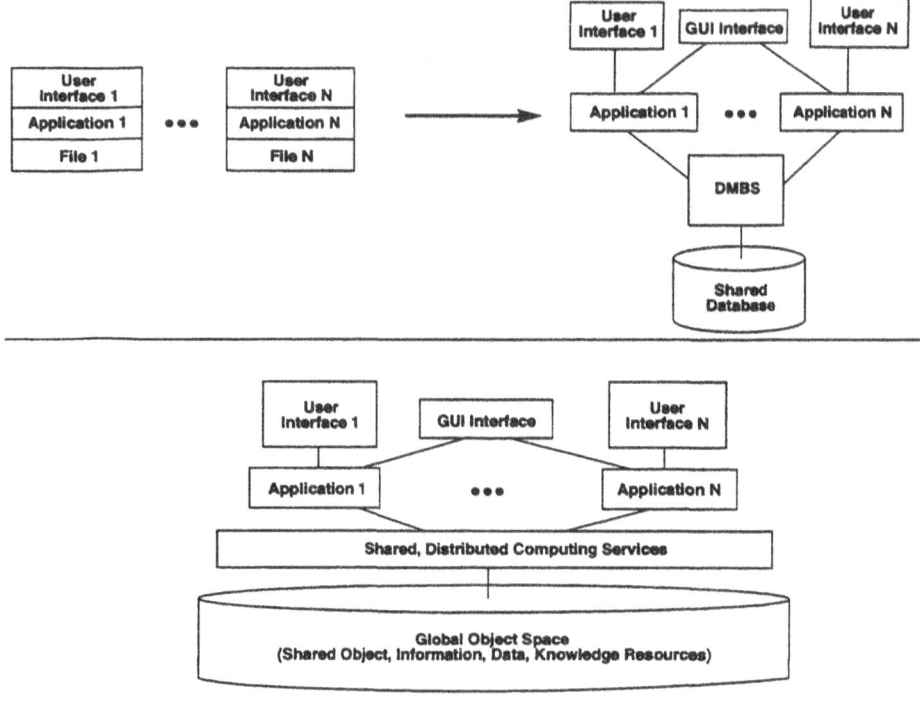

Fig. 6. Distributed computing architecture

computing services. The principle is to provide as many computing services as possible as sharable servers in a distributed computing environment. The services are provided by systems or computing infrastructure technologies such as DBMSs, OSs, user interface management systems, and development environments. This is the home of the global object manager. Collectively, the systems providing infrastructure support are being called **middleware**. Figure 7 illustrates details of the layers of the architecture:

- Human Presentation Interface
- Applications and System Applications Development Environments
- APIs
- Middleware (Distributed Computing Services)
- System Interfaces
- OS, Network, and Hardware and gives examples of the middleware

The distributed computing architectures, middleware, and global object management are much more than visions. The major software vendors have all announced their support of the architectural goals, including the following:

- Open systems (i.e., standard interfaces or architectures)
- Client-server computing
- Distributed computing, including distributed DBMSs

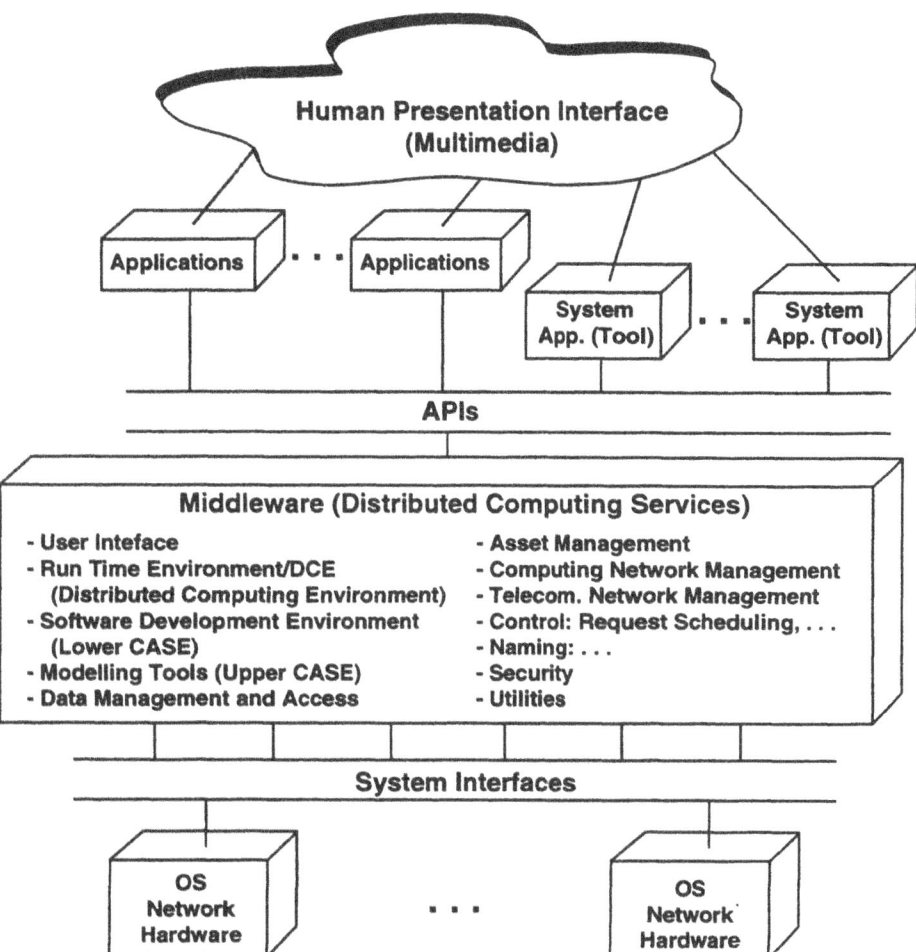

Fig. 7. Enterprise information architecture with middleware

– Advanced flexible user interfaces
– Transparent multivendor interoperability
– Transaction processing
– Structured organization of corporate resources/components
– Reliability and maintainability
– Reduced communication costs
– Single-point program maintenance and upgrading
– Open access to low-cost workstation MIPS

Some vendors have announced and released middleware and related products and strategies, including the following:

– Enterprise Network Architecture (ENA) (Gartner Group terminology)

- Network Application Architecture and Network Application Support products (DEC)
- SAA: System Application Architecture (IBM)
- Information Warehouse Architecture (IBM)
- DRDA: Distributed Relational Database Architecture (IBM)
- Advanced Networked Systems Architecture (ANSA) [Lim89]
- SOE: Systems/Standard Operating Environment (pervasive)
- DCE: Distributed Computing Environment (Open Systems Foundation)
- DME: Distributed Management Environment (Open Systems Foundation)
- GAIA: GUI-based Application Interoperability Architecture (Open Systems Foundation)
- OSI Network Management Forum
- Integration Architecture for the Enterprise (Apple): Data Access Language, Mac-WorkStation, MacAPPC (LU 6.2)
- Open Application Development Architecture and Open Enterprise Networking (Tandem)
- Bull's: Distributed Computing Model (DCM)

There is considerable activity towards achieving interoperability between arbitrary computing services via object-orientation and distributed computing technologies such as distributed databases. There are several research, product, and standards development projects exploring different aspects of global object management. The projects originate in disjoint technologies, including databases (e.g., GTE's Distributed Object Management [MBH+92], Open Systems Liaison's Object Mapper, Stanford's Mediator-based SoD and KSYS, the University of Florida's Federated Information Bases), programming languages (e.g., MIT's Argus), operating systems (e.g., Open Systems Foundation's OSF/1, ANSI's and ISO's Open Distributed Processing, APM Ltd's ANSA [Lim89]), communications (e.g., Open System Liaison's Software Bus), software engineering (e.g., Norway's Eureka Software Factory), and in new technologies that combine features of several technologies (e.g., Yale University's LINDA [CG89]). The use of the object abstraction in integrating heterogeneous and autonomous components is also a characteristic of recent developments in personal computer application integration software, such as Hewlett-Packard's NewWave, Object Linking and Embedding (OLE) in Microsoft[3] Windows[4], and inter-application communication (IAC) facilities in the latest Apple Macintosh[5] operating system.

Perhaps the most notable activity in global object management as a basis for interoperability is that of the Object Management Group (OMG). OMG is an industry consortium of 350 of the major software and hardware vendors around the world. Its goal is the development of a framework of specifications to maximize the portability, reusability, and interoperability of commercial object-oriented software. Within two years, it has proposed a guideline for a Common Object Request Broker Architecture (CORBA) [OMG91a] which provides the core functionality for interoperability to be provided by the global object manager. It facilitates the exchange of messages between

---

[3] Registered by Microsoft Corporation.
[4] Trademark of Microsoft Corporation.
[5] Registered by Apple Computer, Inc.

arbitrary objects in a distributed, heterogeneous computing environment. The broader goal of CORBA is true application integration by providing a common approach to persistence, transactions, security, naming, trading, and object services. The ORB serves as a communications substrate (like RPC) which is intended to support object implementations as diverse as separate processes, code in the same address space, object databases, etc. CORBA's interoperability can be provided to any software that is capable of sending and receiving messages. Hence, it is a basis for interoperability between arbitrary computing systems, whether object-oriented or not. As of mid 1994, over 21 major software vendors have announced CORBA-compliant ORBs. Over 100 OMG members, including IBM, have internally adopted the CORBA specification.

Although object-orientation is in its infancy and is not deployed in practice to any significant degree, it plays a critical role in all of the visions described above. There is a pervasive industry commitment to object-orientation. This is demonstrated by the following strategies and products announced by major vendors:

- IBM's System View (OO is seen as critical to manage large-scale systems)
- IBM-Apple agreement based in part on OO technology
- Apple uses OO in many of its current products
- TINA's commitment to OO (a Telecommunications pre-standards body)
- Multivendor networks based on "Managed Objects"
- Microsoft's Object Linking and Embedding (OLE)
- Microsoft's CAIRO (approach to distributed objects)
- Hewlett-Packard's Distributed Object Computing Program (DOCP)
- Sun's Distributed Objects Everywhere (DOE)
- IBM-Metaphor's Patriot Partner's Constellation Project
- DEC's Trellis OO Application Development Environment
- OODBMSs or DBMS support for OO: Ingres, Oracle, Objectivity/DB (DEC-Objectivity), Ontos (IBM-Ontos), and 13 other OODBMS products
- Object Management Group's (OMG) CORBA, core object model, object services, and common facilities; 15 companies have announced CORBA-compliant products

Another indication of the potential significance of and high expectations for object-orientation is the number of object-orients standards and consortia, including the following:

- ANSI X3H2-SQL (object-oriented support in SQL3)
- ANSI X3H4 Information Resource Dictionary Systems
- ANSI X3H6 CASE Integration Service
- ANSI X3H7 Object Information Management [FKMT91]
- ANSI X3J4 Object COBOL
- ANSI X3J9 Pascal
- ANSI X3J16 C++
- ANSI X3T3-ODP (Open Distributed Processing)
- ANSI X3T1M1.5 (related to ODP)
- ANSI X3T5-TP (Transaction Processing)
- ANSI X3T5-OSI (Open Systems Interconnection)

- ISO's IRDS Information Resource Directory Systems
- OSI/Network Management Forum
- JTC1 SC21/WG4 (Management of Information Services) CCITT's "Managed Objects"
- OSF's Distributed Management Environment
- CCITT's TINA Telecommunications Information Networking Architecture [WA91]
- Object Management Group (OMG)
- OSF Open Systems Foundation
- X/Open
- PCTE: Portable Common Tools Environment

[FKMT91] lists 32 related computing standards efforts in DBMS, transaction processing, object communications and distribution, data interchange, domain-specific data representations, repositories, programming languages, and frameworks and consortia. The TINA 90 and TINA 91 proceedings (see e.g., [WA91]) lists a similar number of standards and framework efforts in telecommunications and computing.

The existence of so many object-oriented standards efforts poses potential problems of inconsistent object-oriented standards, thus hindering interoperability, a goal of object-orientation. The ANSI standards body X3H7 was established, in part, to address these problems in the area of object information management. X3H7 has been chartered to make more consistent the object facilities used in various standards (including those of both official standards bodies and industry consortia), where such consistency would improve their ability to interoperate. One of its initial goals is to produce a reference model which could be the basis of later standards. The group is currently discussing whether it should be producing a new object model (e.g., a *least common denominator model*) [MH94] or just facilities for describing object models. This challenge is directly related to data and object model research in databases.

Next generation computing architectures are well on their way from vision to reality. There is a pervasive agreement on many aspects of the vision, including the architectural notion of middleware, the functionality of (global) object management, and the critical role of object-orientation. There is less agreement on the need or means for integrating technologies so as to draw the greatest benefit from each technology, rather then reinventing the wheel. These trends are led and largely determined by the computing industry and will determine, to a very large degree, computing environments for a long time to come. As described in the next sub-section, basic research challenges must be met to realize the vision. To date, the research community has had little impact on formulating and realizing the vision. This is a major opportunity for the research community to do excellent research and make significant contributions.

From Database to Object Space Management. Global object space management can be seen as a logical extension of database management to the global object space. Database technology contributes such concepts on which to base object models, persistence, sharing, object management and migration, optimization, transactions, recovery, distribution, and heterogeneous database interoperability. However, the global object space poses additional challenges, not only based on the scale of the object space compared with that of a database. Global object management requirements are dramatically different based on the fact that heterogeneous objects are being managed. A critical, new requirement of global object management is support for general-purpose interoperability. This sub-section defines interoperability, outlines and approach to providing interoperability, and lists related basic research challenges.

Next Generation Database Research. ICISs were defined above in terms of the ability of two or more systems to interact to execute tasks jointly. This capability is the intuition underlying interoperability. However, there is no agreement on the functionality implied by the term *interoperability*. Therefore, I provide an initial definition and a discussion of the idea and of related objectives.

Interoperability: Two components (or objects) X and Y can interoperate (are interoperable) if X can send requests for services (or messages) R to Y based on a mutual understanding of R by X and Y, and Y can return responses S to X based on a mutual understanding of S as (respectively) responses to R by X and Y.

This definition addresses the function of interoperability and not aspects of the systems context in which it is provided. For example, two components (or objects) that call each other and that are written in the same language, under the same operating system, and on the same machine illustrate trivial interoperability. Specific systems challenges arise in providing interoperability by a DBMS to applications written using the DBMS. More challenges arise when providing it to applications written over heterogeneous, distributed DBMSs. Even more arise when providing it over arbitrary computer systems that may not support any DBMS functionality.

Interoperability does not require X or Y to provide both *client* and *server* functionality, to be distributed or heterogeneous, or to provide any forms of *transparency* with respect to each other unless such transparency is required to satisfy the above definition. However, given a particular systems context, interoperability may require some or all of these features. Alternatively, interoperability could be improved or its scope increased by advances in technology that increase the ease, efficiency, reliability, and security with which components interoperate. Some of these advances can be expressed in terms of various forms of transparency in which differences are hidden and a single, homogeneous view is provided. The following forms of transparency are generalized from those proposed for distributed databases.

- Resource (e.g., seeing one system or resource provider versus needing to know the individual system(s) providing the service or information)
- Language (i.e., using one language and therefore not needing to know the language of the resource)
- Distribution (i.e., not needing to know the location(s) of the resource(s) or how to transfer to and from them)
- Logical/schema (i.e., having the appearance of one meta-information base describing such things as how features are modelled in individual resources)
- Transaction (i.e., ability to run one, apparently local, transaction over multiple resources that appear as one resource); transactions act the same (atomic, commit, abort) at one, two, or more sites
- Copy/replication (e.g., not needing to know that resources are replicated)

- Performance (i.e., tasks execute efficiently independently of the location of invocation or of participating resources)
- Data representation (i.e., not needing to know how information is stored)
- Fragmentation (i.e., not needing to know that information is fragmented)
- Location (i.e., programs access a single logical database, not needing to know the location of the actual data)
- Advanced application development (i.e., supports the creation of *business rules* to be applied to all distributed processing)
- Local autonomy for participant ICISs (i.e., individual components can access and rely on all resources; local operations are purely local, all components are treated equally)
- Network/communication (i.e., communication protocols are transparent)
- Hardware (i.e., execute components ignoring hardware platform)
- Operating system (i.e., run components ignoring the OS that they will run under)

These and other forms of transparency could be described from a system level perspective, e.g., consistency/integrity of copies of object/data/knowledge; augmenting systems with features to ensure system-wide integrity (e.g., backup and recovery). Interoperability involves far more than transparency. It involves issues that arise when two languages or systems must interact, including those involved with type systems, transaction systems, communication protocols, optimization, and systems architecture. These requirements pose basic research challenges to otherwise manageable database technology challenges.

Interoperability could be characterized as a form of *systems level intelligence* that enhances the cooperation between ICIS components. Consider the intelligence required to provide services, find resources, and cooperate and carry out complex functions across component ISs without the user or component IS needing to know precisely what resources are available, how to acquire them, or how they will be orchestrated to achieve the desired result.

Let's consider an approach to providing global object management. This approach is that of GTE's Distributed Object Management project [MBH$^+$92] and of the OMG [OMG91a]. The scale and distribution of the object space leads to the distribution of global object management functionality into a collection of distributed object managers (DOMs). Figure 8 illustrates, in the Health Care ICIS, that medical agents, possibly assisted or simulated by ICIS components, are interconnected indirectly through DOMs.

In the DOM approach, each resource has a client interface to the DOM, as illustrated in Fig. 9. All DOMs have one common object model. Interfaces between resources and DOMs allow resources to be accessed as objects in the common object model. For clients, interfaces allow access to objects, and translate requests and results between the local type system and the common object model.

Consider as an example interaction a request by an object-oriented DBMS to copy text on what appears to it to be a document object (Fig. 10). The request is routed by DOM of System 1 to the DOM of System 2. The interface to the nonobject-oriented word processor allows its DOM to treat files as document objects. The System 2 DOM invokes the word processor, causes loading of the references text file, and invokes the requested operation via the interface.

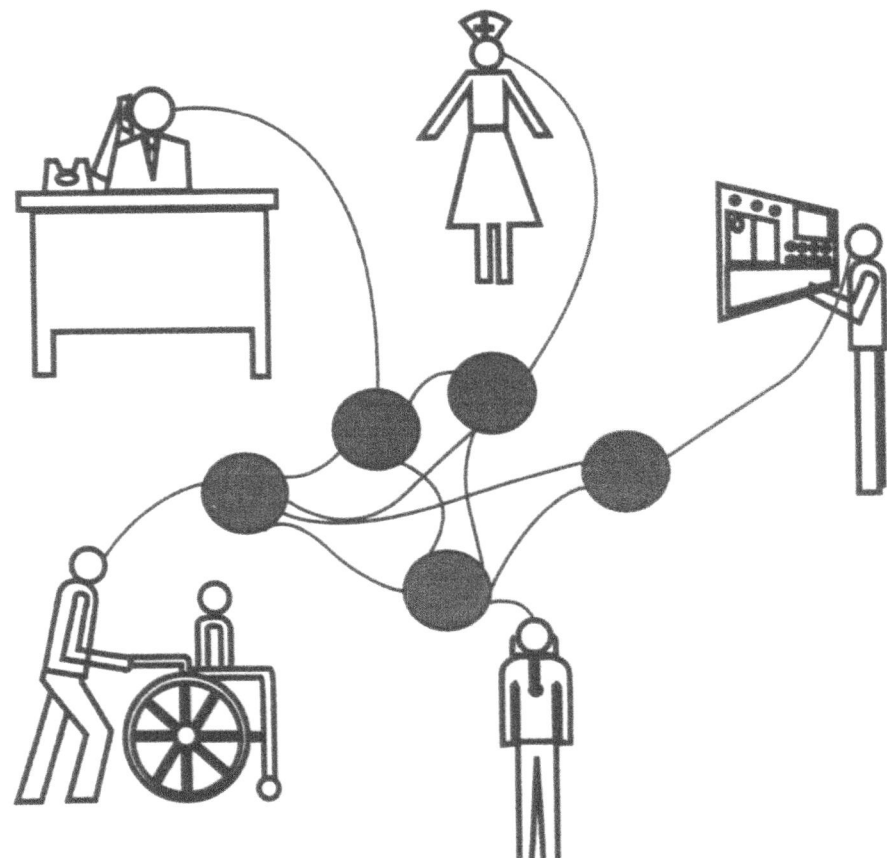

Fig. 8. Health care ICIS interoperability via DOMs

Global object management involves all database research issues except that in the context of the global object space, the challenges are greater. Database solutions may not extrapolate to adequately address global object management requirements. The following is a list of global object management research challenges that appear significantly more difficult than the database counterpart.

- Interoperable object model: It must support all requirements of the multiparadigm, distributed computing environment, not just object manipulation [MB90]. It must provide a basis for mapping between arbitrary computing systems, not just DBMSs [OMG91b]. The proliferation of object model and object model standards leads to a requirement for a *least common denominator* or *RISC* object model [MH94]. A challenge is to develop an object algebra which is for objects what the relational algebra is for relations. This would provide a basis for a theory of objects and for object DBMSs as relational algebra does for relational DBMSs.
- Long-lived, distributed applications (i.e., the ICIS counterpart to database trans-

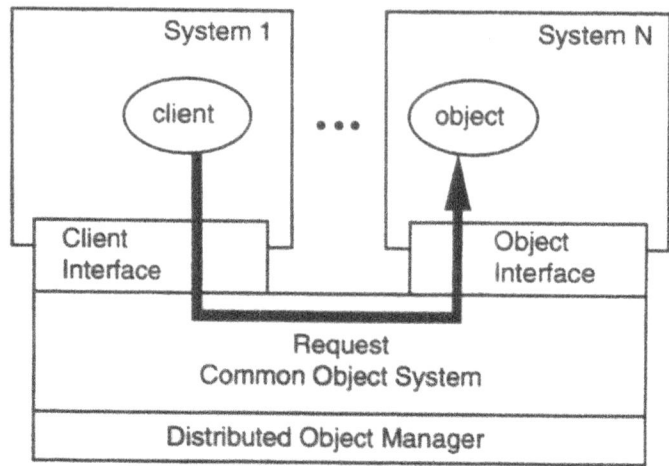

Fig. 9. Role of a DOM

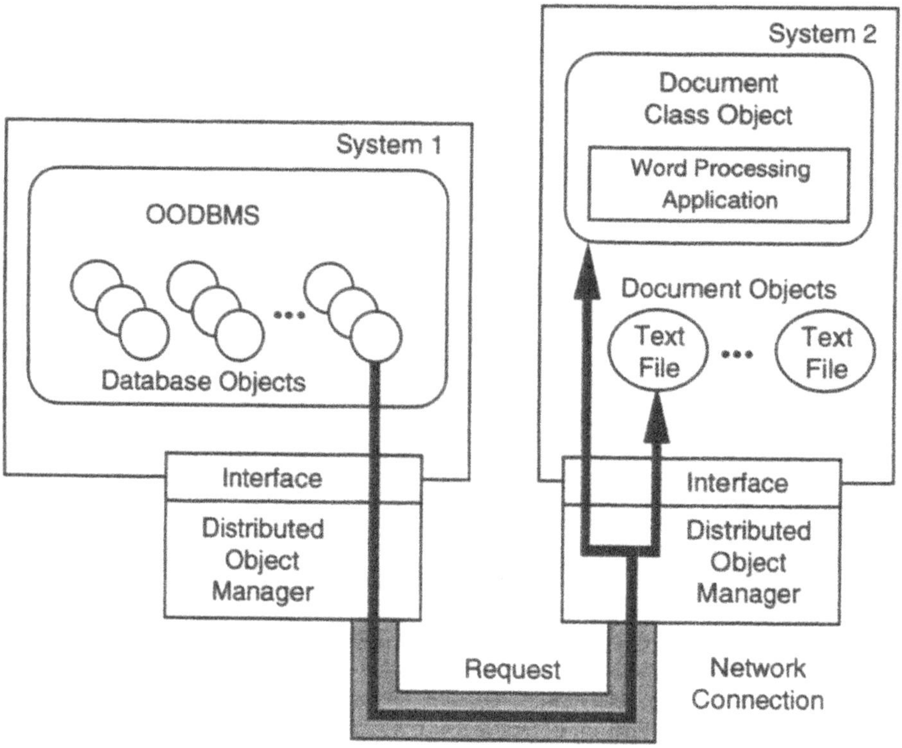

Fig. 10. OODBMS client request of a word processor

actions): An ICIS operation potentially involves operations over many distinct component ISs. Writing transactions corresponds to manipulating entire applications using operations like: start, abort, cancel; suspend, resume, backtrack; migrate computation; and show computational state/history. This requires new abstractions for *programming in the large*, new control mechanisms, new notions of correctness, and compensation. In short, new transaction models (e.g., open, nested, complex, multisystem operations) are needed [GR93, Elm92]. Unlike the conventional transaction model which is orthogonal to the relational data model, the DOM transaction model will have to be integrated with the DOM object model.

Multisystem transactions and workflows are examples of *programming in the large*. They involve programming in which entire ISs are encapsulated and provide functions or services in support of a higher level operation (i.e., the transaction).

- Query optimization: Optimization of queries over the global object space involves optimizing operations over multiple database and nondatabase systems, vastly expanding the scope for optimization by potentially applying database optimization technology to arbitrary computing tasks.

- Global naming: Objects should be uniquely identifiable throughout their life regardless of their system of origin and current location [ZABM92]. Objects or references to them may be embedded in a large number of heterogeneous contexts throughout the global object space. Each context (e.g., IS) will likely have its own unique naming scheme and will require considerable autonomy. A challenge is to provide a mechanism to register a context, including some of its objects, in the global object space that would accommodate many, co-existing, heterogeneous naming schemes within a common (structured) global naming scheme. Another challenge is to develop a migration path that would allow legacy ISs to participate in the naming scheme but permit considerable autonomy. How many objects do you think this might involve?

Naming, as discussed above, involves agreements on what I will call identical concepts. This includes not only identity of values (e.g., Fred's age here is identical to Fred's age there), but also identity of operations (i.e., that the results of executions in the identified context are identical as agreed to by any object that might then reference the result). For example, I want to establish that the *meaning* of PAY(EMPLOYEE) is identical in two contexts (e.g., Fred would get the same pay in two companies if the contexts were identical) except for the differences introduced by the contexts.

- (Object) Views: I assume that complete semantic integration of all ISs is infeasible. Hence, mapping between ISs requires the ability to sub-set the respective ISs so as to present the appropriate information (objects) to the other ISs. This amounts to an object-view (analogous to a relational view). Views in relational databases still pose major challenges, such as view updates. In object-oriented systems, the problems are more difficult [HZ90, SS89].

- Active objects for active ICISs: Cooperative human interaction to achieve jointly agreed upon tasks requires response to conditions, actions, and events in the working environment. Analogously, ICISs must be able to respond to changing conditions, actions, and events. Techniques to facilitate these requirements include rules (If

C, do A), events (When E then If C then Do A), triggers, and alerters. These techniques make systems active in that they now react to changes. These techniques create complex temporal and conditional relationships between objects.

– Modelling: Conceptual modelling has not enjoyed the successes of other database technologies. ICIS complexity, scale, and heterogeneity make the problems dramatically worse. Due to the early stage of development and experience, there are currently no effective, proven concepts, tools, or techniques for object-oriented systems design of the scale being considered here. How do you visualize or conceive of all the objects in a large IS? How do you design their interactions and ensure that all possible combinations of method invocations are meaningful and correct? How do you control the invocation of methods to ensure properties such as integrity, correctness, and recoverability. We have almost no means of *designing in the large* (e.g., design at a level above entire, encapsulated ISs to define multi-IS workflows or transactions). Whereas the semantic aspects of interoperable ISs are not different than conventional ISs (see below), new approaches to modelling are arising from some new aspects of distributed computing including notions of cooperation and agent-oriented computing, object-orientation, advanced transaction models, workflows, active objects (e.g., event-based and rule-based computing), and the necessarily higher level view of ISs.

– Gateways: Gateways will be major components in future IS architectures for both new and legacy ISs. Interoperability involves the interfacing of computing systems. Whenever two systems are required to interact, some interface is required. If the interactions involve anything more than simple message passing, it is often necessary to develop a software interface component. Such a component is called a gateway (i.e., between the two systems). Gateways are an integral part of distributed DBMS architectures for heterogeneous DBMSs. Database gateways are complex, costly, and generally *ad hoc* (i.e., built solely for the two systems being interfaced). They also play a major role in encapsulating legacy ISs when migrating legacy ISs into new software and hardware platforms [BS92]. In this regard, they are sometimes referred to as surround technology. They will become fundamental elements in IS and ICIS architectures (Fig. 5, 7, 9, and 10). Gateways have stringent requirements. For example, those between mission critical systems must be very reliable, robust, and efficient. They cannot impose a significant performance penalty.

Requirements for systems interaction (misleadingly called systems integration) and distributed computing (e.g., client-server) are growing dramatically. Gateways are a frequently proposed solution. Indeed, some proposals for next generation computing [OMG91a, OMG91b, MBH+92, BS92, BC92] are based on gateways, which are related to stubs generated by some compilers; ORBs, adapters, and IDL specifications [OMG91a]; ANSA traders; APIs, and LAIs [MBH+92]. Research is required to develop generic and efficient gateway technology for the automatic generation of gateways between arbitrary computer systems. There are an increasing number of specific (i.e., system to system) and minimal gateway products. General purpose tools are required for constructing gateways, just as DBMSs are generic tools for constructing data-intensive applications.

- Semantic aspects of interoperability[6]: Intuitively, semantic considerations for interaction concern establishing that you and I mean the same thing by the messages
we exchange. In the definition given above for interoperability, this concerns the
mutual agreement of components X and Y on the messages R and S that they
exchange. Interoperability, as defined above, is based on the object-oriented notion
that objects are defined in terms of their interfaces which encapsulate both their
values and methods. In the definition, component, or object, Y has an interface that
includes the methods that can respond to R and that X must understand in order
to interoperate appropriately with Y. Similarly, X has an interface that includes the
methods that can respond to S and that Y must understand in order to interoperate
appropriately with X. That is, the relationships between X and Y are defined by
R and S. Whereas relationships in semantic data models were defined in terms
of structure, predicates, and functions, relationships in object-oriented models are
defined in terms of the messages that the objects can meaningfully exchange (i.e.,
that they mutually understand). Hence, interoperability, as defined above, includes
the semantic relationships between objects.
In general, semantic aspects of interoperability between two interoperable objects
involves establishing, representing, maintaining, and possibly evolving through
time, the relationships between those objects. Operationally in object-oriented environments, relationships are implemented through the messages they exchange and
are manifest in the results of the objects' responses to the messages.

As discussed in detail above, the definition does not address issues such as whether X
or Y are in the same or in different ISs. When X and Y are in different ISs, there are more
issues to address than when they are in the same IS. What can become more difficult is
establishing, representing, implementing, and maintaining relationships. However, the
semantic relationships should be the same in either case. Indeed, from the semantic point
of view, all objects that are registered in the global object space can be considered to
form one object space independently of ISs boundaries. Hence, all of the concepts, tools,
and techniques for dealing with semantic aspects of single or distributed databases or ISs
(e.g., those of conceptual modelling [BMS84]) apply to the semantics of interoperable
ISs (i.e., ICISs). Unfortunately, to date, conceptual modelling has had little impact on ISs
[BC92]. It has not enjoyed the clear progress, over the past 25 years, shared by many
systems areas, including operation systems, databases, and programming languages.
Problems of semantics in ISs are inherently hard and are fundamentally important. No
matter how powerful our computing technology, semantic aspects will remain in the
area of open problems.
This observation does not simplify the semantic problems of interoperable ISs.
Rather, it demonstrates that the problems are at least as hard as individual ISs. No new
semantic problems have been added except scale (i.e., a vastly larger object space),

---

[6] Semantic interoperability presumably refers to the semantic aspects of interoperability. However, interoperability requires that semantic aspects be addressed. Is there another kind of
interoperability in which semantics should not be addressed? What is non-semantic interoperability (c.f., There are other kinds of databases than relational? There are non-relational
databases). Hence, I will use that phrase *semantic aspects of interoperability*, and not the term
semantic interoperability.

and various forms of heterogeneity (e.g., such as those listed above in the discussion of transparency). In addition, the environment is object-oriented, the components may be in separate ISs, and the ISs may be built without a database or schema, in the conventional sense.

I conclude this discussion with one semantic problem in interoperable ISs. It and others are illustrated in the next section. The scale of the global object space for interoperable ISs makes the notion of a global schema infeasible. Indeed, it may be best to have no global anything except a global naming scheme. Interoperability between two objects requires, at a minimum, that the objects be able to reference each other and that when they mutually refer to each other or to a third object using a particular name, they mean the same object. Global naming establishes identity only. When you have identity between two objects, their semantic relationship is trivial. When you cannot establish identity between two objects that you understand to be identical, you have semantic problems. Solutions may involve modifying one or both objects or their contexts until the desired mapping (e.g., identity) can be established. Related problems include schema mapping, and proving programs equivalent. While DOMs or ORBs do not solve semantic integration problems, their type systems and mapping mechanisms (e.g., client interfaces, adapters, stubs) provide powerful tools for mapping between systems. First-order logic also provides powerful means for such mappings.

Requirements for global object management will come, in part, from the applications that require such services, such as ICISs. The following is a list of basic research questions concerning the nature of ICIS [BC92]:

- What forms of cooperation are required between components in an ICIS?
- What ideal architecture (components and interfaces) is required to support ICISs?
- What are the modelling/programming paradigm requirements of an ICIS?
- What languages are required in the life-cycle of an ICIS?
- What does it mean for an ICIS or object to be (re)active?
- What forms of intelligent functionality are required for ICISs?
- What are the requirements for the repository or global directory service?
- What forms of interoperability will ICISs require?
- What are the transaction model requirements of an ICIS?
- What are the key optimization challenges in support of ICISs?
- How can core technology support the inevitable evolution of large-scale ICISs?

Due to the key role of object-orientation, it is important to realize the basic research challenges that exist in that domain. Currently there is no underlying theory comparable to the relational model for databases [Bee90]. Hence, there are not general-purpose means for query or transaction optimization. Further, there are inadequate means for dealing with the complexity and scale of object-oriented systems. There are inadequate concepts, techniques, and tools to model large (e.g., 200+) object systems. In terms of programming and execution, how can you describe and prove that the spreading invocation of operations will achieve some specific functionality? How do you optimally schedule the execution of such operations? Do objects schedule themselves or provide other systems functions such as concurrency control and security, or is this done outside the object?

We may require new ways of thinking. The conventional idea of defining each specific relationship between an object and all potentially related objects can't be right. Consider how bird and fish *objects* interact in nature. Defining every relationship between 100 fish in a small tank may be doable, especially when you can see them all. Do fish really work like that? What happens in a boundless ocean with unlimited fish? Thousands of fish move beautifully in schools, etc., probably without sending messages between every two fish. Similarly, how do large flocks of birds fly in formation?

2 The Challenge of Legacy Information Systems

Most large organizations are deeply mired in their IS *sins of the past*. Typically, their ISs are very large (e.g., 10^7 lines of code), geriatric (e.g., more than 10 years old), written in COBOL, and use a legacy database service (e.g., IBM's IMS or no DBMS at all). These ISs are mission critical (i.e., essential to the organization's business) and must be operational at all times. These characteristics define *legacy information systems*. Today, legacy ISs pose one of the most serious problems for large organizations. Costs due to legacy IS problems often exceed hundreds of millions of dollars per year. They are not only inordinately expensive to maintain, but also inflexible (i.e., difficult to adapt to changing business needs) and *brittle* (i.e., easily broken when modified for any purpose). Perhaps worse is the widespread fear that legacy ISs will, one day, break beyond repair. Such fears combined with a lack of techniques or technology to fix legacy IS problems result in IS apoplexy. That is, legacy ISs consume 90% to 95% of all application systems resources. This prevents organizations from moving to newer software, such as client-server configurations, current generation DBMSs, and fourth generation languages (4GLs), let alone the architectures described above. Consequently, organizations are prevented from *rightsizing*, which involves moving from large mainframe computers to smaller, less expensive computers that fully meet current application systems requirements. This apoplexy, in turn, is a key contributor to the software crisis. New requirements, often called the IS backlog, cannot be met since legacy ISs cannot be extended and new systems cannot be developed with the 5% to 10% remaining resources.

Legacy IS migration involves migrating an existing IS into a target IS. This could mean replacing all of the hardware and the software (i.e., interfaces, applications, and databases). However, under some circumstances, some existing components can, even should, be incorporated into the target IS. I claim that the target environment should, in principle, be the distributed computing and enterprise information architectures described above. In ICIS terms, legacy ISs can be incorporated into the enterprise information architectures as component ISs.

Even if these environments were in place, there are few if any methods for migrating legacy ISs to the new environment (one is proposed in [BS92]). Currently, disjoint and heterogeneous information/computing resources must be made to cooperate efficiently and transparently. Without cooperation (e.g., via interoperability) and increased *intelligence* of these resources, the massive investment may be lost. For example, do you incorporate, into an organization's new distributed computing architecture, a mission critical, multimillion-dollar, multimillion-line COBOL system with all its faults and limitations, or simply replace it with a newly rewritten system? There is technical and economic evidence that legacy ISs cannot be rewritten.

Legacy IS problems are much more compelling and immediate than the vision of distributed computing. No matter how great the vision, it will be of little value if it cannot be integrated into the current IS technology base. A challenge here is to develop technology that permits enhancement and evolution of the current, massive investment in ISs.

2.1 Legacy Information System Case Studies

This section illustrates legacy IS problems via actual legacy IS migration efforts, identifies solution directions, and restates distributed computing research challenges in terms of legacy IS challenges. The message of this section is that the visions described above inadequately address legacy ISs. Researchers and technologists should provide effective means to migrate from legacy ISs and the installed technology base to newly offered technologies. The good news is that the potential cost reductions of the next generation computing and the avoidance of the sins of the past will pay for the vast migration costs. In a competitive environment, you may not be able to afford not to migrate!

Telephone Service Provisioning. Figure 11 illustrates eight very large and very real legacy ISs used in the provisioning of telephone services to telephone customers. When a customer calls to request telephone service, this combination of ISs supports what I call the *service order transaction*. It consists of thirteen steps, each supported by one or more legacy ISs. The steps verify the customer street address, identify an appropriate (e.g., available on your premises, working, not too recently used) cable pair, telephone number, and related equipment (e.g., line equipment, location on a distributing wire frame, jumper wires, special circuits for advanced services, cross connect box) in their available inventory, assign the equipment to you, take it out of inventory, deploy it (i.e., make the necessary connections, update the telephone switch that will serve you), ensure that it works, and inaugurate the service. These steps invoke others not illustrated here, including customer credit validation, account and billing setup, and directory services update. Ideally, service provisioning is completed during the customer contact or within a few hours or days.

As with most legacy ISs, none were originally designed to cooperate with any other to achieve any task or goal. Since telephone service provisioning is a mission critical for the telephone company, the systems were made to interoperate using existing technology. There is no transaction system to support the design, development, testing, and execution of the service order transaction, so it is done using available technology without the value of high-level abstractions, locking mechanisms, transaction-oriented backup and recovery, performance tuning, etc. As you can imagine, such services might dramatically improve IS support for telephone service provisioning.

Major problems in constructing the service order transaction are due to the heterogeneity of the participating systems. They are almost all written in different languages and run on different computers under different operating systems. They all have different interfaces. In some cases, to interact with the system you must simulate a TTY

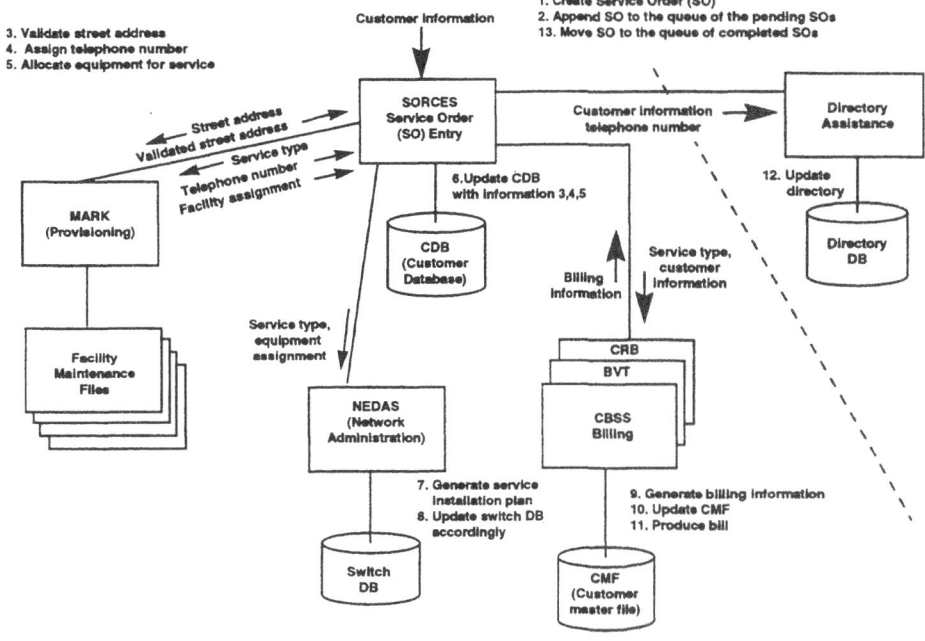

Fig. 11. Service order transaction

terminal to act as an on-line user. Each system has a different information base with naturally arising semantic inconsistencies between definitions and representations of similar concepts (e.g., customer, service order, street address).

Most legacy ISs actually interoperate or have requirements to interoperate in a similar manner. The service order transaction is an excellent illustration of the need for improved technical support for interoperability such as raised in the previous section. It is a real example of *programming in the large* (e.g., the service order transaction involves operations on eight large and distinct ISs) for which there is almost no support such as advanced transaction models [Elm92] that provide some, as yet undefined, notions of transactional integrity in multi-IS tasks, and no high level programming languages to support what are currently called workflows. With eight major ISs and thirteen steps, many things can go wrong. Transaction abort and restart may be infeasible due to the lack of control over component ISs or too costly. In the example, what is a reasonable definition for transactional integrity? What is required to support it?

Gateways provide potential solution to some problems of architecture, systems interaction and interfacing, and heterogeneity via encapsulation. Gateways can be constructed to mediate between the encapsulated IS and requesting IS [MBH⁺92]. They can provide requesting ISs with appropriate views and provide a basis for interoperability. By encapsulating the IS, the gateway provides a means of hiding any modifications to the legacy IS (e.g., the evolutionary replacement of the legacy IS by one or more ISs). The gateway concept is used in all legacy ISs described in this section. Hence, research to facilitate the design, development, deployment, and modification of efficient gateways is critical to both legacy ISs and future distributed computing architectures.

Cash Management System. Like all other legacy ISs described in this section, the CITIBANK Cash Management System (CMS) was believed to be impossible to extend without massive risk and cost. Indeed, several attempts have failed for CMS and for other legacy ISs described here. This sub-section summarizes a potentially successful attempt [BS92].

CMS supports check processing and other specialized services for large corporate customers. It allows a customer to maintain a so-called *zero balance* account (i.e., the bank notifies the customer of all the checks that are processed during a given day, and allows the customer to cover the exact amount of these checks with a single deposit). Hence, the customer applies the minimum possible capital to cover his liabilities and only when the capital is needed. Second, CMS *reconciles* cleared checks. A customer provides the bank with an electronic feed of all the checks written each day. The bank matches issued checks against cleared checks and provides the customer with an electronic feed of all cleared and pending checks. Third, CMS supports electronic funds transfers between customer accounts. When the initiator or recipient of the transfer is another bank, then funds must be electronically received from or transmitted to another bank. This requires connection to several electronic money transfer systems (e.g. Swift, Federal Reserve Bank). Fourth, CMS supports *lock box* operations for customers who receive large numbers of checks in the mail, such as a large landlord or a utility. Mail received in a post office box is opened, the checks deposited for the customer, and an accounting rendered. Such a service is appropriate. Finally, CMS supports customer on-line inquiry and reporting of account status as well as on-line transactions such as the previously discussed transfer of funds.

CMS encompasses 40 separate software modules that perform these and other functions, totaling around 10^7 lines of code. Most of the code runs in a COBOL/CICS/VSAM environment; however, the connection to the Federal Reserve bank is implemented on a Tandem machine using TAL, and lock box operations are provided on a DEC VAX.

The majority of the system was written in 1981, and it has now grown to process 10^6 checks in a batch processing run each night and approximately 300,000 on-line transactions each day. The majority of the systems run on an IBM 3090/400J with 83 spindles of DASD. CMS must continue to operate 24 hours a day, 7 days a week.

The key objective of the migration was that it be an iterative evolution, which we call *Chicken Little*, rather than a complete one-shot replacement, which we call *Cold Turkey*. Management imposed the criteria that each iterative step require less than ten person years of effort, one year in duration, and one further year to payback. The following migration plan was proposed.

1. Peel the Onion: Peel off successive layers of a complex system until only the *core* remained. Upper layers could be moved to a new environment in manageable sized *chunks*. On-line reports and feeds are especially amenable to this treatment.
   In CMS, we were left with a small *core* which had manageable complexity. It is our assertion that most complex systems can be peeled in this fashion. If CMS had been poorly architected, for example, if CITIcash had performed its own updates

instead of calling CITIchecking, then the *core* would have been larger. In this case, we speculate that re-engineering of multiple kernels into a single kernel would have been the appropriate step. This was not required in CMS.

2. Decompose Functionality: When a complex IS implements two or more functions that are logically separable, then the migration plan should untangle the multiple functions and migrate them independently. This is especially valuable when migration steps would otherwise be too large to perform.

3. Design the Target: The target system was designed as a Cash Management ICIS composed of less than ten component ICISs to run on a distributed computing architecture. The resulting design is the target of the migration strategy.

4. Migrate: Completely rewrite the selected components, one at a time, migrating the data and functionality, thereby incrementally constructing the target system.

The key element of the migration plan is that it is an incremental rewrite of CMS and not incremental re-engineering. Although there has been much interest expressed in re-engineering legacy ISs, our case study has indicated that virtually all code would be better re-specified using modern tools, especially fourth generation languages, report writers, and relational DBMS query languages. There may be legacy ISs where re-engineering is a larger part of the migration plan; however, our experience did not indicate any significant use of this technique.

Several research areas emerged from this legacy IS migration exercise [BS92]. First, and foremost, a gateway was seen as critical to legacy IS migration, but its performance was seen as more critical than the other gateways used in other migrations described in this section. Another research area is support for database migration (e.g., from legacy to new) and application cutover. A third area was tools to analyze and extract systems specifications, database designs, and the logical structure of application code. A final research area is an environment for distributed IS design, development, and migration to support not only legacy IS migration but continuous evolution of ISs, ICISs, and support technologies.

Facilities Management System. Many legacy ISs have evolved from simple systems, by adding a small amount of functionality at a time, to become massive systems (e.g., millions of lines of COBOL). Fifteen to twenty years is ample time to embed every conceivable IS blunder deep into an IS. Such ISs are seldom documented. FMS, a telephone facilities management system, is such a legacy IS. I focus here on only a few of the problems and a proposed solution. The vast FMS database is a much more valuable resource than FMS functionality. Many existing systems (i.e., 40 critical systems, over 1,200 lesser systems) depend on accesses to FMS. Many new ISs require access to the data. However, due to the inflexible data structures and the systems interface, the data is largely inaccessible. As a result of this and the construction of new ISs over time, between 40% and 60% of the data is duplicated in other systems. FMS must be in continuous operation, 24 hours a day, 7 days a week.

How do you migrate FMS from its current legacy IS to a facilities management ICIS in a client/server distributed computing environment, following the distributed computing vision? The proposed migration strategy is as follows: First, construct a gateway to encapsulate FMS and the new IS so that changes are transparent to ISs that depend on FMS. Figure 12 illustrates the migration architecture, including the legacy user (UI_i) and systems interfaces to the legacy IS and the new user interfaces (GUI_i) and applications modules (M_i) on the new DBMS. Second, design new databases that include necessary FMS data as well as meet current requirements. Due to FMS' structure and a lack of documentation, this will require, in part, treating FMS as a black box and studying its behaviour externally. Populating the new databases is a challenge. Slowly migrate FMS functionality from FMS to the new databases using the gateway to direct requests to the appropriate ISs (e.g., old FMS, the new IS, or both). Due to potential internal dependencies in FMS, it may be necessary to continue to maintain FMS in its full form even when functionality has been migrated to new systems. Eventually, throw FMS away.

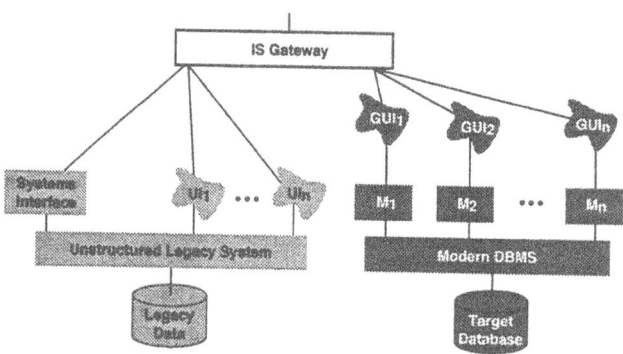

Fig. 12. Legacy IS migration architecture

Under cover of the gateway, any IS architecture can be used, including ones consistent with the distributed computing vision. The requirement to support over 1,200 legacy ISs emphasizes the importance of gateway research and technology. A major function of the gateway is to direct requests to the correct system. This provides an opportunity for an intelligent gateway to add view and query optimization. However, powerful transaction management support must be added. There is no choice. Interoperability research should consider such legacy IS migration requirements. Finally, in this legacy IS migration, as with all others in this section, object-oriented technology was not explicitly used due to the lack of adequate concepts, tools, and techniques, let alone experienced staff. However, the migration architecture, the use of message passing between components, and component encapsulation are appropriate steps toward future conversion to object-orientation and a distributed computing architecture. This illustrates the relationship between the vision of future computing, discussed in Sect. 1, and legacy systems. Legacy systems are intended to be encapsulated component ISs in an ICIS.

The Corporate Customer Database. US West, a large American telephone company, has over 1,000 ISs that deal with customer operations, almost none of which were designed to interoperate [HDB92]. Each has its own customer *database*, however over 200 are major customer databases. This is typical of large telephone companies around the world. There are myriad legacy IS problems in such a nexus of customer operations support systems. Most of the systems are inflexible (e.g., data structures cannot be enhanced or modified) and fragile. Bitter experience has taught that large legacy ISs cannot be rewritten from scratch, the cold turkey approach. Stories of the failures of multimillion dollar, multiyear rewrites abound. Organizations feel that "You can't live with them and you can't live without them."

In recent years, many large organizations have investigated the idea of corporate information repositories, also called corporate subject databases. This suggests that all customer data be integrated logically, and possibly physically, into one corporate customer database. The conceptual modelling world has offered the global conceptual schema approach. The distributed database community has offered limited distributed database interoperability. To date, most such projects have failed. Each database has its own definition of customer. The definition is used and depended upon by many applications. Even if the definition could be altered so that the data could be migrated to the new database, there would be a massive problems of dealing with the old applications. Rather than one definition of *customer*, there are good reasons for contextual variations (e.g., regulatory, legal) that are inherently inconsistent. The scale of the customer database completely defeats all proposed global schema, integrated schema, and conceptual modelling solutions. The scale of the ICIS and world-wide computing puts the nail in the coffin. Even if we had the tools with which to conceptually map schemas, the scale of the problem is beyond the manpower possible to be deployed to the task.

Consider semantic challenges that arise in making 200 customer databases interoperable. Interoperability requires that establishing, representing, maintaining, and possibly evolving through time the relationships between interoperable objects. Consider only the concept of *customer*. At the type or schema level, the above example involves at least 200 different definitions of *customer* in the databases and thousands of different definitions in the applications. What should be the relationships between these definitions? At the individual level, what are the actual relationships between the 10^7 customers? Although many definitions may be different, the 1,000 systems are highly redundant. Further, due to the nature of the business, many geographically distributed business customers are treated as separate customers (i.e., have separate accounts) in the same IS and in separate ISs. How do you establish the relationships between individuals? Type information can help but only to a limited degree. Further, semantic information such as we would like at the type level is often missing completely from legacy ISs or is distributed throughout the data and applications.

These legacy IS examples help to focus the earlier identified interoperability research efforts. Such experiences led to the hypothesis of no global anything and the need for more effective means for systems mapping tools such as type systems instead of conceptual models. Rather than pursue the infeasible and costly goal of complete integration, research should identify different forms of interoperability (e.g., powerful transaction and queries that achieve the required interactions). The example also emphasizes the importance of global naming schemes since it is a bad business practice not to be able to find a customer's records, regardless of the IS in which it is stored. Names are the minimum information that needs to be globally available. Global naming poses major problems since most legacy ISs do not have logical or flexible naming schemes, if any, and systems that do are all inconsistent. Global naming schemes must address legacy ISs or they will not be global.

The Repository. A particularly popular current trend in large IS shops is the construction of a repository, in the sense of IBM's AD/Cycle Repository and DEC's Cohesion. Amongst other things, a repository is intended to support an enterprise model, a design model, and a technology model for all ISs in an enterprise. This is sometimes interpreted to include a corporate-wide dictionary or directory. This brief example is intended to question the feasibility of such a repository and illustrate the principle of no global anything, raised above.

A common approach to building a repository is to integrate every schema element in existing ISs into an enterprise model or dictionary. For example, all definitions of *CUSTOMER* would be resolved (i.e., related) and possibly integrated into, for example, a generalization hierarchy. This incurs the problems raised above concerning semantic aspects of interoperability. In this context, resolving elements involves establishing, representing, maintaining, and possibly evolving through time, the relationships between those objects. In one corporate repository development, 27,000 schema elements from 40 major systems, of more than 1,000, are being resolved in this manner. The first step of establishing relationships is currently taking one person day for two elements. At this rate (and assuming, e.g., no resolution tools or techniques), the first-step of this partial corporate repository will take 65 person years!

2.2 Migration Challenges

Migrating from the current installed technology base involves the migration of two aspects. First, the existing systems technology and its architecture must be migrated into the systems technology and architecture for distributed computing, as described in Sect. 1.2. Second, legacy ISs must be migrated, as described in Sect. 2.1. Both aspects of migration were studied in GTE. The resulting observations, summarized below, were compared with experiences in other large corporations and were found to be universal for large legacy ISs. The universal recommendation for addressing these problems was incremental evolution.

Legacy Information Systems Migration Challenges. The following is a list of the most common and important legacy IS migration challenges. The more mission critical an IS is, the more severe the problems. Cold turkey rewrites do not work. There is no clean sheet of paper. You must deal with the existing ISs, management, operations, technology, budgets, environment, people, etc. Half of the problems below (3, 5, and 7) concern embedding the new IS into the existing environment. These problems vastly complicate cold turkey replacement. The other problems (1, 2, 5) involve ensuring that the new IS captures all the functionality of the old IS.

1. That's All Of It, I Think — The development of large, complex ISs requires years to accomplish. While the legacy IS rewrite proceeds, the original legacy IS evolves

in response to maintenance and urgent business requirements. It is a significant problem to evolve the developing replacement IS in step with the evolving legacy IS.

More significant than maintenance and minor *ad hoc* changes are changes in the business processes that the system is intended to support. These are typically in a constant state of flux. The prospect of incorporating support for the new business processes in the replacement system may lead to significant changes to the system's purpose throughout its development. This dramatically increases the risk of failure.

2. Incomplete Specification Leads to Incomplete Functionality — The requirements for the old IS are never complete and are almost impossible to define. Many requirements have been met directly by coding solutions into the old IS without documentation. The old IS is the only real specification. (See also problem 5.) There is never a specification of the legacy IS due, in part, to the constant evolution of requirements and IS changes. Requirements that couldn't be met are replaced with approximations and work-arounds that are seldom documented. The standard life cycle does not have as a deliverable "A complete specification of the current IS."

3. Ripple Effect Problem — An IS that is mission critical naturally invites other ISs to connect to it. When you change the mission-critical IS, you must deal with all ISs that connect to it. How do you embed the new IS into the operational environment? For example, you can't replace one old IS with one or more standard ISs that cover the same functionality if they don't meet the requirements of the old IS provide on which other ISs depend. The more central the IS is to the organization, the greater the ripple effect.

4. Rebuild the Organization — In supporting some business requirements of some organization, an IS mirrors its structure, to some degree. Over 20 years, both the organization and the IS evolve. The relationship between them is complex in terms of business functions and politics. This poses nontechnical barriers to changes to individual ISs, let alone many ISs that might form an ICIS. These problems tend to overwhelm technical challenges.

5. The Outer Tar Baby: Dependencies to External Systems — Throughout the life of the old IS, vast numbers of small procedures or local systems have been developed to depend on the old IS (e.g., utilities, analysis and report programs). Many, if not all, of these have never been documented or identified. First you must find them and then handle the requirement. In one of the above case studies, we found 1,200 undocumented utilities/small systems that use one mission-critical IS.

6. We Want It All — Users will not be satisfied with a new IS unless it offers them substantially more than the old IS. Cost justification and other organizational incentives argue for more than the old IS provided. It is easier to justify continual, expensive fixes than a costly rewrite with projected annual savings.

7. Jus' Load 'Er Up: Migration and Data Conversion — Once the new IS has been successfully implemented, you must migrate it into the operational environment. This requires that all of the data in the old IS be converted into the format of the new IS and that the new and/or old IS continue to support its functions. Once the new IS is fully loaded, it must be embedded into the existing operational environment. All this must be done without interrupting the mission-critical IS which must be

available 99% of the time. How long does it take to download a terabyte database? (Also see problem 3.)

8. The Inner Tar Baby: Dependence Without Modularity — Like so many pre-database systems, the code and data of large, mission-critical ISs are intimately bound together. There is virtually no data independence. The system code and data is not modular, hence it is difficult or impossible to identify a subset of data or functions to extract or address independently from the rest of the system. Even though current documentation can, and often does for expository reasons, describe the old IS in logical groupings, the code is not so structured.

Legacy Information Systems Technology Migration Challenges. Legacy ISs were designed to be supported by the existing, hence, legacy, systems technology and architecture (e.g., simple flat file systems, ridged hierarchical DBMSs, COBOL, TTY interfaces). The new systems technology and architectures (e.g., described in Sect. 1) may not support legacy ISs, and *vice versa*. I see the following problems as some of the most significant problems with the current systems technology base. Although the new technology base may attempt to avoid such problems, there are no known means for migrating from the old to the new, except for cold turkey. Evolutionary, incremental means must be developed.

- Data Liberation — Users and systems cannot easily access or store the necessary, often already existing, information as it is bound to applications in multiple systems.
- Inability of Systems to Interoperate — Systems do not easily or adequately interoperate (e.g., batch vs. on-line/real-time; tasks involve multiple systems that must interact).
- Systems Designed To Be Inflexible — Poor design and development, older technologies, and techniques have resulted in ISs that are difficult to maintain, evolve, and enhance, due to inflexible systems design and development; inter-system dependencies; lack of modularity; lack of access to data; and business rules and policies (the way business is done) embedded in ISs in inaccessible and fixed representations (e.g., difficult to find or change the rules governing billing).
- Inadequate Life Cycle — Current life cycles include requirements gathering, specification, design, development, testing, implementation, maintenance, enhancement, and evolution. They do not adequately address current problems and the long-term requirements. There is almost no life cycle support (e.g., environments or methodologies) for continuous evolution of ISs that last 20 years or more. History says that you build a large, mission-critical IS only once. Thereafter you must support its evolution. We should build ISs to last 100 years!
- Diversity of Information Bases (including data and function definition) — This is a data administration and standardization issue. For reasons such as funding methods, a lack of knowledge of existing systems and data, and inflexible systems (e.g., difficult technical issues in migration, conversion and cutover), there has been a proliferation of independent systems and information bases. In the past, standards were avoided. This has led, in part, to the diversity.
- Diversity of User Interface and Presentation Formats, Tools, and Technology.

- Inadequate System Responsiveness — Current systems performance does/will not meet real time needs. Today's standards concern screen presentation times. They should focus on ensuring that the intended function, or any related to it, meet business requirements to be accomplished within reasonable limits. This means that the right information is accessed and presented in a way appropriate to the viewer and the task.
- Costs Invested in Existing Systems Technology Base — The massive investment in the existing systems technology make modification difficult to justify.
- Proliferation of Independent Systems and Data.
- Inadequate Skills Match To Meet Current and Future Systems Technology Requirements.
- Lack of Focus on Infrastructure in Systems Technology — Legacy IS projects acquired and used their own systems technology. The new view is of distributed resources to be shared by all ISs in the distributed computing environment and supported by a corporate-wide system technology infrastructure. This major change in systems technology leads to radical changes to funding and administration of IS. Consequently, it poses major, nontechnical challenges.
- Inadequate Management Information, Controls, Measures, and Processes — Current metrics (e.g., reliability and up-time) are not adequate to meet current or future business requirements. There is a lack of management information to adequately manage distributed computing environments. There are inadequate tools to manage the versions required in the continuous evolution of large-scale ICISs, including all legacy IS migrations.

As you can see from the above problem list, the legacy problem is far more than the migration of legacy ISs. Legacy ISs depend on legacy IS technology, which depends on legacy concepts, tools, and techniques, which depend on legacy management, which all depends on legacy thinking which often tries to achieve homeostasis. Much of computer science is based on assumptions that are no longer true (e.g., Von Neuman machines, network communications as bottlenecks). The value of the legacy can be argued, but the problems, when you want to move on, can seem to be insurmountable.

3 Killer Applications for World-Wide Computing

The challenges we face in realizing world-wide computing and ICISs are far more than technical. The technical challenges are exciting, but they do not pose the greatest challenges. Legacy problems, ranging from technology to thinking, are also not the greatest challenges. The greatest challenge is to find ways in which computing can solve major human problems and meet compelling human needs.

In telecommunications, computing, and the potential integration of the two, we have solutions in search of problems, on one hand, and a lack of solutions for existing hard problems on the other. The visions are not new. They are progressing very slowly. Again, the central problem is not the technology nor our legacy. The technologies do not yet meet a human need or solve a problem in a way that people would pay anything for. Originally, databases were hard to sell since they violated ways of doing business (e.g., shared data means loss of ownership and control). Distributed databases pose similar threats today. Databases are more acceptable as support for applications within divisions, when ownership is not lost. For nontechnical reasons, amongst others, the original vision of corporate ownership of data is far from reality.

It takes a killer application to overcome the legacy. We have no creative, compelling applications for world-wide computing or ICISs. Lotus 1-2-3, almost on its own, started the PC/minicomputer revolution, which led to the movement of applications to the desktop and the economics (i.e., cheap workstation MIPS) that is leading to distributed computing and the demise of mainframes. Lotus 1-2-3, for less than $500, motivated managers to buy $5000 machines. If I were to offer you everything you currently have on your desktop plus a lot more, for a lot less cost, but on a mainframe, would you take it? I haven't met anyone who has said yes. Hence, the key point was not cost, nor the technology, but rather what Lotus 1-2-3, the application, brought, namely personal autonomy, control, and power which led to personal innovation. It facilitated real work and met real needs in ways that people would pay for. That's what makes revolutions. For both next generation computing and telecommunications, we have no such killer applications.

What do killer applications look like and how do you discover one? They should meet some significant human, business, or societal need in ways that are compelling or even just acceptable to those with the need. Hence, to find it you must understand human or organizational needs. Computer scientists may not be as well suited to this as application domain experts. Computing and communications must be critical enabling elements. Computer scientists can help here. To find killer applications, hence to assist in realizing the visions, you should understand applications and interact with application experts, those people and organizations with the problems.

My current guess is that killer applications may not be individual applications but the result of multiple, possibly pre-existing applications, working in cooperation (e.g., not just spreadsheets, databases, text processors, schedulers, billing programs, etc., but some very useful combination of these). Correspondingly, future technical successes will come not from individual technologies but from the cooperation of multiple technologies.

To get over the legacy, to find killer applications, we may have to use new ways of thinking, new perspectives. I will conclude with one currently popular such method called Process Re-Engineering.

Conventional ISs are designed to support specific functions of some organization. For example, in the service order transaction example, described in Sect. 2.1, eight ISs each provide a specific function. The problem with the service order transaction was that the systems were never built to cooperate. There was little focus on the higher level function that they now collectively support. The perspective was a bottom-up view of the business, focusing on specific functions.

In process re-engineering, the focus is exclusively on the critical business processes, the lifeblood of your organization. In the above example, it is telephone service provisioning. Hence, the service order transaction is important rather than the supporting systems. With this orientation, concern is for the process to ensure that it goes smoothly from beginning to end, and for the role the business process plays in the organization. In turn, we can view such processes as placing requirements on the supporting ISs. When business processes change, the IS requirements change. Function-specific systems may no longer be of use. Hence, IS technology must be considerably more flexible than it is today. Process re-engineering encourages a new way of thinking of ISs. Perhaps a killer application is one that permits the constant recombination of arbitrary IS components to meet the evolving requirements of ever-changing business processes.

It might be possible to imagine extrapolations of current ISs to intelligent and cooperative ISs in a variety of domains, such as health care. It might also be possible to imagine extrapolations of current telecommunications (e.g., plain old telephones, FAX, modems) to the communication of any information, in any form, at any time, to any location. But it is beyond my power to imagine the potential of world-wide computing/communications and what contributions it might bring to make the world a better place.

The ideas presented in this paper can be summarized in one sentence. *The greatest challenge for future ISs and IS technology is their capability to accommodate change.*

Acknowledgments

The author gratefully acknowledges the insightful discussions with Sandra Heiler and Frank Manola concerning topics in this paper.

Appendix: A Personal Statement – Computer Science and Concern for Our Planet

This message comes from my heart, from my spirit. Please consider with me some challenging questions for which I have no clear answers but which provide a source of creativity and inspiration in my professional and personal life:

– What kind of world are we creating with computers?
– What kind of world do you want to live in?
– How can you use computers, amongst other things, to create that world?
– Are you doing those things now? Or, at least, is your work consistent with your desired world view?
– Whatever you are doing with computers, you are changing our world. Is it for the better?

Computers provide an enormous power on our planet. Moment by moment their power affects and influences you, me, nations, the world economy. Their power and influence will continue to grow enormously. Like all potent powers, computers can be used in many ways. As computer scientists, we play a key role in directing the future use of that power.

Computer scientists often accept jobs or funding to achieve tasks without considering whether these jobs or tasks are in keeping with their desired world view. At least, it is difficult for me to imagine that they want their children to live in the world that could result from their work. Such inattention to values and goals leads to monsters, waste of minds, waste of money, or just plain poor computer systems.

There are also computer scientists and detractors of computer science whose world views exclude many or even all applications of computers. Such myopia can prevent the positive deployment of the amazing power of computers. Computer scientists with this positive attitude may be unable to obtain funding for creative, positive applications of computers.

Where do you fall in this spectrum of concern for the effects of your work? What kind of world are you creating? Do you feel good about your work?

I have grown a great deal professionally and personally, in part, by considering these issues. My goal is to align my intellectual, spiritual, and physical beings. I want everything I do, without exception, to contribute to a world that I want to live in. Such a vision has provided me clear direction concerning what I want to do with computers and what I refuse to do with computers. A major consequence of the process is dramatic freedom of thought, inspiration, and creativity. I am more creative now than I have ever been before in my life. I'm having a blast!

I encourage you to align your mind, spirit, and body to consider vigilantly how your work contributes to improving the world for all beings, to find the strength to refuse tasks that do not contribute to your world view, and to delight in the creativity that will come from this alignment. Each of us is capable of these things and much more! Our work in computer science is as important in its way as that of Mother Teresa. Let us strive to make our work worthy of such a comparison.

Object-Orientation and Interoperability

William Kent

Hewlett-Packard Laboratories, Database Technology Department, 1501 Page Mill Road, Palo Alto, CA 94303, USA

Abstract. Interoperability among database management systems to provide access to multiple autonomous databases has been a long-standing concern. As open distributed systems become more prevalent, the importance of interoperability among general system components significantly increases. Object-oriented technology is expected to play an importnat role in facilitating interoperability. In this paper we address this issue, examining the problems and possible solutions.

1 Introduction

Barriers between various sorts of environments in computational systems are being breached. Independently developed applications need to use each other's services and share each other's data despite a host of differences in the ways they were developed and the ways they operate.

Object-orientation offers some tools for solving such problems. Ironically, though, object orientation also introduces interoperability problems of its own. Our examination of object orientation and interoperability will sketch the problems and solutions, focusing in particular on object-oriented database management systems (OODBMS).

2 Dimensions of the Interoperability Problem

Interoperating applications are often developed independently of each other in environments that may differ in the following dimensions:

- Locations.
- Machine architectures.
- Operating systems.
- Programming languages.
- Models of information.

Applications can interoperate along the following dimensions:

- "Horizontal" peer-to-peer sharing of services and information, such as an editor invoking a spreadsheet processor to embed a spreadsheet in a document.

- "Vertical" cascading through levels of implementation. A student registration service may use a DBMS service which in turn uses a file manager which uses a device driver.
- "Time-line" through the life cycle of an application. Enterprise modeling may be done in terms of one set of constructs which are translated into constructs of the application programming language which are compiled into constructs of the run-time environment. Or, a graphical language used to capture a user's conceptual model of a business domain is translated into a computer-executable simulation language, with the results of the simulation then being input either to an analysis tool to allow refinement of the simulation, or to a report generator to produce the final result.
- Others, e.g., the "viewpoints" of the ISO/CCITT Reference Model for Open Distributed Processing (RM-ODP) [ISO93]:

  • Enterprise viewpoint
  • Information viewpoint
  • Computational viewpoint
  • Engineering viewpoint
  • Technology viewpoint

Interoperation is concerned with such things as:

- Application interconnection:

  • Finding services and information in a distributed environment.
  • Coping with operational differences between requesters and providers of services, such as interface/communication protocols, synchronization, exception handling, work coordination, resource management, etc.

- Information compatibility.

3 Application Interconnection

Problems of application interconnection are addressed by distributed application architectures such as the Common Object Request Broker Architecture (CORBA), shown in Fig. 1, being developed by the Object Management Group [SK94, OMG91a, OMG92].

Requests are submitted via a stub or the dynamic invocation interface and interpreted via an object adapter, a skeleton, and an implementation (performer). The ORB Core itself supports a performer model [Sect. 5.2] defined by its Interface Definition Language (IDL) [OMG91a]. Mapping of models is possible on two sides:

- Applications are expected to invoke local routines to generate ORB requests in IDL. Such routines could map various capabilities into IDL form, supported by appropriate interpretations in the application compiler, adapter, skeleton, and implementation to which the requests are routed.
- Specific mechanisms of how an implementation is chosen and activated are determined by specific implementations of ORB cores, adapters, and skeletons.

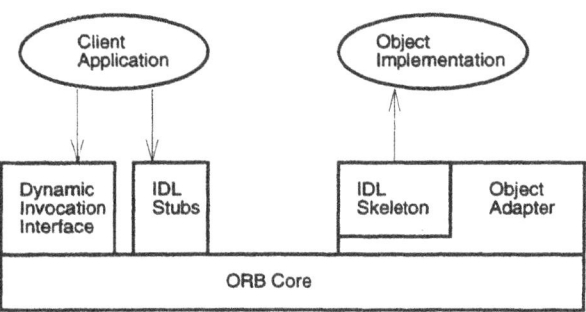

Fig. 1. CORBA

4 Information Compatibility

4.1 Problems

Problems of information compatibility arise in the following dimensions (many are illustrated in [Ken89]):

- Different data models:
    - Traditional data models: relational, hierarchical, network.
    - File systems. Files often don't even have a schema of their own. File format descriptions are buried in applications, allowing different applications to have different views of the same file.
    - Object-oriented models (there are many! [Sect. 5]).
    - New forms: complex structures, spatial data, text, hypertext, blobs, multimedia.
- Differences in enterprise views of similar domains, reflected in data and/or process differences. These might represent local differences in policies or business rules.
    - At the schema level: Some businesses have several salesman per territory, others give several territories to one salesman. Some schools have teaching assistants, others don't. TeachingAssistant is a subtype of Student at some schools, a subtype of GraduateStudent at other schools.
    - Differences in abstraction level/granularity: One source has motor vehicles, the other has cars, trucks, buses, motorcycles, etc.
    - At the instance level: Sales territories are partitioned differently at different companies. Different schools offer different courses.
- Different schemas for the same domain, even within the same model and enterprise view:
    - Different names or spellings for schema elements.
    - Single vs. multiple elements for addresses, dates, names, etc.
    - Cross-level mappings: Jobs are data values in some sources, distinct tables or subtypes in others.
    - Other structural differences.
- Data element (representation) differences:

- • Data types, unit of measure, precision.
- • Notational differences such as spelling, punctuation, capitalization, or omitted parts in names, addresses, document citations, etc.

– Discrepancies in information values:

- • Errors.
- • Out of date information (different currency levels).
- • Different opinions, e.g., ratings of movies or restaurants.
- • Subtle unspecified differences in definition, e.g., distances as airline miles vs. driving miles.

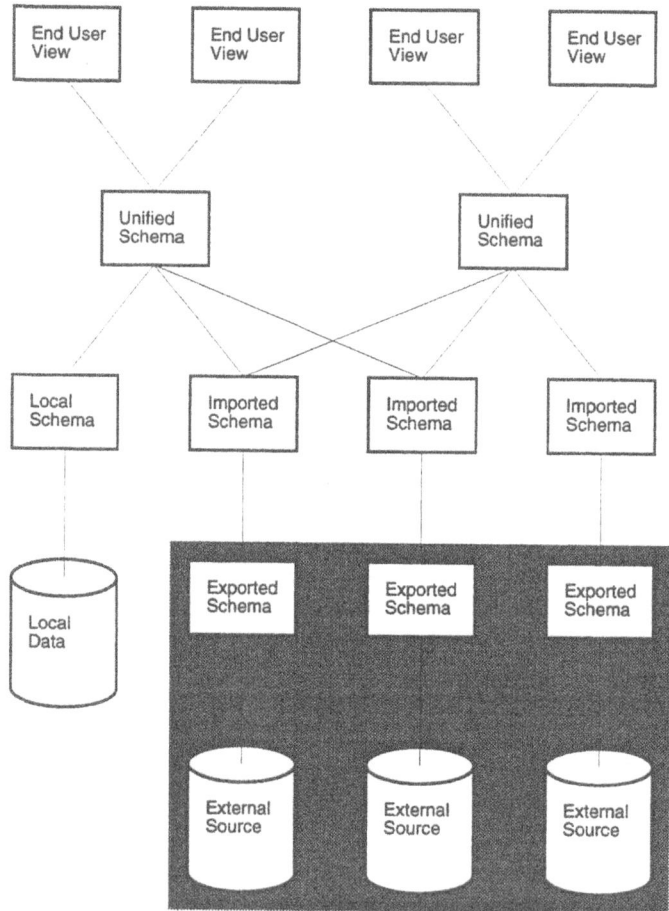

Fig. 2. Integration framework

4.2 A Framework

We focus on peer-to-peer interoperation, and particularly on data sharing, i.e., making data from multiple sources available to an application/user.

A general framework for integrating the information in multiple data sources, such as described in [SL90], involves zero or more of the following components:

- External sources.
- Exported schema of each external data source.
- Imported schema of each source in a common model.
- Locally managed data.
- Unified schemas, reconciling discrepancies of all sorts.
- End user views, possibly in various models.

A sample framework is shown in Fig. 2.

There are many variations on the basic framework, with no clear winners emerging yet. Different situations require different approaches, and it is not clear whether any one paradigm will dominate. Some variations:

- Framework architecture: there might be zero or several of some components.
- Characteristics of external sources:
  - Degree of autonomy.
  - Possible presence of an application serving as an "agent" of the importing system.
  - Degree of heterogeneity.
  - Distribution (physical location and connectivity).
  - Variations in services available, e.g., queries and transactions.
- Inter-component processing:
  - Manual vs. automated import.
  - Query processing/optimization strategies.
  - Transaction management.
  - Propagation of updates, in both directions.
- Integration scope:
  - Across multiple enterprises (least feasible).
  - Across one whole enterprise.
  - Localized application domain (most feasible).
- When the framework is developed:
  - Statically in advance (not practical for large scope).
  - Incrementally as needed, accumulating an expanding framework. (Both of those have to cope with schema evolution.)
  - Ad hoc: as needed, then discarded.
- End user capabilities:
  - Read-only vs. update of external sources.
  - Current vs. snapshot view of external data.
  - Integration with locally maintained data.

We will focus on information mapping concerns.

4.3 Object-Orientation as a Solution

Certain object-oriented features are particularly useful for solving problems of information compatibility:

- Object identity provides a basis for correlating information about "the same thing" from different sources.
- Subtyping allows reconciliation of different levels of abstraction.
- Computationally complete behavior specification (beyond relational view definition) allows complex resolution of information discrepancies.
- The notion of overloaded operators can be extended to help correlate object identities and reconcile information discrepancies.

Note that we are describing language for expressing solutions, not facilities for discovering them. Solutions will be illustrated in terms of a participant model [Sect. 5.2] in order to use its higher level of semantic abstraction [ADD+91, DH84].

Stages. Access to external data in multiple sources involves:

- Discovering/identifying relevant external sources.
- Importing their schemas into a common model. After importing into a common model, the "home" system has a schema of the external data while the external sources serve as underlying "storage managers" for the data. At this stage the imported data from multiple sources is in a common form accessible by end users, but without identities correlated or discrepancies reconciled. The schema is the simple union of the imported schemas, possibly along with schemas for locally maintained data as well.
- Integrating into a unified view:
  - Integrate the schemas.
  - Correlate object identity.
  - Reconcile discrepancies in information content.
- Executing user requests.

We will focus on import and integration, which are the main areas to which object-oriented techniques can be usefully applied. Import and integration correspond to "levels" in the schema, and need not correspond to a chronological sequence. Schemas don't have to be statically pre-defined or persistently maintained [Sect. 4.2]. However, the application/user does need some coherent picture of the information being used. At minimum, what we describe here is a mental model, or some implicit descriptive mechanism transiently created at run time. Renaming (mentioned below) doesn't have to be explicitly specified, but could be inferred from knowledge of synonyms and variant spellings. Of course, the more heuristic the more the risk of error. Algorithms for correlating identities and reconciling information do need to be expressed somewhere.

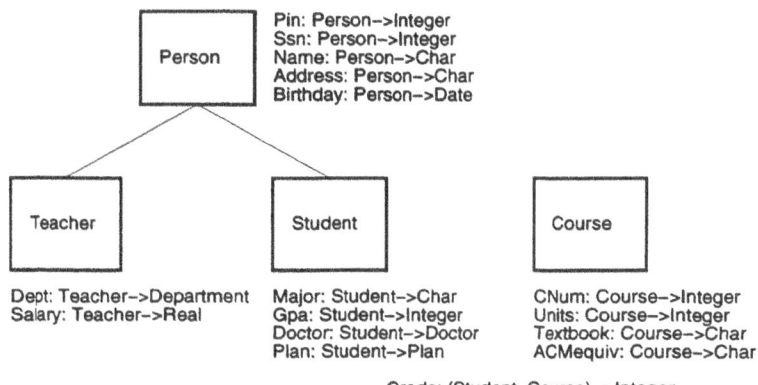

Imported OO Schema

Exported Relational Schema

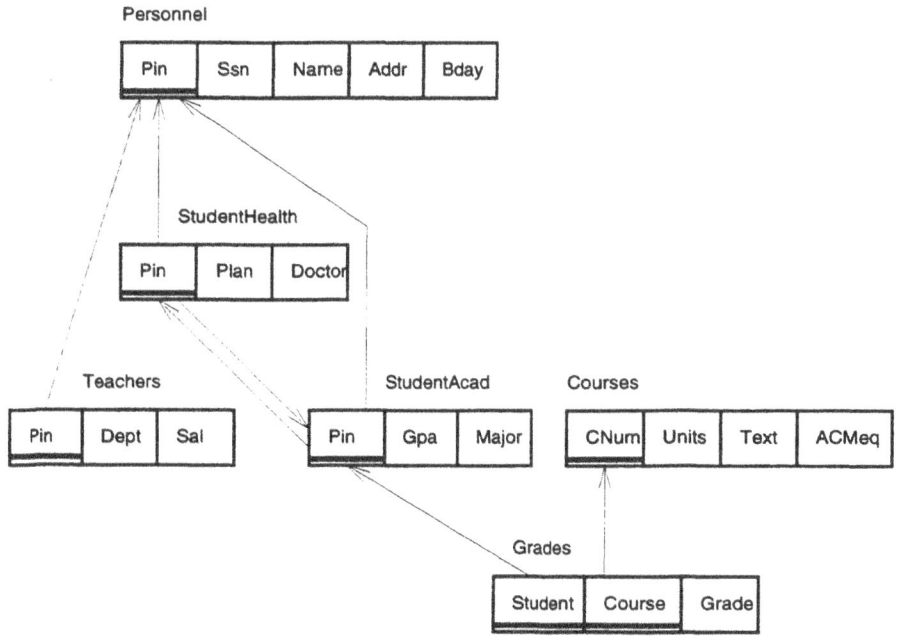

Fig. 3. University data example

Import. Suppose we are accessing information about students, teachers, and courses from various universities. One of the university sources might export a relational schema as shown in Fig. 3.

Type relationships can be inferred from certain inclusion dependencies [AAK+93] (indicated as arrows in Fig. 3). Simple key inclusions imply subtypes, so the Teacher type is imported as a subtype of Person. Mutual key inclusions imply vertical partitioning, so StudentHealth and StudentAcad are recognized as providing data about the same objects, and hence are imported as a single Student type (also a subtype of Person). Courses are imported as a distinct type. Some foreign keys imply that relations represent relationships rather than types, and are imported into whatever mechanism represents relationships in the object model. Thus the Grades relation is imported as a multi-argument function in a functional object model.

The university uses its own "person identification numbers" (Pin) to identify people, since not everybody has a social security number. In the external relational data, a person corresponds to a Pin value, which is an integer. In the object-oriented model, a person has an identity as a distinct object, separate from the integer Pin value which is one of its properties. Put simply, an instance of Person is not an integer.

In a locally managed OODBMS, objects are explicitly created and deleted. An explicit object creation operation provides a semantic basis for object identity: distinct creation events give rise to distinct objects. (In some implementations, creation generates a unique oid for the object as a "birthmark"). An explicit deletion operation allows the DBMS to manage referential integrity, removing all stored references to the deleted object (or disallowing the deletion while there is such stored data). Such facilities are not available for data imported from fully autonomous external sources. The external data will simply contain different numbers of students at different times, with the OODBMS getting no intervening notification of creation or deletion.

Since there are no creation events on which to base object identity, such identity must be based on data in the external source. Essentially, a set of values has to be defined such that an instance of the imported type exists for each value in the set. We can say that an imported type "produces" an instance corresponding to each value in its "producer set". The producer set might be simply defined, as with the Pin numbers used by this university to identify people. In the absence of such simple keys, it might be something more complex, such as a composite key consisting of Name, Address, and Birthday. (In general, imported object types don't have to correspond to primary keys of relations.)

As mentioned, the values in the producer set are not the same things as the instances of the type. Although Pin integer values are not themselves instances of Person, there is a one-to-one correspondence. Whenever a certain Pin value is detected in the external data, a corresponding Person instance exists. When the Pin value vanishes, the corresponding Person instance ceases to exist. If the Pin value reappears, so does the Person instance. Such "produced objects" have their existence defined by a rule, rather than by creation events (like the "imaginary objects" of [AB91]).

Object identity has to be carefully managed among different types. Common values in different producer sets may or may not correspond to the same object. In the university example, course numbers (CNum values) might accidentally match Pin values, yet courses and persons are obviously not the same thing. Furthermore, several universities might use Pin numbers independently.

Different students at different universities might have the same Pin number - and a student who has attended several universities will probably have a different Pin number at each.

A conservative strategy is to assume that, in the absence of other information, all imported types are disjoint from each other, i.e., they have no instances in common. A plausible implementation strategy would be to construct an object identifier as a concatenation of a producer value with a unique "tag" associated with each imported type.

The disjointness assumption can be relaxed, for example, if inclusion dependencies are known for a relational data source [AAK+93]. The disjointness assumption is clearly inapplicable in the case of vertical partitioning, since the underlying relations are imported into a single type. The assumption is also inappropriate for subtypes, as indicated by key inclusion dependencies. It does not make sense to treat Teacher or Student as being disjoint from the Person supertype, since the instances of Teacher or Student are obviously known to be instances of Person. Thus, in implementation terms, these three types should all use the same tag in their produced oid's. (Note that we have no information as to whether or not Teacher and Student are disjoint from each other.)

Naming conventions generally require types to be uniquely named, so types imported from different sources might have to be renamed (e.g., if they are imported from external relations having the same name). Thus, if we are importing data from "Eastern University" and "Western University", the imported types might be named EPerson, WPerson, ETeacher, WTeacher, and so on.

The imported functions (operations) only have to be uniquely named within their argument types, since object systems support overloading (polymorphism). However, we should carefully distinguish between specific and generic functions. Thus, for example, the functions named "Address" which are defined on EPerson and WPerson are two distinct specific functions, corresponding to a single generic function named "Address". Specific functions can be uniquely named by appending their argument types, e.g., EPerson.Address and WPerson.Address.

We will later see that it is very useful to rename functions so that they have the same name if and only if they represent "semantically equivalent" information - a concept which we will not define further. Thus, for example, all functions which provide addresses should be named "Address", and no other function should have that name.

If no further integration is defined, imported data can be made accessible to end users uniformly via the object model of the importing OODBMS. However, it is uncorrelated. Objects imported from different sources appear distinct, so that a person who has attended several universities appears to be several distinct persons. Courses given by one university are different objects from those given at another. The schemas associated with the different sources might be different (though we will assume they are similar for the moment).

For retrieval purposes, imported data can be indistinguishable from locally maintained data. Update may be restricted, depending on the level of interaction supported by the autonomous external source.

Schema Integration. Schema integration is a problem when imported schemas from "similar" domains are structurally different, yet need to be presented as a single schema to the end user [BLN86]. A typical problem is illustrated in Fig. 4.

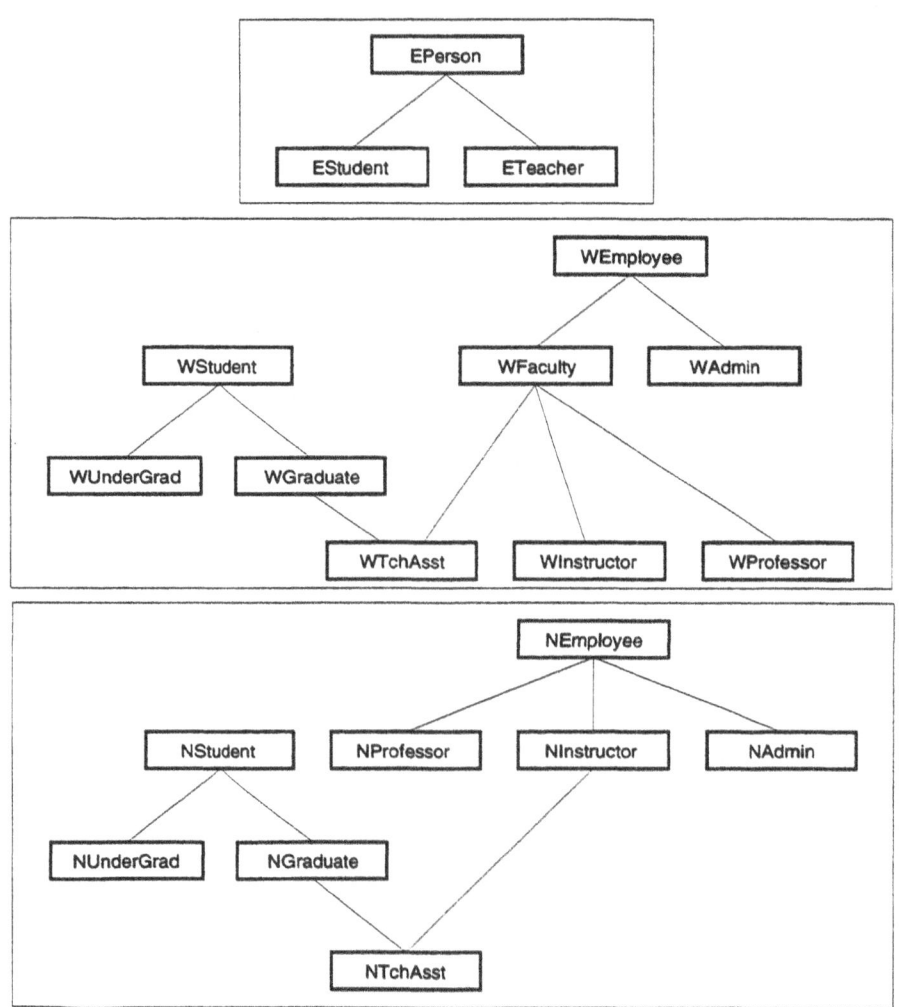

Fig. 4. Non-isomorphic imported schemas·

Object technology is generally useful here to the extent that it is capable of representing various levels of abstraction in a type hierarchy. However, the specific problem of unifying these into a coherent schema for the end user is not in itself facilitated by object oriented techniques. We will not pursue this problem in this paper.

Correlating Identities. Correlating identities requires a mechanism for establishing that several imported things should be treated as being the same object. The problem is simpler when the things being made equal are imported from different sources, but we will later consider cases where things imported from the same source should be considered equal ("localized equivalence") [Sect. 4.3]. In the absence of localized equivalence, identity correlation can be described in terms of a "single-viewpoint" approach, whereby the equal things are immediately treated as the same object on import. Localized equivalence requires a more complex description, involving an "underlying viewpoint" in which the imported things are distinct objects, and an "integrated viewpoint" in which they appear as one. Care need be taken to preserve the semantics of equality when treating things as being the same [Ken91b]. In the single-viewpoint approach, $x = y$ does not have the sense of two objects which become one object. It simply means that the variables x and y refer to one and the same object (whether or not they are implemented as having the same oid).

Equality is an equivalence relation, hence the following axioms hold:

E1: $\forall x, x = x$ (reflexivity).

E2: $\forall x \forall y, x = y \Rightarrow y = x$ (symmetry).

E3: $\forall x \forall y \forall z, x = y \& y = z \Rightarrow x = z$ (transitivity).

Equality implies *substitutability*:

E4: $\forall x \forall y \forall f, x = y \Rightarrow f(x) = f(y)$;

also, $f(x)$ and $f(y)$ cause the same conditions and side effects.

Equality implies *singularity*, i.e., there is just one object:

E5: $\forall x \forall y, x = y \Rightarrow \{x, y\} = \{x\}$, or equivalently, $Card(\{x, y\}) = 1$.

E5 might not be an independent axiom, depending on how set construction is defined in terms of equal elements. But it doesn't hurt to emphasize it here. A typical equality specification might take the form

$$\text{EPerson.Ssn}(x) = \text{WPerson.Ssn}(y) \Rightarrow x = y \qquad (1)$$

An equality specification essentially involves a binary predicate $e(x, y)$ such that

$$\forall x \forall y, e(x, y) \Rightarrow x = y \qquad (2)$$

is added to the list of equality axioms. Note that this is one-way implication, not iff.

Oid-based object systems have an implicit axiom that $x = y$ if they have the same oid. In general, $x = y$ is true if it can be deduced from the full set of equality axioms.

Equality is independent of type. An instance of ETeacher might be equal to an instance of WTeacher because of a rule defined on EPerson and WPerson, or even because of a rule defined on EStudent and WStudent if some teachers were also students.

Criteria for judging whether things are the same object can be quite complex, involving various sorts of heuristics, which we will not investigate here. What we will describe are language facilities for expressing equality once the criteria have been determined.

Equality of objects can be described in terms of matching values of some property. The property might be a simple one such as social security number, or a complex one such as the combination of name, address, and birthday. The property might be an artificial one expressly provided for this purpose; for example, a course can be labeled with its equivalent in the ACM/IEEE standard computer science curriculum, with this property then used for establishing identity.

There can be multiple disjunctive criteria, e.g., persons are the same if they have the same social security number (Ssn) or if they have the same citizenship and passport number (Ppn) (not illustrated in Fig. 3). Equality criteria often constitute a one-way implication rather than an if-and-only-if condition. Thus persons should be considered equal if they have the same Ssn (even if they have different Ppn's) or if they have the same citizenship and Ppn (even if they have different Ssn's).

The general form of an equality specification is thus based on equality of properties, e.g., $f(x) = g(y)$ $x = y$. It really only makes sense to specify equality based on "semantically equivalent" properties, e.g., comparing social security numbers with social security numbers, or passport numbers with passport numbers. If semantically equivalent properties are given the same name, then equality specifications can be described as uniqueness constraints on generic functions.

A uniqueness constraint means that $f(x) = f(y)$ $x = y$, i.e., distinct things can't have the same value of f. Such constraints are typically specified for single specific functions, e.g., EPerson.Ssn is unique-valued over all instances of EPerson, so that distinct instances of EPerson cannot have the same value of Ssn.

Declaring generic functions to be unique-valued extends the constraint across all the types on which the function is defined. Declaring Ssn to be a globally unique generic function essentially says that things having the same value of Ssn, via any of the specific functions named Ssn, must be the same object, i.e.,

$$T_i.\mathrm{Ssn}(x) = T_j.\mathrm{Ssn}(y) \Rightarrow x = y \tag{3}$$

for each of the types T_i and T_j on which Ssn is defined.

Reconciling Discrepancies in Information Content. The essential problem can be described by saying that there are functions which the end user wishes to use whose values may not be consistent in the various external sources. Again, we deal only with facilities for expressing solutions, not for discovering them.

Typically, when only one of the external sources provides a value, this can be taken as the intended result. When there is more than one source, then various strategies might be appropriate:

- If all the sources provide the same value, use it.
- Apply some aggregating operation, such as sum, average, minimum, etc.
- Establish a priority ranking of the sources, returning the value from the most reliable source.
- If the information is dated, return the most recent value.
- Apply conversion routines to reconcile differences in units, precision, or other representation characteristics.
- Return all the values from the various sources, perhaps annotated as to the source of each. This option is only viable if the function is defined to return results of the appropriate structure.
- Other arbitrary procedure.

It should be obvious that none of these is the natural default for all cases. Computationally complete object-oriented languages generally have the power to express such algorithms. What remains to be defined are mechanisms for specifying and invoking the action to be taken.

If we again assume that semantically equivalent functions have the same name, this problem bears a remarkable resemblance to overloaded function resolution. The situations where discrepancies might arise correspond exactly to the cases where an overloaded function call is ambiguous.

As before, let's assume we are importing data from several university sources such as Eastern and Western. A request such as Salary(x) is an invocation of an overloaded function, involving specific Salary functions defined on ETeacher, WTeacher, etc. If x is not an instance of any of these types, we have a type violation. If x is an instance of exactly one of these types, then the value of the corresponding specific function should be returned, e.g., ETeacher.Salary(x). Otherwise, if x is an instance of several of these types, the overloaded function call is ambiguous and should be treated as an error condition - unless a disambiguating procedure has been provided. (An ambiguity exists when more than one specific function is relevant, even if they all yield the same value.) It is not at all self-evident what the disambiguation ought to be. If the sources are providing data about different universities, it may be appropriate to return the sum of the salaries (even if they happen to be equal). If the sources are different databases containing data about the same university, it might be appropriate to take the average, or to use the source considered most reliable, or to use the most recent value if the dates are known.

A fairly natural approach here is to allow explicit definition of generic functions, providing a mechanism for defining the disambiguating algorithm. This also provides a mechanism for declaring uniqueness of generic functions [Sect. 4.3]. Such a definition might, for example, specify that a user-defined function named BestSal should be invoked to return an appropriate result whenever Salary(x) is ambiguous.

Localized Equivalence. Localized equivalence arises when several things from the same source are to be treated as equal. Most often, these things will be instances of the same imported type. The situation often arises when there is an independently defined set of instances to be seen by the end user, and imported things have to be mapped into this set of instances.

As an example, suppose that courses are to be considered equal if they correspond to the same course in the standard ACM/IEEE curriculum, and a university offers several courses having the same ACM equivalent. All those courses should appear to be the same course to the end user. The same situation might arise if courses were to be considered equal if they used the same textbook. It might also arise if courses are to be mapped into the local university's own set of courses.

Similar localized equivalence might occur in connection with job titles, geographic entities, colors, and other such things.

Formally, localized equivalence can arise when:

- Equality specifications are based on non-unique properties, such as the ACM equivalent or textbook of a course.

- There are cycles among equality specifications. Suppose an equality specification correlates EPerson and WPerson by social number, and another correlates them by nationality and passport number. Then, if an instance of ETeacher had the same social security number as one instance of WTeacher and the same nationality and passport number as a different instance of WTeacher, transitivity would force those instances of WTeacher to be equal.

Localized equivalence makes it difficult to even formulate the problem of information discrepancy. It can no longer be handled directly by the mechanisms of overloaded functions.

As an example, let's say that when courses are considered equal, we want Units of a course to be presented to the end user as the average of the Units in the external data sources. Without localized equivalence, a characteristic problem would be that different specific functions had different values for the same argument, e.g., ECourse.Units$(x) \neq$ WCourse.Units(x). We could resolve that with a disambiguator for the overloaded Units function, which would take the average of the values when Units(x) was invoked. The unreconciled values could be seen by the end user by invoking the specific functions ECourse.Units(x) or WCourse.Units(x).

With localized equivalence, we somehow need to have x and y be instances of the same type (say ECourse) with different values of ECourse.Units, and yet also have $x = y$. This simply doesn't work. Under the substitutability principle [Sect. 4.3], it is not possible for ECourse.Units(x) to be different from ECourse.Units(y) if $x = y$, since they are logically one and the same object.

This problem requires the introduction of two distinct "viewpoints" (or "spheres" [Ken91a]). In an *underlying* sphere, x and y appear to be distinct objects, allowing the possibility of ECourse.Units$(x) \neq$ ECourse.Units(y). This sphere should only be visible to an administrator responsible for defining the reconciliation mechanisms. The end user should only see an *integrated* sphere in which $x = y$ and there is only one reconciled value of ECourse.Units(x).

An equality specification $e(x, y)$ now implies that $x = y$ in the integrated sphere, but not necessarily in the underlying sphere. Under these conditions, a type may have fewer instances in the integrated sphere than in the underlying sphere, since x and y count as one object in the former but two in the latter. Logically speaking, an instance in the integrated sphere corresponds to an equivalence class of instances in the underlying sphere.

Disambiguators for overloaded functions dealt with the values of several specific functions for a given argument. Here we need the complementary notion, having to unify the values of a given specific function for several arguments. That is, we have to unify the values of ECourse.Units(x) and ECourse.Units(y).

The solution is similar to the one for disambiguation of overloaded functions, though now it has to span between the integrated and underlying spheres. A "unifier" function could be defined for ECourse.Units, such that an invocation of ECourse.Units(x) in the integrated sphere would apply this unifier to the set of values of ECourse.Units(x_i), where the x_i are the distinct objects in the underlying sphere which are equivalent to x.

5 Object-Orientation is Part of the Problem

Object-orientation is plagued by a diversity of interpretations. There is a variety of object oriented models. Readers will probably have noticed different models assumed in different lectures at this Institute. Various experts have very clear and self-consistent ideas, but they are not consistent with each other. Hence there is a new problem of interoperability of object oriented facilities.

5.1 Common Concepts

There seems to be a fairly common core of concepts shared by most object models [FKMT91, SK94, OMG92], but even these are likely to stir some discussion among experts:

- Identity.
- Behavior (messages/methods/operations).
- State.
- Types/interfaces.
- Subtyping.
- Inheritance.
- Overloaded/polymorphic operations.
- Encapsulation.

5.2 Performer and Participant Models

Perhaps the most fundamental distinction between object models is whether objects are perceived as performers or participants. Suppose that a student counseling service (human or automated) wishes to register Sam in the Algebra course. The user might perceive this as a request for a Register operation in which Sam and Algebra *participate*, perhaps written as Register(Sam,Algebra). The requested service might be *performed* by an object corresponding to Sam, by an object corresponding to Algebra, by a Registrar application object, or directly by a DBMS object which records Sam's registration in Algebra. The requester might not even know that the Registrar or DBMS objects exist.

The "participants" in the user's request are Sam and Algebra. The "performer" might be Sam, Algebra, the Registrar, or the DBMS. Thus, in general, the performer may or may not be one of the participants mentioned in the request. Sometimes the application programming language imposes a "performer-oriented" syntax, e.g., Sam.Register(Algebra) or Algebra.Register(Sam), but even then the actual performer might be something else, i.e., the Registrar or the DBMS rather than Sam or Algebra. Similarly, a user at a graphical interface might drag a document icon to a trashcan icon (the two participants), causing the service to be performed by a file manager object.

Some facility in the system may have to transform a user's request of the form Register(Sam,Algebra) into a performer request such as Registrar.Register(Sam,Algebra) or DBMS.Register(Sam,Algebra). This may even cascade to another level, which recognizes different copies of the Registrar application at different sites as being distinct objects, and selects one copy to service the request. There are thus at least two object models involved in the registration scenario, requiring a cascading of interfaces [SK94, OMG92] to map between them.

A participant model does not distinguish between performers and participants, while a performer model does. The distinction is relative to a particular request; a performer for one request might simply be a participant in another. In a typical performer model, only certain objects can play the role of performer, and most model facilities are oriented toward those objects.

There are a number of other distinctions which roughly parallel the performer/participant distinction as shown in Table 1.

Performer Models	Participant Models
Request Message to one target object (the performer) This is the "classical" object model	Operation applied to one or more participant objects. This is the "generalized" model.
Request Syntax Performer.Operation(Participants)	Operation(Participants)
Objects Represent System components & resources (applications, clients/servers, chunks of code, chunks of storage, files, tables, tuples, data "frames").	Enterprise entities.
Object Granularity Coarse, large.	Fine, small.
Role of Infrastructure Locate performer, deliver request, manage parameters.	Determine performer, then locate it, etc.
Method Ownership Exclusively owned by performer type.	Jointly owned by participant types [Ken92b].
State Disjointly partitioned between objects.	Could be shared among objects.
Relationships Separate constructs.	Could be multi-operand operations.
Localization Object is at one node, state is a contiguous "chunk"	Object can be dispersed, with state and services scattered (not just replicas).

Table 1. Performer/participant distinction

This is not a strict partitioning. Various object models exhibit these characteristics in various degrees and combinations.

Note that both performers and participants can have associated behavior.

The role of OODBMS is ambivalent. Some have performer models, some have participant models.

5.3 Other Significant Differences

The following is a sampling of some other significant differences:

- Which of the following are objects? Literals, aggregates, tables, applications, users, icons, types, classes, operations, methods, attributes, relationship, factories,
- Object introduction:
  - Objects are created, made instances of types, and acquire corresponding interfaces by explicit operations of the object system, or
  - Independently existing objects are accessed by the object system, which has to discover their types and interfaces.
- Identity:
  - Based on oid's? Format? Scope of uniqueness?
  - Can oid's be held outside the object system, with guaranteed meaning on future use?
  - Can objects have several (synonymous) oid's?
  - Is $x = y$ testable?
  - How do oid's relate to naming systems?
- Data structure:
  - Expose more complex data structure, or
  - Hide structure behind behavioral abstraction.
- Behavior: is there a distinction between behavior specification and implementation? Which corresponds to methods?
- Types:
  - One level vs. subtyping.
  - Single vs. multiple (immediate).
  - Changeable?
  - Are extents maintained?
  - Various definitions of the difference between types and classes.
  - Basic data types.
- Various inheritance notions (single/multiple, class/type, blocking, instance vs. property, delegation,)
- Treatment of attributes and relationships.
- Various approaches to containment, aggregates, composite objects.
- Query (yes/no, different query models; is it really an object-orientation issue?).
- Single performer per object?
  - All services for a given object are provided by one performer (e.g., a document is associated with one word processor for all services). All requests involving this object can be routed to the same performer.
  - Services may be provided by different performers (e.g., independent performers for editing, displaying, and printing a document, possibly at different locations). Choice of performer may depend on service requested.

5.4 Why the Differences?

Object models differ for a variety of reasons. Perhaps the most important is that different goals are being pursued by various object-oriented facilities:

- Interoperability.
- Portability.
- Extensibility.
- Code reuse.
- Communication/distribution.
- Complex applications.
- Persistence of program data.
- Enterprise modeling.
- System resource management.

There are also business, political, and cultural reasons. Vendors have vested interests in their products. Users need to protect their investments in legacy applications, hardware, software, and programmer training. Researchers become committed to a certain line of development. People have learned to think in the metaphors of certain languages (C++, Smalltalk, CLOS, SQL, etc.). Nationalism plays a role. People have different views of the role of database, e.g., as a repository of structured data vs. an interface through which users manage information.

5.5 Solution Approaches

There is even diversity in the solutions to the problem, and also in the organizations trying to solve the problem [Ken92a].

One style of reconciliation is to develop a unified super-model, in which each model can be found as a subset or restriction of the general model. The other approach is an interoperability framework in which distinct models can cooperate. Diverse agencies are addressing the problems of object technology. There are companies and consortia in the private sector, as well as government standards bodies, both in the United States and internationally. Some are concerned with the object paradigm in specific technologies, such as programming languages or databases, while others seek a uniform approach to object technology as a whole. Two of the organizations addressing these issues are:

- The Object Management Group (OMG), an industrial consortium trying to reach rapid consensus on shared conventions to promote interoperability of applications using currently available technology.
- X3H7 (Object Information Management), an ANSI technical committee intended to foster harmony in the object-oriented aspects of various information processing standards.

The key steps in such reconciliation will include:

- Recognizing the diversity of fundamental assumptions regarding the nature of objects.

- Identifying and characterizing different models.
- Developing a coherent strategy to reconcile diverse models:
  - Describe the models and their differences in common terminology.
  - Converge to a common model as much as possible.
  - Develop interoperability strategies for reconciling the unavoidable differences.

6 Conclusions

Object-orientation plays a major role in the interoperation of computational systems. Its basic messaging model, and the associated architecture and infrastructure, enable applications to communicate across hardware and software boundaries and to coordinate the execution of their work. Rich semantic features such as identity, generalization and specialization, encapsulation, polymorphism, and computational completeness facilitate the sharing of common information among the applications.

At the same time, the diversity of object-oriented models is raising interoperability problems of its own.

Acknowledgments

Many thanks to my colleagues in the Pegasus project, with whom many of these concepts were developed, and especially to Stephanie Leichner for helping assemble the material for this paper.

SECTION 4

SYSTEMS AND PROTOTYPES

Open OODB: Architecture and Query Processing Overview

José A. Blakeley

Texas Instruments Incorporated, Computer Science Laboratory, P.O. Box 655474, MS 238, Dallas, Texas 75265, USA

Abstract. This paper covers two main aspects of the Open Object-Oriented Database (Open OODB) system. First, it presents an overview of its architecture which consists of an extensible collection of services including address space management, translation, communications, name and type management, persistence, distribution, transaction management, index management, query processing, and versioning. Second, it describes in more detail the query processing service of the Open OODB system. This service includes an SQL-based object query language called OQL[C++], an extensible object query optimizer, and a data model-independent query execution engine. We conclude with a discussion of the development status and future research plans of the Open OODB project.

1 Introduction

The Open OODB project is developing an open, extensible architecture for constructing a family of OODBs. By abstracting orthogonal dimensions of database functionality, the Open OODB system will allow tailoring each of these dimensions for particular applications within a common, incrementally improvable framework, and will also serve as a shared platform for research. Texas Instruments developed the Zeitgeist object-oriented database management system (OODBMS) between 1985 and 1990 [FJL+88]. Zeitgeist was used to support applications in the areas of computer-aided design and manufacturing, software engineering, knowledge representation, and hypermedia systems. We learned that these applications have widely varying database management needs and concluded that such applications would be better served by an open, extensible OODB whose functionality could be tailored, rather than by a single monolithic database management system (DBMS). This is consonant with other research and development efforts [BBG+88, HCL+90].

The Open OODB project goals are to describe the design space of OODBs; build an architectural framework that enables configuring independently useful modules to form an OODB; verify the suitability of this open approach by implementing an OODB to these specifications; and determine areas where consensus exists or is possible. Database functionality (such as transactions, persistence, versioning, etc.) is provided via an extensible set of seamless behavioral extensions of the objects and operations from application programming languages such as C++ and Lisp. The extension model allows developers to instantiate Open OODBs with different collections of extensions as needed, and allows researchers to experiment with alternative semantics for the various database extensions (e.g., different versioning or persistence models). Seamlessness aids this process in several ways: it allows application developers to ignore irrelevant details that often require up to 30% of the application code [ABC+83], it allows new extensions to be applied to existing programs, and it encourages minimalist extensions that can be widely applied.

Section 2 describes the computational model for extensibility in the Open OODB. Section 3 describes the system architecture that implements the computational model. Most of the material in Sect.s 2 and 3 are condensed versions of results previously published in [WB92, WBT92]. Section 4 presents in more detail the query module of the Open OODB. The presentation includes a description of OQL[C++], an SQL-based object query language tightly integrated with C++; a query optimizer; and our plans for building a data model independent query execution engine. The material in Sect. 4 is derived primarily from the following previous publications [Bla94a, BMG93]. Finally, Sect. 5 presents our conclusions, project status, and directions for future research.

2 Computational Model for Extensibility

The Open OODB computational model is based on transparently extending the behavior of normal operations (events) in application programming languages [WBT92]. We use the type systems of conventional object-oriented programming languages, initially C++ and Common Lisp, as alternative data models of the database. The computational model is realized by a meta-architecture module that incorporates four basic concepts: event, sentry, policy manager, and policy performer.

In this computational model, objects reside in a *universe of objects* partitioned into *environments* by a collection of *environmental attributes* not normally visible to applications. Environments and the *boundaries* between them are used to identify circumstances in which extensions will be required. An *event* is the entry point to extensibility in Open OODB. Any operation performed within the context of a programming language can be an event. Object dereference and method invocation are two operations that are often extended in a programming language. A *sentry* monitors the occurrence of extended events and invokes the appropriate *policy performer* (PP) which implements the extended behavior. An example of an environmental attribute is the address space in which an object resides; an extension of the application's language is required to operate on an object in a remote address space. Persistence, distribution, and versioning are examples of policy performers.

3 Open OODB Architecture

The Open OODB *system architecture* is divided into (1) a *meta-architecture* consisting of a collection of *glue* modules and definitions providing the infrastructure for specifying and implementing event extensions, sentries, and normalizing interfaces among modules, and (2) an extensible collection of policy performers.

The meta architecture also contains a collection of support modules including *address space manager* (ASM), *communications, translation,* and *data dictionary*. At least one ASM must allow execution of events. If more than one address space exists, there must be *communications* and *translation* mechanisms to effect object transfer between them. A *data dictionary* serves as a globally known repository of system, object, name, and type information. The *meta-architecture support* module provides the *extension* mechanism and defines necessary *interface* conventions to which policy performers must adhere. Figure 1 illustrates the architecture of the Open OODB.

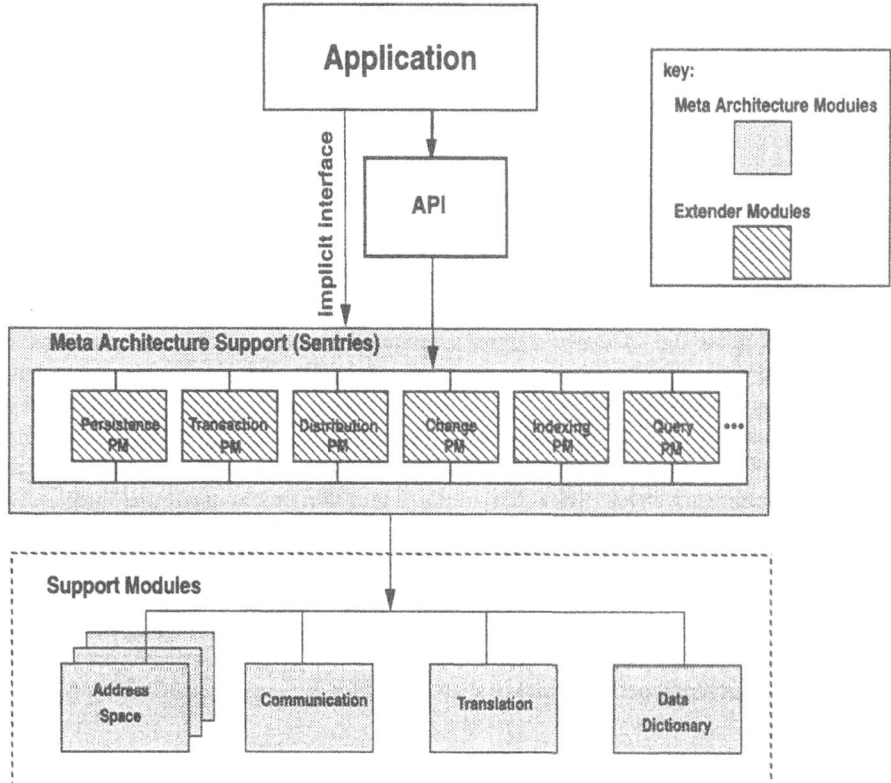

Fig. 1. Open OODB architecture

The set of policy performers in any Open OODB instantiation is flexible; the actual set being determined by the subset of functional requirements being addressed by the instantiation. Since the model supports different extensions, it is possible that systems other than OODBs could be configured in this way. The collection of policy performers for a fully configured Open OODB [Wel91] is summarized in Table 1. Policy performers marked with an asterisk are not supported in the current implementation of Open OODB. The following subsections describe some of the main components of the Open OODB architecture in more detail.

Table 1. Mapping extended behavior to policy performers

Extension	Policy Performer Module
Transactions and controlled sharing	Transaction PP
Distributed (remote) access to objects	Distribution PP
Replicated/partitioned objects	Replication PP*
Indexed sets of objects	Index PP
Object queries	Object Query Processor
Versions of objects	Version PP
Configurations of objects	Configuration PP
Consistency and derived objects	Dependency PP
Object persistence and naming	Persistence PP
Security control over objects	Access Control PP*
Access to objects in foreign databases	Gateway PP*

3.1 Address Space Manager Abstraction

Objects reside in some address space. Address space implementations vary in their representation of objects and their addressing schemes, which allow them to satisfy different functional and performance needs. For example, virtual memories support computation; relational databases support associative access and long term storage; file systems support sequential and perhaps indexed or random access; and archives support long-term storage and recovery. Open OODB can contain address spaces of any of these types (and perhaps others). To allow uniform access to objects from outside an address space, Open OODB defines a module called an Address Space Manager (ASM), which supports mappings between global identifiers and addressing conventions local to an individual address space (see Sect. 3.2).

The address space manager abstraction is orthogonal to physical address spaces. Several address spaces can exist within a single virtual memory; for example a server cache and an application workspace. An address space can also span machine boundaries such as in a client-server model. In this case, the client and server are typically on separate machines, but from the perspective of the OODB, they form a single ASM.

3.2 Object Identifiers and References

Object identifiers (OIDs) and *references* to objects are manipulated by all Open OODB modules. A reference consists of an OID that names the object and a mechanism for mapping the OID to the object's state. An object's state is stored in one or more physical storage locations; the actual collection of storage locations is a function of the object's type, its current representation, and the memory management policies of the address space(s) in which it resides. Many behavioral extensions are modeled or implemented in terms of references to objects rather than operations directed at the objects.

Reference implementations vary on the representation of OIDs, as well as the semantics of pointer following and identity comparison operators. Usually, reference implementations are fixed by the language compiler as a simple resolution to a set of storage locations. However, resolving a reference may be a fairly complex operation outside the norm of resolving an address to a memory location. For example, maintenance of replicas modifies identity comparisons. An application holding references to two different replicas of an object should see them as identical, yet the mechanism maintaining replica consistency has to be aware of their difference. References are modeled as a type lattice having subtypes particular to various extensions of reference semantics.

To make it possible for objects and references to be shared, there is one form of OID called a *global identifier (GID)* that can be interpreted in any environment in which it may be encountered. To allow address space independence and to allow ASMs to locally relocate objects, Open OODB uses a mapping scheme that first determines the current address space of the object globally and then allows the object's current ASM to locate the object locally in its own idiosyncratic manner. Objects can be created in any address space (not necessarily the address space of the creating program).

3.3 Communications

Open OODB's communications module is a veneer that normalizes the interfaces to one or more underlying communications mechanisms. Communications supports the movement of objects, the ability to invoke remote operations, error detection, recovery, and a broadcast capability.

3.4 Translation

The translation module translates objects between the computational, storage, and exchange formats required by the various address spaces, programming languages, programming language implementations, operating systems, communications systems, and hardware platforms present in a particular Open OODB instantiation. Translation allows Open OODB a handle on issues related to the heterogeneity of languages, operating environments, and platforms. It also provides a form of physical data independence. Translation is open to allow new translation routines to be added as the system architecture changes. While the Open OODB is object-oriented, Translation deals with the basic units of transfer in the system, whether they are objects or pages. The Translation process is driven from type information maintained in the Data Dictionary.

3.5 Data Dictionary

The Data Dictionary is a globally known repository of data model and type information, instance information, name mappings (of application-specific names to instances), and possibly system configuration and resource utilization information. The data dictionary also maintains information specific to instances required during query optimization such as cardinalities of collections and distribution of values for members of collections. There are a variety of naming schemes that can be employed in Open OODB. Distribution and persistence use the same naming protocol.

3.6 Meta Architecture Support

The Meta Architecture Support module (MAS) implements the mechanisms to uniformly extend events and defines interface conventions used by other Open OODB modules. The MAS contains one or more sentry implementations to detect and trap events. A variety of sentry implementations with different coverage and selectivity, deployment times, and ability to detect different kinds of events is useful to optimize sentry mechanism costs. To hide this variety of sentry types, the MAS contains a **sentry manager** that serves as the locus for declaring event extensions. To allow any sentry to invoke any policy manager, the MAS defines a common interface presented by all policy managers. Other interface conventions include: (1) a system of pragmas allowing performance hints to be provided to policies without making the system "brittle", (2) a public interface for all reference types, (3) a definition of global object identifiers to be used by all modules, (4) a common exception mechanism, and (5) mechanisms for setting and determining the environment attributes within which the system is operating.

3.7 Persistence Policies

Persistence is the ability of objects to exist beyond the lifetime of the program that created them. The Persistence PM provides applications with an interface through which they can create, access, and manipulate persistent objects. Many OODBs are best characterized as a persistent extension of a programming language. There are many different models of persistent programming, varying in

1. the types of objects that can be made persistent,
2. the times and manner in which objects become persistent,
3. the ways in which persistent objects are bound to programming language constructs,
4. the way object transfer among address spaces is initiated, and
5. the relationship (if any) between persistence and other modules.

Open OODB provides a separate Persistence PM since, in our experience, it is nontrivial to construct a consistent model of persistence given the wide variety of persistence models and interfaces already found.

3.8 Transaction Policies

The Transaction Policy Manager enables *concurrent* access to persistent and transient data and supports *recovery* of changes on these data in the presence of failures. Traditionally transactions satisfy the *atomicity, consistency, isolation,* and *durability* (ACID) properties. Some implementation of ASMs (e.g., Object repositories, relational DBMSs) include some basic support for concurrency control (e.g., two-phase locking) and recovery. In the Open OODB, Transaction Policies built at the level of other policies like persistence represent extended notions of transaction management (e.g., light-weight, nested, long-duration, cooperative) which are built on the basic transactional support provided by some ASMs.

Because Open OODB supports a variety of ASMs within a single system instantiation, it must be possible to not only support distributed transactions, but to do so in a way that allows the use of heterogeneous ASMs. This means that coordination of distributed commit and deadlock detection/prevention must be handled outside of the ASMs via a Transaction Policy Performer, since to do otherwise would require ASMs to know details of other ASMs: this is unreasonable to expect. To participate in a distributed transaction, an ASM must export an interface including `prepare-for-commit`, `commit`, and `waits-for`; the first two being used in two-phase commit, the latter reporting the local waits-for graph for use by a distributed deadlock detector. ASMs not exporting this interface cannot participate in distributed transactions. An ASM that internally supports distribution is compatible with this scheme; it simply appears to the outside world as a single, non-distributed ASM.

3.9 Continuable Policies

Policy performers must have the capability to suspend or delay the execution of a policy and then restart (transparently) on demand. When fetching objects, maintaining indices, creating versions, and many other activities of an OODB, it is often impractical or impossible to perform the entire operation at one time. For instance, incremental object retrieval may be more efficient than eager retrieval when concurrent users access disjoint parts of a graph. Similarly, during automatic index maintenance, an index cannot be maintained when a side-effecting method on an indexed object is trapped because such a side-effect has not occurred yet. In this case, index maintenance needs to be suspended and reactivated at a later time.

4 Extensible Object Query Module

The design of the Open OODB query module has been influenced strongly by the extensibility and modularity goals of the Open OODB project. The Query Module represents an example of intra module extensibility in the Open OODB. The philosophy used in the design of the Open OODB query module can be summarized by the following goals, all of which are equally important.

- *Extensibility.* Currently, there is no widely accepted formal basis for object query processing. Therefore, we wanted to be able to build a query module in such a way that we could "borrow" and experiment with algebraic operators from several existing object algebras, execution algorithms and their transformations, and user query interface paradigms (e.g., different query syntax, visual or graphical) to discover the most effective combination of ideas.
  The query optimizer itself must be extensible to facilitate experimentation with new algebraic operators, new algebraic transformation rules, new execution algorithms, improved statistics and cost models, physical formats and structures (e.g., data compression), enforcer algorithms for physical properties (e.g., sort order, presence in a particular address space), new state space search strategies, and improved quality of plans (e.g., thoroughness of search). An extensible object query module provides us a powerful research workbench on which to try new ideas emerging in the object query processing area.

- *Cost-effective and rapid development*. It is highly desirable to develop a near-production-quality query module within a reasonable amount of time and resources. While our query module is not at production quality yet, the crucial pieces are in already place. The missing functionality can be viewed as refinements of existing pieces, e.g., more accurate selectivity estimation.
- *High performance*. The query module should be able to carry out optimization and execution tasks efficiently. Moderately complex queries should be optimized on today's workstations in less than 1 sec.
- *Effectiveness*. The optimizer should produce plans that substantially improve the efficiency of queries. One of our goals is to ensure that queries over large data collections are executed by the Open OODB system at least as fast as by commercial relational systems.

4.1 Extensible Query Module Architecture

Figure 2 illustrates the extensible architecture of the Open OODB query module. The query module consists of five replaceable submodules: parser and semantic checker, simplification, extensible optimizer, plan generator, and execution. All these submodules use the Data Dictionary of information about types and named collection objects (including estimations on the distribution of values of functions of the members) used by the application. The query compiler processes OQL[C++] query and update statements (see next subsection), and depending on whether the query is embedded in a program or interactive, produces either: (1) equivalent optimized C++ code with appropriate Open OODB query execution function calls (e.g., indexed scan, hash-join) which is subsequently processed by a C++ compiler and executed at a later time (for embedded queries), or (2) query results presented to the user from the immediate execution of the optimized query plan. Our approach is consistent with other concurrent research efforts on object query processing [Mai92a].

To be processed, a OQL[C++] query must first be *parsed* into an internal parse graph representation. Since OQL[C++] allows certain C++ expressions in predicates, this requires a C++-specific parser. Parsing checks the syntax and semantics of the query with the assistance of the data dictionary and name manager. Syntactic and semantic errors (e.g., improper use of set-valued path expressions) are reported to the programmer after this stage. Correct statements are translated by *simplification* into an equivalent logical algebra graph. From this point forward, the actual syntax of the query is irrelevant, which makes it possible to experiment with alternative syntaxes or interactive graphical or visual paradigms. The Open OODB *optimizer*, described in more detail by Blakeley et al. [BMG93], provides a complete optimization framework that includes logical algebra, execution algorithms, logical and physical properties, selectivity and cost estimation, logical transformation rules (e.g., equivalent orders of evaluation), and implementation rules (i.e., a hash-join algorithm implements a pointer traversal). All these components of the optimizer are described below and can be improved incrementally. The optimizer, produced using the Volcano optimizer generator of Graefe and McKenna [GM93], takes the logical algebra expression resulting from simplification and generates an optimal optimal query execution plan. Execution algorithms and implementation rules can be

OQL [C++]
↓ query

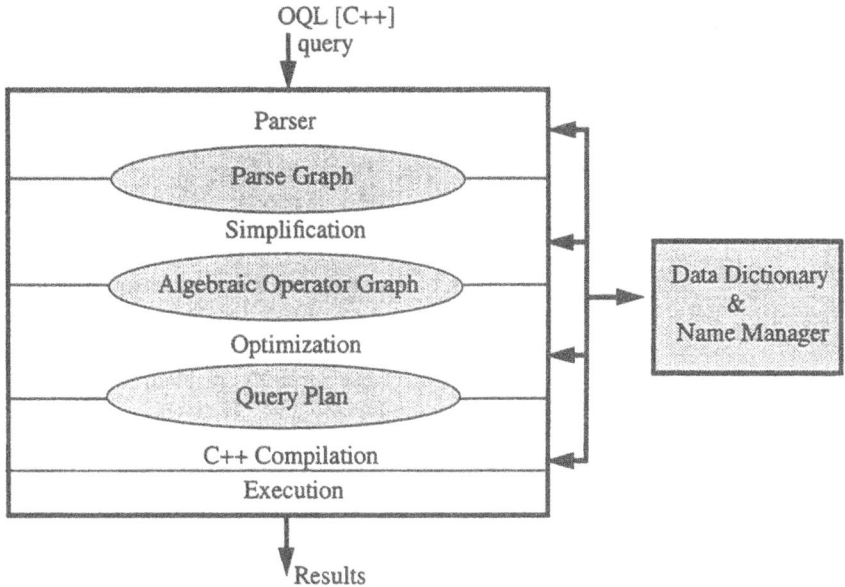

Fig. 2. Extensible query module architecture

added incrementally. The resultant query plan is either *translated* into equivalent C++
code or *executed* directly.

4.2 Object Query Language

This section presents an approach to extending C++ with an object query capability.
The result is a language called OQL[C++] that uses the C++ type system as an object
data model, extends C++ with a query statement that adopts the standard SELECT-FROM-
WHERE structure of SQL, and allows C++ expressions to be used in the formulation of
queries whenever it makes sense. By using the C++ type system as an object data model
instead of inventing yet another object model our approach is able to benefit from the
support of complex objects, inheritance, data abstraction, polymorphism, parameterized
types, and computational completeness already available in C++. OQL[C++] allows
queries on transient or persistent data and permits user-defined functions in the formulation of queries including collection-valued functions and Boolean-valued functions.
OQL[C++] supports queries on semantically different collection types, data abstraction,
inheritance, and complex objects. It also supports uniform type checking of the entire
application including queries and programming language expressions. In OQL[C++],
the notions of type and type extent are distinguished, thus allowing multiple sets of
a type in an application. The above features of OQL[C++] yield a unique integration
between C++ and a query language . A OQL[C++] query statement is an extension of
the SQL query block [Ce76] represented as follows:

```
SELECT  <objects>
FROM    <range variable> IN <collection>
WHERE   <predicate>;
```

We adopted the basic structure of SQL because it has the potential of providing C++ with a well-known model for the formulation of queries that currently enjoys wide use in relational database applications. Also, any syntax of an associative query statement needs to provide a way of specifying the three basic components of the query block above. Therefore, we decided not to design yet another, completely new query syntax that would achieve the same purpose and instead chose to evolve the SQL SELECT statement to an "Object SQL". Clearly, other syntactic approaches are possible (e.g., O++ [AG89a], ObjectStore [LLOW91]).

The SELECT clause identifies the type of the objects in the collection to be returned by the query. The FROM clause declares the range variable and the target collection to be queried. Several variables ranging over several collections may be declared in this clause (e.g., in the case of joins). The WHERE clause specifies the predicate that defines the properties to be satisfied by the objects to be retrieved. The result of the query is assigned to a collection-valued variable in the program.

In addition to adopting the SELECT-FROM-WHERE structure of SQL, OQL[C++] accepts certain C++ expressions when it makes sense within a query. In particular, <objects> specifies objects of the same type as a range variable declared in the FROM clause, or the creation of new objects via C++ class constructors whose type is different than any range variable declared in the query; <range variable> declares a range variable using the same syntax as C++ variable declarations; <collection> can be a named collection-valued object stored in the database, or a collection-valued function or variable defined in the program; <predicate> includes any conditional expression that can be used in a C++ if statement. Such a conditional expression may involve arbitrary user-defined (Boolean) functions or C++ path expressions. In addition, predicates may be formed by connecting conditional C++ expressions with nested subqueries, as in SQL, via the logical operators AND, OR, and NOT. Predicates are defined more formally below.

The following is an example of a OQL[C++] query in a C++ program that obtains the employee name and department of all employees who are at least 32 years old, work in a department on the third floor, and have received a salary increase after January 1, 1993. The query includes the use of a set-valued program variable (i.e., aResult) to hold the result of the query, abstract data type operators (e.g., > for Date), join and projection (i.e., generation of objects of type Newobject with new identity), and data abstraction (i.e., all predicates expressed in terms of the objects' public interface).

```
Set<Newobject> *aResult;
Date aDate(01,01,1993);
aResult = SELECT Newobject( e->name(), d )
          FROM Employee *e IN Employees,
               Department *d IN Departments
          WHERE e->department() == d && e->age() >=32
             && e->last_raise() > aDate && d->floor() == 3;
```

An initial prototype of OQL[C++] was built as part of the Zeitgeist OODB project at Texas Instruments [FJL+88] and further development has continued on the the Open OODB system [BMG93, WBT92]. A commercial implementation by Versant Object

Technologies based on OQL[C++]'s specification is available. An early description of this work is presented in [BTA91].

An important research issue is the definition of criteria for determining a "good integration" between query and programming languages. Blakeley [Bla94a] proposes the following criteria for such an integration which is derived from observation of the deficiencies in existing query language embeddings in PLs:

- *Unification of the programming language's type system and the data model.*
- *Strong typing of the entire application including PL and query statements.*
- *Queries statements must be orthogonal to all programming language and data model extensions (e.g., persistence, distribution, versioning).*
- *Polymorphism of queries over semantically different collection types (e.g., set, bag, array)*
- *Query and programming language statements should be combinable.*
- *Enforce data abstraction in a degree consistent with the underlying data model.*
- *Uniform syntax and semantics of query and PL statements.*

4.3 Extensible Query Optimization Framework

In this section, we discuss how optimization works in the Open OODB query optimizer built using the Volcano optimizer generator. The Volcano optimizer generator translates specifications of algebra operators, transformation rules, and implementation rules into source code (C or C++), combines the generated code with an algebraic search engine, and links it with the support functions provided by the optimizer implementor such as cost functions and with the other DBMS code [GM93]. The essential components of Volcano-generated query optimizers are the logical algebra, the set of execution algorithms, logical and physical properties, the cost model, and the optimization rules. This subsection describes these components for the Open OODB optimizer.

Logical Algebra. In our model of query processing, a logical algebra expression is the input into the query optimizer. The set of execution algorithms defines the query evaluation environment and is discussed in a later subsection. The goal of our optimizer is to map a logical algebra expression to a combination of execution algorithms, optimized by transformations of the logical algebra expression and by choosing the most cost-effective implementation algorithms.

A large number of algebras have been proposed for OODBMSs; most of those are too complex to be manipulated efficiently by an algebraic optimizer, because much of the query semantics is expressed in operator arguments rather than in the actual algebra operators. In fact, the operator arguments (e.g., selection predicates) frequently are more reminiscent of a (non-procedural) calculus language than of an algebra, which is inherently a procedural language. Instead, we have designed our logical algebra so that as much as possible of the query semantics is captured in the algebraic operators and in the algebra expression while the operator arguments are as simple as possible. The optimizer design presumes, therefore, that a preprocessor exists that translates a query's parse tree into an initial algebra expression. This translation, called *simplification*, is

very straightforward because there is no need for optimality and therefore for choices
in this translation.

Since the basic paradigm of Open OODB's query language OQL[C++] is selection
from collections of objects, the foundation of our algebra are the traditional set and
relation operators. *Select, project, join, intersection*, and *union* are defined as in relational
systems. An *unnest* operator is used to manipulate set-valued components. In addition,
we have defined a new logical operator, called *materialize* or *Mat*, that represents
each link of path expressions such as *city.country.president.name*. The purpose of this
operator is to explicitly indicate the use of inter-object references. A single *Mat* operator
can materialize multiple components, or multiple *Mat* operators can be used. Another
way to think of this operator is as a "scope definition," because it lets elements of a
path expression come into scope so that these elements may be used in later operations.
The scoping rules in the optimizer input algebra are very simple. An object component
gets into scope either by being scanned (captured using the logical *Get* operator in
the leaves of expressions trees) or by being referenced (captured in the *Mat* operator).
Components remain in scope until a projection discards them. As an example for the
materialize operator, the query:

```
SELECT Newobject(e.name(),e.dept().name(),e.job().name())
FROM Employee e IN Employees
WHERE e.dept().plant().location() == "Dallas";
```

is translated after parsing into the parse graph shown in Fig. 3 and later into the logical
operator graph shown in Fig. 4. The purpose of the materialize operator is to indicate
to the optimizer where path expressions are used and, therefore, where algebraic transformations can be applied. In the example query, the materialize operators can trade
their positions in the query expression, with the condition that "department" must be
materialized before "plant." We presume that the "name" instance variables are similar
to record fields that need not be explicitly materialized.

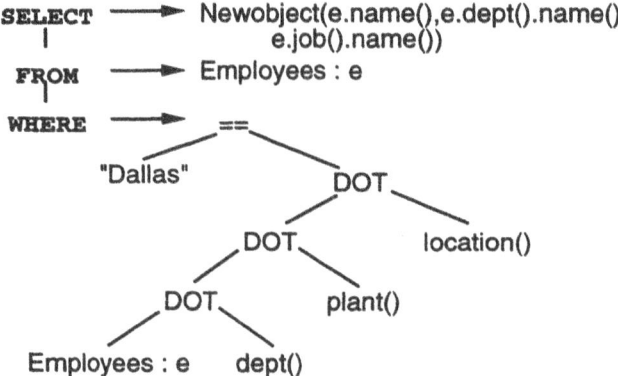

Fig. 3. Example of a query after parsing

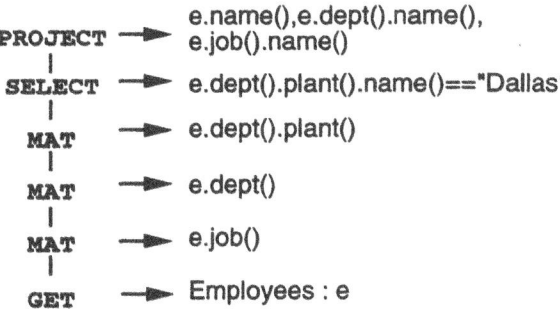

Fig. 4. Example of a query after simplification

Other researchers in object query optimization have used the join operator to logically represent the computation of path expressions [LVZC91, PHH92]. This is possible
in extensible relational database systems that assume that all types (or schemes) have
an extent or scannable collection associated with them. In Open OODB types are orthogonal to extents, therefore, an object may reference a component whose type has no
extent. Representing links of path expressions as joins is possible, but we need to add
exceptions to the join transformation rules (e.g., join commutativity) for this special
case. We decided instead to incorporate a new materialize operator with its own transformation rules to represent links of path expressions that have no extent associated with
them. In cases where the link does have an extent, we allow the logical transformation
from materialize to join. Our materialize operator generalizes previous approaches to
optimizing path expressions.

Query Simplification. The Open OODB query processing model uses a *query simplification* stage to transform OQL[C++] parse trees into an equivalent algebraic operator
graph with simple arguments suitable as input to the Open OODB optimizer. *Complex arguments* are any predicate terms containing path expressions that have not been brought
into scope or collection-valued operations (e.g., an existentially quantified subquery in
the argument of a select).

Currently, simplification has been defined for select-from-where OQL[C++] queries
whose condition involves arbitrary conjunctive Boolean expressions with existentially
quantified nested subqueries, but no aggregates. Interesting simplifications include simplifications for single- and set-valued path expressions as well as existentially quantified
subqueries. A simplification involving a single-valued path expression was illustrated
in the previous subsection when we introduced the materialize operator. Simplification
involving nested subqueries uses tactics similar to the ones used for nested subqueries
in SQL [Day87a].

Consider a query involving a set-valued path *task.team-members* denoting all employees working in a particular project task. This path is translated into a logical algebra
expression shown in Fig. 5. Since the team-members component of a task is a set of references to employee objects, we need to first reveal (unnest) all references to employee
objects that are members of this set. Calling a reference to an employee team member

m, the output of the unnest operator is a set of pairs $[t, m]$. The materialize operator resolves all employee references to employee objects present in memory, producing $[t, e]$ pairs that can be used as the input to subsequent select or other operators.

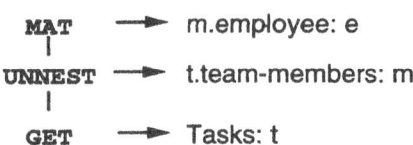

Fig. 5. Algebra expression for set-valued path expression

Properties and Property Enforcement. In order to determine whether a transformation is applicable or whether an algorithm can implement a given logical expression, it is often necessary to inspect the logical and physical properties of intermediate results. *Logical properties* are properties of an expression determined by the logical operators before execution algorithms are chosen (e.g., type or size of intermediate results). *Physical properties* depend on execution algorithms selected. The standard example for a physical property in relational query optimization is the sort order [SAC+79]. In object-oriented query processing, an important property is *presence in memory*. Our optimizer currently does not use merge join for value-based matching, therefore it supports only presence in memory.

Physical properties have no role in the logical algebra but are important in the realm of query execution algorithms. In our framework, execution algorithms implement a logical operator, *enforce* some physical property, or both. For instance, the assembly algorithm is used to enforce the present-in-memory property and to implement the logical materialize operator.

Cost Model. Currently, our cost model is very traditional. We consider both CPU and I/O costs, and "charge" less for sequential than for random I/O. Assembly's I/O cost captures the fact that seek distances are minimized by charging less than for a random I/O operation. Actual assembly performance including the effects of buffer hits can only be studied in the context of a real, working system; therefore, we delay validating and refining assembly's cost function until the query plan executor becomes operational.

While our cost model is not precise yet, the important points are that cost is integrated into our optimizer framework and that query evaluation plans are transformed and compared based on anticipated execution costs, not purely on heuristics. Very little research has been done to-date on cost models and formulas in OODBMSs; however, as such research evolves, we will incorporate it swiftly. Cost is encapsulated in an abstract data type (ADT) and tuning an algorithm's cost formula is a very localized change.

Transformation Rules. Since our logical algebra is based on the relational algebra, our transformation rules include known relational transformations plus some new ones pertaining to the materialize operator. These transformations move materialize operators above and beneath ("through") selection, join, and set operators, provided none of the other operators depends on a scope defined by materialize.

One rule that we believe can be very important and effective in query optimization in OODBMSs transforms materialize operations into joins, not because joins are always a good choice but because joins are an alternative execution strategy that should be chosen or rejected based on anticipated execution costs. If the scope introduced by a materialize operator is actually a scannable object (a set object, file, etc.), the materialize operator can be transformed into a join. For example, if there is a set or file of departments in Fig. 4, the materialize operation bringing e.department() into scope can be replaced by a join operation.

Once a materialize operator has been transformed into a join, all transformation rules and implementation rules for join apply. Join associativity is closely related to the commutativity of multiple materialize operators. Join commutativity permits exploring query plan alternatives that are usually ignored in object query optimization, e.g., traversing single-directional inter-object links (pointers) in their opposite (not pre-computed) direction. Figure 6 illustrates the optimized plan for the query of Fig. 4.

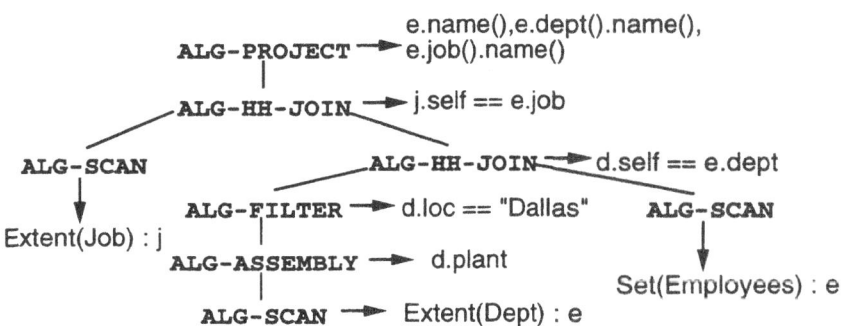

Fig. 6. Optimized plan

Implementation Rules. The implementation rules establish the correspondence between logical algebra expressions and execution algorithms. Algorithm selection is the second important aspect of query optimization, beyond logical equivalence transformations. Query evaluation algorithms are important and still continually improved in the "simpler" relational model, and will have an even larger effect in OODBMSs. The optimizer chooses algorithms based on implementation rules, an algorithm's ability to deliver a logical expression with the desired physical properties, and cost estimations.

4.4 Execution Algorithms

Our research on the Open OODB optimizer provides experimental evidence that set matching operations such as join and intersection and their corresponding algorithms developed in the relational context remain relevant in OODBMSs, not only for operations on sets and for value-based matching, but also as alternative implementation methods for path expressions. Even if precomputed access paths (stored references) exist, naive traversal of such references ("goto's on disk") may result in suboptimal performance. Algebraic equivalence transformations for these operations, including commutativity and associativity, permit significant optimizations. In the case where only uni-directional links exist between objects, we show the need to consider processing operators that resolve the object references in the opposite direction.

Therefore, we believe that it is possible to build a library of data model independent execution algorithms that can support either relational or object-oriented query execution. Since our algebra includes all traditional set operators, our execution engine also includes the traditional set processing algorithms, namely file (extent) and index scan as well as value-based matching (e.g., intersection, union, join) based on hybrid-hash join. Hybird-hash join will also support equality of a reference attribute on one side and object identifiers on the other side.

We are currently implementing (and optimizing for) two algorithms that promise to have a significant performance impact in OODBMSs. *Pointer-based joins*, recently analyzed by Shekita et al. [SC90], are sometimes superior to other join methods; therefore, an optimizer should consider them among the alternative implementations for join.

The second algorithm our optimizer considers is *assembly*, developed in the Revelation project [KGM91]. Assembly generalizes pointer-joins as it permits multiple references, even recursive object references, i.e., transitive closures of sub-component relationships. It achieves higher performance than sequences of traditional operators by maintaining a window of open, unresolved references in order to exploit multiple objects located on a single disk page and to sequence disk read operations into an elevator pattern over physical disk locations.

5 Status and Conclusions

The current Open OODB prototype contains implementations of several policy performers including concurrency control based on two-phase locking, atomic transactions, persistence for CLOS and C++ objects, query processing with optimization, and versioning. The current implementations of the query processor, and the version management modules are detachable from the rest of the Open OODB. Our experiences coupling the query module (without optimization) with Versant, a commercial C++-based OODB; incorporating the Exodus storage manager as an ASM, and using the Volcano optimizer generator to build the open OODB optimizer provide initial evidence that it is possible to enhance the capabilities of an OODB with modules developed independently. In addition to the Exodus storage manager, there are ASM implementations based on a transient ASM, and on Unix files; translation for CLOS and C++ objects; and C++ and CLOS implementations of sentries. Release Alpha 0.2 of the Open OODB (August, 1993), was distributed to 25 ARPA-designated sites. Future research in the Open

OODB project involves continuous validation and improvement of the architecture and module interfaces on real applications such as image understanding, manufacturing, simulation, and software development environments; performance tunning; development of index maintenance, schema evolution, and view policies; and development of a high-performance, data model-independent query execution engine.

Acknowledgements.

This research is sponsored by the Advanced Research Pro-jects Agency under ARPA Order No. A016 and managed by the U.S. Army Research Laboratory under contract DAAB07-90-C-B920. The views and conclusions contained in this document are those of the authors and should not be interpreted as necessarily representing the official policies, either expressed or implied, of the Advanced Research Projects Agency or the United States Government.

The work reported in this paper is a summary of work by many key contributors to the Open OODB project. The Open OODB meta-architecture design is primarily the work of David Wells. The query optimizer was designed and built jointly with William McKenna and Goetz Graefe. The Open OODB system has been developed by José Blakeley, Steve Ford, William McKenna, Aditya Srivastava, Craig Thompson, and David Wells. Craig Thompson is manager of the project. Bob Baltzer, Michael Carey, David DeWitt, Dave Maier, Erik Mettala, Gio Wiederhold, and Stan Zdonik have provided feedback throughout the Open OODB design.

METU Object-Oriented DBMS

Asuman Dogac, Cetin Ozkan, Budak Arpinar, Tansel Okay, Cem Evrendilek

Software Research and Development Center, Scientific and Technical Research Council of Turkey, Middle East Technical University, 06531, Ankara, Turkey

Abstract. METU Object-Oriented DBMS[1] includes the implementation of a database kernel, an object-oriented SQL-like language and a graphical user interface. Kernel functions are divided between a SQL Interpreter and a C++ compiler. Thus the interpretation of functions are avoided increasing the efficiency of the system. The compiled by C++ functions are used by the system through the Function Manager. The system is realized on Exodus Storage Manager (ESM), thus exploiting some of the kernel functions readily provided by ESM. The additional functions provided by the MOOD kernel are the optimization and interpretation of SQL statements, dynamic linking of functions, and catalog management.

An original query optimization strategy based on the object-oriented features of the language is developed. For this purpose formulas for the selectivity of a path expression, and for the cost of forward and backward path traversals are derived, and join sizes are estimated. New strategies for ordering the joins and path expressions are also developed.

A graphical user interface, namely MoodView is implemented on the MOOD kernel. MoodView provides the database programmer with tools and functionalities for every phase of OODBMS application development. Current version of MoodView allows a database user to design, browse, and modify database schema interactively. MoodView can automatically generate graphical displays for complex and multimedia database objects which can be updated through the object browser. Furthermore, a database administration tool, a full screen text-editor, a SQL based query manager, and a graphical indexing tool for the spatial data, i.e., R Trees are also implemented.

1 Introduction

In this paper we describe the METU Object-Oriented DBMS (MOOD). MOOD has a type system derived from C++, eliminating the impedance mismatch between MOOD and C++. It has a SQL-like query language (MOODSQL) and is developed on top of the Exodus Storage Manager (ESM) [Uni92], [CDRS86]. This provides MOOD the following kernel functions available through ESM :

---

[1] The code is available from asuman@vm.cc.metu.edu.tr.

- storage management
- controlling data access and concurrency
- backup and recovery of data.
  Additionally, MOOD kernel [OOD93] provides the following functions :

- optimization and interpretation of SQL statements and dynamic linking of functions
- catalog management.

The main problem in designing a kernel for an object-oriented DBMS is the late binding of methods to the objects. In MOOD we propose to solve this problem by dividing the labor between an object-oriented SQL interpreter and a C++ compiler. Since database environment enforces run-time modification of schema and objects, late binding is essential.

There are two other alternatives that we considered but are not chosen. These are building a system based on a persistent programming language such as C++ or using a full C++ interpreter and extending it with DBMS functionality.

In the first alternative, all other subsystems communicate via the persistent C++ which are compiled externally. The compiled programs may be executed separately, or they may be activated by using dynamic linker (dld). The disadvantage of this alternative is that it is completely orthogonal to the nature of a database management system. A DBMS provides an on-line environment rather than a database tool box where there are calls to separately compiled programs for database operations. The advantage on the other hand, is to be able to use the full power of the chosen programming language.

The second alternative, although it eliminates the previous disadvantage, has the problem of performance decrease due to interpretation. The advantage is again to be able to use the full power of C++.

The proposed approach, on the other hand, is uniform in that interfaces access the database through SQL statements interpreted by the kernel. But the code for the member functions of the classes are not interpreted. They are separately compiled with C++ and executed by SQL interpreter through a dynamic linker(dld). The advantage of this approach is that the interpretation of the functions are avoided increasing the overall efficiency of the system.

MOOD's kernel is described in Sect. 2. Section 3 contains brief descriptions of MOOD data model, MOODSQL and MOOD algebra. In Sect. 4, cost model parameters are given and formulas for the selectivity of path expressions are derived which forms the basis of the cost calculations for the query optimizer. Section 5 summarizes the cost analysis of basic file operations. In Sect. 6, the costs of realizing an implicit join operation through several different techniques are presented. Section 7 contains the general description of the execution of MOODSQL queries. Section 8 describes query optimization in MOOD. MoodView [ADE93], the graphical user interface is then presented in Sect. 9. Finally summary is presented in Sect. 10.

2 MOOD Kernel Implementation

The general structure of the MOOD system is shown in Fig. 1. In MOOD, data can be defined through MOODSQL data definition language or through C++. When data is defined through MOODSQL data definition language, the definitions are stored in the CATALOG and a C++ header file is created for future compilation. To handle the case where data is defined in C++, we have modified cfront such that cfront extracts the catalog information and stores it into the CATALOG.

The basic types supported by the MOOD are Integer, Float, LongInteger, String, Char, and Boolean. The type constructors are Tuple, Set, List, and Reference. A complex type may be created by using basic types and recursive application of the type constructors. A type (or class) in the system has a unique type identifier and name. The functions *typeId(char *typeName)* and *typeName(int typeId)* return type identifier and name of a type (or class) respectively.

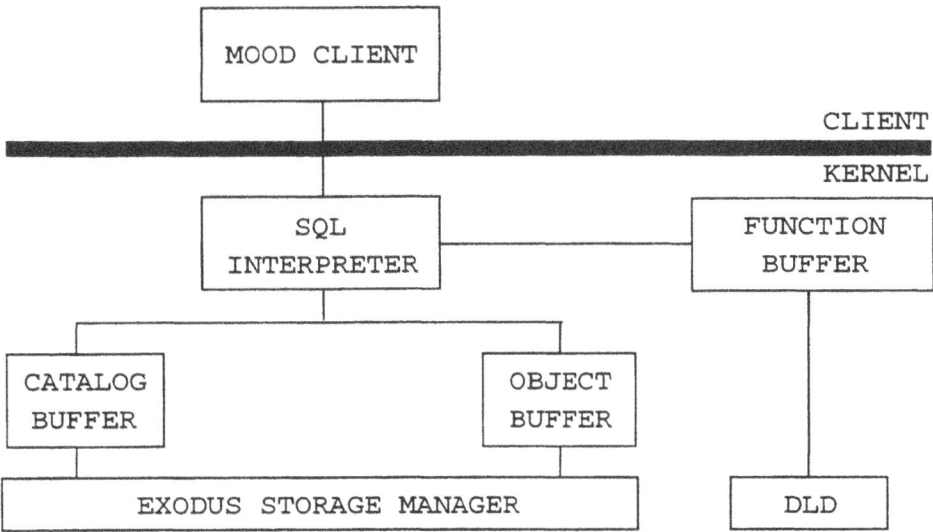

Fig. 1. Overview of the MOOD System

The differences between a type and a class from the implementation point of view are:

 – a class has a default extent that contains the instances created;
 – values which are instances of types have copy semantic;
 – classes are organized into a class hierarchy.

The catalog contains the definition of classes, types, and member functions in a structure similar to a compiler symbol table. In order to achieve late binding at run time, it is necessary to carry compile time information to run time. This is accomplished by the use of the classes *MoodsType*, *MoodsAttribute* and *MoodsFunction*. The *MoodsType* class keeps track of all the types used in the system. The *MoodsAttribute* stores the information about the attributes of these classes. The instances of the *MoodsFunction* class keeps information about the member functions. Figure 2 shows the structure of the catalog on ESM.

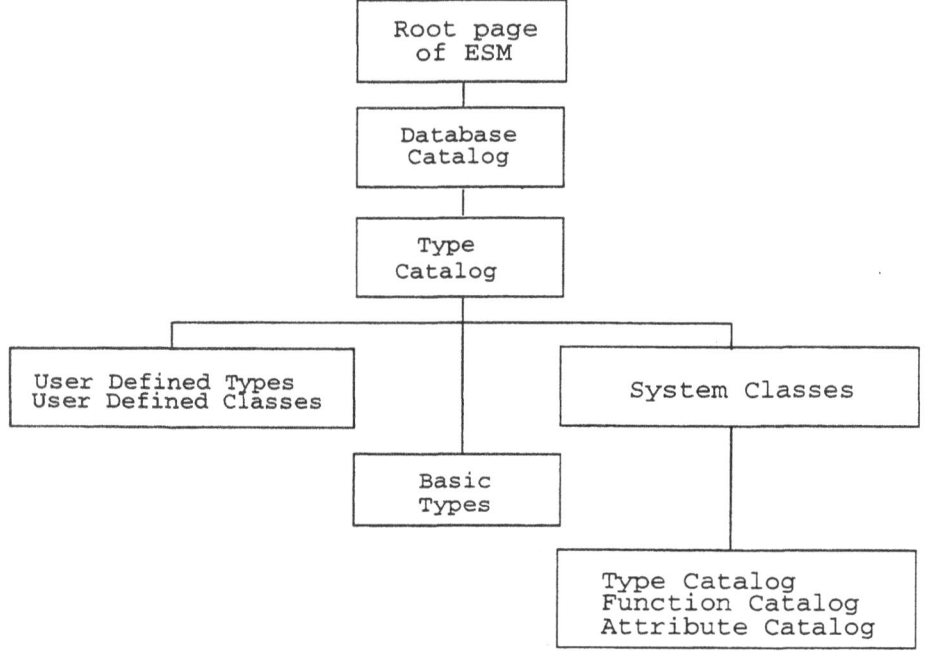

Fig. 2. representation of catalog in ESM

MOODSQL interpreter is responsible for :

– optimization of MOODSQL queries,
– interpretation of arithmetic and Boolean expressions,
– dynamic definition and linking of member functions.

For interpretation of arithmetic and Boolean expressions, the types of operands are necessary at run time. This information is provided by the class *OperandDataType*. As an example :

OperandDataType x(INT16), y(INT32), z (DOUBLE);
x=10;
y=13;
z=(x*3+x%3)*(y/4*5) // this expression can be evaluated and result's
                    // type is casted to double since z is double.

The code for the interpretation of arithmetic and Boolean expressions mainly overloads addition, subtraction, multiplication, division and mode operation operators in the order (+, -,*, /, %) for arithmetic expressions. It evaluates AND, OR, NOT, and comparison operators for Boolean expressions. Type checking and conversion of results are performed at run-time.

The power of object oriented applications lies in the interpretation and late binding which necessitate the system to be an interpreter. Only by interpretation can the user requests be handled dynamically, whereas if the application is static (i.e. compiled) dynamic changes are impossible.

In our approach a Function Manager responsible for adding, updating, deleting and invoking the member functions of the classes is developed. The basic concept is to store the C++ source after some processing into the class hierarchy. In order to compile newly defined functions, MOOD keeps track of the textual definition of classes in the hierarchy. Starting from the root class in a directory hierarchy, every class has its own directory containing its textual definition and function object files and a shared object. A class named FUNCTION handles basic dynamic linking operations by the use of the Shared Object files. All of the basic types (i.e. Integer, Float, LongInteger, String, Char, and Boolean) are automatically replaced with MOOD type classes.

The member function declarations in the source code are extracted and inserted into the CATALOG. The information extracted is the member function signature information.

When a function is invoked through the SQL interpreter, the signature of the function is created by using class name to which the function is applied and its parameter list. This signature is used in locating the function in the CATALOG. When function signature is found in the CATALOG, Shared Object File of the Class is opened and the function is loaded into memory. At the point the function is called, parameters are passed to the function. Function is kept in memory until the scope changes in the program.

At run-time, adding a new function to the system has no effect on the server program, since it is separately pre-processed and compiled. The shared library of the class will be unavailable only during the time it takes to write the new function. We provide locking for this operation.

All system errors, including signals that terminate processes are handled by our Exception class. Thus although the functions are compiled, their error messages are handled as if they are interpreted.

With Function Manager the only cost is the preprocessing and compilation of the added functions for once. It is clear that during this process the server is active; there is no need to recompile the server. This is a dynamic system, where both time and memory are efficiently utilized because the interpretation time is saved and the code is loaded into memory when it is requested.

3 MOODSQL

As part of MOOD, a SQL-like object-oriented query language, MOODSQL, together with a query optimizer has been designed and implemented.

Several SQL like query languages for OODBMSs have been proposed such as CQL++ [DGJ92], O2Query [Deu91b], EXCESS [CDV88], and the query language of ORION [Kim90].

3.1 An Overview of MOOD Data Model and MOODSQL

A detailed description of the MOOD data model and MOODSQL is given in [ODCG93]. In this section the general structure of the data model and the query language are presented briefly.

In the MOOD data model the basic data types are Integer, Float, LongInteger, String, Char, and Boolean. Any complex data type is defined using these types and by the recursive application of the Tuple, Set, List and Reference type constructors. The data model also supports multiple inheritance and strongly typed methods. MOODSQL is designed to support ad-hoc queries in MOOD. General syntax of the query language is as follows:

```
SELECT      projection-list
FROM        class-name r₁,
            class-name r₂,
            ...
            class-name rₙ
[GROUP BY   attribute-list [ HAVING predicate ] ]
[ WHERE     search-expression ]
[ ORDER BY attribute-list ]
```

As an example, consider the database schema given below, which also illustrates the data definition language of MOODSQL. The classes have extensions.

```
CREATE CLASS Vehicle
            TUPLE (
                id Integer,
                weight Integer,
                drivetrain REFERENCE ( VehicleDriveTrain),
                manufacturer REFERENCE ( Company)
            METHODS:
                lbweight () Integer,
                weight () Integer,
            )
CREATE CLASS VehicleDriveTrain
            TUPLE (
                engine REFERENCE (VehicleEngine),
                transmission String(32)
            )
CREATE CLASS VehicleEngine
            TUPLE (
                size Integer,
                cylinders Integer
            )
CREATE CLASS Company
            TUPLE (
                name String(32),
                location String(32),
                president REFERENCE (Employee)
            )
```

```
CREATE CLASS Employee
            TUPLE (
                    ssno Integer,
                    name String(32),
                    age Integer
            )
CREATE CLASS Automobile
            INHERITS FROM Vehicle
CREATE CLASS JapaneseAuto
            INHERITS FROM Automobile
int Vehicle::lbweight()
{ return weight*2.2075; }
int Vehicle::weight()
{ return weight; }
```

MOOD handles the methods only by keeping information on their name, return type, and names and types of their parameters. The body of methods are coded in C++ and dynamically linked through Function Manager.

The following example MOODSQL query finds the automobiles which have automatic transmission, more than 4 cylinders and produced by a non-Japanese company.

SELECT   c
FROM EVERY Automobile - JapaneseAuto c, VehicleEngine v
WHERE   c.drivetrain.transmission = 'AUTOMATIC' AND
                   c.drivetrain.engine = v AND v.cylinders > 4

The minus operator in the FROM clause is used for excluding the instances of a subclass, which would otherwise be included due to an IS-A relationship.

3.2 MOOD Algebra

In this section, the definitions of the MOOD algebra operators are given. In these definitions, the parameter argi denotes a set of objects, or set of object identifiers, or an object itself. The operators are divided into three categories according to their usage:

- general operators
- collection operators
- conversion operators.

General Operators. These operators handle the naming operation in the MOOD kernel and the operations on a single object.

ObjId(o): This operator returns the object identifier of an object *o*.

TypeId(o) : This operator returns the type identifier of an object *o*. Note that every object in MOOD has a typeid associated with it.

Deref(oid): The dereferencing operator which is used in referring to the object with the identifier·*oid*.

isA(path): The input parameter is a path expression that starts with a class name. The return value is the class name of the last attribute of the given path.

Bind(arg, aName) : The naming operator of the algebra. It gives the name *aName* to *arg*.

Collection Operators. The objects can be accessed through the following collections:

- Object identifiers stored in a set object
- Object identifiers stored in a list object
- Objects stored in extents.

Another way to access an object is to give a unique name to an object (Named Objects). Also indices (conventional indices, binary join indices, or path indices) can be used in accessing the objects. In this section we present the operators dealing with these collections.

Select(arg, P): This operator selects the objects from the argument *arg* satisfying the predicate P.

Table 1. The return types of the *Select* operator

arg type	Extent	Set	List	Named Obj.
return type	Extent or Set	Set	List	Named Obj.

The possible types of the argument *arg* are Extent, Set, List and a Named Object, and the returned types are given in Table 1.

IndSel(arg, index_type, P): It selects the set of object identifiers satisfying predicate P from an extent or a group of extents named as *arg* by using the index of type *index_type*. The indexing mechanisms available for simple selection are the B^+-tree indexing and hash indexing supported through the Exodus Storage Manager. The return value of this operation is a set of object identifiers.

Project(aTupleCollection, attribute_list): The project operator is similar to the relational project operator except that *aTupleCollection* may be an extent of tuple type objects, or a list or a set of object identifiers of tuple type objects in our system. In case of a list or a set, the elements are dereferenced. The result of the operator *Project* is the extent of the tuple type values projected onto *attribute_list*. Notice since MOOD allows for dynamic schema changes, it is possible to dynamically define a class for those tuple type values and to make them objects.

Join(arg₁, arg₂, join_method, P): This operator joins *arg₁* and *arg₂* with join predicate P using the join method identified as *join_method*. The return types of this operator are as shown in Table 2. The *join_method* can be one of the following:

- forward traversal
- indexed join (B^+ tree index, binary join index or path index)
- backward traversal
- pointer based hash-partition join

Partition(aTupleCollection, attribute_list): This operator divides the objects in *aTupleCollection* into groups of objects with respect to *attribute_list*. Each group is composed of objects having the same value in their corresponding attribute(s). The return value is the set of groups of objects (partitions).

Sort(aTupleCollection, sort_method, attribute_list): This operator sorts the collection *aTupleCollection* with respect to *attribute_list* by using *sort_method* without duplicate elimination. The only supported *sort_method* for the time being is heap sort with merging. If *aTupleCollection* is a set or a list then the sorted set or list of the object identifiers are the result of the sort operator. In the case of an extent, the result is the sorted extent of the objects. It is clear that the set and list cases require the dereferencing of objects identifiers.

Table 2. The return types of the *Join* operator

arg_1 arg_2	Extent	Set	List	Named Obj.
Extent	Extent	Extent	Extent	Extent
Set	Extent	Set	Set	Set
List	Extent	Set	List	List
Named Obj.	Extent	Set	List	Object

DupElim(arg): This operator eliminates duplicates from the *arg*. The return types of this operator are given in Table 3.

Union(arg$_1$, arg$_2$) : This operator takes the union of *arg$_1$* and *arg$_2$* and returns the set of objects.

Intersection(arg$_1$, arg$_2$) : This operator returns the set of objects common to *arg$_1$* and *arg$_2$*.

Difference(arg$_1$, arg$_2$) : This operator returns the set of objects in *arg$_1$* but not in *arg$_2$*.

Table 3. The return types of *DupElim* operator

type of *arg*	DupElim(arg)
Set	not applicable
List	list of ordered distinct object identifiers
Extent	Extent of the distinct object according to the deep equality check

The types of the arguments for *Union, Intersection, Difference* operators are set or list and the return types are shown in Table 4. If both arguments are lists, union corresponds to array concatenation.

Table 4. The return types *Union, Intersection, Difference* operators

type of arguments	Set	List
Set	Set	Set
List	Set	List

Conversion Operators. The type conversion functions may be carried out as a result of optimization, or their usage may be forced explicitly by the user query.

asSet(arg) : This operator converts *arg* to a set. Table 5 presents the return types for this operator.

Table 5. Return types for *asSet* and *asList* operators

type of *arg*	elements of the resulting set or list
Extent	Object identifiers of the objects in the extent *arg*
Set	Object identifiers of the set *arg*
Set	Object identifiers of the list *arg*
Named Object	Object identifiers of the named object

asList(arg) : This operator converts *arg* to a list. Table 5 presents the return types for this operator.

asExtent(arg) : This operator converts its argument into an extent. The possible types for the *arg* are set and list and the return types are as shown in Table 6.

Table 6. Return types for the *asExtent* operator

type of *arg*	asExtent(arg)
Set	extent of dereferenced objects of the elements of the set
List	extent of dereferenced objects of the elements of the set

Unnest(aTupleCollection) : This operator is borrowed from the 1NF algebra. Its output is also *aTupleCollection*. As an example, consider the extent for the following tuples. $e = \{< o1, \{o2, o3\} >, < o4, \{o5\} >\}$ then $Unnest(e)$ will be a new extent, e', such that $e' = \{< o1, o2 >, < o1, o3 >, < o4, o5 >\}$.

The possible types for *aTupleCollection* for the unnest operation are presented in Table 7. Note that the return type is the extent of the tuples resulting from the unnest operation for all argument types.

Table 7. Possible argument types for the *Unnest* operator

Possible argument types for *aTupleCollection*
Extent for the tuple type objects
Set(object identifiers of tuple type objects)
List(object identifiers of tuple type objects)
A tuple type object

Nest(aTupleCollection) : *Nest* operator functions as the inverse of *Unnest* operator.

Flatten(arg) : This operator is similar to the *unnest* operation in the sense that a set or a list is flattened. The *Flatten* operator converts *arg* into the set of object identifiers. Notice that the result of the Flatten operator is always a set. The following is an example to the *Flatten* operation.

Flatten({oid1, oid2}, {oid3}} = {oid1, oid2, oid3}

4 Cost Model Parameters

In this section cost model parameters are defined and calculated along with the specification of the physical parameters describing the system. These parameters are used in various selectivity calculations which form the basis of the cost function employed in query optimization. Notice that the cost model parameters are analogous to the ones given in [KM90a].

In Table 8, the cost model parameters are presented where C is a class, A is an attribute.

The number of the total references from class C to class D through attribute A is denoted by $totlinks(A, C, D)$ and is given by the following equation :

$$totlinks(A, C, D) = fan(A, C, D) * |C| \qquad (1)$$

The probability that an instance of class D is referenced by the instances of class through attribute A is

$$hitprb(A, C, D) = totref(A, C, D)/|D| \qquad (2)$$

In Table 9, the information kept by the system for a B^+-tree index I is shown.

Physical parameters of the disk, which are used in the cost evaluation process are as shown in Table 10 [Sal88].

4.1 Selectivity

Selectivity is a parameter used with a predicate to denote the ratio of the elements of a collection satisfying a given predicate. When optimizing the queries, selectivity of a predicate is estimated assuming that the values are uniformly distributed. The traditional uniformity and randomness assumptions about value distributions tend to

Table 8. Cost Model Parameters

Parameter	Definition
$|C|$	Total number of instances of C
$nbpages(C)$	Total number of pages in which class C is stored
$size(C)$	Size of an instance of class C
$notnull(A, C)$	The proportion of the instances in class C with attribute A being not null
$fan(A, C, D)$	The average number of instances of class D that are referenced by the instances of class C through attribute A
$totref(A, C, D)$	The total number of objects in class D which are referenced by at least one object in class C through attribute A
$dist(A, C)$	Number of distinct values of the atomic attribute A of class C
$max(A, C)$	The maximum value of the atomic attribute A of class C
$min(A, C)$	The minimum value of the atomic attribute A of class C

Table 9. Parameters for a B^+-tree

Parameter	Definition
v(I)	Order of the B^+ tree
level(I)	Number of levels
leaves(I)	Number of the leaves
keysize(I)	Size of the key value
unique(I)	Unique flag

overestimate costs. However more sophisticated techniques require more statistical information about the database. The question of how to maintain such information within tolerable overhead is not yet fully resolved [JKS85].

A simple predicate in the system is a triplet of the form $< P_1, \theta, oprnd >$, where P_1 is a path expression, θ is a comparison operator $(=, <>, >=, <=, >, <)$, and $oprnd$ is either a constant or another path expression.

Selectivity for Atomic Attributes The well-known selectivity calculations assuming the uniform distribution of the atomic values described in [Ozk90] will be used throughout the derivations presented in this paper.

The selectivity of the expression "$s.A = constant$", denoted f_s, where s is a bind variable of class C, and A is an atomic attribute, is given by the following formula:

$$f_s(s.A) = 1/dist(A, C) \tag{3}$$

The selectivity of the expression "$s.A > constant$" is

$$f_s(s.A) = (max(A, C) - constant)/(max(A, C) - min(A, C)) \tag{4}$$

Table 10. Physical Parameters for hard disk

Parameter	Definition
B	block size
btt	block transfer time
ebt	effective block transfer time
r	average rotational latency
s	average seek time

The selectivity of the expression "$s.A$ BETWEEN $cons_1$ and $cons_2$" is

$$f_s(s.A) = (cons_2 - cons_1)/(max(A,C) - min(A,C)) \tag{5}$$

Selectivity of Path Expressions   Assume that there exists a path expression that contains m attributes, A_1 through A_m, A_1 through A_{m-1} being constructed using set and reference constructors, and A_m is an atomic attribute, A_i being an attribute of class C_i. Then, for the single path expression predicate "$p.A_1.A_2...A_m\theta c$", where θ is a comparison operator and c is a constant, the selectivity, $f_s(p.A_1.A_2...A_m, \theta)$ is to be calculated. For this calculation we define the shorthand notation for some of the previously mentioned parameters as follows:

$$fan_i = fan(A_i, C_i, C_{i+1}) \tag{6}$$

$$totref_i = totref(A_i, C_i, C_{i+1}) \tag{7}$$

$$totlinks_i = totlinks(A_i, C_i, C_{i+1}) \text{ where } 1 \leq i \leq m-1 \tag{8}$$

The calculation of the selectivity of "$A_m\theta c$", $f_s(A_m)$, is clear from the previous section. Therefore the expected number of instances of C_m, denoted by k_m, satisfying "$A_m\theta c$" is:

$$k_m = |C_m| * f_s(A_m) \tag{9}$$

In forward traversal, assuming that we start with k objects of class C_1 and traverse the path $p.A_1.A_2...A_i$ in forward direction, the expected number of objects of class C_{i+1}, denoted by $fref$, is given by the following formula:

$$fref(p.A_1...A_i, k) = \begin{cases} k & ,i = 0 \\ c(totlinks_i, totref_i, fref(p.A_1...A_{i-1}, k) * fan_i) & ,i > 0 \end{cases} \tag{10}$$

where, $c(n, m, r)$ is defined to be an approximation to the number of different colors, when r objects are chosen out of n objects uniformly distributed over m colors given as follows [CP84].

$$c(n, m, r) = \begin{cases} r & , r < \frac{m}{2} \\ \frac{(r+m)}{3} & , \frac{m}{2} \leq r < 2m \\ m & , r \geq 2m \end{cases} \tag{11}$$

Note that better approximations to this problem are given in [Yao77], [Car75]. However it has been validated that $c(n, m, r)$ well serves our purposes. Starting with one instance of class C_1, we denote the number of objects of class C_m obtained at the end of forward path traversal by $fref(p.A_1...A_{m-1}, 1)$. On the other hand, k_m objects have been selected through the predicate $A_m \theta c$. Then the selectivity of a path expression which is assumed to be the probability of at least one object being in common in two sets with cardinalities $fref(p.A_1.A_2...A_{m-1}, 1)$ and $k_m * hitprb(A_{m-1}, C_{m-1}, C_m)$ respectively, is given by

$$f_s(p.A_1.A_2...A_m) = o(totref_{m-1}, fref(p.A_1.A_2...A_{m-1}, 1), k_m * \\ hitprb(A_{m-1}, C_{m-1}, C_m)) \tag{12}$$

where $o(t, x, y)$ is the probability that there exists at least one common object in two sets selected with replacement out of t distinct objects and is defined as

$$o(t, x, y) = 1 - C(t - x, y)/C(t, y) \tag{13}$$

where C stands for combination, and x and y are the cardinalities of the two sets respectively. The term $C(t - x, y)/C(t, y)$ is the probability that the sets with cardinalities x and y never intersect.

5 Cost Analysis of Basic File Operations

In this section the costs of sequential, random and indexed accesses are given. The cost of sequential access to b pages is denoted by $SEQCOST(b)$ and calculated as

$$SEQCOST(b) = s + r + b * ebt \tag{14}$$

The assumption that pages of a file are stored consecutively on disk may not be true in all systems. For example in ESM, a file is stored as a B+ tree and therefore the sequential access cost of a file is equal to its random access cost.

The cost of random access to b pages, denoted by $RNDCOST(b)$ is

$$RNDCOST(b) = b * (s + r + btt) \tag{15}$$

The cost of accessing object identifiers for k random keys from a secondary index I, referred to as $INDCOST(k)$, is

$$INDCOST(k) = (\sum_{i=1}^{level(I)} \lceil c(n_i, m_i, r_i) \rceil) * RNDCOST(1) \tag{16}$$

where $n_i = leaves(I)/(2v(I) * ln2)^{i-2}, m_i = leaves(I)/(2v(I) * ln2)^{i-1}$, and

$$r_i = \begin{cases} k & , i = 1 \\ c(n_{i-1}, m_{i-1}, r_{i-1}) & , otherwise. \end{cases} \tag{17}$$

Finally, the cost of a range query using a B^+-tree index I, $RNGXCOST(fract)$, is obtained by the equation

$$RNGXCOST(fract) = fract * leaves(I) * (s + r + btt) \tag{18}$$

where $fract$ is the proportion of the specified range to the whole domain.

6 Cost of Implicit Join Operation

Throughout the following cost analysis, it is assumed that k_c objects of class C are to be joined (implicitly) through the attribute A of the class C with k_d objects of class D, which can be explicitly shown as $C.A = D$.self. Note that if there are no previous selections $k_c = |C|$ and $k_d = |D|$.

6.1 Cost of Forward Traversal

When there are $k_c * fan(A, C, D)$ number of references from class C to D induced by a group of k_c objects from C, the expected number of pages of class D to be retrieved to realize the join operation is given by the following formula:

$$ftc = RNDCOST(nbpg_c) + RNDCOST(k_c * fan(A, C, D)) \tag{19}$$

where $nbpg_c = nbpages(C) * (1 - (1 - 1/nbpages(C))^{k_c})$.

This is worst case formula where there are no page hits in the buffer allocated for the objects of class D.

6.2 Cost of Backward Traversals

In order to backward traverse k_d objects of the class D into k_c objects of class C, to perform the join $C.A = D$.self, it is necessary to make a sequential scan over the extent of class C. Therefore the cost is given by the following formula:

$$btc = SEQCOST(nbpages(c)) + k_c * fan(A, C, D) * k_d * CPUCOST +$$
$$\begin{cases} 0 & \text{if D is accessed previously} \\ SEQCOST(nbpages(D)) & otherwise \end{cases} \tag{20}$$

6.3 Cost of Using Binary Join Indices

The cost of using a binary join index for k objects of either class C or D is

$$bjc = INDCOST(k) \tag{21}$$

6.4 Cost of Using Pointer-based Hash Partition Join

The cost of hash-partition join in relational databases for two relations is given as [Sal88]:

$$3 * (b + b') * ebt + [1 + (b'/b)] * nsg^2 * (r + s) \tag{22}$$

where b and b' are the number of blocks in outer and inner relations respectively, and nsg denotes the number of segments of the smaller relation.

In case of pointer-based hash-partition join, the referencing class (i.e., class C) is hashed on the pointer field A and partitions are created. Then for each object of class C, the pointer $(C.A)$ is chased to retrieve the object from class D. So the cost of joining k_c objects of class C with the objects of class D by using pointer-based hybrid hash join can be given as follows:

$$hhc = 3 * k_c/|C| * SEQCOST(nbpages(C) + RNDCOST(nbpg)) \tag{23}$$

where $nbpg = nbpages(D) * (1 - (1 - 1/nbpages(D))^\alpha)$ and
$\alpha = c(|C| * fan(A, C, D), totref(A, C, D), k_c * fan(A, C, D))$.

Note that this join technique can only be applied when constructor of attribute A is Reference.

7 General Description of the Execution of MOODSQL Queries

The MOODSQL queries are executed in a predefined order of MOODSQL clauses. The sequence of execution of these clauses is shown in Fig. 3. It should be noted that, this order is, in fact, implied by the nature of the language.

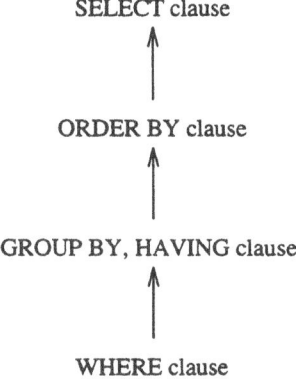

Fig. 3. The sequence of execution of a MOODSQL query

Also within a WHERE clause, there is a predefined order of algebraic operators as shown in Fig. 4. In our implementation, this order is enforced by the nature of our object oriented data model together with the well-accepted query optimization principles in relational DBMSs.

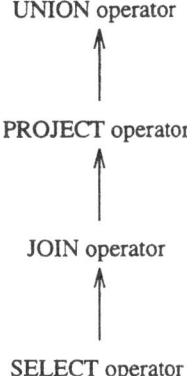

Fig. 4. Order of execution of algebraic operators in a WHERE clause

Usually, after generating the parse tree of a query, it is modified according to the algebraic transformations to obtain the final optimized tree [Ull88]. In our implementation, the final tree structure is created in a single pass with the help of the tables constructed during query parsing, along with the cost calculations performed for optimization. The query processor augmented with the query optimizer works as follows :

– The query is parsed.
– The expressions are simplified.
– The predicates in the WHERE and HAVING clauses in the query are transformed into disjunctive normal form. Such an expression takes the form

$(p_{11}$ AND p_{12} AND ... AND $p_{1m})$ OR $(p_{21}$ AND p_{22} AND ... AND $p_{2r})$ OR ...where each p_{ij} is a predicate and $(p_{i1}$ AND p_{i2} AND ...) is called an AND-term. Thus, the UNION operation is performed after evaluating the predicates for the AND-terms.

We classify the selection predicates into three types.

Immediate Selection : Selection depends on an atomic attribute or a parameterless method. These type of predicates have the following form "$s.A\theta c$", where s, A, θ, and c are a range variable, an atomic attribute or a parameterless method, a comparison operator, and a constant respectively. The information related to these kinds of predicates are kept in a dictionary, called ImmSelInfo. The structure of the ImmSelInfo dictionary is given in Table 11.

Path Selection: Selection depends on a path expression. General form for this type is "$s.A_1...A_m\theta c$", where $s.A_1...A_m$, θ, and c are a path expression, a comparison operator, and a constant respectively. Notice that a path expression implies an implicit join. The structure of PathSelInfo dictionary is given in Table 12.

Other Selections: Other predicates which are not classified as one of the above types. The examples for such predicates include methods and complex predicates. The main

Table 11. Structure of the Dictionary ImmSelInfo

Range Variable	Predicate	Selectivity	Indexed Access Cost	Sequential Access Cost	Access Type

Table 12. Structure of the Dictionary PathSelInfo

Range Variable	Predicate	Selectivity	Forward Traversal Cost

problem for this type is that it is not so easy to calculate the selectivity, and hence, the cost. The related information is stored in the OtherSelInfo dictionary. The data structure for this dictionary is also the same as that of ImmSelInfo.

- The optimal execution order of immediate and path selections are decided as explained in Sect. 8.
- To decide on a near optimal execution plan among feasible alternatives, a new heuristic is developed for ordering joins as explained in Sect. 8. After executing the joins projections are performed.
- Finally, all the subaccess plans generated are combined using the UNION operation.

8 Query Optimization in MOOD

Currently, query optimization for object-oriented database management systems is a challenging research area. The goal of the query optimization is to find an execution plan for a specific query in order to minimize a cost function. The steps involved in this process can be considered at two levels, the logical query optimization (query rewriting) that uses semantic properties of the language in order to find expressions equivalent to the one given by the user and the physical query optimization, that is based on a cost model to choose the best algorithm for evaluating the query [CD92].

In the following, optimization strategies of MOODSQL are presented.

8.1 Ordering of Atomic Selections

For the immediate selection predicates in the ImmSelInfo dictionary, the selectivity of the predicates and the cost of sequential scan for each range variable are calculated. For predicates involving an indexed attribute, indexed access costs are calculated and for each range variable in an AND term these index costs are sorted in the ascending order. Note that for common predicates in AND terms, the cost is calculated only once. Let cost$_i$ denote the indexed access cost of ith item in the sorted order which is calculated as follows:

$$cost_i = \begin{cases} INDCOST(1) & , \text{if } \theta \text{ is "="} \\ RNGXCOST(f_s(P_i)) & , \text{otherwise} \end{cases} \qquad (24)$$

where $f_s(P_i)$ is as given in Sect. 4.1. Then the number of indices to be used is the maximum value k satisfying the inequality

$$\sum_{i=1}^{k} cost_i + RNDCOST(|C| * \prod_{i=1}^{k} f_s(P_i)) < SEQCOST(nbpages(C)) \qquad (25)$$

where C is the class to which the range variable is bound.

The remaining predicates for each range variable in an AND term are sorted in increasing order of their estimated selectivities and applied in this order. The heuristic used here is analogous to short circuiting used in compilers for Boolean expression evaluation: evaluating the predicates from the least selective to the most so that minimum number of predicates are evaluated for each object.

8.2 Determining the Optimum Execution Order of Path Expressions

Given m path expressions in an AND-term :

$p.a_{11}.a_{12}...a_{1n_1}$

$p.a_{21}.a_{22}...a_{2n_2}$

.

.

$p.a_{m1}.a_{m2}...a_{mn_m}$

the problem of finding the least costly execution order of these path expressions can be stated as the following minimization problem:

Find a permutation of the integers 1 through m stored in $i[1]$ through $i[m]$ which minimizes

$$f = F_{i[1]} + s_{i[1]} * F_{i[2]} + s_{i[1]} * s_{i[2]} * F_{i[3]} + ... + s_{i[1]} * s_{i[2]} * ...s_{i[m-1]} * F_{i[m]} \qquad (26)$$

where F_j and s_j, j $i[1]$ through $i[m]$, are the cost of traversing and the selectivity of the jth path expression respectively. In other words, we are trying to minimize the objective function f, denoting the total cost of executing m path expressions in the order induced by the array i.

Assume π denotes a permutation of the integers 1 through m such that path expression indices are sorted in ascending order of $F_i/(1 - s_i)$ values, such that $1 \leq i \leq m$. This π minimizes the objective function f.

The formal treatment of this problem is provided in the Appendix.

Algorithm 8.1. The Evaluation Order of Path Expressions

- Calculate the forward traversal cost F_i for each path expression.
- Calculate the forward traversal selectivity (s_i) for each path expression.

– Order the path expressions by sorting them according to $F_i/(1 - s_i)$ values.

Example 8.1

Let us assume that the statistics given in Tables 13, 14 and 15 have been collected for an example database.

Table 13. Statistics on the example database

Class	$|C|$	nbpages(C)	size(C)
Vehicle	20000	2000	400
VehicleDriveTrain	10000	750	300
VehicleEngine	10000	5000	2000
Company	200000	2500	500

Consider the example query:

SELECT	v
FROM	Vehicle v
WHERE	v.company.name = 'BMW'
AND	v.drivetrain.engine.cylinders = 2

Table 14. Statistics on the example database

Class	Attribute	dist	max	min
VehicleEngine	cylinders	16	32	2
Company	name	200000	-	-

Table 15. Statistics on the example database

Class	Attribute	fan	totref	totlinks	hitprb
Vehicle	drivetrain	1	10000	20000	1
Vehicle	manufacturer	1	20000	20000	0.1
VehicleDriveTrain	engine	1	10000	10000	1

The PathSelInfo dictionary for the example query is given in Table 16.

Table 16. PathSelInfo dictionary contents for Example 8.1

Range Variable	Predicate	f_s	Forward Traversal Cost	cost/(1-f_s)
v	P1:v.drivetrain. engine.cylinders=2	6.25e-2	771.825	823.280
v	P2:v.company. name='BMW'	5.00e-5	520.825	520.851

The order of the path expressions is P2 followed by P1. After applying Algorithm 8.2 given in Sect. 8.3 to the path expression P2, the following subaccess plan is generated.

T1 : JOIN(
    BIND(Vehicle, v),
    SELECT(BIND(Company, c), c.name = 'BMW'), HASH_PARTITION,
    v.company = c.self)

Then applying Algorithm 8.1 by taking into account the effect of the path expression P1, the following access plan is generated.

JOIN(
        JOIN(T1, BIND(VehicleDriveTrain,d),
                        FORWARD_TRAVERSAL, v.drivetrain = d.self),
        SELECT(BIND(VehicleEngine, e), e.cylinder=2),
FORWARD_TRAVERSAL, d.engine = e.self)

8.3 Join Optimization

Join optimization, i.e., deciding on the execution order of join operations is one of the most important decisions that is made by the optimizer. Join optimization does not become a simpler problem due to the precomputed joins (stored references) and path indices; instead, it becomes a more complex problem because the number of join strategies grows with the number of alternative access paths [BMG93]. In this section we propose an algorithm for ordering implicit joins in a path expression. In realizing the implicit joins one of the following join strategies is used.

- Forward traversal
- Backward traversal
- Index-based join (Binary Join Indices)
- Pointer-based hash partition join

Let us assume that there is a path expression $p.a_1.a_2...a_n$ where p is bound to C_0 and a_i references to the instances of the class $C_i (1 \leq i \leq n - 1)$. jc_{ij}, and js_{ij} will denote the individual cost and selectivity of the temporary collection C_{ij} obtained from joining class C_i and class C_j respectively. Δ is the set of all classes which are candidates for join in each iteration of the algorithm.

We use a greedy heuristic in solving this problem such that at each iteration the join pair with lowest cost and highest selectivity are favored at the same time. The function $f(jc, js) = jc/(1 - js)$ where jc is the cost of the join and js is the selectivity of the join, satisfies the required selection criterion.

Algorithm 8.2. Implicit Join Ordering

In this algorithm jc is the minimum cost join technique among the four join algorithms given above.

1. Initialize the list Δ with the classes in the path expression
   $\Delta = \{C_0, C_1, ..., C_{n-1}\}$
2. For $i = 0$ to $n - 2$ compute $jc_{i,i+1}$ and $js_{i,i+1}$.
3. Sort the items with respect to $jc/1 - js$ values in ascending order.
4. Select the minimum pair $< C_i, C_{i+1} >$ in the sort order and name it C_k.
5. Delete i^{th} and $(i + 1)^{st}$ items.
6. Compute $jc_{i-1,k}, js_{i-1,k}, jc_{k,i+2}$, and $js_{k,i+2}$.
7. Insert $< C_{i-1}, C_k >$ and $< C_k, C_{i+2} >$ to the sorted list.
8. If the number of elements in Δ is 1, goto 9 else goto 4.
9. Generate an access plan for this join.

Example 8.2

This example is provided to clarify the implicit join ordering algorithm. Consider the query,

Select v
>From Vehicle v
Where v.drivetrain.engine.cylinders = 2

The initial cost and selectivity estimations for this query are given in Table 17.

Table 17. The initial cost and selectivity estimations for Example 8.2

CLASS	CLASS	ftc	btc	bjc	hhc	f_s	cost/(1-f_s)
Vehicle	VehicleDriveTrain	39.38	24.92	-	11.98	0.0001	11.98
VehicleDriveTrain	VehicleEngine	19.24	10.92	-	5.27	0.0001	5.27

At the end of the first iteration the following subaccess plan is generated:

T1 = JOIN(BIND(VehicleDriveTrain, d),
                    SELECT(BIND(VehicleEngine, e), e.cylinders=2),
                    HASH_PARTITION, d.engine =e.self)

The final execution plan is as follows:
JOIN(BIND(Vehicle, v), T1, HASH_PARTITION, v.drivetrain = d.self).

9 MoodView, the Graphical User Interface

MoodView is the graphical front end to MOOD [ADE93]. It allows the user to browse, edit and query the database schema and the objects. MoodView provides an environment which conforms to the requirements of object-oriented systems. It is a sophisticated, but easy to use interface. It provides visual access to the database without requiring expertise from the database user.

(a)

(b)

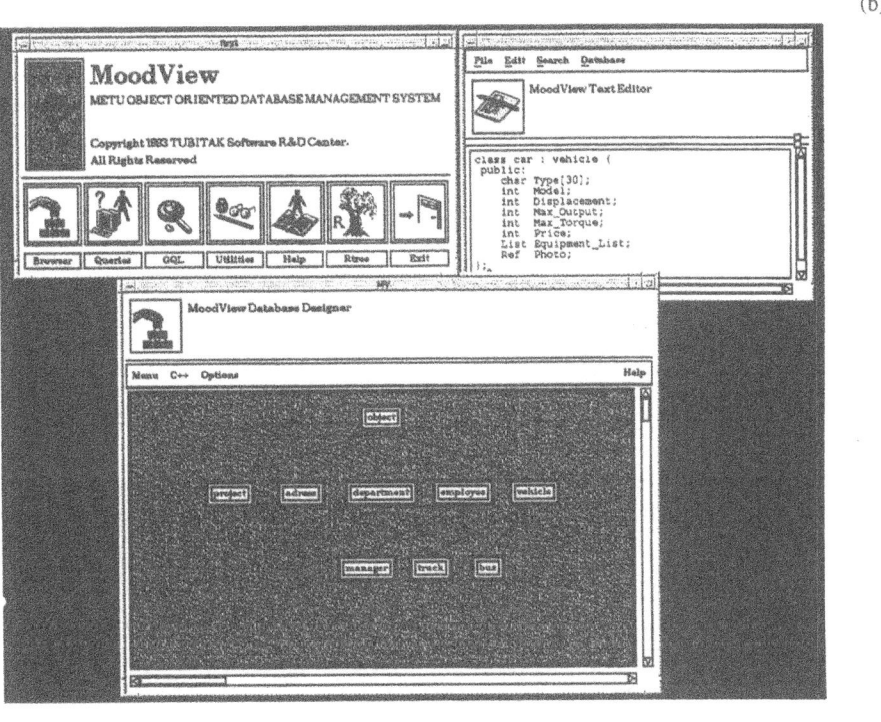

(c)

Fig. 5. (a) Initial MoodView window, (b) Data definition in C++, (c) Class hierarchy browser

9.1 Design Principles

MoodView is based on the graphical direct manipulation paradigm and is implemented in C++ using X Windows/Motif toolkit.

Conventional interfaces such as C++ and SQL are also integrated into the GUI (Graphical User Interface). Class hierarchy of C++ code can be displayed visually and

C++ code can be generated from the visual definitions. MoodView provides a SQL based query formulation tool, that the user can prepare her queries and receive results in a graphical environment.

All the schema information maintained by MoodView is stored in the database catalog through the system defined classes. MoodView actions are performed through execution of the methods by the MOOD Kernel on these data.

9.2 Environment

Upon entering the programming environment, an initial window that contains the icons for each of the MoodView tools is displayed as shown in Fig. 5(a).

Schema Browser. A database schema in MOOD contains class types, their methods and relationships between those classes. Their inheritance relationships is represented as a DAG (Directed Acyclic Graph) and MoodView uses a DAG placement algorithm that minimizes crossovers and makes drawings for graph nodes as shown in Fig. 5(c). It allows the user to design, browse, and modify database schema interactively.

(a)

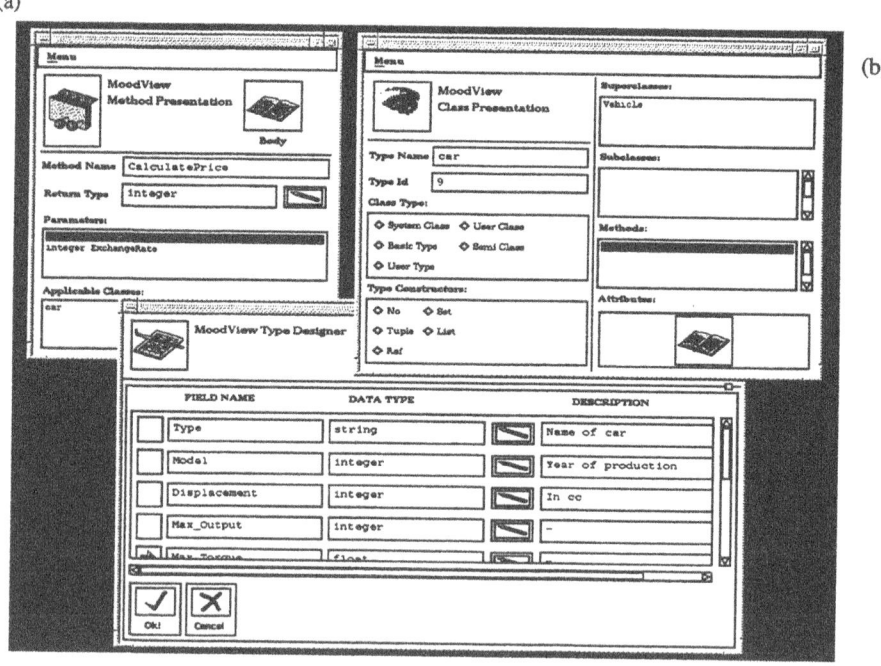

(b)

(c)

Fig. 6. (a) Method presentation, (b) Class presentation, (c) Class designer

Data Definition in C++. MoodView can display a class hierarchy defined in C++ (Fig. 5(b)). Cfront of C++ translator is modified such that, when data is defined through C++, cfront extracts the schema information and MoodView can display class hierarchy graphically using the output of Cfront. MoodView also can convert graphically designed class hierarchy graph into C++ code.

Attributes. Class attributes can be updated through a tool for designing object oriented data types. One can add, drop attributes, change the name or the type of an attribute by using this tool as shown in Fig. 6(c).

(a)

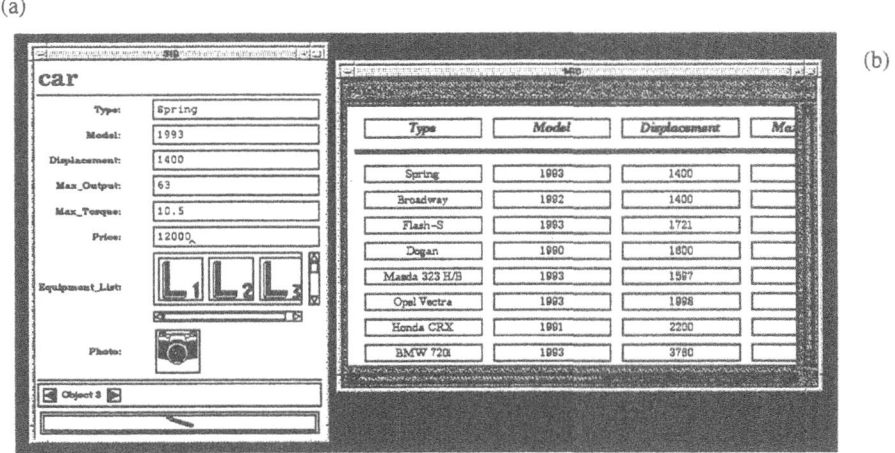

(b)

Fig. 7. (a) Generic presentation for a car object, (b) Generic presentation for the car objects

Methods. MoodView allows creation and deletion of methods and update of existing method bodies and parameters as shown in Fig. 6(a).

9.3 Object Browsing

MoodView allows complex operations against a set of objects. These include creation, deletion, update and automatic display of complex and multimedia objects, and the invocation of methods. Projection, selection and complex query specification can be done on the objects through the SQL based query manager.

Generic Object Presentations. MOOD objects constitute graphs connecting atoms and constructors. MoodView has a generic display algorithm for displaying these object graphs and walking through the referenced objects. Multimedia data such as images in different formats is defined through the system classes.

Updates to Object Presentations. Atomic types such as string or integer can be the widgets representing complex types. Copy, paste operations are also allowed for both atomic and complex types. Dynamic type checking is performed by MoodView to ensure the correctness of updates.

Interactive Method Activation. Methods are attached to object presentations and can be activated interactively.

Query Formulation. Query manager provides a query editor with facilities for accessing previous queries in a session. Through queries, objects with specific characteristics (selection) or selected portions of the objects (projection) can be displayed graphically.

9.4 Implementation

MOOD Kernel interprets provides all the functions needed by MoodView to manage schema and instance levels.

Use of the Catalog. The MOOD catalog contains all of the information required to manage schema through MoodView such as the definition of classes, types, and member functions in a structure similar to a compiler symbol table. The design of MOOD Catalog makes MoodView easily extendible, therefore it can be used in a straightforward manner for new types and objects added to the MOOD. For example, MoodView uses this persistent type catalog to determine how an object of certain type is to be displayed.

SQL Interface Between The Kernel and MoodView. A standard communication protocol is choosen between the database kernel and the GUI. All the database operations performed by the user through MoodView are converted to SQL statements and the interpretation of SQL statements is performed by the Kernel. For example, to create a new instance of employee class, MoodView produces the following SQL statement:

new Employee < "Budak Arpinar", "Computer Engineer", 1969>

Object Presentations. A cursor like mechanism which exists commonly in RDBMSs is designed for displaying objects. It is the Kernel's responsibility to identify type and value of an object in the system at run-time using the MOOD Catalog. The kernel gets the stored representation of the object from the database and returns a pointer to a buffer area each element of which specifies a name, a type and a value of the object's attributes. MoodView synthesizes this information and combines widgets to display an object on the screen. It is also possible to sequence back and forth through the returned objects using the cursor functions provided by the kernel.

10 Summary

We have discussed the design and implementation of an object-oriented DBMS, namely METU Object-Oriented DBMS.

The system includes the following components:

– A database kernel which is responsible from catalog management and dynamic linking of functions.

- An object algebra
- An object-oriented query language, MOODSQL, and its optimizer
- A graphical user interface.

Acknowledgements

The authors wish to gratefully acknowledge the MOOD project implementation team: Mehmet Altinel, Ilker Altintas, Ilker Durusoy, Tolga Gesli, Ismail Tore and Yuksel Saygin.

Appendix

Given m path expressions in an AND-term, the problem of finding the least costly execution order of these path expressions may be stated as the following minimization problem.

Find a permutation of the integers 1 through m stored in $i[1]$ through $i[m]$ which minimizes

$$f = F_{i[1]} + s_{i[1]} * F_{i[2]} + s_{i[1]} * s_{i[2]} * F_{i[3]} + \ldots +$$
$$s_{i[1]} * s_{i[2]} * \ldots s_{i[m-1]} * F_{i[m]} \tag{27}$$

where F_j and s_j, $j \in i[1]$ through $i[m]$, are the cost of traversing and the selectivity of the jth path expression respectively.

Lemma 1. *Assume π denotes a permutation of the integers 1 through m such that path expression indices are sorted in ascending order of $F_i/(1 - s_i)$ values, such that $1 \leq i \leq m$. This π minimizes the objective function f.*

Proof. By induction on the number of path expressions. It is true for 2 path expressions. In this case $f = F_1 + s_1 F_2$ or $f = F_2 + s_2 F_1$. If $F_1 + s_1 F_2 < F_2 + s_2 F_1$ then by simple manipulation, $F_1/(1 - s_1) < F_2/(1 - s_2)$ is found.

Assume it is true for m path expressions and try to show that it is also true for $m + 1$ path expressions. Let us assume that $F_i/(1 - s_i) < F_{i+1}(1 - s_{i+1})$ for $1 \leq i \leq m - 1$, and assume also that $F_j/(1 - s_j) < F_{m+1}/(1 - s_{m+1}) < F_{j+1}/(1 - s_{j+1})$ for some j where $1 < j < m$. We claim that

$$f_1 = F_1 + s_1 F_2 + \ldots + s_1 s_2 \ldots s_{j-1} F_j + s_1 s_2 \ldots s_{j-1} s_j F_{m+1} +$$
$$s_1 s_2 \ldots s_{j-1} s_j s_{m+1} F_{j+1} + \ldots + s_1 s_2 \ldots s_{j-1} s_j s_{m+1} s_{i+1} \ldots s_{m-1} F_m \tag{28}$$

is minimum. Assume on the contrary that,

$$f_2 = F_1 + s_1 F_2 + \ldots + s_1 s_2 \ldots s_{k-1} F_k + s_1 s_2 \ldots s_{k-1} s_k F_{m+1} +$$
$$s_1 s_2 \ldots s_{k-1} s_k s_{m+1} F_{k+1} + \ldots + s_1 s_2 \ldots s_{k-1} s_k s_{m+1} s_{k+1} \ldots s_{m-1} F_m \tag{29}$$

is minimum with the assumption that $k < j$ without loss of generality.

First observe that by the induction hypothesis, it can be shown that with the addition of the $m + 1^{st}$ path expression, the relative order of the previous path expression indices do not change. Therefore, if we parenthesize f_2 by $s_1 s_2 ... s_{k-1} s_k$ starting from the $k + 1^{st}$ term, we observe that the induction hypothesis stating that aforementioned sort order minimizes the objective function for $m + 1 - k \leq m$ path expressions, is violated.

The Ode Object-Oriented Database Management System: An Overview

Narain Gehani

AT&T Bell Labs, 600 Mountain Avenue, Murray Hill, NJ 07974, USA

Abstract. The Ode object-oriented database management system is based on the C++ object paradigm. Ode uses one integrated data model (C++ classes) for both database and general purpose manipulation. Ode provides multiple object-compatible interfaces for accessing the database: (1) the O++ database programming language, which is an extension of C++, (2) OdeView, which is an X-based graphical interface, (3) OdeFS, which is a file-system interface, and (4) CQL++, which in an SQL interface.

In this paper, I will briefly review object-oriented database systems and then discuss Ode. In particular, I will discuss O++ in detail, because it is the primary Ode interface, and summarize the other interfaces. I will also discuss some of the design issues faced by us. I will give a brief summary of Ode's storage manager, describe Ode's proposed active database facilities, and then discuss transaction primitives for allowing users to define their own custom transaction models.

1 Introduction

The Ode object-oriented database management system (OODBMS) [AG89a, AG89b] is based on the C++ [Str91b] object paradigm. Ode uses one integrated data model (C++ classes) for both database and general purpose manipulation. The Ode database is defined, queried and manipulated in the database programming language O++, which provides simple and elegant facilities for manipulating the database. The Ode system architecture can be described as shown in Fig. 1.

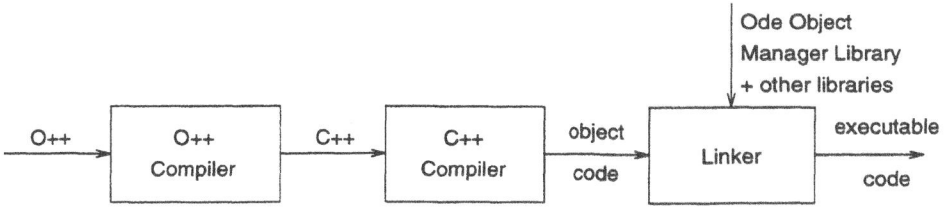

Fig. 1. Ode System Architecture

O++ is an upward-compatible extension of C++ with a few additional facilities to make it into a database programming language. C++ programmers can learn O++ in a very short time. O++ programs can be compiled with C++ programs thus allowing the use of existing C++ code.

Ode offers a simple and elegant notion of persistence which is modeled on the "heap". Specifically, memory is partitioned into *volatile* and *persistent*. Volatile objects are allocated in volatile memory (stack or heap). *Persistent* objects are allocated in persistent store and they continue to exist after the program that created them has terminated.

An Ode database is a collection of persistent objects. Each object is identified by a *unique* object id (i.e., a *persistent pointer*, or to be precise, a *pointer to a persistent object*).

2 Object-Oriented Database Management Systems

Object-oriented programming changes the programming paradigm by shifting focus from control abstractions (functions and procedures) to data abstraction (classes). Users can define data types that model objects in the application domain. Instances of a user-defined type, i.e., objects, can be manipulated using operations defined in the object type definition. These operations parallel operations for manipulating objects in the application domain.

OODBMSs go one step further than object-oriented programming. They allow applications to create, store, retrieve, and update persistent data in terms of the application domain. Some distinguishing characteristics of OODBMSs are: (1) data are stored as objects, (2) data can be interpreted (using methods) only as specified by the class designer, (3) relationship between similar objects is preserved (inheritance), and (4) references between objects are preserved.

2.1 Advantages of OODBMSs

Here is a list of some of the advantages of OODBMSs:

1. **Speed**: Queries can be faster because joins (as in relational databases) are often not needed. This is because an object can be retrieved directly without a search, by dereferencing the object id that refers to the object.
2. **No impedance mismatch**: The same data model is used by both the database programming language and the database. Thus an application does not have to do any format conversions when reading/writing data from/to disk.
3. **Programmers need to learn only one programming language**: The same programming language is used for both data definition and data manipulation.
4. **Complex applications**: The full power of the database programming language's type system can be used to model the data structures of a complex application and the relationship between different data items.
5. **Multimedia applications**: The semantic information stored in the database (class methods) facilitates correct interpretation of the data. For example, an object can be interpreted as an image or as audio using the methods associated with the object.

Storing the semantic information in the database reduces application complexity since applications do not have to be responsible for the correct interpretation of data.

6. **Versions**: OODBMSs typically provide better support for versioning. An object can viewed as the set of all its versions. Also, object versions can be treated as full fledged objects.

7. **Triggers and constraints**: OODBMSs provide systematic support for triggers and constraints which are the basis of active databases.

Most, if not all, object-oriented applications that have database needs will benefit from using an OODBMS. Specifically, C++ applications that have database needs will benefit from using Ode (and O++).

3 Ode

The Ode database [BGL+93] is based on a client-server architecture. Each application runs as a client of the Ode database server. The storage manager used by Ode is EOS [BP93]. Objects in an Ode database can be accessed and manipulated using one or more of the four object-compatible interfaces — O++, OdeView, OdeFS, and CQL++.

1. **O++** [AG89a, AG89b] is a database programming language based on C++. O++ is upward compatible with C++ and it makes minimal changes to C++. O++ offers a simple and elegant notion of persistence which is modeled on the "heap" and provides facilities for defining and querying the database as well as other facilities.

2. **OdeFS** [GJR93] is a file system interface to the Ode OODBMS. OdeFS allows objects to be treated and manipulated like files. For example, on the UNIX[1] system, standard commands such as rm, cp and mv and tools such as vi and grep can be used to manipulate objects in the database.

3. **OdeView** [AGS90] is a graphical X-based interface to the Ode database.

4. **CQL++** [DGJ92] is a C++ variant of SQL for easing the transition from relational DBMSs to OODBMSs such as Ode.

O++ is the primary interface to the Ode database. In the following sections, I will describe O++ in detail and briefly review the other interfaces. I will also discuss some of the design issues faced by us. I will then describe Ode's proposed active database facilities and transaction primitives for allowing users to define their own custom transaction models. Finally, I will give a brief summary of Ode's storage manager.

4 O++

The database programming language O++ [AG89a, AG89b, BGL+93] provides facilities for creating and manipulating the Ode database (e.g., specifying transactions, creating and manipulating persistent objects, querying the database, and creating and manipulating versions). Each O++ source file that uses O++ database facilities must include the file ode.h except when the source file is just a C++ file that doesn't use any O++ facilities.

---

[1] UNIX is a trademark of USL.

4.1 An Example

To give you a flavor of O++, I will write a program that creates employee objects and another program that queries the database for high-salaried employees (those making more than 100,000 dollars). First, here is the definition of the class employee:

```
                                                                    employee.h


#define MAX 128
persistent class employee;
class employee {
public:
    char name[MAX];
    int salary;
    int year, month, day;  //date of birth
    int dept_no;
    employee(char *n, int sal);
    int high_sal();
    int age();
};
```

The following program adds employees to the database (based on input supplied by the user):

```
                                                                        add.c


#include <iostream.h>
#include <stdlib.h>
#include <ode.h>
#include "employee.h"
main()
{
  char name[MAX]; int salary; database *db;
  if ((db = database::open("odedemo")) == NULL)
      ERROR("cannot open database odedemo);
  trans {
    cout << "ADD EMPLOYEES" << endl;
    for (;;) {
      cout << "Name (one word): ";
      cin >> name;
      cout << "Salary: ";
      cin >> salary;
      if (!cin) break;
      pnew employee(name, salary); //create persistent object
    }
  }
  db->close();
}
```

The program first attempts to open a database. If unsuccessful, the program exits after printing an error message. The program then executes a transaction repeatedly which, until it encounters the end of file, reads employee data and creates persistent employee objects by calling the operator pnew with appropriate arguments. Note that the database must be opened (and closed) outside the transaction body.

The following program queries the database for high-salaried employees:

```
                                                            showhigh.c

#include <iostream.h>
#include <stdlib.h>
#include <ode.h>
#include "employee.h"

main()
{
    database *db; persistent employee *pe;

    if ((db = database::open("odedemo")) == NULL)
        ERROR("cannot open database odedemo);

    trans {
        cout << "HIGH SALARY EMPLOYEES IN DATABASE" << endl;

        for (pe in employee) suchthat(pe->high_sal()) {
            cout << "Name=" << pe->name;
            cout << ", salary=" << pe->salary;
            cout << endl;
        }
    }
    db->close();
}
```

The statement of particular interest in this program is the for loop query that looks for all employee objects with a high salary. The "high salary" constraint is specified in the suchthat clause whose expression consists of an employee method call. Note that the loop variable pe is a pointer to a persistent employee object, i.e., its value is an object id that refers to an employee object.

4.2 Database Operations

Class database (which is automatically made available by including the header file ode.h) provides functions for manipulating (closing, opening, etc.) the database and naming persistent objects. A "truncated" version of class database is shown below:

```
                                                         database.h

...
class database {
  ...
public:
  ...

  static database* open( // open (or create) a database
    const char *name,   // the name of the db
    int rdonly = 0,     // if true read only, else r/w
    int create = 1,     // if true & no such db exists,create db
    int trunc = 0       // if true clear the db
    );                  // it returns NULL on failure
  ERR close(void);      // close this database
  ERR remove(void);     // remove this database
  char* name(void);     // the full path name of this database


  // functions for the named object directory

  char* get_name(persistent void *id); // name of obj or NULL
  persistent void * &get_obj(char *name);//null if no such name
  ERR set_name(char *name,persistent void *id,int overwrite=0);
              // give name to this object
  ERR remove_name(persistent void *id);
              //remove name of this obj
};
```

Only the following database operations open, close, and remove can be invoked from outside a transaction body. All other operations must be invoked from within the transaction body.

4.3 Transactions

All code for accessing and manipulating objects must be within a transaction block. Ode synchronizes concurrently running transactions that access shared by using 2-version 2-phase (2V2P) locking[2] scheme. This locking scheme allows multiple transactions to read an object and one transaction to write an object simultaneously.

Currently, there are three flavors of transactions: update, read only, and hypothetical. Update transactions have the form:

    trans { ... }

Read-only transactions have the form

    readonly trans { ... }

---

[2] 2-phase locking will soon be available as a compile-time option.

Read-only transactions are less likely to deadlock because they request only read locks and faster because no log records written.

Hypothetical transactions have the form

```
hypothetical trans {  ...  }
```

Hypothetical transaction allow users to pose "what-if" scenarios (as is often done with spread sheets). Users can change data and see the impact of these changes without changing the database. Only the transaction making the changes sees the changes because these changes are not made visible to other users. No log records are written.

4.4 Transaction Abortion

Transactions can be explicitly aborted by using the `tabort` statement which has the form

```
tabort;
```

In such a case, control simply flows to the statement, if any, following the transaction block.

The Ode system may also abort transactions to break deadlocks. In this case, the client application is terminated.

4.5 Persistent Objects

Objects of any class type and of the primitive types `char`, `short`, `int`, `long`, `float`, and `double` can be made persistent. Definitions of classes whose objects are to be made persistent must be preceded by persistent "forward" declarations which have the form

```
persistent class  class-name;
```

If a class is to be used both in a C++ program and in an O++ program, then the preferred way of declaring a class as persistent is to give a persistent forward declaration. But if a class is to be only used in an O++ program, then instead of giving a forward declaration first and then giving its complete declaration, the class can alternatively be declared to be persistent directly, e.g.,

```
persistent class employee {
    ...
};
```

4.6 Creating and Deleting Persistent Objects

Persistent objects are created and deleted using the operators `pnew` and `pdelete`. Except for the fact that these operators allocate objects in the database, their semantics are similar to those of the C++ operators `new` and `delete`.

Operator `pnew` returns a pointer to persistent object. Such pointers are referred to as *persistent* pointers (object ids). Persistent pointers are declared like ordinary pointers except that the type qualifier persistent is used. Note that the value 0 and the constant NULL are automatically coerced to null persistent pointers.

Persistent objects are referenced using persistent pointers much like heap objects are referenced using volatile pointers.

Consider again the definition of the class employee:

```
                                                                    employee.h


#define MAX 128
persistent class employee;
class employee {
public:
    char name[MAX];
    int salary;
    int year, month, day;   //date of birth
    int dept_no;

    employee(char *n, int sal);
    int high_sal();
    int age();
};
```

Here is some example code illustrating the creation and manipulation of persistent objects:

```
persistent employee *pe;
        ...
pe = pnew employee;
        ...
pe->salary = 40000;
pe->year = 1954;   pe->month = 12; pe->day = 3;
```

"Volatile" pointers embedded within persistent objects will not have legitimate values across transactions. For example, had name been implemented as a pointer to a dynamically allocated array (i.e., of type char *), then it would not have a valid value across transactions.

4.7 Queries

Objects of class types (only!) can be accessed by using the associative for loop as illustrated:

```
for (pe in employee)
    cout << "Name = " << pe->name << ",
                        Age = " < pe->age() << endl;
```

This `for` loop will "iterate" over all the `employees` in the database, i.e., over the `employee` "type extent". After the completion of the loop, `pe` will have the value NULL.

If we are only interested in a subset of objects, then we can use the `suchthat` clause to restrict the set of objects examined. For example, we can look at only employees older than 25 years as follows:

```
for (pe in employee) suchthat(pe->age() > 25)
    cout << "Name = " << pe->name << ",
                    Age = " < pe->age() << endl;
```

We can access a specific `employee` object as follows:

```
for (pe in employee) suchthat(strcmp(pe->name,
                                "O. Shmueli") == 0)
    cout << "Name = " << pe->name << ",
                    Age = " < pe->age() << endl;
```

Joins can be performed using nested `for` loops or a loop with multiple loop variables. For example,

```
for (pe in employee; pd in department) {
    ...
}
```

4.8 Named Persistent Objects

Persistent objects can be given symbolic names. It is not necessary to use the general `for` query statement to access named objects. For example, assume that `db` represents an open database. The persistent `employee` referenced by `pe` whose name field has the value `"OdedShmueli"` can be named oded by using the function `set_name` (defined in class `database` which was shown earlier) as follows:

```
db->set_name("oded", pe);
```

`db->set_name` returns zero if it is successful and a non zero value in case of an error.

In another transaction, this object can be retrieved by using `get_obj` as follows:

```
pe = (persistent employee *) db->get_obj("oded");
```

`get_obj` returns zero (the null persistent pointer) in case of an error. It is the user's responsibility to insure that the type of named object is the one to which it is cast.

The above object could also have been retrieved by using the `for` loop as

```
for (pe in employee) suchthat(strcmp(pe->name,
                                "OdedShmueli") == 0);
```

but this will probably be slower than using named objects.

The member function `get_name` of class `database` is used to retrieve the name of an object:

```
char *name, *p;
...
if (p = db->get_name(pe)) {
    name = new char [strlen(p)+1];
    strcpy(name, p);
}
```

If no name is associated with an object, then get_name returns NULL.

The relationship between names and objects is one-to-one; i.e., an object may have at most one name, and a name may correspond to at most one object. The persistent object naming mechanism is intended for providing fast access to objects that have been stored in the database under a well known name.

4.9 Persistent Arrays

O++ allows the user to allocate and access persistent arrays, in a manner analogous to C++. A persistent array is allocated (dynamically) by specifying it's size. As in C++, a default constructor must exist for the type, and it will be used to initialize each object in the array.

```
persistent employee *pe;
int size;
      ...
pe = pnew employee [size];
```

Individual objects are accessed using the subscript operator []:

```
pe[3].year = 1960;
```

4.10 Large Objects

An object larger than a "page" is classified as large. Such objects are, by default, handled transparently by Ode. However, applications may find it more efficient to manipulate large objects by explicitly accessing portions of such objects. Class large provides functions for efficiently manipulating large objects. Each O++ source file that uses special large object interface provided by the class large must include the file large.h. A "truncated" version of class large, which is defined in the O++ header file large.h, is shown below:

```
                                                              │large.h│

...
class large : ... {
public:
    large();
    ~large(void);
    ERR create(int n, char *buf = NULL, int hint=0,
 const _cluster* c = NULL);
    ERR open(const persistent void *p);
                // open for manipulation as large object
    ERR close(); // close the object
    ERR read(char **p, int b, int n);
    ERR write(char *p, int b, int n);
    ERR append(char *p, int n, int hint=0);
    ERR insert(char *p, int b, int n);
    ERR remove(int b, int n);
    ERR truncate(int b);
    ERR read(char *buf, int b, int n);
    ERR getf(FILE* fp, int n);
    ERR getf(FILE* fp);
    ERR putf(FILE* fp, int b, int n);
    ERR putf(FILE* fp, int b = 0);
    ...
};
```

I will illustrate the use of class large by showing how the contents of a file can be loaded into a large object and then doing the reverse. Member data of an object of type movie is used to point to a large object. Class movie is defined as

```
                                                              │movie.h│

persistent class movie;
struct movie {
    int width, ht;
    persistent char *data;
    movie() {}
    ~movie() {};
};
```

The contents of a file are loaded into a large object as follows:

```
                                                                    store.c

#include <stdio.h>
#include <ode.h>
#include <large.h>
#include "movie.h"
#define MAX 80
int fsize(FILE* fp);      // file size
main()
{
    database *db; persistent movie *pm;
    char name[MAX]; char fname[MAX];
    FILE *fp;
    large lo;  // a large object descriptor

    if ((db = database::open("large_demo")) == NULL)
        ERROR("cannot open large odedemo.");
    trans {
        printf("Name of Movie: "); gets(name);
        printf("Movie File Name: "); gets(fname);

        if ((fp = fopen(fname, "r")) == NULL)
            ERROR("cannot open movie file");

        pm = pnew movie();
        db->set_name(name, pm, 1);

        if (lo.create(0, NULL, fsize(fp)))
            ERROR("cannot make large object.");

        if (lo.getf(fp))
            ERROR("cannot read movie file");

        pm->data = (persistent char *) lo.oid();
        lo.close();
    }
    db->close();
}
```

The above program requests the user to enter the name of the file containing data for the large object and the symbolic name to be given to the movie object. It then creates a movie object and assigns its oid to the persistent pointer pm, gives it the symbolic name, creates a large object using the large object descriptor lo, and initializes it to the contents of the file. Then the object id of the large object is assigned to member data of the movie object referenced by pm.

The following program stores the contents of a large object in a file:

```
                                                              get.c

#include <stdio.h>
#include <ode.h>
#include <large.h>
#include "movie.h"
#define MAX 80
main()
{
    database *db; persistent movie *pm;
    char name[MAX]; char fname[MAX];
    FILE *fp;
    large lo;  // a large object descriptor

    if ((db = database::open("large_demo")) == NULL)
        ERROR("cannot open large odedemo.");

    trans {

        printf("Name of Movie: ");
        gets(name);
        printf("File Name to Put the Movie: ");
        gets(fname);

        if ((fp = fopen(fname, "w+")) == NULL)
            ERROR("cannot open movie file");
        pm = (persistent movie *) db->get_obj(name);
        if (lo.open(pm->data))
            ERROR("cannot open large object.");
        if (lo.putf(fp))
            ERROR("cannot write large object in file.");
        lo.close();
    }
    db->close();
}
```

4.11 Versions

Object versioning in Ode is orthogonal to type, that is, versioning is an object property
and not a type property. Versions of an object can be created without requiring any
change in the corresponding object type definition. All objects in an Ode database can
be versioned and different objects of the same type can have a different number of
versions. O++ tracks both the temporal and derived-from relationships between object
versions.

Suppose p, v1, v2, and v3 are declared as persistent employee pointers:

```
persistent employee *p, *v1, *v2, *v3;
```

Assume that p refers to a valid employee object. Then a new version of this object can be created and its oid stored in v1 as follows:

```
v1 = newvers(p);
```

Ode records the fact that the object referenced by v1 was "derived" from the object referenced by p. Function vdprev (version derived-from previous) can be used to extract this information. The call vdprev(v1) will yield p and the call vdprev(p) will yield NULL (assuming that p is not a version of another employee object).

Ode also records that the fact that object referenced by v1 was created after that referenced by p (assuming that no other versions of this employee object were created in the meantime). Function vtprev (version temporally previous) can be used to extract this information. The call vtprev(v1) will yield p and the call vtprev(p) will yield NULL.

After the following additional statements

```
v2 = newvers(v1);
v3 = newvers(p);
```

have been executed, the relationships between the different versions is described by the "version" graph shown in Fig. 2.

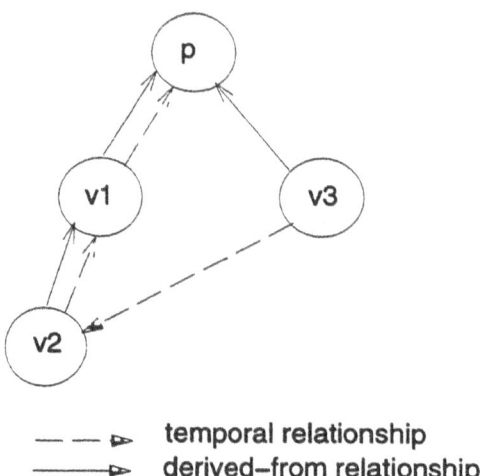

--- ▷   temporal relationship
———▷   derived–from relationship

Fig. 2. Versioning Example

Function vlatest (version latest) is used for finding the most recently derived version of a particular object.

Function vroot (version root) is used to find the initial object that an object is directly or indirectly derived from (the farthest back one can go by applying vdprev to a version repeatedly before hitting NULL).

Other functions are also provided to access nodes of the version graph.

4.12 Flexible Transaction Begin and End

The transaction block

```
trans {  ...  }
```

is the syntactic mechanism for specifying the transaction code. The transaction block clearly demarcates the transaction code. However, this "static" method of specifying the transaction code may not be flexible enough for sophisticated applications such as OdeFS [GJR93]. which may find it necessary to explicitly and dynamically specify transaction begins and commits:

Instead of using a transaction block, a transaction can be begun by calling function

```
_transaction::begin()
```

committed by calling function

```
_transaction::commit()
```

and aborted by calling function

```
_transaction::abort()
```

Using these member functions means that O++ will not be able to detect nested transaction calls (which are not supported), jumping in and out of transaction code, and other potential errors. Also, some facilities such as those for versioning will not be automatically available. In case of trans blocks, the O++ compiler generates code to initialize and close versioning facilities at the beginning and end of a transaction.

4.13 Scanning a Type Extent

A "type extent" refers to the collection of all objects of the same type in the database. Users can examine the objects in a type extent (class types only, no primitive types or arrays!) by using the O++ for statement. Some applications, such as a database browser, may want low-level control for scanning the objects in the database. For example, such an application may want to look at the first object in the database, examine the next object, or examine the previous object.

A "cluster" is a physical concept that refers to where groups of objects are stored. By default, all objects of a type *t* are stored in the cluster named _cluster_t. For example, all employee are stored in the cluster _cluster_employee.

Class scan contains facilities for explicitly scanning the objects in a cluster; these facilities are automatically made available to an application as a result of including the header file ode.h. Here is the definition of class scan:

```
                                                              scan.h

class scan {
    ...
public:
    scan(const _cluster& c);        // make a scan for cluster
    scan(const database& db);       // make a scan for db
    ~scan();
    ERR first(int inpage = 0);
    ERR last(int inpage = 0);
    ERR next(int inpage = 0);
    ERR prev(int inpage = 0);
};
```

Note that ERR is an integer error code type used by many Ode functions to return error values.

4.14 Catalog

The catalog consists of elements of the predefined type metatype, which is automatically made available as a result of including file ode.h. The catalog entries, i.e., type information stored in the database, can be examined by iterating over the metatype type extent. Class metatype is defined as

```
                                                              metatype.h

    ...
class metatype {
public:
    char name[MAX_TYPE_NAME];    // type name
    unsigned int size;            // size of instance of this

    int basecnt;          // how many base classes
    persistent base_spec *base_list; // list of base classes
    ...
};
```

The following program illustrates how information in the catalog can be accessed:

catalog.c

```
#include <ode.h>
#include <iostream.h>
persistent class figure;
persistent class square;
class figure {
public:
    float area;
};
class square: public figure {
public:
    float length;
};
main()
{
    database *db;
    persistent metatype *pm;
    if ((db = database::open("odedemo")) == NULL) {
            cout << "cannot open database odedemo" << endl;
            exit(1);
    }

    trans {
            pnew figure;
            pnew square;
            for (pm in metatype)
                cout << pm->name << endl;
    }
    db->close();
}
```

4.15 Design and Implementation Issues

I will now discuss some issues faced by us in the design and implementation of O++.

Providing DB facilities via libraries or via DBPL We believe that making facilities for manipulating the database available to the user by means of a database programming language (DBPL) is a much better choice than making them available by means library functions or classes:

The main advantage of providing database facilities by defining C++ library functions and classes is that the language does not need to be extended.

On the other hand, a DBPL provides a better user interface (ease of use, readable, smaller, etc.) and its compiler can address the following issues:

– Catalog construction

- Optimization
- Active database support
- Fixing hidden pointers
- Debugging support
- Informing the storage manager when an object is updated, making lock requests
- Index maintenance
- Automatic query plan construction, use of indexes
- View construction and maintenance.

Different Volatile and Persistent Pointer Types O++ has two kinds of pointers: pointers to volatile objects (ordinary C or C++ pointers) and pointers to persistent objects.[3] Using one pointer to refer to either a volatile object or a persistent object has several advantages [AG89b]. For example, all (including existing) code will work with both volatile objects and persistent objects. And having one pointer type makes types strictly orthogonal to persistence.

The one-pointer alternative was rejected mainly on performance grounds. We wanted to have facilities that were easy to port and efficient to implement on general purpose machines and on standard operating systems (particularly on the UNIX system) without requiring special hardware assists.

With the one-pointer alternative, a run-time check must be made to determine whether a pointer refers to a volatile object or a persistent object. Performing this check for every pointer dereference imposes a run-time penalty for references to volatile objects. This overhead is unacceptable in languages such as C and C++ (and therefore O++) which are used for writing efficient programs. Note that in these languages pointers are used heavily, e.g., string and array manipulation are all done using pointers.

One way of avoiding this run-time overhead is to trap references to persistent objects, for example, by using illegal values such as negative values for pointers to persistent objects (assuming that the underlying hardware or operating system provides the appropriate facilities). References to volatile objects then would not incur any penalty. This scheme has several problems:

1. Trapping illegal addresses is like trapping illegal memory references. The trapping mechanism and the resultant actions differ from one machine architecture and operating system to another. On the UNIX system, memory traps can be implemented by catching the segment violation (SIGSEGV) signal. However, interception of this signal is under user control, and the user (or some library routines) may (inadvertently) turn off this signal making persistent object inaccessible.

2. A program may erroneously generate a pointer that refers to a persistent object which can result in the erroneous update of a persistent object. If the database programming language cannot prevent such errors, then it will be hard to write robust applications. Note that illegal pointer references are a common source of errors in C and C++ programs.

---

[3] The original design of O++ envisioned one more type of pointer, a dual pointer, which could be used to point to both persistent and volatile memory. Experience with the use of O++ has shown that if a persistent pointer could be cast to a volatile pointer, then the dual pointers are not really needed.

3. There is no machine-independent way of generating illegal addresses.

Another problem with the one-pointer approach is that it limits the size of pointers to persistent objects to the size of ordinary pointers. This could become a problem for large databases, and it reduces flexibility of the implementation in deciding what information can be stored in a pointer to a persistent object.

These problems do not arise when type information can be used to determine, at compile time, references that involve persistent objects. There is no need to use a memory trap mechanism to differentiate between pointers to volatile and persistent objects and appropriate compile-time checks will ensure that illegal references to persistent objects are not generated inadvertently. Also, the implementation will then not have to limit the size of pointers to persistent objects to the size of ordinary pointers.

Hidden Pointers O++ objects are really C++ objects since the O++ compiler produces C++ as its output. C++ objects of types that have virtual functions or virtual base classes contain volatile ("memory") pointers. We call such pointers "hidden pointers' because they were not specified by the user. When C++ objects are made persistent, then volatile pointers, both hidden pointers and user-defined pointer members, become invalid across program invocations.

In the case of pointer members, the programmer must ensure that the pointers are not used with invalid values. However, in case of hidden pointers it is the responsibility of the system providing persistence to ensure that the objects read from disk do not contain invalid values prior to their use in the program. Otherwise, a reference to a virtual function or a component of a virtual base class will lead to an illegal memory reference.

Making C++ objects persistent is not straightforward. The locations of the hidden pointers within an object are not known to the O++ compiler nor are the values to be assigned to these pointers known.

Our solution [BDG93a] is based on the fact that for every constructor, the C++ compiler adds code to properly initialize the hidden pointers in an object of that type. There are two obstacles to implementing the above scheme. First, C++ does not allow a constructor to be invoked in conjunction with an existing object (as are member functions). However, we can call the constructor indirectly overloading the new operator. For more details, see [BDG93a].

5 Storage Manager

The EOS storage manager [BP93] is the storage engine of Ode. Some features of EOS are

1. Client-server architecture.
2. Efficient and transparent handling of large objects.
3. A file-like interface is also provided for very large objects.
4. Concurrency is based on multi-granularity two-version two-phase locking; it allows many readers and one writer to access the same item simultaneously.

5. A write-ahead redo-only log is maintained. Log records contain only after images of updates, thus making logs small.
6. Recovery from system failures requires one scan over the log resulting in fast restarts.

An Ode database is a collection of EOS files and ordinary objects. EOS files group "related" objects together – i.e., objects that need to be colocated – and provide facilities for sequencing through these objects . For each O++ class defined by the user, an EOS file is created to store all objects of the class, i.e., the type extent. When an object of is created (via pnew), it is automatically placed in its type extent.

Objects ids, which are physical object address, are 8 bytes in size. If an object cannot fit within a page, EOS transparently switches to a different representation suitable for large objects [Bil92a]. Large objects are stored in a sequence of variable-length segments – a number of physically contiguous disk pages. Simulation results show that the EOS technique of managing large objects imposes minimal I/O cost compared to other solutions [Bil92b].

EOS objects are accessed via handles. Having a handle to an object means that the page the object resides on is pinned down in the buffer pool. After an object handle is acquired, the speed of subsequent accesses to the object is comparable to a memory pointer dereference. The in-memory and on-disk representations of an object are the same which allows persistent objects to be manipulated directly on the page on which they reside, without incurring any in-memory copying cost.

6 OdeFS

OdeFS [GJR93] is a file system interface to the Ode OODBMS. OdeFS allows objects to be treated and manipulated like files. Files, called object files, serve as aliases for objects in the Ode database. Standard commands such as rm, cp and mv and tools such as vi and grep can be used to manipulate objects in the database by referring to the corresponding object files. A file-oriented Graphical User Interface (GUI) can display and select Ode objects. Because no code modification or recompilation is required, proprietary applications or applications written in languages such as awk and COBOL applications can also access Ode objects.

Consider a collection of SUN workstations sharing a common file system implemented using the NFS protocol [NFS88]. File requests from client machines are sent to a network file server, called the NFS server, that implements the shared file system. OdeFS is also a network file server. It is "interjected" between the standard NFS server and the client machines.

OdeFS intercepts all file requests sent by the clients to the NFS server. OdeFS passes on all requests for ordinary files to the NFS server and then sends its responses back to the clients. In case of object files, which are aliases for objects in the Ode database, OdeFS transforms the requests appropriately and then interacts with the Ode database and sends responses, as appropriate, back to the client.

The type of a file depends upon its name and the type of directory containing the file. The type of a directory is determined by the "control" files in the directory. The absence of control files in a directory indicates that the directory is an ordinary directory and that the files in it are ordinary files.

For every class whose objects are to be manipulated using OdeFS, the user is expected to define some "interface" functions that will, for example, assist OdeFS in displaying the object and updating the object. If the user does not define such functions, then OdeFS uses default functions which provide little or no functionality. Two interface functions are important for using OdeFS effectively: one function is used for determining the "standard" name of the object file corresponding to an object; the second is used to reading an object for display.

7 OdeView

OdeView [AGS90] is the graphical front end to Ode. OdeView provides facilities for examining the database schema, examining class definitions, accessing and manipulating objects, following chains of references starting from an object, synchronized browsing, displaying selected portions of objects (projection), retrieving objects with specific characteristics (selection), and object updates.

The internals of specific classes are not hardwired into OdeView and new classes can be added to the Ode database without requiring any changes to or recompilation of OdeView. Similarly, class functions (methods) for displaying objects are written without knowing about the specifics of the windowing software used by OdeView or the graphical user interface provided by it.

7.1 Displaying an Object

In a relational DBMS, displaying a tuple is rather straightforward: it is simply a matter of displaying the values of attributes whose types are known to the DBMS. Unfortunately, object displaying is not so straightforward in OODBMSs.

Here are some issues that we encountered:

1. Ode objects arc not simple tuples. Their components can be of arbitrarily complex types: they can be structures, arrays, sets implemented as lists of values, a pair of values representing a point in polar coordinates, so on. However, when these components represent more than just structured values, simple display schemes may not be adequate. For example, it will be unsatisfactory to display a circular buffer simply as a linear list of values.
2. Ode objects can contain references to other objects. When displaying an object, how should the reference be displayed? As a simple value? Or should the referenced object be displayed?
3. Ode classes support data encapsulation. The encapsulated data represents the implementation of the object, and a user sees only the public part of a class. Therefore, if one respects encapsulation, then only the public data and the data made available by calling the public member functions should be displayed. But then how does one decide which member functions should be called? Simply calling all the public member functions will be unacceptable, if not potentially disastrous, because of any potential side effects.

It may also sometimes be beneficial to display the data in the private part, perhaps in a privileged mode, say for debugging. This means that it should be possible to selectively violate the encapsulation.

4. Depending upon the application, an object may be viewed differently or it may simply have multiple views. For example, a document object may be viewed in text form, in Postscript form, or as a bitmap. Thus, it should be possible to display an object in a variety of forms using one or more media.

5. Some components of an object may have embedded semantics. For example, suppose that one of the components of an object is a string that represents the name of the file containing some pictorial description of the object. Displaying the string itself will not be of much value compared to displaying the pictorial representation which may require processing, such as uncompression, of the pictorial description.

In general, it will not possible for a system such as Ode to display an object without some help from the class designer. The class designer knows best how an object is to be displayed. Consequently, we decided that it is the responsibility of class designer to provide a distinguished member function named `display` for displaying objects of the class. If the display function is not provided, then OdeView will synthesize a display function, possibly a rudimentary one.

7.2 Communication Protocol To Separate OdeView from the Class Designer and Vice Versa

We adopted the following "principle of separation":

The class writer should not have to know the specifics of object display (windowing) software and the display software should not have to know about object types.

To realize this separation, we have defined a interface which is understood by both OdeView and the `display` function. Specifically, we have defined a set of generic window types corresponding to the kind of windows that are supported by most windowing systems. Some examples of window types are: static text window, static text window with horizontal and vertical scroll bars, and raster image window.

To display an object, OdeView retrieves the object from the Ode database and then invokes the `display` function associated with the object class. Using the information returned by the `display` function, OdeView creates appropriate windows and displays the object representations. Subsequent scrolling, iconification, movement of these windows is handled by the underlying windowing software.

7.3 Using OdeView

To give you a flavor of OdeView, we will browse through an employee database.

After activating OdeView, clicking on `Database` button and selecting the `LabDB` option, we see the screen shown in Fig. 3

The lab database has a very simple schema as shown in Fig. 4 but it has interesting data.

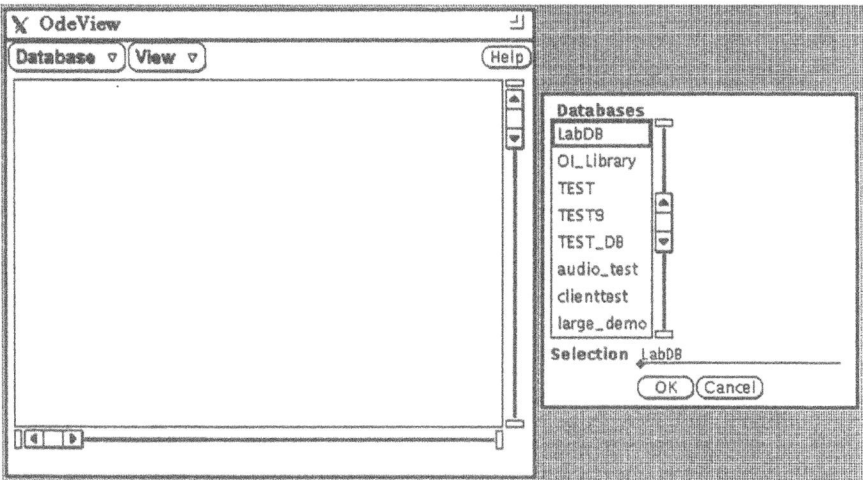

Fig. 3. OdeView Opening Screen

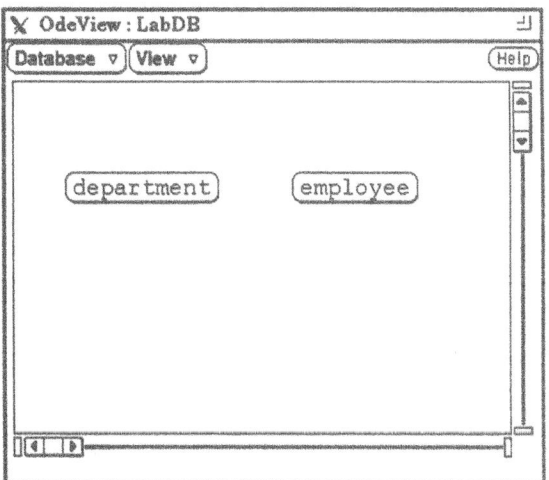

Fig. 4. Schema

Clicking on the employee[4] and then browsing a bit we see the object that stores data about me as shown in Fig. 5.

We can click on the picture button to see author's picture as shown in Fig. 6.

A few more clicks and you see the author's manager Nick Maxemchuk also as shown in Fig. 7.

---

[4] The definition of these employee objects is different from the employee definition shown in Sect. 4.1.

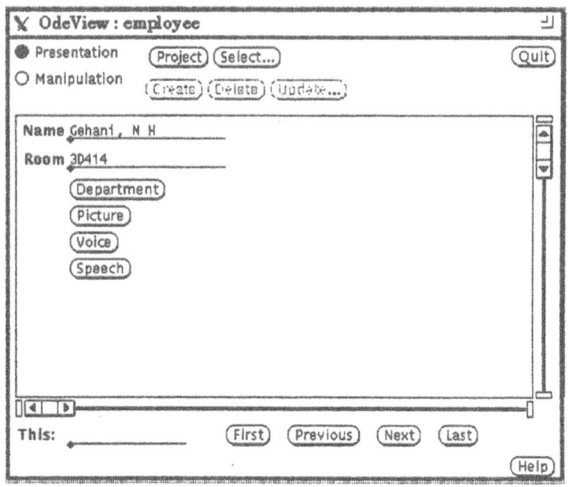

Fig. 5. Gehani employee Object

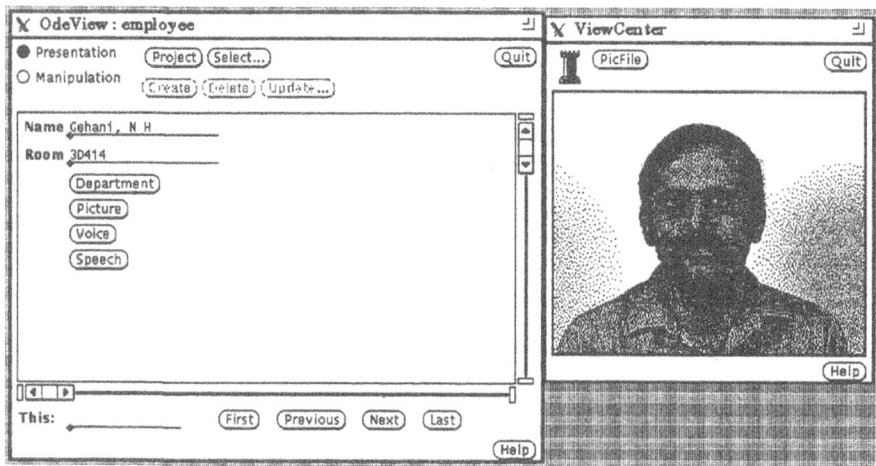

Fig. 6. Gehani employee Object with Picture

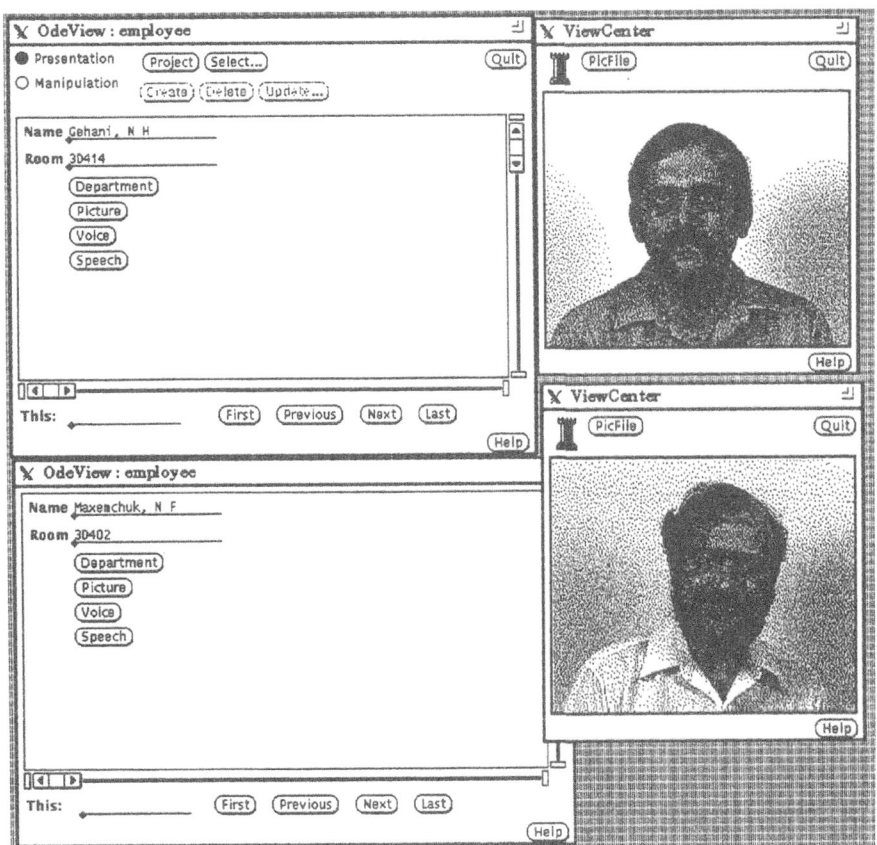

Fig. 7. Gehani and his Manager

Synchronized Browsing OdeView allows a user to start from an object and then explore the related objects in the database by following the embedded chains of references. To speed up such repetitive navigations, OdeView supports synchronized browsing [MDT88]. Once the user has displayed a network of objects and the user applies a sequencing operation to any object in this network, the sequencing operation is automatically propagated over the network. For example, clicking the next button in the window containing the author's picture shows us the next employee, Dwight Hill, and his manager Al Dunlop:

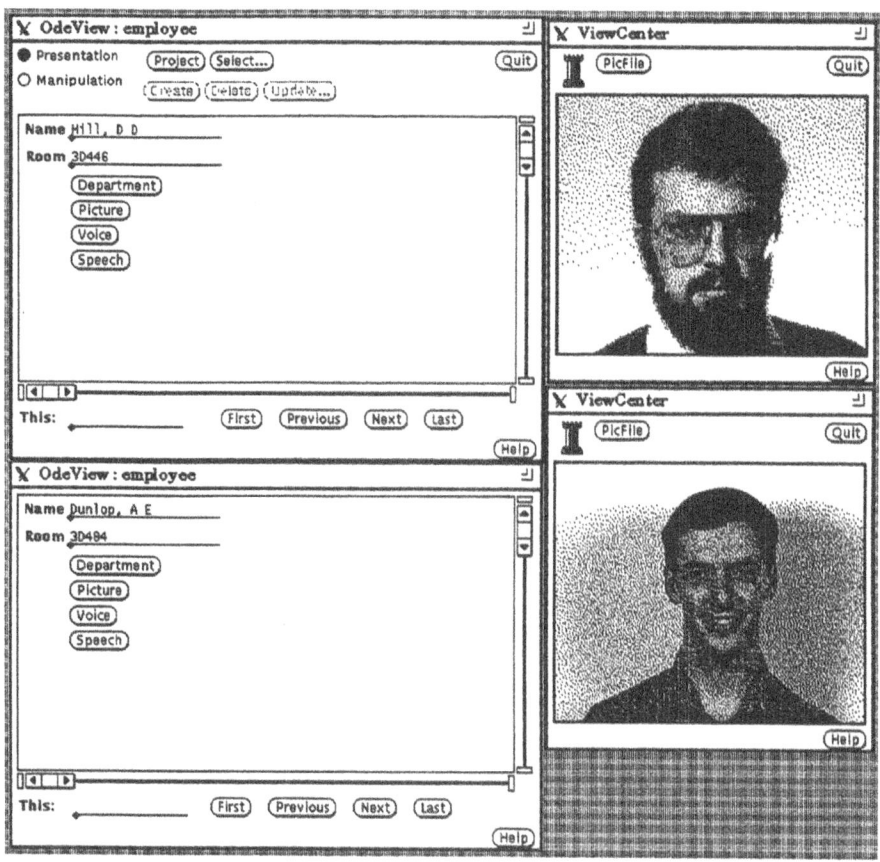

Fig. 8. Synchronized Browsing

Synchronized browsing works even if some of the intermediate windows are closed.

8 cql++

CQL++ [DGJ92] is a declarative front end to the Ode OODBMS that blends an SQL-like syntax with the C++ class model. CQL++ provides facilities for defining classes, and for creating, querying, displaying, and updating objects. CQL++ is designed for SQL users to facilitate a smooth transition from a relational database to the Ode OODBMS.

An important goal in the design of CQL++ is to ensure its integration with O++ (and the other interfaces). Although, CQL++ does not support the full definitional capabilities of O++, it can be used to formulate queries against a database defined and populated using O++. Similarly, O++ users can manipulate objects of classes defined using CQL++. CQL++ tries to minimize the details of the Ode object model it expects its users to know, while maximizing the functionality of O++ available to them. It hides from users such programming language details as object-ids, public and private members of objects, and the implementation (bodies) of member functions.

8.1 Design Goals

Here are some our design goals:

1. CQL++ should "look and feel" like SQL as much as possible.
2. CQL++ and O++ (and the other interfaces) should coexist with each other since they both represent interfaces to Ode. CQL++ may not offer the complete power and flexibility offered by O++, to keep it from becoming too complex.
3. The distinction between objects and object-ids in object-oriented database programming languages, such as O++, should be blurred as far as possible. We believe that pointer (object id) dereferencing is a difficult concept for a non-programmer to learn and that it should not be forced upon a CQL++ user.
4. CQL++ should have the closure property; i.e., it should be possible to use the result of one query in another query.

8.2 Examples

1. Consider the following join query that prints information about all employees under 30 who have the same name as the manager of some department:

   ```
   SELECT employee.name, department.dname
   FROM employee, department
   WHERE employee.name = department.mgr.name
   AND employee.age() < 30
   ```

2. CQL++ supports the definition and use of views, much like SQL. For example, to create a view of all employees who live in New York, we can write

```
CREATE VIEW new_york_emps
AS
SELECT *
FROM Employee
WHERE addr.city = 'New York'
```

3. CQL++, like O++, supports the creation and manipulation of object versions
[ABGS91] tracking both the temporal and derived-from relationships.

   CQL++ provides three modifiers for accessing versions of an object. PREVIOUS
takes a set of objects and returns another set of objects that are the temporally
previous versions, if any, of the objects in the original set. Similarly, PARENT takes
a set of objects and returns another set of objects that are the versions, if any, upon
which the objects in the original set were based. Finally, LATEST takes a set of
objects and returns a the set of logical objects of which the objects in the original
set are versions.

   Assume that a new version of each employee object is created every year to
track changes. The following statements prints the salary earned last year by every
employee more than 55 years old (last year).

```
SELECT salary
FROM PARENT(employee)
WHERE age() > 55
```

9 Active Database Facilities

Triggers, the basic facility of active databases, are specified in O++ class definitions as
event-action pairs of the form

   event-expression ==> action

where an *event-expression* specifies a simple or "composite" event [GJ91, GJS92b,
GJS92a]. An "event" is any happening of interest. Some examples of events are

- The start of a transaction.
- An object read or update.
- AT&T stock price rising to a specified price.
- Credit card transaction authorization.

   Composite events are events composed from simple (basic) events or from other
composite events.

   Finite automata are used to detect event occurrences that satisfy event expressions
Each basic event, that occurs in an event expression, is posted to the corresponding
automaton. We in effect maintain "continuous queries" by advancing the to reflect the
partial occurrence of the (composite) events. A (composite) event is recognized immediately after the basic event satisfying the event expression is posted. The recognition is
immediate because only one state transition is needed to move the automaton to a final
state (in case of a mask, two transitions are required along with the evaluation of the
mask).

An Example — Discount Rate Cut The US Federal Reserve Board changes a key
interest rate, the "discount" rate, to control inflation and economic growth. Three or
more successive discount rate cuts without an intervening increase is a rare phenomenon
and is of interest to the financial community. Many other events can occur, for example,
the prime rate may be cut and the stock market can crash, but these events do not interest
us here. Our problem is to write an event expression that is satisfied by such cuts in the
discount rate.

Figure 9 illustrates the occurrence of events (marked by dots).

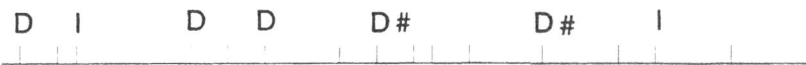

Fig. 9. Discount rate cut

Discount rate cut events are labeled by D (decrease) and increases labeled by I. The
event that interests us occurs at the last two D events (marked with #). This event can be
specified using the following expression:

```
(I || D) | sequence(D, D, D)
```

The left hand operand of the pipe operator |

```
(I || D)
```

specifies that we are only interested in D or I events. The pipe operator filters out all
other events before transmitting these two events to its right operand

```
sequence(D, D, D)
```

which looks for a sequence of three D's.

10 Flexible Transaction Facilities

Ode and other OODBMSs were motivated to support complex applications such as
CAD and software engineering. Transactions in such applications have diverse needs:
they may be long lived and they may need to cooperate.

The traditional atomic transaction model in conjunction with serializability can
be very constraining in advanced database applications that function in distributed,
cooperative, and heterogeneous environments. We have designed a flexible transaction
facility for Ode which consists of a set of transaction modeling primitives for defining
transaction semantics with custom semantics [BDG+93b].

10.1 Basic Transaction Primitives

A transaction that has been registered with the DBMS but which has not begun execution is said to have been *initiated*. A transaction is said to be *running* if it is executing its code, i.e., it has begun but not yet completed. A transaction is said to have *completed* if its code has been executed. A transaction has been *terminated* if it has been *committed* or *aborted*. A transaction is *active* if it has begun executing, and has not terminated yet (it may be running or completed).

In this section, we define transaction primitives found in most transaction processing systems.

- initiate(f_1, f_2, ..., f_n, t_1, t_2, ..., t_n): register n new transactions which are to execute the functions pointed to by f_1, f_2, ..., f_n respectively. That is, the functionality (code) of the n transactions is embedded in the functions f_1, f_2, ..., f_n. If successful, initiate stores in t_1, t_2, ..., t_n the transaction ids of the new transactions and returns 1; otherwise, it stores in t_1, t_2, ..., t_n the null transaction id, and returns 0. The transactions t_1, t_2, ..., t_n do *not* start executing; transaction execution is initiated by calling begin.
- begin(t_1, t_2, ..., t_n): start running the transactions whose ids are t_1, t_2, ..., t_n; it returns 1 if successful; otherwise it returns 0.
- commit(t_1, t_2, ..., t_n): atomically commit all the operations of the transactions whose ids are t_1, t_2, ..., t_n. Atomic commitment of more than one transactions implies that either all these transactions commit or all are aborted. commit returns 1 if all transactions commit; otherwise, it returns 0.
- abort(t_1, t_2, ..., t_n): abort the transactions whose ids are t_1, t_2, ..., t_n. abort returns 1 if successful; otherwise it returns 0.
- self(): returns the id of the executing transaction.
- parent(): returns the id of the parent transaction, that is the transaction that executed the initiate for the current transaction. For top-level transactions, 0 (the null transaction id) is returned.

10.2 Primitives for Specifying New Transaction Semantics

We now introduce two new primitives, delegate and ignore_conflicts. The former allows a transaction to delegate its responsibility to make the effect of (some of) its operations persistent to another transaction. The latter allows a transaction to ignore the effects of executing an operation that conflict with operations of another transaction.

1. delegate(t_j, ob_set): transfer to transaction t_j the responsibility for the operations performed by the invoking transaction, t_i, on objects that are in the set ob_set. These operations are committed if and only if t_j commits (assuming t_j does not delegate them to another transaction). Once t_i delegates an object ob to t_j, all C relations and abort dependencies that were induced by t_i's operations are "transferred" to t_j, i.e., it will be as if t_j, not t_i, performed these operations. One implication is that a subsequent operation on ob performed by t_i can conflict with an operation previously performed by t_i, but since delegated to t_j.
   If an object ob is delegated by t_i, then an object ob', if any, that (recursively) satisfy the following rules must also be delegated at the same time.

(a) An operation by t_i on ob resulted in a nested operation invocation on ob'.

(b) An operation by t_i on ob' resulted in a nested operation invocation on ob.

2. `ignore_conflicts`(t_j, ob_set): when t_j invokes an operation on an object in ob_set, ignore any conflicts that occur with operations of t_i, the transaction issuing this request. In other words, t_j is allowed to execute operations on objects in ob_set even if they conflict with the operations for which t_i is responsible. Operation $op_j[ob]$ is allowed to proceed even though it may conflict with $op_i[ob]$ which was executed by transaction t_i which has not committed as yet.

`ignore_conflicts` allows conflicting operations to proceed without forming dependencies. Consequently, transactions may see a possibly inconsistent state of the database. To preserve global consistency, these transactions still have to guarantee that they will leave the database in a consistent state when they commit.

If t_i ignores conflicts with t_j on some object ob, and then delegates its operations on ob to t_k, then the ignoring of conflicts with respect to ob is delegated as well.

10.3 Using the Transaction Primitives

The above transaction primitives have been used to specify different transaction models. Only a couple are shown here. For more examples, please see [BDG+93b]. Users can use them to define custom transaction models.

10.4 Atomic Transactions

Atomic transactions combine the properties of serializability and failure atomicity. These properties guarantee that concurrent transactions execute without interference as though they executed in some serial order, and that either the transaction executed completely or not at all.

An atomic transaction can be specified as

```
if (initiate(f,t)) {
    if (begin(t)) {
        if (commit(t)) return COMMIT;
    }
}
return ABORT;
```

Leave out the error checks and return codes, an atomic transaction can be specified as

```
initiate(f,t);
begin(t);
commit(t);
```

10.5 Split and Join Transactions

In the split transaction model [PKH88], one transaction can split off another transaction and two transactions can join to form one transaction. At spitting time, operations invoked on a set of objects by the transaction spawning off the split transaction will be delegated to the new transaction. These two transaction can then commit or abort independently.

Consider, for example, a three-level split transaction. t splits off t1, which then splits off t2, which commits by itself. t1 then rejoins with t:

```
initiate(f,t);
begin(t);
commit(t);
```

Function f is defined as

```
void f() {
    ...
    initiate(f1,t1); // splitting off
    delegate(t1, S);
    begin(t1);
    ...
    commit(t1);
}
```

where S is the set of objects on which transaction t has performed operations. Function f1 is defined as

```
void f1() {
    initiate(f2,t2); // splitting off
    delegate(t2, S);
    begin(t2);
    ...
    delegate(parent()); // joining t
}
```

Function f2 is defined as

```
void f2() {
    ...
    commit(self());
}
```

11 Summary

The Ode system is the result of ongoing effort of several researchers at AT&T Bell Laboratories in the area of OODBMSs.

Ode 3.0 is currently being used as the multi-media database engine for AT&T's Interactive TV project. Ode 3.0 has also been distributed to 80+ sites within AT&T and 350+ universities. Currently, O++ is The only Ode interface that is distributed with Ode 3.0. We have also implemented OdeFS and OdeView. OdeFS will be soon ready for distribution.

Appendix: Availability for Universities

Ode 3.0 is now available to Universities. There is no charge for Ode 3.0. However, AT&T does require the signing of a non-disclosure agreement.

For further information and a copy of the Ode system (for SUN Sparcstations only), send mail to Narain Gehani at nhg@allegra.att.com with the following information:

```
Faculty Member Name:
University:
Department:
Postal Address:

Telephone:
Fax no:
Email:
```

Object-Oriented Modeling for Hypermedia Systems Using the VODAK Model Language

Wolfgang Klas, Karl Aberer, Erich Neuhold

GMD-IPSI, Dolivostr. 15, D-64293 Darmstadt, Germany

Abstract. More and more documents become available in electronic form, e.g., in the publishing sector, product design and specification, documentation, medical records, etc. Real applications in industry have a serious problem of handling masses of documents. Therefore, there is a growing demand of database support in the areas of document modelling, in particular hypermedia document modelling, i.e. documents containing multimedia data. As documents represent intrinsically complex structured data object-oriented database management (OODBMS) technology with its ability to handle such kind of information offers itself as a very promising way to tackle this problem as opposed to conventional database technology which was designed to handle simple structured data. OODBMS technology, although fairly developed today, needs to be extended and adapted to meet the specific requirements of hypermedia document modelling. Within the VODAK project at GMD-IPSI we developed an *open* OODBMS. Its data model *VML* can be tailored to the needs of particular applications. In this paper we first present the key principles and main features of the open object-oriented data model VML which can be extended at the meta level. This includes utilizing the concept of metaclasses. By this, system administrators may tailor the kernel data model to the requirements of specific applications and introduce, for example, additional types of links as they can be found in hypertext models at the data-model level. Second we illustrate how this open object-oriented data model can be tailored to the needs of modelling hypermedia documents as they are used in the framework of, e.g., collaborative authoring environments. We incrementally develop a model for hypermedia documents, discuss the advantages and disadvantages as well as the various alternatives.

1 Introduction

Hypertext or hypermedia is an approach to information management in which multimedia data is organized in a network of nodes connected by links. Many hypermedia systems have been designed to support specific tasks, e.g., *Writing Environment (WE)* [SWF+86, SWF87] has been designed specifically to support the professional writer, *Examiner* [Wal87] has been designed specifically for the on-line presentation of technical documents. Other systems provide general hypermedia facilities to be used in a variety of applications, e.g., idea processing and generic authoring (*NoteCards* [HMT87, Hal88]), software engineering (*Neptune* [DS86b], or multi-user interactive education (*Interme-dia* [GSM86, Mey86]). *KMS* [AMY88] is used in a number of applications including project management, electronic publishing, electronic mail, and bulletin boards.

After initial experiments with the management of information through these experimental systems the limitations of traditional modeling and storage concepts used in such systems have become increasingly apparent. The problems reflect fundamental weaknesses in the hypermedia models around which these systems are built. The simple node and link model as well as the conventional database models like the relational data model are not rich and complete enough to support the storage and information management as well as the presentation tasks required by hypermedia applications [Hal88]. File system based storage as in *HAM* [CG88a] also falls short of what is needed. The semantics and the information of how to perform computations over a hypermedia network, e.g., actively deriving new information, or actively controlling the manipulation of the stored information with respect to its meaning, are not captured by the systems. Furthermore, pure navigational access has proven to be insufficient, what is needed are additional query-based access mechanisms.

These approaches do not provide for concepts to extend and tailor the underlying data model to the needs of particular applications. For example, the basic hypermedia model of nodes and links lacks powerful composition mechanisms, i.e., a way of representing and dealing with complexly structured information. Current systems use the two primitive node and link constructs to build up more complex entities.

Some of these limitations may be overcome by employing and extending database technology. Although conventional database systems do not provide the right mechanisms and appropriate concepts for hypermedia systems [Hal88] recent results in research on next generation database systems reduce the gap between the requirements and the available support through database systems. For example, transaction management based on open nested transactions [BSW88, MRKN92, Wei86], object-oriented serializability [RGN90] which has been developed in cooperation with the design of SEPIA (Structured Elicitation and Processing of Ideas for Authoring) [HW92, SHH+92, SHT89], or the concept of *ConTracts* [WR89] may provide appropriate support for the collaborative behavior with respect to the usage of hypermedia systems. The usage of an object-oriented data model will allow to specify more semantics of nodes, link types, and the manipulation and usage of hypermedia networks with the hypermedia system as it provides the encapsulation of structures and operations defined on these structures. Thus, e.g., the information of how to manipulate a hypermedia network consistently can be stored in the database and the hypermedia system can actively support the user according to such information.

Within the VODAK project at GMD-IPSI we developed an *open object-oriented* data model which can be tailored to the needs of particular applications utilizing the concept of *metaclasses*. In this paper we show how this open object-oriented data model can be tailored to the needs of modeling hypermedia documents as they are used in the framework of, e.g., collaborative authoring environments. In this paper we abstract from the multimedia aspects of a hypermedia network. Requirements and solutions for integrating multimedia data in VODAK are described in [AK93, KNS90b, Kla92, RLMN93, TR93a, TR93b].

We propose an open database model which can be extended at the meta level. By this, system administrators may tailor the kernel data model to the requirements of specific applications and introduce, for example, additional types of links at the data-model level. We show how behaviorally object-oriented data models may be employed and extended to meet the special requirements of hypermedia applications.

The remainder of this paper is organized as follows: Section 2 introduces the key principles and main features of the VODAK Model Language VML. Section 3 discusses the application of VML for modeling hypermedia documents. Section 4 concludes the paper and gives an outlook of ongoing developments.

2 The VODAK Model Language VML

2.1 Some Preliminaries

In the VODAK Model Language[1] we distinguish between *data values* and *objects*. Each data value is out of a *domain* determined by a *data type*. Data values themselves exist only *transiently* inside the scope of a program. An object is out of a domain constituted by a *class*. Objects exist *persistently*, i.e., they exist independently of the scope of a program. Each object has assigned exactly one data value, called *object identifier*, which is the unique identifier of the object by a data value through the object's lifetime.

All objects of a class share the description for their *interface* , structure of the object's *state*, and *implementation*. This description constitutes the type of an object and can be defined through *object type definitions*. The *interface* consists of a set of methods, more precisely a set of *method signatures*. The *state* of an object is constituted by a tuple of data values according to property definitions. Access to the object's state is only possible via the execution of the methods in the interface.

Class definitions determine the domains of classes. They refer to object types and define class objects which model the containers of sets of objects, i.e., the *extensions* of classes. Class objects are instances of classes, which are called *metaclasses*. A *VML schema* consist of class definitions, data-type declarations, and object-type declarations.

2.2 Data Types

A data type characterizes a set of values, i.e., a domain, and a set of operations applicable to these values. Data types are built up from *primitive data types*, which include object identifiers, and some basic *type constructors*.

```
datatype ::=
  primitive_type | structured_type | DataType_Identifier |
  Class_Identifier | ClassParam_Identifier
```

Identifiers referring to a class parameter (*ClassParam_Identifier*) can be used only in object-type declarations. Identifiers referring to a class (*Class_Identifier*) can be used only in class definitions. Their usage is explained later in detail in Sect. 2.5.

---

[1] This description refers to VML Version 3, May 1993 [KNB+92]. Only the language features needed in this paper are introduced. Future developments will extend the language by additional concepts, including further support for multimedia applications.

```
primitive_type ::=
  BOOL | INT | REAL | STRING | OID |
  enumeration_type | subrange_type
```

The primitive data types are those types whose values have no components. The operators available for these data types are the usual ones. OID is the type of unique object identifiers. The only relevant operator in this context for OID is the infix operator "=" which tests whether two object identifiers are equal or not. Details about the usage of this data type are given in the subsection on metaclasses in Sect. 2.4. An enumeration type introduces a set of basic values by listing the values, which must be distinct. The subrange type specifies a subset of the integer values.

```
structured_type ::=
  record_type | variant_type | set_type | array_type |
  dictionary_type
```

Structured data types are built from primitive data types, already defined structured data types, object types, and type identifiers using type constructors. In the following we will only describe the most important type constructors for records and sets.

A *record* is a sequence of named variables, called the fields of the record. Different fields can have different types. The name and type of each field is statically determined by a record declaration.

```
record_type   ::=  "[" record_field "," record_field "]"
record_field  ::=  Identifier ":" datatype
```

A field named f in a record r can be access only with the expression r.f. A record value is denoted by the expression [id1:v1, id2:v2, ..., idn:vn]. A set is a collection of values taken from the same type.

```
set_type ::= "{" datatype "}"
```

The values of a set type are all sets whose elements have the type specified by the declaration. Set values can be built either by explicitly enumerating the set members (e.g. {v1, v2,..., vn}), or using the set operators for union, intersection and difference. Set membership can be tested using the **IN** function. Two further operations are provided for set variables. **INSERT** elem **INTO** set inserts an element in a set, and **REMOVE** elem **FROM** set deletes an element from a set variable.

A data type declaration binds types to identifiers. In the following we will use the phrase *named data type* for data types which are bound to an identifier.

```
data_type_declaration ::=
  DATATYPE Identifier"="datatype {"," Identifier "=" datatype}";"
```

Named data types can be used inside a data-type declaration. Recursive type declarations (i.e. where the identifier can be used within datatype) are not allowed.

2.3 Object Types

Object types play a central role in our object-oriented data model, as they define the structure and behavior of the objects stored in the database. An object-type declaration consists of a *public* and a *private part*, thereby separating the interface from the implementation. The interface declaration of an object type consists of a set of *structural property definitions* and a set of *behavioral method definitions*. The implementation definition provides implementations for all methods of the interface definition and may introduce additional structural and behavioral definitions. The values of the structural properties constitute the state of an object. The public methods are the means by which objects can communicate with each other. An object type is declared as follows:

```
object_type_declaration ::= object_complete_declaration

object_complete_declaration ::=
  OBJECTTYPE Identifier ["[" class_parameters "]"] [subtype] ";"
    INTERFACE object_interface
    IMPLEMENTATION object_implementation
  END ";"

class_parameters ::=
    Identifier ":" ObjectType_Identifier {","class_parameters }
```

In the following we explain briefly how the interface and implementation sections of an object type can be defined. The role of the class parameter clause class_parameters is explained later. *Multiple inheritance* allows to build up object-type lattices for modular object-type definitions.

```
subtype   ::= SUBTYPEOF subtypes
subtypes ::=
    ObjectType_Identifier ["[" class_parameters "]"] {"," subtypes}
```

Next we give the object interface definition:

```
object_interface ::=
    [ PROPERTIES
        property_definition {property_definition} ]
                                        /* public properties */
    [ METHODS
        method_signature {method_signature} ]
                                        /* public methods */

property_definition ::= Identifier ":" datatype ";"

method_signature ::=
    Identifier "(" [formal_parameter_list] ")"
    [ ":" datatype][ READONLY ] ";"
```

```
formal_parameter_list ::=
    Identifier ":" datatype ["," formal_parameter_list]
```

In the interface only the signature of the methods is specified. Methods marked as read only are assumed to be side-effect free, so any update of the object (or some other parts of the database) is prohibited in these methods[2]. Updating the object (i.e. changing its internal state by changing the value of an object's property) is performed by non-readonly methods (which may also delegate updates to other objects). We give now a simple example of an interface definition of an object type.

Schema 1. Hypertext nodes interface.

DATATYPE Coordinates = [x: INT, y: INT];

OBJECTTYPE Nodeinfo_type
  INTERFACE
    PROPERTIES
      label: STRING;
      content: STRING
      location: Coordinates;
    METHODS
      newCoordinates(x: INT, y: INT);
  IMPLEMENTATION   /* not shown here */
END;

Next we give the object implementation definition:

```
object_implementation ::=
    [ datatype_declaration {datatype_declaration} ]
                                        /* local data types */
    [ PROPERTIES
        property_definition {property_definition} ]
                                        /* private properties */
    METHODS
        method_definition {method_definition}
                                /* public and private methods */
        [ no_method_clause ]
        [ commuting_definition ]

method_definition ::=
    [ SUBTRANSACTION ] method_signature
    method_body
```

---

[2] This information is used by the compiler and the transaction management for optimization purposes.

```
[ undo_definition ] ";"

method_body ::=
  "{" [variable_declarations] statement_list "}"

no_method_clause ::=
  NOMETHOD  method_body
```

The private part of an object-type declaration consists of the declaration of an object's private properties and the implementation of an object's methods. The optional data-type declarations introduce auxiliary types which are visible only in the implementation part. The implementation part may contain additional methods (which are not defined in the public part). These are private methods which can only be called by other methods of the same object type. Furthermore, the implementation part can specify a **NOMETHOD** clause which allows to specify a dynamic inheritance behavior, details of which will be explained in Sect. 2.4 (subsection on determining the structure and behavior of objects) and Sect. 3.

Method implementations consist of the method heading (specifying the name of the method and its signature), and the method body. The body of a method is an optional list of variable declarations followed by a list of statements. Inside a method body the object's properties are accessed by their name only. The keyword **SELF** is used to denote the actual object. Methods can be specified as subtransactions. In this case an undo definition and a commuting definition have to be specified. For more details on transactions in VML see Sect. 2.6.

Schema 2: Hypertext nodes implementation.

```
OBJECTTYPE Nodeinfo_type
  INTERFACE  /* as defined in Schema 1 */
  IMPLEMENTATION
    METHODS
      newCoordinates(x: INT, y: INT);
      {location.x:=x; location.y:=y};
END;
```

2.4 Objects, Classes, and Metaclasses

Objects represent material or immaterial real world entities, or abstract concepts such as data-model primitives, which are stored persistently in the database. Objects which are similar in their structure and behavior are organized into *classes*. Every object is instance of exactly one class. The only way to operate on an object is by sending it a message which identifies a method defined for the object and arguments for that method.

Objects in VML obey the principle of *object identity*. Object identity is realized by *object identifiers* which are attached to objects. Each object has its own distinct object identifier, which is different from that of any other object and which does not change throughout its lifetime. Object identity is the basis for sharing and updating objects.

A *class* describes the structure and the behavior of a collection of similar objects, called the *extension of a class*. The extension of a class is defined explicitly by creating instances of the class. The definitions needed to define the structure and behavior of instances of a class are specified with object types associated with the class. Due to the distinction of object types and classes, different classes can share the same object type. Details on the relationship between classes and object types are given later in this section and in Sect. 2.5.

Instances of classes are stored persistently in the database and are shared by any application which is allowed to access the database schema and operate on the classes. VML distinguishes between *application classes* and *metaclasses*:

- *Application classes* are defined by an application developer to organize and classify the objects dealt with by the application. They correspond to application specific concepts like DOCUMENT, SECTION, NEWSPAPER, AUTHOR, PERSON, NODE and LINK.
- *Metaclasses* are defined by system administrators together with application developers in order to organize application classes and to tailor the database model to the specific needs of an application, e.g., to meet the requirements of the modeling of complex structured documents, multimedia objects, database integration, or hypertext applications. Metaclasses are used to describe the common structure and behavior of application classes *and* their instances. Every application class has associated exactly one metaclass. A metaclass may have associated many classes.

Classes (application classes and metaclasses) are treated as *first class objects*, i.e., a class C is an instance of its associated class MC (which is called the metaclass of the class C) like an object c is an instance of exactly one class, e.g., the class C. Such a class hierarchy can be of any depth. The root of the class hierarchy is the system predefined metaclass VMLCLASS (see Sect. 2.4, subsection on VML Class System, for a detailed description of this class). VML provides an initial class hierarchy containing a few predefined metaclasses by default. For a detailed description of this initial metaclass system see Sect. 2.4.

Treating classes as first class objects allows the user to operate on classes in the same way as he operates on individual instances of application classes. That is, classes can be retrieved and manipulated in the same manner as individual objects. For example, one can send a method display() to an individual instance representing a hypertext node or one can send it to the class NODE which organizes these individual objects. Depending on the concrete method implementation of display(), in the first case, the properties and property values of the node could be displayed on the screen. In the second case, the characteristic values of the collection of individual nodes like the class definition of the class NODE, the cardinality of the set of individual objects, or any access statistics could be retrieved.

Application Classes. To create an application class one has to specify at least the *name* of the class with the **CLASS** clause, and the *properties* and *methods* defined for the instances of the class with the **INSTTYPE** clause. The syntax for the definition of an application class is as follows:

```
application_class_definition ::=
  CLASS  Class_Identifier [ METACLASS  Class_Identifier]
      [ OWNTYPE object_type]
      INSTTYPE object_type
      [ INIT method_calls]
  END

object_type ::=
  ObjectType_Identifier [ "[" type_to_class_map "]" ] |
                                    /* named object type */
  OBJECTTYPE [ subtypelist ";" ] /* anonymous object type */
      INTERFACE object_interface
      IMPLEMENTATION object_implementation
  END

type_to_class_map ::=
  Class_Identifier { "," type_to_class_map }

subtypelist ::=
  SUBTYPEOF  ObjectType_Identifier
      [ "[" type_to_class_map "]" ]
      {"," ObjectType_Identifier [ "[" type_to_class_map "]" ] }
```

Now we want to discuss in detail the four constituents of an application-class definition, the *metaclass*, the *own type* , the *instance type* and the *initialization*.

An application class is an object, and hence, it must be defined as an instance of a *metaclass*. This is specified by the clause of the form **METACLASS** *Class_*Identifier. The object representing the application class identified by the Identifier is created as an instance of the metaclass identified by *Class_*Identifier. The metaclass can be chosen from a set of classes which contains predefined metaclasses like KERNEL-APPLICATION-CLASS for standard applications or user defined metaclasses provided by a metaclass library. If no metaclass is specified, KERNEL-APPLICATION-CLASS is taken as the default metaclass (see Sect. 2.4, subsection on VML Class System).

An application class may have associated an object type as its *own type*, which defines application specific properties and methods for the object representing the application class. For example, an application class may require a specific object-creation method which initializes the individual new instances of the application class, or it may require a sort method which sorts the individual objects with respect to a specific property. The own type of an application class is specified by the optional clause of the form **OWNTYPE** object_type.

With every application class an object type is associated as its *instance type*, which defines the properties and methods for the individual objects collected by the class. The instance type of an application class is specified by the clause of the form **INSTTYPE** object_type.

Both, own types and instance types, can be specified either by an in-place anonymous object-type definition or by identifying the object type by name and optionally specifying the type-to- class mapping which resolves parametrized object types (see Sect. 2.5).

The application specific initialization of the object representing the application class can optionally be specified with the *init clause* **INIT** method_calls. It consists of the specification of a sequence of method calls which will be executed after the application class has been created as an instance of the associated metaclass during the database creation process.

As an illustration we give a schema for a simple hypertext model (Schema 3). Figure 1 visualizes the database according to the schema and introduces the graphical notation we use in this paper.

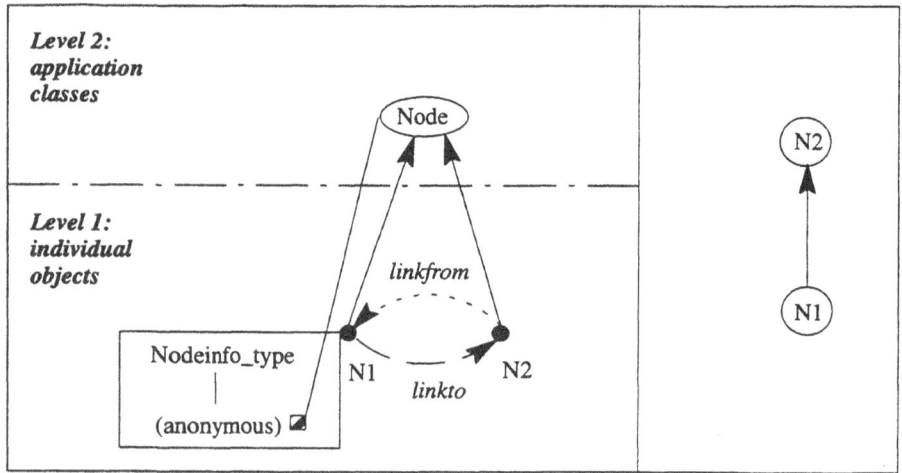

Fig. 1. A simple hypertext database according to Schema 3.

Legend: Left side: Classes are drawn as ellipses, individual objects are drawn as black circles. An unlabeled arrow from one level to another level always specifies an *instance-of* relationship (e.g., *N1* is an instance of *Node*). Object types associated with a class (directly or indirectly via type inheritance) are grouped together by a rectangle. Such a rectangle is attached to an object for which the types define properties/interfaces. A line drawn from a small rectangle (like ▰ at Level 1) to a class (like *Node* at Level 2) specifies the assignment of object types to classes. The pattern ▰ specifies that an (anonymous) object type is assigned as *instance type* to class *Node*. Right side: A hypertext graph that is represented on the left side in the database.

Schema 3.   A simple hypertext model.

```
CLASS Node
  INSTTYPE  OBJECTTYPE  SUBTYPEOF Nodeinfo_type
  INTERFACE
    METHODS        createlink(to : Node);
              /* this method must also update the to-Node */
  IMPLEMENTATION
```

```
    PROPERTIES   linkto: {Node};
                 linkfrom: {Node};
    METHODS      createlink(to : Node);
                     { INSERT to INTO linkto;
                       to->insertfrom(SELF);}
                 insertfrom(from: Node);
                     { INSERT from INTO linkfrom; }
  END;
END;
```

Metaclasses. Metaclasses are used to describe the common structure and behavior of classes and their instances which may not be known at the time a metaclass is defined. This means that the types and the classes of the objects representing the application classes and their instances are not known at the time the properties and methods provided by a metaclass are specified. The designer of a metaclass only knows that the properties and methods provided by the metaclass operate on objects. To overcome this problem, VML provides the primitive data type *object identifier* OID which can be used to refer to an object whose class is not known.

The concept of metaclasses is homogeneously integrated with the other concepts of VML. Metaclasses and application classes are treated uniformly as classes. Hence, the definition of metaclasses follows the same rules as given for application classes. In addition, it is possible to specify the common structure and behavior for the instances of the instances of a metaclass by associating an object type as instance-instance type to the metaclass.

```
meta_class_definition ::=
   CLASS Identifier METACLASS Class_Identifier
       [ OWNTYPE object_type]
       INSTTYPE object_type
       INSTINSTTYPE object_type
       [ INIT method_calls]
   END
```

Additionally to the clauses of an application-class definition, with every metaclass an object type is associated as its *instance-instance type*. This object type defines the common properties and methods for the individual objects collected by the instances of the metaclass, which themselves are classes. The instance-instance type of a metaclass is specified by the clause of the form **INSTINSTTYPE** object_type. Examples for metaclasses will be given in Sect. 3.

Determining the Structure and Behavior of Objects. As previously mentioned, classes determine the structure and behavior of their instances. More precisely, an application class determines

(i) the *application-specific* structure and behavior of its instances which represent the "real world" objects dealt with in an application program, e.g., the content and position of a hypertext node, and

(ii) the *application-specific* structure and behavior of the application class itself, e.g., a specific object creation and initialization method for nodes.

The specification of the structure and the behavior is given with object types which are associated to an application class. In case of (i), an appropriately defined object type is associated with the application class as its *instance type* (as it affects the *instances* of the class). In case of (ii), an appropriately defined object type is associated with the application class as its *own type* (as it affects the *own* structure and behavior of the class as an object).

In this respect, metaclasses are more powerful than application classes. They determine not only the structure and behavior of their instances, but also the structure and behavior of the instances of its instances. That is, a metaclass determines

(i) the structure and the behavior of the metaclass itself, e.g., a specific object creation and initialization method for classes, and

(ii) the *common* structure and behavior of its instances which are classes, i.e., application classes or metaclasses, e.g., the general object creation and initialization method for instances of an application class, which does not consider any application-specific requirements,

(iii) the *common* structure and behavior of the instances of its instances (which are classes), e.g., the common method that returns the class of an instance.

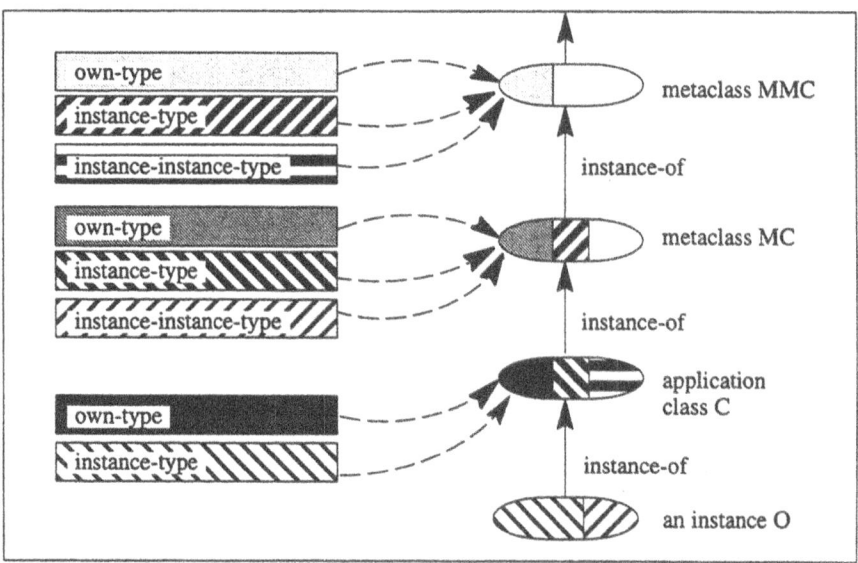

Fig. 2. The general scheme of determining an object's structure and behavior through its class and the class' metaclass.

In case of (i), an appropriately defined object type is associated with the metaclass as its *own type* (as it affects the *own* structure and behavior of the metaclass as an object).

In case of (ii), an appropriately defined object type is associated with the metaclass as its *instance type* (as it affects the *instances* of the metaclass). In case of (iii), an appropriately defined object type is associated with the metaclass as its *instance-instance type* (as it affects the *instances of the instances* of the metaclass).

Figure 2 shows this scheme: The *own type* of the metaclass *MC* affects the structure and behavior of the metaclass itself. The *instance type* of the metaclass *MC* affects the structure and behavior of the instances of the metaclass *MC*, i.e., the class *C*. The *instance-instance type* of the metaclass *MC* affects the structure and behavior of the instances of the class *C*. The *own type* of the class *C* affects the structure and behavior of the application class itself. The *instance type* of the class *C* affects the structure and behavior of the instances of the class *C*.

The *interface* defined for an object is the set of methods which are defined for the object, i.e., which can be executed directly for the object. The interface depends on the definitions given with the object types associated with the object's class and with the class' metaclass. In general, the interface defined for any object consists of

- the methods specified with the *own type* of the object, if this object represents a class, and
- the methods specified with the *instance type* of the object's class, and
- the methods specified with the *instance-instance type* of the metaclass of the object's class.

For any message which specifies a method contained in the interface defined for the receiving object it is guaranteed that the method is executed for this object. A message is sent to an object by executing a statement of the form

receiver_object→m(arglist).

In case the method is not contained in the interface defined for the object, the message handling system of VML tries to delegate the message to another object by executing the method implementation given in the **NOMETHOD** clause. Within the body of the **NOMETHOD** clause two predefined identifiers, currentMethod and arguments are available. The identifier currentMethod is bound to the method name m which has been sent to receiver_object. The identifier arguments is bound to the argument list of the message. If the **NOMETHOD** clause is not defined a run-time error is signalled. The implementation of the body of the **NOMETHOD** clause has to be specified by the user. For example different inheritance strategies can be implemented. Examples of method implementations using the **NOMETHOD** clause are given in Sect. 3.

VML Class System. The class system in VML (see Fig. 3) is logically partitioned into a set of system-internal classes and a set of system-external classes. The latter ones are organized in four levels:

1. the individual object level (level 1),
2. the application class level (level 2),
3. the metaclass level (level 3), and
4. the root level (level 4).

Presumably, an application user will see and use the bottom two levels. He will query, update, create, and remove individual objects of application classes. It is the task of an application developer, working on levels 2 and 3, to define new application classes as instances of some predefined metaclasses. At the metaclass level the system administrator may define new metaclasses and, thus, enhance the modeling capabilities of the predefined kernel model.

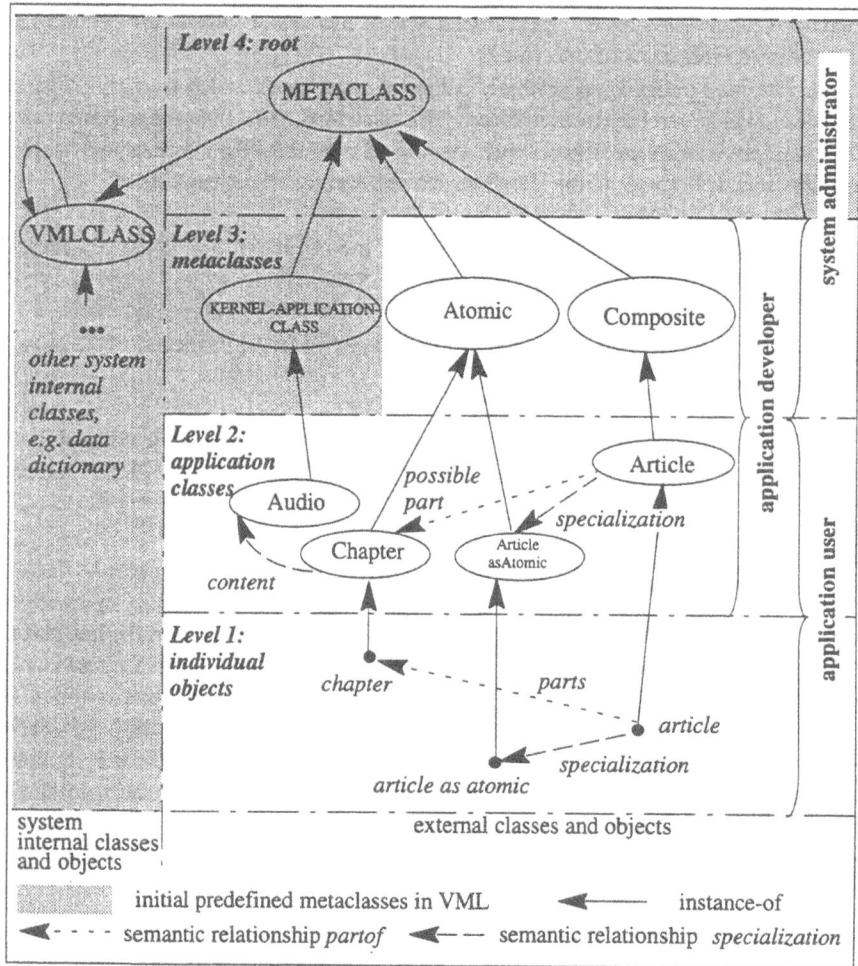

Fig. 3. A sample VML class system including the initial class system of VML.

The initial metaclass system of VML consists of the system-internal class VMLCLASS, METACLASS at the root of the metaclass system, KERNEL-APPLICATION-CLASS at the metaclass level and a few other system-internal metaclasses, which cannot be changed or modified. They are built-in classes[3] and provide for the basic and system inherent capabilities. Changing or extending the definitions for these classes will change the standard modeling capabilities of VML.

In Fig. 3 the initial metaclass system is identified by the shadowed boxes. The system-internal classes provide the basic structures and behavior in order to deal with classes, objects, and the data dictionary of a database. The class VMLCLASS provides capabilities like object creation, object deletion, and object storage. Schema 4 shows the definition of VMLCLASS.

Schema 4. The initial VMLCLASS schema.

```
CLASS VMLCLASS METACLASS  VMLCLASS
  INSTTYPE VML-Class_InstType
  INSTINSTTYPE VML-Class_InstInstType
END;

OBJECTTYPE VML-Object_Type
  INTERFACE
  METHODS        class()   : OID;
END;

OBJECTTYPE  VML-Class_InstType SUBTYPEOF  VML-Object_Type
  INTERFACE
  METHODS
    new() : OID;           /* creates and returns a new object */
    allInstances () : {OID};/* returns the set of instances */
    isInstance (obj: OID) : BOOL;      /* is it an instance? */
    delete (obj: OID);              /* removes an instance  */
END;

OBJECTTYPE VML-Class_InstInstType SUBTYPEOF VML-Object_Type
END;
```

The object type VML-Object_Type defines properties and methods which are in common for all objects. For instance, since every object is defined to be an instance of a class, every object O must be able to respond to the message O->class() which returns the identifier of the object's class, i.e., the method class() must be defined for every object. The object type VML-Class_InstType implements, e.g., a built-in method new() which allows to create a new object. Other methods defined by VML-Class_InstType are typical methods for the management of a set of object identifiers, which stands for the actual set of instances of a class. These methods allow to add a new object identifier to the set of actual instances (needed for the creation of a

---

[3] Following the approach of self-reflective architectures all the VML predefined classes are implemented like other user-defined classes. The boot-strapping problem associated with such an approach is reflected by the fact that VMLCLASS is an instance of itself.

new object), to remove an object identifier from the set of actual instances (needed for
the deletion of an object), to test whether a given object identifier identifies an instance
of the class. The object type VML-Class_InstInstType is defined as a subtype of
VML-Object_Type but implements no further public methods. However, it provides for
a homogeneous object-type hierarchy and for further extensions.

The class METACLASS serves as the container for any metaclass introduced and
defined by a system administrator. The class KERNEL-APPLICATION-CLASS is the
default metaclass for user-defined application classes. The instance types and instance-
instance types corresponding to these two initial classes are derived from the instance
type and instance-instance types of VMLCLASS according to Fig. 4. This figure illustrates
the initial object type hierarchy. All object types in the system are organized by that type
hierarchy. The root of this subtype hierarchy is the type Θ. This type does not define
any properties and methods. Every object type is either a direct subtype of Θ (which is
the default when no explicit supertype is specified) or it is a subtype of another object
type, i.e., it is an indirect subtype of Θ.

Every database schema contains this initial metaclass system. All object types,
application classes and metaclasses are built up using this initial metaclass system.

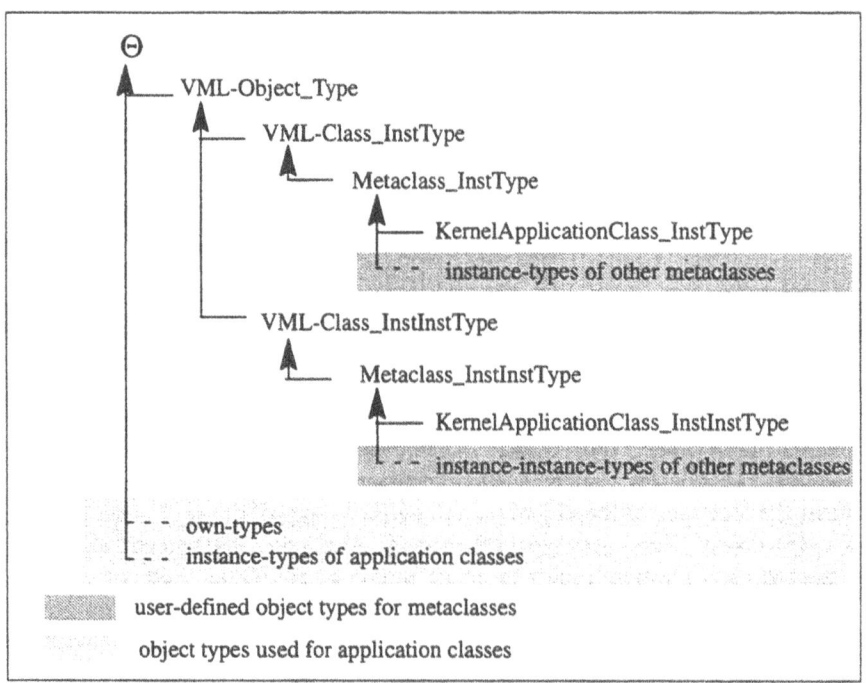

Fig. 4. The initial subtype hierarchy.

2.5 Parameterizing Object Types with Classes

In VML a class definition has two roles: it serves as the definition of a container object to model the extension of a class (the extensional aspect) and it provides object-type definitions (intensional aspect) for describing the interface and structural properties of the instances of the class. Note, that the extensional aspect is an orthogonal concept, which does not exist for data values.

Given this framework it is quite obvious to distinguish between type definitions and class definitions. An object-type definition comprises the full type description. A class definition is related to a class domain (i.e., the set of all possible objects defined by a class), refers to object types (e.g., own type, instance type, and instance-instance type), and is related to a class object.

By explicitly distinguishing between class definitions and object-type definitions VML facilitates the modeling of real world situations. Classes are used to organize a set of objects corresponding to real world entities and relationships between them. That is, classes are used to form an ontology of the application domain. Object types define the structure of objects and the operations defined on these structures. They are associated with classes in order to determine the structure and behavior of the class' instances.

VML does not allow the usage of class identifiers (see *Class_Identifier* in Sect. 2.2) as data types in property, parameter, and variable definitions within object-type definitions[4] : This is because object types should be considered without referring to concrete class definitions at all, e.g., for reuse in different schemas or different class definitions in a single schema. Since object types can be associated to various class definitions the class domains (= classes) appearing in the property, parameter, and variable definitions in object types may vary from class to class. If class domains (which depend on other class definitions) will be used in object-type definitions the extensional aspects would not clearly be separated from the intensional aspects.

As VML does not abandon the definition of properties over class domains, it provides *class domain parameters* for object-type definitions. These parameters are substituted by concrete class domains, when the object-type definition is used in a class definition. We call this substitution the *type-to-class-(domain)-mapping* according to [Kla90].

Introducing these class domain parameters without any knowledge about them is not very useful. Therefore we impose object-type constraints on these parameters, which constrain the class domains to be substituted. Let us make an example which illustrates the type-to-class mapping mechanism:

Schema 5. Parametrized hypertext-node object type.

```
OBJECTTYPE Node_type[aNodeClass: Node_type]
   INTERFACE
      METHODS
         createlink(to : aNodeClass);
         insertfrom(from: aNodeClass);
   IMPLEMENTATION
```

---

[4] However, such a restriction does not apply to anonymous object-type definitions within class definitions (see Sect. 2.4, subsection on Application Classes).

```
        PROPERTIES
          linkto: {aNodeClass};
          linkfrom: {aNodeClass};
        METHODS
          createlink(to : aNodeClass);
            { INSERT to INTO linkto;
            to->insertfrom( SELF);}
          insertfrom(from: aNodeClass);
            { INSERT from INTO linkfrom;}
    END;
```

At this point, we defined an object type which is parametrized with a class-domain parameter (or shortly class parameter) aNodeClass. This class parameter is used as a data type to define the properties fromlink and tolink and it is used in the definitions of the methods operating on these properties. So far, no concrete class (domain) is specified by this class parameter and, hence, no concrete domain is defined for the properties fromlink and tolink. The constraint aNodeClass : Node_Type imposed on the class parameter requires that the concrete classes which can be chosen to substitute the parameter aNodeClass must have Node_Type associated directly as instance-type, or Node_Type has to be a supertype of the instance-type.

The parametrized object type can be used for class definitions as follows:

```
CLASS NODE
  INSTTYPE Node_Type [ NODE ]
END;
```

Class NODE now defines objects which can refer (through their properties tolink and fromlink) to instances of class NODE. Class NODE is a valid class for substituting the class parameter aNodeClass of the object type Node_Type as Node_Type is the instance type of class NODE. One can partition the universe of nodes into sets of white and black nodes. In that case one could define

```
CLASS WHITEN
  INSTTYPE Node_Type [ BLACKN]
END;
```

```
CLASS BLACKN
  INSTTYPE Node_Type [ WHITEN ]
END;
```

Class WHITEN defines now objects which can refer (via their properties fromlink and tolink) to instances of class BLACKN and vice versa. Thus one can enforce the constraint that any path in this hypertext network will visit alternating white and black nodes. WHITEN and BLACKN are both valid classes for the class-parameter substitution for type Node_Type because both classes have associated as instance type Node_Type. See Fig. 5 for a visualization of the database. It shows the actual property definitions according to the actual type-to-class-(domain)-mappings.

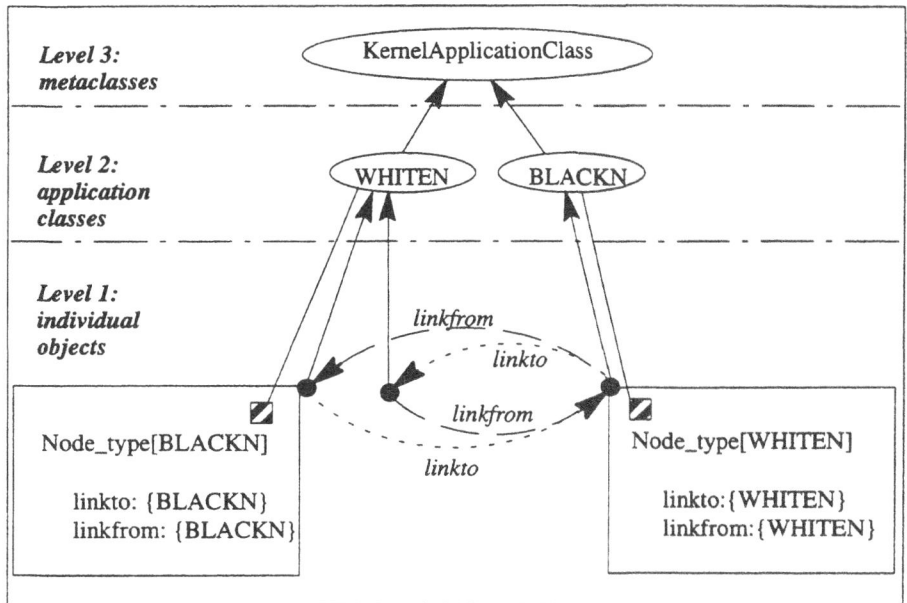

Fig. 5. Parameterization of object types allows for semantic constraints on classes.

2.6 Transactions

In VODAK, we focus on two specific problems of transaction management.

1. Operations to read and edit (hyper)documents are typically complex, interactive and of long duration. A high degree of concurrency is required to reduce the number and length of times a transaction is blocked.
2. A publication environment has to handle existing database systems for using and modifying remote information and documents. Transaction managers of existing systems, i.e. concurrency control and recovery, have to be integrated in a transparent way utilizing the functionality of existing managers.

Our transaction model is based on *open nested transactions*. For a detailed description see [MRKN92, MRW+93, RGN90, WHBM90]. Compared to conventional flat transactions, nested transactions allow more concurrency and are more flexible for recovery. A nested transaction is a tree-like structure, dynamically built up by the call of subtransactions until a bottom implementation level is encountered.

There are two types of nested transactions. Closed nested transactions provide a high degree of concurrency by allowing the concurrent execution of subtransactions. Furthermore, they allow to abort subtransactions independently of the calling transaction. Open nested transactions utilize the semantics of operations, i.e. a commutativity relation is used to define conflicts between operations. By considering the nesting structure, conflicts of subtransactions can be ignored if the calling (sub-) transactions commute and the called subtransactions are executed in a consistent way (i.e. serializably). For example, two increment operations on a counter commute whereas the corresponding update operations on a page conflict. After the update subtransactions are committed, their conflict can be ignored and the calling transactions can be executed concurrently.

We extended the open nested model from a fixed calling hierarchy of operations in a layered system (multi-level transactions) to an arbitrary calling hierarchy of operations in an object-oriented system [RGN90]. Commutativity of operations is applied to system-defined VODAK methods, and to methods of user-defined object types. For the second type of operations, we developed a framework to specify commutativity and inverse operations in VML. The commutativity of methods and the inverse methods are specified in the implementation part of object-type definitions (see the clauses commuting_definition and undo_definition in Sect. 2.3). Their specification is not discussed in this paper.

We also developed an integration model for existing transaction managers. The open nested transaction model has been extended to support distributed transaction execution in a heterogeneous environment. The model provides ACID properties for global transactions if all existing transaction managers also provide these properties [MRKN92]. No assumptions about protocols, e.g. two-phase locking, are made. Subtransactions of existing systems constitute the leaves of our transaction tree. Again, we utilize the semantics of these transactions in order to achieve a high degree of concurrency. Recovery is based on inverse operations, compensating the changes of transactions which have to be aborted. Inverse operations are also used to ensure atomic commitment. Unilateral aborts as well as system crashes can be handled [MKN92, MR91].

2.7 Tailoring the Data Model

One major benefit claimed for OODBMSs is extensibility. Although object-oriented data models allow users to define their own classes, they come with a fixed set of data-model primitives. We consider this a major problem as different application domains have different requirements on a data model. For example, database integration requires the possibility to overcome different representations of the same data. Hypertext applications need flexible concepts for organizing inter- and intra-document references. Multimedia applications need among other features support in handling different sources of data. If a data model is designed to cover many application domains, there are two dangers: On the one hand, the data model may be kept too general and does not fully meet the requirements of specific applications. On the other hand, the data model may be overloaded with too many specialized concepts and is hard to understand. Alternatively, different data models may be developed for specific application domains and thus take into account their needs. This solution, however, leads to disintegrated and isolated applications, each using a different data model.

Metaclasses in VODAK provide a solution to that problem. They can be used to introduce new data-model primitives needed in specific application domains. The VODAK kernel data model contains primitive data types and classes commonly used in many different application domains. To handle specific application domains, such as database integration, multimedia applications, or hypertext applications, the kernel model is extended with additional modeling capabilities through metaclasses. In the following chapter we show how VML can be extended with specific modeling constructs to support the modeling of hypertext structures, hierarchies, object categories, and document versioning. In [Kla92] it is shown how VODAK can be tailored such that a video laser disc providing all the database operations needed to view videos on a screen is transparently integrated into the system. [AK93, KNS90b] show, how multimedia data can be modelled in VODAK. [KNS90a, KFA93] show, how VODAK can be tailored such that an external relational database system can be accessed and integrated into VODAK. In [KN90] we present a database model for argumentative networks (hypertext network according to the semantics of Toulmin schemas) for an authoring environment.

3 Modeling of Hypermedia Documents

In this section we want to illustrate how the open object-oriented data model VML can be used to support the needs of hypermedia applications. We consider the following three aspects of hypermedia document modeling: Hypertext structures, hierarchical document structures and versioning of documents. In concrete applications [Gol91, SS90a, SHH⁺92] these three concepts are needed simultaneously and have therefore to be integrated. In the following we first will discuss alternative VML models for each of these concepts separately, then give a generic VML metaclass schema supporting all of the three concepts and thus extend the VML data model for hypermedia applications. Other aspects like modeling of the multimedia content and presentation of hypermedia documents will be omitted here.

In the course of the subsequent discussion we will emphasize fundamental needs of complex software systems, namely correctness, extensibility, reusability and compatibility and discuss how these aspects are affected by design decisions in VML. Thus we will illustrate several issues of schema design which are particularly relevant when using the VML data model.

We will discuss these issues by developing a series of VML schemas, each of which focusses on a different aspect in the modeling process. An overview of the interdependencies of these schemas can be found in the Appendix.

3.1 Hyperdocument Structures

In the simplest case a hypertext structure can be conceived as a network of nodes which contain some piece of information, about which we do not care at the moment, and which are interconnected by links (Fig. 6). From each node we can navigate through a set of outgoing links to other nodes. This model was captured in the VML class definitions given in Schema 3.

When planning a generic support for modeling of hypermedia documents the approach described in these examples may not be appropriate, as in many cases links should be made available explicitly. Among these reasons are: links may have their own properties and methods, therefore a receiver object for them is needed; links may be referenced by other links; it may be necessary to distinguish different types of links, thus they should be classified by using classes. More abstractly all these reasons are a consequence of the fact that links can carry a substantial amount of application-specific semantics. Thus we consider from now on links as objects and arrive at the following VML definitions (Schema 6 and Fig. 6).

Schema 6. A hypertext model with links as objects.

```
CLASS Node
  INSTTYPE  OBJECTTYPE
    INTERFACE  PROPERTIES
      content: anything;              /* not further specified */
      tolink: {Link};
      fromlink: {Link};
  END;
  OWNTYPE  OBJECTTYPE
    INTERFACE  METHODS
      createnode(): Node;
  END;
END;

CLASS Link
  INSTTYPE  OBJECTTYPE
    INTERFACE  PROPERTIES
      purpose: anything;              /*e.g. meaning of link */
      from: Node;
      to: Node;
  END;
  OWNTYPE  OBJECTTYPE
    INTERFACE  METHODS
      createlink(from: Node, to: Node): Link;
                            /* has to change nodes also */
  END;
END;
```

For object creation the receiver object of the creation method is the class of which a new instance is created. Therefore they are part of the *own type* of the class.

Note that due to space limitations throughout the section we will consider whenever we present VML definitions with a few exceptions only the interfaces of object types and there only methods for object creation. The implementation is described by comments where needed and other methods, e.g. for navigation, retrieval and deletion, have to be added.

In some applications links can behave almost like nodes, as they may have content and they may be referred to by other links (Fig. 7). This amounts to the following two problems: (1) we have to refer to links and nodes by the same property, thus we have to provide a common domain for nodes and links; (2) the interfaces of links and nodes are very similar; thus we want to reuse as much of the type definitions as possible. We discuss two possibilities of how to tackle this in VML.

Possibility 1. As links and nodes are already very similar in structure we just unify their types and use only one generic type. This results in the following class definitions.

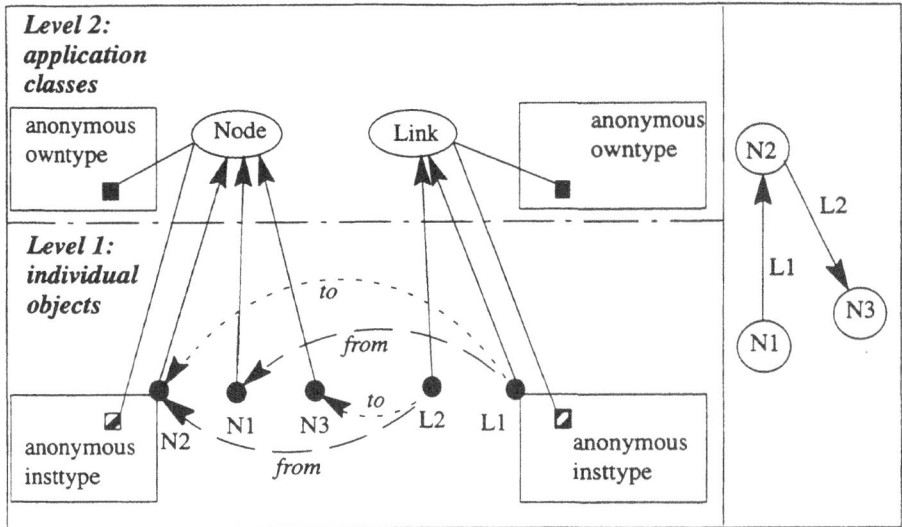

Fig. 6. A hypertext database with links as objects according to Schema 6.

Legend (in addition to the legend given in Figure 1): Rectangles surrounding own-type definitions are attached to classes for which the types define properties/interfaces. The pattern ▦
specifies that object types are assigned as *own types* to classes.

Schema 7. A hypertext model unifying nodes and links.

```
CLASS NLobject
  INSTTYPE  OBJECTTYPE
    INTERFACE
      PROPERTIES
        content:  anything;
        from: NLobject;
        to: NLobject;
        fromlink: {NLobject};
        tolink: {NLobject};
  END;
  OWNTYPE  OBJECTTYPE
    INTERFACE
      METHODS
        createnode(): NLobject;
        createlink(from: NLobject, to: NLobject): NLobject;
  END;
END;
```

Objects, which are considered as nodes will have null values in the properties from
and to. All other properties are used equally by links and nodes. Note that the knowledge
about what is a link and what is a node has moved into the implementation. This is also

reflected by the fact that two different methods for creation of nodes and links are available.

Possibility 2. The idea of the next approach can be described as follows. We introduce two classes, namely a class whose instances represent links as well as nodes with their common features and a special class which represents the particular features of links. Thus we factor out the common part of the structure of links and node and exploit the assumption that links have all the properties of nodes.

Schema 8. A hypertext model using specialization.

```
CLASS Node
  INSTTYPE  OBJECTTYPE
    INTERFACE
      PROPERTIES
        content: anything;
        fromlink: {Link};
        tolink: {Link};
        specialization: Link; /* is NIL for Nodes */
  END;
  OWNTYPE  OBJECTTYPE
    INTERFACE
      METHODS
        createnode(): Node;
        /* creates Nodes which are not specialized to links */
  END;
END;


CLASS Link
  INSTTYPE  OBJECTTYPE
    INTERFACE
      PROPERTIES
        from: Node;
        to: Node;
        generalization: Node; /* never is NIL */
      METHODS
        asnode(): Node; /* returns the generalization node */
    IMPLEMENTATION
      NOMETHOD generalization->currentmethod(args);
  END;
  OWNTYPE  OBJECTTYPE
    INTERFACE
      METHODS
        createlink(from: Node, to: Node): Link;
      /* this method has also to create a generalization node */
  END;
END;
```

An illustration of the instance and the class level of the schema is given in Fig. 7. Now several comments are in place. The method `asnode()` is needed to switch for a link to its node context, for example a link connecting two links is created by the method call `Link->createlink(asnode(link1),asnode(link2))`. The **NOMETHOD** clause in the class `Link` is executed whenever a method is not found in the `Link` interface. In this case the method call is delegated to the node object which is related to the link object via the property `generalization`. Thus an instance of the class `Link` can behave in the same way as an instance of the class `Node`, in other words it *dynamically inherits* the properties and methods of the class `Node`. Alternatively to the class definitions from Schema 8 we could have considered one general class which would capture the common properties of nodes and links with two specializations, namely a link and a node class. This would have been appropriate when the links had not shared all of the properties and methods of nodes. Another design alternative one could consider is to let the link type inherit from the node type via subtyping and thus using *static inheritance* instead of *dynamic inheritance*. Thus a link class will also have the object type of the node class, which solves problem (2), but there exists no generalization for nodes and links for uniform access to them, which was problem (1).

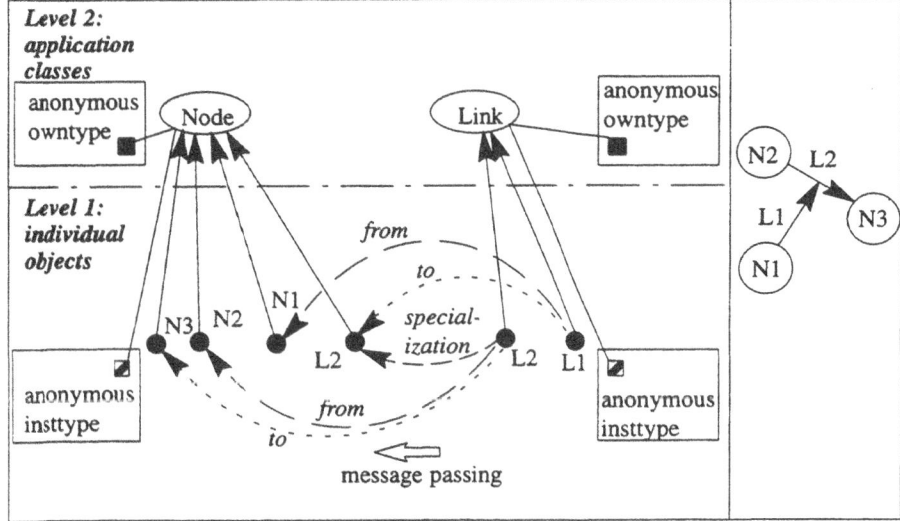

Fig. 7. A hypertext database using specialization according to Schema 8.

In the following we want to discuss the main differences between these two possibilities from the viewpoint of schema design. In the first case, we provide a *pivot model* with a generic structure, where on the one hand more application semantics is represented operationally, e.g., links and nodes have to be distinguished operationally, but on the other hand the structural part of the schema, which is stored persistently, is more flexible and may be used more easily for different hypertext models. In the second case, more of the application semantics is represented in a *declarative* way in the structural part of the schema. Thus more constraints of the data model are hard wired and the application is freed of the responsibility to maintain these constraints. It is also interesting to discuss the differences of these approaches from the viewpoint of complexity. Regarding time complexity, in the first case, more effort has to be spent in determining types of objects while in the second case more pointer-chasing operations are needed. With respect to space complexity in the first case many null values may occur while in the second case references for connecting the different parts of an object in its different contexts are needed.

For the remainder of this section we will assume that we have chosen possibility 2, as it reflects the semantics of hypertext applications in more detail in the structural part of the data model.

3.2 Categorization

The generalization/specialization principle discussed in possibility 2 of the Sect. 3.1 can be considered of course independently of the hypertext modeling issue. It is considered to be a generic *semantic relationship* and such semantic relationships are the prototypical case for using the VML metaclass concept. The typical scenario is given a general class (e.g. node, but also vehicle) and special classes (e.g. link, but also truck, car, van). The special classes are disjoint. In this case we have given a *category generalization* and *specialization* relationship. The classes which participate in this relationship can be considered as instances of particular metaclasses which provide the properties and methods needed to realize the category relationship. We first give the class definitions for the category relationship and, by exploiting the *dual model*, give the object-type declarations later. This is reasonable as we will reuse these type declarations for other purposes later.

Schema 9. Category specialization and generalization.

```
CLASS Specialization METACLASS Metaclass
  INSTTYPE Special_insttype
  INSTINSTTYPE Special_instinsttype
END;

CLASS Generalization METACLASS Metaclass
  INSTTYPE General_insttype
  INSTINSTTYPE General_instinsttype
END;
```

The metaclasses have to control not only the relationship on the class level but also that on the instance level. This is the reason why the metaclass definition also comprises type definitions for the instances of the instances of the metaclasses, the so-called **INSTINSTTYPE**. Next we give the *object types*. These involve explicit object identifiers as we do not know which particular classes will participate in the category relationship.

```
OBJECTTYPE General_instinsttype
  SUBTYPEOF Metaclass_instinsttype
  INTERFACE
    PROPERTIES
      specialization: OID; /* may be NIL */
END;

OBJECTTYPE Special_instinsttype
  SUBTYPEOF Metaclass_instinsttype
  INTERFACE
    PROPERTIES
      generalization: OID;
  IMPLEMENTATION
    NOMETHOD
      generalization->currentMethod(args);
END;

OBJECTTYPE General_insttype
  SUBTYPEOF Metaclass_insttype
  INTERFACE
    PROPERTIES
      specClasses: { OID };
END;

OBJECTTYPE Special_insttype
  SUBTYPEOF Metaclass_insttype
  INTERFACE
    PROPERTIES
      genClass: OID;
    METHODS
      initgen(g: OID);
      createspecial(g: OID): OID;
      /* g is the OID of a generalization class,
      createspecial creates general and special
      object and checks whether g is valid */
END;
```

The semantics of this particular generalization/specialization relationship is partially specified by the structural definitions and partially by the behavioral definitions. For example, the fact that the property specialization may be NIL corresponds to the fact that the categorization is non covering, i.e. not every general object has a specialization. The fact that the property generalization is single-valued implies that the categorization is non-overlapping, i.e. each object has at most one generalization. The **NOMETHOD** clause defines the inheritance behavior of this relationship: the specialized objects inherit the behavior from the general ones.

Application classes for nodes and links, which realize the same model as Schema 8 can then use these relationships as follows.

```
CLASS Node  METACLASS  Generalization
        OWNTYPE Node_owntype
        INSTTYPE Node_insttype
END;

CLASS Link  METACLASS  Specialization
        OWNTYPE Link_owntype
        INSTTYPE Link_insttype
        INIT  SELF->initgen(Node);
END;
```

The **INIT** clause is used to establish the fact that links are a specialization of nodes. The object types Node_owntype, Node_insttype, Link_owntype together with Link_insttype are defined by the application programmer and provide the application-specific properties and methods of nodes and links.

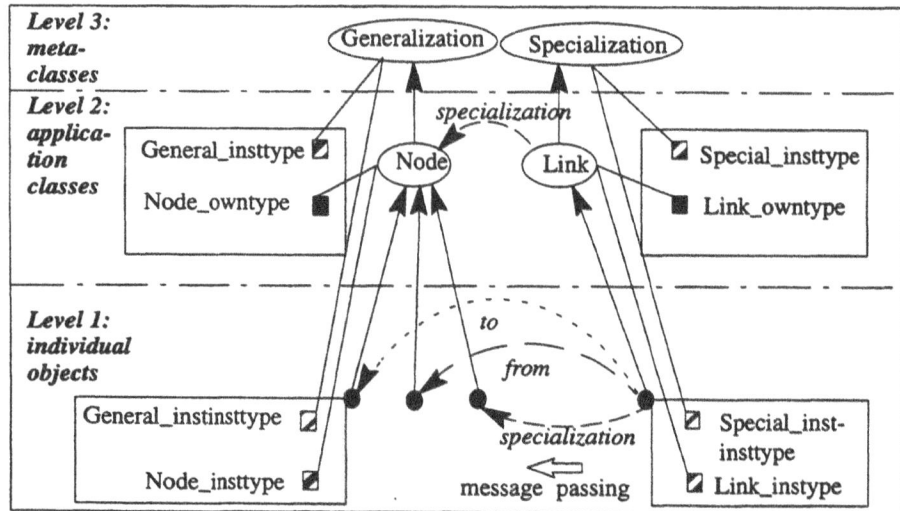

Fig. 8. A hypertext database using specialization introduced by metaclasses (Schema 9). Legend (in addition to the legend given in Figure 6): The pattern ◲ specifies that an object type is assigned as *instance-instance type* to a metaclass.

3.3 Generic Hypertext Modeling

From the viewpoint of reusability the above class definitions for hypertext structures are not satisfying. We want to provide the structure and behavior of hypertext structures in a form such that it can be reused in different applications. We discuss in the following two fundamentally different possibilities of how this is accomplished in VML. For the generic hypertext models we will consider the content of a hypertext node no longer as inherent property. It will be added in the definition of application specific hypertext classes.

A first approach is to exploit the dual model and provide only the *parametrized object types* within a library which can then be reused in different application class definitions. These object-type definitions also inherit all the properties needed to manage a category specialization relationship. Such a library can be given by the following object types (we omit the own types here).

Schema 10. A generic hypertext model using parametrized object types.

```
OBJECTTYPE Node_insttype[Link: Link_insttype]
SUBTYPEOF Generalization_instinsttype
   INTERFACE
      PROPERTIES
         fromlink: {Link};
         tolink: {Link};
END;


OBJECTTYPE Link_insttype[Node: Node_insttype]
SUBTYPEOF Specialization_instinsttype
   INTERFACE
      PROPERTIES
         from: Node;
         to: Node;
END;
```

An application class designer may now use these object types as follows.

```
CLASS MyNode
   INSTTYPE  OBJECTTYPE  SUBTYPEOF Node_insttype[MyLink]
               /* application specific definitions */
   OWNTYPE Node_owntype
END;

CLASS MyLink
   INSTTYPE  OBJECTTYPE  SUBTYPEOF Link_insttype[MyNode]
               /* application specific definitions */
   OWNTYPE Link_owntype[MyNode]
END;
```

We observe the following problem with this approach. When using the object types a constraint has to be observed in order to get a consistent class definition. The parameters used in the class definition of MyLink express the fact that links of this class connect nodes of the class MyNode. Vice versa the parameters used in the class definition of MyNode express the same fact. Thus it is the user's responsibility to substitute these parameters properly in order to use the proper domains for the parameters and thus get a consistent schema.

Relieving the user from the burden to control such constraints is one of the main motivations for the usage of *metaclasses* instead of parametrized object types. Metaclasses allow to control such constraints as they can control simultaneously the behavior of classes and their instances. We illustrate this by giving an alternative generic VML hypertext model based on metaclasses which ensure that the proper domains will be used (see Fig. 9).

Schema 11. A generic hypertext model using metaclasses.

```
CLASS Node  METACLASS Metaclass
   INSTTYPE Node_insttype /* defines behavior of node classes */
   INSTINSTTYPE Node_instinsttype /* defines behavior of nodes */
END;


CLASS Link  METACLASS Metaclass
   INSTTYPE Link_insttype[Node, Node]
                   /* defines behavior of link classes */
   INSTINSTTYPE Link_instinsttype /* defines behavior of links */
END;


OBJECTTYPE Node_insttype  SUBTYPEOF Generalization_insttype
   INTERFACE
      METHODS
         createnode(): OID;
END;


OBJECTTYPE Link_insttype[C: Theta,  G: Theta]
   SUBTYPEOF Specialization_insttype
     /* C is the metaclass of node classes for connection, */
     /* G is the metaclass of node classes for generalization*/
   INTERFACE
      PROPERTIES
         possiblelink: { [from: C, to: C] };
      METHODS
         isasnode(node: G); /* inits specialization relationship,
                               uses initgen(), checks whether
                               node in G */
         haslinks(link: {[ from: C, to: C ]} );
                          /* sets possible link classes */
```

```
        createlink(from: C, to: C): OID;
                    /* creates a corresponding node instance
                    in the appropriate generalization class
END;                G, from/to may be node or link */
```

OBJECTTYPE Node_instinsttype
  SUBTYPEOF Generalization_instinsttype
  INTERFACE
    PROPERTIES
      fromlink: { OID };
      tolink: { OID };
END;

OBJECTTYPE Link_instinsttype
  SUBTYPEOF Specialization_instinsttype
  INTERFACE
    PROPERTIES
      from: OID;
      to: OID;
END;

In the above schema the control over the relationship between node and link classes and their instances is maintained by the methods provided for example in Link_insttype. The relation between the Link metaclass and the Node metaclass is established by the parameters of Link_insttype. The domains of properties at the instance-instance level are of the data type OID, as the particular classes to which the property values will belong are not known at the time of definition of the metaclasses. The domains of properties at the instance level are specified by the class parameters C and G. C is used for specifying the kind of nodes that a particular kind of link connects. G is used for specifying the kind of nodes of which the links are specializations. This distinction will prove valuable when introducing versioning of hypertext structures in Sect. 3.6. The type restrictions on the instance types of C and G are specified as the empty object type Θ, which was introduced in Sect. 2.4, subsection on VML Class System, and which is denoted in the VML language by Theta.

Once the metaclasses are defined an application designer who creates application classes as instances of these metaclasses cannot violate the consistency constraints of hypertext structures. A sample application of the metaclasses would be

CLASS MyNode **METACLASS** Node;
  INSTTYPE MyNode_type;
        /* application specific definitions for MyNode */
END;

CLASS MyLink **METACLASS** Link;
  INSTTYPE MyLink_type;
        /* application specific definitions for MyLink */

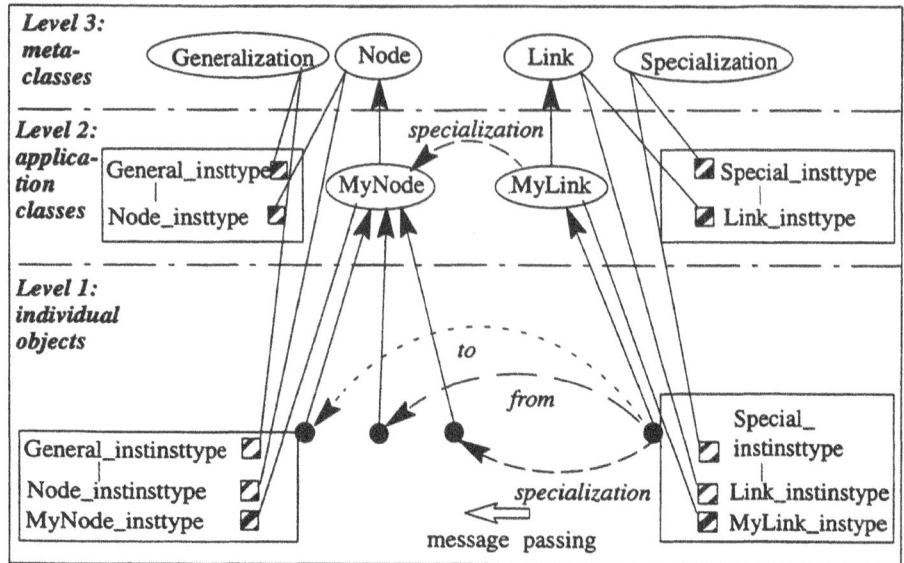

Fig. 9. Usage of the hypertext metaclasses.

```
       INIT  SELF->haslinks({ [from: MyNode, to: MyNode] });
             SELF->isasnode(MyNode);
END;
```

With the above metaclass schema we got something more for free. We can now introduce different kinds of links and nodes and specify connectivity constraints between them, i.e., constraints on the kind of nodes a class of links may connect. For example it is very natural to distinguish between a node class for nodes that cannot be links and one for those that can represent links.

```
CLASS MyNode  METACLASS Node;
  INSTTYPE MyNode_type;
          /* application specific behavior of this node class */
END;

CLASS MyLinkasNode  METACLASS Node;
  INSTTYPE MyLinkasNode_type;
              /* application specific behavior of MyLink*/
END;

CLASS MyLink  METACLASS Link;
  INSTTYPE MyLink_type;
  INIT  SELF->haslinks({ [from: MyNode, to: MyNode],
                         [from: MyNode, to: MyLinkasNode] });
      SELF->isasnode(MyLinkasNode);
END;
```

Thus we have a *categorization principle* for nodes and links working together with a mechanism to maintain connectivity constraints. But note that this categorization principle is very different from that introduced in the previous section used to model links as a specialization of nodes. The categorization is not realized by relating an instance of a generalization class with an instance of a specialization class, which represents the category, but by relating the classes that represent the categories to one metaclass. As a consequence this kind of categorization is not visible at the application level - no generalization class is available there - but only at the metaclass level.

In some cases it may be favorable to hide some of the complexity of the above metaclass schema from the user. For example it may not be necessary that the user is aware of the fact that each link object is related to a node object, but that he simply wants to talk about links and nodes. This can be done by introducing anonymous classes. To this extent we introduce new metaclasses Nodeanonymous and Linkanonymous which are derived from the schema for the metaclasses Node and Link by adding additional behavior.

Schema 12. A generic hypertext model with anonymous classes.

```
CLASS Nodeanonymous METACLASS Metaclass
  OWNTYPE Node_owntype[Nodeanonymous]
  INSTTYPE Node_insttype
  INSTINSTTYPE Node_instinsttype
END;


CLASS Linkanonymous METACLASS Metaclass
  INSTTYPE Linkanonymous_insttype[Node, Nodeanonymous]
  INSTINSTTYPE Link_instinsttype
END;


OBJECTTYPE Node_owntype[N: Theta]
  INTERFACE
    METHODS
      createnodeclass(): N;
END;

OBJECTTYPE Linkanonymous_insttype[C: Theta, G: Theta]
  SUBTYPEOF Link_insttype
  /* C is the connected metaclass, G is the generalization
     metaclass */
  INTERFACE
    METHODS
      initall(link: {[ from: C, to: C ]});
  IMPLEMENTATION
    METHODS
      initall(link: {[ from: C, to: C ]});
      { haslinks(link);
```

```
        g:=G->createnodeclass(); SELF->isasnode(g); };
        /* this method creates an anonymous node class and
           instantiates it as the generalization class of the
           link class, receiving the method */
END;
```

Then the application programmer can write the class definitions this way.

```
CLASS MyNode  METACLASS Node;
  INSTTYPE MyNode_type;
     /* application specific behavior of this node class */
END;
```

```
CLASS MyLink  METACLASS Linkanonymous;
  INSTTYPE  MyLink_type;
  INIT SELF->initall({ [from: MyNode, to: MyNode]
                               [from: MyNode, to: MyLink] });
END;
```

The method call `initall` in the **INIT** clause of the class definition of `MyLink` instantiates an anonymous node class of which the link class `MyLink` is a specialization. The implementation of the method initall is shown in the declaration of the object type `Linkanonymous_insttype`. Note that this way of hiding structture from the user leads to additional constraints on the hypertext model. In this model node classes can either be named node classes with metaclass `Node` that contain "real" nodes or anonymous node classes with metaclass `Nodeanonymous` that contain "link" nodes. Classes that contain both are no longer definable.

3.4 Aggregation Hierarchies

A concept which is even more fundamental in document structures than the concept of hypertext structures is the concept of *hierarchical aggregation*, as it is used, e.g., in [ISO86]. Each document consists of parts which in turn are composed of simpler parts and so on until one arrives at atomic units. For example, a paper consists of title and text, the text consists of sections, and the sections in turn consist of paragraphs of plain text. Of course parts of documents may also be hypertext structures, thus we will have to consider later the integration of the concepts of hypertext and hierarchical aggregation. But first we want to introduce hierarchical aggregation as an isolated concept, and restricted to a very simplified form. We do not consider the internal ordering of the document parts, nor do we consider sharing of document parts by different documents.

We can distinguish two kinds of document parts. Those which are composed of others and which we call *composite*, and those which are not and which we call *atomic*. The relationship between composites and atomics is very similar to that between links and nodes. Composites refer to atomics and they can share all the properties atomics have. The main difference is that composites can exist without referring to any parts, while for a link the source and sink node always have to exist. We do not consider here all the design possibilities for aggregation hierarchies as they are quite similar to those for hypertext structures. Therefore we just present a complete schema for modeling aggregation hierarchies, which is based on the analogous design decisions that we took for hypertext structures. An application of this metaclass schema with one atomic and two composite document types is illustrated in Fig. 10.

Schema 13: A generic aggregation hierarchy model using metaclasses.

```
CLASS Atomic METACLASS Metaclass
  INSTTYPE Atomic_insttype
  INSTINSTTYPE Atomic_instinsttype
END;


CLASS Composite METACLASS Metaclass
  INSTTYPE Composite_insttype[Atomic, Atomic]
  INSTINSTTYPE Composite_instinsttype
END;

OBJECTTYPE Atomic_insttype
  SUBTYPEOF Generalization_insttype
  INTERFACE
    METHODS
      createatom(): OID;
END;

OBJECTTYPE Composite_insttype[C: Theta, G: Theta]
  SUBTYPEOF Specialization_insttype
  INTERFACE
    PROPERTIES
      possiblepart: { C };
    METHODS
      isasnode(n: G);
       /* inits specialization relationship, uses initgen() */
      hasparts(p: { C } );            /*sets part classes */
      createcomposite(): OID; /*create with empty set of parts*/
END;

OBJECTTYPE Atomic_instinsttype
  SUBTYPEOF Generalization_instinsttype
  INTERFACE
    PROPERTIES
      partof: OID;      /* may be NIL, no sharing of parts*/
END;

OBJECTTYPE Composite_instinsttype
  SUBTYPEOF Specialization_instinsttype
```

```
INTERFACE
    PROPERTIES
        parts: { OID };                          /* may be empty */
    METHODS
        insertpart(p: OID);          /* checks whether allowed */
END;
```

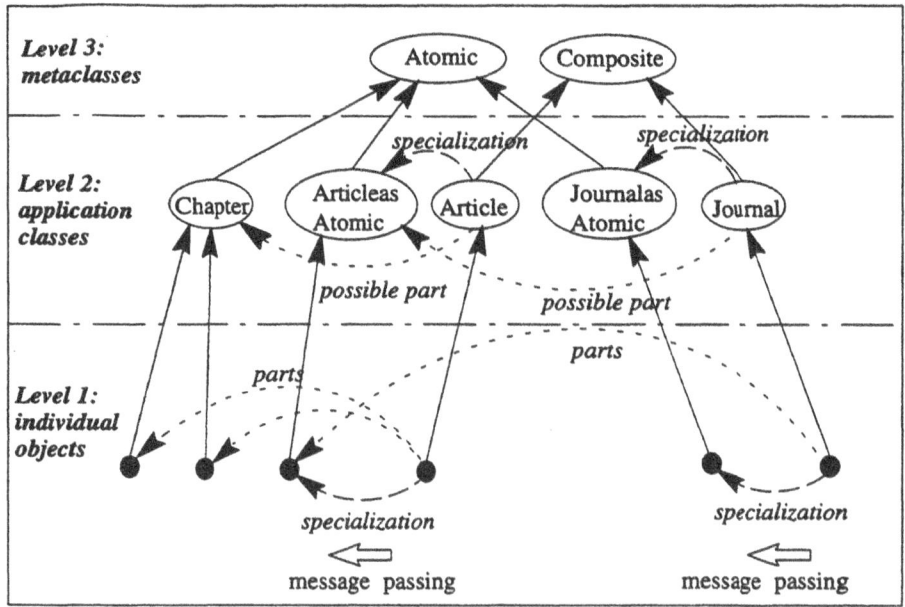

Fig. 10. Usage of the aggregation hierarchy metaclasses.

The metaclasses `Composite` and `Atomic` are used much in the same way as the metaclasses `Node` and `Link`. Thus we skip an explicit example of an application schema here and illustrate the application classes only within Fig. 10.

3.5 Versioning

Versioning is a fundamental issue in any document model. Here we will consider only one aspect of versioning, namely the aspect that a document or an arbitrary part of a document can have *multiple states* due to versioning. This is for example the starting point of a full document-versioning model presented in [HW91], for which a complete VML implementation will be given in [Haa93]. There, also the concept of tasks is introduced. This concept is important in order to describe the work flow that leads to the different states of document parts and thus is crucial for deriving views on documents versions. As a further simplification of the subsequent discussion of versioning and its integration with the other document concepts we restrict ourselves mainly to the structural aspects.

The model we want to consider is described as follows: in document structures any part can consist of multiple states. We do not care about the semantics of these states, i.e., whether they carry a version number or can be related to a particular task within a work flow. We also do not consider the relationships between the different states of different document parts as these will be derived from the relationship of states to tasks and relationships between tasks. Thus we obtain for example for hypertext structures the following simple model derived from the hypertext model introduced in Schema 8.

Schema 14. A hypertext model with versioning at application class level.

```
CLASS VersionedNode
  INSTTYPE  OBJECTTYPE
    INTERFACE
      PROPERTIES
         versions:  {VersionableNode};
    IMPLEMENTATION
      NOMETHOD
        /* delegate each message to an appropriate subset of
           {versionableNode} depending on the context,
           specified e.g. by a query or a task */
  END;
END;


CLASS VersionableNode
  INSTTYPE  OBJECTTYPE
    INTERFACE
      PROPERTIES
         content: anything;
         tolink: {LinkVersions};
         fromlink: {LinkVersions};
         specialization: LinkVersions;
         versionof: VersionedNode;
  END;
END;

CLASS LinkVersion
  INSTTYPE  OBJECTTYPE
    INTERFACE
      PROPERTIES
         from: VersionedNode;
         to: VersionedNode;
         generalization: VersionableNode;
  END;
END;
```

Note that we could not reuse the class Node due to the different types of backward links and we had therefore to introduce the class VersionableNode. This implies

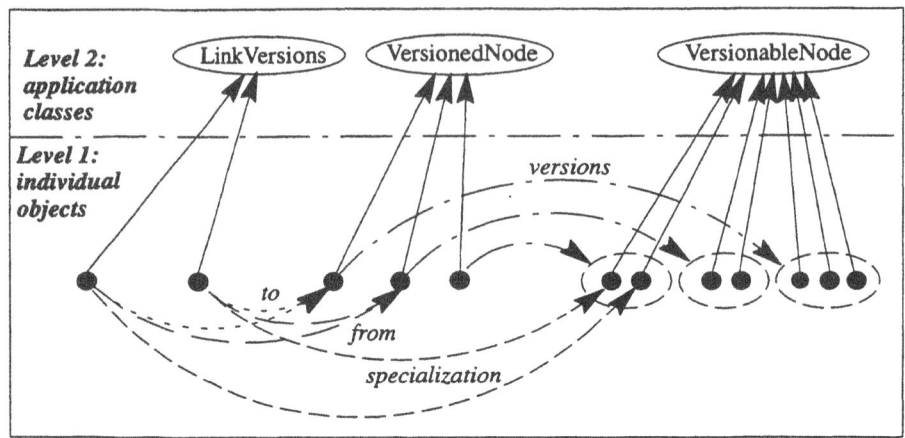

Fig. 11. Introducing versioning at the application class level (compare Schema 14).

that some import-export facility will be needed when creating a version of a non-versioned document. We will later see a way to avoid this. The class VersionedNode uses a **NOMETHOD** clause to delegate all document-specific method calls to the corresponding non-versioned document class. This step may depend upon a context which has to be defined by a query or a task which selects a subset of the different document versions.

We have to observe the following restriction on versions of nodes: two instances of the class VersionedNode have to have disjoint sets in the versions property. Versions of a link object are obtained by versioning the versionableNode object which represents the generalization of the link object. However, there is also a restriction to observe on versions of links: in the case, that the value of the property versions of an instance of VersionedNode consists of instances of versionableNode which are generalizations of link objects, all these instances of versionableNode have the same instance of LinkVersion as specialization. In other words, versions of a link cannot connect different (versioned) nodes. Both constraints have to be maintained operationally.

Versions in aggregation hierarchies are a little bit different as a constraint similar to that formulated for links does not exist for composite objects. In other words, versions of composite objects may consist of different (versioned) parts. Otherwise things are not very different from versioning in hypertext structures.

```
CLASS VersionableAtomic
  INSTTYPE  OBJECTTYPE
    INTERFACE
      PROPERTIES
        content: anything
        specialization: CompositeVersion;
  END;
END;
```

```
CLASS VersionedAtomic
  INSTTYPE  OBJECTTYPE
    INTERFACE
      PROPERTIES
        versions:  {VersionableAtomic};
    IMPLEMENTATION
      NOMETHOD /* delegate each message to an appropriate
                   subset of {VersionableAtomic} depending
                   on the context, specified e.g. by a
                   query or a task */
  END;
END;


CLASS CompositeVersion
  INSTTYPE  OBJECTTYPE
    INTERFACE
      PROPERTIES
        parts: {VersionedAtomic};
        generalization: VersionableAtomic;
  END;
END;
```

If one introduces versioning on an existing document schema in the way illustrated in this section this requires a *schema translation* process. That means from a given non-versioned document schema a new schema has to be generated, either by hand or automatically, according to certain translation rules, some of which should be clear from the above discussion. This new schema models versions of the documents which are structured in the same way as described in the non-versioned document schema. This contradicts again to our goal of a generic support for document modeling. Therefore we will discuss in the following section the modeling of the versioning concept at the metaclass level and how to integrate this with the other modeling primitives introduced at the metaclass layer earlier.

3.6 Integration of document concepts

The goal of this section is to provide a metaclass system that integrates all of the three concepts introduced up to now, namely hypertext, aggregation and versioning. One important design decision we have made earlier, namely separating links and nodes, respectively atomics and composites. This separation will prove valuable in the integration step. It allows to distinguish the different behavior of nodes and links, respectively of atomics and composites with respect to versioning. More precisely, nodes and atomics are not so different at all and thus we unify them in one metaclass called DocObject, links and composites of which will be specializations. The second important decision we take is to derive the connectivity constraints for the versioned classes from the non-versioned classes. Thus we can avoid translation of document schemas for producing the schemas of versioned documents.

We have to point out an observation which is fundamental for the process of integrating different concepts, where each of it is already existent in form of metaclass schemas (in our case the metaclasses generalization/specialization, nodes/links, and atomic/composite). In the VML data model it is not possible to instantiate classes which belong to several metaclasses at a time. So we have first to integrate the object types corresponding to the different concepts by exploiting multiple inheritance and then to produce one *integrated metaclass* which carries the merged semantics. This appears to be an unnecessary complication, however, it is unavoidable: whenever we mix up different concepts we also have to think about the *interdependencies* between them. And these are exactly described in the integrated metaclass. For example, in our case one such dependency is exactly the identification of nodes and atomics.

First we give the integrated schema for hypertext structures and aggregation without versioning. DocObject is the class that integrates nodes and atomics.

Schema 15. An integrated hypermedia document model with versioning.

```
CLASS DocObject METACLASS Metaclass
  INSTTYPE OBJECTTYPE
    SUBTYPEOF Node_insttype, Atomic_insttype
    INTERFACE METHODS createdocobject() DocObject;
    END;
  INSTINSTTYPE OBJECTTYPE
    SUBTYPEOF Node_instinsttype, Atomic_instinsttype
    END;
END;

CLASS Link METACLASS Metaclass
  INSTTYPE   Link_insttype[DocObject, DocObject]
  INSTINSTTYPE   Link_instinsttype
END;

CLASS Composite METACLASS Metaclass
  INSTTYPE   Composite_insttype[DocObject, DocObject]
  INSTINSTTYPE Composite_instinsttype
END;
```

In Schema 15, the types Node-, Atomic-, Link- and Composite_insttype (resp. instinsttype) are the same as defined for Schemas 11 and 13. In order to deal with versioning we introduce classes that model objects that represent versions of nodes and atomics.

```
CLASS VersionedDocObject METACLASS Metaclass
  INSTTYPE Versioned_insttype[DocObject]
  INSTINSTTYPE Versioned_instinsttype
END;
```

```
CLASS LinkVersions METACLASS Metaclass
  INSTTYPE Link_insttype[VersionedDocObject, DocObject]
  INSTINSTTYPE  Link_instinsttype
END;


CLASS CompositeVersions METACLASS Metaclass
  INSTTYPE Composite_insttype[VersionedDocObject, DocObject]
  INSTINSTTYPE Composite_instinsttype
END;


OBJECTTYPE Versioned_instinsttype
  INTERFACE  PROPERTIES
      versions: { OID }
  IMPLEMENTATION
    NOMETHOD
      /* select subset of versions according to context
         and delegate message call to it */
END;


OBJECTTYPE Versioned_insttype[C: Theta]
  INTERFACE
    PROPERTIES
      versionclassof: C;
    METHODS
      versionof(n: C); /* sets versionclassof */
      createversion(n: OID): OID;
                  /* creates a versioned object for nonversioned
                     object n, checks if correct version class */
  IMPLEMENTATION
    NOMETHOD
      {versionclassof->currentmethod(arg);}
END;
```

Note how the parametrization of Link_insttype and Composite_insttype is used. The relationships between the classes and metaclasses of versioned and non-versioned hierarchical document structures is illustrated in Fig. 12. We remark that a distinction as it is made between Atomic and VersionableAtomic in Schema 14 is no longer needed as the references used in the atomic objects, i.e. Chapter, in order to refer to their version objects, i.e. versionedChapter, are object identifiers when introducing these classes via metaclasses. With regard to composites, i.e. Article, two different classes are introduced for versioning. One is ArticlewithVersionedChapter, which models composites holding versioned parts, and the other is versionedArticleasDoc, which models versions of composites.

We now give a sample schema making use of the metaclass schema, under the assumption that the user is aware of the difference between versioned and non-versioned documents.

```
CLASS Chapter METACLASS DocObject
  INSTTYPE Chapter_type
END;


CLASS versionedChapter METACLASS VersionedDocObject
  INIT SELF->versionof(Chapter);
END;


CLASS Article METACLASS Composite
  INSTTYPE Article_type;
  INIT SELF->hasparts({ Chapter });
       SELF->isasnode(ArticleasDoc)
END;


CLASS ArticleasDoc METACLASS DocObject
  INSTTYPE ArticleasDoc_type
END;


CLASS versionedArticle METACLASS VersionedDocObject
  INIT SELF->versionof(ArticleasDoc);
END;


CLASS ArticlewithVersionedChapter METACLASS CompositeVersions
  INIT SELF->hasparts({ versionedChapter });
       SELF->isasnode(ArticleasDoc);
END;
```

This schema finishes our discussion of design alternatives in hypermedia document modeling. As a continuation we could consider to build upon this basic metaclass schema additional operations which make certain classes anonymous in order to hide some of the complexity of the underlying structures from the user. However this would be out of the scope of this presentation. Also we do not consider here the issues of how to control the different constraints explained earlier for versioned links and composites.

4 Conclusion

In this paper we presented the VODAK Model Language VML and its application in the area of hypermedia systems. Only the most important features of VML have been introduced. The main principle we showed was the usage of metaclasses, the separation of object types and classes, the concept of instance-instance types, and the method delegation via the **NOMETHOD** clause for the construction of specific semantic data models for individual applications. The separation of types and classes, called the dual model, was not only used at the level of application classes, but also at the level of metaclasses. In combination with the concept of metaclasses and the parameterization of object types we demonstrated how modeling primitives and modeling constraints can be introduced into the data model.

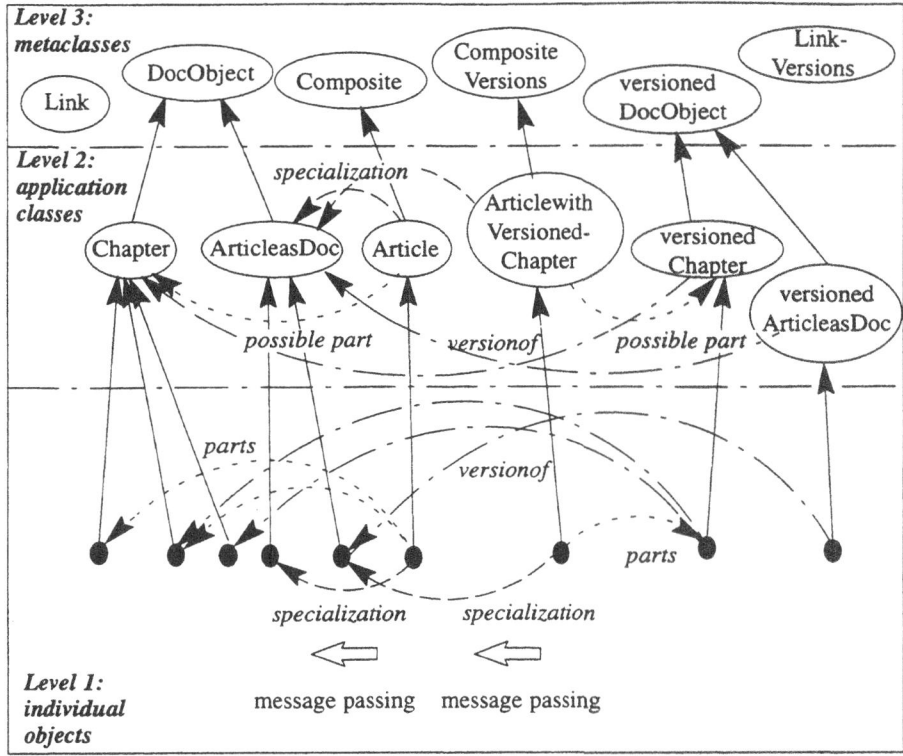

Fig. 12. An integrated hypermedia document database including versioning and part-of relationships

This approach tries to overcome the limitations of existing models, which come with a fixed set of predefined modeling primitives, which fit well into the original application domain the models have been developed in. But they provide neither adequate modeling primitives for other application domains nor extension or adaption mechanisms which would allow a designer to extend or adapt the model such that it meets specific application requirements. VML has been developed as a database programming language which allows to construct individual semantic data models based on a kernel object-oriented data model.

The examples we used for the purpose of demonstrating the VML concepts come from real applications which have been prototyped at the institute: the cooperative authoring system SEPIA [SHH+92] which is based on the hypertext approach, the multimedia electronic news magazine *Multimedia Forum* which uses a SGML-based document database and which makes use of a document-versioning model, and a multimedia document archive which organizes all the documents in a hierarchical way according to the DFR standard [ISO91]. These applications served as a test bed and evaluation framework for our concepts and have shown that VML meets the requirements of constructing adequate modeling primitives and of defining the concrete database schemas.

The examples have also demonstrated some of the numerous design principles which have to be considered when developing data models for VML. Some of them are of a general nature, like the principle of semantic-free associations and the trade off between declarative and operational specifications in the data model. Others are specific for the different features of the VML data model, like the usage of metaclasses for introducing semantic relationships and their integration, the trade off between using parametrized object types and metaclasses, which emerges from using a dual model, or the dynamic creation of anonymous classes, which is possible by treating classes as first class objects.

Further developments with respect to VML include extensions for modeling multimedia data. So far, VML provides built-in data types for audio and video, and a prototype has been built which allows to transparently manage digital and analog video databases [RM93]. Extensions will include mechanisms to describe time dependency between multimedia data, or mechanisms to handle the interactive aspects of data like videos and audios. The VODAK prototype itself is currently extended by new modules, like a continuous object manager, which allows a real integration of multimedia data.

Acknowledgement

We like to thank A. Haake and H. Schütt for fruitful discussions of which we benefitted greatly to become familiar with the document-versioning model developed within the thesis of A. Haake and the SEPIA prototype developed in the WIBAS group of GMD-IPSI. We also would like to thank A. Biliris for supporting us to convert the final version produced with a high-end publishing system to LaTeX.

Appendix: Interdependencies of the Hypermedia Schemas

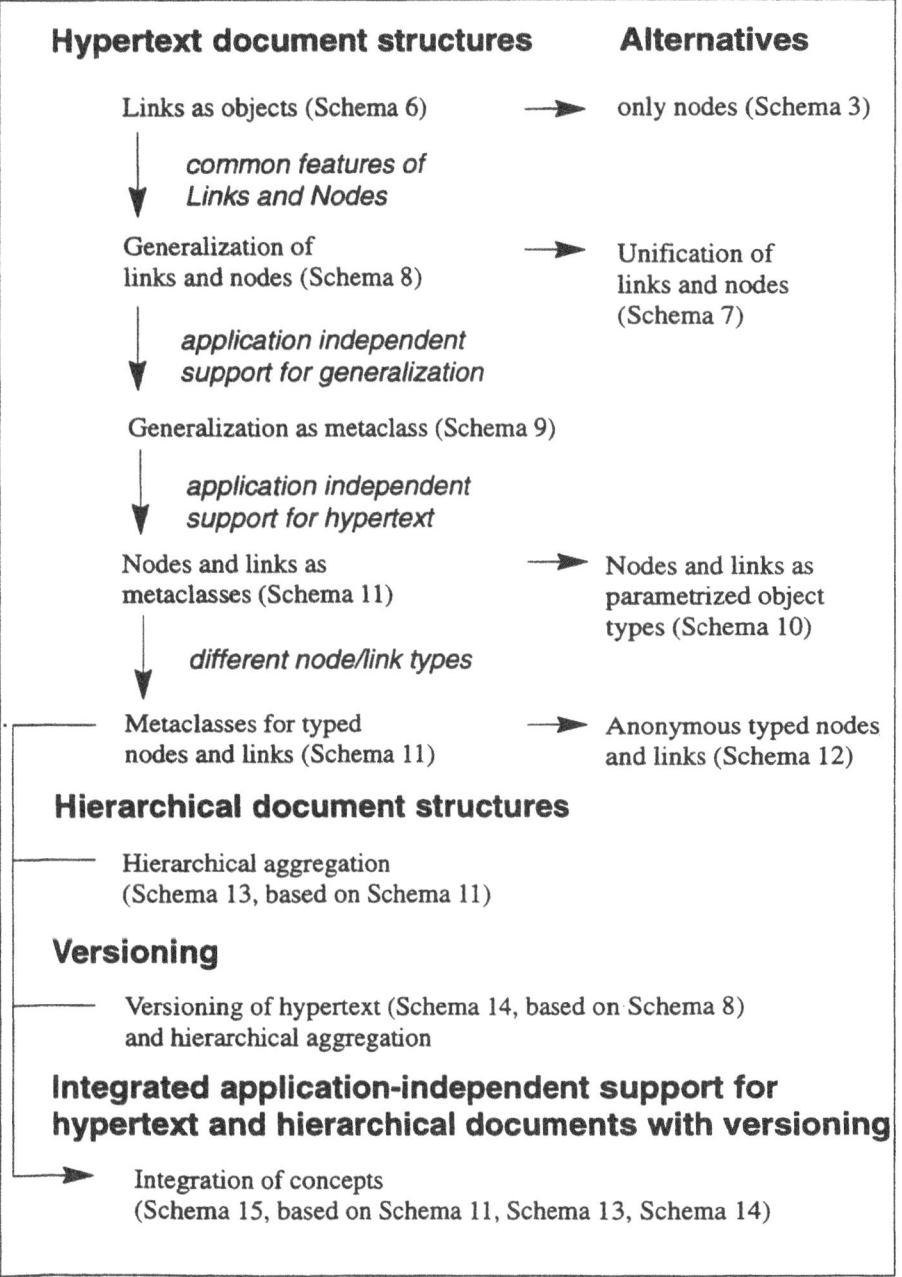

Hypertext document structures   **Alternatives**

Links as objects (Schema 6)   ⟶   only nodes (Schema 3)

common features of
Links and Nodes

Generalization of   ⟶   Unification of
links and nodes (Schema 8)   links and nodes
                                  (Schema 7)

application independent
support for generalization

Generalization as metaclass (Schema 9)

application independent
support for hypertext

Nodes and links as   ⟶   Nodes and links as
metaclasses (Schema 11)   parametrized object
                                 types (Schema 10)

different node/link types

Metaclasses for typed   ⟶   Anonymous typed nodes
nodes and links (Schema 11)   and links (Schema 12)

Hierarchical document structures

Hierarchical aggregation
(Schema 13, based on Schema 11)

Versioning

Versioning of hypertext (Schema 14, based on Schema 8)
and hierarchical aggregation

**Integrated application-independent support for
hypertext and hierarchical documents with versioning**

Integration of concepts
(Schema 15, based on Schema 11, Schema 13, Schema 14)

Object Modeling Using Classification in CANDIDE and its Applications

Shamkant Navathe[1], Ashoka Savasere[1], Tarek Anwar[2], Howard Beck[3], Sunit Gala[4]

[1] Georgia Institute of Technology, School of Information and Computer Science, Atlanta, GA 30332, USA
[2] Computer Sciences Corporation, 304 W. Route 38, P.O. Box N, Moorestown, NJ 08057, USA
[3] University of Florida, College of Engineering, Gainesville, FL 32611, USA
[4] UniSQL Inc., 9390 Research Blvd. Austin, TX 78759, USA

Abstract. CANDIDE is a semantic object model based on the FL-, KANDOR and BACK frame-based knowledge representation languages. A novel feature of this model is that the DDL and DML are identical, thus providing uniform treatment of data objects, query objects and view objects. The classification algorithm finds the correct placement for a data object at definition time and query object at querying time in a given object taxonomy. The fundamental criterion for such correct placement is the subsumption relationship between two object classes. The extensions make CANDIDE a viable data model. Classification can be applied effectively to many database problems. Here we describe two such applications. The first is integration of a set of heterogeneous database systems. In this approach classification is used for schema integration as well as query evaluation. The global schema is automatically generated by repeatedly applying classification to each object of the component schemas ensuring the correctness of the global schema. Deductive reasoning provided by classification offers many unique advantages to global query evaluation, such as validating the correctness of queries before evaluation. The second application is a document retrieval system. In this approach, the knowledge representation capability of CANDIDE is used to capture the structural and conceptual information from a document. The inexact querying capability based on classification makes continuous query refinement unnecessary. The expressiveness of CANDIDE also makes it extremely suitable for natural language query interfaces. Natural language queries are mapped into CANDIDE objects which also act as query objects. Additionally, the semantics of the database objects are directly used by the language processor leading to better language understanding.

1 Introduction

This section is largely based on [BGN89]. Much has been said of the semantic inadequacies of the three classical data models, namely, the hierarchical, network and relational models. These inadequacies have spawned a large number of proposed semantic or object-oriented data models [Nav92]. At first these models were used by designers for describing a database at a conceptual level. This conceptual schema was then translated into a relational, network or hierarchical schema. There is an increasing awareness that we need to supplement the database management systems with knowledge or meta-information so that (i) access to such information is facilitated; and (ii) users get a better idea of what an underlying database contains so that they can ask intelligent queries and use the information effectively.

In this chapter we describe one such attempt at capturing the semantics of a database through an object model based on the properties of subsumption and classification. The resulting data model has a very clear structural object orientation. So far we have not added any behavioral attachments to this model.

Similar efforts to CANDIDE which we first published in early 1989 [BGN89] have been going on in the last several years. For example, the CLASSIC DBMS system at Bell Laboratories [BBMR89] has had a similar goal and has been well developed into a pragmatic knowledge engineering methodology. McGregor et al. [Mac91a, MB92] at USC–ISI have developed the LOOM system with a description classifier, again as a way of representing the knowledge contained in a database. In general, frame representation systems [Kar92], description logics [Bor92], etc are aiming at superimposing the knowledge representation world on top of database systems for better inferencing and reasoning with data.

The query languages being proposed for most semantic data models are usually based on some algebra and tend to have an SQL or QUEL-like syntax [Mac85, PS84a, Zan83]. Queries expressed in these languages cannot be described by the underlying data models. The DDL is used to define the schemas. The DML specifies manipulations to be performed on the database, which is internally translated into a sequence of algebraic operations. It does not exploit the structural relationships or domain constraints which are specified in the schema of the semantic data model. The associated problems of this approach are:

1. the query language syntax has no bearing on the underlying data model;
2. the structural and semantic constraints of the model are not exploited to aid in query interpretation, query reuse or query reformulation;
3. being a fragmented approach, it is difficult to treat data objects, queries and views homogeneously through a single language;
4. view definitions in these languages lead to serious update problems;
5. even though the query language may be declarative, the user still has to think of how (in terms of algebraic operations) and from where (logical access paths, plus exact names of attributes and objects) to get the desired data before specifying the query.

We believe that the *DDL and DML dichotomy* in these database systems, coupled with a *lack of reflection of the model semantics in the query languages or DMLs*, is at the core of the above problems. This has been somewhat alleviated in the relational model by marrying it with logic as exemplified by the so-called deductive databases [GMN84]. But we are unaware of any such marriage between a semantic data model and logic. Thus, we would like to see a more homogeneous specification and behavior of objects, queries and views. This necessarily means collapsing the DDL and DML into a single coherent language. Further, this language must be formally specified so as to reflect the semantics of the data model. *Ideally, this data model should be a correct, complete and tractable model of computation, and yet be expressive enough to be useful.*

With this objective in mind, we propose that one way to enforce database integrity and also process queries is based on deductive reasoning about object definitions.

Classification and subsumption functions are used for such reasoning about structural relationships among objects. Subsumption relationships determine if one object is a special case of another. Classification is a search technique which correctly places new objects into an existing taxonomy by repeatedly applying a subsumption function. These have also been described as terminological reasoning since structural relationships represent object definitions and the terms for describing data [Neb88].

The notions of classification and subsumption have been formally developed in a series of frame-based knowledge representation languages which explore the computational complexity of subsumption. These include FL and FL- [LB85], BACK [Neb88], KL-ONE [BS85], NIKL [KBR86], and KANDOR [PS84b, PS86]. The disappointing conclusion of these studies is that subsumption becomes intractable unless the constructs of the language are *carefully* and *narrowly* constrained. Semantic data models have not been concerned with these issues because they either rely on operational query languages, or just serve as conceptual modeling tools which do not support queries at all. Few are capable of supporting terminological reasoning, and we know of none which address the tractability requirement.

Of these frame-based languages, FL-, KANDOR, and BACK explore the limit of expressibility and tractability, but out of these restricted languages only FL- has a subsumption function which can be executed in polynomial time [Neb88]. We have developed CANDIDE based on extensions of these language in order to facilitate their applicability to data modeling. CANDIDE illustrates that querying by classification is a viable technique for querying semantic data models. In particular, we wish to emphasize the following:

1. The DDL and DML become a single language. Thus, the semantics of the database schema is automatically exploited for query processing.
2. Since query and view objects are treated as new class definitions, they are represented as object definitions and behave in the same way as data objects.
3. The approach lends itself to building an integrated natural language processor that derives information from the database in order to resolve a natural language query.
4. It is possible to couple this approach as a semantic layer on top of existing databases under various scenarios.

1.1 Overview of the CANDIDE Data Model

We have extended FL-, KANDOR, and BACK to make them more suitable for data modeling. We use a notation which conforms with the more common data modeling terms. Also, additional constructs have been added to simplify representing standard data types. For example, we have added the type constructors RANGE, SET, and COMPOSITE domain, and allowed for additional built-in types such as REAL. These do not really increase the expressiveness of the model or affect computational complexity, but they simplify the applicability of the model. The same concepts could be represented in the original models, but with great difficulty. For example, in the original KANDOR, the concept of "21 or older" would have to be represented by creating one instance of age for each integer from 21 up to some arbitrarily large value, and placing them all under a special class. With the extensions, this can be handled by simply using the

"RANGE [21,NIL" construct. We have been careful not to introduce any constructs which would adversely affect computational complexity. This was done by requiring any new construct to be reducible to the original constructs. These extensions make it easier to state queries, as will be illustrated in Sect. 1.4. In this section, we give a brief overview of the CANDIDE data model. One can see that it is at least as expressive as most semantic data models.

Structural Aspect of the Data Model. The Extended BNF of the data definition and manipulation language of the CANDIDE data model is shown in Appendix A. The model explicitly supports the abstractions of aggregation, generalization [SS77], identification, and classification (not to be confused with the classification algorithm described below). The association abstraction can be treated as a special case of aggregation, and is not explicitly supported. An association between two or more object classes is modeled as a class which is the aggregation of attributes referencing each member class (of the association), in addition to other attributes which the association may have. The model has four semantic categories: classes, attributes, instances and disjoint classes. The literals ⟨classname⟩, ⟨attr-name⟩, ⟨inst-name⟩ and ⟨disjoint-name⟩ are strings that uniquely identify objects in each category. Strings, integers and real numbers are system built-in atomic types or classes.

The database schema consists of two partially ordered lattices, one for the *class taxonomy*, and the other for the *attribute hierarchy*. The root of the class taxonomy is a universal class called "Thing." In the attribute hierarchy, which has a root called "Top," each attribute can have at most one parent attribute along with an associated domain. This domain is either an instance, or a set of instances typified by an object class described in the class taxonomy. The domain of an attribute must be a subclass of the domain of its parent attribute. A separate attribute hierarchy also gives the user more flexibility in object or query specification, as we shall see in Sect. 1.4.

An attribute appearing in a class description can be qualified by additional value constraints on its domain specified within the class description. Further, these attribute constraints in a class must logically imply the constraints on each attribute of each of its superclass. They also specify requirements for instances to be members of the class. An object class can have many superclasses, subclasses, and instances. A *disjoint class* means that the named subclasses of a given class cannot have any common instance.

A class can be either primitive or defined [BS85]. *Primitive classes* represent concepts which cannot be fully specified, that is, the attribute constraints are necessary but not sufficient conditions for class membership. They generally occur at the top of a taxonomy. There are two interesting kinds of primitive classes or concepts. The first kind includes concepts such as Schank's conceptual dependencies [SI74] "action," "agent," "object," which are used to define other classes but cannot be defined themselves. For the second kind of primitive classes, it may be impossible to express the sufficient conditions in the language of the data model. For example, a polygon can be described as a set of line segments, but it may not be possible to express the requirements of closure and non-intersection on this set. Thus, a user is forced to declare a polygon as a primitive class. Users must explicitly specify which subclasses and instances belong to a given primitive class. In contrast, the attribute constraints of a *defined class* are necessary and sufficient conditions for class membership. This means defined classes represent concepts that can be fully specified and therefore, class membership in defined classes can be automatically decided.

Similarly, an instance which can also have more than one parent class, must have attributes and values which satisfy the attribute constraints of its parents. An instance can have more attributes than defined in its parent classes, and the values for these additional attributes are constrained only by the domains specified in the attribute hierarchy. Thus, the immediate or most specific parent classes of the instance can be automatically deduced.

1.2 Constraint Specification

So far we have seen that a class description comprises its superclasses, subclasses, instances and attributes. One can specify additional constraints on these attributes. There are four kinds of constraints: "max," "some," "exactly" and "all." The "max" constraint means that an attribute can have at most a specified number of value fillers. The "some" constraint means that there exist at least a specified number of value fillers, each value belonging to a certain domain qualified by value constraints, $\langle vc \rangle$ (see Appendix A for EBNF). The "exactly" constraint says that exactly a specified number of attribute fillers must satisfy a value constraint; it is the combination of "some" and "max" The "all" constraint specifies that all values of an attribute must belong to a domain qualified by $\langle vc \rangle$. Note the similarity of the all and some constraints to the universal and existential quantifiers of first order predicate calculus [LB85].

Value constraints on attributes specify domains (DOMAIN $\langle type\text{-}c \rangle$) or actual values (VALUE $\langle type\text{-}i \rangle$). Domains may be specified by naming the class or type as in CLASS, STRING, INTEGER or REAL, or by using the type constructors RANGE, SET, SETDIF, and COMPOSITE. RANGE specifies a range of values between some upper and lower bounds which may be inclusive, exclusive, or NIL (+/- Infinity). RANGE is currently typed over reals and integers. The SET construct allows a set of domains to be specified such that the attribute values must belong to the union of these domains. A SET may recursively include any construct defined in $\langle type\text{-}c \rangle$. SETDIF allows a special form of negation (set difference) to be handled in a safe way. For instance, "SETDIF f g" where f is a class and g is its subclass (or an instance which belongs to f), means a set consisting of only those instances belonging to f and not to g. The COMPOSITE domain is the aggregation of other (possibly complex) domains, in which each component domain is labeled by an attribute name along with its constraints. For instance, a COMPOSITE domain for an attribute called Date would have component attributes of Month, Day and Year. The type constructors RANGE, SET, SETDIF, and COMPOSITE make it possible to describe complex domains without having to create additional classes and instances as would have been required in the original models.

1.3 Classification and Subsumption

As mentioned earlier, a significant departure from traditional database querying techniques is that we treat a query just as any other object described in the database schema. An object definition is *prescriptive* [ZM88] in the sense that :

1. it provides the minimal class description for any object to be considered a member of the corresponding type set, i.e., an object instance can have additional attributes beyond what is prescribed in each parent class, thus relaxing the fixed arity constraint;
2. typing information is attached to the object class in terms of its superclasses, subclasses, and domain restrictions on its attribute labels (this is similarly true for object instances);
3. since the attributes are labeled, we can relax a traditional constraint such as fixed position (ordering of attributes);
4. object class definitions can provide necessary and sufficient conditions for class membership which can be used to deduce additional relationships among objects not specified by the user.

This interpretation must be based on the semantics of the subsumption relationship. A class F *subsumes* a class G if and only if every instance of G is also an instance of F, i.e., F is a superclass of G. This subsumption relationship is computed on the basis of whether the attribute constraints for class F logically imply the attribute constraints for class G. The classification operation can compute the missing relationships by controlled application of the subsumption function, and completely specify the class lattice.

We propose using this same classification process to compute the results of a query. *Classification* can be viewed as the process of correctly locating a new object in an existing lattice. The correct location is immediately below the most specific classes which subsume the new class and immediately above the most general classes subsumed by this new class. Classification involves a combination of depth-first/breadth-first search of the class lattice, beginning at known superclasses of the object to be classified, and applying the subsumption function, continuing as long as it succeeds. Thus, a query object specification is classified against the complete lattice. The required object instances are obtained from the union of the set of instances of all the superclasses of the query object, subject to additional attribute constraints of the query object.

Class definitions for an example database is shown below. The corresponding class and attribute hierarchies are shown in Fig. 1 and Fig. 2.

In the next section we illustrate how classification is exploited to maintain the class taxonomy, enforce constraints, and process queries.

1.4 Classification as a Query Processing Technique

Comparison with Previous Approaches. The use of subsumption and classification for querying databases is a form of concept matching. Concept matching has its roots in the frame matching retrieval methods of systems such as KRL [BW77], pattern matching in logic databases [RF87, ZM88] and graph matching [Sow84]. Various approaches to classification are described in [BS85, PS84b, PS86, FS86, Neb88]. We are applying the approach for formally computing database queries, and suggest that it can be used as a viable way for querying semantic data models.

Querying by classification is the process of specifying a query object in the same notation as data objects, and then searching for objects which are structurally related to this query object. Query processing is based on deductive inferencing about object

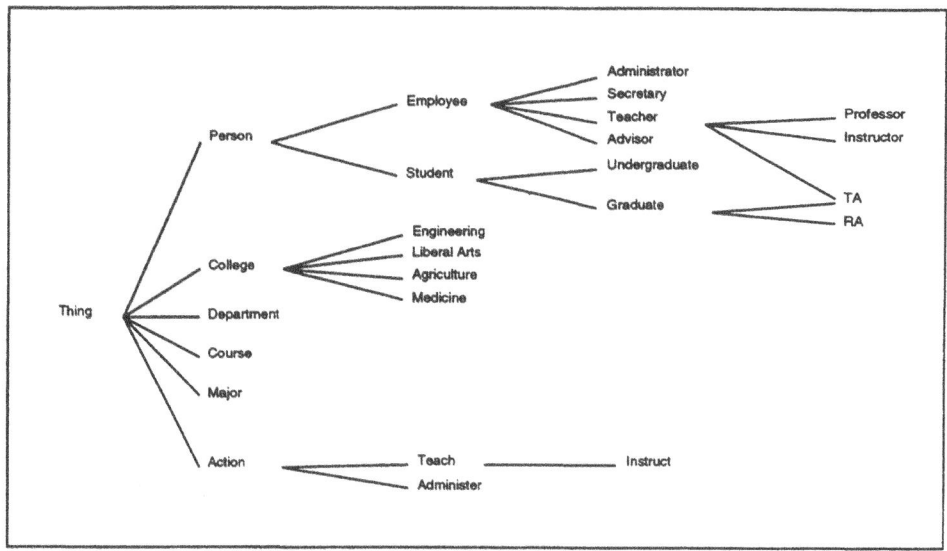

Fig. 1. Class lattice

structures rather than a procedural specification of operations. Query specification is entirely declarative in that the user need not provide any information on how the query is to be executed. The user concentrates on describing the desired information. Inferencing techniques for matching are defined formally by the subsumption function which determines whether one object class is a subclass of another. Since subsumption is a form of terminological reasoning [Neb88], *the user can describe a query in terms which may be different from the exact terms under which the desired information is stored*, so long as the meaning is similar. This contrasts with the SQL-type queries in which names of relations and attributes must be precisely specified. Dealing with concepts also implies that the database objects are not only descriptors for physical data, but must also represent the meaning of terms used to describe the data. Although semantic data models are capable of expressing these meanings, this aspect has not been exploited for query processing.

Querying using classification can be contrasted with the operational approach exemplified by SQL-type query languages. In the operational approach, a query is mapped into a sequence of algebraic operations applied to the objects in the database. Internally, this is a procedural approach since the plan of query execution involves an exact sequence of operations. Externally, high-level data manipulation languages are used which are more declarative in that the user need not specify these steps. However, the user must still have a thorough understanding of the database schema, and must know the names of objects and attributes. Also, the user must be able to conceptualize the operations in general. For example, the user must specify access paths, or describe which relations need to be joined. A number of data manipulation languages based on the operational approach have been proposed for semantic data models including GEM [Zan83], ARIEL [Mac85] and entity-relationship algebra [PS84a].

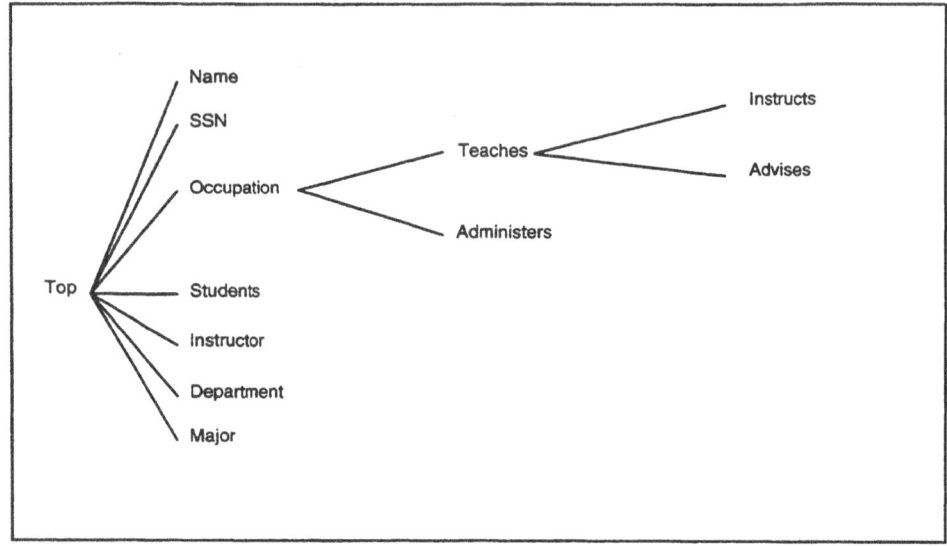

Fig. 2. Attribute hierarchy

Person
    CLASS DEFINED
    SUPERCLASS Thing
    ATTRIBUTE CONSTRAINTS
        Name: EXACTLY 1 DOMAIN STRING
        Ssno: EXACTLY 1 DOMAIN STRING
Employee
    CLASS DEFINED
    SUPERCLASS Person
    ATTRIBUTE CONSTRAINTS
        Occupation: ALL DOMAIN CLASS Occupation
        Department: ALL DOMAIN CLASS Department
Student
    CLASS DEFINED
    SUPERCLASS Person
    ATTRIBUTE CONSTRAINTS
        Courses: ALL DOMAIN CLASS Course
        Advisor: ALL DOMAIN CLASS Advisor
        Major: ALL DOMAIN CLASS College
        GPA: EXACTLY 1 DOMAIN RANGE [0.0,4.0]

Advisor
    CLASS DEFINED
    SUPERCLASS Employee
    ATTRIBUTE CONSTRAINTS
        Students: ALL DOMAIN CLASS Student
Course
    CLASS DEFINED
    SUPERCLASS Thing
    ATTRIBUTE CONSTRAINTS
        Instructor: ALL DOMAIN CLASS Teacher
        Department: ALL DOMAIN CLASS Department
        Students: ALL DOMAIN CLASS Student
Instruct
    CLASS DEFINED
    SUPERCLASS Teach
    ATTRIBUTE CONSTRAINTS
        Teacher: ALL DOMAIN CLASS Teacher
        Course: ALL DOMAIN CLASS Course

Fig. 3. Example class definitions

Other non-operational or declarative approaches to querying semantic data models have been proposed. Zhu and Maier [ZM88] describe abstract objects for TEDM. These abstract objects take a form which is very similar to other TEDM database objects, and they are a part of the database, acting as views. They can be matched with other database objects through isomorphic relations defined on their attributes and values. In our approach, there is no distinction between permanent query objects and database objects. Also, the subsumption function plays a stronger role, for example, by enforcing constraints on insert operations. It is able to identify complex relationships in addition to the type-preserving isomorphic mappings (for example, it can determine that a male child is a son).

ARGON [PSBL84] is an information retrieval system built on top of KANDOR, but it still had to process some queries outside the classifier. It was the same case with RABBIT [TWF+82]. But due to the extensions in CANDIDE as described above, we are able to handle certain queries which otherwise had to be processed by operations outside the classifier.

Finally, the concept matching approach can be contrasted with querying in logic databases. The search by the classifier is directed by the taxonomical relationships among objects, and the terms being unified can be complex objects, but the subsumption function is much less powerful than full first-order logic. Essentially, subsumption can be viewed as a *constrained inferencing technique* compared with logical queries. In the remainder of this Section, we explain the details of query specification and processing based on classification.

1.5 Query Specification and Processing

We will illustrate the specification of query objects and the steps involved in processing queries using the university database with the class and attribute hierarchy shown in Fig. 1 and Fig. 2. The structure of some of the data objects is shown in Fig. 3. Query objects are created using the same EBNF notation as data objects (Fig. 3). Complex queries may be decomposed into several nested query objects.

Once a query object has been specified, classification is used for query processing. In classification, all the superclasses, subclasses, and instances of the query object are identified. The result of the query is the instances and subclasses of the query object. The query object may, if so desired, be inserted permanently into the database.

Example 1. What courses offered by the college of engineering are taught by Smith.

    Query
        SUPERCLASS Course
        ATTRIBUTE CONSTRAINTS
            Instructor: EXACTLY 1 VALUE INSTANCE Smith
            Department: EXACTLY 1 DOMAIN CLASS Engineering

This Query object is a special class of Course in which the Instructor is Smith and the Department is an Engineering department such as Electrical or Mechanical. Smith (an instance) and Engineering (a class) are objects which are already part of the database.

To process this query, the classifier would begin at class Course, and try to find more specialized classes which subsume the Query class. Since there are no classes more specialized than Course (Fig. 1), there is no additional searching in this example. The next step is to test each instance of Course to see which can meet the attribute constraints of the Query object, namely those in which the value for the Instructor attribute is exactly "Smith" and for which the Department is some instance of Engineering.

Example 2. Find all courses which have at least 10 Engineering students enrolled.

    Query1
        SUPERCLASS Course
        ATTRIBUTE CONSTRAINTS
            Students: ATLEAST 10 DOMAIN CLASS Query2   (a)
    Query2
        SUPERCLASS Student
        ATTRIBUTE CONSTRAINTS
            Major: EXACTLY 1 DOMAIN CLASS Engineering   (b)

This is a nested query. Query1 is a specialization of Course in which at least 10 students are instances of class Query2. The value of 10 for the ATLEAST constraint [line (a)] is used to express cardinality. Query2 describes the class of all students majoring in an Engineering department [line (b)]. Query2 would first be classified to temporarily create a new class having as its instances those Students majoring in Engineering.

Query1 is then classified to find courses with at least ten Students that are instances of Query2.

Example 3. Find persons who instruct courses taken by persons majoring in Computer Science.

```
Query1
    CLASS DEFINED
    SUPERCLASS Person
    ATTRIBUTE CONSTRAINTS
        Instructs ATLEAST 1 DOMAIN CLASS Query2
Query2
    CLASS DEFINED
    SUPERCLASS Course
    ATTRIBUTE CONSTRAINTS
        Students ATLEAST 1 DOMAIN CLASS Query3                          (a)
Query3
    CLASS DEFINED
    SUPERCLASS Person
    ATTRIBUTE CONSTRAINTS
        Major ATLEAST 1 VALUE INSTANCE Computer Science                (b)
```

This example illustrates aspects of *terminological reasoning* in that the Teacher and Student classes are not mentioned directly in the query. They are located *automatically* by the classifier. The objects are classified in a nested fashion which is similar to nesting select-from-where blocks in SQL. Notice that the nesting also provides a form of path specification which is similar to a natural join in relational algebra.

Query3 represents the concept "persons majoring in Computer Science." Query3 is classified first, beginning the search at "Person" which is listed in the SUPERCLASS list. Since Employee does not have a Major attribute, the subsumption function fails on Employee (see Fig. 1 and Fig. 2). It succeeds for Student, but cannot satisfy any of the attribute constraints for Graduate or Undergraduate (Since there is now information provided which is specific to these subclasses). So, the classification step ends for Query3 with its being subsumed by Student. Next, all instances of student are tested to see which can meet the constraint in line (b) of Query3, resulting in the set of instances which contains all students majoring in Computer Science.

Query2 is the set of all courses containing at least one student who is an instance of Query3 [line (a)]. Since there are no classes below Course, the classifier cannot find any more specific classes. All instances of Course are tested against Query2, resulting in the desired set of instances.

Finally, Query1 is classified beginning at Person. Since Instructs is an Occupation according to the attribute hierarchy, Employee subsumes Query1, but Query1 cannot satisfy the Student attribute constraints. Similarly, subsumption fails for Administrator, and Secretary. It succeeds for Teacher since Instructs is below Teaches in the attribute hierarchy. It cannot proceed further because the attribute constraints for Professor and Instructor are not satisfied. All instances of teacher (which includes all instances of

Professor and Instructor) are tested against Query1, resulting in the set of instances of teachers who teach at least one course which is an instance of Query2. This final set satisfies the query.

Example 4. Find all students who do not have advisors from engineering, but who have taken either at least 2 engineering courses or one engineering and one liberal arts course.

    Query1
        CLASS DEFINED
        SUPERCLASSES Student
        SUBCLASSES Query2, Query3   (a)
        ATTRIBUTE CONSTRAINTS
            Advisor: EXACTLY 1 DOMAIN COMPOSITE
                Department: ALL DOMAIN SETDIF   (b)
                              {CLASS College,
                              CLASS Engineering}
    Query2
        CLASS DEFINED
        SUPERCLASSES Query1
        ATTRIBUTE CONSTRAINTS
            Courses: ATLEAST 2 DOMAIN CLASS Engineering
    Query3
        CLASS DEFINED
        SUPERCLASSES Query1
        ATTRIBUTE CONSTRAINTS
            Courses: ATLEAST 1 DOMAIN CLASS Engineering
                  ATLEAST 1 DOMAIN CLASS Liberal Arts

The "or" requirement is handled by creating two subclasses [line (a)] in Query1. Alternately, this could also have been modeled by the SET construct. This is the equivalent of a relational union. The negation for advisor is treated as a set difference [line (b)], resulting in the set of values for advisor's department which includes every College except Engineering. That is, negation is taken as the set of instances which does not include the instances of the negated class. Query2 and Query3 are classified first, creating temporary classes which are used in the classification of Query1. The SETDIF construct is evaluated by checking the value of the Advisor attribute to see that its Department is an instance of College but not an instance of Engineering.

Example 5. Find all students who teach other students with a GPA greater than 3.5.

    Query
        CLASS DEFINED
        SUPERCLASS: Student
        ATTRIBUTE CONSTRAINTS
            Teaches: ATLEAST 1 DOMAIN COMPOSITE   (a)
                Students: ATLEAST 1 DOMAIN COMPOSITE   (b)
                    GPA: EXACTLY 1 DOMAIN RANGE (3.5,4.0]

Here the Query object is of class Student. The attribute constraints are also constraints on the Student domain, resulting in a *recursive query*. The nested constraints on Students [line (b)] requires at least one student with GPA greater than 3.5. The constraints on Teaches [line (a)] require at least one such course to be taught which contains one such student. Although Student is not defined to have a Teaches attribute in the database definition (Fig. 3), TA which is a subclass of Student has such an attribute. In query processing, this Query class would be subsumed by TA. Thus only instances which are both Students and Teachers will be tested for the additional constraints.

Example 6. This example illustrates *view creation*. Suppose we wish to define a new concept called "Honors Student" which is a student with GPA greater than 3.5.

    Honors Student
        CLASS DEFINED
        SUPERCLASS Student
        ATTRIBUTE CONSTRAINTS
            GPA: EXACTLY 1 DOMAIN RANGE (3.5,4.0]

This query object will retrieve all honors students by checking all instances of student and retrieving those meeting the constraints. This object could be made a permanent part of the database resulting in view creation. Any student instance with GPA greater than 3.5 would then automatically become an instance of this class during insert or modify operations. This view object could have been used to compute the result of Example 5, by rephrasing the query as "Find all students who teach honors students," which is shown below:

    Query
        CLASS DEFINED
        SUPERCLASS: Student
        ATTRIBUTE CONSTRAINTS
            Teaches: ATLEAST 1 DOMAIN COMPOSITE
                Students: ATLEAST 1 DOMAIN CLASS Honors Student

Summary of Query Processing Features. With respect to the above examples, we would like to highlight the following features:

1. The declarative nature of query specification is evident in all examples.
2. We can compare these queries with relational algebra in the sense that:
    (a) a "join" is illustrated in Examples 2, 3, and 4,
    (b) "selection" is illustrated in Examples 1 and 5,
    (c) 'Student.GPA' is "projected" in Example 5 [line (b)],
    (d) set union and set difference is shown in Example 4, and
    (e) Examples 2, 3 and 4 illustrate nested queries.

    However, this approach cannot support arbitrary joins since the classes must be related through some navigation path.

3. View definition (Example 6), query reuse (Examples 5 and 6 together), and a type of recursive query (Example 5) are supported.
4. Example 4 also illustrates query combination, which is simply the generalization of subqueries into a "superquery"
5. Most of these queries can be represented in other equivalent ways.

1.6 Relationship to Relational Databases

In this section, we briefly show the mapping between a relational database and its equivalent representation in CANDIDE.

1. Map an **extract** of an RDB onto a CANDIDE database (CDB). Provide all query processing through CDB. To make it viable, the classification process should be optimized. This is a workable solution for retrieval intensive databases where updates can be applied periodically, and a new extract created after each update.
2. Do a **total** mapping of an RDB into a CDB and support queries simultaneously on both databases. This again requires that classification be optimized. Furthermore, if on-line updating is supported, then each update must be correctly reflected in both the databases.
3. A third option, which coincides with the current trend in optimizing logic queries, is to map the queries in CDB after going through the classifier into appropriate **minimal** SQL queries. The execution of such queries is then left to the optimizer within the RDB.

The steps involved in mapping a relational schema into the CANDIDE data model are:

1. Each relation becomes a class, the attributes of the relation each become an attribute constraint with the EXACTLY 1 constraint to the domain of the attribute.
2. Tuples are mapped into instances of a class.
3. Add one additional attribute constraint to the class for a relation per every association to another relation via a foreign key.
4. The key of a relation is associated with the class name.
5. A class for a relation can have subclasses to express generalization and specialization.
6. The values within an attribute domain become instances of a class representing that attribute (except for primitive values such as integer or string). This enables complex domains to be built for the relational attributes.

With the above mapping, a semantic layer is created on top of an underlying relational database to simplify the end-user interface. Note that the inverse process of mapping our data model into the relational model cannot be done without loss of information. We are currently interfacing our model with the ORACLE relational database.

In the following sections we describe the application of CANDIDE object model to integrating a set of heterogeneous databases and to a document retrieval system.

2 Application to Heterogeneous Database Integration

This section discusses our efforts in applying the CANDIDE object model for integrating and querying a set of autonomous databases. A novel feature of this approach is that classification is used for schema integration as well as query evaluation.

2.1 Background Work in Heterogeneous Database Management

The need for shared access to autonomous and heterogeneous databases is discussed extensively in the literature [SL90]. Over the last several years numerous experimental and prototype systems have been built. The most important of these are Mermaid [TBC+87], MULTIBASE [LR82], CALIDA [JPSL+88], SIRIUS-DELTA [LBE+82], etc. These systems can be further categorized into tightly coupled systems and loosely coupled systems or federated systems depending on such issues as to who maintains and controls the global database and the degree of autonomy of the local databases. Several research efforts are also in progress currently. For example, Pegasus at HP [AAD+93], Carnot at MCC [WCH+93, CKRS91], etc. The excellent survey paper [SL90] discusses the terminology and concepts of federated database systems. In the present paper we discuss the motivation and implementation of a federated database system integrating a set of pre-existing and heterogeneous database systems.

During the past decade, significant progress has been made along many dimensions in this area. For example, the problems of interconnectivity involving heterogeneity at the hardware and systems level and access to remote data are no longer considered important. The problems of interoperability, distributed transaction management, recovery management, query optimization, etc., are well understood. However, experience in building heterogeneous database systems has shown that the problems due to semantic interoperability are much more difficult and are likely to become the main bottleneck in implementing fully operational federated database systems [She91].

The Federated Information Bases (FIB) project was motivated by the need to study the semantic interoperability problems encountered in federated systems and to provide solutions to these problems. We have chosen to ignore the issues of transaction management, cost based query optimization, etc, as many other research projects have devoted considerable attention to these aspects. FIB is based on the CANDIDE object model [BGN89]. It offers many unique advantages when applied to integration of databases. A novel feature of FIB is that classification is used to perform query validation, query evaluation and also schema integration.

2.2 Motivation

We discuss below some of the semantic interoperability problems in federated database systems. We give an overview of our approach to solving these problems and compare them with those discussed in the literature.

1. The main problem with real life database schemas is the lack of sufficient information contained explicitly within the schema. This can be attributed to two facts: (1) many of the data models such as the relational. hierarchical. and network models,

lack the power of abstraction necessary to express complex relationships between objects as well as structural and semantic constraints; (2) very often there is implicitly assumed information which is clear to the local users but must be explicitly specified for the global users. To overcome these problems, it is necessary to choose a global data model that has sufficient expressive power and clear semantics.

2. Another problem faced during database integration is that of capturing the interschema constraints. Most of these constraints are implicit or irrelevant in the component schemas but become evident when the database schemas are being merged. Traditionally, structural and semantic constraints have been contained in the application programs in database systems. However, owing to the complexity and size of the federated database systems it is most desirable to capture the constraints at the schema level, so that they are not only explicitly stated but can also be enforced during query processing.

3. A federated database system comprises many independent operational database systems. The component databases themselves undergo constant changes and modifications, with the result that the federated environment may become highly dynamic and may need frequent modifications. Owing to the difficulty of reintegrating the database systems, it is extremely important that the federated system be able to handle changes gracefully without necessitating a complex and expensive reintegration.

4. Schema integration is one of the most difficult problems to be handled during database integration due to the large number of schema objects and the lack of complete information in the database schemas. It is an expensive and cumbersome process for which no satisfactory solutions exist. We believe that the global data model should assist the system integrators in performing this function. We have developed a novel method for this operation by employing classification as a schema integration technique.

5. It has been pointed out that the most important future issues in heterogeneous database systems are not how efficiently data is processed but in determining what data is relevant and how to locate that data [She91]. With the ever increasing complexity in the data and applications, it is important for the future federated systems to provide support to the users in locating and retrieving the data in an intelligent manner.

2.3 Our Approach

In FIB, the problems arising due to semantic heterogeneity described above are solved by choosing a powerful global data model CANDIDE with reasoning capabilities. We capture the semantics and the complex relationships among the data objects by applying a more expressive model of information than the conventional semantic data models and uniformly exploit this richer semantic information to support a truly non-procedural and powerful query processing technique. The information contained in the underlying databases is automatically integrated into a taxonomy representing the global schema. Therefore the problems of semantic heterogeneity and semantic relativism present in the conventional approaches are alleviated. Further the structural integrity rules can be directly represented in the global schema, which captures both the intra-schema and inter-schema constraints. Since we can automatically organize the schema information, the problem of schema changes and modifications at the component database level, as well as schema integration are handled very gracefully by applying classification.

In the following sections, we discuss in more detail how the choice of the data model has helped alleviate the problems of semantic heterogeneity in FIB.

Capturing More Semantic Information. The global schema in a federated database system consists of all the underlying schemas. The underlying schemas by themselves are usually quite complex schemas. When such schemas are integrated, the resulting schema becomes highly complex. Some of the reasons for this are as below:

1. The component schemas model overlapping domains with possibly very different perspectives. These different perspectives are required to be reconciled. For example, one component database may contain customer credit data and the other may contain customer shopping data. However, there may be considerable overlap in the customer information they store.
2. The component schemas may model the the same domains at widely different levels of granularity, or different levels of abstraction. For example, two component databases may contain exports information. One of them may store it by the industry and the other may store it by the products.
3. The information in the component schemas may be disjoint but related to each other in complex ways. The global schema should contain these types of inter-schema relationships. For example, travel guides by say, Michelin and Fodor, may contain disjoint but related information.

Therefore it is necessary that the global data model be expressive enough to capture the above conceptual information explicitly so that the global users can understand the total information in the federation and exploit this understanding to query the federated system in a more intelligent form.

Schema Integration. In the context of FIB, we have developed a novel technique for schema integration based on the subsumption paradigm supported by CANDIDE. Schema integration is generally considered one of the important tasks in database integration. Numerous techniques have been proposed in the literature for database schema integration. The survey paper [BLN86] discusses a number of these methodologies. In most of these approaches, the schema integration is performed by the database administrator by specifying object relationships often in an *ad hoc* manner. The disadvantages of this approach are that the "correctness" of the resulting integrated schema cannot be guaranteed with the consequence that the structural information contained in the global schema cannot be used to deduce how a global query is to be processed.

In FIB, the global schema lattice is automatically generated guided by the attribute relationships provided by the database administrator. The resulting schema structure is "correct" with respect to the input to the schema integration module. A significant part of the difficult task of schema integration is now partially automated removing the burden from the database administrator.

The schema integration process is divided into two distinct phases. In the first phase, the user input in the form of attribute relationships is provided to the integration module. In the second phase, the classification and the subsumption techniques are employed to correctly deduce the object relationships automatically, and thus create the integrated schema. The relationships that are identified are: equivalent, overlap, subsume, disjoint, and unrelated. Schema merging operations are automatically applied to pairs of classes according to the nature of relationship between them to generate the merged schema.

Changes in the Global Schema. Since the federated database is a collection of loosely coupled databases, the global schema undergoes frequent changes. These changes are due to following reasons: (1) changes in the schemas of the underlying databases; (2) new component databases may be added to the federation or existing component databases may leave the federation. The federated database system must accommodate these constant changes in the global schema with as little disruption to the global users as possible. Accommodating frequent changes is also very important for scalability of the federated architecture.

In conventional approaches, any change in the underlying database schema necessitates re-integrating the component schemas again, since the effects of the change on the overall global schema cannot be determined precisely. This may be time-consuming and cumbersome and possibly require lengthy down time of the federated system.

In the case of FIB, the object relationships are automatically detected. Therefore, any changes in the underlying component schemas require only re-classification of the entire global schema along with any new attribute correspondences. This requires very little amount of work since specifying the attribute correspondences for the changed schema is expected to be quite small and classification is an entirely automatic process.

Querying the Global Schema. The classification based query processing technique in CANDIDE solves the problem of querying the global database by providing a reasoning capability which does not depend on the explicit target class names but rather on the structural description of the object being requested. The user states the intensional properties of the query object and the system automatically decides what classes if any satisfy the specified properties.

This paradigm provides a powerful capability to hide the schematic complexity of the underlying databases. The user does not have to be familiar with the details of the integrated schema of the federation. Together with a directory of the entire federation, all the data satisfying a given query are automatically retrieved from the component databases and presented to the user.

Rejection of Null Queries. Query evaluation in a federated database system is considerably expensive compared to a centralized database. The global query is decomposed into subqueries, translated into queries in the DML of the component databases, executed against the respective component databases, the resulting data formats are translated into a common format and the results are combined which may involve some expensive operations like join. The communication overhead incurred is also considerable. The response time for global queries suffers further if the component databases are geographically dispersed.

In FIB, all queries are validated against the global schema and those queries which potentially have null results are not considered further. This saves substantial amount of work and time if the given query happens to be logically inconsistent. A valid query object has to be subsumed by at least one class in the global class lattice.

We shall show later in Section 3.2 under inexact querying how by successive generalization, a query may be modified so as to produce answers (possibly intensional) to queries that are an approximation of the original query. That kind of "knowledge discovery" approach may be superimposed on top of the existing FIB query processor.

2.4 Schema Integration Using CANDIDE

The subsumption and classification functions supported by the global data model are also used for performing schema integration. In most other systems schema integration is treated as a separate process. However, for the reasons of scalability and schema modification mentioned above, we consider schema integration as an integral part of the federated database system. In this section we describe the extensions to classification for performing schema integration.

Two classes c_1 and c_2 can be related by one of the following relationship types: c_1 **equals** c_2, c_1 **includes** (or **is-included-in**) c_2, c_1 **overlaps** c_2, and c_1 **is-disjoint-with** c_2. It can be seen that the **subsume** function described above computes **includes** relationship. That is,

subsume$(c_1, c_2) \equiv$ **includes**$(c_1, c_2) \equiv$ **is-included-in**(c_2, c_1).

The other relationships can be computed as follows:

equals$(c_1, c_2) =$ **subsume**$(c_1, c_2) \wedge$ **subsume**(c_2, c_1).

overlaps$(c_1, c_2) = \neg$**subsume**$(c_1, c_2) \wedge \neg$**subsume**$(c_2, c_1) \wedge \neg$ **is-disjoint-with**(c_1, c_2).

Two classes are defined as disjoint if the intersection of all possible extensions of the two classes is empty. That is, there cannot exist an object which is an instance of both the classes. This is computed as shown below:

is-disjoint-with$(c_1, c_2) =$ **incoherent**(**conjunction**(c_1, c_2)).

Where **conjunction** is a function that returns a new class such that the extension of the new class is the intersection of the possible extensions of the given classes. **incoherent** is a boolean function which tests for the logical consistency of the constraints on the attributes of a given class [PS84b]. It essentially means tha the extension of the given class is null. The incoherency of a class is computed by checking if the given class is subsumed by a system defined incoherent class.

All the functions described above are boolean functions which are defined in terms of the subsumption function. Depending on the class relationships computed as described above, restructuring operators are applied to the classes. The following restructuring operators are defined: **delete**(c_1), **generalize_1**(c_1, c_2), **generalize_2**(c_1, c_2), **specialize_1**(c_1, c_2), and **specialize_2**(c_1, c_2). The **delete** operator deletes the given class from the integrated schema and checks the resulting schema for consistency. The **generalize** operators create a new class such that the extension of this class is a union of the extensions of the given classes by choosing only the common attributes of the given classes and taking a logical disjunction of the constraints on them. The resulting class is checked for incoherency. **generalize_2** is same as **generalize_1** except that the given classes are deleted from the integrated schema. The **specialize** operators create a new class such that its extension is an intersection of the extensions of the given classes by choosing the union of the attributes of the given classes and the constraints on the common attributes are logical conjunction of the constraints in the given classes. The resulting class is checked for incoherency. **specialize_2** is same as **specialize_1** except that the given classes are deleted from the integrated schema.

The schema integration process is driven by the attribute relationships provided by the database administrator. Two attributes a_1 and a_2 may be related as follows: a_1 **is-equivalent-to** a_2, a_1 **is-above** a_2, a_1 **is-below** a_2 or they may be unrelated. These attribute relationships cannot be determined automatically, hence they are specified during schema integration. The attribute relationships between individual pairs of attributes are used to generate the attribute hierarchy for the integrated schema. The integrated schema is a lattice where each descending node of a given node (i.e., the subclasses of a given class) can belong to a different component database.

A detailed discussion of the approach to schema integration based on capturing the semantics of the underlying databases is given in [SGN93]. A schema integration tool based on this approach has been implemented as discussed in [Sav90, SSG+91].

2.5 System Architecture

There are two kinds of users in FIB, namely, local users and universal users. Each IS has its own local users, and the universal user can virtually access any portion of the FIB subject to schema constraints (i.e., constraints implied by the underlying integrated schema). The FIB system architecture is shown in Fig. 4.

The user interface allows a global user to browse the global schema and formulate queries in the Request Description Language (RDL). RDL is an extension of the CANDIDE DDL and includes constructs to specify additional information for executing global queries. The global query is decomposed into a number of subqueries each of which is an independent query against a component database. The results of the subquery must be combined to generate the final results. The result combination phase may involve complex operations such as joins, etc. In FIB, the result combination is performed by one of the component databases by creating temporary tables for the subquery results. We have adapted the Distributed Operations Language (DOL) and the Transaction Execution Supervisor [ROE+90] for coordinating the execution of the subqueries. The functions of different components of FIB are discussed below.

The query processor is responsible for accepting the user queries and generating the subqueries. It performs the following tasks.

1. Validates whether a user request is meaningful by classifying the query object against the global schema. If the request is found to be invalid or valid but null, it is rejected. This operation is performed by the query validation processor.
2. The global query is decomposed into a number of subqueries. Each subquery can be independently executed against a component database. The query decomposition processor performs this task with the help of the global catalog.

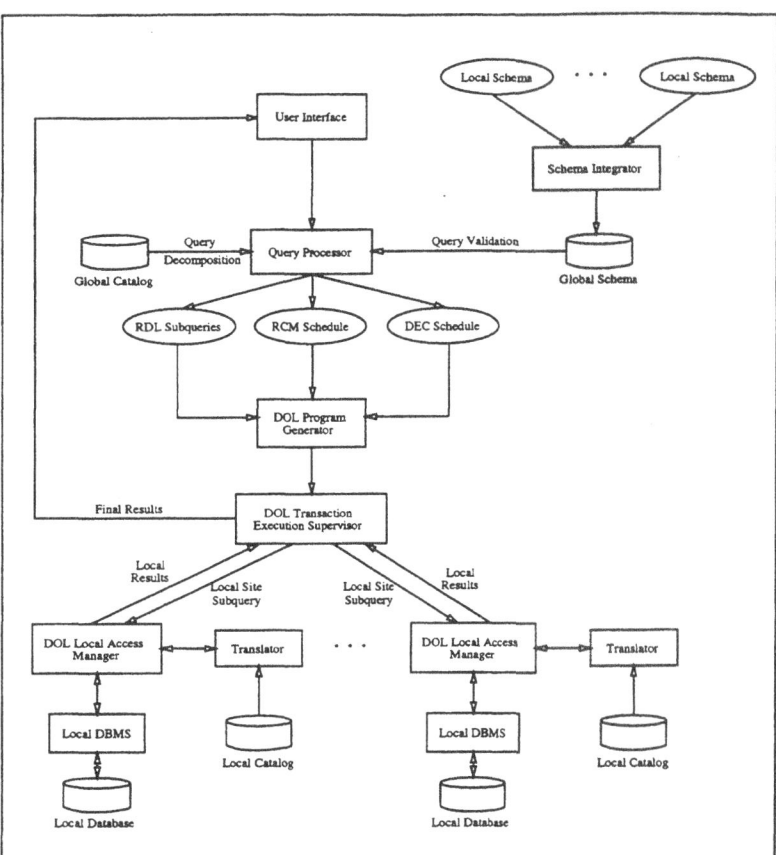

Fig. 4. FIB system architecture

3. The subqueries contain dependencies among them (e.g., some subrequest must be executed before another) as well as parallelism. The scheduling processor detects the dependencies and parallelism, if any and generates a schedule for all the subqueries.
4. The results of subqueries must be combined to generate the final results for the global query. The result combination may include operations such as joins, etc. The result combination is performed by one of the component databases. The scheduling processor generates a schedule for the result combination operations.

The DOL program generator module generates the DOL program to be executed by the DOL transaction execution supervisor. The subquery requests as well as the result combination operations are embedded in the generated DOL program. The execution order of subqueries and the sequencing information is encoded in the DOL program.

The DOL transaction execution supervisor coordinates the execution of the subrequests as specified by the DOL program. First it sets up connections with the DOL Local Access Managers (LAM) residing at the component database sites. Next, it sends the subrequests to the specified LAMs in the specified order. It also sets up connections between different LAMs for receiving the subrequest results.

The subrequest received by a LAM is also in RDL. This subrequest must be translated into a query against the local database. The translator residing locally at each component database site accepts an RDL subquery and translates it into a query in the local DBMS DML. The local catalog contains information necessary for this translation. The LAM executes the translated query against the local database and accepts the results. The subquery results are then translated into the standard data format and sent to the result combination site as specified by the DOL program.

The result combination is performed at a suitable site. The LAM executes the result combination operations as it would execute a subquery. First, it waits for the partial results from all the local databases against which the subqueries are issued. It then creates temporary tables for the partial results and performs result combination operations. The final results are sent to the user interface.

3 The Storage and Retrieval of Structured Documents

Documents, such as technical manuals, memoranda, circulars, fact sheets and handbooks are substantial sources of information. In recent years there has been an increasing need to find alternate techniques to manage the plethora of documents controlled by organizations. This has led to the conversion of documents into electronic format for ease of management. The establishment of two sets of international standards, the ODA (Office Document Architecture) and SGML (Standard Generalized Markup Language), have significantly impacted the way documents are modeled and managed. As documents conforming to these standards are converted into electronic form, the resulting electronic library provides not only more efficient document storage and retrieval techniques, but also a potential for greater utilization of structural knowledge contained in the documents. The document analysis is a knowledge extraction and acquisition activity which can lend to the representation of that knowledge in a knowledge representation language. It yields two benefits:

1. The knowledge contained in the document can be better represented.
2. The *ad hoc* document search and retrieval process can be improved by applying some reasoning techniques to the knowledge.

In this section we will point out the utility of CANDIDE as a knowledge representation and data modeling language in this context.

Conventional text retrieval systems do not have the flexibility to handle the more complex view of documents as proposed by the ISO standards mentioned above. Moreover, record-oriented database systems such as the relational data model cannot adequately model the hierarchical structure of a document because this structure does not conform to the tabular format expected by such data models. Consequently, it seems apparent that any future document management should be based on the semantic or object-oriented data models rather than on extensions to conventional database management systems.

In this section we demonstrate the use of CANDIDE for the storage and retrieval of documents. All structural details of the document as marked by SGML can be reflected by defining the structure of the database in CANDIDE. The content and attributes of a document are uniformly modeled within CANDIDE. Moreover, an inexact querying capability has been implemented that assists the user in retrieving information from the database that is subjective and is based on incomplete specification. This spares the user from continuously refining the original query until retrieval results are satisfactory. Such a facility is critical for naive users or users who are unfamiliar with the contents of the database.

The remainder of this section is organized as follows. Section 5.1 overviews the two relevant ISO standards. Section 5.2 surveys some popular document retrieval systems. Section 5.3 illustrates the application of CANDIDE to document databases. Section 5.4 illustrates the use of inexact querying in the retrieval of documents. Conclusions and implementation status appear in Sect. 5.5.

3.1 ISO Document Standards

The establishment of two sets of international standards, the ODA (Office Document Architecture) [ISO86] and SGML (Standard Generalized Markup Language) [Org6E], have significantly impacted the way documents are viewed. The two most important aspects of these standards relate to the organization of documents and their components and to the structuring of information within documents, respectively.

The SGML standard deals with document content. It views documents as a hierarchic structure. So instead of a document being viewed as an ordered list of terms, it is considered to consist of certain elements which may in turn consist of other elements, and so on. For example, a document may consist of a title, information about the authors, date of publication, and a set of sections. Each section may in turn consist of several subsections and so on. Moreover, attributes may be associated with certain elements of the document to further qualify them. Such a structure is captured by a *document type definition* (DTD). Consider the document type definition of a simple memorandum in Fig. 5.

This DTD indicates that a memorandum consists of a "front," "body" and possibly a "close." The "front" consists of a "to," "from," "date" and "subject" component, in any particular order. The memo has an attribute "status" which indicates whether this is a confidential or public memo. The "body" consists of one or more paragraphs ("para") An example of a memorandum that conforms to this DTD is given in Fig. 6.

The ODA standard deals with the existence of a logical view of a document; a view in the sense of its abstract components which may or may not correspond to the elements described in the SGML standard. Thus, documents are defined by means of their generic logical structure with a specific logical structure for individual documents. The generic structure is the template that guides the creation of a document, similar to the way that a DTD guides the markup of a document. This structure consists of components called objects. Objects are classified as either basic, in the sense that they are indivisible, or as composite which in turn consist of other (possibly composite) objects. Each object may have several attributes associated with it. These attributes express a characteristic of an object or a relationship with one or more other objects. Moreover, these objects

```
⟨!DOCTYPE memo  [
    ⟨!ELEMENT    memo    - -  (front, body, close?)                    ⟩
    ⟨!ELEMENT    front   - -  (to & from & date & subj)                ⟩
    ⟨!ELEMENT    body    - -  ( para + )                               ⟩
    ⟨!ELEMENT    to      - O  (#PCDATA)                                ⟩
    ⟨!ELEMENT    from    - O  (#PCDATA)                                ⟩
    ⟨!ELEMENT    date    - O  (#PCDATA)                                ⟩
    ⟨!ELEMENT    subj    - O  (#PCDATA)                                ⟩
    ⟨!ELEMENT    para    - O  (#PCDATA)                                ⟩
    ⟨!ELEMENT    close   - O  (salut | #PCDATA)                        ⟩
    ⟨!ELEMENT    salut   - O  (#PCDATA)                                ⟩
    ⟨!ATTLIST    memo    status (confidential | public) "public"       ⟩
]⟩
```

Fig. 5. A simple memorandum DTD

are classified into groups of similar objects; that is, object classes. These object classes are specifications of the set of properties that are common to its members. Such a specification consists of a set of rules to determine attribute values that specify the common properties. These rules can be used to control the consistency among objects.

The structure that is particular to a document is called the specific logical structure. This structure identifies the objects that constitute a particular document instance. Therefore, the generic logical structure of a document can be used as a set of rules from which a specific logical structure can be derived or validated.

Conventional Text Retrieval Systems. In conventional systems, Documents are retrieved on the basis of the correspondence between search terms expressed in a query and index terms of the document. The query language of these systems are geared toward this one purpose. Conventional text retrieval systems search for exact matches in the text. These systems have no knowledge of the meaning of text (other than the possible synonyms that might be stored in the thesaurus). Moreover, such systems cannot interpret grammatical constructs like words or phrases.

While the approach utilized by conventional text retrieval systems is very attractive because of its simplicity, it has the following shortcomings:

– There is a very restrictive view of content as an ordered list of terms, each of which can be looked up in an index. Such a scheme does not capture document structure as modeled in an SGML application.
– It does not permit the establishment of relationships that originate between documents and other objects. Relationships such as citations and graphics which might appear in a document cannot be modeled in this environment.
– Conventional systems utilize query languages that are geared for simple text retrieval of either whole documents or portions thereof. This level of functionality

```
⟨memo status="public"⟩
⟨front⟩
⟨to⟩            Distribution      ⟨/to⟩
⟨from⟩          President         ⟨/from⟩
⟨date⟩          May 1, 1993       ⟨/date⟩
⟨subject⟩       Workplace Attire ⟨/subject⟩ ⟨/front⟩
⟨body⟩ ⟨para⟩   In accordance with Human Resource Management Policy, all
                employees are required to conduct and present themselves
                at all times in a highly professional manner. Our University
                takes great pride in its professional image and considers
                certain attire unacceptable. This includes, but is not
                limited to: shorts, tank tops, halter tops, T shirts and
                torn clothing. ⟨/para⟩
⟨para⟩          If there are any questions regarding this matter please
                contact your respective Department Chairman. ⟨/para⟩ ⟨/body⟩
⟨close⟩         John Smith ⟨/close⟩
⟨/memo⟩
```

Fig. 6. An example marked-up memo

is not powerful enough for retrieval operations or as a basis for applications other than pure retrieval.

Using The Relational Data Model. The relational data model presumes *horizontal* and *vertical* homogeneity in data. That is, each record of a given type contains the same fields (horizontal homogeneity) and a given field contains the same type of information (vertical homogeneity)[Ken79]. Record-based systems provide an excellent tool for processing information that fits a certain pattern; in the case of the relational data model this pattern is tabular. Moreover, each entry in a relation must represent a single atomic piece of data (if the relation is to be in first normal form). Typically, documents have a complex hierarchical structure that does not naturally map to a relational representation. Consequently, the following shortcomings exist [Ken79, Mac90, Mac91b]:

- **Primary Key**. All instances (tuples) within a relational database are uniquely identified by one or more attribute values (primary key). Document attributes do not generally possess attributes that uniquely identify a document and thus an artificial key must be introduced. This will entail maintaining yet another attribute by the user.
- **Multi-valued Data**. A significant problem in the relational model arises when multi-valued attributes are part of a single real world object. The object gets decomposed into a number of distinct parts each of which is stored as a row in some table. The only way to eliminate such repeated data is through normalization. This will require the information to be split over more than one table. Unfortunately, the result of this decomposition is to make the retrieval of documents more difficult because

of the more complicated queries. Because textual information does not lend itself
to normalization, a compromise position is to create views of the fully normalized
data which permit the data to be viewed more simply.

- **Textual Attributes**. Text differs from other attributes in that while a body of text
  may be the value of a single attribute in its own right, the ordering of words
  within the text must also be preserved and utilized. To efficiently access individual
  words within the string data type, it is necessary to build a relation capturing the
  ordinal relationship existing between words and the strings containing them. This
  retrieval process then will require an extensive use of join operations which are
  very expensive computationally.
- **Hierarchical Structure**. Documents typically have complex hierarchical structures. This view can be modeled relationally at the cost of some query complexity
  and is not practical. The basic problem with the relational data model is that the
  internal representation of a document can often be quite different from the external representation. Because the structure of the data is not naturally tabular, a
  consequence of the normalization process is to cause components of the object to
  be dispersed over several relations. To retrieve the original document, the disjoint
  pieces must be explicitly reassembled which requires knowledge of the underlying
  organization of the database. In all cases, the use of record structures depends on
  supplementary information, often reflected only in special-purpose application programs which may or may not be known by the users of the data and therefore do
  not provide the semantically self-describing base needed for conceptual schemas.
- **Ordering**. A key issue in capturing the structure of the document is the ordering of
  its components, not just at the text level but the subcomponent level. By definition,
  a relation is a set of tuples; that is, there is no order associated with tuples in
  a relation. While the relational data model does not directly support ordering of
  information, ordering can be specified in a relation by maintaining an extra field in
  the relational representation. Such a solution will necessarily complicate document
  representation.

3.2 Document Databases in CANDIDE

Schema Design Issues. There are a number of design issues peculiar to a document
database. To design a database specifically for storing documents, it must be structured
in a way reflecting the structure of the documents. Tagged documents by themselves
are not suitable as a database since searching through tags would be cumbersome
and inefficient. The database makes the tagged structure of the document explicit and
provides a way to rapidly access parts of the document, or search and retrieve over a large
collection of documents. The translation process of SGML documents into CANDIDE
is described more fully in [BWA92]. To share SGML documents the database should
support the following functions [BWA92]:

- All structural details of the document as marked by SGML must be reflected in the
  structure of the database. That is, rather than store each document in the database
  as an SGML file, tagged information is extracted from he document as stored in
  database objects. These complex objects reflect the structure of the document while
  providing greater flexibility in manipulating documents.

- The ability to reconstruct a complete document and identify its structure from the information stored in the database. This ensures that the document's integrity is maintained during translation.
- The ability to store the DTD rules in the database. This facilitates the use of the DTD. It also facilitates the comparison of different DTDs, such as a specialization of a particular DTD for use in a particular class of documents for a specific organization.
- To provide an appropriate level of granularity and identifiable information units for retrieval. A document is typically decomposed into a number of smaller units. This "chunking" is typical of hypertext systems in which pieces of the document must be retrieved. If the level of granularity is too coarse, too much information is retrieved at once, and the user must spend additional time searching within the retrieved unit. If the level of granularity is too fine, an explosion occurs in the number of units to be tracked. Moreover, each unit must be referenced and identified in some way. This permits units to be retrieved in response to a query.

To illustrate these criteria, we now show how the memorandum DTD of Fig. 5 may be represented in CANDIDE in Fig. 7 and how a memo DTD may be represented in CANDIDE in Fig. 8.

Memorandum
    PRIMITIVE
    SUPERCLASSES: Document
    INSTANCES: Memo_1
    ATTRIBUTE RESTRICTIONS:
        FROM: EXACT 1 CLASS Employee
        TO: SOME 1 CLASS Person
        DATE: EXACT 1 DOMAIN STRING
        SUBJECT: EXACT 1 DOMAIN STRING
        STATUS: EXACT 1 SET "Public," "Confidential"
        CLOSE: MAX 1 SET
            {DOMAIN STRING,
            COMPOSITE (SALUT: EXACT 1 DOMAIN STRING)}
        BODY: SOME 1 ORDERED_SET CLASS Para
Para
    PRIMITIVE
    SUPERCLASSES: Document Component
    INSTANCES: Para_1, Para_2
    ATTRIBUTE RESTRICTIONS:
        PARTOF: EXACT 1 CLASS Document
        BODY: EXACT 1 DOMAIN STRING

Fig. 7. A model for a document database corresponding to the Memo DTD

Example_Memo
    PARENTS: Memorandum
    ATTRIBUTES:
        FROM: President
        TO: CLASS Employee
        DATE: "May 1, 1993"
        SUBJECT: "Workplace Attire"
        CLOSE: "John Smith"
        STATUS: "Public"
        BODY: ORDERED_SET(Para_1, Para_2)

Para_1
    PARENTS: Document Component
    ATTRIBUTES:
        PARTOF: Example_Memo
        BODY: "In accordance with Human Resource......."

Para_2
    PARENTS: Document Component
    ATTRIBUTES:
        PARTOF: Example_Memo
        BODY:"If there are any ...."

Fig. 8. Objects representing the Example_Memo in CANDIDE

More formally, a memorandum is broken down into two objects. One object represents the top level of the memorandum. This object contains the attributes FROM, TO, DATE, SUBJECT, CLOSE, STATUS and BODY. The domain of FROM and TO is the class Employee; that is, only instances from this class can instantiate this attribute. Moreover, the FROM attribute must have *exactly one* (EXACT 1) value from the class Employee while the TO attribute must have at *least one* (SOME 1) instance from the class Person. DATE and SUBJECT accept exactly one value of type string. The CLOSE attribute accepts *at most* one value of type string or a composite attribute SALUT. Thus, the CLOSE attribute may be NULL. The SALUT attribute accepts exactly one value of type string. The STATUS attribute can accept one of two possible values from the set {"Public", "Confidential"} The BODY attribute of this object is an ordered set (ORDERED_SET) of at least one instance from the class Para. Thus, the value of the BODY attribute contains references to the paragraph instances that constitute the memorandum. The Para class contains all instances of paragraph objects in the database. Instances of the class Para contain two attributes. The first attribute, PARTOF, determines which document this particular paragraph belongs to. Notice that the domain of this attribute is the class Document. This indicates that this type of object may be used in more than one document class, not only that of Memorandum. The BODY attribute of Para has exactly one value of type string.

While the memorandum DTD is a simple one, it contains the three different contexts which can be modeled in a DTD (ordered, unordered, optional) which were successfully modeled by the two object classes (as shown in Fig. 7). Moreover, CANDIDE objects are declarative in the sense that they reflect the actual structure of the memorandum in contrast to hiding this structure within application programs that manipulate relational tables mentioned earlier. In addition, the attribute/content dichotomy does not exist in CANDIDE; all information concerning a document is uniformly modeled within a CANDIDE database.

Querying. To illustrate the use of CANDIDE in querying a document database, consider the following query class:

Query 1
    SUPERCLASSES: Para
    ATTRIBUTE RESTRICTIONS:
        PARTOF: EXACT 1 Memorandum
        BODY: "Professional image"

This query is a subclass of Para and its instances are all those paragraphs that are contained in exactly one memorandum and contain the phrase "professional image" To process this query the classifier (using the subsumption function) would begin at class Para and attempt to find other subclasses of Para that subsume the Query 1 class. Since there are no classes more specialized than Para, no additional searching is required. The next step is to test each instance of the class Para to see if it meets the attribute constraints of the Query object (realization). The result of the query is a set of instances that satisfy the conditions specified in the query class. The query class may, if so desired, be inserted permanently into the database. Special attention must be paid to the subsumption function and the way it interprets the ORDERED_SET type constructor. We define that, an ordered set A subsumes another ordered set B if every element in B is in A and the relative ordering of each element in B is preserved in A. Thus, under this definition, the ordered set $\{a, b, c, d\}$ subsumes the ordered set $\{b, d\}$, but not $\{c, a\}$, for example. Formally,

$$SUBSUME(A, B) = \text{TRUE iff } B \subseteq A \ \wedge \ \{\forall x, y \mid x \in B, y \in B, x \neq y,$$
$$REL\_ORD(x, y, B) = REL\_ORD(x, y, A)\} \qquad (1)$$

where $REL\_ORD(x, y, Z)$ is a binary function (relative order) that returns TRUE if element x precedes element y in the ordered set Z, otherwise it is FALSE. Under this implementation, a string is considered to be a special case of the ordered set construct. Thus the string "This is a string" would subsume the string "this string" "a string" and so on, but, would not subsume the string "is this" because the relative ordering of the two words is not the same in the two strings.

Inexact Querying. Conventional queries manipulate databases to retrieve sets of instances that completely satisfy the conditions specified in a query. Recently, more attention has been given to inexact queries in which instances are retrieved that partially match a query [Mot88, Mot90, ABN92, ABN91, BGN89]. Such a facility improves user-system interaction by providing more informative answers to queries that do not match any instance in the database. Rather than returning a null answer to such a query, the system retrieves instances that are somehow similar to the conditions specified in the query. Moreover, users may prefer or be forced to formulate their queries in such a way in which an inexact match is preferred. For example, it might be advantageous to find all documents that most closely match a request submitted by a user, even though no one document would completely satisfy the request. Without this capability the user will be forced to emulate such a request by repeatedly submitting that query with alternative values. If these alternative values are not known, even this approach becomes infeasible. Thus, the need for such a facility is greater for naive users of a database.

A facility for inexact querying has been implemented which retrieves instances that are structurally (correspondence between object components), semantically (correspondences in meaning), and pragmatically (relevancy to the goal, query object) similar to the query even though they may not match the query exactly [ABN92, ABN91, BGN89]. The query processor has a deductive and inductive component. The deductive component finds exact matches in the traditional sense as mentioned in the previous section. A query object is specified in the same notation as other database class objects. As we know, query processing occurs in CANDIDE by classifying the query object to determine its correct place in the class taxonomy. The classifier deductively finds the most specific classes that logically subsume the new class and the most general classes subsumed by the new class. A realization function is used to determine whether an instance meets an existing class description. Only instances of the immediate superclasses are considered.

The inductive component identifies ways in which inexact matches may be generated. The inductive component generates new class descriptions from the original query. This is done by generalizing the constraints specified in the query in different *directions* and to different *levels*. The inexact querying algorithm thus automatically generates a class taxonomy and groups instances into classes. The inexact query algorithm is triggered by a null answer in response to the initial query. That is, if no instances in the database satisfy the conditions stated in the query, the system will try to find instances that partially satisfy the query.

The algorithm consists of the following steps:

– The original query is generalized by relaxing the attribute restrictions stated in the query. This is done by selectively relaxing the value set constraints and the cardinality constraints stated in attribute restrictions. Several new query objects can be generated.

– These generalized query objects are then classified in the taxonomy and the realization function is used to determine whether instances satisfy these query objects.

– If no instances satisfy these generalized queries, the process is repeated for each generalized query until either all conditions are dropped (last step of generalization) or instances satisfy any of the queries.

Essentially, this technique follows up the failed query with several more general queries. This process is continued until a match is found. To illustrate this process consider the following query:

Query2
    SUPERCLASSES: Memorandum
    ATTRIBUTE RESTRICTIONS:
        FROM: SOME 1 CLASS Professor
        TO: SOME 2 CLASS Grad

This query is a subclass of Memorandum and will retrieve all instances of Memorandum that are issued by at least one Professor to at least two graduate students. If no instances of Memorandum satisfy these conditions, the previous query will be generalized into three other query objects shown below. Notice that all these query objects will necessarily subsume the original query.

Query3
    SUPERCLASSES: Memorandum
    ATTRIBUTE RESTRICTIONS:
        FROM: SOME 1 CLASS Faculty
        TO: SOME 2 CLASS Grad
Query4
    SUPERCLASSES: Memorandum
    ATTRIBUTE RESTRICTIONS:
        FROM: SOME 1 CLASS Professor
        TO: SOME 1 CLASS Grad
Query5
    SUPERCLASSES: Memorandum
    ATTRIBUTE RESTRICTIONS:
        FROM: SOME 1 CLASS Professor
        TO: SOME 2 CLASS Student

Query3 was generated by generalizing the value set domain of the first attribute restriction without modifying any other restriction. Therefore, this query will retrieve all instances of the Memorandum class that were issued by at least one *faculty member* to at least two graduate students. The class Faculty subsumes and is therefore more general than the class Professor. Notice that the cardinality constraint of the first attribute restriction (SOME 1) cannot be generalized any further. Query4 was generated by generalizing the cardinality constraint of the second attribute restriction and it will retrieve all instances of Memorandum that were issued by at least one Professor to *at least* one graduate student (instead of two). Query5 was obtained by relaxing the value set constraint of the second attribute restriction. Hence, Query5 will retrieve all instances of Memorandum that were issued by at least one Professor to at least two *students* (Student subsumes Grad).

The result of the inexact querying process is not only a set of instances but also a schema that describes those data instances. This is an *intensional answer* to a query [ABN92, ABN91]. The resultant schema can be regarded as an 'abstracted answer' to the query. Conceptually, this abstracted answer is much more informative, in the sense that it is easier to comprehend by the user, than to abstract an intension from a set of instances. A distinct feature of this approach is that the intensional answer is specified in the data definition language (in the form of a schema) as opposed to predicates in other techniques. Therefore, we are able to utilize the full expressive power of the semantic data model to describe these instances.

Concluding Remarks on CANDIDE for Document Processing. A document ana- lyzer has been incorporated which extracts structural and conceptual information (i.e. syntactic and semantic information) from a document and represents this information using structural knowledge representation language of CANDIDE. The document an- alyzer and database have been implemented from the point where WordPerfect files are created containing tags, these tagged documents are converted to an SGML format and then these SGML files are translated into database objects. So far documents are obtained after being generated using this word processing package. Tags are inserted into the document as they are created on the word processor. The first service provided by the document analyzer is to convert tagged documents into database objects. This is accomplished by using a software tool we call "the translator". The translator parses documents by using the rules contained in the DTD. The resulting parse tree is then mapped onto the database objects. Any errors in tagging, such as omitting a tag or placing a sub-section tag out of sequence, are trapped by the translator in much the same way as a compiler catches errors in the source code of a program. A commercial software package, XGML [Cor91] is being used for document translation.

At the University of Florida's Institute of Food and Agricultural Sciences (IFAS), CD-ROM technology is used as a primary vehicle for electronic dissemination of exten- sion information to agricultural extension centers. Most significant reduction of labor required to build text databases has resulted from the work reported here. The manual processing (chunking, referencing) of documents has practically been eliminated by au- tomatic document analysis. This will greatly reduce a major bottleneck in development of CD-ROM text databases, and increase the flow of information from printed text into electronic libraries.

In conclusion, the use of the CANDIDE has enabled us to model all structural details of the document as required by the ODA and SGML international standards. The ensuing database objects reflect the structure of the document while providing greater flexibility in manipulating documents. Moreover, the DDL and DML of CANDIDE are unified into one which will allow the query language to utilize the semantics of the schema in the processing of queries. In addition, an inexact querying capability has been implemented that assists the user in retrieving information from the database that is subjective. This spares the user from continuously refining the original query until retrieval results are satisfactory. Such a facility is critical for naive users.

Further research is currently being conducted to enhance the retrieval capabilities of the system by incorporating a natural language component. We consider this to be the next step in document analysis. The knowledge of the structure of the document fails to help in concept-based retrieval in which the text is analyzed for semantic concepts not just syntactic structure [BGN89]. Such an enhancement will necessarily be more computationally intensive and a compromise must be reached between the processing requirements and the quality of answers generated.

4 Natural Language Query Interface to CANDIDE

Much of the material in this section is derived from [BGN89]. Traditionally, natural language query systems are interfaced to a database management system via an intermediate query language. Even in the most recent systems such as KID [IIY+87] which do support a rich model for domain semantics, the objective is to translate the natural language query into a formal query language such as SQL. There are a number of disadvantages to this approach. The sentences accepted by the system can be no more expressive than the formal language, thus the interface is limited to the scope of SQL expressions. Also, there is poor integration between the database and the language understanding subsystems. This means that much of the semantic information in the database structure cannot be used to interpret sentences. Finally, translation into the formal query language may be an awkward task since most database query languages are not designed for representing natural language expressions.

In contrast, it is easier to map the structure of natural language sentences into the objects of a data model such as the one we have presented than to map into query languages like SQL. Since the objects also act as the query language, the additional step of converting into another formal query language is eliminated. Furthermore, database objects can be used by the language processor to interpret sentences. Thus *the semantics of the database play an active and direct role in language understanding.*

Our approach to natural language understanding is based on *integrating syntax, semantics, and world knowledge.* This integration allows many sources of information to be applied to understanding queries, reducing ambiguity and enhancing meaning. In order to achieve this integration, we have coupled a natural language grammar formalism known as the lexical-functional grammar, or LFG [KB82] with the data model. This enables the LFG parsing algorithm to incorporate data objects which can be used for enforcing word meanings. Thus the objects in the database must represent word meanings as well as physical data.

LFG consists of standard context-free grammar rules augmented by functional forms which act as constraints. In addition, a lexicon includes the terminal symbols (words), their possible pre-terminals (parts of speech), and functional forms which couple words to objects in the database and add additional constraints. Parse trees are generated subject to the constraints of the functional forms. These constraints include agreement with the structure of objects in the database. For example, a verb may have case arguments (subject, direct object, indirect object) which map into the attributes of a class object for the verb as specified in the lexicon. Values for these arguments must satisfy the constraints on these attributes.

Each word in the sentence is associated with a database object, and may have more than one lexical entry, corresponding to different word senses, parts of speech, and other grammatical functions. For example, the verb "teach" would have lexical entries such as:

    teach, verb,   tense = present
      predicate = Instruct(subject: Teacher, object: Course)

    teach, verb,   tense = present
      predicate = Instruct(subject: Teacher, object: Student)

    teach, verb,   tense = present
      predicate = Instruct(subject: Teacher, object: Level)

In this example, each entry corresponds to a present tense verb. The first entry corresponds to the sense of a teacher teaching a course as in "Mr. Smith teaches physics," the second to a teacher teaching a student as in "Mr. Smith teaches Judy," and the third to teaching a grade level as in "Mr Smith teaches third grade." Each entry is associated with a database object. As shown in the predicate associated with each word, "teach" is mapped to the database object Instruct. A predicate can also have arguments. In this case, "subject" and "object" refer to the subject and object of the sentence which are identified by grammar rules. In addition, the arguments are labeled with database objects. The values for the arguments must correspond to the domains of these objects. Thus, in each case the subject must be an instance of Teacher. The following example shows the steps in mapping an English sentence into query objects:

Example 7. Which professors teach courses in engineering?

The phrase structure analysis for this sentence produced by the LFG parser is:

    SENTENCE
        NOUN PHRASE
            ADJECTIVE Which
            NOUN Professor
        VERB PHRASE
            VERB Teach NOUN PHRASE
                NOUN Course
                PREPOSITIONAL PHRASE
                PREPOSITION In
                NOUN Engineering

The subject noun phrase "which professors" and object noun phrase "courses in engineering" are identified by the grammar rules. The sense of the main verb "teach" corresponds with the first lexical entry given above since the subject "professor" fills the domain of Teacher, and the object "courses" fills the domain for Course. The other lexical entries would be rejected since the object cannot fill the domain for Student or Level. Since the verb "teach" is associated with the database object Instruct, a query class can be created by using Instruct as a template. The labels for the subject and object of the predicate are matched with attribute constraints:

Query1
    CLASS DEFINED
    SUPERCLASS Instruct
    ATTRIBUTE CONSTRAINTS
        Teacher: ATLEAST 1 DOMAIN CLASS Professor
        Course: ATLEAST 1 DOMAIN CLASS Query2

where the concept Course is expanded into Query2. The prepositional phrase "in engineering" modifies "course" so Engineering must be related to Course. Since Engineering is in the domain for the Department attribute of Course (i.e., the Course is being offered by a Department in the Engineering), Query2 can be created:

Query2
    CLASS DEFINED
    SUPERCLASS Course
    ATTRIBUTE CONSTRAINTS
        Department: ATLEAST 1 DOMAIN CLASS Engineering

This example illustrates how query objects can be generated from the natural language sentence, and how the database objects play a direct role in interpreting the sentence.

5 Implementation of CANDIDE on Secondary Storage

5.1 Requirements

Large information retrieval systems containing heterogeneous information place great demands on secondary storage systems. In addition to storing large number of objects, the secondary storage manager must support the efficient implementation of advanced object manipulation techniques such as parsing, query processing, automatic classification, and induction. In fact, the speed at which these manipulations can be performed is severely limited by the speed of the secondary storage manager which must quickly move objects between disk and main memory where they are processed.

A storage manager has been designed to meet the specific needs of a database management system based on CANDIDE. It is designed to support the predominant manipulation specific to CANDIDE, namely automatic classification. The main approach is to physically cluster objects on the disk so that objects belonging in the same class are in the same region on the disk. This provides rapid sequential access to objects in the same class, resulting in faster classification and query processing. The storage manager has been implemented for use in delivering information retrieval systems via CD-ROM (read only), and for application development purposes (read and write). The following sections describe data structures used to physically represent objects, evaluates the use of the decomposition storage model, and proposes an object-oriented virtual memory approach including the description of a physical clustering algorithm.

5.2 Physical Object Representation

Each CANDIDE object is physically represented in two different forms: relocatable and instantiated. The relocatable object is simply a variable length block of bytes. Relocatable objects are designed to provide maximum compaction and speed. Relocatable objects can be rapidly swapped between storage devices (especially between main memory and disk). The term "relocatable" means that the objects can be located physically at any memory address. Because of the complex internal structure of objects, object representations make extensive use of memory pointers. For example, there is a pointer to indicate where inside the object the attribute section begins.

Because relocatable objects are compacted binary data structures, they are very difficult to manipulate. The second representation, instantiated objects, was created to make it easier for application programmers to create and modify complex objects. Instantiated objects use C++ classes and structures to represent all the components of an object. There is a C++ class for every construct in CANDIDE. Relocatable objects can be transformed to instantiated objects by picking apart the object internals and instantiating each component into a C++ instance. Although instantiated objects are easier to manipulate, they are not relocatable (pointers are absolute memory locations), they take up a great deal of space, and the process of instantiation is very slow. When rapid object manipulation is desired, relocatable objects must be used.

Another strategy for physical object representation would be to use an existing relational database system for secondary storage. Rather than store objects physically as relocatable objects, the decomposition storage model [CK85] uses an underlying relational database for secondary storage and decomposes each object into many different relational tables. This increases not only the amount of data to be stored, but also the join operations required to recompose the data. Hence this alternative is discarded.

5.3 Object-Oriented Virtual Memory Manager

The object storage manager is designed to optimize two frequently performed operations. One, sequential access, is retrieving all the objects within a particular class. The other, taxonomic subsumption, is determining whether object B is below object A in the class taxonomy (A subsumes B). Sequential access to all the objects in a class is used extensively during classification for query processing. Taxonomic subsumption is used in determining object type. Note that determining subsumption in an existing taxonomy is different from determining the class membership of a new object (classification).

Determining subsumption relationships for existing objects can be done by climbing the taxonomy. Since this is very inefficient, another approach is to store ancestor lists for each object. We have chosen to do this for classes but not for instances (instances can quickly examine the lists for their parent classes). Updating the ancestor list is problematic, but mostly for updates occuring high in the taxonomy. Approaches based on the use of numerical indexes are being examined as an alternative, but these also can lead to updating problems.

To speed sequential access within a class, the secondary storage manager uses a physical clustering algorithm which attempts to locate objects which are logically clustered in the same class near the same physical location on disk. The secondary storage manager is an object-oriented virtual memory manager (OOVMM). Objects are cached in main memory, and when a request is made for an object that is not in main memory, an "object-fault" occurs, and the disk is accessed to retrieve that object. The unit of memory transfer is an object instead of a page. The relocatable object is the smallest unit of access. Whole objects are transferred between the database manager and the application program (the database manager cannot serve up part of an object). The secondary storage manager is not concerned with object internals. Instantiated objects are not used much by the secondary storage manager (although some update methods are implemented at the level of instantiated objects), rather instantiated objects may be generated once a relocatable object is obtained from storage.

Three levels of memory are identified; main memory, memory cache, and disk. The main memory contains the application program which is the source and destination of objects generated or stored. Memory cache is the main memory set aside for buffering objects. The disk is the secondary storage manager. There is no provision for caching between CD-ROM and secondary storage, although such a layer may be added. The database can be segmented into multiple files, some of which can be stored on CD-ROM, and others on magnetic disks, possibly on different servers.

An example of retrieval from the OOVMM is as follows. The function fclass(oid) is called to retrieve the relocatable form of the object with identifier oid. A request to fclass first causes a search of an OID_Table. The OID_Table contains one entry for each object, and is keyed on oid. The OID_Table returns a structure, OID_Pointer, containing information on the location of the object. Specifically, it includes an address for the object consisting of a file id and bucket number.

The database on disk is contained in one or more object files. A particular object can exist in one and only one object file which is identified by the file id. A File_Index translates file ids to physical file names. Multiple object files are supported to allow for multiple projects. That is, a particular project can store all of its objects in one file.

An object file consists of a set of fixed-sized buckets. These buckets are identified sequentially by bucket number. The bucket is the unit of transfer between disk and main memory. The bucket size corresponds to the disk sector size. A bucket contains a number of relocatable objects and, according to the physical clustering algorithm, all these objects are members of the same class. Thus, when the bucket containing the desired object is loaded into memory, many of the neighboring objects are loaded as well. This is intended to speed sequential access since it increases the probability of the next object requested already being in memory.

Buckets are cached into main memory (the memory cache), using a bucket buffer. An LRU replacement policy is activated for fetching buckets into the buffer. Requests from the information retrieval system tend to be ad hoc and do not follow any consistent pattern; hence it is difficult to devise a new buffer replacement strategy. Thus, the process of reading an object from disk involves first specifying the OID. An entry in the OID_Table returns the file id and bucket number. The File_Index provides the physical file name, and the bucket number identifies the bucket within that file. The bucket is read into main memory and stored in the bucket buffer. At the same time, the desired object is retrieved from the bucket. If the object is already in the memory cache the process is simply to retrieve the bucket from the bucket buffer in memory, and then retrieve the object from that buffer. Once retrieved, the relocatable object may be instantiated.

Multiple identical copies of an object are stored to speed sequential access. In CANDIDE an object may belong to more than one class. One copy of an object is stored for each of its parent classes, according to guidelines specified in the physical clustering algorithm. Though this speeds up sequential access, it has the disadvantage of slowing updating since all copies of the object must be updated. It was desired to accept this tradeoff since slow updating times could be tolerated in exchange for fast query processing. The strategy works as long as there is a high read to write ration, as is the case in general information retrieval applications. A structure called OID_Copies keeps track of all copies of an object. Given an oid, OID_Copies returns a list of all locations of copies of the object.

5.4 Physical Clustering

The OOVMM is based on fixed sized buckets, where each bucket contains a number of relocatable objects (objects larger than a bucket are handled specially by breaking them into several buckets). The purpose of the physical clustering algorithm is to allocate objects to buckets such that all the objects in a bucket are members of the same class.

Here the algorithm is presented for initial clustering to illustrate the procedure. This is used on existing databases which have not yet been physically clustered. The algorithm uses a recursive function pcluster() which physically clusters the subtree rooted at class oid. Initially pcluster() is called with the root of the taxonomy. The parameters, α and β, are the lowest and highest levels that a bucket can be filled. Buckets will be filled to at least α, and β is the size of the bucket.

Procedure main()
Input: A database consisting of classes and instances arranged logically in a
          generalization taxonomy. The taxonomy has a single root.
Output: A set of buckets containing relocatable objects (classes and instances)
          which are physically clustered so that members of the
          same class are placed in the same buckets.

          pcluster(root_oid)

          Procedure pcluster(oid)
          {
              Get size of subtree rooted at oid.
              While (size > β)
                  {
                      Create a list containing the subtrees rooted at each
                      subclass of object oid.
                      If the size of one of these subtrees is > β, call
                      pcluster(s_oid) where s_oid is the subclass of oid which
                      is the root of this subtree.
                      Else keep removing the smallest subtrees until the
                      combined size of the remaining subtrees is between
                      α and β. Then store the remaining subtrees in a bucket.

```
        }
        If oid is the root of the taxonomy, then store the remaining
        subtree rooted at oid in a bucket and return.
        Else return without storing (remaining subtree passed to
        next higher class).
}
```

Once the database has been physically clustered, it is desirable that updates on this database (adding, modifying, deleting objects) attempt to maintain an optimal distribution of objects in buckets. Strategies for doing this include:

1. Recluster a subtree containing the updated object plus all of its ancestors.
2. Recluster the taxonomy only in the immediate neighborhood of the updated object.

Currently the first strategy has been implemented, but is much too slow for updates (too many buckets are effected). The second strategy, which uses techniques such as bucket splitting, is currently being implemented and promises to result in updates which are very rapid (requiring only a few buckets to be written). It depends on updates filling in unused space in existing buckets.

6 Conclusion

We have presented the CANDIDE semantic data model and its applications to very diverse problems.

The main features of the CANDIDE data model can be summarized as follows.

1. It provides a uniform treatment of objects, queries and views,
2. Query computation is based on deductive reasoning about the structural relationships between objects. This involves the computation of subsumption and classification.

An important consequence of our approach is that the subsume function is essentially a theorem prover. Thus, *we are at the confluence of semantic data modeling and logic databases*. The user still views object definitions in the same way as in other semantic data models, but specifies queries (and views) in terms of object definitions. The query processing can be viewed as the translation of the object definition into equivalent logic statements, which are then processed by the "subsumption" theorem prover. Therefore, results from logic databases can inspire further extensions to our model, and query evaluation strategies can be exploited for optimization.

CANDIDE was originally developed to support an intelligent multi-media information retrieval system with a natural language query interface at the University of Florida. We have later applied this object model to two other research projects: the first, called the FIB (Federated Information Bases) project supported by the U. S. West Corporation, involved a federation of loosely coupled databases. The second, a document database retrieval project was done based on the same model to deal with agricultural manuals tagged in SGML.

A An Extended BNF Grammar for the DDL and DML in CANDIDE

```
<class> ::= <classname> CLASS <primitive-flag>
                [SUPERCLASSES <superclass>+]
                [SUBCLASSES <subclass>+]
                [INSTANCE-LIST <inst>+]
                [ATTR-CONSTRAINTS <attr-constraint>+]

<instance> ::= <inst-name> INSTANCE [<iparent>+]
                [ATTR <attr-value>+]

<attr> ::= <attr-name> ATTR [<attr-parent>] <vc>

<disjoint-class> ::= <disjoint-name> DISJOINT
                        <classname> <disj>+

<primitive-flag> ::= PRIMITIVE | DEFINED
<attr-constraint> ::= <attr-name> <constraint>+
<attr-value> ::= <attr-name> <type-i>+
<constraint> ::= <max> | <some> | <exactly> | <all>
<max> ::= ATMOST <integer>
<some> ::= ATLEAST <integer> <vc>
<exactly> ::= EXACTLY <integer> <vc>
<all> ::= ALL <vc>
<vc> ::= (DOMAIN <type-c>) | (VALUE <type-i>) | NIL

<type-c> ::= (CLASS <classname>) | STRING | INTEGER |
                | REAL | (RANGE <range>) | (SET <type-c>+) |
                (SETDIF <classname> ',' <classname>) |
                (COMPOSITE <attr-constraint>+)

<type-i> ::= (CLASS <classname>) |
                (INSTANCE <inst-name>) |
                STRING <string>) |
                (INTEGER <integer>) | REAL <real>) |
                (RANGE <range>) | (SET <type-i>+) |
                (SETDIF <classname> ',' <classname>) |
                (COMPOSITE <attr-value>+)

<range> ::= ( ( '(' | '[' ) <num> | NIL ) ','
        ( NIL | <num> ( ')' | ']' ) ) )
<num> ::= <real> | <integer>

<superclass> ::= <classname>
<subclass> ::= <classname>
```

```
<inst> ::= <inst-name>
<iparent> ::= <classname>
<attr-parent> ::= <attr-name>
<disj> ::= <classname>
<classname> ::= <string>
<inst-name> ::= <string>
<attr-name> ::= <string>
<disjoint-name> ::= <string>
```

B An Extensional Semantics for the CANDIDE Semantic Data Model

Here we present a semantics for CANDIDE which are a trivial extension of that for KANDOR [PS84b]. It is a correct and complete model of computation, and the complexity of computing subsumption is co-NP-hard [Neb88].

B.1 Model

In a CANDIDE database, let C be the set of classes defined in it, let A be the set of attributes defined in it, let R be the set of restrictions or constraints defined in it, and let I be the set of instances defined in it. A partial model for a Candide database is then a set D the set of all instances, plus a function $\mathcal{E}$ such that:

$\mathcal{E} : C \to 2^D$

$\mathcal{E} : A \to (D \to 2^{D+})$ where $D+$ is the disjoint union of D, numbers and strings

$\mathcal{E} : R \to 2^D$

$\mathcal{E} : I \to D$

$\mathcal{E}$: numerals $\to$ integers

$\mathcal{E}$: realnumerals $\to$ real

$\mathcal{E}$: strings $\to$ strings

where $\mathcal{E}$ must satisfy the following condition

1. for restrictions
   (a) $\mathcal{E}[\text{a: all } c] = \{x \in D \mid \text{if } y \in \mathcal{E}[a](x) \text{ then } y \in \mathcal{E}[c]\}$
   (b) $\mathcal{E}[\text{a: atmost } n] = \{x \in D \mid |\mathcal{E}[a](x)| \leq n\}$
   (c) $\mathcal{E}[\text{a: atleast } n \ c] = \{x \in D \mid |\mathcal{E}[a](x) \cap \mathcal{E}[c]| \geq n\}$
   (d) $\mathcal{E}[\text{a: exactly } n \ c] = \mathcal{E}[\text{a: atmost } n] \cap \mathcal{E}[\text{a: atleast } n \ c]$
2. for classes c
   (a) $\mathcal{E}[c] = \bigcap_{i=1}^{n} \mathcal{E}[c_i] \cap \bigcap_{i=1}^{m} \mathcal{E}[r_i]$
       where the class c has superclasses $c_1 \dots c_i$ and has attribute restrictions $r_1 \dots r_m$
   (b) $\mathcal{E}[c_1] \cap \mathcal{E}[c_2] = \{\}$ if c_1 and c_2 are disjoint

This type of model is called a partial model because it does not take into account the definitions of instances. The reason for this is that the definitions of instances are not important for determining class subsumption, because class subsumption does not depend on a particular model but on the entire set of models. Class subsumption is defined as follows:

for any two classes c_1 and c_2 in a CANDIDE database, c_1 subsumes c_2 iff for any partial model of that database, $\mathcal{E}[c_2] \subseteq \mathcal{E}[c_1]$. This is expressed as subsume(c_1, c_2).

B.2 Rules for Computing Subsumption

The above semantics mean that one class c_1 subsumes another c_2 if the superclasses and attribute restrictions attached to c_2 imply the superclasses and attribute restrictions attached to c_1. Therefore, when the CANDIDE classifier classifies a new class it has to perform certain inferences to determine if the restrictions on one class imply those on another, i.e., compute subsumption.

The inference rules for computing subsumption can be grouped together based on the type of restriction they deduce.

1. Rules for deducing the **atmost** constraint
    [a: **atmost** n] $\wedge$ m $>$ n $\rightarrow$ [a: **atmost** m]
    [a: **atmost** n] $\wedge$ [a: **atleast** m c_1] $\wedge$ [a: **all** c_2] $\wedge$ disjoint(c_1, c_2) $\rightarrow$ [a: **atmost** n−m]
2. Rules for deducing the **all** constraint
    [a: **all** c_1] $\wedge$ subsume(c_2, c_1) $\rightarrow$
    [a: **all** c_2]
    [a: **all** c_1] $\wedge$ [a: **all** c_2] $\wedge$ c = conjunction(c_1, c_2) $\rightarrow$ [a: **all** c]
    [a: **atmost** n] $\wedge$ [a: **atleast** n c] $\rightarrow$ [a: **all** c]
3. Rules for deducing the **atleast** constraint
    [a: **atleast** n c_1] $\wedge$ subsume(c_2, c_1) $\rightarrow$ [a: **atleast** c_2]
    [a: **atleast** n c] $\wedge$ m $<$ n $\rightarrow$ [a: **atleast** m c]
    [a: **atleast** n c_1] $\wedge$ [a: **all** c_2] $\wedge$ c = conjunction(c_1, c_2) $\rightarrow$ [a: **atleast** n c]
    [a: **atleast** n c_1] $\wedge$ [a: **atleast** m c_2] $\wedge$ c = join(c_1, c_2) $\wedge$ disjoint(c_1, c_2) $\rightarrow$
    [a: **atleast** n+m c]

Note that c = conjunction(c_1, c_2) iff subsume(c_1, c) and subsume(c_2, c); c = join(c_1, c_2) iff subsume(c, c_1) and subsume(c, c_2). CANDIDE deduces that two classes are disjoint in one of two ways. First, the classes themselves may be defined to be disjoint by the user or they may have ancestors in the class taxonomy that are disjoint. Second, an attribute restriction (or constraint) on one class may be logically incompatible with some restriction on the other class. The following restrictions are recognized as incompatible:

[a: **atmost** n] is incompatible with [a: **atleast** m c], where m $>$ n, and c is any class.
[a: **all** c_1] is incompatible with [a: **atleast** n c_2], where n is any positive integer and disjoint(c_1, c_2) = TRUE.

References

[AA92]   R. Alhajj and M.E. Arkun. A formal data model and object algebra for object-oriented databases. *Applied Mathematics and Computer Science*, 2(1):49–63, 1992.

[AA93a]   R. Alhajj and M.E. Arkun. An object algebra for object-oriented database systems. *The ACM SIGBIT Journal of Data Base*, 1993. Accepted for publication.

[AA93b]   R. Alhajj and M.E. Arkun. Object-oriented query language. *Journal of Information and Software Technology*, 1993. Accepted for publication.

[AA93c]   R. Alhajj and M.E. Arkun. Queries in object-oriented database systems. In T.W. Finin, C.K. Nicholas, and Y. Yesha, editors, *Information and Knowledge Management*, volume 752 of *Lecture Notes in Computer Science*, pages 36–52. Springer-Verlag, 1993.

[AA93d]   R. Alhajj and M.E. Arkun. A query model for object-oriented database systems. In *Proc. 9th Int. Conf. on Data Engineering*, pages 163–172, 1993.

[AAD⁺93]   R. Ahmed, J. Albert, W. Du, W. Kent, W. Litwin, and M.C. Shan. A overview of Pegasus. In *Proc. IEEE 3rd Int. Workshop on Research Issues on Data Engineering - Interoperability in Multidatabase Systems (RIDE-IMS)*, pages 273–277, 1993.

[AAK⁺93]   J. Albert, R. Ahmed, M. Ketabchi, W. Kent, and M.C. Shan. Automatic importation of relational schemas in Pegasus. In *Proc. IEEE 3rd Int. Workshop on Research Issues on Data Engineering - Interoperability in Multidatabase Systems (RIDE-IMS)*, pages 19–20, 1993.

[AB88]   S. Abiteboul and C. Beeri. On the power of languages for the manipulation of complex objects. Technical Report Technical Report 846, INRIA, 1988. Revised October 1992.

[AB91]   S. Abiteboul and A. Bonner. Objects and views. In *Proc. ACM SIGMOD Int. Conf. on Management of Data*, pages 238–247, 1991.

[ABC⁺76]   M.M. Astrahan, M.W. Blasgen, D.D. Chamberlin, K.P. Eswaran, J.N. Gray, P.P. Griffiths, W.F. King, R.A. Lorie, P.R. McJones, J.W. Mehl, G.R. Putzolu, I.L. Traiger, B.W. Wade, and V. Watson. System R: Relational approach to database management. *ACM Transactions on Database Systems*, 1(2):97–137, June 1976.

[ABC⁺83]   M. P. Atkinson, P. J. Bailey, K. J. Chisholm, P. W. Cockshott, and R. Morrison. An approach to persistent programming. *Computer*, 26(4):360–365, 1983.

[ABD⁺89]   M. Atkinson, F. Bancilhon, D.J. DeWitt, K. Dittrich, D. Maier, and S. Zdonik. The object-oriented database system manifesto. In *Proc. 1st Int. Conf. on Deductive and Object-Oriented Databases*, pages 40–57, 1989.

[ABGS91]   R. Agrawal, S.J. Buroff, N. H. Gehani, and D. Shasha. Object versioning in Ode. In *Proc. 7th Int. Conf. on Data Engineering*, pages 446–455, 1991.

[Abi90]   S. Abiteboul. Towards a deductive object-oriented database language. *Data & Knowledge Engineering*, 5(4), 1990.

[ABN91]   T.M. Anwar, H.W. Beck, and S.B. Navathe. Conceptual clustering in database systems. In *Proc. American Soc. for Inf. Sys. Workshop on Classification Research*, 1991.

[ABN92]   T.M. Anwar, H.W. Beck, and S. B. Navathe. Knowledge mining by imprecise querying: A classification-based approach. In *Proc. 8th Int. Conf. on Data Engineering*, pages 622–630, 1992.

[ACM91]   Special Issue on Digital Multimedia Systems. *Comm. of the ACM*, 34(4), April 1991.

[ACO85]   A. Albano, L. Cardelli, and R. Orsini. Gelileo: A strongly-typed interactive conceptual language. *ACM Transactions on Database Systems*, 10(2):230–260, 1985.

[ADD+91]   R. Ahmed, P. DeSmedt, W. Du, W. Kent, M. Ketabchi, W. Litwin, A. Rafii, and M.-C. Shan. The Pegasus heterogeneous multidatabase system. *IEEE Computer*, December 1991.

[ADE93]   I.B. Arpinar, A. Dogac, and C. Evrendilek. MoodView: An advanced graphical user interface for OODBMSs. *ACM SIGMOD Record*, 22(4):11–17, December 1993.

[AE90]   D. Agrawal and A. El Abbadi. Locks with constrained sharing. In *Proc. ACM SIGACT-SIGMOD Symp. on Principles of Database Systems*, pages 85–93, 1990.

[AE94]   D. Agrawal and A. El Abbadi. A nonrestrictive concurrency control protocol for object-oriented databases. *Distributed and Parallel Database Systems*, 2(1):7–31, January 1994.

[AG89a]   R. Agrawal and N. H. Gehani. ODE (Object Database and Environment): The language and the data model. In *Proc. ACM SIGMOD Int. Conf. on Management of Data*, pages 36–45, 1989.

[AG89b]   R. Agrawal and N.H. Gehani. Rationale for the design of persistence and query processing facilities in the database programming language O++. In *Proc. Second Int. Workshop on Database Programming Languages*, pages 25–40, 1989.

[AGS90]   R. Agrawal, N. H. Gehani, and J. Srinivasan. OdeView: The graphical interface to Ode. In *Proc. ACM SIGMOD Int. Conf. on Management of Data*, pages 34–43, 1990.

[AH87]   T. Andrews and C. Harris. Combining language and database advances in an object-oriented development environment. In *OOPSLA '87 Conf. Proc.*, pages 430–440, 1987.

[AH87a]   G. Agha and C. Hewitt. Actors: A conceptual foundation for concurrent object-oriented programming. In B. Shriver and P. Wegner, editors, *Research Directions in Object-Oriented Programming*, pages 49–74. MIT Press, 1987.

[AH87b]   G. Agha and C. Hewitt. *Concurrent Programming Using Actors*. MIT Press, Cambridge, 1987.

[AK89]   S. Abiteboul and P. Kanellakis. Object identity as a query language primitive. In *Proc. ACM SIGMOD Int. Conf. on Management of Data*, pages 159–173, 1989.

[AK90]   S. Abiteboul and P. Kanellakis. Database theory column: Query languages for complex object databases. *SIGACT News*, 21:9–18, 1990.

[AK93]   K. Aberer and W. Klas. The impact of multimedia data on database management systems. In *Proc. IEEE Workshop on Multimedia Computing*, pages 21–31, 1993.

[AKRW92]   S. Abiteboul, P. Kanellakis, S. Ramaswamy, and E. Waller. Method schemas. Technical Report CS-92-33, Brown University, Providence, RI, 1992. An earlier version appeared in *Proc. 9th ACM Symposium on Principles of Database Systems*.

[Alh92]   R. Alhajj. *A Query Model and an Object Algebra for Object-Oriented Databases*. PhD thesis, Department of Computer Engineering and Information Sciences, Bilkent University, Fall 1992.

[ALUW93] S. Abiteboul, G. Lausen, H. Uphoff, and E. Waller. Methods and rules. In *Proc. ACM SIGMOD Int. Conf. on Management of Data*, pages 32–41, 1993.

[AMP73] E. Ashcroft, Z. Manna, and A. Pnueli. Decidable properties of monadic functional schemas. *J. ACM*, 20:489–499, 1973.

[AMY88] R. Akscyn, D.L. McCracken, and E. Yoder. A distributed hypertext for sharing knowledge in organizations. *Comm. of the ACM*, 31(7):820–835, 1988.

[AR88] N. Adams and J. Rees. Object-oriented programming in Scheme. In *Proc. ACM Symp. on Lisp and Functional Programming*, pages 277–288, 1988.

[ASL89] A. Alashqur, S.Y. Su, and H. Lam. OQL: A query language for manipulating object-oriented databases. In *Proc. 15th Int. Conf. on Very Large Databases*, pages 433–442, 1989.

[AV91] S. Abiteboul and V. Vianu. Datalog extensions for database queries and updates. *Journal of Computer and System Sciences*, 43:62–124, 1991.

[AWHJ92] A. Aiken, J. Widom, J.M. Hellerstein. Behavior of database production rules: Termination, confluence, and observable determinism,. In *Proc. ACM SIGMOD Int. Conf. on Management of Data*, pages 59–68, 1992.

[Bac78] J. Backus. Can programming be liberated from the von neuman style? A functional style of programming and its algebra of programs. *Comm. of the ACM*, 21(8):613–641, August 1978.

[Ban88] F. Bancilhon. Object-oriented database systems. In *Proc. 7th ACM SIGACT-SIGMOD-SIGART Symp. on Principles of Database Systems*, pages 152–162, 1988.

[Bar84] H. Barendregt. *The Lambda Calculus: Its Syntax and Semantics*. North-Holland, 1984.

[Bar90] H. Barendregt. Functional programming and lambda calculus. In J. van Leeuwen, editor, *Handbook of Theoretical Computer Science*, volume B, pages 321–363. Elsevier Science Publishers, 1990.

[BB84] D. Batory and A. Buchmann. Molecular objexts, abstract data types, and data models: A framework. In *Proc. 10th Int. Conf. on Very Large Databases*, pages 172–184, 1984.

[BBG+88] D.S. Batory, J.R. Barnett, J.F. Garza, K.P. Smith, K. Tsukuda, B.C. Twichell, and T.E. Wise. GENESIS: An Extensible Database Management System. *IEEE Transactions on Software Eng.*, 14(11):1711–1730, November 1988.

[BBG89] C. Beeri, P.A. Bernstein, and N. Goodman. A model for concurrency in nested transaction systems. *J. ACM*, 36(2):230–269, 1989.

[BBKV87] F. Bancilhon, T. Briggs, S. Knoshafian, and P. Valduriez. FAD: A powerful and simple database language. In *Proc. 13th Int. Conf. on Very Large Databases*, pages 97–105, 1987.

[BBKZ92] A. Buchmann, H. Branding, T. Kudrass, and J. Zimmermann. REACH: a REal-time, ACtive and Heterogeneous mediator system. *Q. Bull. IEEE TC on Data Engineering*, December 1992.

[BBKZ93] H. Branding, A. Buchmann, T. Kudrass, and J. Zimmermann. Rules in an open system: The REACH rule system,. In *Proc. 1st Int. Workshop on Rules in Database Systems*, 1993.

[BBMR89] A. Borgida, R. J. Brachman, D. L. McGuinness, and Alperin Resnick. CLASSIC: A structural data model for objects. *ACM SIGMOD Record*, 18(2):58–67, June 1989.

[BC92] M.L. Brodie and S. Ceri. On intelligent and cooperative information systems. *Int. Jour. Intelligent and Cooperative Information Systems*, 1(2), 1992.

[BCG+87] J. Banerjee, H-T. Chou, J.F. Garza, W. Kim, D. Woelk, N. Ballau, and H.J. Kim. Data model issues for object-oriented applications. *ACM Transactions on Office Information Systems*, 5(1):3–26, 1987.

[BD90]   V. Benzaken and C. Delobel. Enhancing performance in a persistent object store: Clustering strategies in O_2. In A. Dearle, G.M. Shaw, and S.B. Zdonik, editors, *Implementing Persistent Object Bases: Principles and Practice. Proc. Fourth Int. Workshop on Persistent Object Systems*, pages 403–412. Morgan Kaufmann, 1990.

[BDG93a]   A. Biliris, S. Dar, and N. Gehani. Making C++ objects persistent: Hidden pointers. *Software — Practice & Experience*, 23(12):1285–1303, December 1993.

[BDG+93b]   A. Biliris, S. Dar, N. Gehani, H. V. Jagadish, and K. Ramamritham. A flexible transaction facility for an object-oriented database, 1993. Unpublished manuscript.

[BDK92]   F. Bancilhon, C. Delobel, and P. Kanellakis. *Building an Object-Oriented Database System, The Story of O_2*. Morgan Kaufmann, 1992.

[Bee90]   C. Beeri. A formal approach to object-oriented databases. *Data & Knowledge Engineering*, 5:353–382, 1990.

[Bee93]   C. Beeri. Some thoughts on the future evolution of object-oriented database concepts. In W. Stucky and A. Oberweis, editors, *Proc. BTW '93 - GI-Fachtagung: Datenbanksysteme fuer Buero. Technik und Wissenschaft*, Informatik aktuell, pages 18–32. Springer-Verlag, 1993.

[Ber91]   E. Bertino. Method precomputation in object-oriented databases. *SIGOIS Bulletin*, 12(2,3):199–212, 1991.

[Ber93]   E. Bertino. A survey of indexing techniques for object-oriented databases. In J.C. Freytag, G. Vossen, and D. Maier, editors, *Query Processing for Advanced Database Applications*. Morgan Kaufmann, 1993.

[BF92]   E. Bertino and P. Foscoli. An analytical model of object-oriented query costs. In *Proc. of the Fifth Int. Workshop on Persistent Object Systems*, pages 241–261. Springer-Verlag, 1992.

[BFKM85]   L. Brownston, R. Farrell, E. Kant, and N. Martin. *Programming Expert Systems in OPS5: An Introduction to Rule-Based Programming*. Addison Wesley, 1985.

[BFN82]   P. Buneman, R. Frankel, and R. Nikhil. An implementation technique for database query languages. *ACM Transactions on Database Systems*, 7:164–186, 1982.

[BGL+93]   A. Biliris, N. Gehani, D. Lieuwen, E. Panagos, and T. Roycraft. Ode 2.0 user's manual. Technical report, AT&T Bell Laboratories, 1993.

[BGN89]   H.W. Beck, S. Gala, and S.B. Navathe. Classification as a query processing technique in the CANDIDE semantic data model. In *Proc. 5th Int. Conf. on Data Engineering*, pages 572–581, 1989.

[BH86]   D. Bryce and R. Hull. SNAP: A graphics-based schema manager. In *Proc. 2nd Int. Conf. on Data Engineering*, pages 151–164, 1986.

[BHG87]   P.A. Bernstein, V. Hadzilacos, and N. Goodman. *Concurrency Control and Recovery in Database Systems*. Addison Wesley, Reading, MA, 1987.

[Bid91]   N. Bidoit. Negation in rule-based database languages : A survey. *Theoretical Computer Science*, 78(1), 1991.

[Bil92a]   A. Biliris. An efficient database storage structure for large dynamic objects. In *Proc. 8th Int. Conf. on Data Engineering*, pages 301–308, 1992.

[Bil92b]   A. Biliris. The performance of three database storage structures for managing large objects. In *Proc. ACM SIGMOD Int. Conf. on Management of Data*, pages 276–285, 1992.

[BJ91]   O. Boucelma and Le Maiter J. An extensible functional query language for an object-oriented database system. In C. Delobel, M. Kifer, and Y. Masunaga, editors, *Proc. 2nd Int. Conf. on Deductive and Object-Oriented Databases*, volume 566 of *Lecture Notes in Computer Science*. Springer-Verlag, 1991.

[BK86]   F. Bancilhon and S. Khoshafian. A calculus for complex objects. In *Proc. ACM SIGACT-SIGMOD Symp. on Principles of Database Systems*, pages 53–60, 1986.

[BK89]   E. Bertino and W. Kim. Indexing techniques for queries on nested objects. *IEEE Transactions on Knowledge and Data Eng.*, 1(2):196–214, June 1989.

[BK90]   C. Beeri and Y. Kornatzky. Algebraic optimization of object-oriented query languages. In *Proc. 3rd Int. Conf. on Database Theory*, pages 72–88. Springer-Verlag, 1990.

[BKK85]   F. Bancilhon, W. Kim, and H. Korth. A model of CAD transactions. In *Proc. 11th Int. Conf. on Very Large Databases*, pages 25–33, 1985.

[BKK88]   J. Banerjee, W. Kim, and K.C. Kim. Queries in object-oriented databases. In *Proc. 4th Int. Conf. on Data Engineering*, pages 31–38, 1988.

[BKKK87] J. Banerjee, W. Kim, H. Kim, and H. Korth. Semantics and implementation of schema evolution in object-oriented databases. In *Proc. ACM SIGMOD Int. Conf. on Management of Data*, pages 311–322, May 1987.

[Bla94a] J.A. Blakeley. OQL[C++]: Extending the C++ language with an object query capability. In W. Kim, editor, *Modern Database Management – Object-Oriented and Multidatabase Technologies*. ACM Press/Addison-Wesley, 1994. In press.

[Bla94b] J. Blakeley. Open OODB: Architecture and query processing overview, 1994. In this volume.

[BLN86]   C. Batini, M. Lenzerini, and S.B. Navathe. A comparative analysis of methodologies for database schema integration. *ACM Computing Surveys*, 18(4):323–364, December 1986.

[BM92]   E. Bertino and D. Montesi. Towards a logical object-oriented programming language for databases. In A. Pirotte, C. Delobel, and G. Gottlob, editors, *Advances in Database Technology — EDBT'92*, volume 580 of *Lecture Notes in Computer Science*, pages 241–580. Springer-Verlag, 1992.

[BMG93]   J.A. Blakeley, W.J. McKenna, and G. Graefe. Experiences building the Open OODB query optimizer. In *Proc. ACM SIGMOD Int. Conf. on Management of Data*, pages 287–296, 1993.

[BMS84]   M.L. Brodie, J. Mylopoulos, and J.W. Schmidt, editors. *On Conceptual Modelling: Perspectives from Artificial Intelligence, Databases, and Programming Languages*. Springer-Verlag, 1984.

[BMSU86] F. Bancilhon, D. Maier, Y. Sagiv, and J.D. Ullman. Magic sets and other strange ways to implement logic programs. In *Proc. ACM SIGACT-SIGMOD Symp. on Principles of Database Systems*, pages 1–15, 1986.

[BÖ90]   K. Barker and M.T. Özsu. Concurrent transaction execution in multidatabase systems. In *Proc. COMPSAC90 – The 14th. Annual Int. Computer Software and Applications Conference*, pages 224–233, October 1990.

[BÖG91]   A. Buchmann, M.T. Özsu, and D. Georgakopoulos. Towards a transaction management system for DOM. Technical Report TR-0146-06-91-165, GTE Laboratories Incorporated, June 1991.

[BÖH+92] A. Buchmann, M.T. Özsu, M. Hornick, D. Georgakopoulos, and F.A. Manola. A transaction model for active distributed object systems. In A.K. Elmagarmid, editor, *Transaction Models for Advanced Database Applications*, pages 123–158. Morgan Kaufmann, 1992.

[Bor92]   A. Borgida. From type systems to knowledge representation: Natural semantics specifications for decription logics. *Int. J. of Intelligent & Cooperative Inf. Sys.*, 1(1):93–126, March 1992.

[BOS91]   P. Butterworth, A. Otis, and J. Stein. The GemStone object database management system. *Comm. of the ACM*, 34(10):51–63, October 1991.

[BP93]   A. Biliris and E. Panagos. EOS User's Guide, Release 2.0. Technical report, AT&T Bell Laboratories, May 1993.

[BR87a]   C. Beeri and R. Ramakrishnan. On the power of magic. In *Proc. ACM SIGACT-SIGMOD Symp. on Principles of Database Systems*, pages 269–283, 1987.

[BR87b]   B. R. Badrinath and K. Ramamritham. Semantics-based concurrency control: Beyond commutativity. In *Proc. 3th Int. Conf. on Data Engineering*, pages 304–311, February 1987.

[BR88]   B. R. Badrinath and K. Ramamritham. Synchronizing transactions on objects. *IEEE Transactions on Computers*, 37(5):541–547, May 1988.

[Bro84]   M.L. Brodie. On the development of data models. In Brodie. M.L., J. Mylopoulos, and J.W. Schmidt, editors, *On Conceptual Modelling*, pages 19–47. Springer-Verlag, 1984.

[BS85]   R. J. Brachman and J. G. Schmolze. An overview of KL-ONE knowledge representation system. *Cognitive Science*, 9(2):171–216, April 1985.

[BS91]   V. Breazu-Tannen and R. Subrahmanyan. Logical and computational aspects of programming with sets/bags/lists. In *Proc. 18th Int. Colloquium on Automata, Languages, and Programming*, volume 510 of *Lecture Notes in Computer Science*. Springer-Verlag, 1991.

[BS92]   M.L. Brodie and M. Stonebraker. DARWIN: On the incremental migration of legacy information systems. Technical Report DOM Technical Report, TM-0588-10-92-165, GTE Laboratories Incorporated, Waltham, MA, USA, November 1992.

[BSR80]   P.A. Bernstein, D.W. Shipman, and J.B. Rothnie. Concurrency control in a system for distributed databases (SDD-1). *ACM Transactions on Database Systems*, 5(1):18–51, 1980.

[BSW88]   C. Beeri, H.-J. Schek, and G. Weikum. Multi-level transaction management, theoretical art or practical need? In J.W. Schmidt, S. Ceri, and M. Missikof, editors, *Advances in Database Technology — EDBT'88*, volume 303 of *Lecture Notes in Computer Science*, pages 134–154. Springer-Verlag, 1988.

[BTA91]   J.A. Blakeley, C.W. Thompson, and A. Alashqur. A Strawman Reference Model for Object Query Languages. *Computer Standards & Interfaces*, 13:185–199, 1991.

[BTBN92]   V. Breazu-Tannen, P. Buneman, and S. Naqvi. Structural recursion as a query language. In *Proc. 3rd Int. Workshop on Database Programming Languages*, pages 9–19, 1992.

[BTBW92]   V. Breazu-Tannen, P. Buneman, and L. Wong. Naturally embedded query languages. In *Proc. 4th Int. Conf. on Database Theory*, 1992.

[Buc90]   A. Buchmann. Modelling heterogeneous systems as an active object space. In A. Dearle, G.M. Shaw, and S.B. Zdonik, editors, *Implementing Persistent Object Bases: Principles and Practice. Proc. Fourth Int. Workshop on Persistent Object Systems*, pages 279–290. Morgan Kaufmann, 1990.

[Buc94]   A.P. Buchmann. Active object systems, 1994. In this volume.

[BW77]   D. Bobrow and T. Winograd. An overview of KRL, a knowledge representation language. *Cognitive Science*, 1(1):3–46, 1977.

[BWA92]   H. W. Beck, D. Watson, and T. Anwar. From SGML documents to databases. In *Proc. 4th International Conference on Computers in Agricultural Extension Programs*, 1992.

[Car75]   A.F. Cardenas. Analysis and performance of inverted data base structured. *Comm. of the ACM*, 18(5), May 1975.

[Cat91]   R.G.G. Cattell. *Object Data Management - Object-Oriented and Extended Relational Database Systems*. Addison Wesley, 1991.

[CBB+89]   S. Chakravarthy, B. Blaustein, A. Buchmann, M. Carey, U. Dayal, D. Goldhirsch, M. Hsu, R. Jauhari, R. Ladin, M. Livny, D. McCarthy, R. Mckee, and

A. Rosenthal. HiPAC: A research project in active, time-constrained database management. Technical report, Xerox Advanced Information Technology, July 1989.

[CCCR+90] F. Cacace, S. Ceri, S. Crespi-Reghizzi, L. Tanca, and R. Zicari. The Logres project: Integrating object-oriented data modeling with a rule-based programming paradigm. In *Proc. ACM SIGMOD Int. Conf. on Management of Data*, pages 225–236, 1990.

[CD92] S. Cluet and C. Delobel. A general framework for the optimization of object-oriented queries. In *Proc. ACM SIGMOD Int. Conf. on Management of Data*, pages 383–392, 1992.

[CDF+86] M. Carey, D.J. DeWitt, D. Frank, G. Graefe, M. Muralikrishna, J.E. Richardson, and E.J. Shekita. The architecture of the EXODUS extensible DBMS. In *Proc. of the 1st Int. Workshop on Object-Oriented Database Systems*, pages 52–65, 1986.

[CDKK85] H-T. Chou, D.J. DeWitt, R.H. Katz, and A.C. Klug. Design and implementation of the Wisconsin storage system. *Software — Practice & Experience*, 15(10):943–962, October 1985.

[CDLR90] S. Cluet, C. Delobel, C. Lecluse, and P. Richard. Reloop, an algebra based query language for an object-oriented database system. *Data & Knowledge Engineering*, 5:333–352, 1990.

[CDN93] M. J. Carey, D. J. DeWitt, and J. F. Naughton. The OO7 benchmark. In *Proc. ACM SIGMOD Int. Conf. on Management of Data*, pages 12–21, 1993.

[CDRS86] M.J. Carey, D.J. DeWitt, J.E. Richardson, and E.J. Shekita. Object and file management in the EXODUS extensible database system. In *Proc. 12th Int. Conf. on Very Large Databases*, pages 91–100, 1986.

[CDV88] M. Carey, D. DeWitt, and S. Vandenberg. A data model and query language for EXODUS. In *Proc. ACM SIGMOD Int. Conf. on Management of Data*, pages 413–423, 1988.

[Ce76] D.D. Chamberlin and et.al. SEQUEL 2: A Unified Approach to Data Definition, Manipulation and Control. *IBM Journal of Research and Development*, 20(6):560–575, November 1976.

[CF90] M. Cart and J. Ferrie. Integrating concurrency control into an object-oriented database system. In *Advances in Database Technology — EDBT'90*, pages 363–377. Springer-Verlag, 1990.

[CFLS91] M. J. Carey, M. Franklin, M. Linvy, and Shekita. Data caching tradeoffs in client-server DBMS architectures. In *Proc. ACM SIGMOD Int. Conf. on Management of Data*, pages 357–366, 1991.

[CG88a] B. Campbell and J.M. Goodman. HAM: A general purpose hypertext abstract machine. *Comm. of the ACM*, 31(7):856–861, 1988.

[CG88b] Q. Chen and G. Gardarin. An implementation model for reasoning with complex objects. In *Proc. ACM SIGMOD Int. Conf. on Management of Data*, pages 164–172, 1988.

[CG89] N. Carriero and D. Gelernter. Linda in context. *Comm. of the ACM*, 32(4), 1989.

[CGL86] S. Ceri, G. Gottlob, and L. Lavazza. Translation and optimization of logic queries: the algebraic approach. In *Proc. 12th Int. Conf. on Very Large Databases*, pages 395–402, 1986.

[CGT90] S. Ceri, G. Gottlob, and L. Tanca. *Logic Programming and Databases*. Springer-Verlag, 1990.

[CH80] A. Chandra and D. Harel. Computable queries for relational databases. *Journal of Computer and System Sciences*, 21:156–178, 1980.

[CH82] A. Chandra and D. Harel. Structure and complexity of relational queries. *Journal of Computer and System Sciences*, 25:99–128, 1982.

[CH85]   A. Chandra and D. Harel. Horn clause queries and generalizations. *Journal of Logic Programming*, 2:1–15, 1985.

[CH90]   M. Carey and L. Haas. Extensible database management systems. *ACM SIGMOD Record*, 19(4):54–60, December 1990.

[Cha92]   E.P.F. Chan. Containment and minimization of positive conjunctive queries in OODB's. In *Proc. ACM SIGACT-SIGMOD Symp. on Principles of Database Systems*, pages 202–211, 1992.

[Chu41]   A. Church. *The Calculi of Lambda-Conversion*. Princeton University Press, 1941.

[CK85]   G. Copeland and S. Khoshafian. A decomposition storage model. In *Proc. ACM SIGMOD Int. Conf. on Management of Data*, pages 268–279, 1985.

[CK86]   H.T. Chou and W. Kim. A unifying framework for version control in a CAD environment. In *Proc. 12th Int. Conf. on Very Large Databases*, pages 336–344, 1986.

[CK89]   E.E. Chang and R.H. Katz. Exploiting inheritance and structure semantics for effective clustering and buffering in an object-oriented DBMS. In *Proc. ACM SIGMOD Int. Conf. on Management of Data*, pages 348–357, 1989.

[CKRS91] P. E. Cannata, Y. Kambayashi, M. Rusinkiewicz, and A. Sheth. The irresistible move towards interoperable database systems. In *Proc. 1st Int. Workshop on Interoperability in Multidatabase Systems (IMS'91)*, pages 2–5, 1991.

[CKV93]   K.M. Curewitz, P. Krishnan, and J.S. Vitter. Practical prefetching via data compression. In *Proc. ACM SIGMOD Int. Conf. on Management of Data*, pages 257–266, 1993.

[Clu91]   S. Cluet. *Langages et imisation de Requêtes pour Systèmes de Gestion de Base de Données Orientés-Objet*. PhD thesis, Université de Paris-Sud - Centre d'Orsay, Paris, France, 1991.

[CM84]   G. P. Copeland and D. Maier. Making Smalltalk a database system. In *Proc. ACM SIGMOD Int. Conf. on Management of Data*, 1984.

[CM91]   S. Chakravarthy and D. Mishra. An event specification language (SNOOP) for active databases and its detection. Technical Report TR-91-23, University of Florida, Gainesville, Florida, September 1991.

[Cod72]   E.F. Codd. Relational completeness of relational languages. In R. Rustin, editor, *Data Base Systems*, pages 65–98. Prentice-Hall, 1972.

[Col90]   L.S. Colby. A recursive algebra for nested relations. *Information Systems*, 15(5):567–582, 1990.

[Cor91]   Software Exoterica Corporation. *XGML*. Ottawa, Ontario Canada, 1991.

[Cou90]   B. Courcelle. Recursive applicative program schemes. In J. van Leeuwen, editor, *Handbook of Theoretical Computer Science*, volume B, pages 459–492. Elsevier Science Publishers, 1990.

[CP84]   J. Ceri and G. Pelagatti. *Distributed Databases Principles and Systems*. McGraw-Hill, 1984.

[CR90]   P.K. Chrysanthis and K. Ramamritham. ACTA: A framework for specifying and reasoning about transaction structure and behavior. In *Proc. ACM SIGMOD Int. Conf. on Management of Data*, pages 194–203, 1990.

[Cru92]   I.F. Cruz. DOODLE: A visual language for object-oriented databases. In *Proc. ACM SIGMOD Int. Conf. on Management of Data*, pages 71–80, 1992.

[CW93]   W. Cellary and W. Wieczerzycki. Locking objects and classes in multiversion object-oriented databses. In *Proc. 2nd Int. Conf. on Information and Knowledge Management*, pages 586–595, November 1993.

[Dan91]   S. Daniels, et al. Query optimization in Revelation, an overview. *Q. Bull. IEEE TC on Data Engineering*, 14(2):58–62, June 1991.

[Dat84]   C.J. Date. A critique of the SQL database language. *ACM SIGMOD Record*, 14(3):8–54, November 1984.

[Dat90a]   C.J. Date. *An Introduction to Database Systems, Volume 1*. Addison Wesley, 1990.

[Dat90b]   C.J. Date. *An Intoduction to Database Systems, Volume 2*. Addison Wesley, 1990.

[Day87a]   U. Dayal. Of nests and trees: A unified approach to processing queries that contain nested subqueries, aggregates, and quantifiers. In *Proc. 13th Int. Conf. on Very Large Databases*, pages 197–208, 1987.

[Day87b]   U. Dayal. Simplifying complex objects: The PROBE approach to modelling and querying them. In *Proc. German Database Conference, Burg Technik und Wissenschafts*, 1987.

[Day88]   U. Dayal. Active database management systems. In *Proc. 3rd Int. Conf. on Data and Knowledge Bases: Improving Usability and Responsiveness*, pages 150–169, 1988.

[Day89]   U. Dayal. Queries and views in an object-oriented data model. In *Proc. Second Int. Workshop on Database Programming Languages*, pages 80–102, 1989.

[DBM88]   U. Dayal, A. Buchmann, and D. McCarthy. Rules are objects too: A knowledge model for an active object-oriented database system. In *Advances in Object-Oriented Database Systems. Proc. of the 2nd Int. Workshop on Object-Oriented Database Systems*, pages 129–143, 1988.

[DDB91]   K.R. Dittrich, U. Dayal, and A.P. Buchmann, editors. *On Object-Oriented Database Systems*. Springer-Verlag, 1991.

[DE89]   W. Du and A.K. Elmagarmid. Quasi serializability: a correctness criterion for global concurrency control in InterBase. In *Proc. 15th Int. Conf. on Very Large Databases*, pages 347–355, 1989.

[DOA+94]   A. Dogac, C. Ozkan, B. Arpinar, T. Okay, and C. Evrendilek. METU object-oriented DBMS, 1994. In this volume.

[Deu91a]   L.P. Deutsch. Object-oriented software technology. *Computer*, pages 112–113, September 1991.

[Deu91b]   O. Deux et al. The O_2 system. *Comm. of the ACM*, 34(10):34–48, October 1991.

[DGJ92]   S. Dar, N.H. Gehani, and H.V. Jagadish. CQL++: A SQL for the Ode object-oriented DBMS. In A. Pirotte, C. Delobel, and G. Gottlob, editors, *Advances in Database Technology — EDBT'92*, volume 580 of *Lecture Notes in Computer Science*, pages 201–216. Springer-Verlag, 1992.

[DGL90]   K.R. Dittrich, W. Gotthard, and P.C. Lockemann. Complex entities for engineering applications. In A.F. Cárdenas and D. McLeod, editors, *Object-Oriented and Semantic Database Systems*, pages 303–321. Prentice-Hall, 1990.

[DH84]   U. Dayal and H.-Y. Hwang. View definition and generalization for database integration in a multidatabase system. *IEEE Transactions on Software Eng.*, SE-10(6):628–645, November 1984.

[DHL90]   U. Dayal, M. Hsu, and R. Ladin. Organizing long-running activities with triggers and transactions. In *Proc. ACM SIGMOD Int. Conf. on Management of Data*, pages 204–214, 1990.

[DHL91]   U. Dayal, M. Hsu, and R. Ladin. A transactional model for long-running activities. In *Proc. 17th Int. Conf. on Very Large Databases*, pages 113–122, 1991.

[Dit90]   K.R. Dittrich. Object-oriented database systems: The next miles of the marathon. *Information Systems*, 15(1):161–167, September 1990.

[Dit91]   K.R. Dittrich. Object-oriented database systems - the notion and the issues. In K.R. Dittrich, U. Dayal, and A.P. Buchmann, editors, *On Object-Oriented Database Systems*, pages 3–10. Springer-Verlag, 1991.

[Dit94]   K.R. Dittrich. Object-oriented data model concepts, 1994. In this volume.

[DJP93]   O. Diaz, A. Jaime, and N.W. Paton. DEAR: A Debugger for Active Rules in an object-oriented context. In *Proc. 1st Int. Workshop on Rules in Database Systems*, 1993.

[DKA⁺86]   P. Dadam, K. Kuespert, F. Andersen, H. Blanken, R. Erbe, J. Guenauer, V. Lum, P. Pistor, and G. Walch. A DBMS prototype to support extended NF^2 relations: An integrated view on flat tables and hierarchies. In *Proc. ACM SIGMOD Int. Conf. on Management of Data*, pages 356–367, 1986.

[DMFV90]   D. J. DeWitt, D. Maier, P. Futtersack, and F. Velez. A Study of Three Alternative Workstation-Server Architectures for Object-Oriented Database Systems. In *Proc. 16th Int. Conf. on Very Large Databases*, pages 107–121, 1990.

[DPG91]   O. Diaz, N.W Paton, and P. Gray. Rule management in object-oriented databases: A uniform approach. In *Proc. 17th Int. Conf. on Very Large Databases*, 1991.

[DS86a]   U. Dayal and J.M. Smith. PROBE: A knowledge-oriented database management system. In M.L. Brodie and J. Mylopoulos, editors, *On Knowledge Base Management Systems*, pages 227–257. Springer-Verlag, 1986.

[DS86b]   N. Delisle and M. Schwartz. Neptune: A hypertext system for CAD applications. In *Proc. ACM SIGMOD Int. Conf. on Management of Data*, pages 132–142, 1986.

[EGLT76]   K.P. Eswaran, K.P. Gray, J.N. Lorie, and I.L. Traiger. The notions of consistency and predicate locks in a database system. *Comm. of the ACM*, 19(11):624–633, November 1976.

[ELLR90]   A. Elmagarmid, Y. Leu, W. Litwin, and M. Rusinkiewicz. A multidatabase transaction model for InterBase. In *Proc. 16th Int. Conf. on Very Large Databases*, pages 507–518, 1990.

[Elm92]   A.K. Elmagarmid (ed.). *Transaction Models for Advanced Database Applications*. Morgan Kaufmann, 1992.

[EMS91]   J.L. Eppinger, L.B. Mummert, and A.Z. Spector. *Camelot and Avalon – A Distributed Transaction Facility*. Morgan Kaufmann, 1991.

[EN89]   R. Elmasri and S.B. Navathe. *Fundamentals of Database Systems*. Benjamin/Cummings, 1989.

[Etz90]   O. Etzion. PARDES - An active semantic database model. Technical report, Technion, Israel, December 1990. Technical Reports on Information Systems Engineering.

[Fag74]   R. Fagin. Generalized first-order spectra and polynomial-time recognizable sets. *SIAM-AMS Proceedings*, 7:43–73, 1974.

[FBC⁺87]   D.H. Fishman, D. Beech, H.P. Cate, E.C. Chow, T. Conners, J.W. Davis, N. Dennett, C.G. Hoch, W. Kent, P. Lyngbaek, B. Mahbod, M.A. Neimat, T.A. Ryan, and M.C. Shan. Iris: An object-oriented database management system. *ACM Transactions on Office Information Systems*, 5(1), 1987.

[FCL92]   M. Franklin, M. Carey, and M. Livny. Global memory management in client-server DBMS architectures. In *Proc. 18th Int. Conf. on Very Large Databases*, pages 596–609, 1992.

[FG91]   B. Finance and G. Gardarin. A rule-based query rewriter in an extensible DBMS. In *Proc. 7th Int. Conf. on Data Engineering*, pages 248–256, 1991.

[FJL⁺88]   S. Ford, J. Joseph, D.E. Langworthy, D. F. Lively, G. Pathak, E.R. Perez, R.W. Peterson, D.M. Sparacin, S.M. Thatte, D.L. Wells, and S. Agarwala. ZEITGEIST: Database Support for Object-Oriented Programming. In *Advances in Object-Oriented Database Systems. Proc. of the 2nd Int. Workshop on Object-Oriented Database Systems*, pages 23–42. Springer-Verlag, 1988.

[FKMT91]   E. Fong, W. Kent, K. Moore, and C. Thompson. X3/SPARC/DBSSG/OODBTG Final Report. Technical report, NIST, September 1991.

[FLMW89] A. Fekete, N. Lynch, M. Merritt, and W. Weihl. Commutativity-based locking for nested transactions. Technical Report MIT/LCS/TM-370.b, Massachusetts Institute of Technology, Laboratory for Computer Science, Cambridge, MA), October 1989.

[FÖ89] A.A. Farrag and M.T. Özsu. Using semantic knowledge of transactions to increase concurrency. *ACM Transactions on Database Systems*, 14(4):503–525, December 1989.

[For82] C. Forgy. Rete, a fast algorithm for the many patterns many objects match problem. *Artificial Intelligence*, 19(241):17–37, 1982.

[FRS92] F. Fabret, M. Régnier, and E. Simon. Optimizing incremental computation of datalog programs with non-deterministic semantics. In *Proc. 4th Int. Conf. on Database Theory*, 1992.

[FS86] T. Finin and D. Silverman. Interactive classification as a knowledge acquisition tool. In *Proc. 1st Int. Conf. on Expert Database Systems*, 1986.

[FT83] P. Fischer and S. Thomas. Operators for non-first-normal-form relations. In *Proc. 7th COMPSAC*, 1983.

[G. 86] G. Gardarin and et al. Sabrina, a relational database system developed in a research environment. *Technology and Sciences of Informatics*, 1986.

[Gal92] L.J. Gallagher. Object SQL: Language extensions for object data management. In *Project: ISO/IEC JTC 1.21.3.4 (SQL3)*. ISO/IEC JTC1/SC21/WG3 DBL Rapporteur Group, 1992.

[Gar93] G. Gardarin. Object-oriented rule languages and optimization techniques, 1993. This volume.

[GCD+93] G. Graefe, R.L. Cole, D.L. Davison, W.J. McKenna, and R.H. Wolniewicz. Extensible query optimization and parallel execution in Volcano. In J.C. Freytag, G. Vossen, and D. Maier, editors, *Query Processing for Advanced Database Applications*, pages 305–335. Morgan Kaufmann, 1993.

[GD87] G. Graefe and D.J. DeWitt. The EXODUS optimizer generator. In *Proc. ACM SIGMOD Int. Conf. on Management of Data*, pages 160–172, 1987.

[GD93a] S. Gatziu and K.R. Dittrich. Eine ereignissprache für das aktive, objektorientierte datenbanksystem samos. In *Proc. Datenbanksysteme in Büro,Technik und Wissenschaft*, 1993.

[GD93b] S. Gatziu and K.R. Dittrich. Events in an active object-oriented database system. In *Proc. 1st Int. Workshop on Rules in Database Systems*, 1993.

[Geo90] D. Georgakopoulos. *Transaction Management in Multidatabase Systems*. PhD thesis, Department of Computer Science, University of Houston, 1990.

[GF92] G. Gardarin and F. Fabret. Query optimization in a deductive object-oriented DBMS. In *Logic and Database Workshop*, 1992.

[GGKZ85] K.J. Goldman, S.A. Goldman, P.C. Kanellakis, and S.B. Zdonik. ISIS: Interface for a semantic information system. In *Proc. ACM SIGMOD Int. Conf. on Management of Data*, pages 328–342, 1985.

[GJ91] N.H. Gehani and H. V. Jagadish. Ode as an active database: Constraints and triggers. In *Proc. 17th Int. Conf. on Very Large Databases*, pages 327–336, 1991.

[GJR93] N. H. Gehani, H. V. Jagadish, and W. D. Roome. Odefs: a file system interface to an object-oriented database, 1993. Unpublished manuscript.

[GJS92a] N. H. Gehani, H. V. Jagadish, and O. Shmueli. Composite event specification in active databases: Model & implementation. In *Proc. 18th Int. Conf. on Very Large Databases*, pages 327–338, 1992.

[GJS92b] N. H. Gehani, H. V. Jagadish, and O. Shmueli. Event specification in an active object-oriented database. In *Proc. ACM SIGMOD Int. Conf. on Management of Data*, pages 81–90, 1992.

[GK88]   J. F. Garza and W. Kim. Transaction management in an object-oriented database system. In *Proc. ACM SIGMOD Int. Conf. on Management of Data*, pages 37–45, September 1988.

[GL92a]   G. Gardarin and R. Lanzelotte. Optimizing object-oriented database queries using cost-controlled rewriting. In A. Pirotte, C. Delobel, and G. Gottlob, editors, *Advances in Database Technology — EDBT'92*, volume 580 of *Lecture Notes in Computer Science*, pages 534–549. Springer-Verlag, 1992.

[GL92b]   V. Gottemukkala and T. Lehman. Locking and latching in a memory-resident database system. In *Proc. 18th Int. Conf. on Very Large Databases*, pages 533–544, 1992.

[GLB89]   C. Galindo-Legaria and R. Barrera. A rule-based query optimizer. Technical Report 92, Centro de Investigacion y de Estudios Avanzados Del IPN, 1989.

[GLR92]   C. Galindo-Legaria and A. Rosenthal. How to extend a conventional optimizer to handle one- and two-sided outerjoin. In *Proc. 8th Int. Conf. on Data Engineering*, pages 402–409, 1992.

[GM83]   H. Garcia-Molina. Using semantic knowledge for transaction processing in a distributed database. *ACM Transactions on Database Systems*, 18(2):186–213, June 1983.

[GM88]   G. Graefe and D. Maier. Query optimization in object-oriented database systems: A prospectus. In K.R. Dittrich, editor, *Advances in Object-Oriented Database Systems. Proc. of the 2nd Int. Workshop on Object-Oriented Database Systems*, volume 334 of *Lecture Notes in Computer Science*, pages 358–363. Springer-Verlag, 1988.

[GM93]   G. Graefe and W.J. McKenna. The Volcano optimizer generator. In *Proc. 9th Int. Conf. on Data Engineering*, pages 209–218, 1993.

[GMGK⁺90] H. Garcia-Molina, D. Gawlick, J. Klein, K. Kleissner, and K. Salem. Coordinating multi-transaction activities. Technical Report Technical Report CS-TR-247-90, Department of Computer Science, Princeton University, February 1990.

[GMK87]   H. Garcia-Molina and K.Salem. Sagas. In *Proc. ACM SIGMOD Int. Conf. on Management of Data*, pages 249–259, 1987.

[GMN84]   H. Gallaire, J. Minker, and J. Nicolas. Logic and databases: A deductive approach. *ACM Computing Surveys*, 16(2), June 1984.

[Gol91]   C. F. Goldfarb. HyTime: A standard for structured hypermedia interchange. *IEEE Computer*, 24(8):81–84, 1991.

[GR83]   A. Goldberg and D. Robson. *Smalltalk-80: The Language and Its Implementation*. Addison Wesley, 1983.

[GR93]   J. Gray and A. Reuter. *Transaction Processing: Concepts and Techniques*. Morgan Kaufmann, 1993.

[Gra79]   J.N. Gray. Notes on database operating systems. In R. Bayer, R.M. Graham, and G. Seegmüller, editors, *Operating Systems, An Advanced Course*, pages 393–481. Springer-Verlag, New York, 1979.

[Gra87]   G. Graefe. *Rule-Based Query Optimization in Extensible Database Systems*. PhD thesis, University of Wisconsin-Madison, Wisconsin, Madison, 1987.

[Gre75]   S. Greibach. *Theory of Program Structures: Schemes, Semantics, Verification*. LNCS Vol. 36. Springer-Verlag, 1975.

[GRS88]   A. Van Gelder, K. Ross, and J.S. Schlipf. Unfounded sets and well-founded semantics for general logic programs. In *Proc. ACM SIGACT-SIGMOD Symp. on Principles of Database Systems*, pages 221–230, 1988.

[GRS91]   D. Georgakopoulos, M. Rusinkiewicz, and A. Sheth. On serializability of multidatabase transactions through forced local conflicts. In *Proc. 7th Int. Conf. on Data Engineering*, pages 314–323, 1991.

[GSM86] L.N. Garret, K.E. Smith, and N. Meyrowitz. Intermedia: Issues, strategies, and tactics in the design of a hypermedia document system. In *Proc. Conference on Computer-Supported Cooperative Work*, pages 163–174, 1986.

[Gur83] Y. Gurevich. Algebras of feasible functions. In *Proc. 24th IEEE Conf. on Foundations of Computer Science*, pages 210–214, 1983.

[GV89] G. Gardarin and P. Valduriez. *Relational Databases and Knowledge Bases*. Addison Wesley, 1989.

[GV91] S. Grumbach and V. Vianu. Tractable query languages for complex object databases. In *Proc. ACM SIGACT-SIGMOD Symp. on Principles of Database Systems*, pages 315–327, 1991.

[GW87] R.A. Ganski and H.K.T. Wong. Optimization of nested SQL queries revisited. In *Proc. ACM SIGMOD Int. Conf. on Management of Data*, pages 23–33, 1987.

[GW89] G. Graefe and K. Ward. Dynamic query evaluation plans. In *Proc. ACM SIGMOD Int. Conf. on Management of Data*, pages 358–366, 1989.

[H+88] J.H. Howard et al. Scale and Performance in a Distributed File System. *ACM Transactions on Computer Systems*, 6(1):51–81, February 1988.

[Haa93] A. Haake. *TBA*. PhD thesis, Univ. Darmstadt, 1993. Private communication.

[Had88] V. Hadzilacos. A theory of reliability in database systems. *J. ACM*, 35(1), January 1988.

[Hal88] F.G. Halasz. Reflections on NoteCards: Seven issues for the next generation of hypermedia systems. *Comm. of the ACM*, 31(7), 1988.

[HC88] M. Hsu and T Cheatham. Rule execution in CPLEX: A persistent objectbase. In *Advances in Object-Oriented Database Systems. Proc. of the 2nd Int. Workshop on Object-Oriented Database Systems*, pages 150–155, 1988.

[HCF+89] L.M. Haas, W.F. Cody, J.C. Freytag, G. Lapis, B.G. Lindsay, G.M. Lohman, K. Ono, and H. Pirahesh. Extensible query processing in Starburst. In *Proc. ACM SIGMOD Int. Conf. on Management of Data*, pages 377–388, 1989.

[HCL+90] L.M. Haas, W. Chang, G.M. Lohman, J. McPherson, P.F. Wilms, G. Lapis, B. Lindsay, H. Pirahesh, M.J. Carey, and E. Shekita. Starburst midflight: As the dust clears. *IEEE Transactions on Knowledge and Data Eng.*, 2(1):143–160, March 1990.

[HDB92] *Proc. Workshop On Heterogeneous Databases and Semantic Interoperability*, Boulder, CO, USA, 1992.

[HDK+90] U. Herrmann, P. Dadam, K Küspert, E.A. Roman, and G. Schlageter. A lock technique for disjoint and non-disjoint complex objects. In *Advances in Database Technology — EDBT'90*, pages 219–237. Springer-Verlag, 1990.

[Her86] M. Herlihy. Optimistic concurrency control for abstract data types. In *Proc. 5th Symp. on the Principles of Distributed Computing*, pages 206–217, Vancouver (Canada), August 1986. ACM.

[Her90] M. Herlihy. Apologizing versus asking permission: Optimistic concurrency control for abstract data types. *ACM Transactions on Database Systems*, 15(1):96–124, 1990.

[HGP92] M. Halper, J. Geller, and Y. Perl. "Part" relations for object-oriented databases. Research report CIS-92-11, Institute for Integrated Systems, CIS Department and Center for Manufacturing Systems, New Jersey Institute of Technology, Newark, N.J., 1992.

[HH91] T. Hadzilacos and V. Hadzilacos. Transaction synchroniation in object bases. *Journal of Computer and System Sciences*, 43(1):2–24, August 1991.

[HKM93] G. Hillebrand, P. Kanellakis, and H. Mairson. Database query languages embedded in the typed lambda calculus. In *Proc. 8th IEE Conf. on LICS*, pages 332–343, 1993.

[HL82]   R. L. Haskin and R. A. Lorie. On extending the relational database system. In *Proc. ACM SIGMOD Int. Conf. on Management of Data*, pages 207–212, 1982.

[HLM88]   M. Hsu, R. Ladin, and D. McCarthy. An execution model for active database management systems. In *Proc. 3rd Int. Conf. on Data and Knowledge Bases: Improving Usability and Responsiveness*, pages 171–179, 1988.

[HM81]   M. Hammer and D. McLeod. Database description with a semantic data model: SDM. *ACM Transactions on Database Systems*, 6(3):351–386, September 1981.

[HMT87]   F.G. Halasz, T.P. Moran, and R.H. Trigg. NoteCards in a nutshell. In *Proc. ACM Conference of Human Factors in Computer Systems*, pages 45–52, 1987.

[HOV93]   M. Hsu, R. Obermarck, and R. Vuurboom. Workflow model and execution. *Q. Bull. IEEE TC on Data Engineering*, 16(2):45–48, June 1993.

[HR83]   T. Haerder and A. Reuter. Principles of transaction-oriented database recovery. *ACM Computing Surveys*, 15(4):287–317, December 1983.

[HS91a]   A. Heuer and M.H. Scholl. Principles of object-oriented query languages. In *Proc. GI Conf. on Database Systems for Office, Engineering, and Scientific Applications*, March 1991.

[HS91b]   R. Hull and J. Su. On the expressive power of database queries with intermediate types. *Journal of Computer and System Sciences*, 43:219–267, 1991.

[Hsu93]   M. Hsu, editor. *Special Issue on Workflow and Extended Transaction Systems*, volume 16 of *Q. Bull. IEEE TC on Data Engineering*, June 1993.

[HTY89]   R. Hull, K. Tanaka, and M. Yoshikawa. Behavior analysis of object-oriented databases: Method structure, execution trees and reachability. In *Proc. 3rd Int. Conf. on Foundations of Data Organization and Algorithms*, 1989.

[HW88]   M. Herlihy and W. Weihl. Hybrid concurrency control for abstract data types. In *Proc. ACM SIGACT-SIGMOD Symp. on Principles of Database Systems*, pages 201–210, 1988.

[HW91]   A. Haake-Weber. Publishing tools need both: State-oriented and task-oriented version support. In *Proc. 15th Annual International Computer Software and Applications Conference (COMPSAC-91*, pages 633–639, 1991.

[HW92]   J. Haake and B. Wilson. Supporting collaborative writing of hyperdocuments in SEPIA. In *Proc. Conference on Computer-Supported Cooperative Work*, pages 138–146, 1992.

[HZ80]   M. Hammer and S.B. Zdonik. Knowledge-based query processing. In *Proc. 6th Int. Conf. on Very Large Databases*, pages 137–147, 1980.

[HZ87]   M. F. Hornick and S. B. Zdonik. A shared, segmented memory system for an object-oriented database. *ACM Transactions on Office Information Systems*, 5(1):70–95, January 1987.

[HZ90]   S. Heiler and S. Zdonik. Object Views: Extending the vision. In *Proc. 6th Int. Conf. on Data Engineering*, pages 86–93, 1990.

[IC90]   Y. Ioannidis and Y. Cha Kang. Randomized algorithms for optimizing large join queries. In *Proc. ACM SIGMOD Int. Conf. on Management of Data*, pages 312–321, 1990.

[IIY+87]   H. Ishikawa, Y. Izumida, T. Yoshino, T. Hoshaiai, and A. Makinouchi. Kid: Designing knowledge-based natural language interface. *IEEE Expert*, 2(2):57–71, 1987.

[Imm86]   N. Immerman. Relational queries computable in polynomial time. *Information and Computing*, 68:86–104, 1986.

[Ing89]   *INGRES 6.3 Reference Manual*, 1989. Ingres Corporation.

[INSS92]   Y.E. Ioannidis, R.T Ng, K. Shim, and T.K. Sellis. Parametric query optimization. In *Proc. 18th Int. Conf. on Very Large Databases*, pages 103–114, 1992.

[ISO86]   ISO/IEC International Standard 8879-1986. *Information Technology - Text and Office Systems - Standard Generalized Markup Language (SGML)*, 1986.

[ISO91]   ISO/IEC International Standard 10166-1. *Information Technology - Text and Office Systems - Document Filing and Retrieval (DFR) - Part 1 and Part 2*, 1991. First edition.

[ISO93]   ISO/IEC CD 10746-2.2. *Information Technology - Basic Reference Model of Open Distributed Processing - Part 2: Descriptive Model*, April 1993.

[IT86]   Y. Ishikawa and M. Tokoro. A concurrent object-oriented representation language Orient84/K: Its features and implementation. In *Proc. OOPSLA '86 Conf.*, pages 232–241, 1986.

[IT87]   Y. Ishikawa and M. Tokoro. Orient84/K: An object-oriented concurrent programming language for knowledge representation. In A. Yonezawa and M. Tokoro, editors, *Object-Oriented Concurrent Programming*. MIT Press, 1987.

[IW87]   Y. Ioannidis and E. Wong. Query optimization by simulated annealing. In *Proc. ACM SIGMOD Int. Conf. on Management of Data*, pages 9–22, 1987.

[JK84]   M. Jarke and J. Koch. Query optimization in database systems. *ACM Computing Surveys*, 16(2):111–152, 1984.

[JKS85]   M. Jarke, J. Koch, and J.W. Schmidt. Introduction to query processing. In W. Kim, D. Reiner, and D. Batory, editors, *Query Processing in Database Systems*, pages 3–28. Springer-Verlag, 1985.

[Jos91]   A. Joshi. Adaptive locking strategies in a multi-node data sharing environment. In *Proc. 17th Int. Conf. on Very Large Databases*, pages 181–191, 1991.

[JPSL+88]   G. Jakobson, G. Piatesky-Shapiro, C. Lafond, M. Rajinikanth, and J. Hernandez. CALIDA: A knowledge-based system for integrating multiple heterogeneous databases. In *Proc. 3rd Int. Conf. on Data and Knowledge Bases: Improving Usability and Responsiveness*, pages 3–18, 1988.

[JS82]   G. Jaeschke and H. Schek. Remarks on the algebra of non first normal form relations. In *Proc. ACM SIGACT-SIGMOD Symp. on Principles of Database Systems*, pages 124–137, 1982.

[JWKL90]   B.P. Jenq, D. Woelk, W. Kim, and W-L. Lee. Query processing in distributed ORION. In F. Bancilhon, C. Thanos, and D. Tsichritzis, editors, *Advances in Database Technology — EDBT'90*, volume 416 of *Lecture Notes in Computer Science*, pages 169–187. Springer-Verlag, 1990.

[Kai89]   G.E. Kaiser. Transactions for concurrent object-oriented programming systems. In *Proc. ACM SIGPLAN Workshop on Object-Based Concurrent Programming*, pages 136–138, 1989.

[Kan90]   P. Kanellakis. Elements of relational database theory. In J. van Leeuwen, editor, *Handbook of Theoretical Computer Science*, pages 1073–1156. Elsevier Science Publishers, 1990.

[Kap92]   B.A. Kaplan et al. Communicopia: A digital communication bounty. Technical Report Investment Research Report, Goldman Sachs, New York, NY, USA, 1992.

[Kar92]   P. D. Karp. The design space of frame knowledge representation systems. Technical Note 520, SRI International, Artificial Intelligence Center, Computing and Engineering Sciences Division, 1992.

[Kat90]   R.H. Katz. Toward a unified framework for version modeling in engineering databases. *ACM Computing Surveys*, 22(4):375–408, 1990.

[KB82]   R. Kaplan and J. Bresnan. Lexical-functional grammar: A formal system for grammatical representation. In J. Bresnan, editor, *The Mental Representation of Grammatical Relations*. MIT Press, 1982.

[KBC⁺87]   W. Kim, J. Banerjee, H.T. Chou, J.F. Garza, and D. Woelk. Composite object sup-
           port in an object-oriented database system. In *OOPSLA '87 Conf. Proc.*, pages
           118–125, 1987.

[KBR86]   T. S. Kaczmarek, R. Bates, and G. Robbins. Recent developments in NIKL. In
           Proc. 5th National Conf. on Artificial Intelligence (AAAI'92), pages 978–985, 1986.

[KC86]   S. N. Khoshafian and G. P. Copeland. Object identity. In *Proc. OOPSLA '86 Conf.*,
           pages 406–416, 1986.

[KC87]   R.H. Katz and E. Chang. Managing change in a computer-aided design database.
           In *Proc. 13th Int. Conf. on Very Large Databases*, pages 455–462, 1987.

[KDM88]   A.M. Kotz, K.R. Dittrich, and J.A. Mulle. Supporting semantic rules by a ggener-
           alized event/trigger mechanism. In *Advances in Database Technology — EDBT'88*,
           pages 76–91. Springer-Verlag, 1988.

[Ken79]   W. Kent. Limitations of record-based information models. *ACM Transactions on
           Database Systems*, 4(1):107–131, March 1979.

[Ken89]   W. Kent. The many forms of a single fact. In *Digest of Papers — IEEE COMPCON*,
           1989.

[Ken91a]   W. Kent. The breakdown of the information model in multi-database systems. *ACM
           SIGMOD Record*, 20(4):10–15, December 1991.

[Ken91b]   W. Kent. A rigorous model of object reference, identity, and existence. *Journal of
           Object-Oriented Programming*, 4(3):28–38, June 1991.

[Ken92a]   W. Kent. The state of object technology. *Canadian Information Processing*,
           July/August 1992.

[Ken92b]   W. Kent. User object model. *ACM OOPS Messenger*, 3(1), January 1992.

[KFA93]   W. Klas, G. Fischer, and K. Aberer. Integrating a relational database system into
           VODAK using its metaclass concept. Technical report, Arbeitspapiere der GMD,
           No 738, 1993.

[KGBW90]   W. Kim, J. Garza, N. Ballou, and D. Woelk. Architecture of the ORION next-
           generation database system. *IEEE Transactions on Knowledge and Data Eng.*, 2(1),
           March 1990.

[KGM91]   T. Keller, G. Graefe, and D. Maier. Efficient Assembly of Complex Objects. In
           Proc. ACM SIGMOD Int. Conf. on Management of Data, pages 148–157, 1991.

[Kim82]   W. Kim. On optimizing an SQL-like nested query. *ACM Transactions on Database
           Systems*, 7(3):443–469, September 1982.

[Kim89]   W. Kim. A model of queries for object-oriented databases. In *Proc. 15th Int. Conf.
           on Very Large Databases*, pages 423–432, 1989.

[Kim90]   W. Kim. *Introduction to Object-Oriented Databases*. MIT Press, 1990.

[Kin81]   J.J. King. QUIST: A system for semantic query optimization in relational databases.
           In *Proc. 7th Int. Conf. on Very Large Databases*, pages 510–517, 1981.

[Kin86]   R. King. A database management system based on an object-oriented model. In
           L. Kerschberg, editor, *Proc. 1st Int. Conf. on Expert Database Systems*, pages 443–
           468, 1986.

[KKM91]   A. Kemper, C. Kilger, and G. Moerkotte. Function materialization in object bases.
           In *Proc. ACM SIGMOD Int. Conf. on Management of Data*, pages 258–267, 1991.

[KL84]   R. Katz and T. Lehman. Database support for versions and alternatives of large
           design files. *IEEE Transactions on Software Eng.*, 10(2), 1984.

[KL89]   M. Kifer and G. Lausen. F-logic: A higher-order language for reasoning about
           objects, inheritance and scheme. In *Proc. ACM SIGMOD Int. Conf. on Management
           of Data*, pages 134–146, 1989.

[KL89]   W. Kim and F. Lochovsky. *Object-Oriented Concepts, Applications, and
           Databases*. Addison Wesley, 1989.

[Kla90]   W. Klas. *A Metaclass System for Open Object-Oriented Data Models*. PhD thesis,
           Technical University of Vienna, Vienna, Austria, 1990.

[Kla92]   W. Klas. Tailoring an object-oriented database system to integrate external multime-
           dia devices. In *Workshop on Heterogeneous Databases & Semantic Interoperability*,
           1992.

[KLR92]   P. Kanellakis, C. Lécluse, and P. Richard. Introduction to the data model. In
           F. Bancilhon, C. Delobel, and P. Kanellakis, editors, *Building an Object-Oriented
           Database System, The Story of* O_2. Morgan Kaufmann, 1992.

[KLS90]   H.F. Korth, E. Levy, and A. Silberschatz. Compensating transctions: A new recov-
           ery paradigm. In *Proc. 16th Int. Conf. on Very Large Databases*, pages 95–106,
           1990.

[KM90a]   A. Kemper and G. Moerkotte. Access support in object bases. In *Proc. ACM
           SIGMOD Int. Conf. on Management of Data*, pages 364–374, 1990.

[KM90b]   A. Kemper and G. Moerkotte. Advanced query processing in object bases using
           access support relations. In *Proc. 16th Int. Conf. on Very Large Databases*, pages
           290–301, 1990.

[KMM91]   P. Kanellakis, J. Mitchell, and H. Mairson. Unification and ml-type reconstruction.
           In J-L. Lassez and G. Plotkin, editors, *Computational Logic: Essays in Honor of
           Alan Robinson*, pages 444–479. MIT Press, 1991. Also in *Proc. 16th ACM Conf.
           on Principles of Programming Languages*, 1989 and *Proc. 17th ACM Conf. on
           Principles on Programming Languages*, 1990.

[KMP93]   A. Kemper, G. Moerkotte, and K. Peithner. A blackboard architecture for query
           optimization in object bases. In *Proc. 19th Int. Conf. on Very Large Databases*,
           pages 543–554, 1993.

[KMS90]   G. Kiernan, C. De Maindreville, and E. Simon. Making deductive database a prac-
           tical technology: a step forward. In *Proc. ACM SIGMOD Int. Conf. on Management
           of Data*, pages 237–246, 1990.

[KN90]   W. Klas and E.J. Neuhold. Designing intelligent hypertext systems using an open
           object-oriented database model. In *Arbeitspapiere der GMD, No 489*, 1990.

[KNB$^+$92] W. Klas, E.J. Neuhold, R. Bahlke, P. Fankhauser, G. Fischer, M. Kaul, P. Muth,
           T. Rakow, and V. Turau. VODAK design specification document, VML-VODAK
           model language, version 3.0. Technical report, University of Stuttgart, FRG, 1992.
           Working paper GMD.

[KNP88]   D. Konstantas, O. Nierstrasz, and M. Papathomas. An implementation of Hybrid:
           A concurrent, object-oriented language. In D. Tsichritzis, editor, *Active Object
           Environments*. Universite de Geneve, 1988.

[KNS90a]   W. Klas, E.J. Neuhold, and M. Schrefl. Metaclasses in vodak and their application
           in database integration. In *Arbeitspapiere der GMD, No 462*, 1990.

[KNS90b]   W. Klas, E.J. Neuhold, and M. Schrefl. Using an object-oriented approach to model
           multimedia data. *Computer Communications, Special Issue on Multimedia Systems*,
           13(4):204–216, 1990.

[Kor88]   H. F. Korth. Optimization of object-retrieval queries. In K. R. Dittrich, editor,
           Advances in Object-Oriented Database Systems, volume 334 of *Lecture Notes in
           Computer Science*, pages 352–357. Springer-Verlag, 1988.

[Kot87]   P.D. Kotch. Disk file allocation based on the buddy system. *ACM Transactions on
           Computer Systems*, 5(4), November 1987.

[Kot93]   A. Kotz-Dittrich. Adding active functionality to an object-oriented database system
           - a layered approach. In *Proc. Datenbanksysteme in Büro, Technik und Wissenschaft*,
           1993.

[KP88]   P. Kolaitis and C. Papadimitriou. Why not negation by fixpoint. In *Proc. ACM SIGACT-SIGMOD Symp. on Principles of Database Systems*, pages 231–239, 1988.

[KS88]   H.F. Korth and G.D. Speegle. Formal model of correctness without serializability. In *Proc. ACM SIGMOD Int. Conf. on Management of Data*, pages 379–386, 1988.

[KSW86]   P. Klahold, G. Schlageter, and W. Wilkes. A general model for version management in databases. In *Proc. 12th Int. Conf. on Very Large Databases*, pages 319–327, 1986.

[Kup87]   G. Kuper. Logic programming with sets. In *Proc. ACM SIGACT-SIGMOD Symp. on Principles of Database Systems*, pages 11–20, 1987.

[KV84]   G. Kuper and M. Vardi. A new approach to database logic. In *Proc. ACM SIGACT-SIGMOD Symp. on Principles of Database Systems*, pages 86–96, 1984.

[L⁺93]   M.E.S. Loomis et al. The ODMG object model. *Journal of Object-Oriented Programming*, pages 64–69, June 1993.

[LB85]   H. J. Levesque and R. J. Brachman. A fundamental tradeoff in knowledge representation and reasoning (revised version). In R.J. Brachman and H.J. Levesque, editors, *Readings in Knowledge Representation*. Morgan Kaufmann, Los Altos, CA, 1985.

[LBE⁺82]   W. Litwin, J. Boudenant, C. Esculier, A. Ferrier, A. Glorieux, J. La Chimia, K. Kabbaz, C. Moulinoux, P. Rolin, and C. Stangret. Sirius system for distributed data management. In H.-J. Schneider, editor, *Distributed Databases*, pages 311–366. North-Holland, 1982.

[LGJS90]   B. Liskov, R. Gruber, P. Johnson, and L. Shrira. A highly available object repository for use in a heterogeneous distributed system. In A. Dearle, G.M. Shaw, and S.B. Zdonik, editors, *Implementing Persistent Object Bases: Principles and Practice. Proc. Fourth Int. Workshop on Persistent Object Systems*, pages 255–266. Morgan Kaufmann, 1990.

[Lie87]   H. Lieberman. Concurrent object-oriented programming in Act1. In A. Yonezawa and M. Tokoro, editors, *Object-Oriented Concurrent Programming*. MIT Press, 1987.

[Lim89]   Architecture Projects Management Limited. *The ANSA Reference Manual*. Architecture Projects Management Limited, Castle Park, Cambridge, U.K., 1989.

[Lis88]   B. Liskov. Distributed programming in ARGUS. *Comm. of the ACM*, 31(3):300–312, March 1988.

[LK86]   P. Lyngbaek and W. Kent. A data modeling methodology for the design and implementation of information systems. In *Proc. of the 1st Int. Workshop on Object-Oriented Database Systems*, pages 6–17, 1986.

[LL89]   T.J. Lehman and B.G. Lindsay. The Starburst long field manager. In *Proc. 15th Int. Conf. on Very Large Databases*, pages 375–384, 1989.

[Llo87]   J. Lloyd. *Foundations of Logic Programming*. Springer-Verlag, 2nd edition, 1987.

[LLOW91]   C. Lamb, G. Landis, J. Orenstein, and D. Weinreb. The ObjectStore Database System. *Comm. of the ACM*, 34(10):50–63, October 1991.

[LM93]   D. Leivant and J.-Y. Marion. Lambda calculus characterizations of poly-time. In *Proc. Int. Conf. on Typed Lambda Calculi and Applications*, 1993. To appear in *Fundamenta Informaticae*.

[LP93]   R. Lorie and W. Plouffe. Complex objects and their use in design transactions. In *Proc. Engineering Design Applications Stream of ACM-IEEE Database Week*, pages 115–122, San Jose, 1993. ACM press.

[LPP70]   D. Luckham, D. Park, and M. Paterson. On formalized computer programs. *Journal of Computer and System Sciences*, 4:220–249, 1970.

[LR82]   T. Landers and R. Rosenberg. An overview of multibase. In H.-J. Schneider, editor, *Distributed Databases*, pages 153–184. North-Holland, 1982.

[LRV88]   C. Lecluse, P. Richard, and F. Velez. O$_2$, an Object-Oriented Data Model. In *Proc. ACM SIGMOD Int. Conf. on Management of Data*, pages 424–433, 1988.

[LV91]   R. Lanzelotte and P. Valduriez. Extending the search strategy in a query optimizer. In *Proc. 17th Int. Conf. on Very Large Databases*, pages 363–373, 1991.

[LVZ92]   R.S.G. Lanzelotte, P. Valduriez, and M. Zaït. Optimization of object-oriented recursive queries using cost-controlled strategies. In *Proc. ACM SIGMOD Int. Conf. on Management of Data*, pages 256–265, 1992.

[LVZC91] R. Lanzelotte, P. Valduriez, M. Ziane, and J.-P. Cheiney. Optimization of nonrecursive queries in OODBs. In C. Delobel, M. Kifer, and Y. Masunaga, editors, *Proc. 2nd Int. Conf. on Deductive and Object-Oriented Databases*, volume 566 of *Lecture Notes in Computer Science*, pages 1–21. Springer-Verlag, 1991.

[Lyn83]   N. Lynch. Multilevel atomicity: A new correctness criterion for database concurrency control. *ACM Transactions on Database Systems*, 8(4):484–502, 1983.

[Lyn91]   P. Lyngbaek, et al. OSQL: A language for object databases. Technical Report HPL-DTD-91-4, HP Laboratories, Palo Alto, CA, 1991.

[Mac85]   R. M. MacGregor. Ariel - a semantic front-end to relational dbmss. In *Proc. 11th Int. Conf. on Very Large Databases*, 1985.

[Mac90]   I.A. Macleod. Storage and retrieval of strcutured documents. *Information Processing and Management*, 26(2):197–208, 1990.

[Mac91a]   R. MacGregor. Using a description classifier to enhance deductive inference. In *Proc. 7th IEEE Conference on Artificial Intelligence Applications*, pages 141–147, 1991.

[Mac91b]   I.A. Macleod. Text retrieval and the relational data model. *Journal of the American Society for Information Science*, 42(2), 1991.

[Mai86]   D. Maier. A logic for objects. In *Int. Workshop on Foundations of Deductive Database and Logic Programming*, 1986.

[Mai89]   D. Maier. Making database systems fast enough for CAD applications. In W. Kim and F. Lochovsky, editors, *Object-Oriented Concepts, Applications and Databases*, pages 573–582. ACM and Addison-Wesley, 1989.

[Mai92a]   D. Maier. Specifying a database system to itself. In D.J. Harper and M.C. Norrie, editors, *Specifications of Database Systems*. Springer-Verlag, 1992.

[Mai92b]   H. Mairson. A simple proof of a theorem of statman. *Theoretical Computer Science*, 103:387–394, 1992.

[MB90]   F. Manola and A.P. Buchmann. A functional/relational object-oriented model for distributed object management – Preliminary description. Technical Report TM-0331-11-90-165, GTE Laboratories, December 1990.

[MB92]   R. M. MacGregor and D. Brill. Recognition algorithms for the LOOM classifier. In *Proc. 10th National Conf. on Artificial Intelligence (AAAI'92)*, pages 774–779, 1992.

[MBH$^+$92] F. Manola, M.L. Brodie, S. Heiler, M. Hornick, and D. Georgakopoulos. Distributed object management. *Int. Jour. Intelligent and Cooperative Information Systems*, 1(1), 1992.

[MBW80]   J. Mylopoulos, P. Bernstein, and H.K.T. Wong. A language facility for designing interactive database-intensive systems. *ACM Transactions on Database Systems*, 5(2):185–207, June 1980.

[MD86]   F. Manola and U. Dayal. PDM: An object-oriented data model. In *Proc. of the 1st Int. Workshop on Object-Oriented Database Systems*, pages 18–25, 1986.

[MDT88]   A. Motro, A. D'Atri, and L. Tarantino. The design of KIVIEW: An object-oriented browser. In *Proc. 2nd Int. Conf. on Expert Database Systems*, pages 17–31, 1988.

[MDZ93]   G. Mitchell, U. Dayal, and S.B. Zdonik. Control of an extensible query optimizer: A planning-based approach. In *Proc. 19th Int. Conf. on Very Large Databases*, pages 517–528, 1993.

[MDZ94]   G. Mitchell, U. Dayal, and S.B. Zdonik. Optimization of object-oriented queries: Problems and approaches, 1994. In this volume.

[Mey86]   N. Meyrowitz. Intermedia: The architecture and construction of an object-oriented hypermedia system and applications framework. In *Proc. OOPSLA '86 Conf.*, 1986.

[MH94]   F. Manola and S. Heiler. An approach to interoperable object models. In M.T. Özsu, U. Dayal, and P. Valduriez, editors, *Distributed Object Management*, pages 304–308. Morgan Kaufmann, 1994.

[MHF93]   J.C. Mitchell, F. Honsell, and K. Fisher. A lambda calculus of objects and method specialization. In *Proc. 8th IEE Conf. on LICS*, pages 26–38, 1993.

[Mil78]   R. Milner. A theory of type polymorphism in programming. *Journal of Computer and System Sciences*, 103:348–375, 1978.

[Mir87]   D.P. Miranker. Treat: A better match algorithm for AI production systems. In *Proc. National Conf. on Artificial Intelligence*, 1987.

[Mit90]   J.C. Mitchell. Toward a typed foundation for method specialization and inheritance. In *Proc. 17th ACM Conf. on Principles of Programming Languages*, pages 109–124, 1990.

[Mit93]   G.A. Mitchell. *Extensible Query Processing in an Object-Oriented Database*. PhD thesis, Brown University, Providence, RI, 1993. Available as Technical Report CS-93-16.

[MKN92]   P. Muth, W. Klas, and E.J. Neuhold. How to handle global transactions in heterogeneous database systems. In *Proc. IEEE 2nd Int. Workshop on Research Issues on Data Engineering - Transaction and Query Processing (RIDE-TQP)*, pages 192–198, 1992.

[MMWF93] R. Medina-Mora, H.K.T. Wong, and P. Flores. Action Workflow as the enterprise integration technology. *Q. Bull. IEEE TC on Data Engineering*, 16(2):49–52, 1993.

[MN91]   C. Mohan and I. Narang. Recovery and coherency-control protocols for fast intersystem page transfer and fine-granularity locking in a shared disks transaction environment. In *Proc. 17th Int. Conf. on Very Large Databases*, pages 193–207, 1991.

[Mos85]   E. Moss. *Nested Transactions*. The MIT Press, Cambridge, MA, 1985.

[Mos90]   J.E.B. Moss. Design of the Mneme persistent object store. *ACM Transactions on Information Systems*, 8(2):103–139, April 1990.

[Mos92]   J.E.B. Moss. Working with persistent objects: To swizzle or not to swizzle. *IEEE Transactions on Software Eng.*, 18(8):657–673, August 1992.

[Mot88]   A. Motro. Vague: A user interface to relational databases that permits vague queries. *ACM Transactions on Office Information Systems*, 6(3):187–214, July 1988.

[Mot90]   A. Motro. Accommodating imprecision in database systems. *ACM SIGMOD Record*, 19(4):69–74, December 1990.

[MP94]   B. Martin and C.H. Pedersen. Long-lived concurrent activities. In M.T. Özsu, U. Dayal, and P. Valduriez, editors, *Distributed Object Management*, pages 188–211. Morgan Kaufmann, 1994.

[MR91]   P. Muth and T.C Rakow. Atomic commitment for integrated database systems. In *Proc. 7th Int. Conf. on Data Engineering*, 1991.

[MRKN92] P. Muth, T.C. Rakow, W. Klas, and E.J. Neuhold. A transaction model for an open publication environment. In A.K. Elmagarmid, editor, *Transaction Models for Advanced Database Applications*. Morgan Kaufmann, 1992.

[MRW+93]   P. Muth, T.C. Rakow, G. Weikum, P. Brössler, and C. Hasse. Semantic concurrency control in object-oriented database systems. In *Proc. 9th Int. Conf. on Data Engineering*, pages 233–242, 1993.

[MS86]   D. Maier and J. Stein. Indexing in an object-oriented DBMS. In *Proc. of the 1st Int. Workshop on Object-Oriented Database Systems*, pages 171–182, 1986.

[MS88]   D. Maier and J. Stein. Development and implementation of an object-oriented DBMS. In B. Shriver and P. Wegner, editors, *Research Directions in Object-Oriented Programming*, pages 355–392. MIT Press, 1988.

[MS91]   F. Matthes and J.W. Schmidt. Bulk types: Built-in or add-on? In *Proc. 3rd Int. Workshop on Database Programming Lang.*, pages 33–54. Morgan Kaufmann, 1991.

[MSOP86]   D. Maier, J. Stein, A. Otis, and A. Purdy. Development of an object-oriented DBMS. In *Proc. OOPSLA '86 Conf.*, pages 472–482, 1986.

[Mur92]   M. Muralikrishna. Improved unnesting algorithms for join aggregate SQL queries. In *Proc. 18th Int. Conf. on Very Large Databases*, pages 91–102, 1992.

[MZ87]   C.V. Malley and S.B. Zdonik. A knowledge-based approach to query optimization. In *Proc. 1st Int. Conf. on Expert Database Systems*, pages 329–344. Addison Wesley, 1987.

[MZD92]   G. Mitchell, S.B. Zdonik, and U. Dayal. An architecture for query processing in persistent object stores. In *Proc. Hawaii Int. Conf. on System Sciences*, volume II, pages 787–798, 1992.

[Nak94]   T. Nakajima. Commutativity based concurrency control for multiversion objects. In M.T. Özsu, U. Dayal, and P. Valduriez, editors, *Distributed Object Management*, pages 231–247. Morgan Kaufmann, 1994.

[Nav92]   S. B. Navathe. Evolution of data modeling for databases. *Comm. of the ACM*, 35(9):112–123, September 1992.

[Neb88]   B. Nebel. Computational complexity of terminological reasoning in back. *Artificial Intelligence*, 34(3):371–383, 1988.

[NFS88]   *Network File System: Version 2 Protocol Specification*. Sun Microsystems, Inc., Mountain View, California, 1988.

[Nie87]   O.M. Nierstrasz. Active objects in Hybrid. In *Proc. OOPSLA '87 Conf.*, pages 243–253, 1987.

[Not87]   J.D. Nothcutt. *Mechanisms for Reliable Distributed Real-Time Operating Systems, The Alpha Kernel*. Academic Press, 1987.

[NRZ92]   M.H. Nodine, S.R. Ramaswamy, and S.B. Zdonik. A cooperative transaction model for design databases. In A.K. Elmagarmid, editor, *Database Transaction Models for Advanced Applications*, pages 53–86. Morgan Kaufmann, 1992.

[NS88]   E. Neuhold and M. Stonebraker. Future directions in dbms research. Technical report, Technical Report 88-001, Intl. Computer Science Inst. Berkeley, May 1988.

[NT89]   S. Naqvi and S. Tsur. *A Logic Language for Data and Knowledge Bases*. Computer Science Press, 1989.

[NZ90]   M. Nodine and S. Zdonik. Cooperative transaction hierarchies: A transaction model to support design applications. In *Proc. 16th Int. Conf. on Very Large Databases*, pages 83–94, 1990.

[Obj93]   Objectivity Inc. *Objectivity/DB Documentation V2*, 1993.

[ODCG93]   C. Ozkan, A. Dogac, C.Evrendilek, and T. Gesli. Efficient ordering of path traversals in object-oriented query optimization. In *Proc. Int. Symp. on Computer and Information Sciences*, Istanbul, Turkey, 1993.

[OHMS92]   J. Orenstein, S. Haradvala, B. Margulies, and D. Sakahara. Query processing in the ObjectStore database system. In *Proc. ACM SIGMOD Int. Conf. on Management of Data*, pages 403–412, 1992.

[OMG91a]   OMG. *The Commmon Object Request Broker: Architecture and Specification*. Object Management Group, 1991.

[OMG91b]   OMG. The OMG object model, draft 0.9. Technical Report OMG Document Number 91.9.1, Object Management Group, Framingham, MA, USA, September 1991.

[OMG92]   OMG. *Object Management Architecture Guide*. Framingham, MA, USA, 1992. Second Edition.

[ONT92]   ONTOS Inc., Burlington, Massachusetts. *Ontos DB 2.2 Reference Manual*, 1992.

[OOD93]   T. Okay, C. Ozkan, and A. Dogac. Design and implementation of a database kernel. Technical Report 15, TUBITAK Software Research and Development Center, March 1993.

[Org87]   International Standards Organization. Information processing systems — document filing and retrieval (DFR), Part 2: Protocol specification, iso/tc 97/sc 18/wg 4, version 1, 1987.

[Osb88]   S. L. Osborn. Identity, equality and query optimization. In K.R. Dittrich, editor, *Advances in Object-Oriented Database Systems*, volume 334 of *Lecture Notes in Computer Science*, pages 346–351. Springer-Verlag, 1988.

[Ozk90]   E. Ozkarahan. *Database Management Concepts, Design and Practice*. Prentice-Hall, 1990.

[ÖDV94]   M. T. Özsu, U. Dayal, and P. Valduriez. An introduction to distributed object management. In M.T. Özsu, U. Dayal, and P. Valduriez, editors, *Distributed Object Management*, pages 1–24. Morgan Kaufmann, San Mateo, California, 1994.

[ÖV91]   M.T. Özsu and P. Valduriez. *Principles of Distributed Database Systems*. Prentice-Hall, 1991.

[Özs94]   M.T. Özsu. Transaction models and transaction management in object-oriented database management systems, 1994. In this volume.

[Pap86]   C. Papadimitriou. *The Theory of Database Concurrency Control*. Computer Science Press, Rockville, MD, 1986.

[Pey87]   S.L. Peyton Jones. *The implementation of functional programming languages*. Prentice-Hall, 1987.

[PHH92]   H. Pirahesh, J.M. Hellerstein, and W. Hasan. Extensible/rule based query rewrite optimization in Starburst. In *Proc. ACM SIGMOD Int. Conf. on Management of Data*, pages 39–48, 1992.

[PKH88]   C. Pu, G. Kaiser, and N. Hutchinson. Split-transactions for open-ended activities. In *Proc. 14th Int. Conf. on Very Large Databases*, pages 26–37, 1988.

[PM93]   R.J. Peters and M.T.Özsu. Reflection in a uniform behavioral object model. In *Proc. 12th Int. Conf. on Entity-Relaionship Approach*, pages 37–49, December 1993.

[PÖS94]   M.T. Özsu, R.J. Peters, D. Szafron, B. Irani, A. Munoz, and A. Lipka. TIGUKAT: A uniform behavioral objectbase management system. *VLDB Journal*. To appear.

[PS84a]   C. Parent and S. Spaccapietra. An entity-relationship algebra. In *Proc. 1st Int. Conf. on Data Engineering*, pages 501–507, 1984.

[PS84b]   P. F. Patel-Schneider. Small can be beautiful in knowledge representation. Technical Report Fairchild Technical Report 37, FLAIR, October 1984.

[PS86]   P. F. Patel-Schneider. A four valued semantics for frame-based description languages. In *Proc. 5th National Conf. on Artificial Intelligence (AAAI'92)*, pages 344–348, 1986.

[PSBL84]   P. F. Patel-Schneider, R. J. Brachman, and H. J. Levesque. ARGON: Knowledge representation meets information retrieval. Technical Report Fairchild Technical Report 654, FLAIR, 1984.

[PZ91]   M. Palmer and S.B. Zdonik. Fido: A cache that learns to fetch. In *Proc. 17th Int. Conf. on Very Large Databases*, pages 255–264, 1991.

[Rei82]   S.P. Reiss. Eris: The design and implementation of an experimental relational information system. Unpublished manuscript, December 1982.

[RF87]   A. S. Rao and N. Foo. CONGRESS: Conceptual graph reasoning system. In *Proc. 3rd Conf. on Artificial Intelligence Applications*, pages 87–92, 1987.

[RGL90]   A. Rosenthal and C. Galindo-Legaria. Query graphs, implementing trees, and freely-reorderable outerjoins. In *Proc. ACM SIGMOD Int. Conf. on Management of Data*, pages 291–299, 1990.

[RGN90]   T. Rakow, J. Gu, and E.J. Neuhold. Serializability in object-oriented database systems. In *Proc. 6th Int. Conf. on Data Engineering*, 1990.

[Rie83]   D.R. Ries, et al. Decompilation and optimization for ADAPLEX: A procedural database language. Technical Report CCA-82-04, Computer Corporation of America, Cambridge, MA, September 1983.

[RLK86]   J. Rohmer, R. Lescoeur, and J.M. Kerisit. The alexander-method, a technique for processing of recursive axioms in deductive databases. *New Generation Computing*, pages 273–285, 1986.

[RLMN93]   T.C. Rakow, M. Löhr, F. Moser, and E.J. Neuhold. Using object-oriented database systems for multimedia applications. *it+it (Special Issue on Hypermedia/Multimedia*, 35(3):4–17, June 1993. In German.

[RM93]   T.C. Rakow and P. Muth. The V3 video server - managing analog and digital video clips. In *Proc. ACM SIGMOD Int. Conf. on Management of Data*, 1993.

[ROE+90]   M. Rusinkiewicz, S. Ostermann, A. K. Elmagarmid, K. Loa, P. A. Ng, C. V. Ramamoorthy, L. C. Seifert, and R. T. Yeh. The distributed operation language for specifying multi-system applications. In *Systems Integration '90. Proc. 1st Int. Conf. on Systems Integration*, pages 337–345, 1990.

[RR84]   A. Rosenthal and D. Reiner. Extending the algebraic framework of query processing to handle outerjoins. In *Proc. 10th Int. Conf. on Very Large Databases*, pages 334–343, 1984.

[RR85]   A. Rosenthal and D.S. Reiner. Querying relational views of networks. In W. Kim, D.S. Reiner, and D.S. Batory, editors, *Query Processing in Database Systems*, pages 109–124. Springer-Verlag, 1985.

[RS87]   L.A. Rowe and M.R. Stonebraker. The Postgres data model. In *Proc. 13th Int. Conf. on Very Large Databases*, pages 83–96, 1987.

[Rud92]   E.A. Rudensteiner. Multiview: A methodology for supporting multiple views in object-oriented databases. In *Proc. 18th Int. Conf. on Very Large Databases*, pages 187–198, 1992.

[Saa89]   G. Saake, et al. Sorting, grouping and duplicate elimination in the advanced information management prototype. In *Proc. 15th Int. Conf. on Very Large Databases*, pages 307–316, 1989.

[SAC+79]   P.G. Selinger, M.M. Astrahan, D.D. Chamberlin, R.A. Lorie, and T.G. Price. Access path selection in a relational database management system. In *Proc. ACM SIGMOD Int. Conf. on Management of Data*, pages 23–34, 1979.

[Sal88]   B. Salzberg. *File Structures, An Analytic Approach*. Prentice-Hall, 1988.

[Sav90]   A. Savasere. An approach to schema integration using classification. Master's thesis, University of Florida, Gainesville, Fl 32611, 1990.

[SB86]   M. Stefik and D.G. Bobrow. Object-oriented programming: Themes and variations. *AI Magazine*, January 1986.

[SC90]   E.J. Shekita and M.J. Carey. A performance evaluation of pointer-based joins. In *Proc. ACM SIGMOD Int. Conf. on Management of Data*, pages 300–311, 1990.

[SCB+86] C. Schaffert, T. Cooper, B. Bullis, M. Kilian, and C. Wilpolt. An introduction to trellis/owl. In *OOPSLA '86 Conf. Proc.*, pages 9–16, 1986.

[Sch86]   P. Schwarz, et al. Extensibility in the Starburst database system. In *Proc. of the 1st Int. Workshop on Object-Oriented Database Systems*, pages 85–92, 1986.

[SG88]   A. Swami and A. Gupta. Optimization of large join queries. In *Proc. ACM SIGMOD Int. Conf. on Management of Data*, pages 8–17, 1988.

[SGN93]   A. P. Sheth, S. K. Gala, and S. B. Navathe. On automatic reasoning for shema integration. *Int. Jour. Intelligent and Cooperative Information Systems*, 2(1):23–50, March 1993.

[She91]   A. Sheth. Preface by the special issue editor. *ACM SIGMOD Record*, 20(4):5–9, December 1991.

[SHH+92] N. Streitz, J. Haake, J. Hannemann, A. Lemke, W. Schuler, H. Schütt, and M. Thüring. SEPIA: A cooperative hypermedia authoring environment. In *Proc. ACM Conf. on Hypertext*, pages 343–364, 1992.

[Shi81]   D.W. Shipman. The functional data model and the language DAPLEX. *ACM Transactions on Database Systems*, 6(1):140–173, March 1981.

[SHP88]   M. Stonebraker, E. Hanson, and S. Potamianos. The POSTGRES rule manager. *IEEE Transactions on Software Eng.*, 14(7):897–907, July 1988.

[SHP89]   M. Stonebraker, M. Hearst, and S. Potamianos. A commentary on the POSTGRES rules system. *ACM SIGMOD Record*, 18(3):5–11, September 1989.

[SHT89]   N. Steitz, J. Hannemann, and M. Thüring. From ideas and arguments to hyper-documents: Travelling through activity spaces. In *Proc. Hypertext'89 Workshop*, 1989.

[SI74]   R. Schank and C. J. Rieger III. Inference and the computer understanding of natural language. *Artificial Intelligence*, 5(4):373–412, 1974.

[SJGP90] M. Stonebraker, A. Jhingran, J. Goh, and S. Potamianos. On rules, procedures, caching and views in data base systems. In *Proc. ACM SIGMOD Int. Conf. on Management of Data*, pages 281–290, 1990.

[SK94]   R. Soley and W. Kent. The OMG object model. In W. Kim, editor, *Modern Database Management – Object-Oriented and Multidatabase Technologies*. Addison Wesley, 1994. (in press).

[Ska89]   A. Skarra. Concurrency control for cooperating transactions in an object-oriented database. In *Proc. ACM SIGPLAN Workshop on Object-Based Concurrent Programming*, pages 145–147, 1989.

[Ska91]   A.H. Skarra. Localized correctness specifications for cooperating transactions in an object-oriented database. *Office Knowledge Engineering*, 4(1):79–105, February 1991.

[SKW92]   V. Singhal, S.V. Kakkad, and P.R. Wilson. Texas: An Efficient, Portable Persistent Store. In *Proc. of the Fifth Int. Workshop on Persistent Object Systems*, pages 11–33, 1992.

[SL90]   A. P. Sheth and J. A. Larson. Federated database systems for managing distributed, heterogeneous, and autonomous databases. *ACM Computing Surveys*, 22(3):183–236, September 1990.

[SL90]   A. P. Sheth and J. A. Larson. Federated database systems for managing distributed, heterogeneous, and autonomous databases. *ACM Computing Surveys*, 22(3):183–236, September 1990.

[SLPW89] G. Saake, V. Linnemann, P. Pistor, and L. Wegner. Sorting, grouping and duplicate elimination in the advanced information managment prototype. In *Proc. 15th Int. Conf. on Very Large Databases*, pages 307–316, 1989.

[SLR88]   T. Sellis, C. Lin, and L. Raschid. Implementing large production systems in a dbms environement: Concepts and algorithms. In *Proc. ACM SIGMOD Int. Conf. on Management of Data*, pages 404–412, 1988.

[SO87]   S. Shenoy and Z. Ozsoyoglu. A system for semantic query optimization. In *Proc. ACM SIGMOD Int. Conf. on Management of Data*, pages 181–195, 1987.

[SÖ89]   D.D. Straube and M.T. Özsu. Query transformation rules for an object algebra. Technical Report TR 89–23, Department of Computing Science, University of Alberta, September 1989.

[SÖ90a]   D.D. Straube and M.T. Özsu. Queries and query processing in object-oriented database systems. *ACM Transactions on Information Systems*, 8(4):387–430, October 1990.

[SÖ90b]   D.D. Straube and M.T. Özsu. Type consistency of queries in an object-oriented database system. In *Proc. ECOOP/OOPSLA '90 Conf.*, pages 224–233, 1990.

[Sow84]   J. Sowa. *Conceptual Structures: Information Processing in Mind and Machine*. Addison Wesley, 1984.

[SR86]   M. Stonebraker and L. Rowe. The design of POSTGRES. In *Proc. ACM SIGMOD Int. Conf. on Management of Data*, pages 340–355, 1986.

[SRL⁺90]   M. Stonebraker, L.A. Rowe, B. Lindsay, J. Gray, M. Carey, M. Brodie, P. Bernstein, and D. Beech. Third-generation data base system manifesto. *ACM SIGMOD Record*, 19(3):31–44, September 1990.

[SS77]   J. M. Smith and D. C. P. Smith. Database abstractions: Aggregation and generalization. *ACM Transactions on Database Systems*, 2(2):105–133, June 1977.

[SS84]   P. Schwartz and A. Spector. Synchronizing shared abstract types. *ACM Transactions on Computer Systems*, 2(3):223–250, August 1984.

[SS86]   H.-J. Schek and M. Scholl. An algebra for the relational model with relation-valued attributes. *Information Systems*, 11(2):137–147, 1986.

[SS89]   J.J. Shilling and P.F. Sweeney. Three steps to views: Extending the object-oriented paradigm. In *Proc. OOPSLA '89 Conf.*, pages 353–361, 1989.

[SS90a]   H. Schütt and N. Streitz. HyperBase: A hypermedia engine based on a relational database management system. In A. Rizk, N. Streitz, and J André, editors, *Hypertext: Concepts, Systems, and Applications: Proceedings of the First European Conference on Hypertext*, pages 95–108. Cambridge University Press, 1990.

[SS90b]   K. Shannon and R. Snodgrass. Semantic clustering. In A. Dearle, G.M. Shaw, and S.B. Zdonik, editors, *Implementing Persistent Object Bases: Principles and Practice. Proc. Fourth Int. Workshop on Persistent Object Systems*, pages 389–402. Morgan Kaufmann, 1990.

[SSG⁺91]   A. Savasere, A. P. Sheth, S. K. Gala, S. B. Navathe, and H. Marcus. On applying classification to schema integration. In *Proc. 1st Int. Workshop on Interoperability in Multidatabase Systems (IMS'91)*, pages 258–261, 1991.

[Sta79]   R. Statman. The typed λ-calculus is not elementary recursive. *Theoretical Computer Science*, 9:73–81, 1979.

[Str91a]   D.D. Straube. *Queries and Query Processing in Object-Oriented Database Systems*. PhD thesis, University of Alberta, 1991.

[Str91b]   B. Stroustrup. *The C++ Programming Language (2nd Ed.)*. Addison-Wesley, 1991.

[SW91]   Frank Schmuck and Jim Wyllie. Experience with transactions in QuickSilver. In *Proc. 13th ACM Symp. on Operating Systems Principles*, pages 239–253, October 1991.

[SWF⁺86]   J.B. Smith, S.F. Weiss, G.J. Ferguson, J.D. Bolter, M. Lansman, and D.V. Bea. WE: A writing environment for professionals. Technical Report 86-025, Dept. of Computer Science, University of North Carolina, August 1986.

[SWF87]   J.B. Smith, S.F. Weiss, and G.J. Ferguson. A hypertext writing environment and its cognitive basis. In *Proc. Hypertext'87 Workshop*, pages 195–214, 1987.

[SWKH76]   M. Stonebraker, E. Wong, P. Kreps, and G. Held. The design and implementations of Ingres. *ACM Transactions on Database Systems*, 1(3):189–222, September 1976.

[Syb89]   *SYBASE Reference Manual*, 1989. Sybase Corporation.

[SZ87]   A. Skarra and S. Zdonik. Type evolution in an object-oriented database. In B. Shriver and P. Wegner, editors, *Research Directions in Object-Oriented Programming*, pages 393–416. MIT Press, 1987.

[SZ89]   G.M. Shaw and S.B. Zdonik. Object-oriented queries: Equivalence and optimization. In *Proc. 1st Int. Conf. on Deductive and Object-Oriented Databases*, pages 264–278, 1989.

[SZ90]   G. Shaw and S. Zdonik. A query algebra for object-oriented databases. In *Proc. 6th Int. Conf. on Data Engineering*, pages 154–162, 1990.

[SZR86]   A.H. Skarra, S.B. Zdonik, and S.P. Reiss. An object server for an object-oriented database system. In *Proc. of the 1st Int. Workshop on Object-Oriented Database Systems*, pages 196–204, September 1986.

[TBC+87]   M. Templeton, D. Brill, A. Chen, S. Dao, E. Lund, R. McGregor, and P. Ward. Mermaid: A front end to distributed heterogeneous databases. *Proc. IEEE*, 75(5):695–708, May 1987.

[TFGN87]   D. Tsichritzis, E. Fiume, S. Gibbs, and O. Nierstrasz. KNOs: Knowledge acquisition, dissemination, and manipulation objects. *ACM Transactions on Information Systems*, 5(1):96–112, January 1987.

[The83]   D.G. Theriault. Issues in the design and implementation of Act2. Technical Report 728, MIT Artificial Intelligence Laboratory, Cambridge, MA, June 1983.

[TI86]   M. Tokoro and Y. Ishikawa. Orient84/K: A language with multiple paradigms in the object framework. In *Proc. 19th Annual Hawaii Conf. on System Sciences*, 1986.

[TR93a]   H. Thimm and T.C. Rakow. Upgrading multimedia data handling services of a database management system by an interaction manager. In *Arbeitspapiere der GMD, No 729*, 1993.

[TR93b]   V. Turau and T.C. Rakow. A schema partition for multimedia database management systems. In *Arbeitspapiere der GMD, No 729*, 1993.

[Tri91]   P. Trinder. Comprehensions, a query notation for DBPLs. In *Proc. 3rd Int. Workshop on Database Programming Languages*, pages 55–68. Morgan Kaufmann, 1991.

[TWF+82]   F. Tou, M. Williams, F. Fikes, A. Henderson, and T. Malone. RABBIT: An intelligent database assistant. In *Proc. 1st National Conf. on Artificial Intelligence (AAAI'82)*, 1982.

[UA79]   J.D. Ullman and A.V. Aho. Universality of data retrievial languages. In *Proc. ACM Conf. on Principles of Programming Languages*, 1979.

[Ull82]   J.D. Ullman. *Principles of Database Systems*. Computer Science Press, 2nd edition, 1982.

[Ull88]   J.D. Ullman. *Principles of Database and Knowledge Base Systems*. Computer Science Press, 1988.

[Uni92]   University of Wisconsin. *Using the EXODUS storage manager, V2.1.1*, June 1992.

[US92]   R. Unland and G. Schlageter. Object-oriented database systems - state of the art and research problems. In K. Jeffery, editor, *Expert Database Systems*, pages 117–222. Academic Press, 1992.

[Var82]   M. Vardi. The complexity of relational query languages. In *Proc. Fourteenth Annual ACM Symp. on Theory of Computing*, pages 137–146, 1982.

[VBD89]   F. Velez, G. Bernard, and V. Darnis. The O2 object manager: an overview. In *Proc. 15th Int. Conf. on Very Large Databases*, pages 357–366, 1989.

[VD91]   S.L. Vandenberg and D.J. DeWitt. Algebraic support for complex objects with arrays, identity and inheritance. In *Proc. ACM SIGMOD Int. Conf. on Management of Data*, pages 158–167, 1991.

[Ver91]   Versant Object Technology, Menlo Park, California. *VERSTANT System Reference Manual, Release 1.6*, 1991.

[Vie86]   L. Vieille. Recursive axioms in deductive databases : the query-subquery approach. In *Proc. 1st Int. Conf. on Expert Database Systems*, pages 253–267, 1986.

[Vie90]   L. Vieille. Eks-v1, a short overview. In *Proc. AAAI Workshop on Knowledge Base Management System*, 1990.

[VK91]   J.S. Vitter and P. Krishnan. Optimal prefetching via data compression. In *Proc. 32nd Annual Symp. on Foundations of Computer Science*, 1991.

[VKC86]   P. Valduriez, S. Khoshafian, and G. Copeland. Implementation techniques of complex objects. In *Proc. 12th Int. Conf. on Very Large Databases*, pages 101–110, August 1986.

[W+88]   D. Weinreb et al. An Object-Oriented Database System to Support an Integrated Programming Environment. *Q. Bull. IEEE TC on Data Eng.*, 11(2):33–43, June 1988.

[WA91]   G.I. Williamson and M. Asmoodeh. The application of information modeling in the telecommunications management network (tmn). In *Proc. Telecommunications Information Networking Architecture Workshop (TINA91)*, 1991.

[Wal87]   J. Walker. Document examiner: Delivery interface to hypertext documents. In *Proc. Hypertext'87 Workshop*, 1987.

[Wal91]   E. Waller. Schema updates and consistency. In *Proc. 2nd Int. Conf. on Deductive and Object-Oriented Databases*, pages 167–188. Springer-Verlag, 1991.

[WB92]   D.L. Wells and J.A. Blakeley. Distribution and persistence in the open object-oriented database system. In M.T. Özsu, U. Dayal, and P. Valduriez, editors, *Distributed Object Management*, pages 51–56. Morgan Kaufmann, 1992.

[WBT92]   D.L. Wells, J.A. Blakeley, and C.W. Thompson. Architecture of an open object-oriented database management system. *Computer*, 25(10):74–82, October 1992.

[WCH+93]   D. Woelk, P. Cannata, M. Huhns, W.-M. Shen, and C. Tomlinson. Using Carnot for enterprise information integration. In *Proc. 2nd Int. Conf. on Parallel and Distributed Information Systems*, pages 133–136, 1993.

[Wei86]   G. Weikum. A theoretical foundation of multi-level concurrency control. In *Proc. 5th ACM SIGACT-SIGMOD Symp. on Principles of Database Systems*, pages 31–42, 1986.

[Wei88]   W. Weihl. Commutativity-based concurrency control for abstract data types. *IEEE Transactions on Computers*, 37(12):1488–1505, 1988.

[Wei89]   W. Weihl. Local atomicity properties: Modular concurrency controlf or abstract data types. *ACM Trans. on Programming Languages and Systems*, 11(2):249–281, 1989.

[Wei91]   G. Weikum. Principles and realization strategies of multilevel transaction management. *ACM Transactions on Database Systems*, 16(1):132–180, March 1991.

[Wel91]   D.L. Wells. DARPA Open Object-Oriented Database Architecture Specification. Technical Report Version 6, Computer Science Laboratory, Texas Instruments, Inc., November 1991.

[WF90]   J. Widom and S.J. Finkelstein. Set-oriental production rules in relational database systems. In *Proc. ACM SIGMOD Int. Conf. on Management of Data*, pages 259–270, 1990.

[WH93]   G. Weikum and C. Hasse. Multi-level transaction management for complex objects: Implementation, performance, parallelism. *The VLDB Journal*, 2(4):407–454, October 1993.

[WHBM90] G. Weikum, C. Hasse, P. Broessler, and P Muth. Multi level recovery. In *Proc. 9th ACM SIGACT-SIGMOD-SIGART Symp. on Principles of Database Systems*, 1990.

[WN90]   K. Wilkinson and M.-A. Neimat. Maintaining Consistency of Client-Cached Data. In *Proc. 16th Int. Conf. on Very Large Databases*, pages 122–133, 1990.

[WR89]   H. Wächter and A. Reuter. Transaction concepts and recovery mechanisms for object bases. Technical Report Technical Report 322 672, Re 660/2-1, University of Stuttgart, FRG, 1989.

[WR91]   Y. Wang and L. A. Rowe. Cache consistency and concurrency control in client/server DBMS architecture. In *Proc. ACM SIGMOD Int. Conf. on Management of Data*, pages 367–376, 1991.

[WS84]   G. Weikum and H.-J. Schek. Architectural issues of transaction management in layered systems. In *Proc. 10th Int. Conf. on Very Large Databases*, pages 454–465, 1984.

[WZ88]   P. Wegner and S.B. Zdonik. Type similarity, inheritance, and evolution. In *Proc. 2nd European Conf. on Object-Oriented Programming*, 1988.

[Yao77]   S.B. Yao. Approximating block accesses in database orginizations. *Comm. of the ACM*, 20(4):260–261, April 1977.

[YBS86]   A. Yonezawa, J.P. Briot, and E. Shibayama. Object-oriented programming in ABCL/1. In *Proc. OOPSLA '86 Conf.*, pages 258–268, 1986.

[YSTH87] A. Yonezawa, E. Shibayama, T. Takada, and Y. Honda. *Modelling and Programming in an Object-Oriented Concurrent Language ABCL/1*. MIT Press, 1987.

[ZABM92] S. Zatti, J. Ashfield, J. Baker, and E. Miller. Naming and registration for ibm distributed systems. *IBM Systems Journal*, 31(2), 1992.

[Zan83]   C. Zaniolo. The database language GEM. In *Proc. ACM SIGMOD Int. Conf. on Management of Data*, pages 207–218, 1983.

[Zan88]   C. Zaniolo. Design and implementation of a logic based language for data intensive applications. In *Proc. Int. Conf. on Logic Programming*, 1988.

[Zdo86]   S.B. Zdonik. Query processing in an object-oriented database. In *Proc. Int. Workshop on Advanced Programming Environments for Programming in the Large*, Trondheim, Norway, 1986. Springer-Verlag.

[Zdo89]   S.B. Zdonik. Query optimization in object-oriented database systems. In *Proc. of the 22nd Annual Hawaii Int. Conf. on System Sciences*, 1989.

[Zdo94]   S.B. Zdonik. What makes object-oriented database management systems different?, 1994. In this volume.

[Zic92]   R. Zicari. A framework for schema updates in an object-oriented database system. In F. Bancilhon, C. Delobel, and P. Kanellakis, editors, *Building an Object-Oriented Database System, The Story of O₂*, pages 146–182. Morgan Kaufmann, 1992.

[ZM88]   J. Zhu and D. Maier. Abstract objects in an object-oriented data model. In *Proc. 2nd Int. Conf. on Expert Database Systems*, pages 73–105, 1988.

[ZM90a]   S.B. Zdonik and D. Maier. Fundamentals of object-oriented databases. In S.B. Zdonik and D. Maier, editors, *Readings in Object-Oriented Database Systems*, pages 1–32. Morgan Kaufmann, 1990.

[ZM90b]   S.B. Zdonik and D. Maier, editors. *Readings in Object-Oriented Database Systems*. Morgan Kaufmann, 1990.

[ZM91]   S.B. Zdonik and G. Mitchell. ENCORE: An object-oriented approach to database modelling and querying. *Q. Bull. IEEE TC on Data Engineering*, 14(2):53–57, June 1991.

[ZW86]   S.B. Zdonik and P. Wegner. Language and methodology for object-oriented database environments. In *Proc. of the 19th Annual Hawaii Int. Conf. on System Sciences*, 1986.

Index

NATO ASI Series F

NATO ASI Series F

NATO ASI Series F

Including Special Programmes on Sensory Systems for Robotic Control (ROB) and on Advanced Educational Technology (AET)

NATO ASI Series F

Including Special Programmes on Sensory Systems for Robotic Control (ROB) and on Advanced Educational Technology (AET)

NATO ASI Series F

Including Special Programmes on Sensory Systems for Robotic Control (ROB) and on Advanced Educational Technology (AET)

Vol. 94: Logic and Algebra of Specification. Edited by F. L. Bauer, W. Brauer, and H. Schwichtenberg. VII, 442 pages. 1993.

Vol. 95: Comprehensive Systems Design: A New Educational Technology. Edited by C. M. Reigeluth, B. H. Banathy, and J. R. Olson. IX, 437 pages. 1993. *(AET)*

Vol. 96: New Directions in Educational Technology. Edited by E. Scanlon and T. O'Shea. VIII, 251 pages. 1992. *(AET)*

Vol. 97: Advanced Models of Cognition for Medical Training and Practice. Edited by D. A. Evans and V. L. Patel. XI, 372 pages. 1992. *(AET)*

Vol. 98: Medical Images: Formation, Handling and Evaluation. Edited by A. E. Todd-Pokropek and M. A. Viergever. IX, 700 pages. 1992.

Vol. 99: Multisensor Fusion for Computer Vision. Edited by J. K. Aggarwal. XI, 456 pages. 1993. *(ROB)*

Vol. 100: Communication from an Artificial Intelligence Perspective. Theoretical and Applied Issues. Edited by A. Ortony, J. Slack and O. Stock. XII, 260 pages. 1992.

Vol. 101: Recent Developments in Decision Support Systems. Edited by C. W. Holsapple and A. B. Whinston. XI, 618 pages. 1993.

Vol. 102: Robots and Biological Systems: Towards a New Bionics? Edited by P. Dario, G. Sandini and P. Aebischer. XII, 786 pages. 1993.

Vol. 103: Parallel Computing on Distributed Memory Multiprocessors. Edited by F. Özgüner and F. Erçal. VIII, 332 pages. 1993.

Vol. 104: Instructional Models in Computer-Based Learning Environments. Edited by S. Dijkstra, H. P. M. Krammer and J. J. G. van Merriënboer. X, 510 pages. 1993. *(AET)*

Vol. 105: Designing Environments for Constructive Learning. Edited by T. M. Duffy, J. Lowyck and D. H. Jonassen. VIII, 374 pages. 1993. *(AET)*

Vol. 106: Software for Parallel Computation. Edited by J. S. Kowalik and L. Grandinetti. IX, 363 pages. 1993.

Vol. 107: Advanced Educational Technologies for Mathematics and Science. Edited by D. L. Ferguson. XII, 749 pages. 1993. *(AET)*

Vol. 108: Concurrent Engineering: Tools and Technologies for Mechanical System Design. Edited by E. J. Haug. XIII, 998 pages. 1993.

Vol. 109: Advanced Educational Technology in Technology Education. Edited by A. Gordon, M. Hacker and M. de Vries. VIII, 253 pages. 1993. *(AET)*

Vol. 110: Verification and Validation of Complex Systems: Human Factors Issues. Edited by J. A. Wise, V. D. Hopkin and P. Stager. XIII, 704 pages. 1993.

Vol. 111: Cognitive Models and Intelligent Environments for Learning Programming. Edited by E. Lemut, B. du Boulay and G. Dettori. VIII, 305 pages. 1993. *(AET)*

Vol. 112: Item Banking: Interactive Testing and Self-Assessment. Edited by D. A. Leclercq and J. E. Bruno. VIII, 261 pages. 1993. *(AET)*

Vol. 113: Interactive Learning Technology for the Deaf. Edited by B. A. G. Elsendoorn and F. Coninx. XIII, 285 pages. 1993. *(AET)*

Vol. 114: Intelligent Systems: Safety, Reliability and Maintainability Issues. Edited by O. Kaynak, G. Honderd and E. Grant. XI, 340 pages. 1993.

Vol. 115: Learning Electricity and Electronics with Advanced Educational Technology. Edited by M. Caillot. VII, 329 pages. 1993. *(AET)*

NATO ASI Series F

Springer-Verlag
and the Environment

We at Springer-Verlag firmly believe that an international science publisher has a special obligation to the environment, and our corporate policies consistently reflect this conviction.

We also expect our business partners – paper mills, printers, packaging manufacturers, etc. – to commit themselves to using environmentally friendly materials and production processes.

The paper in this book is made from low- or no-chlorine pulp and is acid free, in conformance with international standards for paper permanency.

The manufacturer's authorised representative in the EU is Springer
Nature Customer Service Centre GmbH, Europaplatz 3, 69115 Heidelberg,
Germany. If you have any concerns regarding our products, please
contact ProductSafety@springernature.com

Printed and bound by CPI Group (UK) Ltd, Croydon, CR0 4YY

28/04/2026

02098497-0001